THE McGRAW-HILL
DICTIONARY OF
MODERN
ECONOMICS

DOUGLAS GREENWALD *Chief Economist and Head of the Department of Economics, McGraw-Hill Publications*

In collaboration with:

HENRY C. F. ARNOLD *Professor, Rutgers University*

WILLIAM J. BROWN *Director of Business Research, Northern Illinois University, College of Business*

LEWIS I. KOFLOWITZ *Economist, Department of Economics, McGraw-Hill Publications*

JACK L. McCROSKEY *Professor of Economics and Finance, University of Denver's College of Business Administration*

GUENTER H. MATTERSDORFF *Chairman, Department of Economics, and Professor, Lewis and Clark College*

EDWARD G. MAYERS *Senior Economist, Department of Economics, McGraw-Hill Publications*

THE McGRAW-HILL DICTIONARY OF MODERN ECONOMICS

A Handbook of Terms and Organizations

SECOND EDITION

McGRAW-HILL BOOK COMPANY

New York   St. Louis   San Francisco   Düsseldorf   Johannesburg
Kuala Lumpur   London   Mexico   Montreal   New Delhi
Panama   Rio de Janeiro   Singapore   Sydney   Toronto

Library of Congress Cataloging in Publication Data

Main entry under title:

The McGraw-Hill dictionary of modern economics.

 1. Economics—Dictionaries. I. Greenwald, Douglas.
II. Title: Dictionary of modern economics.
HB61.M16 1973   330′.03   72-11813
ISBN 0-07-024369-7

67890BPBP7

*The editors for this book were W. Hodson Mogan and Lila M. Gardner,
the designer was Naomi Auerbach, and its production
was supervised by Teresa F. Leaden. It was set in Caledonia
by Brown Brothers Linotypers, Inc.
It was printed and bound by The Book Press.*

Contents

Preface

In the first edition of *The McGraw-Hill Dictionary of Modern Economics* we stated, "Unfortunately for all authors of economic dictionaries, economic terms change with changing societies. Furthermore, economics is the study of dynamic forces whose changes require new assumptions and theories." The period from 1965, when our first edition was published, to 1972, when we completed our revised edition, has been one of evolution or revolution in economics in the U.S. We have gone from the New Economics to the New Economic Program. And for some time a major war has been going on between Keynesians and monetarists. Now coming forth from the ashes of that battle are the proponents of the planned, or controlled, economy.

Thus during this very hectic period for economists of all types, definitions of economic terms, which have long been accepted by the profession, have been altered drastically, some old terms have even been discarded completely, and some new ones have just become part of our language. However, the omission of some particular terms in this dictionary could be an oversight on our part. It does not necessarily mean that they have been eliminated from the economist's vocabulary.

None of the terms included in the dictionary embodies any formal or official expression of McGraw-Hill policy, nor does the company necessarily endorse the programs of any of the private research organizations listed. The authors are solely responsible for the selection of terms and organizations for inclusion or exclusion.

The decisions we had to make with regard to changing, eliminating, and adding definitions involved considerable research, effort, and time. Thus a revision which we expected at the outset would take less than a year to complete actually took about two years, approximately one-half the time it took us to put together the first edition.

For this edition of the dictionary, we have revised the definitions of many of our original 1,300 economic terms and the descriptions of nearly all the economic and research organizations included. We have added more than 125 definitions of economic terms, including 75 econometrics terms. We have also included descriptions of 25 additional economic and research organizations. We have updated many of our references, and we have replaced many others. Finally, we have updated all the charts and tables.

As in our first edition, we have striven to explain clearly and concisely the key points of each concept. We have tried hard to write simple and lucid definitions of the many difficult technical and econometric terms that form the basis of much theoretical and mathematical analysis currently being propounded.

In addition to the listed authors, James A. Carlson, Herbert F. Harbach, and Dennis M. Heydenek, graduate assistants at Northern Illinois University, helped considerably in completing this revision. I must also thank my department's administrative assistant, Elaine Bogart, and our staff secretary, Dianne Brennan, for their excellent cooperation, hard work, and overtime hours spent to get the revised manuscript, including updated charts, into shape. I must also thank my wife Sylvia for allowing me to devote so much of my so-called leisure time to this project.

Douglas Greenwald

What the dictionary provides

1 A simple definition of approximately 1,400 frequently used modern economic terms.

2 A description of approximately 225 private, public, and nonprofit agencies, associations, and research organizations concerned with economics and marketing, including important agencies and organizations outside the U.S.

3 References to both current and original sources of information which provide a more detailed explanation of the terms.

4 References to sources of economic data.

5 Charts, tables, and diagrams when necessary to enhance the definitions.

6 Whenever a definition might be subject to controversy, we have tried to present both sides of the issue.

Who can use the dictionary

1 Students who need an auxiliary reference work for courses in economics and business.
2 Students who are working in applied courses and whose background in economics may be limited or out of date.
3 Students of American history and government.
4 College engineering students who are taking a first course in economics.
5 Women who are family managers and investors who must understand financial and economic reports.
6 Libraries.
7 Instructors.
8 Foreign students who are unfamiliar with American practice and terminology.
9 High school students.
10 Students who are taking evening courses.
11 Editors of newspapers and periodicals of all types.
12 Businessmen.
13 The man on the street who would like to know a little bit about a lot of economics.

How they can use it

1 Teachers, students, and the general public can consult it as a reference work.
2 Readers can use the dictionary to develop increased interest in economics and to stimulate a desire to learn more about a specific area of economics.
3 Students and nonstudents of economics can use it to bring their economic thinking up to date.

Contributors

DOUGLAS GREENWALD Chief economist, McGraw-Hill Publications, and head of its Department of Economics. Mr. Greenwald is a fellow of the American Statistical Association and the National Association of Business Economists. He was a member of the board of directors of the American Statistical Association (ASA), chairman of the Business and Economics Statistics Section of the ASA, and a president of the New York chapter of the ASA. He was a president of the Metropolitan Economic Association and a vice president for economists in the Business Advisory Professions Society. He was chairman of the Federal Statistics Users' Conference, a member of the Regional Accounts Committee, and an adviser to the National Wealth Planning Committee of George Washington University. He was a member of the Census Advisory Committee of the ASA. He is a member of the Business Research Advisory Committee to the Bureau of Labor Statistics, concerned particularly with economic growth and productivity, and a member of the Advisory Committee on Statistical Policy to the Statistical Policy Division of the Office of Management and Budget. He is coauthor with Dexter Keezer of *New Forces in American Business.* He is the contributor of the chapter entitled "Forecasting Capital Expenditures" for the National Association of Business Economists' *How Business Economists Forecast.*

HENRY C. F. ARNOLD B.A. and M.A., University of Michigan. Mr. Arnold is finishing his doctoral work at the New School for Social Research. Prior to joining McGraw-Hill Publications' Department of Economics, he worked in the research departments of the Federal Reserve Bank of New York and the New York Stock Exchange. After leaving McGraw-Hill, he worked for four years as an economist for the Chase Manhattan Bank and then moved to Rutgers University in Newark, where he is currently teaching economics. He is a member of the American Economic Association, the American Finance Association, and the Royal Economic Society.

WILLIAM J. BROWN A.B., Bowdoin College; M.A., University of Chicago; Ph.D., New York University. Dr. Brown is currently serving as Director of Business Research in the College of Business, Northern Illinois University. He was an economist for the American Bankers Association and prior to that was with the Department of Economics of McGraw-Hill Publications. He serves both private industry and government agencies as a consultant and is the author of numerous scholarly and popular articles in the field of economics.

LEWIS I. KOFLOWITZ M.B.A. in business economics, Columbia University Graduate Business School. Mr. Koflowitz is an honors graduate in economics from New York University. Prior to joining the Department of Economics in 1969, he was economics editor on Engineering News-Record, a McGraw-Hill publication. He has also been a research assistant specializing in management, with Business International, Inc. He is a member of the New York Association of Business Economists, the American Economic Association, and the Metropolitan Economic Association

JACK L. McCROSKEY B.A , Southern Methodist University; M.A. and Ph.D., Indiana University Dr. McCroskey was a senior economist in the McGraw-Hill Publications' Department of Economics and is a former business economist for Chase Manhattan Bank, New York. He joined the University of Denver's College of Business Administration faculty in 1967 as an associate professor of economics and finance. He is currently a full professor of economics and finance and holds the Denver Clearinghouse Chair of Finance at DU. He is the author of numerous articles in the field of economics and is the past editor of *Business Economics,* the journal of the National Association of Business Economists.

GUENTER H. MATTERSDORFF Ph.D. in economics, Harvard Graduate School of Public Administration. Before coming to McGraw-Hill Publications' Department of Economics as senior economist, Dr. Mattersdorff was an instructor at Yale University, the University of Massachusetts and Connecticut College. Currently he is a professor at Lewis and Clark College and chairman of the department of economics. He holds an Ayres Fellowship to the Stonier Graduate School of Banking at Rutgers, granted by the American Bankers Association, and is currently holding a Senior Science Faculty Fellowship granted by the National Science Foundation. He serves in a consulting capacity as regional economist for the thirteenth national bank region.

EDWARD G. MAYERS B.Sci.B.A., M.A. in economics, Ohio State University. He is currently senior economist in the McGraw-Hill Department of Economics. Prior to joining McGraw-Hill, Mr. Mayers was an associate economist of the American Cyanamid Company and associate professor of economics at the U.S. Merchant Marine Academy, Kings Point, L.I. He is the author of two monographs commissioned by the Joint Council on Economic Education and has contributed to several textbooks on business and economics. He is a member of the American Statistical Association and the National Association of Business Economists.

Part 1

TERMS

A

Ability-to-Pay Principle of Taxation The theory that the tax burden should be distributed according to the individual's ability to pay. It is based on the assumption that those who possess more wealth than others should contribute a relatively larger amount to the support of the government. The obligation to pay is seen as a social or collective responsibility rather than as a personal one. Employing the concept of a diminishing utility of income, the ability-to-pay principle tries to equalize the sacrifice made by each individual in paying his taxes. The determination of a tax base capable of measuring an individual's ability to pay is a major problem of this theory. Generally, net money income (with deductions for minimal survival needs) is used as the best measure of this ability. This measure ignores differences in financial commitments, in expectations of future income, and in habits of consumption, however, and thus may not reflect the individual's real ability to pay the tax. Another problem is the determination of a rate schedule which truly equalizes the sacrifices involved in paying a tax. The concept of diminishing marginal utility indicates that a tax based on the ability to pay should be progressive (or at least proportional), but there is no way of determining how steep rate increases should be. Furthermore, the application of a uniform rate to all taxpayers ignores differences among persons in the utility of income. The ability-to-pay principle, regarded by many as the most equitable and just theory of taxation, is incorporated into most of the important U.S. taxes, such as the progressive personal income tax and the inheritance tax. For additional information, see Richard A. Musgrave, *The Theory of Public Finance*, McGraw-Hill Book Company, New York, 1959, chap. 5; Edwin Seligman, *Progressive Taxation in Theory and Practice*, 2d ed., Princeton University Press, Princeton, N.J., 1908; M. Slade Kendrick, "Ability to Pay Theory of Taxation," *American Economic Review*, vol. XXIX, pp. 92–101, American Economic Association, Evanston, Ill., March, 1939.

Absolute Advantage   The ability of a particular country, firm, or worker to supply a product or service at a cost lower than that of a competitor. Most of the world's trade is carried on because of differences in absolute advantage: bananas are bought from Honduras instead of Canada, nylon is purchased from Du Pont rather than General Motors, and even in a small village the watchmaker buys his bread from the baker instead of making it himself. This division of labor is generally advantageous because it forces every country, firm, and worker to specialize and thus to acquire cost-cutting skills. Nevertheless, competitors faced with the prospect of going out of business sometimes react by requesting government regulations that give them a new lease on life. Such regulations, which reduce the gain obtained from an absolute advantage, are sometimes defended in the name of the infant-industry argument. According to this argument, a protected industry, if allowed to live and grow even when at a competitive disadvantage, may have a chance to develop new markets and new methods that will give it an absolute advantage in the future. See Gottfried Haberler, *The Theory of International Trade*, The Macmillan Company, New York, 1950, pp. 127–129; Richard I. Leighton, *Economics of International Trade*, McGraw-Hill Book Company, New York, 1970.

Accelerated Depreciation   A faster-than-historical rate of depreciation of a fixed asset for income tax purposes. It is a method of depreciation that makes the depreciation allowance, and hence the tax allowance, available earlier in the life of the asset. By using the liberalized provisions for computing depreciation allowances introduced in the U.S. Internal Revenue Code of 1954, a business can recapture almost 50% more of its investment in a new fixed asset during the first half of the asset's useful life than it could when it was limited to straight-line depreciation. In addition, rapid tax amortization certificates, introduced during World War II and the Korean conflict to stimulate defense and defense-supporting investment, permitted companies to depreciate within five years assets that would normally have been depreciated over a longer period. Accelerated depreciation in any form does not increase the total tax-free allowance for capital consumption. For additional details, see George Terborgh, *Realistic Depreciation Policy*, Machinery and Allied Products Institute, Washington, D.C., 1954; for the effect of accelerated depreciation on the economy, see Dexter M. Keezer and Associates, *New Forces in American Business*, McGraw-Hill Book Company, New York, 1959; for an appraisal of accelerated depreciation methods, see Robert Feinschreiber, "Accelerated Depreciation: A Proposed New Method," *Journal of Accounting Research*, vol. 7, no. 1, pp. 17–21, Spring, 1969; Norman B. Ture, *Accelerated Depreciation in the United States*,

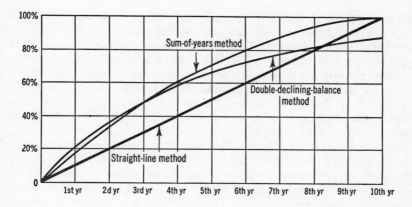

1954–1960, National Bureau of Economic Research, Inc., New York, 1967.

Accelerator Theory   The theory that a change in the demand for goods induces a change in the amount of machinery needed to produce those goods. Let us assume that a manufacturer of radios needs $3 of capital for $1 of production, and that he has annual replacement costs equal to 10% of the preceding year's capital stock. The table below shows that his output rises between periods I and II by $5, and that he must expand his capacity by spending $15, plus a replacement cost of $30. Thus, a 5% rise in demand induces a 50% increase in investment spending. The accelerator can also cause a violent collapse of investment spending, as shown between periods III and IV.

Period	Output of Goods	Capital Stock Required	Addition to Capacity	Replacement	Total Spending for Investment
I	100	300	0	30	30
II	105	315	15	30	45
III	115	345	30	32	62
IV	110	330	−15	35	20

The accelerator is particularly important in assessing the business outlook when industry is operating near capacity. At such a time, a small increase in demand can raise investment spending enormously. Five limitations to the accelerator theory should be considered before applying it to practical problems. (1) The theory assumes full-capacity operation at all times. This assumption is obviously untrue in practice, and this is one of the main reasons that capacity statistics have been developed for the economy. (2) The theory, as stated, breaks down because it assumes that gross investment can fall below zero, which is impossible. When the derived demand for capital equipment falls so rapidly that depreciation does not dispose of all the equipment not needed, excess capacity is created. (3) The model does not explicitly include expectations as a factor which may raise or lower capital investment. (4) All the foregoing are limitations to be borne in mind, but they do not destroy the theory. More important is the fact that investment sometimes requires years to be completed, a fact that the theory ignores. Because of this time factor, actual investment may fluctuate less markedly than the theory allows when business goes through the cycle. (5) The principle assumes fixed proportions between output and capital stock. This may not necessarily be true if capital can be worked three shifts during periods of unusually heavy demand instead of the normal one shift. The accelerator principle was introduced by John M. Clark in 1917 to explain proportionately larger variations in investment over the course of a business cycle than had occurred in the output of consumer goods. Interest in the accelerator as a theoretical tool increased after 1936, when it was discovered that it could be combined with the Keynesian consumption function to formulate self-generating models of the business cycle. For an example of a model of the business cycle based on the combination of the accelerator and the consumption function, see Paul A. Samuelson, "Interactions between the Multiplier Analysis and the Principle of Acceleration," *Review of Economics and Statistics*, vol. 21, pp. 78–88, Harvard University Press, Cambridge, Mass., 1939; see also John M. Clark, "Business Acceleration and the Law of Demand: A Technical Factor in Economic Cycles," *Journal of Political Economy*, The University of Chicago Press, Chicago; reprinted in *Readings in Business Cycles*, McGraw-Hill Book Company, New York, 1951; Thomas F. Dernburg and Duncan M. McDougall, *Macroeconomics*, McGraw-Hill Book Company, New York, 1968, pp. 316–323.

Accession Rate (Hiring Rate)   The number of additional employees hired during a specific period, expressed as a percentage of total employment. The additions cover all types of employees, including both new and rehired workers on either a permanent or a temporary basis. A significant indicator of overall business activity, the accession rate is classified by the National Bureau of Economic Research as one of its leading indicators. When the rate begins to fall, business may be moving into a recession; when it rises, business may be on the road to recovery. For industry statistics and a more detailed definition of accession rate, see

U.S. Department of Labor, *Employment and Earnings,* monthly; for a discussion of the accession rate as an indicator of turning points of business cycles, see R. C. Mendelssohn, "Three BLS Series as Business Cycle Turn Signals," *Monthly Labor Review,* U.S. Department of Labor, September, 1959.

Accession Rate (Per 100 employees)

Source: U.S. Department of Labor.

Accord, Treasury–Federal Reserve An agreement by the U.S. Secretary of the Treasury and the Board of Governors of the Federal Reserve System on the "debt management and monetary policies to be pursued in furthering their common purpose to assure the successful financing of the government's requirements and, at the same time, to minimize the monetization of the public debt." The announcement on March 4, 1951, that the Treasury and the Federal Reserve had reached "full accord" in these matters marked the official end of one of the most controversial disputes on monetary policy in the Federal Reserve's history. This dispute concerned the continuation into the 1950s, at the Treasury's behest, of the World War II policy of supporting at par the prices of U.S. government bonds. Before the accord, financial institutions wishing to expand their private lending operations were able to sell their accumulated government bond holdings to the Federal Reserve at par. As a result, the Federal Reserve's ability to employ monetary policy as a weapon against postwar inflation was severely restricted. The additional inflationary pressures created by mobilization for the Korean conflict led to the announced accord and to a decision to abandon the unconditional support of government security prices. For a discussion of the basic questions involved in the controversy, see Lester V. Chandler, *The Economics of Money and Banking*, 5th ed., Harper & Row, Publishers, Incorporated, New York, 1969, pp. 491–493; for an account of events surrounding the accord, see Herbert Stein, *The Fiscal Revolution in America*, The University of Chicago Press, Chicago, 1969, chap. 10.

Accounts Payable   Liabilities owed by a firm to trade creditors. Usually, accounts payable are limited to the unpaid amounts of goods and services purchased as part of a firm's everyday transactions. The accounts payable are most often listed on the balance sheet under the heading of current liabilities. According to statistics of the Federal Trade Commission and the Securities and Exchange Commission, trade accounts and notes payable of manufacturing corporations totaled $45.6 billion in the first quarter of 1970. For further discussion, see J. Fred Weston and Eugene F. Brigham, *Managerial Finance*, Holt, Rinehart and Winston, Inc., New York, 1966; Walter B. Meigs and Charles E. Johnson, *Accounting*, 2d ed., McGraw-Hill Book Company, New York, 1967.

Accounts Receivable   Amounts owed to a nonfinancial enterprise by its customers. Accounts receivable arise from the widespread business practice of shipping customers' merchandise on credit which calls for payment at a later date, usually within ten to ninety days. Accounts receivable average about 8 to 10% of sales and about 16 to 20% of total assets. Because of varying customs in different lines of business, however, these percentages range widely from one firm to another. For a discussion of accounts receivable and their management, see J. Fred Weston and Eugene F. Brigham, *Managerial Finance*, 2d ed., Holt, Rinehart and Winston, Inc., New York, 1966; Walter B. Meigs and Charles E. Johnson, *Accounting*, 2d ed., McGraw-Hill Book Company, New York, 1967. Statistics on total receivables for manufacturing are carried in U.S. Federal Trade Commission and Securities and Exchange Commission, *Quarterly Financial Report for Manufacturing Corporations*.

Accounts Receivable Financing   A type of business financing in which firms either sell their accounts receivable or pledge them as collateral for loans. The sale of accounts receivable is called factoring, and the pledging of such accounts is called discounting. In the U.S., accounts receivable financing usually involves an interest rate of 6 to 8%, plus an additional 0.5 to 2% when the accounts are sold to a factor. The advantages of such financing include: (1) flexibility, since the volume of credit can expand and contract in direct proportion to the total sales volume; and (2) access to credit that many firms, particularly small firms, might not be able to obtain on an unsecured basis. Among the disadvantages are the following: (1) accounts receivable financing frequently tends to be relatively expensive; and (2) some observers consider it an indication of an unsound financial position. See J. Fred Weston and Eugene F. Brigham, *Managerial Finance*, 2d ed., Holt, Rinehart and Winston, Inc., New York, 1966, chap. 14; see also Clyde William Phelps, *Accounts Receivable as a Method of Securing Business Loans*, Commercial Credit Corporation, Baltimore, 1962.

Accrual Basis A method of accounting in which revenue is recorded in the period in which it is earned (whether or not it is collected in that period), and expenses are reported in the period when they are incurred (no matter when the disbursements are made). This method differs from the cash basis of accounting, in which income is considered earned when received and expenses are recorded when paid. On the accrual basis, all sales of merchandise are recorded as income even if payment is not received until the following year. The accrual method is used by most firms and by almost all large ones. All corporations in which inventories are an income-determining factor (this provision includes all merchandising and manufacturing firms) must prepare their income tax returns according to the accrual method, and only corporations selling services may report income on the cash basis. For additional information, see H. A. Finney and H. E. Miller, *Principles of Accounting*, 6th ed., Prentice-Hall, Inc., Englewood Cliffs, N.J., 1965.

Acid-Test Ratio (Quick Ratio) A ratio of a firm's current liquid assets (cash, trade receivables, and readily marketable securities) to its current liabilities. For example, if the current liquid assets amount to $175,000 and the total current debt to $125,000, the acid-test ratio is 1.4 to 1, which means that the firm has $1.40 of current liquid assets for each $1 of current debt. This ratio provides a better check on a firm's current operations than the current ratio, which includes inventories that may not prove to be liquid enough to meet current debts. See H. A. Finney and H. E. Miller, *Principles of Accounting*, 6th ed., Prentice-Hall, Inc., Englewood Cliffs, N.J., 1965.

Acquisition The taking over of one firm by another. The acquisition of a corporation is usually carried out by the purchase of a controlling portion of its common stock. The acquisition form of merger differs from consolidation, which is a joining of firms into a single consolidated company. It is easier to merge small firms by acquisition, since the capital needed for the take-over is within the resources of the acquiring firm. Consolidation is more common in the merger of large firms, especially since new sources of capital may sometimes be required in merging the given firms into a more highly capitalized corporation. A series of acquisitions by one company may be part of an attempt to secure market control, particularly if legal or other restrictions prevent the consolidation of a large number of firms at one time. For additional details, see Betty Bock, *Mergers and Markets: 7*, National Industrial Conference Board, Inc., Studies in Business Economics, no. 105, New York, 1969; *Corporate Mergers and Acquisitions*, American Management Association, New York, 1958; Ralph L. Nelson, *Merger Movements in American Industry, 1895–1956*, Princeton University Press, Princeton, N.J., 1959; for statistics on acquisitions in manufacturing, see U.S. Bureau of the Census, "Acquisitions and Disposals of Manufacturing Facilities, 1959 and 1960," *Annual Survey of Manufacturers: 1959 and 1960*, M60 (AS)-S1, 1963; see also *Mergers and Superconcentration: Acquisitions of the 500 Largest Industrial and 50 Largest Merchandising Firms*, staff report of the Select Committee on Small Business, U.S. House of Representatives, Nov. 8, 1962.

Acreage Allotment A program to cut farm production by limiting plant acreage. The Agricultural Adjustment Act of 1933 established acreage limits for farms growing specified crops (corn, wheat, cotton, tobacco). The Agricultural Adjustment Administration (AAA) first determined the total acreage to be devoted to each crop. Part of the total was then allotted to each state and to each farm in the state where the crop was produced. The total acreage was set each year in accordance with carry-overs from previous years, prospective demand, and the parity price. The allotment for each farm was based on its customary production. Direct benefits offered to the farmers to induce them to participate in the program comprised AAA payments, crop loans, reduced prices for fertilizers and other materials, and a crop insurance program. The acreage allotment program was not successful. Although acreage was cut, production did not decline by a corresponding amount, since farmers curtailed the use of their least productive acres and increased the use of their most productive ones. See Theodore W. Schultz, *The Economic Organization of Agriculture*, McGraw-Hill Book Company, New York, 1953; Murray R. Benedict, *Can We Solve the Farm Problem?* The Twentieth Century Fund, New York, 1955.

Actuary A highly skilled mathematician in the business community who determines the annual retirement of plants and equipment on the basis of statistical techniques. He also provides estimates of the average life of facilities on the basis of detailed company records of each unit of plant and equipment. His computational methods are generally similar to those developed by life insurance actuaries in the study of human mortality.

Administered-Price Theory   A theory that the prices of goods or services are allegedly established by agreement among the executives of large firms and maintained despite changes in market conditions. Thus, the market forces of supply and demand play little or no role in determining prices. When the demand for a particular product declines, prices remain the same. Because economic activity no longer declines sharply in recession periods, those persons who supposedly administer prices are not under strong pressure to reduce them. Rather, the incentive is to maintain prices, since the pressures from cost-push and from the demand side are generally prevalent. Before World War II, the inflexibility of administered prices was accepted by some economists and government authorities, but it was not until after the war that this inflexibility was considered to be closely related to the degree of market concentration. For further discussion, see Gardiner C. Means, *The Corporate Revolution in America*, Crowell-Collier Publishing Co., New York, 1962; for administered prices in specific industries, see "Administered Prices: Steel," *Report of the Subcommittee on Antitrust and Monopoly to the Senate Judiciary Committee*, Senate Report 1387, 85th Cong., 2d Sess., 1958; "Administered Prices: Drugs," *Report of the Subcommittee on Antitrust and Monopoly to the Senate Judiciary Committee*, Senate Report 448, 87th Cong., 1st Sess., 1961; John S. Gambs and Jerome B. Komisar, *Economics and Man*, 3d ed., Richard D. Irwin, Inc., Homewood, Ill., 1968, pp. 324–326.

Administrative Budget   The traditional method of budgeting Federal expenditures and receipts in the U.S. until 1969. The administrative budget includes the collection and distribution of all funds of which the government considers itself the sole owner. The administrative budget concept is roughly consistent with the concept of Federal debt subject to limitation and the Federal funds part of the unified budget. There are a number of trust accounts, such as those used to finance social security programs, of which the government does not consider itself full owner, and transactions for these accounts are not included in the administrative budget. Certain highway and housing trust funds are also regarded as outside the administrative accounts and are excluded from the administrative budget. The result of these exclusions is that the administrative budget does not present a complete picture of Federal government transactions. In the fiscal year 1967, for example, the difference between Fed-

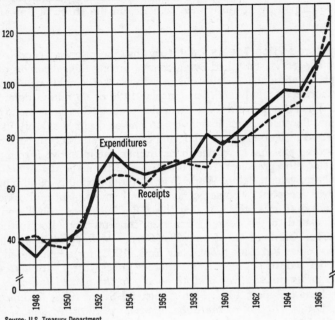

Federal Administrative Budget, Receipts and Expenditures for the Fiscal Years, 1947-1967 (Billions of dollars)

Source: U.S. Treasury Department.

eral government expenditures according to the administrative budget and the cash budget (which includes the trust funds) was $29.4 billion, and the difference in receipts was $37.8 billion. For additional details, see Gerhard Colm, *The Federal Budget and the National Economy*, National Planning Association, Washington, D.C., 1955.

Ad Valorem Tax   A levy based on a fixed percentage of an item's dollar value. Ad valorem is a Latin term meaning "depending on the value of the item." The great advantages of an ad valorem tax over a specific tax (for example, 4 cents per gallon of gasoline) are that it does not erode during inflationary times and that its direct relationship to an item's value makes it more equitable. A disadvantage is that the need to determine the value of the taxable item makes this tax more difficult to compute. Ad valorem taxes include sales taxes, property taxes, and the majority of import duties. See Richard A. Musgrave, *The Theory of Public Finance*, McGraw-Hill Book Company, New York, 1959; Philip E. Taylor, *The Economics of Public Policy*, The Macmillan Company, New York, 1953;

Robert H. Haveman, *The Economics of the Public Sector,* John Wiley &
Sons, Inc., New York, 1970, pp. 67–68.

Advance Refunding   A term used in connection with the refinancing of
the public debt. Under this system, which was initiated by the Eisenhower administration in June, 1960, holders of an issue of government
securities falling due in the near future are given the opportunity of
turning in their securities, before they come due, for others of a later
maturity. Advance-refunding procedures have helped stretch out the
national debt while keeping it in the hands of noncommercial banking
institutions, such as insurance companies and pension funds, which tend
to hold bonds for the long pull. To make the advance-refunding operation a success (that is, to induce holders to take an issue of longer maturity), a higher rate of return than that offered by the previous issue is
given to all holders who accept the refunding terms. For further information, see Douglas Dillon, "Advance Refundings as a Debt Management
Tool," *Commercial and Financial Chronicle,* New York, Mar. 29, 1962,
p. 3.

Advertising   A method of providing private consumers, businesses, and
governments with information about specific goods, services, or opportunities with the ultimate goal of increasing sales. Advertisements convey
news about goods and services, including details to show what they are,
what they are used for, where they are, and what they cost. Advertising
has become an important sales aid, especially for nationally and internationally distributed items. It may be considered one step in the process of
automated selling, in which fewer salesmen are needed to inform potential purchasers about a product. The dollar volume of advertising in all
media in the U.S. in 1970 exceeded $19.5 billion, or more than 2% of the
dollar volume of all goods and services produced in the nation. Most
businessmen believe that advertising helps move billions of dollars' worth
of goods and services off the shelves of manufacturers, wholesalers, retailers, and service establishments to the consumers of the world. On the
other hand, some economists believe that advertising results in a misuse
of resources, that it creates undesirable wants at the expense of public
needs, and that its benefits rarely justify the costs involved. Despite a
popular belief prior to the 1950s that advertising contributes to economic
instability, postwar evidence suggests that it may be a stabilizing economic force. In the business recessions of 1948–1949, 1953–1954, and
1957–1958, advertising did not follow the downward course of business
activity, and in the recession of 1960–1961 it declined much less than
general business. See David M. Potter, *People of Plenty,* The University
of Chicago Press, Chicago, 1954; Martin Mayer, *Madison Avenue, U.S.A.,*

Total Advertising Dollar Volume and Total Corporate Sales (Billions of dollars)

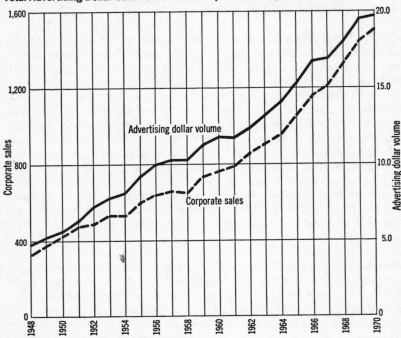

Source: U.S. Department of Commerce; Marketing/Communications.

Harper & Row, Publishers, Incorporated, New York, 1958; Neil Borden, *Economic Effects of Advertising*, Richard D. Irwin, Inc., Homewood, Ill., 1942.

Advertising Agency   A service firm whose principal function is the planning and execution of advertising programs for its clients. The agency aids the individual firm in the planning, preparation, and placing of its advertising. An important service is the design of advertisements, including the preparation of material, written or oral, and the arrangement of layouts. The advertising agency helps formulate the short- and long-range strategy of advertising campaigns and provides research services, such as market and product surveys. It also recommends to its client the most effective media (e.g., newspapers, magazines, or television). In addition, agencies are often responsible for the mechanical production of advertisements (setting type, photoengraving, etc.) and, in radio and television advertising, for the writing and production of commercials. Many large agencies also provide advice on the overall merchandising strategy of clients. There are approximately 6,000 advertising agencies in the U.S., ranging from one-man firms to those employing more than 2,000 persons. The volume of advertising handled by all advertising agencies in the U.S. in 1967 was about $7.6 billion, or 45% of total advertising. For additional details on the structure and services of advertising agencies, see Roger Barton, *Advertising Agency Operations and Management,* McGraw-Hill Book Company, New York, 1955; Martin Mayer, *Madison Avenue, U.S.A.,* Harper & Row, Publishers, Incorporated, New York, 1958; Frederic Gamble, *What Advertising Agencies Are: What They Do and How They Do It,* 2d ed., American Association of Advertising Agencies, New York, 1960.

Advertising Media The means of communication by which an advertiser informs consumers about his goods, services, or opportunities. The selection and use of advertising media form a key part of a company's marketing strategy. Major types of media include outdoor advertising, newspapers, magazines, farm and business periodicals, radio and tele-

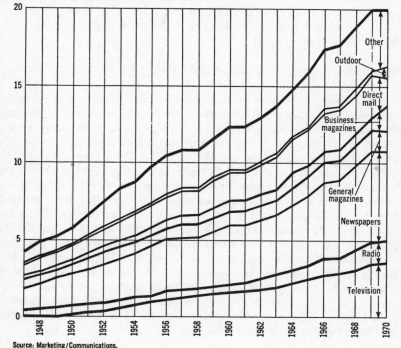

Advertising by Media (Billions of dollars)

Source: Marketing/Communications.

vision, and direct mail. Newspapers account for about 30% of the dollar volume of advertising, television for 19%, and direct mail for 16%. For a discussion of creative planning in the selection of media, see Lyndon O. Brown et al., *Advertising Media,* The Ronald Press Company, New York, 1957.

Affluent Society A wealthy nation in which most persons enjoy an abundance of material things. Popularized by John Kenneth Galbraith in *The Affluent Society,* the term is frequently used to describe the U.S., where, at the end of 1970, 67 million families and individuals owned more than 89 million automobiles, 90 million television sets, 59 million vacuum cleaners, and 20 million home freezers. The U.S. has grown so prosperous, Galbraith argues, that it no longer needs to increase the output of consumer products, but it can and should improve the quality of life by shifting emphasis from the private to the public sector of the economy. For example, resources could be used to create better schools, cleaner streets, a greater number of parks, and a variety of other social services. Many U.S. economists disagree with this argument. They reject the idea that most consumer wants have been satisfied and oppose the promotion of government services at the expense of private consumption. For Galbraith's view, see J. K. Galbraith, *The Affluent Society,* Houghton Mifflin Company, Boston, 1958.

Agency Marketing *See Investment Banking.*

Agency Shop A plant or establishment in which a union and the management have an arrangement that all employees who elect not to join the union shall pay, as a condition of employment, a monthly service charge (usually equal to regular union dues) to the union. Although agency shop agreements are included in only a small proportion of U.S. collective bargaining contracts, because only a few unions have been willing to accept this arrangement as a substitute for the union shop, interest in the agency shop has increased. In states that have enacted laws banning union membership as a condition of employment (right-to-work laws), the agency shop is established unless it, too, is specifically prohibited by state law. For statistics, see *Union Security and Checkoff Provisions in Major Union Contracts 1958–59,* U.S. Department of Labor Bulletin 1272; for discussion, see Sumner H. Slichter et al., *The Impact of Collective Bargaining on Management,* The Brookings Institution, Washington, D.C., 1960; Joseph Shister, *The Economics of the Labor Market,* J. B. Lippincott Company, Philadelphia, 1956; Melvin W. Reder, *Labor in a Growing Economy,* John Wiley & Sons, Inc., New York, 1957.

Aggregate The familiar type of summary series shown in most statistical reports. Generally, it is a total, such as the gross national product or retail sales, but sometimes it is an average, such as the index of industrial production or the index of wholesale prices. For a discussion of how aggregates are used in diffusion indices, see Geoffrey H. Moore and Julius Shiskin, "Variable Span Diffusion Indexes and Economic Forecasting," a paper presented at the Sixth Annual Forecasting Conference, American Statistical Association, New York Chapter, Apr. 17, 1964.

Aggregative Model An econometric model involving variables whose individual observations represent aggregates. For example, total income and total expenditures are both aggregates. Similarly, an index number may depict the behavior of groups of individual observations. It follows that peculiarities of the individual observations that are grouped as well as the peculiarities of possible subgroups are not encompassed by such models. For additional information, see Stefan Valavanis, *Econometrics*, McGraw-Hill Book Company, New York, 1959.

Agio An exchange premium or discount. An agio arises when two currencies, supposedly equal in value, actually differ. It consists of the premium paid when one exchanges the cheaper for the dearer currency. Speculation may either reduce the agio (if it is believed that the value of the two currencies will become equal again) or increase it (if it is believed that the difference in value will become greater). Such a trading agio arises most often when a nation suffers from a balance-of-payments deficit, thus reducing the exchange value of its currency in relation to that of other nations.

Agribusiness The production, processing, and marketing of farm commodities, including both food and nonfood items. It includes the production and sale of such supplies as machinery, feed, and fertilizers, as well as the manufacture and distribution of agricultural products, including meatpacking, grocery sales, and the production of textiles made from natural fibers. In 1961, U.S. agribusiness produced an estimated $120 billion of consumer goods and employed 35% of the nation's labor force. See John H. Davis and Ray A. Goldberg, *A Concept of Agribusiness*, Harvard Graduate School of Business Administration, Boston, 1957.

Agricultural Revolution The introduction of new productive techniques into farming, transforming agricultural methods from medieval to modern conditions. The Agricultural Revolution occurred in England from the latter half of the eighteenth century to the first half of the nineteenth century. It was characterized by the consolidation of landholdings, by introduction of new lands into cultivation, and, most important, by the use of new techniques. Among the pioneers of the English Agricultural Revolution were the 2d Viscount Townshend, Jethro Tull, Robert Bakewell, and Arthur Young, who introduced such advances as crop rotation and systematic animal breeding. The revolution resulted in an increased specialization of agricultural production by region, a greater use of machinery, an increased division of labor, and a larger investment of capital in soil and in farm equipment. The English Agricultural Revolution not only made possible a great increase in food production, but also laid the foundations for the further application of science and technology to farming that occurred in the late nineteenth and twentieth centuries. For additional details on the Agricultural Revolution, see N. S. B. Gras, *A History of Agriculture in Europe and America,* Appleton-Century-Crofts, Inc., New York, 1940; Shepard B. Clough, *Economic Development of Western Civilization,* McGraw-Hill Book Company, New York, 1959, chap. 14.

Agricultural Revolution, Modern The rapid rise in farm output per man-hour and in crop output per acre, accompanied by a sharp decline in the number of farm workers, since the 1940s. Because of the introduction of new and improved agricultural machinery, the development of better soil-utilization methods, and the marked improvement in farm chemicals, such as fertilizers, weed killers, and insecticides, farm production per man-hour rose by 323% and output per acre by 51% between 1950 and 1970, while the number of farm workers declined from 6 million to 3.5 million. Although the main impact of the modern agricultural revolution has been felt in the U.S., its effects have been worldwide. For statistics showing the magnitude of the agricultural revolution in the U.S., see *Farm Production and Efficiency,* U.S. Department of Agriculture Bulletin 233, 1962.

Allocation of Resources The distribution of resources among different uses and users. A basic problem of every economic system is the means of achieving an allocation of resources that will result in maximum efficiency. Resources must be channeled into the production of goods that consumers want most and must be prevented from entering the production of goods that consumers want least. In addition, they must be allocated to the most productive industries. The optimum allocation of resources is achieved through the workings of the free-price system, in which resources move from less profitable to more profitable uses and

Measures of Farm Productivity (1950 = 100)

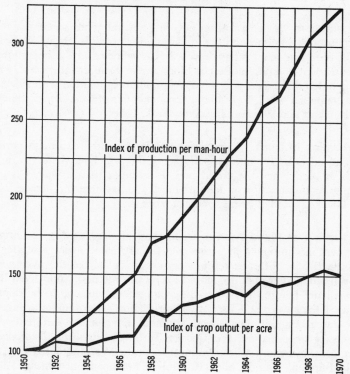

Index of production per man-hour

Index of crop output per acre

Source: U.S. Department of Agriculture.

from less important to more important uses. A necessary condition for an optimum allocation of resources is that the marginal product of any resource be the same for all its alternative uses. With pure competition in all product and resource markets, an optimum allocation is achieved automatically, but monopoly or monopsony leads to different marginal products with different uses and thus to misallocation. Other impediments to optimum resource allocation are ignorance of profitable opportunities, sociological and psychological factors (e.g., lack of factor mobility), and institutional restrictions (e.g., labor unions and patents). For further information, see Richard H. Leftwich, *The Price System and Resource Allocation,* 3d ed., Holt, Rinehart and Winston, Inc., New York, 1966; D. S. Watson, *Price Theory and Its Uses,* 2d ed., Houghton Mifflin Company, Boston, 1968; Joe S. Bain, *Industrial Organization,* 2d ed., John Wiley & Sons, Inc., New York, 1968.

Alternative Costs   *See Opportunity Costs.*

Amalgamation   A general term covering several types of combinations of corporations (merger and consolidation, for example) in which one or more of the fusing companies drop out of existence and the operations of the constituent companies are combined under centralized control. For a more detailed discussion of types of corporate combination with reference to amalgamation, see J. F. Bradley, *Fundamentals of Corporation Finance,* Holt, Rinehart and Winston, Inc., New York, 1955.

Amortization of Debt   A gradual reduction of a debt through periodic payments covering the interest and part of the principal. Generally, amortization is used when the credit period is longer than a year. Common examples of amortization of debt are mortgage payments on homes, which extend over a period of twenty years or more.

Amortization of Fixed Assets   A method of depreciating the original investment in equipment or plants over the estimated average service life of an asset. Mortalities or retirements occurring before the average life has been attained are not accounted for by this method. Short-lived items that wear out before the end of the average life continue to be depreciated as if they were still present. Depreciation is terminated altogether when the average life has been attained. For further information on methods of depreciation, see George Terborgh, *Realistic Depreciation Policy,* Machinery and Allied Products Institute, Washington, D.C., 1954; Harold Burman, Jr., and Allan R. Drebin, *Financial Accounting: An Introduction,* The Macmillan Company, New York, 1968, pp. 214–226.

Anarchism   A political philosophy that advocates the abolition of government administration by revolutionary means if necessary. It holds that people are basically good and would live in harmony with one another if the artificial apparatus of the state were abolished. Although anarchism is sometimes confused with socialism, the two are quite different. Anarchism has very little to do with economics; its philosophers generally ignore the problems of interpersonal economic relations that would arise with the abolition of the state. Socialism, on the other hand, is concerned mainly with economics. Through state ownership of all the means of production, it attempts to bring about a new order that would advance the economic welfare of the whole society. In the sense that true anarchy would eliminate all forms of coercion over the individual, anarchism is the eventual goal of most Socialists who are motivated by the desire to improve the welfare of mankind and to ensure individual freedom. For further discussion, see Earl R. Sykes, *Contemporary Economic Systems,* Holt, Rinehart and Winston, Inc., New York, 1951, chap. 6.

Angell Plan   A program proposed by James W. Angell for expanding international liquidity to meet balance-of-payments problems. The plan calls for changing the International Monetary Fund into a world central bank which would create and issue an international currency. National currencies would still be used as a means of international settlement and as a store of values, but their use would be controlled indirectly by the new IMF. The new international currency would provide additional international liquidity. For additional information, see James W. Angell, "The Reorganization of the International Monetary System," *The Economic Journal,* vol. LXXI, pp. 691–708, December, 1961.

Annual Improvement Factor   A provision written into a collective bargaining agreement for wage increases tied to increases in productivity. Often called the productivity clause, the annual improvement factor provides for wage increases in addition to those resulting from the operation of an escalator clause, which keeps real wages in line with rising consumer prices. The annual improvement provision originated in the contract agreement signed by General Motors and the United Automobile Workers in 1948. The annual improvement factor is based on the theory that employees should periodically receive wage or salary increases in addition to those connected with promotions. In the *Economic Report of the President* of January, 1962, an administration for the first time advanced guidelines for noninflationary wage increases. These equated the rate of increase in wage rates (including fringe benefits) in each industry to the trend rate of overall productivity increases. By the end of 1967, the Council of Economic Advisers no longer thought it appropriate to set the trend of productivity as a numerical target for wage increases. See Albert Rees, *The Economics of Trade Unions,* The University of Chicago Press, Chicago, 1962; U.S. Bureau of Labor Statistics, *Guide to Labor Management in the United States,* 1958.

Annual Rate   The result of expanding an economic or accounting statistic relating to a time period shorter than a year into its yearly equivalent. For example, retail sales, seasonally adjusted, totaled $30 billion in January, 1970. On an annual-rate basis, this figure becomes $360 billion. Similarly, in the second quarter of 1970, the new orders of machinery and equipment manufacturers, seasonally adjusted, totaled $18.5 billion, which, when converted to an annual-rate basis, equals $74 billion.

Annuity   A payment made yearly, quarterly, or at some other regular interval for either a specified or an uncertain length of time (such as a specified number of years, for life, or in perpetuity). An annuity that lasts for a fixed number of years is an annuity certain; one for which the length of payments is not fixed is a contingent annuity. An annuity may be arranged either for another person or for oneself. The first type used was the annuity established for another person, generally in place of a lump gift or legacy, to guarantee continuation of support over a period of time. The annuity set up for oneself is now the more usual type. The most important modern annuities are certain forms of life insurance, other annuity contracts offered by insurance companies, and retirement and disability pension plans. For further information, see William J. Matteson and E. C. Harwood, *Life Insurance and Annuities from the Buyer's Point of View*, American Institute for Economic Research, Great Barrington, Mass., 1954.

Anticipation Survey   A survey of the expectations of business firms and consumers. The use of anticipations data from surveys has become an important element in the forecasting of short-term business conditions. Anticipations data are divided into two broad classes. First, there are expectations relating to the future behavior of business as a whole, such as sales or the climate of the financial markets, which are beyond the individual firm's control. These expectations are called market anticipations. Second, there are anticipations about the future actions of the economic unit (firm or household), such as plans to install capital equipment or to make certain consumer purchases. These anticipations, over which the individual or firm has control, are known as intentions or plans. The two types of expectations are closely related, since business or consumer intentions are highly dependent on the relevant market anticipations. Since World War II, the systematic collection of anticipations data through survey methods has greatly expanded, and information on many aspects of consumer and business expectations is now compiled periodically. Perhaps the most useful anticipations data collected are those of capital spending plans and sales expectations. The two main sources of these data are the *Annual Survey of Business Anticipations in Plant and Equipment Expenditures*, compiled jointly by the U.S. Department of Commerce and the Securities and Exchange Commission; and the McGraw-Hill Department of Economics surveys, *Business' Plans for New Plants and Equipment*. The two principal sources of information on consumer anticipations of purchases, finances, etc., are the Survey Research Center of the University of Michigan and the U.S. Bureau of the Census. For additional details on the use of anticipation surveys in forecasting, see

National Bureau of Economic Research, Inc., *The Quality and Economic Significance of Anticipations Data,* Princeton University Press, Princeton, N.J., 1960; Conference on Research in Income and Wealth, *Short-term Economic Forecasting,* Studies in Income and Wealth, vol. 12, Princeton University Press, Princeton, N.J., 1955; Franco Modigliani and H. Weingartner, "Forecasting Uses of Anticipatory Data on Investment and Sales," *Quarterly Journal of Economics,* pp. 23–55, Harvard University Press, Cambridge, Mass., February, 1958.

Antitrust Legislation   Legislation that prohibits monopoly, restraints of trade, and conspiracies to inhibit competition. Laws of this type are based on common law originating in the opposition of British courts to illegal grants of monopoly by the Crown during the seventeenth century, and on the long-standing resistance to conspiracy and to contracts that restrict the freedom to choose and pursue one's trade. The first U.S. antitrust laws were enacted in Kansas in 1889; some forty states now enforce them. The first Federal law, the Sherman Antitrust Act of 1890, outlawed monopolies, restraints of trade, and every contract, combination, trust, or conspiracy to achieve them, but without defining these terms. It was followed by the Federal Trade Commission Act of September 26, 1914, which created the Commission and empowered it to prevent persons, partnerships, or corporations (except banks and common carriers otherwise controlled) from using unfair methods of competition and unfair deceptive acts or practices in commerce. This law was strengthened by the Clayton Antitrust Act of October 15, 1914, which outlawed price discrimination, exclusive or tying contracts, intercorporate stockholdings, interlocking directorates, and, by amendment in 1950, direct or indirect acquisition of a competitor's assets if this action substantially lessened competition. The Robinson-Patman Act of 1936 amended the Clayton Act with regard to price discrimination. Specifically, it prohibited suppliers from soliciting business from large customer firms, such as chain stores and mail-order houses, by offering terms more favorable than the real savings in cost that would result from handling a large order. It also enjoined large integrated companies from making traditional charges (such as brokerage fees, advertising allowances, and fees for other services) unless the costs were actually incurred. This act, which is often said to aim as much at preserving small firms as at curbing restraints of trade, symbolizes the dilemma of the Antitrust Division in the Department of Justice and of the Federal Trade Commission. They must find the means to prevent a firm from acquiring great market power without destroying its incentive to prosper and grow more than its competitors, and also to avoid penalizing a large firm, which can often be much more efficient than its smaller competitors. See Corwin Edwards, *Big Business and the Policy of Competition,* Western Reserve University Press, Cleveland, 1956; ————, *Foreign Anti-trust Laws in the 1960's,* The Brookings Institution, Washington, D.C., 1962.

Application for FHA Insurance   *See Request for VA Appraisal.*

Applied Research   Scientific investigation aimed at discovering new products and processes, usually with specific profit-making objectives. Applied research differs from basic research, which has no specific profit-making objectives, chiefly in terms of economic purpose. In methods and procedures, however, it is often difficult to distinguish between the two. As of 1970, about $6 billion was being spent annually on applied research in the U.S., compared with less than $500 million at the end of World War II. Statistics on applied research are published by the National Science Foundation, Washington, D.C., in its periodic *Reviews of Data on Research and Development.* For a forecast of applied research expenditures, see Dexter M. Keezer et al., "The Outlook for Expenditures on Research and Development during the Next Decade," Papers and Proceedings, 72d annual meeting of the American Economic Association, *American Economic Review,* Evanston, Ill., May, 1960.

Applied Research Expenditures in U.S. (Billions of dollars)

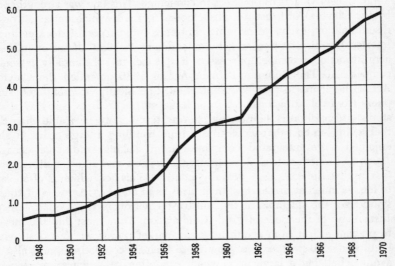

Source: National Science Foundation.

Appreciation An increase in the market value of an asset (stocks, bonds, plant and equipment, real estate, and the like) above its value at some prior period. It is the opposite of depreciation. Generally, appreciation is not recognized until it has actually been realized through the sale of the asset. For example, a private home in a fine location was purchased for $35,000 in 1960, but within a decade the value of the location and the house appreciated until it was worth $50,000. When the owner sold the house for $50,000 in 1970, the appreciation on his original investment was $15,000. Current accounting practice frowns on the writing up of business assets. For current accounting practice, see Walter B. Meigs and Charles E. Johnson, *Accounting*, McGraw-Hill Book Company, New York, 1967.

Appropriation, Federal A financial grant by the Congress of the U.S. for a stated purpose, such as permitting a Federal agency to place an order, to award a contract, or to buy goods and services and thus to commit the government to expenditure in the future. The rates at which appropriations are obligated and expenditures carried out are determined by the various Federal departments and agencies, subject to the control of the U.S. Bureau of the Budget. The appropriation is the most important form of new obligational authority. For details of the process by which the Federal government reaches decisions on expenditure, see Arthur Smithies, *The Budgetary Process in the United States*, McGraw-Hill Book Company, New York, 1955; see also Murray L. Weidenbaum, "The Federal Government Spending Process," in U.S. Joint Economic Committee, *Federal Expenditure Policy for Economic Growth and Stability*, Government Printing Office, Washington, D.C., 1957; for current statistics, see U.S. Bureau of the Budget, *The Federal Budget in Brief* and *The Budget Review*, annual reports.

A Priori Estimates *See Extraneous Estimates.*

Arbitrage The act of simultaneously purchasing foreign exchange, securities, commodities, or other goods in one market and selling them in another market at a higher price. The following example, using foreign exchange, best shows the operation. Let us suppose that at a given moment one British pound (£1) is trading for $2.62 in London and that at the same time £1 is trading for $2.58 in New York. This difference in exchange rates (prices) between the two markets allows a nimble arbitrager to buy pounds in New York at $2.58 per pound and sell them in London for $2.62, thus making a profit of 4 cents per pound, less any costs arising from the transaction. An arbitrager can profit whenever the price differential between the two markets exceeds the cost of the transactions. Generally the act of arbitraging tends to decrease any price differential between the two markets. See Lester V. Chandler, *The Economics of Money and Banking,* Harper & Row, Publishers, Incorporated, New York, 1964, pp. 437–438; Alan R. Holmes, *The New York Foreign Exchange Market,* Federal Reserve Bank of New York, New York, 1959, pp. 42–54.

Arbitration The settlement of differences between two parties—usually labor and management—by a third party known as an arbitrator. Arbitration in labor disputes is divided into two types. The first, called arbitration of rights, involves a dispute arising during the life of a contract between union and management. This type of arbitration is provided for in more than 90% of all U.S. collective bargaining agreements. Unions and managements are willing to accept this kind of arbitration because it involves only the interpretation of the principles and rules governing the relationships between them, which have already been established in the collective bargaining process. This type of arbitration often involves a worker's claim that he has been treated unfairly in promotion or layoff procedures. The second type, called arbitration of interests, consists of the negotiation of a new contract. In such an arbitration, which is much less common, wages and working conditions are usually at issue. The arbitration in 1963–1964 of featherbedding on railroads by a committee composed of public, private, and interested parties brought this type of arbitration into prominence in the U.S. See Joseph Shister, *The Economics of the Labor Market,* J. B. Lippincott Company, Philadelphia, 1956; Melvin W. Reder, *Labor in a Growing Economy,* John Wiley & Sons, Inc., New York, 1957.

Area Redevelopment Program A Federal government program to stimulate industry and employment in economically depressed areas. It was enacted into law in the Area Redevelopment Act of 1961. The act provides for a Federal program of loans, grants, and technical assistance to private enterprises and public communities to attract new industries to depressed areas. It also includes provisions for the retraining of unemployed persons in these areas and for the payment of an allowance to such individuals while they are training for new jobs.

Arrival Draft *See Draft.*

Assessed Valuation The value placed on privately owned property by local public officials, such as boards of assessors, as a basis for computing local property taxes. Although assessors are supposed to appraise property at its fair market value, in practice they generally appraise it at less than this value. The result of this official underevaluation of property is a higher local tax rate. For general information on property valuation, see Alfred A. Ring, *The Valuation of Real Estate*, Prentice-Hall, Inc., Englewood Cliffs, N.J., 1963.

Asset   A physical property or intangible right, owned by a business or an individual, that has a value. An asset is useful to its owner, either because it is the source of future services or because it can be used to secure future benefits. Business assets are usually divided into two categories, current and fixed. Current assets, which are those that can readily be turned into cash, include cash on hand, accounts receivable, inventories, and marketable securities. Fixed, or noncurrent, assets, which are those that cannot readily be turned into cash without disrupting the business operations and which are generally held for more than one year, include land, buildings, equipment, and long-term investments. Another type of fixed assets, called intangible assets, consist of certain nonmaterial rights and benefits of a firm, such as patents, copyrights, trademarks, and goodwill. For additional information see George MacFarland et al., *Accounting Fundamentals*, 3d ed., McGraw-Hill Book Company, New York, 1957; William A. Paton and Robert L. Dixon, *Essentials of Accounting*, The Macmillan Company, New York, 1958.

Assignment   A written transfer of property or rights from one person or company to another. The term is generally used in connection with two specific transfers, assignment of contracts and assignment for the benefit of creditors. Contracts calling for a money payment can be assigned without consultation with, or approval by, the person obliged to pay. Assignment for the benefit of creditors is a method of settlement whereby a debtor assigns his property to a trustee who administers and liquidates it so as to pay off the debtor's obligations in the best way possible. This method is falling into disuse because the Federal Bankruptcy Act considers this type of assignment an act of bankruptcy, and any creditor who has not agreed to the assignment can have it set aside by instituting bankruptcy proceedings. See Jules I. Bogen (ed.), *Financial Handbook*, The Ronald Press Company, New York, 1952; Charles W. Gerstenberg, *Financial Organization and Management of Business*, 4th ed., Prentice-Hall, Inc., Englewood Cliffs, N.J., 1959.

Atomistic Economy   An economy in which many small independent producers compete in each industry. In an atomistic industry, the theoretical models of pure competition are approximately valid. Each seller is so small that he accepts the selling price for his goods as more or less given and adjusts his output to this market price. No seller (or buyer) acting independently in an atomistic industry can perceptibly influence price, and the large number of firms rules out the possibility of collusive restraint of output. The U.S. had a more or less atomistic economy in the first half of the nineteenth century before the widespread emergence of large-scale production and big business. Among industries that have approached the atomistic model in recent times are agriculture, coal mining, and cotton textile manufacturing. For additional information, see Joe S. Bain, *Industrial Organization*, 2d ed., John Wiley & Sons, Inc., New York, 1968.

Attachment A legal means taken by a creditor to stop financial loss to him. Attachment is a temporary expedient for use in an emergency situation. It could result from an action on the part of a debtor, such as fraud, insolvency while goods are in transit, or assignment of goods to a third party. In order to satisfy his claim, the creditor must obtain a writ of seizure of property. This writ is served on the debtor by a sheriff or other levying officer. For additional details, see William J. Shultz and Hedwig Reinhardt, *Credit and Collection Management*, 3d ed., Prentice-Hall, Inc., Englewood Cliffs, N.J., 1962, pp. 323–325.

Austerity Program A government program designed to reduce temporarily the level of consumption in a country, undertaken in order to free resources for greater capital investment, to reduce imports and help balance international payments, or to make a larger proportion of resources available for other purposes, such as the prosecution of a war. It can be achieved by raising taxes or tariffs, by instituting government controls over the output of certain industries or of the nation as a whole, or by regulating consumption directly. The United Kingdom, in particular, has carried out austerity programs at various times in its history to attain desired goals. For additional details on austerity in the United Kingdom, see Sir Roy F. Harrod, *The British Economy*, McGraw-Hill Book Company, New York, 1963, pp. 63–64; C. T. Sandford, *Economics of Public Finance*, Pergamon Press, London, 1969.

Austrian School The name applied to a group of late nineteenth-century Austrian economists, led by Karl Menger, Friedrich von Wieser, and Eugen von Böhm-Bawerk, who adopted a more subjective approach to economics than earlier economists had, emphasizing the concepts of demand and utility and changing the previous emphasis on production and supply. Basic to their analysis was the theory of diminishing marginal utility, whereby a diminishing quantity of satisfaction is derived from successive units of a good, given an unchanging demand. These economists believed that the value of a good depends on the pleasure or utility derived from it and thus varies directly with the strength of the demand and inversely with the supply of the good. Besides its theory of value, the school was noted for its theory of interest and capital. Böhm-Bawerk, the principal exponent of the theory, treated capital as a commodity and interest as the price paid for the use of capital. The rate of interest was determined by consumers' preferences for present over future goods, and by the possibility of increasing the productivity of a given process through an increase in its roundaboutness, or period of production. For additional details, see Joseph A. Schumpeter, *History of Economic Analysis*, Oxford University Press, Fair Lawn, N.J., 1954; Mark Blaug, *Economic Theory in Retrospect*, Richard D. Irwin, Inc., Homewood, Ill., 1962; Eugen von Böhm-Bawerk, *The Positive Theory of Capital*, G. E. Stechert & Company, New York, 1923.

Autarchy   The economic self-sufficiency of a nation or group of nations. A policy of national autarchy requires extensive government controls to ensure economic isolation from the rest of the world. Among these controls are tight restrictions on foreign trade, especially limitations of imports and capital movements; exchange controls; and planning of domestic production to provide the economy with all the goods it needs. Nations usually pursue a policy of autarchy for political rather than economic reasons: to achieve self-sufficiency for military considerations or to protect themselves against hostile nations unwilling to trade with them. Programs of autarchy were undertaken by Soviet Russia in the early years after the revolution as well as by the fascist economies of Germany and Italy in the 1930s. Since World War II the Communist countries of Eastern Europe have pursued a policy of bloc autarchy, maintaining the economic self-sufficiency of the entire bloc while expanding trade within it. For further information, see C. S. Tippets, *Autarchy: National Self-sufficiency*, Public Policy Pamphlet 5, The University of Chicago Press, Chicago, 1933; J. M. Keynes, "National Self-sufficiency," *Yale Review*, New Haven, Conn., Summer, 1933.

Authorized Stock   The maximum amount of all classes of stock that can be issued by a corporation. The authorization is contained in the certificate of incorporation, which may be amended by the corporation's stockholders according to statute. Not all authorized stock may be issued; that part which is not issued is kept in reserve for possible future financing. For further information, see Jules I. Bogen (ed.), *Financial Handbook*, 4th ed., The Ronald Press Company, New York, 1968.

Autocorrelation   A situation in regression analysis that exists when the historical actual data that constitute a *dependent* variable are not randomly distributed around the calculated regression line. In practice, in the case of the equation $\hat{Y} = a + bX$, it is not required that observations constituting the independent variable X be random. Neither is it required that successive values of the dependent variable Y be random. However, deviations of actual from computed values (Y minus $\hat{Y}$) should be random if the squared standard error of estimate $\bar{S}_{yx}{}^2$ and the coefficient of determination $\bar{R}_{yx}{}^2$ are to be unbiased. Autocorrelation, when detected, can be reduced or eliminated by converting the dependent variable to first differences. For additional information, see Karl A. Fox, *Intermediate Economic Statistics,* John Wiley & Sons, Inc., New York, 1968; Lawrence R. Klein, *A Textbook of Econometrics,* Row, Peterson & Company, Evanston, Ill., 1953.

Automatic Stabilizer (Built-in Stabilizer)   An economic shock absorber that helps smooth the swings of incomes and prices without constant changes in government policy. Personal and corporate income taxes and unemployment insurance are among the most important automatic stabilizers in the U.S. When business begins to sag, the government's income tax receipts immediately decline by a larger proportion than personal income, and payments to the unemployed rise. Thus, consumer buying power is strengthened, and recessionary pressures are tempered. Social security and farm-aid programs also act as built-in stabilizers. In combination, these stabilizers have been credited with a key role in the prompt reversal of U.S. recessions since World War II. This point is discussed by M. O. Clement, "The Quantitative Impact of Automatic Stabilizers," *Review of Economics and Statistics,* Harvard University Press, Cambridge, Mass., February, 1960; see also Sumner H. Slichter, "Thinking Ahead: Break Up of the Business Cycle," *Harvard Business Review,* Harvard Graduate School of Business Administration, Boston, January–February, 1955; Alvin H. Hansen, *Economic Issues of the 1960's,* McGraw-Hill Book Company, New York, 1960, pp. 140–150; Thomas F. Dernburg and Duncan M. McDougall, *Macroeconomics,* McGraw-Hill Book Company, New York, 1968.

Automation   The use of advanced mechanical equipment, especially in combination with high-speed computers and other self-regulating controls. The word, which is an abbreviation of "automatization," was first used by D. S. Harder in the General Motors Fisher Body Division in 1935, when he set up an automation engineering department and a manufacturing department in the Grand Rapids plant. Automation includes almost every operation that dispenses with human assistance or control, whether because of the newly developed control machinery or because of mechanical improvements on the assembly line. Although automation is credited with much of the increase in productivity that industrial nations throughout the world have experienced since World War II, its full economic impact is difficult to assess. On the one hand, its introduction has permitted significant cost reductions and made feasible tasks that would have been impractical without it. On the other hand, it has helped aggravate the problem of unemployment by reducing the need for labor, especially unskilled labor. See U.S. Joint Economic Committee, *New Views on Automation,* Government Printing Office, Washington, D.C., 1960; for further discussion of the problems and potentials of automation, see John Diebold, *Automation: The Advent of the Automatic Factory,* D. Van Nostrand Company, Inc., Princeton, N.J., 1953; Norbert Wiener, *The Human Use of Human Beings,* Houghton Mifflin Company, Boston, 1954, especially chap. 9; Paul Einzig, *The Economic Consequences of Automation,* W. W. Norton & Company, Inc., New York, 1957; for current statistics on automated equipment bought by industry, see *How Modern Is American Industry?,* McGraw-Hill Department of Economics, New York, November, 1970.

**Expenditures for Automated
Equipment (Billions of dollars)**

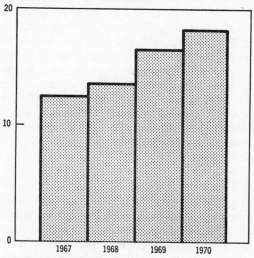

Source: McGraw-Hill Department of Economics.

Autonomous Investment   Investment that is determined independently of existing economic conditions, such as the level of national income or consumption. Induced investment, in contrast, depends on existing and anticipated economic conditions. The development of new products and new production techniques is a major force underlying autonomous investment. Investment induced by sociological, psychological, and political conditions also is considered autonomous. Thus, investment in Western railroads in the U.S. in the nineteenth century was investment of the autonomous type. See G. H. Fisher, "Endogenous and Exogenous Investment in Macro-economic Models," *Review of Economics and Statistics,* vol. 35, pp. 211–220, Harvard University Press, Cambridge, Mass., May, 1953; D. Hamburg and Charles L. Schultze, "Autonomous Investment vs. Induced Investment," *Economic Journal,* Royal Economic Society, London, March, 1961.

Autonomous Variable A variable in statistics and econometrics that is not wholly dependent on economic factors. Its movement cannot be predicted from a correlation with business activity. Usually, it is a variable the structure of which does not change freely in the short run. Investment expenditures are generally considered an autonomous variable. See Elmer C. Bratt, *Business Cycles and Forecasting,* Richard D. Irwin, Inc., Homewood, Ill., 1948.

Autoregression The possibility that the error term in an econometric equation may be correlated with one or more lagged endogenous variables included in the equation. The lagged endogenous variables are, in effect, predetermined values, each standing in a regression relationship with one or more of the immediately preceding terms. Econometric equations involving lags of an endogenous variable are called autoregressive. The inclusion of such variables nullifies any assumption that the error inherent in the estimating equation is not correlated with any predetermined value. For additional information, see Lawrence R. Klein, *A Textbook of Econometrics,* Row, Peterson & Company, Evanston, Ill., 1953; Stefan Valavanis, *Econometrics,* McGraw-Hill Book Company, New York, 1959.

Autoregressive Transformation The procedure whereby the original variables in an autoregressive system where there is autocorrelation in the error term are restated in such form that the error term is uncorrelated. For example, the conversion of variables to first differences may have the desired result. For additional information, see Lawrence R. Klein, *A Textbook of Econometrics,* Row, Peterson & Company, Evanston, Ill., 1953.

Average A figure describing the typical or characteristic value of a group of numbers. It usually refers to the arithmetic mean, which is the sum of all values divided by the number of values included. Arithmetic means are commonly used in expressing baseball players' batting averages and stock-market averages. Although widely employed, the arithmetic mean is limited in utility by the fact that it is influenced by extremely high or low values in a group, whereas the median and the mode are not influenced in the same way. The term average includes a group of statistical measures besides the mean that indicate the typical or characteristic value. One of these measures is the median, which is the middle value in an array of values from high to low. Another is the mode, the most frequently occurring value in a group of values. See Frederick E. Croxton et al., *Applied General Statistics*, 3d ed., Prentice-Hall, Inc., Englewood Cliffs, N.J., 1967.

B

Backdoor Financing   A method of financing Federal programs by bypassing usual congressional appropriations procedures. It eliminates review by appropriations committees. Known also as the public debt transaction, the device authorizes a government agency to borrow from the Treasury rather than depend on congressional appropriations. The justification for this method is that it merely involves a lending program; since the Treasury will be repaid, there is no need for outright appropriations. Theoretically, the borrowed sums must be repaid, but in the past Congress has canceled the larger part of a debt when an agency has been unable to repay it. Backdoor financing was first used in the depression of the 1930s, when the Reconstruction Finance Corporation (RFC) was established to revitalize business. To accelerate operations, Congress gave the RFC borrowing power and thus avoided the necessity for yearly appropriations. Originally, loans were to be repaid, but by the time the RFC closed its books in 1957, Congress had canceled $12.8 billion of the $26.6 billion that the RFC had borrowed from the Treasury. Since then the technique has spread rapidly. For further information, see Charles B. Seib, "Backdoor Spending Dodges Congress' Control," *Nation's Business*, October, 1958, pp. 48–57.

Backlog of Unfilled Orders An accumulation of orders received by manufacturers for products to be shipped at a later date. Manufacturers' backlogs depend on both the rate at which new orders are received and the rate at which they are shipped. In the period 1968–1971, U.S. manufacturers added producing capacity more rapidly than the volume of new orders grew. As a result, the time elapsing between the receipt of an order and shipment of the goods declined, and the backlog of unfilled orders generally dwindled. To the business economist, short-run fluctuations in backlog volume are an important tool for forecasting short-term business trends. A rapidly growing backlog suggests a steadily rising production level; a declining backlog suggests cutbacks. The level of unfilled orders for major industries is reported in U.S. Department of Commerce, *Survey of Current Business,* monthly.

Manufacturers Unfilled Orders, New Orders, and Shipments
(Billions of dollars, monthly average)

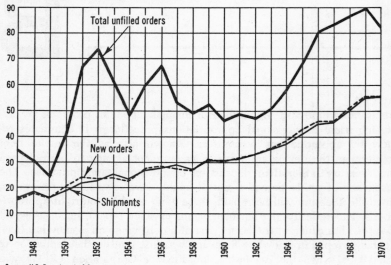

Source: U.S. Department of Commerce.

Backwash Effect An unfavorable condition arising in underdeveloped countries as a result of the emphasis placed on export trade (usually only raw materials) at the expense of the growth of domestic manufacturing and the industrialization of rural areas. Some economists claim that the backwash effect of trade has been stronger than the spread effect. By slowing down much-needed industrialization in underdeveloped countries, the backwash effect presents a major obstacle to development and results in increasing disparities in productivity between advanced and underdeveloped countries. For additional information, see Gunnar Myrdal, *Economic Theory and the Underdeveloped Regions,* Gerald Duckworth & Co., Ltd., London, 1957.

Bailout An attempt to use corporate funds to provide payments to shareholders which are taxable at favorable capital gains rates and do not adversely affect the shareholders' relative interest in the corporation. Among types of bailouts are additional stock dividends and debt financing. For a discussion, see J. H. Alexander and W. B. Landis, Jr., "Bail Outs and the Internal Revenue Code," *Yale Law Journal,* New Haven, Conn., June, 1956, p. 909.

Balanced Budget The equalization of revenues and expenditures over a period of time. Traditionally, the annually balanced budget has been the basis of sound government fiscal policy, since it serves as an important check to irresponsible action and promotes business confidence. Whereas political support for increased government spending and lower taxes is easy to secure, adherence to a balanced budget limits the use of these steps. Seen in this light, the balanced budget has come to mean any surplus of government revenues over expenditures. Although balancing the budget is the long-standing method of ensuring fiscal responsibility, according to many economists it runs counter to the goal of economic growth and stability. During a period of recession, tax revenues fall; taxes may be raised and/or expenditures reduced, or both may take place, to eliminate the resulting deficit. Such measures generally aggravate the recession, however, causing income and tax revenues to fall still further. Similarly, during a period of inflation, a balanced-budget program requires that rising tax revenues be offset by lowered taxes or by increased government expenditures, both of which steps accelerate inflation. For this reason, some economists argue that the conventional wisdom of the balanced budget is outmoded and that government deficits and surpluses ought to be used as part of a planned compensatory fiscal policy to stabilize the fluctuations of the business cycle. For additional information, see Alvin H. Hansen, *Fiscal Policy and Business Cycles,* W. W. Norton & Company, Inc., New York, 1941; Walter Heller, *New Dimensions of Political Economy,* Harvard University Press, Cambridge, Mass., 1966; Herbert Stein, *The Fiscal Revolution in America,* The University of Chicago Press, Chicago, 1969.

Balanced Growth A program of coordinated growth of all sectors of the economy. Usually, developing countries plan a balanced growth for their economies. Thus, in an undeveloped nation, the success of a program of capital formation depends on complementary production. Goods produced by the new production facilities must be demanded by consumers, and the productive factors required for expanded manufacturing must be available. Balanced growth requires that investment take place in clusters. For example, a plan for the construction of a steel mill should include coal and iron ore mines, a transportation system, and a market for the finished output. The basic purpose of a program of balanced growth is to minimize the occurrence of bottlenecks and gluts in the various sectors of the economy. It usually requires some planning by the central government to ensure the undertaking of the necessary projects. For further information, see Benjamin Higgins, *Economic Development,* W. W. Norton & Company, Inc., New York, 1968; Hans Singer, *The Concept of Balanced Growth and Economic Development: Theory and Facts,* University of Texas Conference on Economic Development, Austin, Tex., April, 1958.

Balanced Sample   A purposive sample drawn in such a way that the sample mean value of some known characteristic approximates or is identical to a known population mean for the same characteristic. The sample is then used to derive estimates of characteristics whose values are not known. The notion that such a sample will be more representative in respect to some unknown characteristic than a random sample has not received unanimous expert endorsement.

Balance of Payments   A systematic record of all the economic transactions between one country and the rest of the world in a given period, usually one year. Among the principal international economic transactions are the movement of goods, services, interest and dividends, gifts, and short- and long-term investments, currency shipments, and gold movements. Each transaction gives rise either to a foreign claim for payment, recorded as a debit (e.g., from imports, capital outflows), or a foreign obligation to pay, recorded as a credit (e.g., from exports, capital inflows). Each debit transaction in the balance of payments of one country is automatically accompanied by a credit entry in that of another. By totaling all debit and credit transactions between the residents (individuals, business firms, and government) of one country and the residents of all other countries, a statement of the international economic relationships of an individual country is provided. The balance of payments is generally divided into three accounts: current, capital, and gold. The current account includes the flow of goods and services and thus represents payments for and receipts from imports and exports, including interest and dividends. The capital account, which includes the transfer of short- and long-term investments, represents all additions to or subtractions from a stock of investment. The third major account is that of compensatory gold movements. In recent years the U.S. balance-of-payments presentation has focused on two official definitions of the overall surplus or deficit—the balance on liquidity and the balance on official reserve transactions. In 1971, the presentation was altered to give emphasis to six balances: the balance on goods and services; the balance on goods, services, and remittances; the balance on current account; the balance on current account and long-term capital; the net liquidity balance; and the official reserve transactions balance. As an accounting method, the balance of payments must balance over a given period; because of its double entry nature, debits must always equal credits. If a country's receipts (credits) fall short of its payments (debits), it has a balance-of-payments deficit and must export gold to meet its obligations for the remaining payments. If, on the other hand, credits exceed debits, the country has a balance-of-payments surplus, and an inflow of gold will take place to bring the accounting statement into balance. For quarterly data on the U.S. balance of payments, see U.S. Department of Commerce, *Survey of Current Business*, March, June, September, and December issues; for a more comprehensive collection of balance-of-payments data for different regions and countries, see International Monetary Fund, *Balance of Payments Yearbook*, Washington, D.C.; see also Donald Badger, "The Balance of Payments: A Toll of Economic Analysis," *International Monetary Fund Staff Papers*, Washington, D.C., September, 1951, vol. 2, pp. 86–197; J. E. Meade, *The Balance of Payments*, Oxford University Press, Fair Lawn, N.J., 1951.

Balance of Trade (Merchandise Balance)   The difference between the value of the goods that a nation exports and the value of the goods that it imports. The balance of trade differs from the balance of payments in that it excludes capital transactions, payments for services, and shipments of gold. When a country has an export surplus, its balance is favorable; when it has a deficit, its balance is unfavorable. The balance-of-trade concept is losing much of its usefulness because of the growing volume of capital transactions and payments for services. For example, in every year during the 1950s and 1960s, the U.S. enjoyed a surplus in its balance of trade but suffered an almost uninterrupted succession of deficits in its balance of payments. Merchandise trade statistics for Western countries are reported in Statistical Office of the United Nations, *Monthly Bulletin of Statistics*, New York; those for the U.S. are reported in great detail in *Department of Commerce Report FT110* (for imports) and *Department* *of Commerce Report FT410* (for exports); see Walter S. Salant and Associates, *The United States Balance of Payments in 1968,* The Brookings Institution, Washington, D.C., 1963.

U.S. Balance of Trade
(In millions of dollars)

	Merchandise Exports	Merchandise Imports	Balance of Trade
1951	14,123	11,202	+2,921
1952	13,319	10,838	+2,481
1953	12,281	10,990	+1,291
1954	12,799	10,354	+2,445
1955	14,280	11,527	+2,753
1956	17,379	12,804	+4,575
1957	19,390	13,291	+6,099
1958	16,264	12,952	+3,312
1959	16,295	15,310	+ 985
1960	19,489	14,732	+3,757
1961	19,954	14,510	+5,444
1962	20,976	16,392	+4,584
1963	22,428	17,136	+5,292
1964	25,836	18,744	+7,092
1965	26,748	21,432	+5,316
1966	29,496	25,620	+3,876
1967	31,032	26,892	+4,140
1968	34,068	33,228	+ 840
1969	37,332	36,048	+1,284
1970	42,660	39,960	+2,700

SOURCE: U.S. Department of Commerce.

Balance Sheet   A statement of a firm's financial position on a particular day of the year; as of that moment, it provides a complete picture of what the firm owns (its assets), what it owes (its liabilities), and its net worth. The balance sheet should not be confused with the income statement, which is a record of a year's operations. Assets are customarily divided into two parts, current assets and fixed assets. Current assets include cash on hand, investment in government securities, accounts receivable (the amount owed to the company by its customers), inventories, and other short-term investments. Fixed assets include land, buildings, and equipment. Liabilities are divided into current obligations, which fall due within a year, and long-term debt. Current liabilities consist of accounts payable (what the company owes to its suppliers), short-term loans, interest, and accrued taxes. Long-term liabilities include such items as long-term bank loans, bonds, and mortgages. By subtracting total liabilities from total assets, a company's net worth or a stockholder's share in the business may be ascertained. Net worth is the value of all outstanding stock, usually listed at par value or the issue price, plus any surpluses. A balance sheet always balances in total, but no individual item necessarily matches another. See H. A. Finney and H. E. Miller, *Principles of Accounting,* 6th ed., Prentice-Hall, Inc., Englewood Cliffs, N.J., 1965.

Bank Credit Proxy   A rough daily estimate of movements in commercial bank loans and investments. This is a measure of bank credit from the liability side. The proxy is composed of all deposits at member banks and is adjusted to include nondeposit liabilities such as bank-related commercial paper, loan participations and sales, and Euro-dollar deposits. The bank credit proxy was developed to assist the Federal Reserve operate monetary policy. Some economists view bank credit as having a more direct effect on spending than money or money-related variables. Since credit can be identified with outlays by particular economic sectors, the use of the bank credit proxy allows analysis of the quality and distribution of credit. See "Monetary Aggregates and Money Market Conditions in Open Market Policy," *Federal Reserve Bulletin,* February, 1971.

Bank Debits   The total dollar value of checks which depositors write on their bank accounts during a certain period. Because the ratio of bank debits to demand deposits measures the use of deposit money, it is an important indicator of business activity. The figures on the volume of bank debits and demand deposits are compiled by the Federal Reserve System from reports by approximately 1,600 banks in 232 centers in the U.S. (New York City, where bank debits are heavily weighted by securities transactions, is not included). Excluded from this statistical series are debits to U.S. government accounts and interbank transactions, which are not directly related to business activity. For further information on bank debits, see George Garvy, *Debits and Clearings Statistics and Their Use,* Board of Governors of the Federal Reserve System, Washington, D.C., 1959; for statistics on debits to demand deposits, see *Federal Reserve Bulletin,* Washington, D.C., monthly.

Bank Deposit   The money in an account of a depositor (either an individual or a firm) in a bank. A bank deposit arises when (1) an individual or a firm puts cash in a bank, (2) some other asset is sold to a bank, or (3) a bank lends money to an individual. It is a bookkeeping item, constituting an asset for an individual and a liability for a bank. There are two types of bank deposits: demand deposits (money payable on demand)

Bank Debits Outside of New York City 232 Centers* (Billions of dollars)

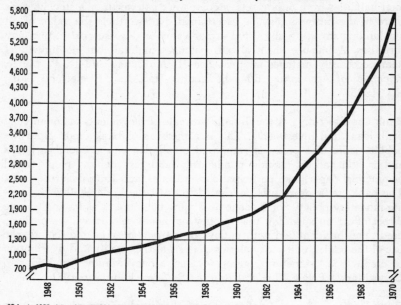

*Prior to 1955, data relates to 344 centers outside New York City, between 1956 and
  1963 data relates to 343 centers, and between 1964 and the present 232 centers.

Source: Board of Governors, Federal Reserve System.

and time deposits (money payable after a fixed period of time). As of
December 30, 1970, bank deposits in the U.S. totaled nearly $468 billion
($167 billion in demand deposits and $301 billion in time deposits),
exclusive of interbank and U.S. government deposits. See Lester V.
Chandler, *The Economics of Money and Banking*, 5th ed., Harper &
Row, Publishers, Incorporated, New York, 1969; for statistics on the
amounts and kinds of bank deposits, see *Federal Reserve Bulletin*, Washington, D.C., monthly.

Bank Discount   The difference between the face amount of a bank loan
and the amount credited to the borrower. It is the total amount of interest
paid by a borrower to a bank in advance rather than at fixed intervals or
at maturity. The interest is deducted at a fixed rate from the face amount
of the loan, and the remaining balance is credited to the borrower.

Banker's Acceptance   An agreement by a bank to pay specific bills for
one of its customers when the bills come due. It is usually used in international trade. For example, an American clothing firm might ask its bank

Total Bank Deposits (Billions of dollars)

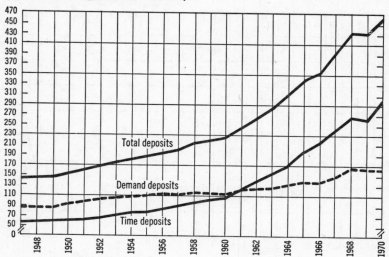

Source: Board of Governors, Federal Reserve System.

to accept a demand for payment from an Italian exporter. The obligation for payment is thus shifted from the importer to his bank, and the Italian exporter knows that the bank will pay. When the time draft drawn by the Italian exporter is stamped "accepted" by the American bank, it is known as a banker's acceptance. The exporter may discount the accepted draft, or he may hold it to maturity and collect the face value of the acceptance. Acceptance financing of international trade has grown steadily since World War II, in 1960 surpassing the previous record year of 1929. For a detailed discussion, see Federal Reserve Bank of New York, *Monthly Review,* June, 1961, pp. 94–100.

Banking School The name given to a group of nineteenth-century economists who argued that a mixed currency (bank notes and demand deposits) would expand and contract with the needs of business. Whereas the currency school held that only gold and redeemable notes were money, the banking school, led by Thomas Tooke and J. Fullarton, stressed the variety of sources of credit and emphasized the aspect of demand deposits as part of the money supply. Adherents of the banking school considered it more important to control the lending policies of the central bank, and so influence the quantity of demand deposits, than to try to limit the quantity of currency in circulation. They also adhered to the real-bills doctrine, which held that if banks limited their loans to self-liquidating

Bankers' Acceptances (Millions of dollars)

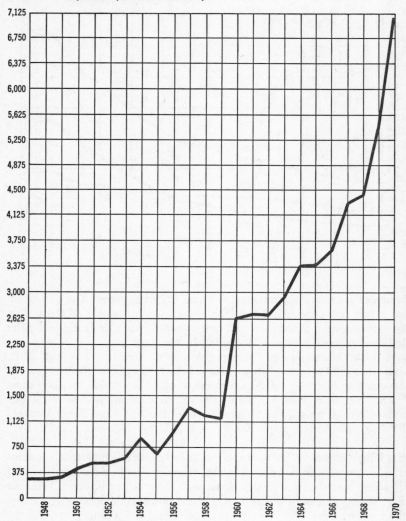

Source: Board of Governors, Federal Reserve System.

commercial paper (real bills), the money supply would adjust itself so as to be exactly adequate for business needs. If the banks ignored the policy of real bills only, the resulting rise in prices would lead to a *pari passu* increase in the money supply, so that there was no possibility of an inflation produced by the overexpansion of bank credit. For additional details on the controversy between the currency and banking schools, see Jacob Viner, *Studies in the Theory of International Trade*, Harper & Row, Publishers, Incorporated, New York, 1937; see also M. R. Dougherty, "The Currency-Banking Controversy," *Southern Journal of Economics*, Southern Economic Association and University of North Carolina, Chapel Hill, N.C., October, 1942, and January, 1943.

Banking System   The establishment of a group of financial institutions which foster a flow of credit and money that will facilitate orderly economic growth. Early banking systems served mainly as depositories for funds, while the more modern systems have considered the supplying of credit their main purpose. A system of banks now serves three main functions: (1) It lends money, (2) it accepts money on deposit, and (3) it creates and lends its own credit. The National Banking Act, passed on February 25, 1863, and amended many times thereafter, has served as the basis for the national banks of the U.S. Because of the defects and inefficiencies of the decentralized nation-state system, the act was further amended on December 23, 1913, when President Woodrow Wilson signed the Federal Reserve Act, establishing the Federal Reserve System and requiring all national banks to become members of it. For a discussion of the banking systems of sixteen countries, see Benjamin Haggott Beckhart, *Banking Systems*, Columbia University Press, New York, 1954; for information on the Federal Reserve System, see *The Federal Reserve System: Purposes and Functions*, Board of Governors of the Federal Reserve System, Washington, D.C., 1964.

Bankruptcy   A condition, legally declared by a court of law, of insolvency of individuals, partnerships, or corporations. Its purpose is to discharge the debtor from his debts and to protect his creditors by providing an orderly procedure for liquidation. The bankrupt debtor relinquishes all his property to a court-appointed receiver, who then transfers the assets to an elected trustee for disposal for creditors' benefits. Bankruptcy proceedings are of two types: (1) voluntary, in which the debtor submits a petition to a Federal district court requesting that he be declared bankrupt; and (2) involuntary, in which the creditors take the initiative and submit the petition to the court requesting that the debtor be declared bankrupt. Under the bankruptcy law, an individual, a partnership, or a corporation (except railroads, municipalities, and financial corporations) may be voluntary bankrupts. Any person (except farmers and wage earners) and any corporation (except railroads, municipalities, and financial corporations) can be declared an involuntary bankrupt. For further information, see Lincoln A. Lavine, *A Handbook on Bankruptcy*, Professional Publications, New York, 1941.

Bargaining Agent A union chosen by the employees of an appropriate bargaining unit to act as their representative and certified as such by the National Labor Relations Board. Controversies have arisen over the selection of a craft or an industrial union as the bargaining agent. Prior to the early 1940s, the Board has shown a preference for industrial unions over craft unions, but subsequently it has permitted skilled crafts to vote separately whenever they have wished to do so. This policy has not, however, been applied to steel, aluminum, and other mass-output industries, where the Board has maintained that production is so highly integrated that separation of crafts is not practical. For a general discussion of bargaining agents, see Lloyd G. Reynolds, *Labor Economics and Labor Relations*, 5th ed., Prentice-Hall, Inc., Englewood Cliffs, N.J., 1970; Neil W. Chamberlain and James W. Kuhn, *Collective Bargaining*, 2d ed., McGraw-Hill Book Company, New York, 1965.

Bargaining Theory of Wages A theory which holds that wages are determined by the relative bargaining strength of employers and employees. When workers join unions, wages rise because the relative strength of the labor rises. On the other hand, as the size of business enterprises grows, wages are pushed below the level which they would otherwise attain because the strength of employers rises. In general, the bargaining theory attempts to explain how wages are determined in the short run and not how they are determined over long periods of time. For a classic statement of the theory, see John R. Commons, *History of Labor in the United States*, The Macmillan Company, New York, 1951; J. K. Galbraith, *American Capitalism: The Theory of Countervailing Power*, Houghton Mifflin Company, Boston, 1952; for a critique, see Albert Rees, *The Economics of Trade Unions*, The University of Chicago Press, Chicago, 1962.

Bargaining Unit A group of employees with sufficiently similar interests (as members of the same craft or the same industry) so that it can be classed as a unit for purposes of negotiating a labor contract with management. At one extreme, a single employer may negotiate with representatives of a single skilled craft. At the other extreme, an employers' association may negotiate with an industrial union representing all employees in the industry throughout the nation. According to the U.S. Bureau of Labor Statistics, the great bulk of bargaining units in the U.S. include employees of a single company. For a general discussion of bargaining units, see Lloyd G. Reynolds, *Labor Economics and Labor Relations*, 5th ed., Prentice-Hall, Inc., Englewood Cliffs, N.J., 1970; Neil

W. Chamberlain and J. W. Kuhn, *Collective Bargaining*, 2d ed., McGraw-Hill Book Company, New York, 1965.

Base Period A point in time used as a reference point for business and economic data. It may be a selected month, year, or set of years. A month is generally too short, however, and is apt to be unusual because of seasonal factors; a year is a better period, and an average of several years is best. Whatever its length, a well-chosen base period should be sufficiently normal to provide a good basis of comparison; that is, it should not be at the bottom of a recession or at the peak of a boom. Until 1961, the average for 1947, 1948, and 1949 was used as the base period for most official U.S. government statistics. Then, beginning in 1962, there was a general shift to the average for 1957, 1958, and 1959 as the base period. In 1971, most official U.S. government statistics were shifted to a one-year base, 1967. In the calculation of index numbers, such as those for prices, production, and sales, the figures for the base period are usually averaged, and the average is made to equal 100. For additional details on the selection of base periods, see John E. Freund and Frank J. Williams, *Elementary Business Statistics*, Prentice-Hall, Inc., Englewood Cliffs, N.J., 1964, pp. 73–74.

Basic Research Original scientific investigation undertaken for the advancement of knowledge rather than immediate financial return. Basic research differs from applied research, which usually has specific profit-making objectives, in terms of economic progress. In methods and procedures, however, it is often difficult to distinguish between the two. As of 1970, more than $3.8 billion was being spent annually on basic research in the U.S., compared with less than $200 million at the end of World War II. Statistics on basic research expenditures are published in National Science Foundation, *Reviews of Data on Research and Development*, Washington, D.C., periodically; for a forecast of basic research expenditures, see Dexter M. Keezer et al., "The Outlook for Expenditures on Research and Development during the Next Decade," *Papers and Proceedings*, 72d annual meeting of the American Economic Association, *American Economic Review*, Evanston, Ill., May, 1960.

Basing-Point System A pricing system in which the seller sets his price by adding to a list price transportation costs between a fixed base, which is not necessarily the seller's plant, and the buyer's plant. An extreme illustration of this practice is the Pittsburgh-plus system formerly used by steel producers. Under this system, the price of steel was set by taking the Pittsburgh price and adding the cost of freight from Pittsburgh to the market regardless of the location of the shipping plant. If, for example,

Basic Research Expenditures in U.S. (Billions of dollars)

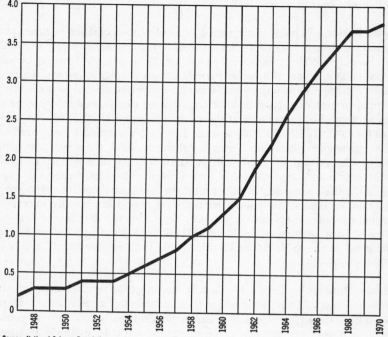

Source: National Science Foundation.

the price of a ton of steel in Pittsburgh was $50 and the freight to a Chicago customer was $10, the delivered price in Chicago was $60 no matter whether the steel came from a Chicago mill or a Pittsburgh mill. The basing-point system was most effective in industries in which transportation costs were high in relation to price. The arguments against the system are that it eliminates price competition, introduces geographical price discrimination, and results in wasteful crosshauling and uneconomic location of plants. Some economists disagree, suggesting that the practice is only one element in a complex economic system. For further information, see Fritz Machlup, *The Basing-Point System: An Economic Analysis of a Controversial Pricing Practice*, McGraw-Hill Book Company, New York, 1949.

Basis Point   A unit of measure used to express interest rates and bond yields. One basis point is equal to one-hundredth of a percent. Small-point differences in percentage rates of return are extremely significant in the bond markets because huge sums of money are involved. A 6% rate on a $100-million bond issue means that the borrower must pay $6 million a year in interest charges. An increase of only 15 basis points to 6.15% brings the interest cost to $6.15 million, an increase of $150,000. That is why yields are generally expressed in graduations of one-hundredth of a point.

Bayesian Statistics The translation of subjective forecasts into mathematical probability curves. Traditionally, statisticians use probabilities based on exhaustive empirical research. For example, if a coin were flipped an infinite number of times, the proportion of heads should be 0.5. In many business situations, however, there are no probabilities available because the process in question has not been in operation. Instead of a firmly tested probability, then, Bayesian statistics uses the best estimate of the given circumstances as if it were a firm probability. Named for Thomas Bayes, an eighteenth-century English clergyman who invented the first formula for using subjective probabilities, Bayesian statistics has become an important decision tool for modern business. For further information, see Röbert Schlaifer, *Probability and Statistics for Business Decisions*, McGraw-Hill Book Company, New York, 1959; ———, "Math Plus Intuition Equals Decision," *Business Week*, Mar. 24, 1962; for the application of Bayesian statistics to marketing problems, see Paul E. Green and Donald S. Tull, *Research for Marketing Decisions*, Prentice-Hall, Inc., Englewood Cliffs, N.J., 1966.

Bear A person who believes that the prices of stocks, bonds, commodities, or foreign exchange are going to decline and generally acts on this belief by selling short and hoping to buy back (cover) at a lower price. The term dates back to the early eighteenth century, when dealers on the London Stock Exchange were called bears if they thought the trend of stock and bond prices was down and bulls if they thought it was up. Why the more pessimistic dealers were called bears is difficult to say, but there are two plausible stories. First, the old proverb "to sell a bear's skin before one has caught the bear" describes what the bear on the stock exchange is doing, because the short seller does not own the stock he is selling—he has borrowed it. Second, "bear" may be a perversion of "bare," so that the "bear" seller is "bare" of the securities he has sold. See "Bulls and Bears," *Wall Street Journal*, Aug. 27, 1940; F. E. Armstrong, *The Book of the Stock Exchange*, Sir Isaac Pitman & Sons, Ltd., London, 1934, pp. 102–105.

Bear Market A market in which the prices of most of the items traded are declining. The term generally refers to falling stock, bond, or commodity markets. No precise origin of the term is known, but it is likely that someone coined it to refer to the London Stock Exchange when the "bears" (dealers who thought that prices were going to fall and sold stocks or bonds short) were dominant.

Bear Raid   Heavy short selling of a stock by one or more big traders who hoped to drive its price down far and fast so that they could profit by covering their short sales at lower prices. Bear raiders, who usually formed a pool, selected stocks that were in technically weak positions, stocks that had little popularity with investors. By flooding the market with sell orders, they were usually successful in pushing the price down. Bear raiding ended with the securities legislation of the 1930s, particularly the U.S. Securities and Exchange Commission's so-called 1939 rule, which states that a person can sell stock short under only two conditions. (1) The short sale price is higher than the price of the last sale. (2) If the short sale price is the same as that of the last sale, it must be higher than the last different price. This rule makes it impossible to "hammer the price down" because no short sale is executed in a declining market. See George L. Leffler and L. C. Farwell, *The Stock Market,* The Ronald Press Company, New York, 1963.

Beggar-My-Neighbor Tactics   Methods of increasing the exports of one country at the expense of those of other countries. Such actions as unnecessary currency depreciation or unprovoked tariff increases, especially in times of domestic unemployment, are generally considered beggar-my-neighbor tactics. It is argued that such tariff increases or currency depreciations increase domestic income and employment by causing a rise in the demand for domestic products since imports are reduced. However valid such an argument may be theoretically, in the real world beggar-my-neighbor policies induce swift retaliation by foreign countries who see their markets shrinking. Thus, beggar-my-neighbor tactics rarely produce much good and often result in competitive tariff increases or currency depreciation, causing a decrease in total world trade. For additional details, see Joan Robinson, "Beggar-My-Neighbor Remedies for Unemployment," in American Economic Association, *Readings in the Theory of International Trade,* Richard D. Irwin, Inc., Homewood, Ill., 1950.

Behavior Equations   These are based largely on what economic theory indicates that an individual or group of individuals acting as agents will do when faced with an economic decision. Theory suggests first which variables should be included in the analysis (that is, the conditions surrounding the decision) and second, given the conditions, the direction that the decision will take. Behavior equations may be contrasted with institutional equations where the pattern of action is prescribed by law, rule, or custom. For additional information, see T. C. Koopmans (ed.), *Statistical Inference in Dynamic Economic Models,* Cowles Commission Monograph no. 10, John Wiley & Sons, Inc., New York, 1950.

Bench Mark   An actual measurement of economic data in a specific time period that is used as a base for comparative purposes with comparable data. For example, figures for earlier U.S. censuses of business provide the base for current estimates of wholesale trade. Current data are derived by extrapolating bench-mark figures from the 1967 *Census of Business* on the basis of monthly reports of merchant wholesalers to the Bureau of the Census. For a discussion of bench marks and how they are used in the national income accounts, see Richard Ruggles and Nancy D. Ruggles, *National Income Accounts and Income Analysis,* McGraw-Hill Book Company, New York, 1956, pp. 160–162.

Benefits of Large-Scale Production   Economies in the productive process made possible because of the large scale on which the firm operates. For example, small firms must buy in less-than-carload lots, while larger firms may buy in carload lots or possibly in trainload lots, both of which lessen the transportation costs of purchased factors of production. In addition, technological methods which may be impractical at low levels of production become economically beneficial at higher levels. Small amounts of by-products may not be economically salable, but large and continuous quantities may find a ready market. Large purchasers of labor and other productive factors may find themselves in a position to dominate the economic lives of their suppliers and thus bargain for prices which smaller purchasers could not obtain. One of the most familiar advantages of large size is the ability to issue unsecured promissory notes to the public (known as commercial paper), on which the interest cost is considerably less than it is on commercial bank loans. None of these pecuniary benefits are to be confused with returns to scale in production, which involves the firm's production function. See Campbell R. McConnell, *Economics,* 4th ed., McGraw-Hill Book Company, New York, 1969, chap. 8.

Benefit Theory of Taxation   The principle that tax payments should be based on the amount of benefits received from government services. Thus, the cost of government services should be apportioned among individuals according to the relative benefits that they enjoy. Although the benefit theory may be applicable to certain fields in which the government functions as a commercial enterprise (e.g., the postal system, public power projects, etc.), it is generally very difficult to allocate the costs or benefits of the majority of government services among citizens with any degree of accuracy. Most services of modern governments are provided in the interest of group rather than individual welfare; thus, the cost of these activities cannot be divided and assigned logically to the recipients of the benefits. For example, there is no fair way of dividing the cost or benefit derived from the operation of a police force or from the workings of the judicial system. The benefit theory would also restrict the performance of certain socially desirable government services, such as relief to the needy and free public education, since the primary beneficiaries cannot afford the full cost of these programs. Application of the benefit theory of taxation is not widespread today, but it is used in such taxes as highway tolls, gas taxation, fishing and hunting licenses, and property taxation. For further information, see Richard A. Musgrave, *The Theory of Public Finance*, McGraw-Hill Book Company, New York, 1959, chap. 4; John F. Due, *Government Finance*, 4th ed., Richard D. Irwin, Inc., Homewood, Ill., 1968.

Bernstein Plan   A proposal by Edward M. Bernstein for a new international monetary reserve unit. The plan was to create reserve units each of which would be equal to one gold dollar and would consist of the eleven leading currencies in agreed-upon proportions. Participating countries could hold their reserves in any form—gold, foreign exchange, or reserve units. The Bernstein Plan does not increase the amount of international resources to finance expanding world trade. It merely substitutes an international unit for an equivalent amount of convertible currencies. For additional information, see E. M. Bernstein, "A Practical Program for International Monetary Reserves," *Quarterly Review and Investment Surveys*, Model, Roland and Company, New York, fourth quarter, 1963.

Best-Efforts Selling   *See Investment Banking.*

Beveridge Plan   A program designed to achieve a high standard of social security for Great Britain. Developed by Sir William Beveridge, it was to be carried out by a redistribution of income through social insurance and children's allowances. Benefits were to vary only on the basis of the size of the family and the age and sex of the family members, and they were to be paid for an unlimited time. The costs of the program were to be widely distributed, half of the support coming from general taxes and the other half from employer and employee contributions. For a detailed discussion of the plan, see Sir William Beveridge, *Social Insurance and Allied Services: The Beveridge Report*, The Macmillan Company, New York, 1942.

Bias In forecasting, the situation that exists when a set of forecasts typically understates or overstates the corresponding actual values. A strong pessimistic bias would be demonstrated by forecasts that consistently underestimated the actual level or changes for a series. A strong optimistic bias would be illustrated by forecasts that consistently overshot the actual level or changes for a series. A simple measure of bias is the mean error. A measure of the overall accuracy of forecasts, which can be used to separate the bias from the remaining error, is the mean square error. For additional information, see Victor Zarnowitz, *An Appraisal of Short-Term Economic Forecasts,* National Bureau of Economic Research Occasional Paper 104, Columbia University Press, New York, 1967.

Big Business Any business enterprise which is large in relation to the market it serves. The term is, however, most frequently identified with industrial corporations that control a large share of the *national* market for their product and large absolute amounts of capital and labor. American Telephone and Telegraph, Standard Oil (New Jersey), General Motors, and United States Steel are good examples of big business. Big business has been a feature of the U.S. economy since the Civil War. National markets grew as the nation moved westward, and big enterprises arose to satisfy the ensuing demand for industrial products. This expansion was made possible by the nation's rich supply of natural resources, labor, and venturesome entrepreneurs. In economic theory, the size of a business enterprise in relation to its market is an important criterion of determining the degree of monopoly or competition present in an industry. Size can be measured by the amount of total sales, the value of total assets, the number of employees, or the amount of income generated by a given firm. For additional information, see A. A. Berle, *The Twentieth Century Capitalist Revolution,* Harcourt, Brace & World, Inc., New York, 1954; A. D. H. Kaplan, *Big Enterprise in a Competitive System,* The Brookings Institution, Washington, D.C., 1954; for a listing of the largest corporations measured by sales, assets, net income, stockholders' equity, and employees, see *Fortune,* May, 1971, pp. 172–204.

Big Steel A designation of the large integrated steel companies in the U.S., as distinguished from the smaller integrated, semi-integrated, and specialty steel companies. The companies which are generally considered to constitute Big Steel are United States Steel, Bethlehem, Republic, National, Armco, Jones and Laughlin, Inland Steel, and Youngstown Sheet and Tube. Together, these eight companies account for about 80% of the total steel ingot capacity. United States Steel, which alone accounts for about 30% of the total capacity, is often referred to as Big Steel.

Big Three A designation of the three leading producers of passenger cars in the U.S., which together accounted for about 96% of U.S. automobile production in the calendar year 1970. The share of General Motors was 45%, that of Ford was 31%, and that of Chrysler was more than 19%.

Bilateral Negotiations and Agreements Transactions and agreements between two parties. The term is generally used to refer to trade agreements between two countries. There are bilateral clearing agreements, bilateral payments agreements, and bilateral trade agreements. Bilateral trade and payments agreements are substitutes for more efficient and economic multilateral trade. Except for limited advantages in periods of disturbance, bilateral agreements are usually harmful to world trade and to the countries participating in them. When trade between any two countries is conducted through bilateral agreements, it tends to be reduced to a level at which the value of goods moving in one direction exactly equals the value of goods moving in the other direction. As a result, less effective use is made of the world's resources, since there are fewer opportunities to take advantage of international specialization. Moreover, trade is diverted from its normal channels into channels that are determined by the control system and not by market forces. Many countries lacking foreign exchange seek bilateral agreements to overcome this shortage. Once bilateral trade begins, it has a tendency to spread. Thus, nations placed at a disadvantage because of exchange controls adopt controls themselves as a means of striking back at other countries. For additional information, see Raymond F. Mikesell, *Foreign Exchange in the Postwar World,* The Twentieth Century Fund, New York, 1954; see also Henry Chalmers, *World Trade Policies,* University of California Press, Berkeley, Calif., 1953.

Bills-Only Policy The policy of confining Federal Reserve open-market operations to short-term securities, especially ninety-one-day Treasury bills. The Federal Open Market Committee felt that limitation of its transactions to Treasury bills would have less of a disrupting influence on the money market, since the market for short-term securities is more fluid than other markets. It believed that the policy of bills only would increase the "depth, breadth, and resiliency" of the government bond market, whereas intervention in all maturity sections of government securities might destroy the private market in these securities, leaving a market in which the Federal Reserve alone would establish prices and yields. It has been argued, however, that the actual operation of the policy has not had the desired effects on the government bond market. Furthermore, critics assert that the interest structure of government securities is an important tool of monetary policy and should be influenced more effectively by the Federal Reserve. In reply, the Federal Open Market Committee has stated that it is the central bank's business to control only bank reserves and the money supply, leaving the determination of interest rates to the free market; the bills-only policy has enabled it to do that. In 1960 the committee relaxed its bills-only stand to a policy of bills preferably, opening the way for possible Federal Reserve transactions in longer-term government securities. For additional details, see Dudley Luckett, "Bills Only: A Critical Appraisal," *Review of Economics and Statistics,* Harvard University Press, Cambridge, Mass., August, 1960, p. 301; Ralph Young and Charles Yager, "The Economics of Bills Preferably," *Quarterly Journal of Economics,* Harvard University Press, Cambridge, Mass., August, 1960, p. 341; Daniel Ahearn, *Federal Reserve Policy Reappraised, 1951–1959,* Columbia University Press, New York, 1963, chaps. 4, 5, and 6; U.S. Joint Committee on the Economic Report, *U.S. Monetary Policy: Recent Thinking and Experience,* hearings before the Subcommittee on Economic Stabilization, Government Printing Office, Washington, D.C., 1954, pp. 257–331.

Bills-Preferably Policy   *See Bills-Only Policy.*

Bimetallism   The policy of defining the value of the monetary unit of a country in terms of two different metals, usually gold and silver, by making both legal tender and setting the ratio of the coined value of one metal to the other. It represented an attempt to increase the circulating money supply of a country by allowing both gold and silver, or money backed by either of these metals, to circulate. The policy was practiced in the late eighteenth century and the nineteenth century by France, the United States, and several other countries. Because of the fluctuating market values of the two metals with respect to each other, it has since been abandoned. For example, when the market price of silver fell in relation to gold, silver was overvalued by the fixed ratio in the value of silver and gold coins to each other. As a result, only silver money was circulated, and gold was hoarded or exported. It proved impossible to stabilize the market ratio of gold to silver, and countries attempting to follow a bimetallic system eventually found themselves in fact on either a gold or a silver standard. By 1900 a single metal standard, generally gold, was the accepted norm. See Paul B. Trescott, *Money, Banking, and Economic Welfare,* 2d ed., McGraw-Hill Book Company, New York, 1963, for classic discussions of bimetallism, see James L. Laughlin, *The History of Bimetallism in the United States,* D. Appleton & Company, Inc., New York, 1896; Francis A. Walker, *International Bimetallism,* Henry Holt & Company, Inc., New York, 1896.

Birthrate The number of births per 1,000 population. This is the crude birthrate. The crude birthrate of the U.S. has declined over the years and in 1968, at 17.5 per 1,000, reached the lowest ratio in well over a decade. It increased in 1969 and 1970. Refined birthrates are calculated to allow for differences in the population's composition, such as age or color, in varying time periods. A knowledge of birthrate trends is important in projecting future population growth. Historical and current statistics on birthrates and fertility rates (births per 1,000 females from fifteen to forty-four years old) are found in U.S. Department of Health, Education and Welfare, *Health, Education and Welfare Indicators,* monthly.

Birthrate (Per 1,000 population)

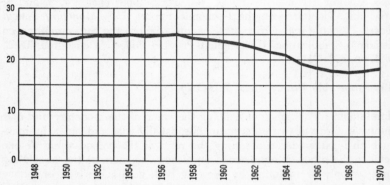

Source: U.S. Department of Health, Education, and Welfare, Public Health Service, National Vital Statistics Division.

Blighted Area An area that is on the verge of becoming a slum. It is a section in which owners are either unwilling or unable to maintain or renovate their property because of faulty civic planning or economic or environmental changes. Blighted areas flourish in less desirable locations, such as industrial waterfronts, the vicinity of polluted rivers, and urban areas that have become undesirable because of sharply growing population. For a discussion of the treatment of blighted areas under urban renewal programs, see John W. Dyckman and Reginald R. Isaacs, *Capital Requirements for Urban Development and Renewal,* McGraw-Hill Book Company, New York, 1961, particularly chap. 5.

Blocked Account A bank account of a foreigner that is made unavailable to its owner by means of governmental action. In this manner, the government restricts the use of its currency by foreigners. The blocked-account technique may be used when a government is concerned about inflation and wishes to dampen excess demand for goods by restricting purchases by foreigners. One way to do so is to cut off the financing of exports by blocking foreigners' accounts and by limiting the rate at which foreigners can draw on their bank accounts. After World War II, when Great Britain had little industrial output to sell, she used this method to restrict foreign industrial purchases. In wartime, the accounts of enemy nationals are restricted in this manner.

Blue Chip   The common stock of a large, well-known corporation, whose earnings and dividend records have been stable or have been growing slowly but steadily. Because of this stability, which reduces the risk of loss, typical blue-chip stocks are high-priced in relation to a corporation's earnings.

Blue-Collar Workers   Production, maintenance, and service workers, whether they are skilled, semiskilled, or unskilled. Craftsmen, foremen, operatives, service workers (except for private household workers), farm laborers and foremen, and other laborers are generally considered blue-collar workers. In 1950 there were 31 million employed persons classified as blue-collar workers in the U.S. By 1971 there were 5 million fewer blue-collar workers, whereas total employment had grown by about 20 million in this period. Thus, the share of blue-collar workers in the employed labor force had declined substantially. For data on the number of blue-collar workers in the U.S., see U.S. Department of Labor, *Employment and Earnings,* monthly.

Boiler Room   Headquarters from which high-pressure salesmen sell securities of dubious value by telephone. In the 1920s, boiler-room operators took advantage of the public's interest in the stock market and flourished, but such operations were outlawed by the securities legislation of the 1930s and the establishment of the U.S. Securities and Exchange Commission. The boiler rooms that are set up now serve as the retail arms of elaborate stock swindles. The operation itself has changed little; although the securities offered for sale are rarely worthless, as they frequently were in the 1920s, they never have the value the salesman claims. A boiler room works like this: Promotional literature with teaser titles is sent to "sucker lists," lists of persons who own securities and have some familiarity with stocks. If these persons want additional information, it is supplied. A salesman, who is called an "opener" or "coxey," gets in touch by telephone with anyone who requests information and whets the rienced boiler-room salesman, who is called a "loader" or a "dynamiter" potential customer's interest. If the person shows interest, a more expe-takes over and sells hard. He tells the person that, since the stock is about ready to "take off," the customer should send his money in immediately to get in on the ground floor. Unfortunately, many persons do send in money and invariably pay much more than the stock is worth. See Spencer Klaw, "The Great Sweet Grass Swindle," *Fortune*, August, 1957.

Bond   A written promise to pay a specified sum of money (principal) at a certain date in the future or periodically over the course of a loan, during which time interest is paid at a fixed rate on specified dates. Bonds are issued by corporations, states, localities (municipal bonds), foreign governments, and the U.S. government, usually for long terms (more than ten years), although any security issued by the U.S. government for more than five years is defined as a bond. The quality of bonds of U.S. and foreign governments rests on the ability of these entities to tax citizens to gain revenue. State and local government bonds, which are exempt from Federal income taxes, can be classified as general or limited-obligation bonds. The former rest on the "full faith and credit" of the issuer, that is, the taxing ability; the latter depend on the revenue gained from a specific asset, such as a bridge or a tunnel, for payment of interest and principal. Corporate bonds may be unsecured (debenture) or secured by the assets of the corporation. In the latter case, the corporation usually executes a mortgage to a trustee who represents the rights of the bondholders. In all cases, the safety of a corporate bond depends on the earning power of the corporation. For further information, see Charles W. Gerstenberg, *Financial Organization and Management of Business*, 4th ed., Prentice-Hall, Inc., Englewood Cliffs, N.J., 1959; Jules I. Bogen (ed.), *Financial Handbook*, 4th ed., The Ronald Press Company, New York, 1968; for a brief description of the many kinds of bonds, see Joseph H. Bonneville et al., *Organizing and Financing Business*, Prentice-Hall, Inc., Englewood Cliffs, N.J., 1959.

Bond Yield   The rate of return on an investment in bonds. The yield of a bond is one of the principal determinants of its attractiveness. Concepts of yield used to judge bonds include yield to maturity and nominal current yield. Yield to maturity, the most common measure of yield on good bonds, is the percentage which the combined annual gain bears to the average investment. It is used when the purchase price of a bond differs from its maturity value, and the computation of yield must therefore take into account any changes in the size of the principal at maturity. To compute the net yield at maturity, the amortization of the increase or decrease in the average annual investment must be added to the basic interest rate. Generally, longer-term bonds have a higher yield, and the more speculative the bond, the higher its rate of return. The nominal yield, or the coupon rate, is the ratio of interest to principal, as expressed on the face of the bond. The current yield generally used in describing speculative bonds whose repayment at maturity is doubtful expresses the annual interest payment as a percentage of the actual purchase price of the bond (not its face value). For additional details, see T. M. Simpson et al., *Mathematics of Finance*, 3d ed., Prentice-Hall, Inc., Englewood Cliffs, N.J., 1951; W. L. Hart, *Mathematics of Investment*, 3d ed., D. C. Heath and Company, Boston, 1946; *Yield and Interest Tables: Bonds and Stocks,* Financial Publishing Co., Boston, 1938.

Book Account   *See Open Account.*

Book Value   The value of a corporation according to its accounting records. It is computed by subtracting all debts from assets; the remainder represents total book value. Total book value is also referred to as net assets. If a corporation has assets of $300,000 and debts of $100,000, its total book value is $200,000. In reports of corporations, the book value is usually represented on a per-share basis. This is done by dividing the total book value by the number of shares. In the example given above, if the corporation had 10,000 shares outstanding, its book value would be $20 per share. The book value differs from the par value of the shares and also from the market value. For information concerning the relation of book value to security analysis, see Benjamin Graham et al., *Security Analysis,* 4th ed., McGraw-Hill Book Company, New York, 1962.

Boom   A rapid expansion in business activity to new high marks, resulting in low unemployment, high profits, and high stock and commodity prices. Since booms cannot be sustained for long periods of time, busts may follow them. The U.S. economy has experienced few booms and no busts since World War II.

Boomerang   A system to discourage the practice of dumping goods, devised by the Action Committee for a United States of Europe, which is headed by Jean Monnet. Under this system, goods that have been dumped are liable to be returned to the country that had dumped them, free of customs duties and exempt from restrictions on quantities. This system could be very costly for the country that had dumped the goods. According to the customs services of the member countries, however, the system is technically unenforceable. For additional details, see Emile Benoit, *Europe at Sixes and Sevens,* Columbia University Press, New York, 1961.

Boom Year   A year in which the physical volume of goods and services and industrial production rises sharply (more than 4.5%), when consumer money income after taxes increases more than 6% per year, and when unemployment drops below 4.5% of the labor force. In a boom year, there are very large purchases of consumer durable goods and capital goods. The criteria given above are now generally used by many business economists in describing a boom business year. Of the post-World War II years, only 1955, 1966, and 1968 satisfied all these requirements.

Bourgeoisie The upper-middle-class group which includes professional persons and businessmen. The *bourgeoisie* emerged as a class at the end of the Middle Ages, and by the Industrial Revolution had become very influential in public life, business, and culture. Since then, it has continued to grow as an important element in modern society. The term *bourgeoisie* is applied more narrowly by Socialists and Communists to include anyone with significant property interests. For further information, see C. Wright Mills, *White Collar: The American Middle Classes*, Oxford University Press, Fair Lawn, N.J., 1951; Roy Lewis and Angus Maude, *The English Middle Classes*, Alfred A. Knopf, Inc., New York, 1950.

Bourse The French word for an exchange, such as a stock or a commodity exchange. In Europe most stock exchanges are termed bourses.

Branch Banking The operation of one or more suboffices by a single bank. Unlike many other countries, such as Great Britain and Canada, in which a few large banks with hundreds of branches dominate the financial scene, the U.S. has traditionally relied on independent banking units. Nevertheless, branch banking has expanded in the U.S., and by the end of 1970, nearly 4,300 American banks (about 30% of the total) owned branches, or more than twice as many as in 1949. The number and location of branches are regulated by state laws; sixteen states severely limit branches, and fifteen prohibit them altogether. The advocates of branch banking claim that it offers great credit mobility (funds can flow from one branch to another) and permits individual banks to grow large enough to serve large corporations. Those opposed to branch banking believe that it leads to a dangerous concentration of economic power. For further information on this type of banking, see C. E. Coyle, *Branch, Group and Chain Banking*, Banking Studies, Board of Governors of the Federal Reserve System, Washington, D.C., 1941; for branch banking data, see *Federal Reserve Bulletin*, Washington, D.C., usually the April issue.

Branch Store A store located in an area other than that of the parent store. In most instances, branches of central city department stores are located in suburban shopping centers. With the growth of these centers as a result of the substantial rise in suburban population, the number of branch stores is increasing rapidly.

Brand Name Any combination of letters or words which is used by a manufacturer to identify his goods and services and to distinguish them from the products of other firms. It may be the company's name or the name given to a particular product. Its principal purpose is identity, but it also protects the buyer, who can expect standards of the same quality that have been associated with the product in the past. Furthermore, brand names give producers a measure of control over demand by garnering consumer preference for their brands. Brand names play an important role in advertising and in facilitating the introduction of new products. There are two distinct types of brands, manufacturers', or national, brands and private, or distributors', brands. Manufacturers' brands are those adopted by producers themselves for their products, whereas private brands are those sponsored by distributors, such as wholesalers and retailers. A single brand name used by a manufacturer for all his goods is a blanket or family brand. When a producer markets his products under different brands, they are known as individual or multiple brand names. For additional details, see Theodore Beckman and William Davidson, *Marketing*, 8th ed., The Ronald Press Company, New York, 1967; D. M. Phelps, *Sales Management*, Richard D. Irwin, Inc., Homewood, Ill., 1953; Burleigh Gardner and Sidney Levy, "The Product and the Brand," *Harvard Business Review*, vol. XXXIII, no. 2, Harvard Graduate School of Business Administration, Boston, March, 1955.

Brassage *See Seigniorage.*

Breakeven Point The specific volume of sales with which a firm neither makes nor loses money. Above this point, a firm begins to show a profit; below it, a loss. Breakeven point analysis is used to compute the approximate profit or loss that will be experienced at various levels of production. In carrying out this analysis, each expense item is classified as either fixed (constant at any reasonable level of output) or variable (increasing as output increases and decreasing as output declines). For a more comprehensive analysis of breakeven point examples, see Edison E. Easton and Byron L. Newton, *Accounting and the Analysis of Financial Data*, McGraw-Hill Book Company, New York, 1958.

Broker Any person who brings others together to negotiate a contract. For this service, the broker receives a commission. In finance and real estate, the broker brings together in a physical or financial sense the buyer and the seller of an asset. The distinction between a stockbroker and a dealer is important legally. In brokerage transactions, a stockbroker can hold his customer liable for damages arising from the execution of an

Breakeven Point Analysis

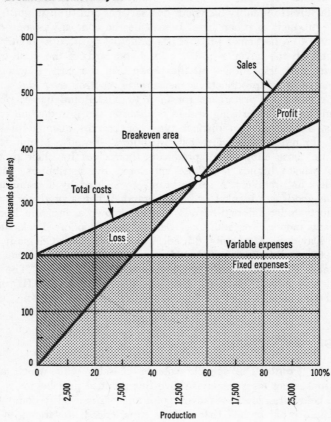

oral order. The reason is that the legal relationship between the broker and the customer is that of principal and agent.

Bucket Shop An illegal establishment that masqueraded as a stock-brokerage office, but in reality was a gambling house the operator of which bet against the customer on the trend of stock prices. Not knowing the true nature of the bucket shop, a customer would place an order to buy a stock. The bucket-shop operator would accept the money and either hold it or sell an equivalent amount of the stock short. If the price of the stock declined and the customer told the operator to sell, the operator won the bet because he returned a smaller amount of money to the customer. If, on the other hand, the price of the stock rose and the customer told the operator to sell, the operator lost the bet because he had to return a larger sum of money to the customer. The New York Stock Exchange, by controlling the selection of those who could possess ticker tapes and therefore get stock price information quickly, put virtually all bucket shops out of existence. See *The Security Markets,* The Twentieth Century Fund, New York, 1935.

Budget   A schedule of all the revenues and expenditures that an individual, group, government, or organization expects to receive and plans to spend during some future time period, usually the following year. Budgets range from very simple and casual ones, like the typical family budget, to extremely complex and sophisticated ones, like the Federal government's annual 14-pound endeavor. All contain estimates of anticipated revenues from sales, taxes, gifts, and so on, and they specify what expenditures are planned during the time period. If revenues exceed expenditures, a budget surplus is expected. If, on the other hand, expenses are expected to be greater than revenues, a budget deficit must be confronted, and some method of financing it must be planned. A budget usually is used to control the allocation of revenues so that spending is rational. For additional information, see J. K. Lasser, Tax Institute, *J. K. Lasser's Managing Your Family Finances,* Doubleday & Company, Inc., Garden City, N.Y., 1968; R. K. Mikesell and Leon Etting, *Governmental Accounting,* 4th ed., Richard D. Irwin, Inc., Homewood, Ill., 1969; I. Wayne Keller and William L. Ferrara, *Management Accounting for Profit Control,* 2d ed., McGraw-Hill Book Company, New York, 1966.

Budget Deficit   An excess of expenditures over revenues. Although no individual or business firm can incur deficits over an indefinite period, some economists believe that the Federal government is in a different category and that budget deficts year after year are acceptable and sometimes recommendable. They point out that a balanced budget is unstabilizing in recessions, aggravating the effects of a drop in national income, and suggest instead a deliberate unbalancing of the budget to create a deficit. This will increase total spending, which, in turn, will increase national income. Because of the operation of the national income multiplier, the increase in income will be larger than the deficit. The budget deficit can be achieved by lowering taxes, raising government expenditures, or adopting both measures. Although an increase in government spending may be more effective in raising national income, since it has a higher income multiplier, a tax cut may be preferable, since it can be made effective more quickly. Government budget deficits are generally financed by borrowing through the sale of bonds. The sale of such bonds to Federal Reserve banks and private commercial banks tends to maximize the expansionary effects of the deficit, while the sale of bonds to individuals and nonfinancial business firms has less of an expansionary (and, possibly, an inflationary) effect. For additional details, see Alvin H. Hansen, *Fiscal Policy and Business Cycles*, W. W. Norton & Company, Inc., New York, 1941; for a recent review, see Herbert Stein, *The Fiscal Revolution in America*, The University of Chicago Press, Chicago, 1969.

Unified Budget, Deficit and Surplus for Fiscal Years 1954-1970 (Billions of dollars)

Source: Bureau of the Budget.

Budget Surplus   An excess of revenues over expenditures. The use of the government budget surplus is an important part of countercyclical fiscal policy. During periods of inflation, it is desirable to reduce total spending in the economy, diminishing the excess demand which is forcing up prices. At such times, the government budget can be adjusted to produce a surplus and achieve the desired lowering of income. This may be accomplished by lowering government expenditures, raising taxes, or adopting both measures. The reduction of government expenditures is more effective than a tax increase as an anti-inflationary measure, since its negative income multiplier is greater, but it is generally harder to put into effect, especially when the budget consists of many large items. For the budget surplus to be effective, the surplus money must not find its way back into the spending stream. The surplus funds may be used to retire part of the outstanding Federal debt or to build up the balance of the Treasury account. If debt retirement is undertaken, the purchase of government bonds held by banks has a greater anti-inflationary effect than the refunding of bonds held by private citizens and nonfinancial business firms. For further information, see Alvin H. Hansen, *Fiscal Policy and Business Cycles,* W. W. Norton & Company, Inc., New York, 1941; for a recent view, see Herbert Stein, *The Fiscal Revolution in America,* The University of Chicago Press, Chicago, 1969.

Building Cycle   An alternate expansion and contraction of fairly long duration in building construction activity. It may be caused by a sharp increase in population, speculation, or the lifting of building restrictions which had been imposed in wartime. In each of these cases, a relatively sudden increase in the demand for new buildings leads to construction of boom proportions that gradually declines as building needs are filled. Some authorities have estimated the duration of building cycles in the U.S. at about 18 years, but others deny the existence of a regular pattern of fluctuations in construction activity. For a fuller treatment of building cycles in theory and fact, see Clarence D. Long, Jr., *Building Cycles and the Theory of Investment,* Princeton University Press, Princeton, N.J., 1940; for a discussion of the causes and consequences of fluctuations in building activity and a critique of Long's findings, see Miles L. Colean and Robinson Newcomb, *Stabilizing Construction: The Record and Potential,* McGraw-Hill Book Company, New York, 1952; for historical data on building activity in the U.S., see *Construction during Five Decades,* U.S. Department of Labor Bulletin 1146, 1953; U.S. Department of Commerce, *Construction Volume and Costs 1915–1956, A Statistical Supplement to Construction Review,* 1958.

Built-in Stabilizer   *See Automatic Stabilizer.*

Bull   A person who believes that the prices of stocks, bonds, commodities, or foreign exchange are going to rise and generally acts on this belief by buying and hoping to sell at a higher price. The term dates back to the early eighteenth century, when dealers on the London Stock Exchange were called bulls if they thought the trend of stock and bond prices was up and bears if they thought it was down. Why the more optimistic dealers were called bulls is difficult to say, but one story is that the way in which a bull tosses things up with its horns describes the action of the bull on the exchange. See "Bulls and Bears," *Wall Street Journal,* Aug. 27, 1940; F. E. Armstrong, *The Book of the Stock Exchange,* Sir Isaac Pitman & Sons, Ltd., London, 1934, pp. 102–105.

Bullion   Gold, silver, or other precious metals in nonmonetary (uncoined) form. For convenience of handling, bullion is usually cast into bars or ingots of a specified weight. Today, silver bullion is important mainly for industrial and decorative purposes, such as jewelry or tableware, but gold bullion plays an important role as an international medium of exchange and store of value as well as a partial reserve (backing) for many currencies. Some economists believe, however, that gold is unnecessary as a monetary reserve. In mid-1971 the U.S. had a monetary gold stock of less than $11 billion, compared with $20 billion at the end of 1958 (valued at the price fixed by the government of $35 per ounce). The decline in the gold stock after 1958 resulted from the payment of gold to other countries in partial settlement of the U.S. balance-of-payments deficit. The increase in the price of gold to $38 per ounce at the end of 1971 resulted in an 8.57% increase in the value of the U.S. gold stock.

Bull Market   A market in which the prices of most of the items traded are increasing. The term usually refers to rising stock, bond, or commodity markets. No precise origin of the term is known, but it is likely that someone coined it to refer to the London Stock Exchange at times when the "bulls" (those dealers who thought the prices were going to rise and bought stocks or bonds) were dominant.

Bumping   The practice whereby one worker, because of his greater seniority, is allowed to displace another worker in a similar job. The purpose of bumping may be to avoid a layoff, to secure more desirable working conditions, or to obtain more desirable working hours. In the U.S., bumping is a common practice in industries covered by labor contracts with strong seniority provisions. See Sumner A. Slichter, James J. Healy, and E. Robert Livernash, *The Impact of Collective Bargaining on Management*, The Brookings Institution, Washington, D.C., 1960, pp. 158–160.

Bunch-Map Analysis   A graphic technique for studying relationships between coefficients of correlation for simple and multiple regressions. It employs the familiar coordinates with the horizontal axis corresponding to the independent variable, the vertical axis corresponding to the dependent variable, and the origin at zero. The scales range from 0 to ±1, that is, from zero correlation to perfect correlation. Points are plotted at the intersection of values for coefficients of correlation—for example, $R_{21}:R_{22}$, $R_{11}:R_{12}$, and $R_{31}:R_{32}$—and a line (beam) is drawn to connect each such point with the origin. A separate bunch map is drawn for each of several (or all the possible) different combinations of variables, and the analysis consists of studying the length and direction of beams and changes therein depending upon the variables involved. This permits a graphic distinction between variables that are significant and should be included in a predictive model and those which should be eliminated. A variable is considered significant if it changes the general slope of the bunch (of beams) or tightens it. For additional information, see Earl F. Beach, *Economic Models: An Exposition,* John Wiley & Sons, Inc., New York, 1957; Stefan Valavanis, *Econometrics,* McGraw-Hill Book Company, New York, 1959.

Business Barometer   A weighted average of a variety of economic indicators, such as steel production, coal production, oil production, electric power generation, and carloadings, that measures the level of general business activity. A business barometer provides relatively current information on business activity which can be directly related by businessmen to their own operations. There are weekly, monthly, and quarterly business barometers. The *Business Week* index is an example of a weekly business barometer widely used by the business community. For a detailed listing of business barometers compiled by business organizations or government agencies, see Arthur A. Cole, *Measures of Business Change,* Richard D. Irwin, Inc., Homewood, Ill., 1952.

Business Cycles   An alternate expansion and contraction in overall business activity, evidenced by fluctuations in measures of aggregate economic activity, such as the gross national product, the index of industrial production, and employment and income. A business cycle may be divided into four phases: expansion, during which business activity is successively reaching new high points; leveling out, during which business activity reaches a high point and remains at that level for a short period of time; contraction, during which business volume recedes from the peak level for a sustained period until the bottom is reached; and recovery, during which business activity resumes after the low point has been reached and continues to rise to the previous high mark. Unlike many cycles observed in nature, business cycles are not uniform in frequency, amplitude, or duration. Joseph A. Schumpeter classified business cycles into three categories on the basis of their duration: Kondratieff cycles, or long waves, lasting from fifty-four to sixty years; Juglar cycles, having a duration of nine to ten years; and Kitchin cycles, spanning a forty-month interval. The National Bureau of Economic Research, which has carried out extensive investigations of the empirical evidence of business cycles, counts twenty-seven distinct business cycles in the U.S. during the period 1854–1971, measured from trough to trough; their average duration is fifty-two months. Many theories have been advanced to explain business cycles. Some economists blame inadequate levels of investment or consumption. Schumpeter saw a principal cause in the disruptions created by such major innovations as railroads. Wesley C. Mitchell's analysis centered around the prices, costs, and profits theory. He also took the position that fluctuations are due to the very nature of the free-enterprise business system but that no single explanation of their causes is adequate. Other economists have felt that fluctuations in the stock of money cause business fluctuations. In attempting to postulate theories of the business cycle, economists have not as yet been able fully to explain the variety of factors that underlie business fluctuations, but most of them have made valuable contributions to the understanding of the changes that business undergoes. Among the many works on business cycles are Wesley C. Mitchell, *Business Cycles and Their Causes,* University of California Press, Berkeley, Calif., 1959; Joseph A. Schumpeter, *Business Cycles,* 2 vols., McGraw-Hill Book Company, New York, 1939; James S. Duesenberry, *Business Cycles and Economic Growth,* McGraw-Hill Book Company, New York, 1958; Gottfried Haberler, *Prosperity and Depression,* Harvard University Press, Cambridge, Mass., 1958; for a collection of some of the major theoretical writings on business cycles, see Robert A. Gordon and Lawrence R. Klein, *Readings in Business Cycles,* Richard D. Irwin, Inc., Homewood, Ill.,1965; for recent work of the National Bureau of Economic Research, see Geoffrey H. Moore and Julius Shiskin, *Indicators of Business Expansions and Contractions,* Columbia University Press, New York, 1967. An excellent general text is Thomas F. Dernberg and Duncan M. McDougall, *Macroeconomics,* McGraw-Hill Book Company, New York, 1968.

Business Equipment   A term comprising the capital asset units, such as machinery, fixtures, and vehicles, used by industry and commercial business. It excludes capital items purchased by farmers and professional persons, such as physicians and dentists. These items are included, however, in producers' durable equipment. Spending for business equipment accounted for roughly 75% of capital expenditures by manufacturers during the 1950s. In the 1960s and early 1970s, because of emphasis placed by industry on modernization rather than expansion, the percentage was even higher. For estimates of annual expenditures on business equipment, see *Annual Surveys of Business' Plans for New Plants and Equipment,* McGraw-Hill Department of Economics, New York.

Business Failures   The cessation of operations by a business concern because of involvement in court procedures or voluntary actions which will result in loss to its creditors. The statistics of business failures compiled by Dun and Bradstreet include only firms involved in court procedures, such as receivership, reorganization, and assignment, or voluntary actions which will result in loss to their creditors. They do not take into account firms which were liquidated, merged, or sold to avoid loss. For the most part, these statistics cover commercial and industrial businesses. The Dun and Bradstreet series differs from that of discontinued businesses, which refers to all firms that go out of business for any reason. The number of business failures is a significant indicator of overall business activity, classified by the National Bureau of Economic Research as one of its thirty leading indicators. Business failures generally increase when business recedes and decrease when business expands. In 1970 business failures in the U.S. totaled 10,748. For current statistics, see *Business Trends News: Monthly Business Failures;* for cyclical changes in business failures, see Victor Zarnowitz and Lionel J. Lerner, "Cyclical Changes in Business Failures and Corporate Profits," in Geoffrey H. Moore (ed.), *Business Cycle Indicators,* Princeton University Press, Princeton, N.J., 1961, chap. 12.

Business Failures (Number)

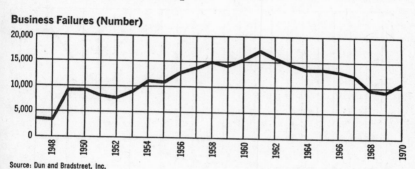

Source: Dun and Bradstreet, Inc.

Business Forecasting   The art of predicting future business conditions. Short-term forecasts run from one to as many as six quarters ahead, and long-term forecasts from five to fifteen years or more. Only a few U.S. companies make medium-term forecasts covering from two to three years. Short-term forecasts, which are strongly influenced by current business levels, usually serve to support decisions on inventory purchasing, operating rates, and sales activity; their vista is too short to form a good basis for capital investment plans. In long-term forecasts, on the other hand, the potential growth of the economy is the important consideration. These forecasts form the basis for an intelligent financial plan, in which decisions on capital investment can be made with regard to new capacity and the distribution of the new capacity among new products and regions of the nation and the world. For methods of business forecasting, see Elmer C. Bratt, *Business Forecasting,* McGraw-Hill Book Company, New York, 1958; Leonard S. Silk and Louise Curley, *Forecasting Business Trends,* McGraw-Hill Book Company, New York, 1956; William F. Butler and Robert A. Kavesh (eds.), *How Business Economists Forecast,* Prentice-Hall, Inc., Englewood Cliffs, N.J., 1966.

Business Loan   A loan to a commercial or an industrial enterprise for business purposes. Such a loan is used to increase the volume of production and the distribution of goods or to accumulate inventories. Business loans are distinguished from loans to financial institutions and other non-commercial enterprises. The amount of such loans is studied closely as an indicator of business activity. For a study of bank loans to businesses, see Neil H. Jacoby and Raymond J. Saulnier, *Business Finance and Banking*, National Bureau of Economic Research, Inc., New York, 1947; for current weekly or monthly data, see *Federal Reserve Bulletin*, Washington, D.C.

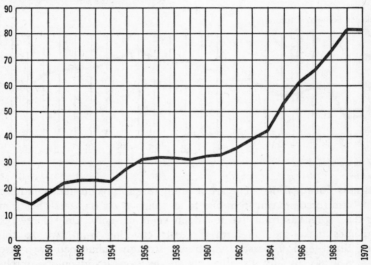

Business Loans (Billions of dollars)

Source: Board of Governors, Federal Reserve System.

Business Unionism   A term applied to labor unions whose primary concern is the improvement of wages, hours, and working conditions. Such a union may also be interested in broader programs of social reform, but this is a secondary concern. Business unionism may be contrasted with "radical," or "uplift," unionism, which has as its primary goals new legislation, changes in the economic system, or producer cooperation. Labor unions in the U.S. today, unlike many in other countries, are of the business type. The International Workers of the World, founded in 1905, was the last major union in the U.S. that placed primary emphasis on changes in the economic system. With a rapid decline in their strength after World War I, all major U.S. labor unions emphasized the establishment of their own members' wages, hours, and working conditions. For a discussion of business unionism in the U.S., see Albert Rees, *The Economics of Trade Unions,* The University of Chicago Press, Chicago, 1962; for the classic statement of business unionism in the U.S., see Selig Perlman, *A Theory of the Labor Movement,* The Macmillan Company, New York, 1928.

Bust A drop in business activity to an extremely low level, resulting in high unemployment, low incomes, low profits, and low stock and commodity prices. Historically, busts have usually followed booms. Automatic stabilizers have helped prevent the U.S. economy from experiencing a bust during the postwar years.

Buyers' Market A market situation in which, at current prices that would cover a representative producer's average costs, supply is greater than demand. Because of the excess short-run supply, buyers have a bargaining advantage, and prices are forced below average costs. To reduce their excess stocks, sellers must accept lower prices. The existence of a buyers' market determines the direction of longer-run movements in production and price, indicating a fall in production or price or a combination of the two.

Buy-Now Campaign A plan, urged usually by the national government or part of the business community, to spur recovery through an increase in current consumer purchases. Timed correctly, a buy-now campaign can give a depressed economy the needed impetus to start it moving upward.

By-product A secondary product obtained in the production process of a principal product. Although it is produced incidentally, it does represent a source of revenue. Common examples of by-products are the glycerin produced in the making of soap and the coke obtained in the production of illuminating gas. For important by-products of various industries, see John G. Glover and Rudolph Lagai, *The Development of American Industries,* 4th ed., Simmons-Boardman Publishing Corporation, New York, 1959.

C

Calendar Variations Fluctuations in monthly economic time series that arise from the structure of the calendar. The variations consist of *length-of-month variation,* which is attributable to the fact that some months are longer than others; and *trading-day (working-day) variation,* which is explained by different patterns of economic activity on different days of the week. The trading-day variation is removed from the time series by a trading-day adjustment, and a length-of-month adjustment may be incorporated into either the seasonal index or the trading-day adjustment. For further discussion, see Julius Shiskin, *Electronic Computers and Business Indicators,* National Bureau of Economic Research, Inc., Occasional Paper 57, New York, 1957.

Call An option, or contract, which gives the holder the right to buy a certain amount of stock at a specified price for a designated time period. It is the opposite of a put. There are four parties to every call: the holder (buyer); the maker (seller); the broker who brought them together; and the endorser, a New York Stock Exchange member firm, which guarantees that the maker will comply with the agreement. Calls are usually written for thirty, sixty, or ninety days or for six months, but any time period longer than 21 days (a New York Stock Exchange rule) to which the parties agree is acceptable. For the right to buy the stock, the buyer pays a premium to the seller of the call. The seller, in turn, pays a small commission to the put and call broker. Four factors affect the price of a call: (1) the period covered by the contract, (2) the price of the stock at the time the call is written, (3) the ability of the call to be exercised at that price or at a higher price, and (4) the volatility of past price movements of the stock. For further information, see George L. Leffler and L. C. Farwell, *The Stock Market,* The Ronald Press Company, New York, 1963, pp. 310–329; for the only recent extensive study of puts and calls, see Division of Trading and Exchanges, U.S. Securities and Exchange Commission, *Report on Put and Call Options,* August, 1961.

Callable Loan (Call Loan) A commercial bank loan payable on demand by the lender and repayable at any time by the borrower. The greater part of broker borrowing has been on a call-loan basis, repayable on demand in clearinghouse funds on one day's notice. Stocks, bonds, and other forms of property are put up as collateral for a call loan. The call-loan agreement between the bank and the broker stipulates the margin, the difference between the market value of the pledged securities and the amount of the loan; provides for the substitution of collateral deemed adequate to the bank; and empowers the bank to sell the securities in case of default or failure to keep collateral at the required level of margin. Because the call loan tends to deter rational business planning, it is rarely used by manufacturers or distributors. Before the 1930s, the callable loan market was the most important segment of the

Stock Exchange Call Loans, Going Rate (Percent)

Source: New York Stock Exchange.

New York money market because commercial banks used call loans a:
secondary reserves. Individual banks considered these loans highly liquid
and had no compunction in demanding repayment. After the 1929 market
crash had shown how illiquid these loans actually were, however, bank
no longer regarded them in the same light. For further information, see
D. K. Eiteman, C. A. Dice, and W. J. Eiteman, *The Stock Market*, 4th ed.
McGraw-Hill Book Company, New York, 1966, pp. 310–327; Sipa Heller
and Samuel S. Shipman, *The Money Market and Its Institutions*, The
Ronald Press Company, New York, 1955; W. H. Steiner and Eli Shapiro
Money and Banking, Holt, Rinehart and Winston, Inc., New York, 1955

Cambridge School   A school of economic thought of the late nineteenth
and twentieth centuries, based largely on the works of Alfred Marshall
Arthur C. Pigou, and D. H. Robertson. The Cambridge school, so named
because many of its adherents taught at the University of Cambridge
borrowed much from earlier schools of economic analysis, combining the
classical concepts of real cost as the basis of value, rent, and the basic
theory of money and foreign trade with the German historical approach
of the institutional study of economic forces and the contributions of the
marginal-utility theorists. Economists of this school concentrated their
study on value and distribution theory, analyzing the pricing and alloca
tive processes of the economic system while largely neglecting the prob
lems of aggregative output, income, and economic growth and develop
ment. The unifying factor in their approach was the concept of economic
equilibrium. Their basic tool was partial-equilibrium analysis, or the
analysis of phenomena in one industry at a time, holding all other prices
outputs, and demands unchanged. The value of a particular commodity
was determined by the equilibrium of the forces of supply and demand
The theory of money and foreign trade was treated in a similar manner
by studying the equilibrium of supply and demand. For fuller details on
the approach of the Cambridge school, see Alfred Marshall, *Principle
of Economics*, 8th ed., Macmillan & Co., Ltd., London, 1922; Mark
Blaug, *Economic Theory in Retrospect*, Richard D. Irwin, Inc., Home
wood, Ill., 1968; R. Frisch, "Alfred Marshall's Theory of Value," *Quar
terly Journal of Economics*, vol. LXIV, pp. 495–524, Harvard University
Press, Cambridge, Mass., November, 1950.

Cameralism   A form of mercantilism popular in Germany and Austria
in the middle of the eighteenth century. It was a broad system of public
administration, technology, and the management of financial affairs. In
contrast to the Western mercantilists, the cameralists stressed domestic
industrial centralization rather than commercial expansion. Their aim
was to foster home industry and a self-sufficient economy. They favored

a growing population as a means of increasing national production and encouraged the consumption of domestic products. They also designated the revenues of the central government as the most important index of a nation's wealth. See A. Small, *The Cameralists: The Pioneers of German Social Polity,* Burt Franklin, New York, 1909.

Canons of Taxation Principles or maxims used in the establishment or evaluation of a tax system. Adam Smith, the celebrated eighteenth-century British economist, was one of the first to set forth such principles. He said that taxes should (1) be levied on individuals according to their ability to pay as reflected by income, (2) be certain as to amount and condition of payment, (3) be payable at a time and in a manner convenient to the taxpayer, and (4) be collectible at a low cost. Later writers changed the emphasis on these principles, and greater attention is now generally paid to considerations of (1) equity between taxpayers, (2) the effect of the tax system on economic growth and efficiency, and (3) its effect on economic stability. For Adam Smith's classic statement, see *The Wealth of Nations,* Random House, Inc., New York, 1937, book V.

Capacity The largest output that a firm or industry can produce while operating on its customary schedule and using existing plants and equipment. The concept of capacity is different for each industry. It may vary with the number of shifts customarily worked and with allowances for repairs and maintenance. For example, continuous-processing industries, such as paper and steel, work around the clock, while most other industries operate on a one- or two-shift basis. Capacity figures expressed in such units as tons, barrels, pounds, and yards are available for basic industries, including primary aluminum, refined copper, cotton yarn, synthetic fibers, cement, wood pulp, paper, petroleum products, and coke. Capacity indices for major manufacturing industries from 1950 on are found in *Annual Surveys of Business' Plans for New Plants and Equipment,* McGraw-Hill Department of Economics, New York; for various measures of capacity and evaluations, see *Measures of Productive Capacity,* Hearings before the Subcommittee on Economic Statistics of the U.S. Joint Economic Committee, May 14, 22, 23, and 24, 1962, Government Printing Office, Washington, D.C., 1962.

Capacity Utilization Rate *See Operating Rate.*

Capital The designation applied to all goods used in the production of other goods, including plants and machinery. It is one of the three major factors of production, the other two being land and labor. In a business sense, capital is the total wealth or assets of a firm and thus includes not

Index of Manufacturers' Capacity (1957-1959 = 100)

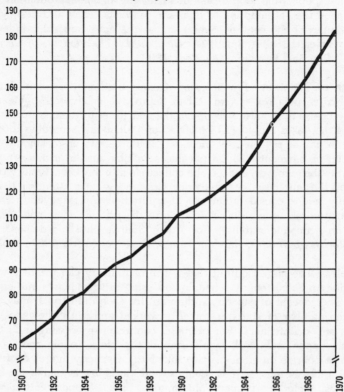

Source: McGraw-Hill Department of Economics.

only capital goods (tangible assets), but also trademarks, goodwill, patents, etc. As an accounting term, it represents all the money secured from stockholders, plus all earnings retained for use in the business. For a fuller discussion of capital and capital formation, see Simon Kuznets, *Capital in the American Economy*, Princeton University Press, Princeton, N.J., 1961; J. R. Hicks, *Value and Capital*, 2d ed., Oxford University Press, Fair Lawn, N.J., 1946; F. A. von Hayek, *Pure Theory of Capital*, The Macmillan Company of Canada, Limited, Toronto, Canada, 1941.

Capital Account, Balance-of-Payments   A group of entries appearing in the balance-of-payments account which provide a measure of all international capital transactions. The term refers to the long- and short-term loans that private citizens make or receive from foreign private citizens.

and the long- and short-term loans and credits that the government makes through various direct or intermediate channels. The capital account is shown in terms of net increases or decreases in assets and liabilities. Assets represent the reporting country's investments abroad; liabilities, the investment of foreigners in the reporting country. Increases in assets and decreases in liabilities indicate an outflow of capital (debit); decreases in assets and increases in liabilities, an inflow of capital (credit). It is the transactions in this account that presented the U.S. with the greatest difficulties in balancing its international payments in the 1957–1964 years. The deficits in capital movements abroad have more than offset the surpluses on current account, thus placing pressure on U.S. gold reserves. For additional information, see International Monetary Fund, *Balance of Payments Manual*, Washington, D.C., January, 1950; see also Geoffrey Crowther, *Balance and Imbalances of Payments*, Harvard Graduate School of Business Administration, Boston, 1957.

Capital Account, Firm   An accounting record of expenditures for assets to be capitalized, such as machines, vehicles, and buildings. Usually, an account is set up for each capital project, expenditures being broken down into two subaccounts, one for capital items and the other for items to be expended. For information on this subject, see *Managing Capital Expenditures*, National Industrial Conference Board, Inc., Studies in Business Policy, no. 107, New York, 1963; Joel Dean, *Capital Budgeting*, Columbia University Press, New York, 1951.

Capital Appropriations   The term applied to a firm's plans to buy new plants and equipment which have been formally approved by its board of directors or other responsible officials. Cumulative appropriations figures serve as a yardstick of future investment, but the measure is only approximate, since appropriations may be advanced or canceled. On the average, nine months elapse from appropriation to actual expenditure. The Con-

Estimated Capital Appropriations for the Thousand Largest Manufacturing Companies
(In millions of dollars, quarters 1967–1969)

	1967				1968				1969			
	IQ	IIQ	IIIQ	IVQ	IQ	IIQ	IIIQ	IVQ	IQ	IIQ	IIIQ	IVQ
All manufacturing newly approved	7.34	5.60	5.13	5.85	7.19	5.37	5.54	6.70	8.04	7.28	6.68	7.49
Durable goods newly approved	3.29	3.02	2.67	3.02	3.03	2.83	2.87	3.86	3.54	3.70	3.72	4.05
Nondurable goods newly approved	4.05	2.58	2.46	2.83	4.16	2.54	2.67	2.84	4.50	3.58	2.96	3.44

SOURCE: National Industrial Conference Board, Inc.

ference Board collects and publishes quarterly data on the capital appropriations of large U.S. manufacturing corporations and utilities; see *The Conference Board Business Record*, Conference Board, Inc., New York.

Capital Budget   That part of a firm's budget which is concerned with the planning and control of capital expenditures. The budgeting of capital outlays is usually undertaken as part of a long-range program and is then transformed into an annual planning budget. Basic considerations in capital-outlay budgeting are the need for capital expenditures during the period in question; the money available for investment, including sources of financing; the rationing of funds among projects; and the timing of capital expenditures in relation to general business conditions. Each project is considered a separate venture and evaluated on the basis of total expenditure involved, the income required to cover the expenditure, the ultimate gain to be derived from the project, and the degree of urgency of the project. Among the steps involved in capital-outlay budgeting are general approval of the project, an estimate of cost and profitability, budget authorization of the project, and a follow-up study to determine the benefits derived from the capital expenditure. For additional details, see Joel Dean, *Capital Budgeting*, Columbia University Press, New York, 1951.

Capital Coefficient   *See Capital-Output Ratio.*

Capital Consumption Allowance   An entry in the national income accounts that reflects the depreciation suffered by business production equipment and plants in a given period. It also includes the value of capital equipment accidentally destroyed and certain expenditures incurred in finding new resources, such as the cost of gas and oil well drilling. The allowance is based primarily on tax reports of depreciation, although these do not necessarily approximate the physical deterioration of productive facilities and do not include the depreciation of hand tools and similar equipment which is not amortized in current tax-accounting practice. The capital consumption allowance, which totaled over $84 billion in the U.S. in 1970, is subtracted from the gross national product in order to give a more accurate measure (the net national product) of a country's economic growth. Historical data on capital consumption allowances are published annually in U.S. Department of Commerce, *Survey of Current Business*, national income number (July issue).

Capital Expenditure (Capital Investment)   The amount of money spent for a fixed asset, such as a plant, a piece of machinery, or a truck. Business capital expenditures constitute a key factor in a nation's economic activity.

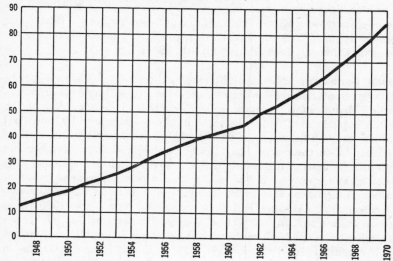

Capital Consumption Allowance (Billions of dollars)

Source: U.S. Department of Commerce.

Historically, capital expenditures in the U.S. have fluctuated widely. The low rate of U.S. economic growth from 1958 to 1964 has been blamed on the low rate of capital expenditure, which approximated less than 7% of the gross national product during that period, whereas in earlier and later periods of prosperity it ran as high as 8% or more. For further discussion of capital expenditure and its relationship to the nation's economy, see Dexter M. Keezer and Associates, *Making Capitalism Work*, McGraw-Hill Book Company, New York, 1950; ———, *New Forces in American Business*, McGraw-Hill Book Company, New York, 1959.

Capital Flight   A massive transfer of currency from one country to another in search of protection against adverse economic, political, or military developments. During the late 1930s, for example, the threat of war sent billions of dollars of private European funds to Switzerland, the U.S., and other countries likely to maintain neutrality and continued political and economic stability. These transfers, which initially were unrelated to economic developments, created considerable turbulence in the international flow of funds and caused the countries of their origin to suffer large balance-of-payments deficits, which, in turn, gave rise to massives waves of currency speculation and to government regulations and controls designed to stem the outflow. The International Monetary Fund now makes short-term loans to countries that have temporary balance-of-payments deficits, thus discouraging currency speculation and softening the effects of capital flight due to unstable political conditions. For a detailed account of postwar episodes of capital flight, see Arthur I. Bloomfield, *Speculative or Flight Movements in Post-War International Finance,* Princeton University Press, Princeton, N.J., 1954.

Capital Formation   The net addition to total capital stock in a given period. It represents the addition of new capital stock to existing stock after subtracting depreciation, damage, and other physical deterioration of the existing capital stock. This is the accounting procedure used by individual business firms, but nations often include human knowledge as well as fixed capital in their accounts. Capital formation is important because capital is the basis of future production. Moreover, gross investment fluctuates greatly from year to year and is thus a prime ingredient of minor business cycles. See Thomas F. Dernburg and Duncan M. McDougall, *Macroeconomics,* McGraw-Hill Book Company, New York, 1960; Conference on Research in Income and Wealth, *Problems of Capital Formation,* a Report of the National Bureau of Economic Research, Inc., Princeton University Press, Princeton, N.J., 1957; Simon Kuznets, *Capital in the American Economy,* National Bureau of Economic Research, Princeton University Press, Princeton, N.J., 1961.

Capital Gains Tax   A tax on that portion of personal income earned through the sale of such capital items as stocks, bonds, and real estate. The capital gain is measured by the difference between the acquisition price and the final sale price of the capital item. If the asset is held for more than six months, the income from its sale is classified as a long-term capital gain and is subject to special taxation by the Federal government and most state governments. The maximum rate is 25% for Federal taxation of long-term capital gains. Much controversy has arisen over whether or not capital gains should be taxed and whether they should receive special tax treatment. Since appreciation on capital items is accumulated over several years, the employment of a progressive tax rate on capital gains may result in overtaxation at the time when the gain is realized. It is also argued that high taxation of capital gains distorts the stock market and investment decisions, since sales are discouraged as capital values rise. In periods of rising prices, a capital gain may merely represent an increase in the price of a capital item and not an increase in the value. Those who favor capital gains taxation argue that capital gains represent unearned increments in income and should be included in income taxation. If capital gains were not subject to taxation, individuals with large incomes would convert substantial parts of their funds into investments on which the return would be in the form of capital gains rather than dividends or ordinary income. Thus, unless capital gains are taxed, they provide a loophole for avoiding personal income taxation. For additional information, see Lawrence H. Seltzer, *The Nature and Tax Treatment of Capital Gains and Losses*, National Bureau of Economic Research, Inc., New York, 1951; U.S. Treasury Department, Tax Advisory Staff, *Federal Income Taxation Treatment of Capital Gains and Losses*, 1951.

Capital Goods Economic goods used in the production of other goods. They include factory buildings, machinery, locomotives, trucks, and tractors. Land and money are not usually considered capital goods. In the U.S. during the period 1959–1971, the share of business' expenditures devoted to machinery and equipment was more than 70%; that devoted to plants and other capital construction, less than 30%. For further information, see Simon Kuznets, *Capital in the American Economy*, Princeton University Press, Princeton, N.J., 1961; for statistics on business' expenditures for capital goods, see U.S. Department of Commerce, *Annual Surveys of Expenditures for New Plants and Equipment; Annual Surveys of Business' Plans for New Plants and Equipment*, McGraw-Hill Department of Economics, New York.

Capital-Intensive Industry An industry that uses large amounts of capital equipment in relation to its labor force or its output. The capital intensity of an industry can be measured by either capital-labor or capital-output ratios. Examples of industries with high ratios are petroleum, primary metals, chemicals, and paper; those with low ratios are the apparel, leather, and furniture industries. In general, capital-intensive industries predominate in the world's more highly developed nations; in developing countries they are generally found in export industries. Such industries imply efficient production methods and a high output per worker, which, in turn, indicate high real incomes and standards of living. For this reason, less highly developed nations stress the need for capital accumulation, which they consider the path to higher output and wealth. For a discussion of how capital intensity is measured and how it is related to investment theory, see Gardner Ackley, *Macroeconomic Theory*, The Macmillan Company, New York, 1961, pp. 460–472; see also M. Dobb, "Second Thoughts on Capital Intensity of Investment," *Review of Economic Studies*, vol. XXIV, pp. 33–42, Oliver & Boyd Ltd., Edinburgh, 1956–1957; for a study and comparison of capital intensity of industries in underdeveloped and developed economies, see V. V. Bhatt, "Capital Output Ratios of Certain Industries: A Comparative Study of Certain Countries," *Review of Economics and Statistics*, Harvard University Press, Cambridge, Mass., August, 1954.

Capitalism *See Free-Enterprise System.*

Capitalized Value The term applied to a technique used to determine the present value of an asset that promises to produce income in the future. To calculate the present value, the total future income expected must be discounted, that is, offset against the cost (as measured by the current interest rate) of carrying the asset until the income has actually been realized. For example, if the current rate of interest is 4%, the present discounted value of an asset that will yield $1,000 per year is about $960. If the asset promises a stream of income (for example, prospects for $1,000 annual rental income from a house for the next ten years), its capitalized value is calculated by adding together the present discounted values of the income in each year. The general formula for this calculation is

$$\frac{I}{(1+r)^t}$$

where I is the annual income, r is the current rate of interest, and t is the number of years involved. In this manner, an investor confronted with a choice of properties can determine which alternative is the most remunerative, though the formula tells him nothing about the relative risks involved.

Capital Levy A one-time tax on all wealth. Such a tax is used primarily after a war to achieve a drastic reduction in the size of the national debt. The capital levy is said to be a capitalization of ordinary taxes that would have been necessary as an alternative. It attempts to remove in one step the debt burden or the inflationary pressures associated with a large debt, but it may result in deflation because many of the persons taxed cannot meet their obligations from liquid assets. The consequent sale of property depresses prices and causes serious inequities and disorganization in the securities and real estate markets. The capital levy is hard to administer, since it is very difficult to make a uniform determination of a fair value of all the capital in a country in a relatively short period of time. There is a probability of inexact valuation and tax evasion. If payment must be made in the form of money, the necessary large liquidation of assets may disrupt the capital and real estate markets, whereas if any type of asset is acceptable as payment, the government faces the problem of disposing of a large variety of assets. For additional details, see J. R. Hicks et al., *The Taxation of War Wealth,* Oxford University Press, Fair Lawn, N.J., 1941; U. K. Hicks, *Public Finance,* Nesbet and Co., London, 1947; P. Robson, "Capital Levies in Western Europe after the Second World War," *Review of Economic Studies,* Oliver & Boyd Ltd., Edinburgh, October, 1959.

Capital-Output Ratio (Capital Coefficient)   The ratio between the book value (net of depreciation) of plant and equipment and the gross value of output. It is a measure of capacity utilization and the capital intensity of an industry. In economic theory, the capital-output ratio is the amount of capital necessary to produce an additional unit of output. Capital-output coefficients vary tremendously from industry to industry, as the accompanying table indicates. Lumber, nonferrous metal products, iron and steel, paper and allied products, and petroleum have high capital-output coefficients, while apparel, tobacco, leather, and furniture and fixtures have low coefficients.

**Ratio of Fixed Capital to Output in 1963 Prices
(1953, 1957, and 1965) ***

	1965	1957	1953
Petroleum and coal products	0.548	0.712	0.828
Primary metal industries	0.470	0.534	0.496
Paper and allied products	0.454	0.519	0.518
Stone, clay, and glass products	0.408	0.507	0.471
Chemicals and allied products	0.330	0.523	0.549
Lumber and wood products	0.243	0.303	0.402
Instruments and related products	0.212	0.232	0.220
Printing and publishing	0.211	0.258	0.320
Rubber and plastic products, n.e.c.	0.206	0.261	0.223
Textile mill products	0.200	0.281	0.396
Machinery, except electrical	0.191	0.229	0.197
Beverages	0.188	0.251	0.218
Fabricated metal products	0.178	0.237	0.218
Motor vehicles, parts, and accessories	0.155	0.273	0.195
Electrical machinery	0.151	0.218	0.132
Miscellaneous manufacturing	0.138	0.199	0.217
Food and kindred products	0.138	0.156	0.174
Transportation equipment, other than automobiles	0.136	0.141	0.093
Furniture and fixtures	0.117	0.164	0.184
Tobacco manufacturers	0.094	0.081	0.067
Leather and leather products	0.088	0.102	0.108
Apparel and related products	0.056	0.074	0.084

* Fixed capital includes structures and machinery and equipment both owned and rented.
SOURCE: National Industrial Conference Board, Inc.

Capital Stock (Issued Stock)   The aggregate equity or ownership in a corporation. Capital stock is that part of authorized stock which has been issued and is still outstanding, as opposed to treasury stock, which comprises those shares of stock that were issued but were brought back by the corporation. It also represents the permanently invested capital of a corporation. Capital stock can be classified into two broad groups, common stock and preferred stock. The owners of the corporation hold certificates which indicate how many shares of the corporation's capital stock they own and what rights and privileges they have. For further information, see Charles W. Gerstenberg, *Financial Organization and Management of Business*, 4th ed., Prentice-Hall, Inc., Englewood Cliffs, N.J., 1959; Jules I. Bogen (ed.), *Financial Handbook*, 4th ed., The Ronald Press Company, New York, 1968; Joseph H. Bonneville et al., *Organizing and Financing Business*, Prentice-Hall, Inc., Englewood Cliffs, N.J., 1959.

Capital Structure   *See Invested Capital.*

Captive Shop   A mine, quarry, or plant producing ores, metals, or semi-manufactured goods that are used almost exclusively by their producer in an integrated business operation. For example, the large steel and non-ferrous metals manufacturers of the U.S. depend on captive mines for their supply of basic ores. There are numerous captive manufacturing plants among large manufacturing companies which are integrated vertically. For a discussion of costs in captive mines versus commercial mines, see W. E. Fisher and C. M. James, *Minimum Price Fixing in the Bituminous Coal Industry*, Report of the National Bureau of Economic Research, Inc., in cooperation with the Wharton School of Finance and Commerce, Industrial Research Department, Princeton University Press, Princeton, N.J., 1955.

Cartel   An association of independent industrial enterprises producing similar goods that is formed to secure a monopoly in a specific market. In current usage, the term cartel refers to the monopolization of world markets, as opposed to trusts, syndicates, and the like, which are monopolies in more restricted markets. Membership in such associations is usually voluntary, although it may be required by law or by competitive pressures in some instances, and the members maintain their separate identities and financial independence. The distinguishing characteristic of a cartel is that the agreement invariably requires substitution of common policies for independent policies of pricing and production. Cartels are classified into four major categories: (1) associations which attempt to control the conditions of sale; (2) associations which attempt to fix prices; (3) associations which attempt to allocate productive activities, sales territories, and customers among their members; and (4) associations which attempt to award a fixed share of the business to each member. Associations can punish their members by revoking licenses granted under patents and held in a common pool; by imposing fines against money held in deposit; and by withholding payments from equalization pools, profit pools, sales receipt pools, or other funds over which they exert control. They can compel outsiders to join by threatening to put them out of business, by underselling them, or by cutting off their sources of supplies. There has been little interest in cartel activity in the 1950s and 1960s because rapid economic growth in countries that have abetted cartels (European nations and Japan) has encouraged the exploration of new markets instead of the allocation of old ones. Cartels are generally held to be illegal under U.S. antitrust laws, but the Webb-Pomerene Act exempts from prosecution associations entered into solely for the purposes of promoting export trade on the theory that members of such associations should be able to compete on equal terms with cartel members of other countries. See Edward Corwin, *Economic and Political Aspects of International Cartels,* Committee Print 1, Subcommittee on War Mobilization of the Senate Committee on Military Affairs, 1944; Clair Wilcox, *Public Policies toward Business,* Richard D. Irwin, Inc., Homewood, Ill., 1955; George W. Stocking and Myron W. Watkins, *Cartels or Competition: The Economics of International Controls by Business and Government,* The Twentieth Century Fund, New York, 1948.

Cash   In an accounting sense, any type of money, including both currency and demand deposits. For example, the cash entry on the asset side of a firm's balance sheet covers currency on hand and bank demand deposits. In general usage, however, cash sometimes refers to currency alone, as when there is a choice of paying by check or by cash, that is, in bills or coins.

Cash Basis   A method of accounting in which income is considered earned when it is received, and expenses are recorded when they are paid. This method differs from the accrual basis of accounting, in which revenues and expenses are allocated to the periods in which they are applicable regardless of when the actual cash is received or paid out. Only corporations selling services are permitted to use the cash basis in preparing their income tax returns. All corporations in which inventories are an income-determining factor (this provision includes all merchandising and manufacturing firms) must use the accrual basis. Most firms, and almost all large ones, use the accrual basis in preparing their financial statements. For further information, see H. A. Finney and H. E. Miller, *Principles of Accounting,* 6th ed., Prentice-Hall, Inc., Englewood Cliffs, N.J., 1965.

Cash Budget   A method of budgeting Federal expenditures and receipts which includes the transactions in a number of government trust-fund accounts. It is less comprehensive than the unified budget but more comprehensive than the administrative budget, which was the traditional method of Federal budgeting until 1969 and which includes all funds for which the government considers itself the sole owner. The cash budget was devised as a method of including all government accounts, such as those used to finance social security, highway, and housing programs, for which the government does not consider itself the full owner. Since it shows more precisely what is happening to tax collections and how Federal funds are being distributed, it is a better measure of the extent of government fiscal operations in the economy than the administrative

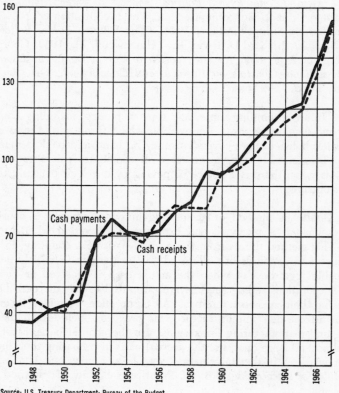

Federal Cash Receipts and Payments for the Fiscal Years, 1947-1966 (Billions of dollars)

Source: U.S. Treasury Department; Bureau of the Budget.

budget. In the fiscal year 1967, for example, the difference between Federal government expenditures according to the cash budget and according to the administrative budget was $29.4 billion, and the difference in receipts was $37.8 billion. For additional details, see Gerhard Colm, *The Federal Budget and the National Economy*, National Planning Association, Washington, D.C., 1955.

Cash Flow The sum of profits and depreciation allowances. (Instead of profits, many economists use retained earnings, which are profits after taxes and after deductions for dividend payments.) Gross cash flow is composed of total profits plus depreciation; net cash flow, of retained earnings plus depreciation. Thus, cash flow represents the total funds that corporations generate internally for investment in the modernization and expansion of plants and equipment and for working capital. The growth of depreciation allowances over the years has made them a much more important part of cash flow than retained earnings. In 1969 cash flow of corporations in the U.S. totaled $73.7 billion, a record high

Corporate Cash Flow (Billions of dollars)

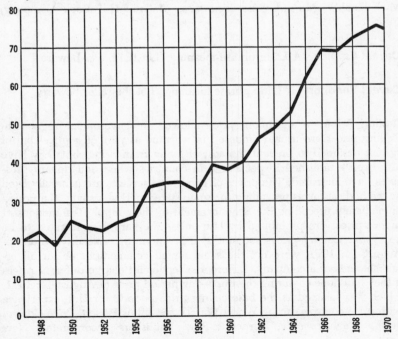

Source: U.S. Department of Commerce; Securities and Exchange Commission.

despite the fact that retained earnings were still well below earlier peaks. Both gross and net cash flow are important tools of financial and economic analysis. For a more detailed explanation of the use of cash flow, see C. Aubrey Smith and Jim Ashburne, *Financial and Administrative Accounting*, McGraw-Hill Book Company, New York, 1960.

Cash Market   *See Spot Market.*

Cash Price   *See Spot Price.*

Casualty Insurance   All insurance except life, fire, and marine insurance. Casualty insurance comprises a variety of types concerned mainly with insurance against losses due to the legal liability of third persons. It includes coverage for loss or liability resulting from accident or mishap. For further information, see Curtis M. Elliott, *Property and Casualty Insurance*, McGraw-Hill Book Company, New York, 1960; John Bainbridge, *Biography of an Idea: The Story of Mutual Fire and Casualty Insurance*, Doubleday & Company, Inc., Garden City, N.Y., 1952; G. F. Michelbacher, *Multiple-Line Insurance*, McGraw-Hill Book Company, New York, 1957.

Caveat Emptor   A Latin phrase meaning "Let the buyer beware."

Caveat Venditor   A Latin phrase meaning "Let the seller beware."

Ceiling Price   A maximum price allowed by government regulation. Ceiling prices are usually imposed in wartime as part of a price-control system designed to prevent the cost of living from rising, but they have also been established in peacetime in countries where inflationary pressures have increased. The prices of goods and services are generally fixed at the highest levels prevailing for some stated period, usually the period immediately preceding the announcement of the control. Transactions at higher prices are prohibited by law unless they are demonstrated to be necessary. Ceiling prices set in the U.S. under the Executive order of August 14, 1971, were not the same for all commodities or for all establishments of a company. Different sellers could charge different prices if they had done so during the thirty-day period prior to August 14, 1971, which was selected as the base ceiling price period. For U.S. experience with price controls during World War II, see Julius Hirsch, *Price Control in the War Economy*, Harper & Row, Publishers, Incorporated, New York, 1943.

Census Tract   A small area of a large city, usually covering a few blocks with about 4,000 residents. There are approximately 23,000 census tracts in 175 places in the U.S. The area generally remains unchanged in its environment, population, and economic status for a long period. Thus, studies made within a tract by the U.S. Bureau of the Census provide comparable statistical and economic information which proves extremely valuable to business and local government planners as well as to advertising agencies and market research organizations. Census tract data are available from the Census Bureau in Washington, D.C.

Central Bank   The most important bank in a country, usually possessing official standing in the government. It regulates the banking system and the supply of money and credit to help promote the public goals of economic growth and high employment with a minimum of inflation. The central bank of England is the Bank of England, that of France is the Banque de France, and that of the Federal Republic of Germany is the Deutsche Bundesbank. The U.S. central bank is the Federal Reserve System, created by act of Congress and placed in operation in 1913. Its tasks are clearly and succinctly set forth in its publication, *The Federal Reserve System: Purposes and Functions,* and statistics pertaining to the System's operations and banks under its aegis are published monthly in the *Federal Reserve Bulletin.* For operations of central banks in other countries, see specific reports of each bank; see also "Comparative Features of Central Banks in Selected Foreign Countries," *Economic Policies and Practices,* Paper I, prepared for the U.S. Joint Economic Committee, Government Printing Office, Washington, D.C., 1963.

Central-Limit Theorem   The sum of n random, independent variables having finite variances will tend to be normally distributed as the number of variables approaches infinity regardless of the manner in which the individual variables are distributed. It is through this theorem that the normal distribution, which occurs frequently in observations of natural and social phenomena, acquires its central importance in the theories of probability and sampling. For additional information, see Gerhard Tintner and Charles B. Millham, *Mathematics and Statistics for Economists,* Holt, Rinehart and Winston, Inc., New York, 1970; Stefan Valavanis, *Econometrics,* McGraw-Hill Book Company, New York, 1959.

Central Reserve Cities   The two largest cities in the United States, New York and Chicago, which account for the greatest amount of banking activity in the nation. The reserve funds held in these areas generally are higher than those of any other city of the Federal Reserve System.

The Board of Governors' authority to classify or reclassify cities as central reserve cities was terminated effective July 28, 1962.

Certificate of Deposit   A certificate for money deposited in a commercial bank for a specified period of time and earning a specified rate of return. The use of certificates has grown rapidly in the U.S. since 1961, when they were introduced to attract time money, especially that of domestic corporations. Until that time, large banks had rarely accepted interest-bearing time deposits from domestic firms. The certificate of deposit, commonly called a CD, is a negotiable instrument and has a secondary market for the sale of outstanding issues. CDs thus compete for idle funds with treasury bills, commercial paper, and other short-term money instruments. The volume of negotiable CDs in the U.S. in May, 1971, was about $27 billion, compared with $1 billion in July, 1961. For a detailed discussion of certificates of deposit, see R. Fieldhouse, *Certificates of Deposit*, The Bankers Publishing Company, Boston, 1962.

Certificate of Necessity   An authorization permitting accelerated depreciation of part or all of new emergency facilities for national defense. First employed in the U.S. during World War I, this accelerated amortization of privately owned defense facilities for Federal tax purposes was reemployed during World War II and the Korean conflict. Its primary purpose was to induce private businessmen to build new facilities essential to the war effort. During the Korean conflict, the Office of Defense Mobilization issued certificates of necessity, which enabled plants and equipment deemed essential to national defense to be amortized on a basis of five years instead of over their natural life. Among the problems raised by such a program are the discrimination involved in a temporary certification period, the difficulty of excluding projects which would have been undertaken without accelerated amortization, and the exclusion of the replacement of expenditures from certification. For additional details, see *Amortization of Defense Facilities*, Machinery and Allied Products Institute, Washington, D.C., 1952.

Certification   An endorsement of standards, qualifications, qualities, and preparation by an authoritative organization or agency. An example of certification in the labor field is the endorsement by a national or state board of a specific union as the bargaining agent for a particular group of employees. An example in banking is the certification of a check, which indicates that the signature of the drawer is genuine and that he has funds in the bank to cover payment. Professional groups, such as acccountants and teachers, have their own organizations that administer certification tests to set qualifications and standards for their professions.

Ceteris Paribus   A Latin phrase meaning "all other things remaining the same" or "all relevant factors being equal." The term is used in the analysis of a variety of economic phenomena. For example, in price theory the analysis of a price change is often carried on under *ceteris paribus* assumptions. Giving a declining demand schedule for a particular consumer good, a reduction in the price of this good will cause a larger quantity to be purchased *ceteris paribus*, meaning that this will be the result if consumer incomes and tastes remain unchanged and the prices of other goods and services also are unchanged.

Chain Banking   The control and operation of three or more independently incorporated banks by one or more individuals. The control is usually exercised by stock ownership or interlocking directorates, but it can take other forms. Usually, such chains are centered at one or a few key banks which are larger and more important than the others in the chain. Chain banking differs from branch banking, which is a form of multiple-office banking in which the bank is a single legal entity and merely operates more than one banking office. It also differs from group banking, in which three or more banks are controlled by a holding company. Usually a looser and less formal arrangement than group banking, chain banking offers the advantage of coordinating the resources and policies of the chain members. In the U.S., chain banking is now significant in only a few Middle Western states where branch banking is prohibited by law, and its general importance in the banking system is declining. For further information on this type of banking, see C. E. Coyle, *Branch, Group and Chain Banking*, Banking Studies, Board of Governors of the Federal Reserve System, Washington, D.C., 1941.

Chain Index   An index number whose value at any given point in time is related to a base in the immediately preceding time period rather than to a fixed base period in the more distant past. The individual index numbers thus constructed may then be linked together (link relatives) in attempting to make comparisons between nonconsecutive periods. The chain index is accurate in measuring changes over relatively short time periods. Its accuracy decreases as the time period between two chain-index numbers that are being compared is extended. A modified form of the chain index is used in deriving the implicit deflator of U.S. gross national product. For additional information, see Leonard J. Kazmier, *Statistical Analysis for Business and Economics*, McGraw-Hill Book Company, New York, 1967.

Chain Stores   A large merchandising organization that consists of many individual units located throughout the nation or in specific areas of a nation. The advantages of large-scale operations (lower costs through purchases in large quantities and cash transactions with consumers) have contributed to the growth of such enterprises. Among well-known national chains in the U.S. are Great Atlantic and Pacific Tea for food, Walgreen for drugs, A. S. Beck for shoes, and Robert Hall for clothing. According to the U.S. Bureau of the Census, chain-store firms (operating eleven or more retail stores) accounted in 1970 for sales of $110 billion out of a total retail business of $365 billion. See G. M. Lebhar, *Chain Stores in America 1859–1959,* Chain Store Publishing Co., New York, 1959; for monthly statistics of chain stores, see U.S. Bureau of the Census, *Monthly Retail Trade Report.*

Chattel Mortgage   A lien against tangible personal property that secures a loan. Chattel mortgages are distinguished from ordinary mortgages in that they are liens against personal property rather than real estate. Unlike security loans, they make use of tangible property as collateral. Chattel mortgages are used by consumers to finance purchases of automobiles, television sets, and other durable goods and by businesses to finance inventories. See E. R. Dillavou et al., *Principles of Business Law,* Prentice-Hall, Inc., Englewood Cliffs, N.J., 1957, chap. 43.

Cheap Money   *See Easy Money.*

Checkbook Money   *See Demand Deposit.*

Checkoff, Automatic   The withholding by an employer of union dues and other assessments from the earnings of workers. Its purpose is to assure the union that dues are paid promptly and regularly by the workers. Before the checkoff became common, unions sometimes had to use a "dues picket line" at plant gates on pay days to enforce the payment of dues. The picket line was composed of union officers and staunch union supporters, and the penalty for crossing the line without payment could be a bloody nose or a cracked skull. Employers tend to consider that the use of the checkoff lessens the likelihood that unions will press grievance claims of dubious validity or attack employers merely to generate enthusiasm for the union and thus collect dues. In the U.S., the checkoff rose rapidly in popularity until 1951. Since that time its use has remained at the same level, the dues of slightly more than three-fourths of all workers under collective bargaining agreements being checked off periodically. Under the provisions of the Taft-Hartley Act of 1947, the checkoff is legal only if the worker gives his permission in writing. For statistics, see *Union Security and Checkoff Provisions in Major Union Contracts 1958–59,* U.S. Department of Labor Bulletin 1272; for discussion, see

Melvin W. Reder, *Labor in a Growing Economy*, John Wiley & Sons, Inc., New York, 1957; Joseph Shister, *Economics of the Labor Market*, J. B. Lippincott Company, Philadelphia, 1956.

Chicago School   The name given to a group of economists adhering to a neoliberal economic philosophy who teach at the University of Chicago. Among them are Henry C. Simons, F. A. von Hayek, Frank Knight, Milton Friedman, and George J. Stigler. All have strong faith in competition and free markets as means of allocating resources in the economy, although they do not agree on the exact nature of the institutional framework that should be used to achieve their goals. In addition, the followers of the Chicago school are generally considered to believe that the behavior of the economy can be explained better by changes in the money supply than by other variables, although this view has been enunciated principally by one member of the Chicago school. Not all professors at the University of Chicago embrace the neoliberal philosophy. For additional details and an explanation of neoliberalism and alternative economic philosophies, see D. S. Watson, *Economic Policy*, Houghton Mifflin Company, Boston, 1961; for views of individuals associated with the Chicago school, see F. A. von Hayek, *The Road to Serfdom*, The University of Chicago Press, Chicago, 1944; Henry C. Simons, *Economic Policy for a Free Society*, The University of Chicago Press, Chicago, 1948; Milton Friedman, *Capitalism and Freedom*, The University of Chicago Press, Chicago, 1962. For a discussion of the ideas and policy implications of the Chicago school, see Harvey D. Shapiro, "The Chicago School: Apostles of the Money Supply," *The Institutional Investor*, February, 1970, pp. 36–40, 127–136.

Child Labor Laws   Legislation designed to protect working children from unhealthy conditions and hazardous labor and to assure them of a minimum amount of school. State regulation of child labor in the U.S. began in 1842, and every state now imposes some measure of restriction on the employment of children. Among the common provisions of state laws are minimum ages for employment, particularly in manufacturing and in hazardous occupations; requirements that young workers obtain employment certificates or work permits; and limitations on the length of the work day or week and the amount of night work. In 1938 limitations on the use of child labor were incorporated in the Federal government's Fair Labor Standards Act. The act prohibits the employment of children in the production of goods in interstate commerce below certain minimum ages (sixteen years is the standard for most jobs, and eighteen years for hazardous occupations). A 1949 amendment imposed further restrictions and provided sanctions to enforce its measures. These sanctions are directed not at the employer but at the goods produced, which become "hot" and are prohibited from distribution in interstate commerce for a thirty-day period while the child labor situation is being corrected. For information on the development of child labor laws, see U.S. Department of Labor, *Growth of Labor Laws in the United States,* 1962, pp. 1–58.

Christian Socialism A movement which attempted to combine the basic aims of socialism with the ethical teachings of Christianity. Begun in England in the 1850s primarily as a result of the writings of Frederick Maurice and Charles Kingsley, Christian socialism did not advocate state ownership of the means of production, but was interested rather in cooperative production and social reform. Egalitarian concepts of equal distribution of wealth and benevolent altruism were largely substituted for the private profit motive, but the supremacy of the economic freedom of the individual was upheld. Since World War II, a number of Christian Socialist parties have arisen in Europe, primarily as right-of-center political forces. For further information, see Harry W. Laidler, *History of Socialism,* Thomas Y. Crowell Company, New York, 1968; G. D. H. Cole, *A History of Socialist Thought,* St. Martin's Press, Inc., New York, 1956–1958.

Chronic Unemployment Unemployment lasting for at least six months as a result of factors other than seasonal slackness in a particular industry or routine job changing and similar causes. A common measure of chronic unemployment is the statistical series of the U.S. Department of Labor covering long-term unemployment. This series shows that in April, 1971, persons unemployed for a period of twenty-seven weeks or longer numbered more than 500,000. Among frequently cited causes of chronic unemployment are structural changes in the economy that render particular skills obsolete; inadequate education for suitable jobs; increasing automation that displaces unskilled and semiskilled workers in a variety of jobs; and an unsatisfactory rate of growth for the economy as a whole, resulting in relatively low demand for the services offered by particular groups of workers. For a discussion of chronic unemployment, see *The Rise of Chronic Unemployment,* National Planning Association, Planning Pamphlet 113, Washington, D.C., 1961; *Employment and Unemployment,* Hearings before the Subcommittee on Economic Statistics of the U.S. Joint Economic Committee, Dec. 18, 19, and 20, 1961, Government Printing Office, Washington, D.C., 1962; for data on long-term unemployment, see U.S. Department of Labor, *Monthly Labor Review.*

Circular Flow The continual circular movement of money and goods in the economy. The concept of the circular flow of income is a simplification which attempts to illustrate the flow of money and goods from households to business enterprises and back to households. As resource owners, individuals sell their resources to businesses; as consumers, they spend the income received from this sale to buy goods and services Businesses buy resources from households and produce finished products, which are sold to the consuming households for money, which is then used to pay for resource costs. Resources and finished goods flow in one direction, and money income and expenditures in the other direction. In the resource markets, the businesses are on the demand side of the market while households are on the supply side. In the product market, these positions are reversed, the households demanding goods and the businesses supplying them. A number of problems arise from the use of this simple circular-flow model. It ignores transactions occurring within the business and household sectors; it assumes that households spend all their income, so that flows of income and expenditures are constant; and it does not explain the determination of resource and product prices but assumes that they are already given. For further information, see Walter W. Haines, *Money, Prices and Policy*, 2d ed., McGraw-Hill Book Company, New York, 1966.

Circular Integration   A fusion of noncompetitive concerns that have the same general market or the ability to benefit from the application of supervised management procedures. (Other types of integration are horizontal and vertical.) A good example of circular integration is the General Foods Corporation, which over the years has merged with many noncompetitive companies in the food industry. Among the advantages of this method of integration are savings on overhead and selling costs as well as most of the economies of large-scale operations. For a more detailed discussion of circular integration, see Joseph H. Bonneville et al., *Organizing and Financing Business,* Prentice-Hall, Inc., Englewood Cliffs, N.J., 1959.

Circulating Capital   Goods which can be used only at one time or over a relatively short period of time. Circulating capital is thus distinguished from fixed capital, which is used over a long period of time. Materials and fuels are considered circulating-capital items.

Classical Liberalism (Nineteenth-Century Liberalism)   An economic philosophy that is characterized by strong faith in the general beneficence of markets largely unfettered by governmental or other restraints. An assumption of classical liberalism is that human wants are best satisfied and productive resources most efficiently employed when goods and services are sold in competitive markets. The social ethics emphasized are the freedom and the self-reliance of the individual. The political framework implied consists of the supremacy of the rule of law and a minimum role for the government in the economy, although the philosophy explicitly recognizes the need for public works projects, defense, and other governmental operations. Classical liberalism emphasizes economic freedom, namely, the right to engage in any occupation without restriction or to produce any good or service. There is a strong presumption that if every individual seeks his own self-interest, the results will be the promotion of social welfare and the creation of economic harmony. The theory developed in England in the late 1700s and early 1800s. Adam Smith, Jeremy Bentham, and John Stuart Mill were among the leaders of classical liberalism. They favored free trade, competition, the gold standard, some public works, relief to the indigent, and work laws protecting women and children. The U.S. version of classical liberalism became known as social Darwinism, or the survival of the fittest in the rough-and-tumble of the free market. Herbert Spencer, a British writer who had greater influence in the U.S. than in England, proposed a form of *laissez faire* that would now be regarded as radical. He favored extreme individualism and even opposed sanitary laws and compulsory free education. For further information, see Overton Taylor, *Economics and Liberalism*, Harvard University Press, Cambridge, Mass., 1955; Lionel Robbins, *The Theory of Economic Policy*, St. Martin's Press, Inc., New York, 1952; for a brief contemporary textbook treatment, see D. S. Watson, *Economic Policy*, Houghton Mifflin Company, Boston, 1960.

Classical School   A late eighteenth- and early nineteenth-century school of political economists who believed that economies function better under free private initiative and vigorous competition than under government control. The school's founder was Adam Smith, and its leaders were David Ricardo, Nassau W. Senior, John Stuart Mill, and Jean Baptiste Say. The classical theory was based on the notion that the production, consumption, and distribution of wealth are determined by economic laws. The classicists considered that the power of competition alone determined prices, wages, profits, and rent. They were opposed to relief for the poor because it promoted instability, but they believed that the government should undertake some type of investment projects which would prove useful to the nation as a whole. Classical theory and analysis were spelled out in relatively clear and systematic statements of common-sensible notions about economics. The school had an intuitive grasp of the important elements and relationships in the development of the real economy, although it was unable to express precisely all the political, social, and economic implications. The main differences between the classical school and the neoclassical school, which evolved later, were the emphasis of the latter on mathematical economics and its stress on the analysis of the psychological background of consumer demands, decisions, and actions. For further discussion of the classical school and classicists, see William Fellner, *Modern Economic Analysis,* McGraw-Hill Book Company, New York, 1960; Overton Taylor, *A History of Economic Thought,* McGraw-Hill Book Company, New York, 1960; for theories of the classicists, see Adam Smith, *The Wealth of Nations,* Random House, Inc., New York, 1937; David Ricardo, *The Principles of Political Economy and Taxation,* Richard D. Irwin, Inc., Homewood, Ill., 1963.

Class I Motor Carrier   A large motor carrier of property and passengers that has annual gross operating revenues of $1 million or more. A large proportion of Class I carriers are common carriers. Among Class I carriers in the U.S. in 1969 were 1,311 carriers of property with combined operating revenues of $10.8 billion (or 80% of the total revenue of Class I, Class II, and Class III motor carriers of property) and 96 carriers of passengers (70 intercity and 26 local and suburban) with combined operating revenues of $836 million. The Class I category is set by the Interstate Commerce Commission. For statistics on Class I motor carriers, see U.S. Interstate Commerce Commission, *Annual Report.*

Class I Railroad   A carrier of property and passengers that has annual operating revenues of $3 million or more when averaged over a three-year period. In 1969, Class I line-haul railroads in the U.S. had operating revenues of $11.5 billion, or more than 95% of the operating revenues of all railroads. The Class I category is set by the Interstate Commerce Commission. For statistics of Class I railroads, see U.S. Interstate Commerce Commission, *Annual Report.*

Class Struggle   The doctrine, usually attributed to Karl Marx, which states that the driving force of historical change lies in antagonisms between social classes. In *The Communist Manifesto* (1848), Marx set forth his proposition as follows: "The history of all hitherto existing society is the history of class struggles. . . . Freeman and slave, patrician and plebeian, lord and serf, guildmaster and journeyman, in a word; oppressor and oppressed, stood in constant opposition to one another, carried on an uninterrupted, now hidden, now open fight, a fight that each time ended, either in a revolutionary reconstitution of society at large, or in the common ruin of the contending classes. . . . Our epoch, the epoch of the bourgeoisie, possesses . . . this distinctive feature; it has simplified the class antagonisms. Society as a whole is more and more splitting up into two great hostile camps, into two great classes directly facing each other: Bourgeoisie and Proletariat." Combined with a second Marxian precept, the economic interpretation of history, this doctrine provides the basis for the Communists' firm belief in the inevitable success of their economic and social systems. A great body of literature has been produced that denies the validity of the Marxian emphasis on the role of class struggles in history. Some historians have denied that the idea was originally Marx's. For a further discussion of the subject, see Karl Marx and Friedrich Engels, *The Communist Manifesto*, Henry Regnery Company, Chicago, 1954; J. A. LeRossignol, *From Marx to Stalin: A Critique of Communism*, Thomas Y. Crowell Company, New York, 1940, chap. 10; H. See, *The Economic Interpretation of History*, Adelphi Publishing Company, New York, 1929; Benedetto Croce, *Historical Materialism and the Economics of Karl Marx*, The Macmillan Company, New York, 1914; Joseph A. Schumpeter, *Capitalism, Socialism and Democracy*, Harper & Row, Publishers, Incorporated, New York, 1950, chap. 11.

Clayton Antitrust Act   A Federal statute prohibiting unfair methods of competition in commerce. Enacted in 1914, it revised and strengthened the Sherman Antitrust Act. The Clayton Act was concerned with methods of preventing the accumulation of monopoly power rather than with the breaking up of established monopolies. Its main purpose was to prevent a business from becoming a monopoly by outlawing unfair practices the effect of which was to lessen competition or to create a monopoly: price discrimination, exclusive-dealing and tying contracts, intercorporate stockholdings, and interlocking directorates. Basically, the act was an attempt to prevent cutthroat competition, by which large firms were able to eliminate their smaller rivals. Only price discrimination made in good faith to meet competition was allowed by the Clayton Act. This and others of the act's nondiscrimination provisions have, however, resulted in difficult problems of judicial interpretation. The act exempted labor from the Sherman Act's provisions, stating that human labor is not a commodity, and thus labor unions cannot be considered conspiracies in restraint of trade. For additional details, see Vernon A Mund, *Government and Business*, 3d ed., Harper & Row, Publishers, Incorporated, New York, 1960; Joel Dirlam and Alfred Kahn, *Fair Competition: The Law and Economics of Antitrust Policy*, Cornell University Press, Ithaca, N.Y., 1954.

Clearinghouse   An association of banks in a given area the representatives of which meet daily to exchange checks drawn on each other. Each participating bank, by settling simultaneously the claims against it and its claims against the other members of the clearinghouse, reduces to a net balance the amount that it must settle. This settlement is a single payment that was originally made in cash, later in clearinghouse loan certificates, and now, in most cases, through entries in the books of the respective Federal Reserve banks (or, in smaller centers, in drafts on correspondent banks). In most cities, clearinghouse associations also exchange drafts on large local business firms, state and county warrants, and a variety of noncash items as well as drafts originating in interbank transactions and payments to or by the Federal Reserve Bank. Nonbank institutions that habitually have frequent and large payments to make to each other—airlines that accept each other's tickets, railroads that use each other's freight cars, etc.—organize clearinghouses of their own to reduce the necessity of settling each transaction individually. For a more explicit explanation of bank clearings, see *Information Regarding the Operation of the New York Clearing House,* The New York Clearing House, New York, 1962; for an example of the usefulness of clearinghouse data in economic analysis, see George Garvy, *Debits and Clearings Statistics and Their Use,* Board of Governors of the Federal Reserve System, Washington, D.C., 1959.

Clearing Union An association of international banking institutions (usually the central banks of various countries) that operates as an international clearinghouse by offsetting a nation's balance-of-payments deficits with one country against its balance-of-payments surpluses with another, leaving only each nation's net surplus or deficit with its trading partners as a group for settlement. No international clearing union has ever existed on a worldwide scale; the nearest thing to it was the London Clearing House, which operated before 1931, when most of the world's major banking institutions held deposits in correspondent banks in London, effected payments to each other through these accounts, and settled their balances in sterling credits or gold. In 1943, John Maynard Keynes suggested a worldwide clearing union that would involve not only clearings but the settlement of net balances with credits financed in "bancor," a proposed international currency under the jurisdiction of an international authority. His suggestion was not accepted at the Bretton Woods Conference of 1944, which agreed instead on the establishment of the International Monetary Fund. The essence of Keynes' plan has reappeared in the European Payments Union, which came into existence in 1950 after the operation of more limited clearing schemes among the participants of the European Recovery Program in 1948 and 1949. The purpose of all clearing unions is to facilitate multilateral trade and payments, giving each participant the opportunity to concentrate on one trading partner for its imports even when its exports go mostly to another one and reducing to a minimum the size of the necessary settlements, whether in gold or in international credits. For a thorough discussion of postwar clearing arrangements, see Robert Triffin, *Europe and the Money Muddle,* Yale University Press, New Haven, Conn., 1957.

Closed Corporation (Private Corporation) A corporation in which all or almost all the stock is owned by the few persons who formed the business; usually it is a family-owned or small business. Generally, the officers of a closed corporation keep control of the operation limited to a few persons, and very few, if any, shares of stock are sold to the general public. The Ford Motor Company was formerly a closed corporation with all its stock held or controlled by the Ford family. Deering Millikin, a textile firm, is an existing example of a closed corporation. For additional details on closed corporations, see Lyman A. Keith and Carlo E. Gubellini, *Introduction to Business Enterprise*, 2d ed., McGraw-Hill Book Company, New York, 1967.

Closed Economy The economy of an isolated area. In a closed economy, no person has any business or trade relationships with anyone outside the area. The term closed economy usually refers to an economy in which no imports, exports, or factor movements are permitted across boundaries.

Closed-End Investment Company An investment company that has a fixed capital structure. Unlike an open-end investment company (mutual fund), whose capital structure is almost constantly changing as people buy and redeem shares, a closed-end investment company raises capital as ordinary corporations do; that is, it sells common and preferred stocks to the public and sometimes floats bonds and borrows from banks. Once issued, these securities are traded in the same manner as other securities; many of the large companies are listed on the New York Stock Exchange, while others are traded in the over-the-counter market. Price is determined by supply and demand, which is obviously related to the net asset value of the fund per share of stock outstanding. (Net asset value equals assets minus liabilities divided by the number of shares outstanding.) Price rarely exactly equals net asset value, being either higher (premium) or lower (discount), depending on the market's appraisal of the stock. Closed-end investment companies can be classified by investment objectives. Common-stock funds, as their name suggests, invest primarily in common stocks, although they reserve the right to hold cash, bonds, or other securities of the defensive type if the market is weak. Some common-stock funds specialize in certain kinds of equity securities, such as growth stocks, blue chips, electronics companies, or chemical companies, while others diversify their holdings. Balanced funds invest in common and preferred stocks and bonds and generally try to keep the proportions of each type of security that they hold close to stated policies. Because balanced funds diversify not only the companies they hold, but also the type of security, they are more conservative than common-stock funds. Finally, fully managed funds are those that invest at the discretion of the managers. They do not have stated investment objectives like those of common-stock and balanced funds. See *Fact Book*, Investment Company Institute, New York, periodically; U.S. Securities and Exchange Commission, *Annual Reports*; T. A. Wise, "The Double Play in Closed-End Funds," *Fortune*, October, 1962; *Report of the S.E.C. on the Public Policy Implications of Investment Company Growth*, Commission on Interstate and Foreign Commerce, Dec. 2, 1966.

Closed Shop   A plant or establishment in which only persons who are already union members may be hired. In 1947 about one-third of all United States workers covered by collective bargaining agreements were employed in closed shops. The Taft-Hartley Act of 1947 made the closed shop illegal for firms engaged in interstate commerce, and by 1959 less than 4% of the workers covered by collective bargaining agreements were employed in such shops. It is estimated, however, that the closed shop exists in fact, even if not in a contract, in a number of industries, notably printing, transportation, and construction. See Lloyd G. Reynolds, *Labor Economics and Labor Relations*, 5th ed., Prentice-Hall, Inc., Englewood Cliffs, N.J., 1970, pp. 567–570; Joseph Shister, *Economics of the Labor Market*, J. B. Lippincott Company, Philadelphia, 1956; Melvin W. Reder, *Labor in a Growing Economy*, John Wiley & Sons, Inc., New York, 1957.

Cobb-Douglas Production Function   A physical relationship between output and various inputs in the form $Y = kL^aC^{(1-a)}$, where Y represents national output, L is the quantity of labor input, C is the quantity of capital employed, and k and a are positive constants (and $a < 1$). This production function is linear and homogeneous of degree 1, implying constant returns to scale. Furthermore, if each of the factors is paid according to its marginal product, it can be shown that this production function will yield relative shares of wages and return to capital which are independent of the variables Y, L, and C. The relative share of wages in total output will be a, the exponent of L, while the relative share of the return to capital will be $1 - a$, the exponent of C. Both relative shares are constant for all variations of the ratio of capital to labor. The Cobb-Douglas production function was proposed as an empirical hypothesis to explain the relative constancy of the share of wages in the national income of the U.S. since the early 1900s. So far, statistical evidence has not contradicted this production function. For additional information about the function and an empirical test of it, see Paul H. Douglas, *The Theory of Wages*, The Macmillan Company, New York, 1934, chaps. 5 to 9; Robert Solow, "Technical Change and the Aggregate Production Function," *Review of Economics and Statistics*, vol. 39, pp. 312–320, Harvard University Press, Cambridge, Mass., August, 1957; Milton H. Spencer,

Managerial Economics, 3d ed., Richard D. Irwin, Inc., Homewood, Ill., 1968.

Cobweb Theorem A theory which attempts to explain the regularly recurring cycles observed in the production and prices of some commodities. Although many economists had attempted to explain cyclical movements, it was not until 1930 that H. Schultze of the U.S., J. Tinbergen of the Netherlands, and U. Ricci of Italy, working independently, presented the theory in three separate articles. N. Kaldor first suggested the name cobweb theorem because the pattern traced by the price movements resembles a cobweb. Classical economic theory assumed that production and prices, if disturbed from equilibrium, would tend to return automatically to equilibrium. The cobweb theorem demonstrates that on classical assumptions of pure competition under static conditions, prices and production, if disturbed, do not necessarily return to equilib-

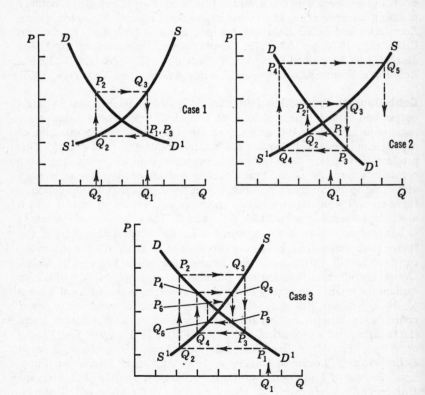

rium. The assumptions on which the theorem is based are (1) pure competition, in which each producer assumes that present prices will continue and that his own production plans will not affect the market (once plans for production are made, they cannot be changed until the next time period); (2) the establishment of price by available supply (price is completely a function of the preceding period's supply); and (3) the perishability of the commodity produced. These assumptions suggest that the theorem has been used mainly in analyzing agricultural commodities. The accompanying three figures show three cases of the cobweb in action. In each case, the first period's price (P_1) is established by supply Q_1; producers use this price to determine their output in period 2. This output, Q_2, determines the price for period 2, which is P_2. The output for period 3, Q_3, is determined by the price of period 2, P_2, etc. The elasticity of demand equals the elasticity of supply in case 1; this leads to constantly and regularly fluctuating prices and outputs. Case 2, in which the elasticity of supply is greater than the elasticity of demand, yields a diverging cobweb and eventually a change in elasticities; if this change did not occur, chaos would result. The elasticity of supply in case 3 is lower than that of demand, leading to a converging cobweb and eventually to an equilibrium price and output. A complete statement of the theorem is given in M. Ezekiel, "The Cobweb Theorem," *Quarterly Journal of Economics*, Harvard University Press, Cambridge, Mass., February, 1938, reprinted in American Economic Association, *Readings in Business Cycle Theory*, McGraw-Hill Book Company, New York, 1951; for a criticism of the theory, see Norman S. Buchanan, "A Reconsideration of the Cobweb Theorem," *Journal of Political Economy*, The University of Chicago Press, Chicago, February, 1939, reprinted in R. Clemence (ed.), *Readings in Economic Analysis*, Addison-Wesley Publishing Company, Inc., Reading, Mass., 1950; Donald S. Watson, *Price Theory and Its Uses*, 2d ed., Houghton Mifflin Company, Boston, 1968.

Coefficient of Determination   In correlation analysis, the squared coefficient of correlation (r^2 or R^2) which may be corrected to take into account the number of observations and constants involved in the analysis. It is interpreted as the ratio of explained variation of the dependent variable to total variation. For additional information, see Karl A. Fox, *Intermediate Economic Statistics*, John Wiley & Sons, Inc., New York, 1968; Gerhard Tintner and Charles B. Millham, *Mathematics and Statistics for Economists*, Holt, Rinehart and Winston, Inc., New York, 1970.

Coincident Indicator   A measure of economic activity that usually moves in the same direction and at the same time as total economic activity. The use of statistical indicators was developed by Wesley Mitchell and Arthur F. Burns, members of the staff of the National Bureau of Economic Research, and Warren Persons of the Harvard Economic Society, to indicate historical changes in the general course of business. Geoffrey H. Moore and Julius Shiskin, also staff members of the Bureau, have carried the indicator method of business-cycle analysis forward to a point at which many economists consider that coincident indicators provide the basis for determining the dates when the general economy reaches peaks or troughs. Other economists merely use the peaks or troughs of either the gross national product or the industrial production index, both of which are included among the coincident indicators, as indications of the top and bottom of the business cycle. *Business Conditions Digest,* a report of the U.S. Bureau of the Census under the direction of Julius Shiskin, lists fifteen coincident indicators and divides them into three major groups for analysis: (1) employment and unemployment, (2) production, and (3) income and trade. For the development and analysis of coincident indicators, see Geoffrey H. Moore (ed.), *Business Cycle Indicators,* Princeton University Press, Princeton, N.J., 1961, vol. 1; for current statistics of the coincident indicators see Bureau of Economic Analysis, *Business Conditions Digest,* monthly. See also J. Shiskin, "Business Cycle Indicators: The Known and the Unknown," *Business Cycle Developments,* U.S. Department of Commerce, Washington, D.C., September, 1963.

Collapsible Corporation A business arrangement in the U.S. that is sometimes used in an effort to avoid ordinary income taxes. The device works as follows: (1) A corporation is formed for the production of a certain property, for example, a motion picture. (2) After production of the property but before the realization of any income, the corporation is liquidated, and the property is distributed to shareholders. (3) The shareholders, after complying with the six-month holding period in order to qualify for capital-gains treatment, sell or otherwise dispose of the property. Thus, ordinary income tax is avoided at both the corporate and the shareholder level. Section 341 of the U.S. Internal Revenue Code provides, however, that if a corporation is founded for the production of property with a view to distribution before realization of substantial part of the income to be derived from such property, the gain shall be treated as ordinary income and not as a capital gain. For a discussion of the legal aspects of the collapsible corporation, see Irving I. Axerad, "Tax Advantages and Pitfalls in Collapsible Corporations and Partnerships," *Taxes,* Commerce Clearing House, Chicago, December, 1956, p. 845.

Collateral Property that is pledged to secure a loan. Any asset can serve as collateral, but commercial banks usually accept such types as commodities, securities, and real estate. Salaries, wages, or durable goods are acceptable for consumer loans. Other lending institutions may accept other assets as collateral; for example, pawnbrokers hold all kinds of goods to secure their loans. In all cases, collateral becomes the property of the lender if the borrower fails to repay the loan.

Collective Bargaining   Negotiations between employees' representatives (usually labor union functionaries) and employers for the purpose of establishing mutually acceptable terms to govern conditions of employment. Collective bargaining covers topics ranging from the obviously important, such as wage rates, hours of work, hiring, and layoff procedures, to the seemingly trivial, such as rest time or time allowed employees for washing and changing clothes at the end of a work day. The terms ultimately arrived at are included in a collective bargaining agreement, or contract, which is binding on both employees and employer. There are now more than 100,000 such agreements in force in the U.S., some governing a single facet of a plant operation, others a firm's entire operations, and some applying to entire industries, such as the giant steel industry. Although collective bargaining has long existed in some form, it owes its vigorous growth since the 1930s to the passage of legislation explicitly permitting workers to organize for purposes of collective bargaining (Norris-La Guardia Act of 1932) and, later, of Federal statutes making it illegal for an employer to refuse to bargain in good faith with employees' representatives (National Labor Relations Act of 1935—the Wagner Act). More recently, 1947, the Labor-Management Relations Act (Taft-Hartley Act) imposed some restrictions on the scope of collective bargaining. Numerous criticisms of the collective bargaining process have arisen. A frequent one has been the argument that the parties directly involved, industry and labor, tend to ignore the interest of the general public in arriving at their agreements. For a discussion of this facet of the subject, see summaries of talks by W. Willard Wirtz, Secretary of Labor in President John F. Kennedy's Cabinet, and Archibald Cox, Solicitor General of the U.S., *Monthly Labor Review,* Government Printing Office, Washington, D.C., November, 1961, pp. 1206–1212; U.S. Department of Labor, *Collective Bargaining in the Basic Steel Industry: A Study of the Public Interest and the Role of Government,* special report, 1961; for a discussion of the broader area of collective bargaining, see Neil W. Chamberlain and James W. Kuhn, *Collective Bargaining,* 2d ed., McGraw-Hill Book Company, New York, 1965; Sumner H. Slichter et al., *The Impact of Collective Bargaining on Management,* The Brookings Institution, Washington, D.C., 1960; Lloyd G. Reynolds, *Labor Economics and Labor Relations,* 5th ed., Prentice-Hall, Inc., Englewood Cliffs, N.J., 1970.

Collective Farm A mode of agricultural organization in Communist countries. Collective farms were first established in the Soviet Union in the 1920s, following the expropriation of farm property. In theory, collective farms are democratic, cooperative associations of farmers who possess charters to work state-owned land. With the exception of land and heavy farm machinery, the means of production on collective farms are owned by the members. Ostensibly democratic, the policies of collective farms are determined by the nation's economic goals, as spelled out in the central government's plan. Crop and livestock production on collective farms thus must fit into the overall economic scheme. Moreover, distribution of the collective farms' annual produce is made on the basis of a government decree, first claim on output belonging to the state rather than to the cooperating farmers. See Harry Schwartz, *Russia's Soviet Economy*, Prentice-Hall, Inc., Englewood Cliffs, N.J., 1954, chap. 8, pp. 297ff.

Collectivism A social and political system which places responsibility for the planning and control of the economy in the hands of a central government. Collectivism is in direct contrast to individualism, which stresses the importance of private property, free competition, and individual initiative and enterprise. In collectivism, other objectives are usually placed before individual economic welfare. The approaches to collectivism are usually divided into three distinct groups, fascism, socialism, and communism. For additional details, see William Fellner, *Modern Economic Analysis*, McGraw-Hill Book Company, New York, 1960.

Command-directed Economy A mode of economic organization in which the three key economic problems—what goods will be produced, how they will be produced, and who will receive them once they have been produced—are solved by the central government or ruler. Communist Russia and Communist China are examples of nations with command-directed economies. Even in these countries, however, some economic decisions are made by private citizens in response to prices rather than by the government. In the U.S., less drastic elements of command are found, such as taxes that preempt a part of private income for public purposes. See Robert H. Heilbroner, *The Making of an Economic Society*, Prentice-Hall, Inc., Englewood Cliffs, N.J., 1962; Alec Nove, *The Soviet Economy*, Frederick A. Praeger, Inc., New York, 1961, p. 143.

Commerce Business activity concerned with the buying, selling, and transportation of goods and services. Commerce, as opposed to industry, usually refers to the trade of large quantities of goods. It may take place between different firms, communities, or countries. In the U.S., intrastate commerce is trade carried on entirely within the borders of a single state, whereas interstate commerce refers to trade between different states and is subject to control by Congress. International commerce refers to any trade between businessmen in different countries. For additional information, see J. B. Condliffe, *The Commerce of Nations*, W. W. Norton & Company, Inc., New York, 1950; Harold Heck, *Foreign Commerce*, McGraw-Hill Book Company, New York, 1953; see also U.S. Department of Commerce, *Annual Report of the Secretary of Commerce*.

Commercial Bank   A financial institution which for the most part makes short-term commercial and industrial loans. It has the power to create and destroy money, within limits, through the use of loans and demand deposits. Commercial banks lend money by creating demand deposits and retire loans by canceling demand deposits. In addition, they carry on functions duplicated by other financial institutions, such as holding time deposits, making loans (including business, mortgage, and consumer short- and long-term loans), operating trust departments, offering safe-deposit boxes, and so forth. Commercial banks may be chartered by Federal or state governments. In the U.S. as of December 30, 1968, there were 13,698 commercial banks, and all but 197 were insured by the Federal Deposit Insurance Corporation. Of the total, 5,978 were members of the Federal Reserve System; these banks controlled 82% of commercial bank assets. For further information, see Lester V. Chandler, *The Economics of Money and Banking*, 5th ed., Harper & Row, Publishers, Incorporated, New York, 1969; for statistics on the number, classes, and forms of assets and liabilities of commercial banks, see *Federal Reserve Bulletin*, Washington, D.C., monthly.

Commercial Credit Company (Sales Finance Company)   A firm engaged in the business of buying installment contracts and accounts receivables from other businesses, especially retailers. Since commercial credit companies are substantial borrowers from banks in order to finance their operations, their discount rate (about 8%) is much higher than the rate that they pay for bank loans. Such companies enable retailers and other business firms to do a large volume of credit or installment sales without tying up their own capital in unpaid balances on goods sold. See J. Fred Weston, *Managerial Finance*, Holt, Rinehart and Winston, Inc., New York, 1962, chap. 14; Clyde William Phelps, *Accounts Receivable as a Method of Securing Business Loans*, Commercial Credit Corporation, Baltimore, 1962.

Commercial Farm   A farm operated as a business unit, generally enjoying sales of $2,500 or more. It is an agricultural producing unit rather than a rural living unit. On farms of this type, capital investment is relatively higher than on family farms. Commercial farms account for about two-thirds of all farms; 7% of them had sales of more than $40,000 in 1964. The largest farms are most numerous in the Pacific states, the western Corn Belt, and the southern Plains states. For detailed definitions and statistics, see U.S. Department of Commerce, *Census of Agriculture,* 1964.

Commercial Paper   Unsecured promissory notes of well-known business concerns having the highest credit ratings. Except for large finance companies, which place their paper directly with investors, corporations usually sell to commercial-paper houses (dealers), which resell the paper to investors, chiefly commercial banks. Commercial paper is generally written in amounts ranging from $5,000 to $1,000,000 or more (notes of less than $50,000 are not common), with maturities of three days to nine months; however, most paper carries an original maturity of less than ninety days. Interest at the prevailing rate and a commission of about 0.25% of the principal amount of the note are deducted in advance by the dealer. As a rule, the interest rate on commercial paper is less than that on an ordinary bank loan. Moreover, commercial paper has a certain prestige value because only the largest and most credit-worthy corporations can issue it. Its major disadvantage is that it does not allow the extension of the loan. The amount of commercial paper outstanding and the prevailing interest rate on commercial paper are published in *Federal Reserve Bulletin,* Washington, D.C., monthly; for further information, see Marcus Nadler et al., *The Money Market and Its Institutions,* The Ronald Press Company, New York, 1955, pp. 82–86; Richard T. Selden, *Trends and Cycles in the Commercial Paper Market,* National Bureau of Economic Research, Inc., Occasional Paper 85, New York, 1963; Nevins D. Baxter, *Commercial Paper Market,* Bankers Publishing Company, Boston, 1966. For developments through mid-1970, see Federal Reserve Bank of New York, *Monthly Review,* pp. 280–291.

Commodity Exchange   An organized association of traders who buy and sell contracts for immediate or future delivery of certain commodities. The commodities are not brought to the exchange; only the promises of immediate delivery, called spots, and the promises of future delivery, futures, are traded. The commodity exchange offers a continuous, stable market on which spots and futures may always be bought and sold. The great bulk of the transactions consists of the trading of futures, with relatively little spot trading. The commodity exchange, through an affiliated clearinghouse, also guarantees that the merchandise traded in the exchange will be delivered at the agree time and that full payment will be made. The continuous existence of a stable and liquid market also facilitates the formal financing of commodity production. In the U.S., the main commodity exchanges exist for wheat, corn, other grains, cotton, sugar, and coffee. For further information on the significance and workings of commodity exchanges, see Julius Baer and E. Olin Saxon, *Commodity Exchanges and Futures Trading*, Harper & Row, Publishers, Incorporated, New York, 1949; Gerald Cold, *Modern Commodity Futures Trading*, Commodity Research Bureau, Inc., New York, 1959; G. Wright Hoffman, *Future Trading upon Organized Commodity Markets in the U.S.*, University of Pennsylvania Press, Philadelphia, 1932.

Commodity Stabilization Agreement A pact concerning the production and trade of a certain commodity that is made between a group of producer and consumer nations. Stabilization measures are usually undertaken to reduce the widely fluctuating prices and volumes of some internationally traded goods (primary goods in particular) whose instability is an important cause of inefficiency in the international economy, especially for developing countries. There are two basic kinds of commodity agreements, the buffer-stock type and the production-market control type. In a buffer-stock agreement, the participating nations attempt to produce a stable flow of a good by establishing an intergovernmental agency to buy the surplus of the good when the price falls below a certain point, store it while the price is normal, and sell it when a shortage causes the price to rise above a fixed point. Buffer-stock schemes involve a number of difficulties, especially problems of storage and the setting of buying and selling prices. The second approach, the production-market control type of agreement, entails restriction programs and marketing-quota systems. It sometimes involves an upper price, at which exporting nations agree to sell a specified amount of the good, and a lower price, at which the importing nations agree to buy a specified amount, with a free market operating between these prices. In other cases, it may incorporate a rigid system of export and import quotas and prices governing trade. The freezing of production involved in the production-market control type of agreement may lead to serious misallocation and maladjustment in the economic system. Commodity agreements among nations are similar to cartels in that they are associations of producers who try to control production. Unlike private cartels, they give the consumer nations a voice in supply and price policies, and they seek to avoid the mere restriction of output and bolstering of prices without removing the basic causes of disequilibrium. The major intergovernmental commodity stabilization agreements effected since World War II have been the International Wheat Agreement and the International Sugar Agreement. For additional information, see Woodrow Wilson Foundation, *The Political Economy of*

American Foreign Policy, Holt, Rinehart and Winston, Inc., New York, 1955, chap. 9; see also UN Department of Economic Affairs, *Commodity Trade and Economic Development,* New York, 1953; J. C. Black and S. S. Tsou, "International Commodity Arrangements," *Quarterly Journal of Economics,* Harvard University Press, Cambridge, Mass., August, 1944. For a discussion of commodity policy issues, see John Pincus, *Trade, Aid and Development,* McGraw-Hill Book Company, New York, 1967, pp. 233–294.

Common Carrier   An individual or company engaged in the public transportation of persons or goods in return for a uniform fee or rate. A carrier of this type usually operates under franchise and is regulated by a governmental agency. Taxicabs, railroads, trucks, and buses are examples of common carriers. For additional information on common carriers and their regulation, status, and duties, see G. Lloyd Wilson, *Interstate Commerce and Traffic Law,* Prentice-Hall, Inc., Englewood Cliffs, N.J., 1947; see also Charles A. Taff, *Commercial Motor Transportation,* Richard D. Irwin, Inc., Homewood, Ill., 1961.

Common Stock   The capital stock of a corporation, which gives the holder an unlimited interest in the corporation's earnings and assets after prior claims have been met. Common stock represents the holder's equity or ownership in the corporation. Common stockholders have certain fundamental legal rights, including preemptive rights; the right, in most cases, to vote for the board of directors, who actually manage the company; the right to transfer any or all shares of stock owned; and the right to receive dividends when they are declared by the board of directors. For monthly information concerning new issues of common stocks, see *Federal Reserve Bulletin,* Washington, D.C.; for technical explanations, see Jules I. Bogen (ed.), *Financial Handbook,* 4th ed., The Ronald Press Company, New York, 1968; Joseph H. Bonneville et al., *Organizing and Financing Business,* Prentice-Hall, Inc., Englewood Cliffs, N.J., 1959; Charles W. Gerstenberg, *Financial Organization and Management of Business,* 4th ed., Prentice-Hall, Inc., Englewood Cliffs, N.J., 1959; D. K. Eiteman, C. A. Dice, and W. J. Eiteman, *The Stock Market,* 4th ed., McGraw-Hill Book Company, New York, 1966, pp. 89–96.

Communism   According to Marxists, the highest and inevitable stage in social development in the historical sequence of slavery, feudalism, capitalism, socialism, and communism. The term is defined not only as the public ownership of productive resources but also as the "withering away" of central governmental authority. Marxists argue that all human relationships are affected by the stage through which society is passing;

therefore, personal relationships will be different, and better, under communism, which will eliminate all social problems. Because these relationships are determined largely by economic factors, Marxists call themselves materialists, and the successive stages of development are called dialectical materialism, meaning that a new stage (synthesis) is reached as a result of the impact of new forces (antithesis) on the original stage (thesis). It is argued that earlier stages of development pass out of existence through internal strains (contradictions) and that communism is brought about by the growing awareness of wage earners (the proletariat) of their political role, leading them to form and support Communist parties. In practice, Communist parties have been imposed by military force on a society weakened by war. Although Communist parties control the U.S.S.R., mainland China, and certain countries in Eastern Europe, these countries are considered to be passing through a period of Socialist development and not to have reached the stage of communism. Despite the original insistence that communism would come about only after society had passed through a capitalist stage of development, Communists have seized power only in predominately agricultural societies. Today, despite an equally strong insistence on the "scientific" nature of communism, Communist practice is essentially pragmatic, relying on military force and rapid technological and industrial growth to demonstrate Communist superiority over other forms of economic practice. For further discussion, see Karl Marx and Friedrich Engels, *The Communist Manifesto,* Henry Regnery Company, Chicago, 1954; J. A. LeRossignol, *From Marx to Stalin: A Critique of Communism,* Thomas Y. Crowell Company, New York, 1940; Joseph A. Schumpeter, *Capitalism, Socialism and Democracy,* Harper & Row, Publishers, Incorporated, New York, 1950; Zbigniew K. Brzezinski, *Ideology and Power in Soviet Politics,* Frederick A. Praeger, Inc., New York, 1967.

Community–Property Principle A concept of property ownership whereby the property acquired by a husband and wife is regarded as owned by both of them in community, each having an equal share. All income earned by either spouse belongs equally to each, and thus a husband and wife may each report one-half of the community income on their individual tax returns. This principle applies in more than a dozen states of the U.S. Since 1948 it has also been accepted in the filing of joint Federal income tax returns for husband and wife.

Company Union An organization of workers limited to those in a given firm. Generally, the officers of a company union are elected from among the employees of the firm and therefore can spend only part of their time working for the union. The employer thus has some control over the union. Organized labor opposes company unions on the ground that only completely independent unions can protect the rights of the workers. For discussion, see Gordon F. Bloom and Herbert R. Northrup, *Economics of Labor Relations,* 6th ed., McGraw-Hill Book Company, New York, 1966.

Comparative Advantage   The special ability of a country to provide one product or service relatively more cheaply than other products or services. This concept is generally used in international trade theory, although it also applies to cost comparisons among firms in an industry and among individual workers. It explains why a country capable of providing a wide range of goods and services at a lower cost than any other country should concentrate on selling that product or service for which its cost advantage is greatest and leave the production of other goods, in which it has a positive but lesser cost advantage, to other countries. The idea of comparative advantage was first formulated by David Ricardo, an English economist. In his model of a two-country, two-commodity world, Ricardo showed that Portugal was better off if it concentrated on producing wine (at a cost of 80 hours of labor per unit, compared with England's 120 hours of labor) instead of expending any of its resources on the production of textiles, in which Portugal had a cost advantage of 90 hours of labor per unit to England's 100. In this example, a unit of domestic wine would, in the absence of international trade, exchange for only eight-ninths of a unit of textiles in Portugal instead of as much as one and one-fifth units of English textiles if the wine were shipped to England in trade. The converse would also be true. The example and its variants explain who producers with an absolute advantage in a number of goods are still best advised to concentrate on producing that good in which their advantage is greatest. For a discussion of the principle of comparative advantage, see David Ricardo, *Principles of Political Economy and Taxation,* Everyman's Library, New York, 1917, chap. 7; see also Gottfried Haberler, *The Theory of International Trade,* The Macmillan Company, New York, 1950; Murray C. Kemp, *Pure Theory of International Trade,* Prentice-Hall, Inc., Englewood Cliffs, N.J., 1964.

Comparative Statics   The comparison of different positions of static equilibrium of the economy. Comparative statics analysis disregards the delays involved in economic changes and is not concerned with the process through which the economy moves from one equilibrium point to another. Instead, it traces the variables from one static equilibrium situation to another, concentrating on the final location of the equilibrium rather than on the transition. In the model first introduced by John Maynard Keynes, comparative statics analysis is used in the determination of national income. A model of this type cannot handle dynamic problems, such as those connected with the movement between equilibrium and stages of change over time, but it can be used to determine the final equilibrium point of national income under a set of given static conditions. For further information, see Martin J. Bailey, *National Income and the Price Level*, McGraw-Hill Book Company, New York, 1962.

Compensating Balance   The minimum percentage (usually from 10 to 20%) of a line of credit that a bank's customer is expected to keep on deposit at all times. Thus, if a manufacturer has a line of credit of $1 million, he might be expected to keep 20% of that amount, or $200,000, on deposit. Since most firms require large working balances, this restriction is normally not particularly significant, and the bank may never make the requirement explicit if the customer keeps the correct amount in his checking account. There was, however, a growing tendency during the 1950s for firms to use their deposits more intensively. As a result, many bankers were forced to remind their customers of compensating balances. If a prospective borrower is not a regular customer of a bank, the compensating-reserve requirement may induce him to become a regular customer, since he will be required to keep a certain portion of his borrowings on deposit. The portion kept on deposit can be used as a normal working balance. Compensating-balance requirements are considerably more common among large banks than among small ones and among large borrowers than among small borrowers. Balance requirements change considerably during business cycles. They may be high when money is tight and low when credit is easy. One result of compensating balances is to make effective bank interest rates higher than conventional statistical measures indicate. In addition, the fluctuation of effective rates is greater over the course of the business cycle than is indicated by the fluctuation of nominal rates. See J. M. Guttentag and R. G. Davis, "Compensating Balances," *Monthly Review*, Federal Reserve Bank of New York, December, 1961.

Compensation of Employees   Income received as remuneration for work. It includes wages and salaries paid to employees including executive salaries and bonuses, commissions, payments in kind, incentive payments, and tips in a given time period irrespective of when they were earned. It also includes supplements to wages and salaries, such as employer contributions for social insurance and employer payments for private pension, health, and welfare funds. Compensation of employees accounts for about 70 to 75% of national income. For a detailed discussion of the concept, coverage, and sources of data, see U.S. Department of Commerce, *National Income Supplement*, 1954; see also Richard Ruggles and Nancy D. Ruggles, *National Income Accounts and Income Analysis*,

2d ed., McGraw-Hill Book Company, New York, 1956; for quarterly and annual data, see U.S. Department of Commerce, *Survey of Current Business*, monthly.

Compensatory Fiscal Policy   The management of government finance to compensate for fluctuations in national income and employment. Compensatory fiscal policy, which combines deficit and surplus financing, attempts to achieve a high level of employment by maintaining a high level of national income. It uses taxation and spending to produce the desired balance. To maintain the desired level of income during a business decline, any decrease in private spending or investment must be balanced by a government policy of either increasing government spending (raising total government purchases from private business) or reducing taxes (increasing the income of consumers, business, or both). To maintain the desired level of income during a period of overexpansion and inflation, government policy would comprise a reduction in Federal spending, a possible increase in taxes, or both steps. If such government action is timely and the amounts involved are large enough, substantial fluctuations in national income and employment may be avoided. Generally, private consumption is relatively stable in the short run, while private investment is relatively volatile. Thus, compensatory fiscal policy is primarily an attempt to counterbalance changes in private investment. For further information, see John M. Culbertson, *Macroeconomic Theory and Stabilization Policy*, McGraw-Hill Book Company, New York, 1968; Campbell R. McConnell, *Economics*, 4th ed., McGraw-Hill Book Company, New York, 1969, chap. 14; Herbert Stein, *The Fiscal Revolution in America*, The University of Chicago Press, Chicago, 1969.

Competition   The condition prevailing in a market in which rival sellers try to increase their profits at one another's expense. In economic theory, the varieties of competition range from perfect competition, in which numerous firms produce or sell identical goods or services, to oligopoly, in which a few large sellers with substantial influence in the market vie with one another for the available business. Early economists envisioned perfect competition as the most effective assurance that consumers would be provided with goods and services at the lowest possible prices. In practice, however, perfect competition is virtually unknown in major industries. Most large industries are dominated by relatively few firms, and competition frequently prevails between substitute goods or services rather than between identical goods or services. In the U.S., since the late nineteenth century the Federal government has played an active role in attempting to preserve and encourage some measure of competition in major industries. Antitrust laws, such as the Sherman Antitrust Act and the Clayton Antitrust Act, are cornerstones of the government's activities in this area. See Fritz Machlup, *The Economics of Sellers' Competition*, Johns Hopkins University, Baltimore, 1952; Edward H. Chamberlin, *The Theory of Monopolistic Competition*, Harvard University Press, Cambridge, Mass., 1931; John M. Clark, *Competition as a Dynamic Process*, The Brookings Institution, Washington, D.C., 1961; Joan Robinson, *The Economics of Imperfect Competition*, St. Martin's Press, Inc., New York, 1953; J. K. Galbraith, *American Capitalism: The Theory of Countervailing Power*, Houghton Mifflin Company, Boston, 1952; Robert E. Kuenne, *Microeconomic Theory of the Market Mechanism*, The Macmillan Company, New York, 1968; Campbell R. McConnell, *Economics*, 4th ed., McGraw-Hill Book Company, New York, 1969.

Competition, Imperfect (Monopolistic Competition)   The market situation that exists when there are many sellers and buyers of a product but each seller has some feature of his product that distinguishes it from other goods, either in fact or in the minds of purchasers. As a result, there are combined features of pure competition and of monopoly in the same firm. The monopolistically competitive firm produces slightly less than a purely competitive firm would, but in the long run it will not earn the excess profits associated with monopoly. Edward H. Chamberlin and Joan Robinson developed the theory independently at about the same time in the 1930s, and it is widely cited as the prevailing condition in retail trade. See Edward H. Chamberlin, *The Theory of Monopolistic Competition*, Harvard University Press, Cambridge, Mass., 1931; Joan Robinson, *The Economics of Imperfect Competition*, St. Martin's Press, Inc., New York, 1953; D. S. Watson, *Price Theory and Its Uses*, 2d ed., Houghton Mifflin Company, Boston, 1968; Robert E. Kuenne (ed.), *Monopolistic Competition Theory*, John Wiley & Sons, Inc., New York, 1967.

Competition, Perfect   The condition prevailing in a market in which, in addition to the conditions prevailing under pure competition (large numbers of sellers, identical products, unrestricted entry of new sellers), there are (1) perfect knowledge among buyers and sellers of existing market conditions; (2) complete interindustry mobility of productive factors, enabling new entrants to set up selling operations; and (3) no differences among firms in the cost of transporting their products to buyers. This is a refinement of theoretically pure competition. Economic theory says that, under conditions of perfect competition, the consumer is assured of the widest availability of goods at the lowest possible price level. In the real world, however, examples of perfect competition are rare. See Paul A. Samuelson, *Economics*, 7th ed., McGraw-Hill Book Company, New York, 1967; Fritz Machlup, *The Economics of Sellers'*

Competition, Johns Hopkins University, Baltimore, 1952; Edward H. Chamberlin, *The Theory of Monopolistic Competition,* Harvard University Press, Cambridge, Mass., 1931; John M. Clark, *Competition as a Dynamic Process,* The Brookings Institution, Washington, D.C., 1961; Joan Robinson, *The Economics of Imperfect Competition,* St. Martin's Press, Inc., New York, 1953; J. K. Galbraith, *American Capitalism: The Theory of Countervailing Power,* Houghton Mifflin Company, Boston, 1952.

Competition, Pure   The condition prevailing in a market in which (1) there are a large number of sellers, (2) the goods or services sold are identical, and (3) additional sellers are free to enter the market. Under these circumstances, no single seller is able to affect significantly the price of the product being sold or the quantity offered for sale. Each seller sells at the established market price. Only under purely (or perfectly) competitive conditions, economic theory says, is the consumer assured the widest availability of goods at the lowest possible price level. In the real world, however, examples of purely competitive markets are scarce. With the possible exception of agricultural products, no major industry in the U.S. meets the criteria of pure competition. John Kenneth Galbraith maintains, however, that certain countervailing powers have developed in the U.S. between large sellers and buyers that provide the economy with many of the benefits associated with theoretically pure competition. See Paul A. Samuelson, *Economics,* 7th ed., McGraw-Hill Book Company, New York, 1967; Fritz Machlup, *The Economics of Sellers' Competition,* Johns Hopkins University, Baltimore, 1952; Edward H. Chamberlin, *The Theory of Monopolistic Competition,* Harvard University Press, Cambridge, Mass., 1931; John M. Clark, *Competition as a Dynamic Process,* The Brookings Institution, Washington, D.C., 1961; Joan Robinson, *The Economics of Imperfect Competition,* St. Martin's Press, Inc., New York, 1953; J. K. Galbraith, *American Capitalism: The Theory of Countervailing Power,* Houghton Mifflin Company, Boston, 1952.

Competition, Workable   The adaptation of businesses to their markets in a way which gives rise to reasonably satisfactory market performance. A satisfactory market performance would include average profit margins which were just large enough to pay for a normal return on investment plus a risk reward, an efficient scale of operation for the producing firms without inefficient, small-scale producers and chronic excess capacity, and a reasonable degree of product quality. Workable competition does not require the standardization of commodities, equally informed firms, equal advantages for all firms, complete independence of action, frictionless movement of resources, free entry, or many of the other requirements of perfect competition. Rather, an attempt is made to prevent the deliberate reduction of output and survival of inefficient firms. Although complete flexibility or optimum use of resources is not achieved under workable competition, the system is an attempt to develop a market structure which offers access to genuine alternatives and protects weaker firms against domination by stronger ones. Workable competition is a less nearly perfect market situation than pure competition, but it is a much more realistic goal for public policy. For further information, See John M. Clark, "Toward a Concept of Workable Competition," *American Economic Review*, pp. 241–256, American Economic Association, Evanston, Ill., June, 1940; Joe Bain, "Workable Competition in Oligopoly," *American Economic Review*, pp. 35–47, American Economic Association, Evanston, Ill, May, 1950.

Complementary Goods Products or commodities so related that a change in the consumption of one will be accompanied by a similar change in the consumption of the other. Thus if the price of tea declines, its consumption would be expected to increase, which in turn will induce an upward shift in the demand for lemons. The degree of this relationship may be measured by the coefficient of cross elasticity, which in this example relates the change in the quantity of lemons purchased to the change in the price of tea. The formula for this coefficient is

$$\text{CE} = \frac{\text{percent change of } Q_1}{\text{percent change of } P_2}$$

where Q_1 is the quantity of commodity 1 and P_2 is the price of commodity 2. (When the prices of one commodity and the quantities of the other commodity move in opposite directions, the sign of the coefficient is minus.) If the goods are substitutes (the prices of one commodity and the quantities of the other move in the same direction), the sign of the coefficient is plus. Independent goods have a zero coefficient of cross elasticity because no relationship exists. See John R. Hicks, *Value and Capital*, 2d ed., Oxford University Press, Fair Lawn, N.J., 1946; Donald S. Watson, *Price Theory and Its Uses*, 2d ed., Houghton Mifflin Company, Boston, 1968.

Complete System of Equations In econometrics, a model or set of equations that includes all equations involved in determining a given economic sector or system. The model is complete if it can be solved for all its endogenous variables. A complete system makes unbiased estimates of parameters possible. For additional information, see Stefan Valavanis, *Econometrics*, McGraw-Hill Book Company, New York, 1959.

Composite Index Number An index number that is based on a combination of dissimilar component series. For example, the Federal Reserve

Board, *Index of Industrial Production,* is a complete index in the sense that it includes all branches of industry in the nation.

Compound Frequency Distribution   A frequency distribution that is created by combining two or more separate distributions—for example, the combination of income distributions for several states that reveals a regional distribution.

Comptroller   The executive officer in charge of the bookkeeping, accounting, and auditing procedures of a large corporation. All reports, internal statistics, and data concerning the financial condition of the corporation are prepared and approved by his department. For information concerning the comptroller's functions, see Jacob Hugh Jackson, *The Comptroller: His Functions and Organization,* Harvard University Press, Cambridge, Mass., 1948.

Concentration Ratio   The percentage of total business in a given industry that is handled by a specified number of the largest firms. This ratio is a relative index, showing to what extent the ownership or control of an industry is concentrated in the hands of a relatively small number of firms. There is no standard way of measuring the degree of industrial concentration, and a number of different indices have been used. Generally, the concentration ratio has been expressed as the percentage of business assets, production, sales, employment, or profits accounted for by the three to eight largest firms. For example, using the percentage of value of shipments accounted for by the four leading manufacturing firms as a measure of industrial concentration in the U.S. in 1958, 6.5% of U.S. manufacturing industries had a concentration ratio of more than 80, 33% had a concentration ratio of more than 50, and 80% had a concentration ratio of more than 20. Concentration refers to both the number and the size distribution of the producers within a given industry. Thus, a market which may be said to be more highly concentrated in the first sense may be relatively less concentrated in the second sense. This ambiguity in the measures of concentration may develop because the standard measures pertain to only the few largest units as a group and do not show whether the firms are dominated by a single firm or whether they share approximately equal market power. Another problem in the use of concentration measures is that these measures do not show the existence of possible competition on the other side of the market: countervailing power. For further information, see Betty Bock and Jack Farkas, *Concentration and Productivity,* National Industrial Conference Board, Inc., Studies in Business Policy, no. 103, New York, 1969; Betty Bock, *Concentration Patterns in Manufacturing,* National Industrial Conference Board,

Inc., Studies in Business Economics, no. 65, New York, 1959; National Bureau of Economic Research, Inc., *Business Concentration and Price Policy*, Princeton University Press, Princeton, N.J., 1955; Joe S. Bain, *Industrial Organization*, 2d ed., John Wiley & Sons, Inc., New York, 1968; for 1958 concentration statistics by industry, see U.S. Bureau of the Census, *Concentration Ratios in Manufacturing Industry, 1958*, a report prepared for the Subcommittee on Antitrust and Monopoly of the Senate Committee on the Judiciary, 1962.

Conciliation   An attempt by a third party to reconcile differences in labor-management disputes. In the narrower sense of the word, conciliation consists in transmitting information to the disputing parties and keeping the negotiations in operation. The conciliator stays aloof from the issues involved, never expressing judgments on the problems or submitting compromise proposals. The term conciliation is, however, often used in its broader sense as a synonym for mediation, which entails more positive and direct intervention in negotiations. In this case, the conciliator advances proposals of his own to resolve differences between the parties and tries to induce both labor and management to agree to the compromise suggestions. The Federal Mediation and Conciliation Service, set up under the Taft-Hartley Act of 1947, offers its conciliation services in any important labor dispute involving interstate commerce. For further information, see Kurt Braun, *Labor Disputes and Their Settlement*, The Johns Hopkins Press, Baltimore, 1955; G. F. Grieve, *Industrial Conciliation and Arbitration*, National Foreman's Institute, Waterford, Conn., 1956; E. Peters, *Conciliation in Action*, National Foreman's Institute, Waterford, Conn., 1952.

Conditional Sale   A sale providing that title to the product or products sold remains with the seller until the full purchase price has been paid. In other words, the buyer does not acquire legal title to the property until he has performed all the conditions of sale, which are usually specified in a conditional sales contract. The contract provides for repossession if the debtor defaults on his payments. In the event that the sale price of the repossessed article is lower than the original purchase price, most conditional sales contracts provide for a deficiency judgment so that the difference in amount may be recovered. For further information on this subject and for forms of conditional sales contracts, see *Credit Manual of Commercial Laws*, National Association of Credit Management, New York, annually.

Confluence   A situation encountered in regression analysis in which there are linear relations between the independent variables or in which errors of observation introduce linear relations in the independent variables. Multicollinearity and underidentification are two special cases of confluence. For example, when multicollinearity appears, one cannot separate the effects of two or more independent variables because they happen to move together. Where confluence exists, it results in the indeterminacy of the coefficients of a regression equation. The technique known as bunch-map analysis was developed by Frisch in 1934 in an effort to cope with the problems of confluence. For additional information, see Stefan Valavanis, *Econometrics,* McGraw-Hill Book Company, New York, 1959.

Conglomerate   A diversified corporation that has grown through mergers that are neither horizontal nor vertical. Conglomerate mergers are classified into three types: product-tension, market-extension, and pure conglomerate mergers. There are those who hold that proliferation of conglomerates is leading to the death of competition, while others argue that the conglomerate is making new forms of competition possible. During the 1969–1970 recession, conglomerates appeared to have lost some of their earlier glamour in the stock market. For additional information, see Betty Bock, "The Conglomerate and the Hippogriff," *The Conference Board Record,* National Industrial Conference Board, Inc., New York, February, 1972; Neil H. Jacoby, "The Conglomerate Corporation," *The Center Magazine,* July, 1969; J. Fred Weston, "Diversification and Merger Trends," *Business Economics,* January, 1970.

Conjugate   In mathematics, two quantities, curves, etc., that present themselves simultaneously and are interchangeable in the enunciation of properties. For example, *conjugate samples* are two samples consecutively drawn from the same time span and are such that the disturbances that brought about corresponding observations have the same absolute value in the two samples. The two samples form a *conjugate set.* For additional information, see Stefan Valavanis, *Econometrics,* McGraw-Hill Book Company, New York, 1959.

Consent Settlement   A method of settling cases before the Federal Trade Commission. By accepting a consent settlement, a business organization charged with a violation of law can avoid a trial by agreeing to the filing of a cease-and-desist order. About 70% of the cases acted on by the Commission are disposed of by consent settlements.

Conservatism   An approach to economics and politics which generally favors the *status quo* and resists change. Conservatism views society and its body of institutions as a phenomenon that has developed over a period of time and cannot arbitrarily be changed. It is wary of broad solutions based on abstract reasoning and places greater reliance on experience and gradual change. Conservatism holds the individual and his freedom as its supreme value. The individual is encouraged to exercise his individuality, creativity, and self-reliance. Thus, the free-enterprise system of free markets, competition, and decentralization of power is basic to economic conservatism. The conservative wishes to limit the role of government, especially the central government, to a few necessary spheres. In his view, the government should not undertake any program which could be undertaken equally well by private enterprise. Government spending should be kept as low as possible, and the traditional rule of the balanced budget should be upheld. Furthermore, wages, prices, and interest rates should be completely free from government influence. For a fuller exposition of the doctrines of economic conservatism, see Milton Friedman, *Capitalism and Freedom*, The University of Chicago Press, Chicago, 1962; Henry C. Wallich, "Conservative Economic Policy," *Yale Review*, New Haven, Conn., Autumn, 1956; National Association of Manufacturers, Economic Principles Committee, *The American Free Enterprise System*, McGraw-Hill Book Company, New York, 1946.

Consolidation A union of two or more companies into a new company. The new corporation takes over the assets and customers of the constituent companies, and the constituent companies are then dissolved. For example, if company A is formed to take over companies X, Y, and Z, only company A remains in existence after the consolidation. Strictly a statutory procedure, consolidation differs from a merger, in which one of the constituent companies remains while the other companies are legally dissolved. Despite this legal difference between a merger and consolidation, the economic consequences of both are the same, permitting operations to be combined under centralized control. For information on the procedure required to effect a consolidation, see Lillian Doris (ed.), *Business Finance Handbook*, Prentice-Hall, Inc., Englewood Cliffs, N.J., 1953, pp. 701–705; Elvin F. Donaldson and John K. Pfahl, *Corporate Finance*, The Ronald Press Company, New York, 1969, pp. 735–738.

Consols Long-term securities issued by the British government. The term consols is an abbreviation of Consolidated Annuities, which were first issued in 1751. Consols pay a fixed amount of interest and thus resemble bonds, but they have no maturity date, and in this sense they are similar to stock, which they are frequently called. Consols are redeemable at the option of the government, and many have been redeemed in the past when refinancing could be accomplished at lower interest rates. As of March 31, 1969, £ 371.5 million of 4% Consols and £ 275.6 million of 2½% Consols were outstanding. For additional information, see R. S. Sayers, *Modern Banking*, 7th ed., Oxford University Press, New York, 1967, pp. 206–207.

Conspicuous Consumption Consumption intended chiefly as an ostentatious display of wealth. Thorstein Veblen, who introduced the concept, maintained that conspicuous consumption exists among all classes of society, even the poorest, who in their own modest way, attempt to outshine their neighbors by purchasing superior goods even though these are beyond their means. Among the wealthy, costly entertainment, such as fancy balls, were, Veblen maintained, a favored means of carrying out conspicuous consumption. To determine whether a particular outlay fell under the heading of conspicuous consumption, the question was "whether, aside from acquired tastes and from the canons of usage and conventional decency, its result is a net gain in comfort or in the fullness of life." Rigidly applied, Veblem's standard would label as conspicuous consumption the overwhelming majority of consumer expenditures in most industrial nations. See Thorstein Veblen, *The Theory of the Leisure Class*, Random House, Inc., New York, 1934, chap. 4.

Constant-Dollar Values (Real-Dollar Values) A series of dollar values, such as gross national product, personal income, sales, or profits, from which the effect of changes in the purchasing power of the dollar has been removed. The resulting series is in real terms and thus indirectly measures physical volume. The process of converting current-dollar values into constant-dollar values is generally called deflating. Different deflators may be used to adjust different sets of data to constant dollars. Among them are the U.S. Department of Commerce's implicit price deflator, which roughly measures the general price level of the whole economy and is used to deflate gross national product to constant-dollar terms; the U.S. Bureau of Labor Statistics' wholesale price index of industrial commodities, which is used to deflate industrial sales; and the U.S. Bureau of Labor Statistics' consumer price index, which is used to deflate consumer income and consumer purchases of goods and services. Usually, dollar figures are expressed in terms of dollars of some selected year, such as 1940, 1950, or 1960, or a set of years, such as the average for 1947, 1948, and 1949 or the average for 1957, 1958, and 1959. For deflating techniques, see Frederick E. Croxton and Dudley J. Cowden, *Applied General Statistics*, Prentice-Hall, Inc., Englewood Cliffs, N.J., 1955.

Constant Returns, Theory of *See Returns to Scale.*

Construction Contract Award   A contract granted to a builder for the completion of specified construction work. Since contracts must be awarded before building activity begins, tabulations of contract award data are valuable aids in business forecasting, serving to indicate the trend of future construction, which is a major item in the nation's total output of goods and services. In the U.S., there is only one widely used measure of contract awards, the Dodge construction contract awards, which measure the dollar value of awards for housing, industrial and commercial buildings, utilities, and public works (farm building is

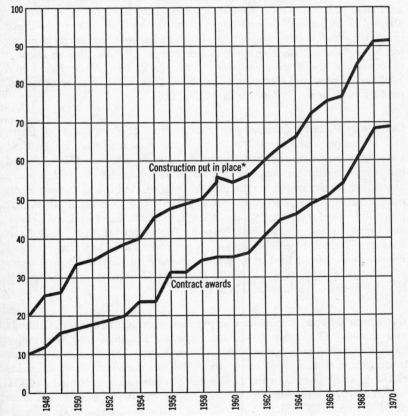

Construction Awards vs. Construction Put in Place (Billions of dollars)

Construction put in place*

Contract awards

*1959-1969 includes Alaska and Hawaii.

Source: U.S. Department of Commerce; F.W. Dodge Division, McGraw-Hill Information Systems Company.

excluded). Monthly contract award data are published in U.S. Department of Commerce, *Survey of Current Business.*

Consumer Credit   An arrangement that enables consumers to buy goods and services immediately and pay for them later. Consumer credit is essentially short-term debt. It includes both installment credit, which is scheduled to be repaid in two or more payments; and noninstallment credit, such as single-payment loans, charge accounts, credit cards, and credit extended by hospitals, physicians, and utilities. It does not include home mortgages, which are long-term loans. In U.S. history, consumer credit has existed since the Pilgrims booked passage on the *Mayflower* and paid for it on the installment plan. From this small beginning, the volume of consumer credit grew to approximately $127 billion in 1970, or about 19% of personal income after taxes. In the U.S., about two-thirds of all cars and about one-half of all television sets, furniture, washing machines, and outboard motorboats are bought on time. For an account of consumer credit practices, see Hillel Black, *Buy Now, Pay Later,* William Morrow and Company, Inc., New York, 1961; for monthy data, see *Federal Reserve Bulletin,* Washington, D.C.

Consumer Finance Company (Personal Finance Company)   A financial institution which specializes in small and personal loans. In the U.S., state laws limit the amount of a single loan to $300 or $500 in most cases and specify the amount of interest that can be charged, usually about 2 to 3% per month on the unpaid balance. As high as these interest rates are, they are low in comparison with the loan-shark rates that prevailed before state regulation of these businesses. For additional details, see Louis Robinson and Rolf Nugent, *Regulation of the Small Loan Business,* Russell Sage Foundation, New York, 1935; see also National Bureau of Economic Research, Inc., Conference on Regulation, *Consumer Installment Credit,* part 1, vol. I, Board of Governors of the Federal Reserve System, Washington, D.C., 1957.

Consumer Goods   Manufactured products used primarily by individuals and families. Consumer goods are generally classified into two major categories according to the degree of durability: (1) *durables,* such as passenger cars and appliances; and (2) *nondurables,* such as food, clothing, and tobacco. In the U.S., sales of consumer goods totaled $355 billion in 1970, with durables accounting for about $90 billion, and nondurables for $265 billion. For historical statistics and methods of estimating consumer goods in the national accounts, see U.S. Department of Commerce, *U.S. Income and Output: A Supplement to the Survey of*

Consumer Credit (Billions of dollars)

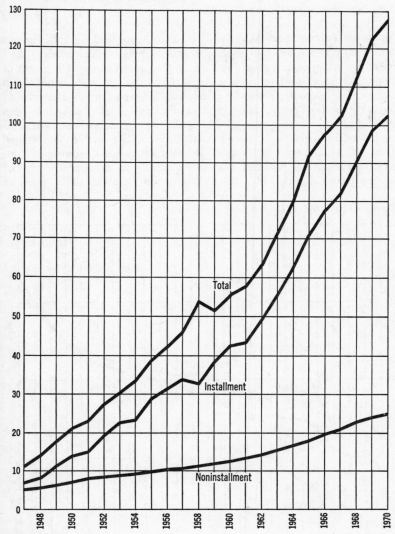

Source: Federal Reserve Board.

Current Business; for the latest quarterly estimates, U.S. Department of Commerce, *Survey of Current Business.*

Consumer Price Index A monthly measure, compiled by U.S. Bureau of Labor Statistics, of changes in the prices of goods and services consumed by urban families and individuals. The index includes a group of about 300 goods and services, ranging from food to automobiles and from rent to haircuts, normally purchased by urban wage earners and clerical consumers representing both families and single persons. It does not include items that are bought primarily by suburban and rural families or by lower- and upper-income families. The relative importance given individual items in the index is based on periodic surveys of consumer expenditures. Current prices are expressed as a percentage of average prices during 1967. For example, the October, 1971, index of

Consumer Price Index (1967 = 100)

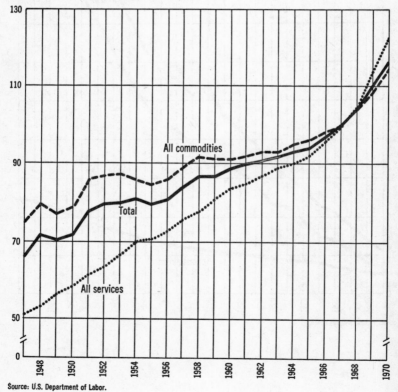

Source: U.S. Department of Labor.

22.6 indicated that prices in that month were 22.6% higher than during 1967. Although the consumer price index is sometimes incorrectly called the cost-of-living index, it fails to measure the cost of living. This is partly because (1) quality changes are not measured precisely, and (2) there are delays in including new goods and services. The monthly index is prepared for the nation as a whole, for each of seventeen large metropolitan areas, for individual items, and for commodity and service groupings. All data are published in U.S. Department of Labor *Monthly Labor Review;* for a detailed critique of concepts and problems, see *The Price Statistics of the Federal Government,* National Bureau of Economic Research, Inc., New York, 1961; for a detailed defense, see Sidney A. Jaffe, "Consumer Price Index: Technical Questions and Practical Answers," a paper delivered before the American Statistical Association, Dec. 27, 1959.

Consumer Sovereignty The dominant role of the consumer in determining the types and quantities of goods produced by an economic system. The principle of consumer sovereignty is a key factor in the organization of production in a free economy. Each consumer purchase is actually the casting of "dollar votes," by which the consumer registers his desires in terms of goods and services. The casting of dollar votes by consumers is translated directly into business profits, the motivating factor in production, so that changes in demand result in corresponding changes in production patterns. As consumer demand for certain goods increases, production of those goods is increased to take advantage of the new potentialities for profit. Many economists believe that consumer sovereignty is limited by such factors as lack of knowledge about products and by monopoly. For further information, see Clark Lee Allen et al., *Prices, Income, and Public Policy,* 2d ed., McGraw-Hill Book Company, New York, 1959, chap. 1; George Katona, *The Powerful Consumer,* McGraw-Hill Book Company, New York, 1960; Alvin H. Hansen, *Economic Issues of the 1960's,* McGraw-Hill Book Company, New York, 1961, pp. 75–76.

Consumer's Surplus The difference between the price that a consumer pays for a good or a service and the amount that he would be willing to pay rather than to do without the purchase. The concept of the consumer's surplus was introduced formally into value theory by Alfred Marshall, who held that it serves as a measure of the satisfaction that a consumer receives from a purchase, above and beyond the sacrifices that he makes to acquire the purchase as measured by its price. For Marshall's statement, see Alfred Marshall, *Principles of Economics,* 8th ed., The Macmillan Company, New York, 1948, book III, chap. 6; see also J. R. Hicks, *Value and Capital,* Oxford University Press, Fair Lawn, N.J., 1946, chap. 2.

Consumption Function   A function relating the level of consumption expenditures to the level of national income. The basis of the formulation introduced by John Maynard Keynes was that real consumption expenditures are a stable function of real income. Keynes felt that the marginal propensity to consume (the percentage of an addition to income which is spent for consumption) is positive but less than unity, that the marginal propensity to consume is less than the average propensity to consume and that it falls as the level of income rises. Empirical studies seem to confirm the stable relationship of consumption to the level of income, the value of the marginal propensity to consume being about 0.75 in the U.S. There is, however, little evidence that the marginal propensity declines with rising income even though it has been found to be lower than the average propensity to consume. It has also been determined that the longer the time period considered, the steeper the consumption function becomes (the higher the marginal propensity to consume). This fact indicates that the consumption function may be related not so closely to current income as to some measure of long-run income or wealth. It has also been proposed that differences in consumption behavior may be due to differences in relative income (income to which one is accustomed) rather than to the level of absolute income. For further information, see J. M. Keynes, *The General Theory of Employment, Interest, and Money,* Harcourt, Brace and World, Inc., New York, 1936, chaps. 8, 9, and 10; see also Gardner Ackley, *Macroecenomic Theory,* The Macmillan Company, New York, 1961, chaps. 10, 11, and 12; Milton Friedman, *A Theory of the Consumption Function,* National Bureau of Economic Research, Inc., New York, 1955; James S. Duesenberry, *Income, Savings, and the Theory of Consumer Behavior,* Harvard University Press, Cambridge, Mass, 1949. For a brief summary of important findings pertaining to research on the consumption function, see Milton H. Spencer, *Managerial Economics,* Richard D. Irwin, Inc., Homewood, Ill., 1968, pp. 146–149.

Consumption Product   A designation of any product which is consumed for personal satisfaction. Such a product differs from raw materials, industrial products, and farm products.

Consumption Tax   A levy on consumer goods. The base of a consumption tax levied on the buyers or sellers of products is the amount or value of goods bought or sold. Not all consumption taxes are levied originally on consumers, but those that are levied on manufacturers and distributors can be shifted forward by including the amount of the tax in the price of the consumer good, so that the consumer bears the final burden. The amount of the tax for each individual varies with the level of his expenditures. The most common forms of consumption taxes are the retail sales tax, the turnover tax, taxes on the production, sale, and use of particular goods (taxes on business gross receipts, use taxes, and excise taxes), and import duties. Although consumption taxes are considered to be regressive, placing a larger burden on the poor than on the rich, they offer the advantages of stable revenues (since consumption is usually more stable than income), relatively low cost of collection, ability to produce revenue immediately, and utility in regulating consumption (e.g., consumption of luxuries). The regressive nature of such consumption taxes as the sales tax can be reduced by exempting certain necessities, such as food. For additional information, see Philip E. Taylor, *The Economics of Public Finance*, rev. ed., The Macmillan Company, New York, 1953, chap. 20; Harold Groves, *Financing Government*, 6th ed., Holt, Rinehart and Winston, Inc., New York, 1964; Alfred G. Buehler, *General Sales Taxation*, The Business Bourse, New York, 1932.

Contract Authorization A financial grant by the Congress of the U.S., empowering Federal agencies to incur obligations, usually for construction projects which will take a considerable time to complete, before appropriations have been made to cover them. Most authorizations are enacted for a one- or two-year period; if they are not obligated during that time, they usually expire. Before money may be disbursed to pay a Federal obligation incurred under authorization, an appropriation of funds is necessary. For details of the process by which the Federal government reaches decisions on expenditures, see Arthur Smithies, *The Budgetary Process in the United States*, McGraw-Hill Book Company, New York, 1955; see also Murray L. Weidenbaum, "The Federal Government Spending Process," in U.S. Joint Economic Committee, *Federal Expenditure Policy for Economic Growth and Stability*, Government Printing Office, Washington, D.C., 1957; for current statistics, see U.S. Bureau of the Budget, *The Federal Budget in Brief* and *The Budget Review*, annual reports.

Contract Curve The locus of optimal points in a trading situation with one buyer and one seller. The contract curve is derived with the help of the Edgeworth box, introduced by the English economist F. Y. Edgeworth. In the situation analyzed by the contract curve, there is one seller (the input supplier) and one buyer (the input purchaser). First, an indifference map between money and X (the quantity of input sold) is drawn for each of the two individuals (see the accompanying figure). The two indifference maps are combined by rotating one (the seller's) by 180° and joining the ends of the axes (see figure). The length of the vertical axis (money) is determined by the buyer's money supply; the length of the horizontal axis (output sold), by the productive capacity of the seller. Every point in the box can be interpreted as a trade of a certain number of dollars (e.g., 1 at point A) for a certain number of input units (e.g., 3 at point A). Whatever input does not remain in the hands of the seller after the trade has been completed must have gone to the buyer; whatever money the buyer does not have after the trade must be in the hands of the seller. The contract curve (CC') is the locus of all points of tangency between the buyer's and the seller's indifference curves. For every trading point not on the contract curve, there exists a point on the curve which is mutually advantageous to both buyer and seller. For example, if the trade first agreed on by both buyer and seller is represented by point A, they could not move to point B and both be better off. Thus, the actual trading point should finally be located some-

Buyer's Indifference Map   **Seller's Indifference Map**

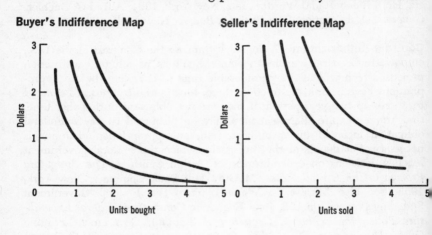

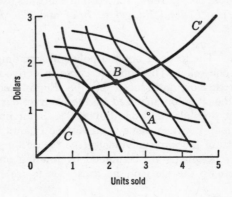

where along the contract curve (the actual location along the curve is indeterminate); otherwise, it would be to the advantage of both buyer and seller to renegotiate the deal and move to a point on the curve where no further mutually advantageous renegotiation would be possible. For a fuller explanation of the contract curve, see William Baumol, *Economic Theory and Operations Analysis*, 2d ed., Prentice-Hall, Inc., Englewood Cliffs, N.J., 1965, chap. 11; F. Y. Edgeworth, *Mathematical Psychics*, Augustus M. Kelley, Publishers, New York, 1881, pp. 17ff.

Contraction   A widespread decline in economic activity. The term covers both depressions and recessions. A contraction begins after the peak in economic activity has been attained and continues until the trough has been reached. Contractions vary widely in the degree and duration of the decline. Between 1854 and 1971 there were twenty-seven contractions in the U.S.; the shortest (1917–1918) lasted seven months, and the longest (1873–1879) sixty-five months. The 1929–1933 contraction lasted forty-five months. For more detailed information on contractions, see Geoffrey H. Moore (ed.), *Business Cycle Indicators*, Princeton University Press, Princeton, N.J., 1961.

Controller   *See Comptroller.*

Convenience Goods   Items which the consumer generally desires to purchase frequently, immediately, and with a minimum of effort. Convenience goods are usually inexpensive items which generally may be bought near the consumer's home or place of business. Example are cigarettes, candy, and such staple grocery items as milk, cream, and butter.

Conversion   The exchange of one security for another. The term usually applies to the exchange of preferred stock for common stock or of bonds or debentures (unsecured bonds) for common or preferred stock. All convertible securities are restricted by the terms of conversion, which are contained in the certificate of incorporation in the case of stocks and in the indenture in the case of bonds. The terms of conversion stipulate the kind of security which the bondholder or stockholder can convert to, the conversion rate, and the period during which the holder is allowed to exchange the securities. For example, a holder of a debenture worth $1,000 may be allowed to convert it into fifty shares of common stock of the same corporation at $20 per share at any time during a ten-year period. As long as the market prices of the debenture and the stock are at $1,000 and $20, respectively, it makes little difference which security he holds (except for any difference between dividend and interest yields). Generally, when the price of the common stock increases, the price of the convertible debenture also rises. See Charles W. Gerstenberg, *Financial Organization and Management of Business,* 4th ed., Prentice-Hall, Inc., Englewood Cliffs, N.J., 1959; Elvin F. Donaldson and John K. Pfahl, *Corporate Finance,* The Ronald Press Company, New York, 1969, pp. 218–243; J. Fred Weston and Eugene F. Brigham, *Essentials of Managerial Finance,* Holt, Rinehart and Winston, Inc., New York, 1968.

Convertible Debenture A certificate issued by a corporation as evidence of debt that can be converted at the option of the holder into other securities (usually common stock, but sometimes preferred stock) of the same corporation. Each debenture can be converted into a specified number of shares of stock at a stipulated price for a certain period. There are two advantages to convertible debentures for the issuing corporation: (1) The conversion privilege makes the debentures more attractive to investors and tends to reduce interest costs. (2) The debentures facilitate the extinction of debt because debt declines and equity (stock) increases as holders convert their debentures. The major disadvantage is discrimination against the company's stockholders, whose equity is diluted as the holders of debentures convert them. At all times during the conversion period, there is a price relationship between the debenture and the stock. It is based on the conversion price, the number of shares into which each debenture can be converted, and the value that the market puts on the conversion privilege. For example, a $1,000 debenture that can be converted into fifty shares of common stock at $20 per share will normally trade in the market at a price higher than $1,000 because of the conversion privilege. Moreover, the price of the convertible debenture will change as the price of the stock changes because of the conversion feature. Convertible debentures appeal to investors because they yield a fixed income (interest) without limiting the holder's participation in the growth of the company; if the company grows, the price of the common stock will increase. Speculators favor convertible debentures because the law allows them to borrow more money to purchase and carry debentures than common or preferred stocks, thus giving them more leverage. See Charles W. Gerstenberg, *Financial Organization and Management of Business,* 4th ed., Prentice-Hall, Inc., Englewood Cliffs, N.J., 1959, pp. 166–172; Joseph H. Bonneville et al., *Organizing and Financing Business,* Prentice-Hall, Inc., Englewood Cliffs, N.J., 1959; C. J. Pilcher, *Raising Capital with Convertible Securities,* University of Michigan, Bureau of Business Research, Ann Arbor, Mich., 1955.

Cooling-Off Period A period during which employees cannot strike and employers cannot engage in a lockout. It is fixed by Federal or state law or, occasionally, by contract. An important U.S. example of the cooling-off period is found in the Taft-Hartley Act, which authorizes the President to direct the Attorney General to seek an injunction from the Federal courts, forbidding a strike or lockout for eighty days. During this time, a three-man board of inquiry studies the issue and reports to the President. If at the end of eighty days labor is still unwilling to accept management's last offer, the court removes the injunction and the strike may proceed. During the cooling-off period, wages and conditions of work are usually frozen under conditions set by the previous contract. See U.S. Code, subchapter III, title 29; see also Albert Rees, *The Economics of Trade Unions,* The University of Chicago Press, Chicago, 1962.

Cooperative   A voluntary organization engaged in an economic activity which is established, owned, and operated by those persons who together will share the total benefit. The theory is that cooperatives can reduce costs, thus raising the incomes of their members, and eliminating the profits of the middleman or, in the case of producers' cooperatives, the capitalist. In addition, the theory involves the realization that individuals united have greater power than a single individual. A cooperative can engage in production, financing, or marketing. Among producers' cooperatives, only agricultural marketing cooperatives, which often involve the processing of the agricultural output as well as its collective marketing, have ever had much success and significance in the United States or Europe. Other important types of cooperatives are the credit union, the consumer cooperative, and residential cooperatives. A consumer cooperative is a retail establishment, which sometimes includes a wholesale business, that is operated by some or all of its customers to save marketing costs. In such a cooperative, savings take the form of a patronage dividend distributed to members from the net earnings on the basis of the amount that each member spent in the store since the last dividend. In a residential cooperative, each tenant is a stockholder by virtue of having bought the property, usually an apartment, that he occupies; he generally profits from the cooperative handling of maintenance and interest costs. See Henry H. Bakken and Marvin A. Schaars, *The Economics of Cooperative Marketing,* McGraw-Hill Book Company, New York, 1937; William N. Loucks, *Comparative Economic Systems,* Harper & Row, Publishers, Incorporated, New York, 1957.

Corner   A virtual monopoly in the supply of a company's stock for sale in security markets. In such a situation, buyers of the stock (generally speculators who have sold it short and must eventually purchase and deliver it) are often forced by the controlling interests to pay exorbitant prices. Under modern security and commodity market regulations, there are almost no opportunities to create a corner. In the nineteenth and early twentieth centuries, however, corners arose frequently, sometimes unintentionally as by-products of struggles for control of a company, but often as a result of devious manipulations. They developed when a group of operators who hoped to engineer a corner began to buy all the available stock of a company, thereby raising its price. In time, the price trend encouraged other traders to sell the overpriced stock short in the expectation that the price would decline again. If the original operators could buy and hold enough stock to force short sellers to buy from them in order to make good on the short sellers' promise to deliver the stock, they could extort very high prices for it. Through this same mechanism, corners have also occasionally been attempted, and a few times have succeeded, in the market for commodity futures. See George L. Leffler and L. C. Farwell, *The Stock Market,* The Ronald Press Company, New York, 1963.

Corporate Income Tax   A tax levied on the earnings of corporations. It was first instituted on the Federal level in the U.S. in 1901. Since 1936, when it became progressive, the tax has applied to undistributed net income as well as to income distributed as dividends. As of January, 1965, corporations pay a normal tax of 22% on the first $25,000 of taxable income and 26% on any taxable income over $25,000. A 10% surcharge on normal corporate tax and surtax became effective on January 1, 1968. The tax reform act of 1969 extended the surcharge on corporate tax liabilities at a 5% annual rate for the period January 1, 1970, to June 30,

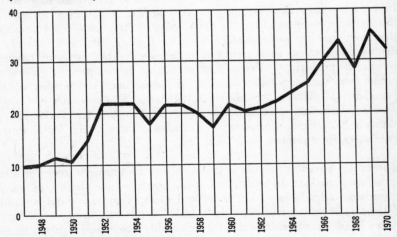

Federal Receipts from Corporate Income Taxes, 1947-1970 Fiscal Years (Billions of dollars)

Source: U.S. Treasury Department; Bureau of the Budget.

1970. In the fiscal year 1970, the corporate income tax accounted for nearly 17% of Federal budget receipts. The tax is regarded as a companion measure to the personal income tax, constituting an extension of that tax to corporate income, but it differs from the latter in several important respects. The corporate income tax does not provide for a minimum exemption to cover the cost of equity capital. The rate of the tax depends on the size of the corporation's total income rather than on the net income of its owners, and the dividends distributed by the corporation are taxed twice, once as corporate earnings and again as shareholders' dividend income. Many experts believe that this double taxation of distributed corporate profits, without regard for the individual shareholder's ability to pay the tax, is the most objectionable part of the corporate tax structure. For further information on the Federal corporate income tax, see Richard Goode, *The Corporation Income Tax,* John Wiley & Sons, Inc., New York, 1951; see also J. K. Lasser Tax Institute, *Standard Handbook of Business Tax Techniques,* McGraw-Hill Book Company, New York, 1957; J. G. Smith, "Economic Significance of the Undistributed Profits Tax," *American Economic Review,* vol. XXVIII, pp. 305ff., American Economic Association, Evanston, Ill., June, 1938.

Corporation, Business A voluntary organization of persons, either actual individuals or legal entities, legally bound together to form a business enterprise. Industrial corporations became significant in the U.S. after the Civil War, when it was necessary to raise large amounts of capital for reconstruction. About 25% of U.S. businesses is now in the corporate form, and corporations clearly dominate the economy. For the fiscal year 1968, 1,547,000 corporations reported $1,495 billion of receipts to the Internal Revenue Service. The advantages of the corporate form of business enterprise are as follows: (1) It is by far the most effective form of business organization for the raising of capital funds. (2) It has limited liability. The owners (stockholders) risk only what they paid for the stock; their personal assets are not at stake if the corporation goes bankrupt. Creditors can sue the corporation as a legal person but not the owners of that corporation as individuals. (3) As a legal entity, the corporation has a perpetual life independent of its owners or of its individual officials. Proprietorships and partnerships, on the other hand, are subject to sudden and unpredictable demise. (4) Because of its size, the corporation can secure more specialized and more efficient management than can proprietorships and partnerships and can take full advantage of any gains to be had from large-scale production. (5) Incorporation may provide tax advantage when net profits are sizable. The maximum tax rate of 48% on a corporation is preferable to the maximum personal income tax rate of 70%. There are also disadvantages to the corporate form: (1)

The corporation is difficult to form because of legal complications and expense in obtaining a corporate charter from the state. (2) Corporate operations are limited to those enumerated in the charter, thus making the corporation seem less flexible than other forms in its business activities. (This shortcoming is, however, more apparent than real.) (3) Whereas in the sole proprietorship and partnership forms, the persons who own the real and financial assets of the firm also manage and control these assets, corporate ownership is widely scattered among relatively small owners. Thus, real control is likely to rest not with those who own a majority of the stock but rather with the management (the board of directors). (4) Corporate income paid out as dividends to stockholders is taxed twice, once as part of corporate profits and again as part of the stockholders' personal incomes. See Lyman A. Keith and Carlo E. Gubellini, *Introduction to Business Enterprise*, McGraw-Hill Book Company, New York, 1962, pp. 66–71.

Correlation The statistical technique which relates a dependent economic variable to one or more independent variables over a period of time in order to determine how close the relationship between the variables is. This technique may be used for business forecasting. When more than one independent variable is used, the relationship is called a multiple correlation. Thus, a forecaster may relate disposable personal income and time, in units of a year, to consumer expenditures to derive a mathematical formula which will predict the future level of consumer spending. A single business or industry can use similar relationships to predict its own sales. Gross national product, disposable income, and industrial production are commonly used as the independent variables. For information concerning correlation methodology, see Frederick E. Croxton and Dudley J. Cowden, *Applied General Statistics*, Prentice-Hall, Inc., Englewood Cliffs, N.J., 1967.

Correlogram The graph of the serial correlation of order k as ordinate against k as abscissa; a chart technique that may help to identify the type of econometric model to which a given time series conforms. In the nonstochastic case, if a trendless or detrended time series is cyclical (or periodic), its nature can be determined by the unaided eye observing a faithful pattern. In the stochastic case, if a series oscillates (is neither random nor periodic), the true pattern may be obscured by superimposed random effects. A strictly periodic time series has a periodic correlogram. In contrast, the correlogram of a moving average of random terms reveals no fixed periodicity. The larger the random element in a time series, the less reliable that time series' correlogram is. The term correlogram was coined by Wold in 1938, but the technique was used earlier by Yule.

Department of State, Agency for International Development, *Counterpart Funds and Aid Foreign Currency Accounts;* for a discussion, see Robert Asher, *Grants, Loans, and Local Currency Transactions: Their Role in Foreign Aid,* The Brookings Institution, Washington, D.C., 1961.

Countervailing Duty   An import tax levied on a commodity on which exporters have been paid a subsidy or an export bounty. The main purpose of a countervailing duty is to offset the special advantage of subsidized exports, placing them on an equal footing with other imports and with domestic products. The amount of the countervailing duty usually equals the amount of the subsidy. The use of the countervailing duty is a method of counteracting subsidized dumping operations by foreign countries.

Countervailing Power   The term applied to the forces that arise in an economy to offset some of the bargaining power enjoyed by large buyers and sellers in the marketplace. Countervailing power thus acts as a substitute for some of the forces normally expected in a competitive economy. Among the countervailing powers that have evolved in the U.S. are, on the one hand, powerful labor unions, which influence the prices that large corporations must pay for an important natural resource, labor; and, on the other hand, large retail chains (such as Sears, Roebuck and Company or the A & P) which through their purchasing policies can influence the prices that large manufacturing firms receive for their products. The theory of countervailing power is advanced by John Kenneth Galbraith in *American Capitalism: The Theory of Countervailing Power,* Houghton Mifflin Company, Boston, 1952; for a criticism of Galbraith's theory, see George J. Stigler, "The Economist Plays with Blocs," Papers and Proceedings, 66th annual meeting of the American Economic Association, *American Economic Review,* Evanston, Ill., 1954.

Covariance   The first product moment of two variates about their mean values. The econometric formulation measures the degree of intercorrelation between the independent variables in multiple correlation analysis. For additional information, see Karl A. Fox, *Intermediate Economic Statistics,* John Wiley & Sons, Inc., New York, 1968; Stefan Valavanis, *Econometrics,* McGraw-Hill Book Company, New York, 1959.

Craft Union   A labor union that limits its membership to a particular craft or skilled trade. It was in this form that trade unionism first made its appearance in the U.S. Most modern craft unions, however, have broadened their jurisdiction to include occupations and skills not closely related to the originally designated craft. Thus, the International Association of Machinists, a craft union, has brought production workers in the aircraft industry into its union and, in effect, has become an industrial union. In most craft unions, the local has a geographical jurisdiction, that is, the members of a craft in a given city or county. The craft basis of a local is often finer than that of its national union. Thus, the bricklayers, masons, and plasterers, all members of the same national union, have separate locals in most U.S. cities. Despite the long-run trend toward the narrowing of pay differentials among occupations in the economy as a whole, some unions of highly paid craftsmen have been successful in limiting the narrowing of differentials in their industries. When several crafts are represented in one craft union, the highest-paid crafts often dominate the internal politics of the union. See G. D. H. Cole, *An Introduction to Trade Unionism*, George Allen & Unwin, Ltd., London, 1953; Albert Rees, *The Economics of Trade Unions*, The University of Chicago Press, Chicago, 1962.

Cramer's Rule   A rule for solving multivariate, simultaneous linear equations. It is based on the fact that all terms in simultaneous equations, except coefficients of regression, are known numbers. The coefficients of regression may be solved for by using Cramer's rule: the ratio of two determinants that yield each unknown value. The determinants are always square, and their numerical values can be determined. For a detailed set of instructions, consult Karl A. Fox, *Intermediate Economic Statistics*, John Wiley & Sons, Inc., New York, 1968.

Crawling Peg (Sliding Peg)   A technique for allowing exchange rates to drift slowly and steadily by weekly, monthly, or quarterly alterations up to a maximum annual rate of 2 to 3%, either automatically or with deliberate guidance. This type of limited exchange-rate flexibility is thought to be small enough to discourage speculation in foreign-exchange markets. It would also provide relative stability for international trade and payments and sufficient scope for long-run exchange-rate adjustments. Some economists believe this technique would be appropriate for offsetting differences in the rate at which different countries' cost levels are rising, but they have doubts that it would discourage speculation. For additional information, see Paul A. Samuelson, *Economics*, 8th ed., McGraw-Hill Book Company, New York, 1970, pp. 643–644.

Credit   An exchange of goods or services for a promise of future payment. Credit is necessary in a dynamic economy because of the time that elapses between the production of a good and its ultimate sale and consumption. Credit bridges this gap. About 90% of the sales made by manufacturers and wholesalers and 30% of the retail sales involve the use of credit. Credit in manufacturing industries is called business credit, and credit extended by retail stores is called consumer credit. A common form of credit used in business is the open, or book, account, in which the seller keeps a record of the credit extended to the buyer and bills him when payment is due. Written business credit instruments include promissory notes, trade acceptances, and letters of credit. Consumer credit, which facilitates the immediate purchase of goods and services, usually takes the form of charge accounts, installment accounts, and personal loans. The risk in extending credit is the possibility that future payment by the buyer will not be made. For additional details, see Theodore Beckman, *Credits and Collections: Management and Theory*, 7th ed., McGraw-Hill Book Company, New York, 1962; Albert F. Chapin and George E. Hassett, *Credit and Collection Principles and Practice*, 7th ed., McGraw-Hill Book Company, New York, 1960; *Credit Management Handbook*, Richard D. Irwin, Inc., Credit Research Foundation, Homewood, Ill., 1958.

Credit Card   A card of identification which allows the holder to purchase goods and services in the present and pay for them in the future. Credit cards are issued by banks, hotels, travel organizations, dining groups, and many other organizations to individuals who are classified as good credit risks. A small fee must be paid in advance by the individual to obtain certain credit cards, such as Hilton Carte Blanche, Diners' Club, and American Express, but none is required for the cards issued by Hilton Hotel, Hotel Sheraton, oil companies, railroads, air travel organizations, and automobile rental companies.

Credit Control   Regulation of the flow of new credit into the economy, either to curb inflationary pressures or to help stimulate economic activity. Several different levers are available for this regulation: (1) The Federal Reserve System can raise or reduce the rediscount rate, which is the price that commercial banks must pay for borrowing from the central bank. (2) It can engage in open-market operations in the government securities market to absorb or increase the supply of idle funds. (3) It can raise or lower the level of reserves that commercial banks must keep immobile. (4) With congressional authorization, it can set limits on the credit terms offered in loans on securities, mortgages, and consumer credit. The first three of these levers limit or augment the volume of funds available to the commercial banking system for credit expansion. They also have an indirect impact on the price (interest rate) charged for new credit, and they influence indirectly the size and quality of the new loans that can be made by the banks. Only the specific controls on securities, mortgages, and consumer credit can be called direct rationing. Some observers believe that the fiscal policies of the U.S. Treasury Department also represent a form of credit control, in that they may add to or relieve the strain on capital markets. See National Bureau of Economic Research, Inc., Conference on Regulation, *Consumer Installment Credit,* part 2, vols. I and II, Board of Governors of the Federal Reserve System, Washington, D.C., 1957.

Credit Union A cooperative association organized for the purpose of making small short-term loans at low interest rates to members. It obtains the necessary funds for lending by receiving members' savings through selling shares. In the U.S., credit unions are chartered and regulated either by the Federal government or by the states. They are nonprofit organizations, and all earnings are paid to members as dividends. Credit unions were started to make consumer credit more widely available and cheaper than was possible through other financial intermediaries. The fact that credit unions are responsible for only a small percentage of total loans outstanding in the U.S. does not mean that they are unimportant. They make credit available to low-income families who might not otherwise be able to obtain short-terms personal loans except at exorbitant interest rates. At the end of 1968, there were 23,480 credit unions in the U.S., with combined assets of $14.2 billion and loans outstanding of $11.2 billion. See *Credit Unions,* American Bankers Association, New York, 1958; for figures and up-to-date information on credit unions, see *Credit Union Yearbook,* Credit Union National Association, Madison, Wis.

Creeping Inflation A slow but persistent upward movement in the general price level of as much as 2.5% per year. Sumner H. Slichter of Harvard University argued that a gradually rising price level is a stimulant for the economy and for increasing incomes. Other economists disagree and point out that economic gains have been made in times of stable and falling prices as well as in times of rising prices. Furthermore, a gradual price increase, averaging 2.5% per year, would cut the purchasing power of the dollar by nearly one half in twenty-five years. See Arthur F. Burns, *Prosperity Without Inflation,* Fordham University Press, New York, 1957; Sumner H. Slichter, statement before the U.S. Joint Committee on the Economic Report, March 20, 1959; see also Neil H. Jacoby, "The Problem of Creeping Inflation," *Economics and the Policy Maker,* Brookings Lectures, 1958–1959, The Brookings Institution, Washington, D.C., 1959.

Creeping Socialism A term referring to the gradual enroachment of the government on the private sector of the economy. Coined by President Dwight D. Eisenhower in an informal speech on June 11, 1953, it has come into popular usage to describe the increasing activity of the government, usually the Federal government, in areas traditionally left to private enterprise and initiative. The term is sometimes used in a derogatory manner to express the feeling that the continued growth of the governmental sphere will lead eventually to full-fledged socialism and complete government ownership and operation of industry. Among government activities often cited as examples of creeping socialism are government-run power projects, such as those of the Tennessee Valley Authority.

Cross Elasticity A measure of the influence of the price of one good on the demand for another. The cross elasticity of demand for good X in terms of the price of good Y is the percentage change in the quantity bought of X divided by the percentage change in the price of Y, consumer tastes, money incomes, and all other prices being constant. The cross elasticity measures the degree of relationship between the two goods; the higher the cross elasticity between X and Y, the greater the interdependence between them. If a fall in the price of Y causes the demand for good X to rise (e.g., a fall in the price of tennis rackets causes a greater number of tennis balls to be demanded), the cross elasticity of demand is negative (since the numerator and denominator have different algebraic signs), and the two goods—tennis balls and tennis rackets—are complementary goods. A decline in the price of one of the complementary goods, by stimulating an increased use of the good, will raise the marginal utility of the other good and thus increase the quantity of the second good that is bought. If, however, a reduction in the price of Y causes the demand for X to fall (e.g., a fall in the price of coffee causes the demand for tea to fall), then the cross elasticity of demand between coffee and tea is positive, and the two goods are rival commodities, or substitute goods. The fall in the price of one good, by stimulating an increased use of the good, lowers the marginal utility of the other good and thus decreases the quantity of the second good that is bought. Cross elasticity is a pure measure of complementarity and the ability of goods to be substituted only if the commodities in question account for a very small proportion of the total budget, so that the income effect of the price change can be ignored. For further information, see George J. Stigler, *The Theory of Price*, rev. ed., The Macmillan Company, New York, 1952; Milton H. Spencer, *Managerial Economics*, Richard D. Irwin, Inc., Homewood, Ill. 1968, pp. 139–141.

Cross-Section Analysis The analysis of variation arising from interindividual differences with respect to one or more characteristics at a given point in time or during a short time interval—for example, the analysis of family budgets showing expenditures in combination with information on income and a variety of demographic characteristics. The involved information is usually collected according to a rigorous sample design that is based on probability calculations and is intended to produce a sample that is representative of some universe. For additional information, see Karl A. Fox, *Intermediate Economic Statistics,* John Wiley & Sons, Inc., New York, 1968; Lawrence A. Klein, *An Introduction to Econometrics,* Prentice-Hall, Inc., Englewood Cliffs, N.J., 1962.

Cultural Lag   The difference in the rate at which different parts of the same culture change. In current terms, cultural lag refers to the relatively slow rate of change in political, social, and economic ideas and practices, compared with the rapid growth of inventions and technology in the mid-twentieth century. For example, few politicians, sociologists, and economists recognized the political, social, and economic implications of the widespread introduction of automation into business fields. Another example may be seen in education, in which the number of scientists and engineers trained in the schools lags far behind the needs of a rapidly advancing technology. For additional discussion, see William F. Ogburn, *Social Change,* The Viking Press, Inc., New York, 1950.

Cumulative Diffusion Index   A synthetic measure, resembling an aggregate, which is built up from a diffusion index just as an aggregate can be built up from a rate-of-change series. It is computed by subtracting 50 percentage points from a diffusion index (the percentage series rising) and accumulating the remainder from month to month, starting at an arbitrary date. Alternatively, the index may be computed by subtracting the percentage of series declining from the percentage of series rising and accumulating the difference from month to month. For further discussion, see Geoffrey H. Moore and Julius Shiskin, *Variable Span Diffusion Indexes and Economic Forecasting,* a paper presented at the Sixth Annual Forecasting Conference, American Statistical Association, New York Chapter, Apr. 17, 1964.

Currency   The tangible, circulating portion of a nation's money supply, composed of bank notes, government notes, and coins. The term is sometimes used to refer to paper money only. Currency constitutes about 23% of the U.S. money supply, narrowly defined; paper money alone accounts for about 20%. The rest of the money supply is in the form of demand deposits or checking accounts. Currency alone is legal tender in the United States. It is used chiefly for retail purchases and the payment of wages. The currency of the U.S. consists of Federal Reserve notes and treasury notes and coins. This currency is put into circulation when the Federal Reserve banks supply vault cash to commercial banks. The latter, in turn, need it for their customers and pay for it by drawing on their reserve on deposit at the Federal Reserve banks. See Paul B. Trescott, *Money, Banking, and Economic Welfare*, 2d ed., McGraw-Hill Book Company, New York, 1963; for monthly data on the total amounts of currency in circulation, see *Federal Reserve Bulletin*, Washington, D.C.; for data on weekly changes in the amount of currency in circulation, see Federal Reserve Bank of New York, *Monthly Review*.

Currency Convertibility The privilege extended to a holder of a nation's currency to exchange his holdings, at the rate of exchange, for the currency of another nation for any purpose. Under a condition of full currency convertibility, any holder of any national currency is guaranteed unrestricted currency exchange privileges even in times of balance-of-payments deficits. The major advantage of currency convertibility is that it permits consumers or producers to transact their business in the markets most satisfactory to themselves. Consumers, for example, can purchase goods or services in a foreign market when those available in the home market are unsatisfactory and pay for them in their national currency, which the seller abroad may, in turn, exchange for an equivalent value of his own nation's currency. Currency convertibility is thus an essential element in the workings of international economic competition. Because of inadequate holdings of foreign currencies, a nation may be forced to suspend currency convertibility. Some nations have used such suspensions as a discriminatory weapon for political or other purposes. The International Monetary Fund attempts to prevent the involuntary rupture of currency convertibility by lending sufficient funds in appropriate national currencies to nations faced with a sudden rise in the demand for foreign currency. For a fuller discussion of the question, see Gottfried Haberler, *Currency Convertibility*, American Enterprise Association, Washington, D.C., 1954; for a detailed discussion of currency restrictions, see International Monetary Fund, *Thirteenth Annual Report: Exchange Restrictions*, Washington, D.C., 1962.

Currency School A school of economic thought that was prominent in England in the first half of the nineteenth century. At that time there was a public debate on the proper role of the Bank of England in the issuance of currency and the currency needs of the economy. The railroad boom and the subsequent panic of 1837 led to a controversy between the currency school and the banking school. The former advocated a regulated supply of money, letting it vary as a purely metallic currency so that it responded automatically to any inflow or outflow of gold. The Bank of England leaned toward this view and followed the rule of maintaining a constant ratio of security holdings, loans, investments, and discounted paper to total liabilities. In contrast, members of the banking school denied that it was possible to overissue convertible-currency paper, inasmuch as "the needs of trade" automatically regu-lated the volume of issued notes. They argued that there was no need for statutory control of the currency, provided convertibility was maintained. Underlying the debate was the definition of money supply. The currency school insisted that only bank notes and coin were money. Therefore, bank lending policies did not need to be regulated, and if the monetary system could be tied directly to gold, all monetary problems would be avoided. For further information, see M. R. Daugherty, "The Currency-Banking Controversy," *Southern Journal of Economics,* Southern Economic Association and University of North Carolina, Chapel Hill, N.C., October, 1942, and January, 1943; see also E. V. Morgan, *The Theory and Practice of Central Banking 1797–1913,* The Macmillan Company, New York, 1943, chaps. 5 and 6.

Current Account, Balance-of-Payments   Entries in the balance-of-payments account which summarize all international current account transactions. These include exports and imports of goods and services by individuals and government. Thus, current account transactions cover both visible items (merchandise) and invisible items (services). Among the invisible items are shipping and air transportation, travel expenditures, interest and dividends on investments, private and governmental gifts, and miscellaneous services. For additional information, see International Monetary Fund, *Balance of Payments Manual,* Washington, D.C., January, 1950; see also Geoffrey Crowther, *Balances and Imbalances of Payments,* Harvard Graduate School of Business Administration, Boston, 1957.

Current Assets   Cash or other items that will normally be turned into cash within one year, and assets that will be used up in the operation of a firm within one year. The term current assets includes cash on hand and in the bank, accounts receivable, materials, supplies, inventories, market-able securities, and prepaid expenses. If a firm is to remain solvent, current assets must be greater than current liabilities. The excess of current assets over current liabilities is known as working capital and represents the funds that the businessman has at his disposal to carry on the current operation of the business. For further information, see George MacFarland et al., *Accounting Fundamentals,* 3d ed., McGraw-Hill Book Company, New York, 1957; and Jacob Hugh Jackson, *Accounting Principles,* 3d ed., McGraw-Hill Book Company, New York, 1951.

Current Liabilities   Amounts owed that will ordinarily be paid by a firm within one year. The most common types of current liabilities are accounts payable, wages payable, taxes payaable, and interest and dividends payable. Since current liabilities fall due quickly, the firm must have an excess of current assets over current liabilities if it is to remain solvent. The excess of current assets over current liabilities is known as working capital and represents the funds that the businessman has at his disposal to carry on the current operation of the business. For additional details, see George MacFarland et al., *Accounting Fundamentals,* 3d ed., McGraw-Hill Book Company, New York, 1957; Jacob Hugh Jackson, *Accounting Principles,* 3d ed., McGraw-Hill Book Company, New York, 1951.

Current Ratio   A ratio of a firm's current assets to its current liabilities. For example, if the current assets amount to $250,000 and the current liabilities to $125,000, the current ratio is 2 to 1. This means that the firm has $2 of current assets for each $1 of debt. This ratio, also called the banker's ratio because U.S. commercial bankers originated the concept, is used to evaluate a firm's current operations. Since the current ratio includes the value of inventories which have not yet been sold, however, it is not the best indication of the current status of the firm. The acid-test ratio, which covers only the most liquid of current assets, provides a better evaluation of a firm's current operation. See Edison E. Easton and Byron L. Newton, *Accounting and the Analysis of Financial Data,* McGraw-Hill Book Company, New York, 1958.

Customs Duty   *See Tariff.*

Customs Union   An agreement between countries to abolish all tariffs between the members of the union and to adopt a uniform tariff vis-à-vis other nations. The agreement may refer not only to import and export duties, but also to any charges or quotas tending to restrict trade. Thus, in order to be able to sell to a larger market, individual countries surrender their right to protect domestic industry from other members of the union through the traditional devices of trade restriction. The term customs union may refer to one group of products (iron and steel, for example) or to complete economic integration, such as now exists in the European Common Market. A customs union differs from a free-trade area, which does not include a uniform external tariff, each country maintaining autonomy in its relations with third countries. In general, the higher the barriers removed, the greater will be the expansion of trade; the lower the external trade barriers, the less diversion there will be. Domestic producers tend to resist tariff reductions that threaten to increase total imports, but they are much more amenable to tariff reductions which merely shift the source of imports from one outside supplier to another foreign supplier within the preferential area. The classic works in this field are Jacob Viner, *The Customs Union Issue,* Carnegie Endowment for International Peace, New York, 1950; J. E. Meade, *The Theory of Customs Unions,* North Holland Publishing Company, Amsterdam, 1955; see also Emile Benoit, *Europe at Sixes and Sevens,* Columbia University Press, New York, 1961.

Cutthroat Competition   A term designating discriminatory price reductions made by a large seller for the purpose of injuring smaller competitors. The large seller may often cut his price only in the area in which rival firms are operating and maintain the normal price elsewhere. From 1870 to 1890, the dominant firms in a number of U.S. industries, such as oil, sugar, salt, copper, lead, tobacco, and iron and steel, used methods of cutthroat competition ruthlessly to drive competing firms out of business and to expand their private monopoly power. After the Sherman Antitrust Act was passed in 1890, many of these dominant companies were forced to adopt a policy of live and let live, allowing independent sellers to stay in the market if they followed the leader on price policy. In 1914, Congress passed the Federal Trade Commission Act and the Clayton Antitrust Act, both of which outlawed cutthroat competition in interstate commerce and largely put an end to the vicious practices of earlier years. For additional details, see John P. Miller, *Unfair Competition,* Harvard University Press, Cambridge, Mass., 1941; Rudolph Callman, *The Law of Unfair Competition and Trade Marks,* Callaghan & Company, Chicago, 1945; Lloyd G. Reynolds, "Cutthroat Competition," *American Economic Review,* p. 736, American Economic Association, Evanston, Ill., December, 1940.

Cybernetics   The study of communication and control in living organisms and in machines. Originally formulated by Norbert Wiener in the 1940s, cybernetics is an attempt to describe and analyze the workings of the human organism and to simulate its behavior through mechanical devices, concentrating on the automatic control of machines. It includes information and communication theory and the general theory of feedback control systems (the control of an operating machine on the basis of its actual performance). The findings of cybernetics have important applications in the problems of automation and the use of computers. For further information, see Norbert Wiener, *Cybernetics,* 2d ed., John Wiley & Sons, Inc., New York, 1961; W. Ross Ashley, *An Introduction to Cybernetics,* John Wiley & Sons, Inc., New York, 1956; Stafford Beer, *Cybernetics and Management,* John Wiley & Sons, Inc., New York, 1959.

Cyclical Unemployment   Unemployment that results from the depression period of the business cycle. Its immediate cause is a lack of demand for labor due to the downward swing in the economy. Cyclical unemployment is hard to predict, since it is irregular in occurrence and variable in duration and intensity. In the U.S., it has varied in severity from 6% of the labor force in the 1949–1950, 1953–1954, and 1969–1970 recessions to 25% in 1934, and in length from one year in the 1957–1958 recession to the twelve years of depression from 1930 to 1941. Cyclical unemployment affects different industries and workers in different ways. The capital goods industries are usually the most susceptible, since the demand for their goods fluctuates widely with the swings in the business cycle. The burden of cyclical unemployment is concentrated in low-paid, unskilled workers, especially in recessions of short duration. To reduce cyclical unemployment, it is necessary to attack the basic cause and to smooth out the fluctuations in the business cycle. For further information, see Paul Casselman, *Economics of Employment and Unemployment,* Public Affairs Press, Washington, D.C., 1955; Lloyd A. Metzler, "Business Cycles and the Modern Theory of Employment," *American Economic Review,* vol. 36, no. 3, pp. 278–291, American Economic Association, Evanston, Ill., June, 1946.

Dealer Any person who buys (or sells) an asset, hoping to sell (or buy) that asset at a higher (or lower) price than that at which he bought (or sold) it. In finance, dealers take positions by purchasing long or selling short securities, commodities, or foreign exchange, profiting on the spread, or differential, between the buying and the selling price. Legally, the distinction between dealer and broker is important. A dealer cannot hold a customer liable for damages arising from the execution of oral orders.

Dear Money *See Tight Money.*

Death Rate The number of deaths per 1,000 population. This is the crude death rate. The crude death rate of the U.S. has been declining over the years, but it has not dropped below the low of 9.2 per 1,000 attained in 1954. Refined death rates are calculated to allow for differences in the population's composition, such as age or color, in different time periods. A knowledge of death-rate trends is important in projecting future population growth. Historical and current statistics on death rates in total, by age groups, and by causes are found in U.S. Department of Health, Education and Welfare, *Health, Education and Welfare Indicators,* monthly.

Death Rate (Deaths per 1,000 population)

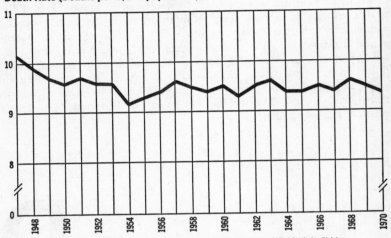

Source: U.S. Department of Health, Education, and Welfare, Public Health Service, National Vital Statistics Division.

Debasement   The act of reducing the metallic content of a coin below its face value. It presupposed a full-bodied coinage and was accomplished by the issuing authority, usually the government. The reason for debasement was generally the government's desire to have a greater amount of money to spend than its tax receipts supplied. If a government took every coin that it minted and added to the valuable metal enough baser metal so as to have two coins for every one, it had twice as much money to spend. Since debasement resulted in inflation, it was not generally considered an ethical or a responsible governmental activity. Debasement is not a practice today, since in most countries money does not derive its value from its metallic content. See Walter W. Haines, *Money, Prices and Policy,* 2d ed., McGraw-Hill Book Company, New York, 1966.

Debenture   A bond which is not protected by a specific lien or mortgage on property. Debentures (debts), which are issued by corporations, are promises to pay a specific amount of money (principal) at a specified date or periodically over the course of the loan, during which time interest is paid at a fixed rate on specified dates. The distinction between a debenture and a note of a corporation is that the debenture, like a bond, is issued under an indenture or deed of trust. Since the safety of a bond or debenture depends ultimately on the earning power of the issuing corporation, a bond is more secure than a debenture (because of the lien) only if the bonds and debentures of the same corporation are compared. Debentures were not issued in the U.S. until after the Civil War, and they became an important type of security only after 1900. Three types of corporations issue debentures: (1) service corporations that have a small proportion of their assets in tangible form, which means that they have little property that can be mortgaged; (2) large, blue-chip companies that enjoy high credit ratings and do not need to mortgage property to entice the investor; and (3) corporations that have mortgaged all their available assets. See Charles W. Gerstenberg, *Financial Organization and Management of Business,* 4th ed., Prentice-Hall, Inc., Englewood Cliffs, N.J., 1959; Joseph H. Bonneville et al., *Organizing and Financing Business,* Prentice-Hall, Inc., Englewood Cliffs, N.J., 1959.

Debit   An accountng term designating any increase in assets or decrease in liabilities and equity. Because, in U.S. accounting procedure, bookkeeping entries for transactions of this type are made on the left side of an account, a debit is also defined as any entry on the left side of an account. In the accounting sense, the word debit carries no moral connotation of good or evil, since for every debit there must be an equal and offsetting credit. Thus, when a bill is paid to a company, cash (an asset which has increased) is debited, and accounts payable (an asset which has decreased) is credited. See Harold Bierman, *Managerial Accounting,* The Macmillan Company, New York, 1959.

Debt Limit   A legislative provision placing a ceiling on the amount of debt that may be outstanding at any one time. The term is usually used in public finance, in which it refers to debt limitations placed on Federal, state, and local governments. The purpose of such debt limitations is to restrict current governmental expenditures to a limited amount in excess of current revenue collections. States impose debt limits on local governments, while state debt itself is usually limited by state constitutions. The Federal government operates under limitations imposed by section 21 of the Second Liberty Bond Act, passed in 1917 and amended many times. Through June 30, 1972, the Federal debt limit stands at $430 billion. Most state governments have debt limits calculated in dollar amounts, but a few have limits calculated as a percentage of the valuation of property within the state. Debt limits for local governments are most frequently stated as percentages of property valuation. For further information on the Federal debt limit, see John F. Due, *Government Finance*, 4th ed., Richard D. Irwin, Inc., Homewood, Ill., 1968.

Debt Management A term applied to the operations of the U.S. Treasury Department which determine the composition and nature of the national debt. Debt management consists primarily of the manipulation of three aspects of the outstanding debt: the level of interest rates, the pattern of ownership of debt, and the maturity schedule. Both the financing of new government debt and the replacement of maturing debt with new securities are included. A government debt-management policy may have a number of different objectives, including the minimizing of the interest burden of the debt, stabilization of the business cycle, gradual reduction of the debt, and support of general growth policies. Since the public debt is a reliable and controllable part of the liquidity base of the economy, its management can have an important impact on economic conditions. The most significant role of debt-management policy is in the area of stabilization, in which the nature of the maturity of the debt is the most important factor. The shorter the maturity of an issue, the more liquid it is, since it can be turned into cash more easily. Thus, by varying the length of the maturities of the national debt, the Treasury can exercise some control over the liquidity base of the economy. For example, during a period of excessive expansionary forces, the Treasury could increase its use of long-term securities and reduce outstanding short-term bills, thus tightening conditions in the capital market and slowing down the inflationary forces. Similarly, in times of recession, a Treasury shift toward shorter-term issues adds liquidity to the economy and stimulates recovery. For additional information, see Richard A. Musgrave, *The Theory of Public Finance*, McGraw-Hill Book Company, New York, 1959; Henry C. Murphy, "Debt Management," in K. E. Poole, *Fiscal Policies and the American Economy*, Prentice-Hall, Inc., Englewood Cliffs, N.J., 1951, chap. 4; J. M. Culbertson, "A Positive Debt Management Program," *Review of Economics and Statistics*, vol. XLI, no. 2, p. 89, Harvard University Press, Cambridge, Mass., 1959.

Debt-to-Net-Worth Ratio The ratio of the total liabilities of a firm to its net worth. A firm with total liabilities of $600,000 and a net worth of $500,000 has a debt-to-net-worth ratio of 1.2, meaning that the creditors have 20% more money in the business than have the owners. The ratio can be used by investors as a check on the working capital of a firm. Working capital can be increased by increasing current assets, reducing current liabilities, or shifting current liabilities into funded-debt obligations.

Decision Making The whole range of activities involved in establishing a corporate or governmental policy or an effective means of executing an existing policy, including the collection of facts needed to make judgments on a specific proposal and the analysis of alternative means of achieving a desired goal. The introduction of mathematical techniques, such as linear programming, and the availability of electronic computers and other innovations have tended to formalize decision-making procedures and to put them on a more scientific footing. In general, however, these advances have provided means of determining more clearly the consequences of alternative courses of action, and the final choice of appropriate corporate policies remains with the business executive. See J. D. Cooper, *The Art of Decision Making*, Doubleday & Company, Inc., Garden City, N.Y., 1961; Norman N. Barish, *Economic Analysis for Engineering and Managerial Decision Making*, McGraw-Hill Book Company, New York, 1962.

Decreasing Returns, Theory of *See Returns to Scale.*

Dedicating of Revenues *See Earmarking of Taxes.*

Deductive Method A method of analyzing an economic problem which works from the general to the particular, starting with a premise accepted as true and arriving at a conclusion based on this premise. It is an alternative to the inductive method. Lacking much important data that would serve as a basis for scientific generalizations, the early economic thinkers, particularly members of the classical school, adopted the deductive method. Critics of this method considered that its use led to abstraction, extreme conclusions, and beliefs at variance with reality. They argued that use of the deductive method produced an abstract economic thinker who reached conclusions that were formally true but could not be applied in practice. Overemphasis on deduction results in fixed assumptions which, taken as premises, prove unsound in dealing with evolving social and economic conditions. For additional history, explanation, and examples, see William Fellner, *Modern Economic Analysis*, McGraw-Hill Book Company, New York, 1960, chap. 1.

Defense Expenditures Money spent by Federal government agencies to provide for national security. In the U.S., these expenditures cover military and civilian personnel, procurement, maintenance, research and development, military construction, civil defense, military assistance to allies, atomic energy, and defense-related activities. U.S. defense expenditures amount to 75% of total Federal expenditures and to about 9% of the dollar value of national output. The high level of defense spending contributes to budget deficits and to an unfavorable balance of payments. Progress in military technology is so rapid that the rate of obsolescence is extremely high, and replacement with new equipment is very expensive. For the destabilizing effects of defense spending on the economy and for an outlook for defense spending, see Dexter M. Keezer and Associates, *New Forces in American Business*, McGraw-Hill Book Company, New York, 1959, pp. 125–137; for details of defense expenditures see U.S. Bureau of the Budget, *The Budget of the United States Government*.

**National Defense
(In billions of dollars)**

	Actual 1970	Estimate 1971	Estimate 1972
Department of Defense—military: *			
Military personnel	23.0	21.7	20.1
Retired military personnel	2.8	3.4	3.7
Operation and maintenance	21.6	20.4	20.2
Procurement	21.6	18.4	17.9
Research, development, test, and evaluation	7.2	7.3	7.5
Military construction and other	1.1	1.4	2.0
Allowances	....	0.9	3.6
Deductions for offsetting receipts	−0.1	−0.2	−0.1
Subtotal, military †	77.2	73.4	75.0
Military assistance ‡	0.7	1.1	1.0
Atomic energy	2.4	2.3	2.3
Defense-related activities	0.1	−0.1	0.1
Deductions for offsetting receipts §	−0.1	−0.3	−0.9
Total	80.3	76.4	77.5

* May not add up because of rounding.
† Entries net of offsetting receipts.
‡ Excludes support to other nations funded directly by the Department of Defense.
§ Excludes offsetting receipts deducted by subfunction above: 1970, $1.0 billion; 1971, $1.2 billion; 1972, $1.1 billion.
SOURCE: *The Budget of the U.S. Government*, fiscal year 1972, U.S. Government Printing Office, Washington, D.C., 1971.

Deficit Financing A practice by a government of spending more money than it receives in revenue. In the U. S., deficit financing has been the rule rather than the exception since the early 1930s. The practice is still highly controversial, however, some observers arguing that expenditures and revenues should balance every year, while others contend that they need never balance. According to surveys of economists working both in business and in universities, the majority of them seem to think that the most prudent policy is to have expenditures and revenues balance over the span of the business cycle. For a favorable view of deficit financing, see Alvin H. Hansen, *Economic Issues of the 1960's,* McGraw-Hill Book Company, New York, 1960; for the opposite view, see William Fellner, *Trends and Cycles in Economic Activity: An Introduction to Problems of Economic Growth,* Holt, Rinehart and Winston, Inc., New York, 1956; for an analysis of recent developments, see Herbert Stein, *The Fiscal Revolution in America,* The University of Chicago Press, Chicago, 1969.

Deflation   A fall in the general price level associated with a contraction of the supply of money and credit. A drop in prices, usually accompanied by declining levels of output and increasing unemployment, is associated with the downturn stage of the business cycle. Although not all economists agree on the exact cause of a deflation, it is generally believed that a spiraling contraction in the volume of bank credit and a deficiency in total spending are important factors in causing a fall in the price level. Most prices fall in a deflation, but not all prices fall evenly. Since the earnings of fixed-income groups probably fall less than those of other groups, they stand to gain from a deflation. This remains true, however, only if they can retain their sources of income. The threat of unemployment during such periods is so great that all gains are precarious, and few groups actually gain during a deflation and depression. For this reason, modern governments have undertaken various contra-cyclical programs to try to reduce the force of the deflationary spiral. These policies include government deficit spending for public works, relief expenditures, and easy-money programs. For a fuller discussion of deflation, see Gottfried Haberler, *Prosperity and Depression,* League of Nations, Geneva, 1939; Asher Achinstein, *Introduction to Business Cycles,* Thomas Y. Crowell Company, New York, 1950; see also G. F. Warren and F. A. Pearson, *Gold and Prices,* John Wiley & Sons, Inc., New York, 1935.

Deflationary Gap   A descriptive term for the deficiency between actual investment and savings. In a full-employment economy, it is the value of demand for goods and services below that which can be produced under full employment. For example, national income in the U.S. at the full-employment level totals $850 billion, but consumers and investors spend only $780 billion. This means that there is a $70-billion gap. Through the multiplier principle, the $70-billion gap could develop into an even larger drop in income. On the other hand, by use of this principle much less than a $70-billion increase in investment would bring the economy to full employment. For a brief explanation of the deflationary gap and its relation to the theory of income determination, see Paul A. Samuelson, *Economics*, 8th ed., McGraw-Hill Book Company, New York, 1970, pp. 226–227.

Degressive Tax   A progressive tax which increases at a decreasing rate. A degressive tax is progressive, since the tax rate increases as the size of the tax base increases, but for each additional increase in the size of the base, the increase in the tax rate is lower. In practice, most income tax schedules are degressive, since as the rates increase, they apply to wider and wider income brackets until all income above a certain amount is taxed at a constant (proportional) rate. For additional details on types of taxes, see Harold Groves, *Financing Government*, 6th ed., Holt, Rinehart and Winston, Inc., New York, 1964; Hugh Dalton, *Principles of Public Finance*, 10th ed., Routledge & Kegan Paul, Ltd., London, 1939.

Demand   The desire, ability, and willingness of an individual to pur-chase a good or service. Desire by itself is not equivalent to demand: the consumer must also have the funds or the ability to obtain funds in order to convert the desire into demand. The demand of a buyer for a certain good is a schedule of the quantites of that good which the indi-vidual would buy at possible alternative prices at a given moment in time. The demand schedule, or the listing of quantities that would be bought at different prices, can be shown graphically by means of the demand curve. The term demand refers to the entire schedule of possi-bilities and not only to one point on the schedule. It is an instantaneous concept, expressing the relationship of price and the quantity that is desired to be bought, all other factors being constant. By adding the quantities demanded by each consumer at the various possible prices, the schedule of demand for all consumers, or the market demand, can be derived. A fundamental characteristic of individual and market demand is that as the price rises, the quantity demanded falls, and as price falls, the corres-ponding quantity demanded rises. This inverse relationship between the price of a good and the quantity demanded is known as the law of demand and is represented graphically by the downward slope of the demand curve. The reasons for this inverse relationship are as follows: (1) The lowering of prices brings new buyers into the market. (2) Each reduction in price may induce each of the good's consumers to make additional pur-chases, since an attempt is made to substitute the good for other goods as its price falls in relation to those of other goods. (3) As the price falls, real income rises, so that the individual's consumption of all goods rises proportionately. The basic determinants of the level of market demand are the tastes and preferences of the consumers, consumers' money incomes, the prices of other related goods (substitute goods), consumer expectations with respect to future prices and income, and the number of consumers in the market. Any change in these factors results in a change in demand or a shifting of the entire demand curve. This change should not be confused with a change in the quantity demanded, which merely describes the movement from one point to another along a given demand curve. For further information, see Hubert Henderson, *Supply and Demand*, The University of Chicago Press, Chicago, 1958; Ruby Norris, *The Theory of Consumer's Demand*, Yale University Press, New Haven, Conn., 1941; George J. Stigler, *The Theory of Price*, 3d ed., The Macmillan Company, New York, 1966. For an explanation of econometric techniques applicable to statistical demand estimation, see Herman Wold, *Demand Analysis*, John Wiley & Sons, Inc., New York, 1953.

Demand Deposit (Checkbook Money)   A bank deposit which can be withdrawn by the depositor without previous notice to the bank. Demand deposits do not earn interest, as do time deposits, but they can be withdrawn by check and therefore possess many of the liquid character-

Demand Deposits (Billions of dollars)

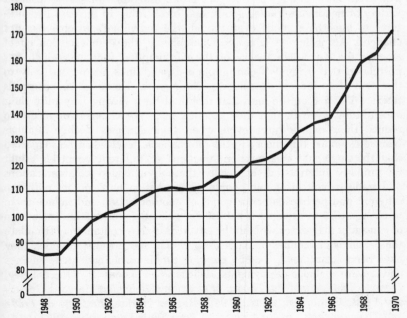

Source: Board of Governors, Federal Reserve System.

istics of circulating currency. For this reason, demand deposits are sometimes called checkbook money and are counted as part of the total money supply. Demand deposits can be classified into two categories: primary deposits, which arise from a deposit of cash in a bank account; and derived deposits, which are created by the bank through the making of loans. It is through the creation of derived demand deposits that banks are able to increase the money supply to meet the needs of business. In December, 1970, there was $1,761 billion worth of demand deposits in the U.S., accounting for almost 80% of the total money supply. For additional details, see Eli Shapiro, Ezra Solomon, and William L. White, *Money and Banking*, 5th ed., Holt, Rinehart and Winston, Inc., New York, 1968, pp. 83–89; Major B. Foster et al., *Money and Banking*, Prentice-Hall, Inc., Englewood Cliffs, N.J., 1953; Walter W. Haines, *Money, Prices and Policy*, McGraw-Hill Book Company, New York, 1961; *Principles of Bank Operations*, American Institute of Banking, New York, 1956. For monthly data on demand deposits, see *Federal Reserve Bulletin*, Washington, D.C.

Demand Schedule   *See Demand.*

Demonstration Effect   The impact on an individual of seeing a larger variety of goods or superior goods, and of deciding to increase expenditures to buy these goods even though the individual's income has not changed. According to James S. Duesenberry, the demonstration effect amends the Keynesian theory of the consumption function, which has postulated that a family's consumption expenditures are related only to the level of its income. Consumers who have a chance to inspect goods that are better than the ones that they had been buying may raise their expenditures even though their incomes have not changed or refuse to reduce their expenditures even when their incomes decline. Ragnar Nürkse extended this theory to the international level when he suggested that the aggregate consumption functions of different countries might be similarly interrelated, especially through extended communications and trade, which bring the people of one nation into contact with the different and perhaps superior goods of another nation and induce them to change their consumption habits. For example, worldwide distribution of consumer magazines with all the advertising they contain may stimulate the demands of families in India to levels far above those to which they have been accustomed, thereby creating problems of inadequate savings and severe balance-of-payments deficits. See James S. Duesenberry, *Income, Savings, and the Theory of Consumer Behavior*, Harvard University Press, Cambridge, Mass., 1949; Ragnar Nurkse, *Patterns of Trade and Development*, Oxford University Press, Fair Lawn, N.J., 1961.

Department Store A large retail establishment consisting of multiple departments that sell a wide assortment of products. According to the definition of the U.S. Bureau of the Census, a department store is an establishment that normally employs 25 or more persons and is engaged in selling some items in each of the following lines of merchandise: (1) furniture, home furnishings, appliances, and radios and television sets; (2) a general line of apparel for the family; and (3) household linens and dry goods. Before the major shift in population to suburban areas, large department stores were located in the downtown areas of cities. Since World War II, however, many department stores have established branches along a city's perimeter to service these suburban centers of population. R. H. Macy in New York, Harrod's in London, and Au Printemps in Paris are examples of large downtown department stores. For the origin, evolution, and economics of the department store, see H. Pasdermadjian, *The Department Store*, Newman Books, London, 1954; for a discussion of the problems and prospects of department stores, see *The Tobé Lectures in Retail Distribution 1957–1958*, Harvard Graduate School of Business Administration, Boston, 1959.

Depletion A decrease in the value of land or other natural resources due to the extraction of minerals or other natural wealth. Depletion resembles depreciation in that both are reductions in the value of fixed assets. Whereas depreciation is a reduction in the quality and usefulness of an asset because of physical deterioration, depletion is the reduction of the physical quantities of a fixed asset. Although both the passage of time and use cause depreciation, in almost all cases depletion is not affected by the passage of time but only by the removal of the asset for use. Depletion occurs in such natural resources, or wasting assets, as they are sometimes known, as mines, oil wells, and timber, which are constantly being removed and sold, so that the proportion of the asset remaining declines from period to period. The depletion for a given period is usually determined by multiplying the unit depletion charge (the total cost of the asset divided by the estimated number of resource units, such as barrels of oil, that it will produce in its lifetime) by the number of units produced in the period.

Depletion Allowance A tax allowance extended to the owners of exhaustible natural resources. The return from the sale of natural resources partly represents a return to the owner on his investment in resource property. If the income from these sales were taxed, this would be, in effect, a tax on the return to capital, or a capital levy. The primary purpose of a depletion allowance is to prevent the imposition of a capital levy on the owners of natural resources. In addition, it encourages the investment of risk capital in the development of unused resources. The depletion allowance permits the owner to deduct from his income part of the cost of his investment in natural resources as the property becomes exhausted or depleted. There are two methods of computing depletion allowance, cost depletion and percentage depletion. Under the cost-depletion method, the value of the depletion deduction is calculated by dividing the number of resource units (e.g., barrels of oil) by the total number of units present at the beginning of the accounting period and multiplying this figure by the total value of the resources, so that the deduction represents the value of the depleted resources. Under the percentage-depletion method, a specified percentage of the gross income from the property is deductible. For example, the depletion allowance in 1970 for oil and gas wells was 22.5% of gross income, provided that this deduction did not result in a deduction of more than 50% of the total net income before deduction. For additional information, see Robert H. Montgomery et al., "Deductions for Depletion," *Montgomery's Federal Taxes: Corporations and Partnerships,* The Ronald Press Company, New York, 1951, vol. I.

Deposit Turnover   The ratio of bank debits to bank deposits. This ratio is used as (1) a fairly accurate indicator of the total velocity of money, since commercial bank deposits account for 77% of the nation's money

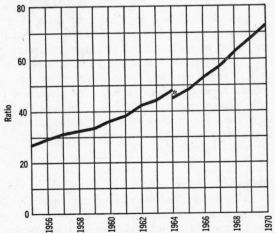

Deposit Turnover — All Reporting Centers

*Beginning with 1964 data, a major change was introduced in this series: the geographic coverage for most reporting centers was increased from the city to the Standard Metropolitan Statistical Area.

Source: Board of Governors, Federal Reserve System.

supply (M_1) (currency accounts for 23%) and (2) a business-cycle indicator, since fluctuations in the rate of turnover of bank deposits generally coincide with fluctuations of the business cycle. For a discussion of the usefulness of statistics on bank debt in economic analysis, see George Garvy, *Debits and Clearings Statistics and Their Use,* Board of Governors of Federal Reserve System, Washington, D.C., 1959; for monthly statistics on the ratio of debits to deposits, see *Federal Reserve Bulletin,* Washington, D.C.

Depreciation A reduction in the value of fixed assets. The most important causes of depreciation are wear and tear (loss of value caused by the use of an asset), the effect of the elements (i.e., decay or corrosion), and gradual obsolescence, which makes it unprofitable to continue using some assets until they have been fully exhausted. The annual amount of depreciation of an asset depends on its original purchase price, its estimated useful life, and its estimated salvage value. A number of different methods of figuring the amount of depreciation have been developed. Using the simple straight-line method, which considers depreciation a function of time, the annual depreciation cost is calculated by dividing the cost of the asset (original minus salvage cost) equally over its entire life. When the life of a fixed asset is a function of activity (use) rather than of time, industry employs the production method, in which depreciation is charged to periods in proportion to the use (generally expressed in terms of hours of operation or units produced) which has been made of the asset. There are also a number of decreasing-charge methods, such as the diminishing-value method and the sum-of-the-digits method, which allocate higher depreciation costs to the beginning years of the operation of an asset and lower depreciation costs to the later years. These methods assign the greatest depreciation loss to the earlier years of the asset's life, when the greatest decrease in resale value normally occurs. Such accelerated-depreciation methods can be used in accordance with the tax laws to reduce the overall cost of new capital investment. For additional details, see George Terborgh, *Realistic Depreciation Policy,* Machinery and Allied Products Institute, Washington, D.C., 1954; Eugene Grant and Paul Horton, Jr., *Depreciation,* The Ronald Press Company, New York, 1949.

Depreciation Reserve A valuation-reserve account used to record depreciation charges. The use of the word reserve does not mean that a fund of cash has been set aside; rather, the word is employed to stand for a valuation reserve, in which credits are made to show the reduced valuation of an asset. The depreciation reserve is shown on the asset side of the balance sheet as a deduction from its corresponding fixed-asset account. As the asset depreciates, periodic additions are made to the reserve for depreciation, thus reducing the stated valuation of the asset Because of the common misinterpretation of the term reserve, terms such as allowance for depreciation and accumulated depreciation are coming into use. For additional details, see H. A. Finney and H. E. Miller *Principles of Accounting*, 6th ed., Prentice-Hall, Inc., Englewood Cliffs N.J., 1965; Harold Bierman, Jr., and Allen R. Drebin, *Managerial Accounting*, The Macmillan Company, New York, 1969.

Depreciation-Reserve Ratio   The ratio of the total depreciation reserve for a specific class of fixed assets to the original cost of the total capital assets still in use. The concept of the depreciation-reserve ratio was introduced as part of the reserve-ratio test by the U.S. Treasury Department in 1962 in its liberalization of business depreciation procedures According to this revision of procedures, a firm can determine whether or not its depreciation policy for a certain class of assets is justified by calculating the reserve ratio for that class and ascertaining that the ratio does not exceed the upper limit of the range of ratios which the Treasury has set as acceptable. For additional discussion of the procedures and problems connected with the depreciation-reserve ratio, see *Depreciation Guidelines and Rules*, U.S. Treasury Department Publication 456 (7–62) R. Slitor et al., "Depreciation: A Special Report," *Journal of Taxation* New York, May, 1963.

Depreciation-Reserve-Ratio Test   An objective test designed to show whether a company's claims for depreciation are in line with its ratio of replacement and modernization. First, the depreciation-reserve ratio that is, the ratio of the total depreciation reserve for a specific class of fixed assets to the original cost of the total capital assets still in use, must be calculated. If the stock of capital equipment has the same value as it had in a given base year (preferably an entire replacement cycle earlier), the reserve-ratio figure may be tested against the reserve-ratio tables prepared by the U.S. Treasury Department. If the stock of capital equipment has grown or declined from the base year to the time of the test, however, an additional computation is necessary. This is the calculation of the capital-growth rate over the period in question, obtained by dividing the original cost of present facilities by the cost of facilities used in the base year and converting this overall capital-growth rate into an annual growth rate. Using these two figures, the depreciation-reserve ratio and the annual capital-growth rate, it is possible to make a check against the Treasury's reserve-ratio tables. The tables cover all methods of depreciation, including straight-line, double-declining-balance, sum-of-the-digits, and 150%-declining-balance depreciation. The actual test works as follows: A company that has been depreciating its assets in specific guideline class over a period of ten years checks its reserve-ratio figure against the range of figures in the tables for a test life of ten years. If the ratio falls within the given range, it is assumed that the company is using the correct life. If it falls below the range, the company is entitled to a shorter life. If it is above the range, presumably the company should be using a longer life, but a company will not be forced into a longer life for the depreciation of equipment on the basis of the test alone. For further discussion of the procedures and problems connected with the depreciation-reserve-ratio test, see *Depreciation Guidelines and Rules,* U.S. Treasury Department Publication 456 (7–62); R. Slitor et al., "Deprecation: A Special Report," *Journal of Taxation,* New York, May, 1963.

Depressed Area (Distressed Area)   A locality that is not participating in a nation's overall economic growth and, as a result, has an exceptional amount of unemployed resources, particularly unemployed manpower. A depressed area may be the result of a variety of developments. In some cases, changes in consumer demand have sharply reduced the market for the products that an area has specialized in producing. Among other possible causes are the exhaustion of the natural resources on which an area's economy has been dependent, the loss of an area's markets to competitive products imported from abroad, and the migration of established industries to other localities. As of August, 1970, there were 575 areas (24 major centers and 551 smaller areas) officially classified by the U.S. Department of Labor as areas of substantial and persistent unemployment. Prime examples of these depressed areas are the coal mining towns of Pennsylvania and West Virginia, whose economic decline is the result of the widespread adoption of new energy sources, particularly gas and oil, in markets long served by coal. Other examples are New England milling towns that have seen their economic viability affected by the migration of textile mills to other areas in the U.S. and by competition from imported products. To help overcome the economic difficulties of depressed areas, Congress in 1961 enacted the Area Redevelopment Act, which includes provisions designed to encourage new business investment in such areas and to assist unemployed workers to develop new skills in order to improve their chances of employment. For further discussion of the problems of depressed areas, see *Employment, Growth and Price Levels,* Hearings before the U.S. Joint Economic Committee, Government Printing Office, Washington, D.C., pp. 535–537, 589–591, 602–604, Apr. 25, 27, and 28, 1959; see also *The Rise of Chronic Unemployment,* National Planning Association, Planning Pamphlet 113, Washington, D.C., 1961; for current statistics on depressed areas, see U.S. Department of Labor, *Area Trends in Employment and Unemployment,* monthly.

Depression A protracted period in which business activity is far below normal and the pessimism of business and consumers is great. It is characterized by a sharp curtailment of production, little capital investment, a contraction of credit, falling prices, mass unemployment and low employment, and a very high rate of business failures. The two longest depressions in U.S. history were those of 1873–1879 (65 months) and 1929–1933 (45 months). One of the key problems of modern times is the prevention of severe depressions. The reason for the great concern in the U.S. and the free world about severe depressions is that these represent a grave threat to the democratic way of life in both political and economic terms. For a measurement of the length and depth of depressions, see Geoffrey H. Moore (ed.), *Business Cycle Indicators,* Princeton University Press, Princeton, N.J., 1961.

Depth Interview *See Qualitative Interview.*

Derived Demand The demand for a factor of production that results from the demand for a final good which it helps produce. The shape of the demand curve for a factor of production, steel, is derived from the demand curve of the final product, automobiles, for which it is used. If we assume profit maximization by the steel producer, the demand curve for steel is its marginal-revenue curve. This demonstrates the fallacy of advocating a rise in steel prices because the price of automobiles is high. The principle of derived demand shows that such a price rise is not a solution, since the demand for steel is derived from the demand for automobiles. A higher price for steel would raise profits for steel companies in the short run, but the price of automobiles might also rise, and the demand for both automobiles and steel would therefore decline. See Paul A. Samuelson, *Economics,* 7th ed., McGraw-Hill Book Company, New York, 1967; J. R. Hicks, *Value and Capital,* Oxford University Press, Fair Lawn, N.J., 1947.

Derived Demand Deposit *See Demand Deposit.*

Derived Statistics Numbers that are obtained from raw data by means of some mathematical operation. In common usage, this term usually refers to numerical series resulting from combining other series in order to reveal more information. For example, the restatement of data for gross national product and population as GNP per capita.

Devaluation The lowering of the value of a nation's currency relative to gold or to the currency of other countries. Devaluation usually occurs when a country is having serious balance-of-payment difficulties, that is, when the relative prices of its goods and services are such that the value of its imports far exceeds the value of the goods and services that it exports. Devaluation of the currency, providing other countries do not follow suit, helps increase a country's physical exports and decrease its physical imports. For example, the U.S., faced with a sizable trade deficit in 1971, devalued the dollar by 7.88% at the end of that year through increasing the price of gold 8.57%, from $35 to $38 per ounce. At the same time, the British and French kept their price per ounce of gold at the previous levels. Thus the dollar depreciated in relation to the pound and the franc: $100 would buy 38.38 pounds or 511.6 francs, as compared with 41.67 pounds or 555.4 francs prior to the devaluation. The outcome of the devaluation would be an increase of American exports to Britain and France and a reduction of American imports. For further information, see S. S. Alexander, "Effects of Devaluation: Simplified Synthesis of Elasticities and Absorption Approaches," *American Economic Review,* vol. XLIX, pp. 22–42, American Economic Association, Evanston, Ill., March, 1959; E. Sohmen, "The Effect of Devaluation on the Price Level," *Quarterly Journal of Economics,* vol. LXXII, pp. 273–283, Harvard University Press, Cambridge, Mass., May, 1958.

Developing Nation   A nation whose people are beginning to utilize available resources in order to bring about a sustained increase in per capita production of goods and services. In general, a developing nation is a country that is capable of greater substantial improvements in its income level and is in process of achieving this improvement. For additional information on economic development, see Benjamin Higgins, *Economic Development,* W. W. Norton & Company, Inc., New York, 1968.

Difference Equation   An equation that involves a variable y and the first differences of the same variable. A first difference is the value obtained by subtracting an observation $y(x)$ from the value following it in a series $y(x + 1)$. Autoregressive, linear difference equations are useful in the econometric analysis of business cycles. For additional information, see Lawrence R. Klein, *A Textbook of Econometrics,* Row, Peterson & Company, Evanston, Ill., 1953; Gerhard Tintner and Charles B. Millham, *Mathematics and Statistics for Economists,* Holt, Rinehart and Winston, Inc., New York, 1970.

Diffusion Index   A statistical device used to summarize in one figure the proportion of a group of series that has increased in a given time interval. The index gives the percentage expanding: if a greater number of series is rising than is declining, the index will be above 50; if fewer are rising than are declining, it will be below 50. A common form of this index is the ratio of stocks whose prices have risen in a day to the total number of stocks traded on the New York Stock Exchange. A more complex form consists of the diffusion indices of business indicators. For a more detailed explanation of diffusion indices, see Geoffrey H. Moore (ed.), *Business Cycle Indicators,* Princeton University Press, Princeton, N.J., 1961.

A Diffusion Index of Eight Roughly Coincident Indicators, 1959-1961

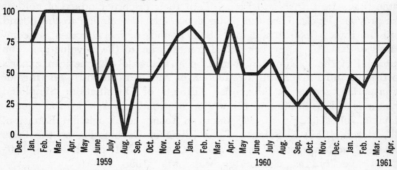

Source: J. Shiskin, Signals of Recession and Recovery, Occasional Paper 77, N.B.E.R., New York, 1961, p. 74.

Dillon Round   The fifth round of tariff negotiations under GATT during the period 1960–1962. The major work of the Dillon round was aimed at transforming the tariff rates of the six EEC members into a common schedule applied by all six toward nonmembers. The U.S. ended the Dillon round by allowing a certain number of its previously obtained rights to bindings of common rates on a certain number of its major agricultural exports to be defaulted. The decision was made that it was more important for the EEC to continue to grow than it was for the U.S. to have assured agricultural export markets. Many experts believe that the U.S. paid a high price, in terms of export markets, for its Dillon round decision. For additional details, see Thomas B. Curtis and John R. Vastine, Jr., *The Kennedy Round and the Future of American Trade,* Frederick A. Praeger, Inc., New York, 1971.

Diminishing Returns, Law of (Law of Variable Proportions)   The economic principle which states that successive additions of quantities of variable factors of production to other fixed factors of production will result in diminishing marginal productivity, at least after some point. Thus, successive additions of capital to a fixed quantity of labor will result in an increase in output, but subsequently the marginal output and then the average production associated with the variable factor will begin to drop. The fixed factor decreases in proportion to the variable factor, so that each unit of the variable factor has a diminishing quantity of the fixed factor to work with. Anne Robert Jacques Turgot, influenced by the physiocrats' system, provided a clear statement of this law in the eighteenth century. Under the influence of David Ricardo, statements of the law were prevalent among classical economists in the early nineteenth century. For further discussion, see Donald S. Watson, *Price Theory and Its Uses*, 2d ed., Houghton Mifflin Company, Boston, 1968; William Fellner, *Modern Economic Analysis*, McGraw-Hill Book Company, New York, 1960, chaps. 4 and 6; John M. Cassals, "On the Law of Variable Proportions," in *Readings in the Theory of Income Distribution*, McGraw-Hill Book Company, New York, 1950.

Direct Cost A cost which can be consistently identified with a specific unit of output. Direct, or variable, costs consist of two types: (1) direct materials, or supplies which can be connected directly with an individual product; and (2) direct labor, which is that portion of wages and salaries that can be identified with a specific product. As a rule, all materials and supplies which are related specifically to the product are classified as direct materials. Thus, the raw materials used in a given production process are classified as direct-cost items, whereas the cost of lighting facilities for an area in which a number of goods are being produced is considered an indirect cost. Labor which changes the form of materials in the productive process is usually called direct, or productive, labor. Thus, the wages of machine operators and welders are examples of direct-labor costs, whereas the wages of supervisors and maintenance men are examples of indirect-labor costs. There is, however, wide leeway in deciding whether a given material or job can be identified with a specific product. This is especially true for labor. For further information, see "Report of Committee on Cost Concepts and Standards," *Accounting Review*, American Accounting Association, Menasha, Wis., April, 1952.

Direct Investment Investment by U.S. business firms or individuals in overseas business operations over which the investor has a considerable measure of control. Direct investment differs somewhat from portfolio investment, which includes holdings intended primarily for their income yields. U.S. direct investment abroad has grown substantially since World War II, and for 1970 was estimated at $75 billion. Much U.S. direct investment takes the form of investment in overseas subsidiaries of U.S. business firms. For a discussion of direct investment and the flow of international capital in general, see D. B. Marsh, *World Trade and Investment*, Harcourt, Brace & World, Inc., New York, 1951; for data on U.S. overseas investment, see U.S. Department of Commerce, *U.S. Business Investment in Foreign Countries: A Supplement to the Survey* *of Current Business,* 1960; for annual data on U.S. holdings abroad, see U.S. Department of Commerce, *Survey of Current Business.*

Direct Labor   Labor expended directly on the actual production of a firm's finished goods or services. It is thus directly identifiable with product costs. For example, employees who work on a product with tools or operate machines in the production process are considered to constitute direct labor. Direct labor is distinguishable from indirect labor, which includes those activities that are not applied specifically to the production of goods or services but are applicable to production activities in general. Sometimes, the distinction between direct and indirect labor becomes difficult to draw, as in the case when fully automatic machinery is used and the worker becomes, in effect, a machine tender. For additional details, see *Accounting for Labor Costs and Labor Related Costs,* National Association of Accountants, Research Series, no. 32, New York, 1957.

Direct Tax   A tax that cannot be shifted from the original payer to the ultimate consumer of the good or service taxed. Poll taxes, property taxes, and income taxes are generally considered direct taxes, although many economists believe that it is possible to pass on property taxes and certain income taxes, especially those levied on corporate incomes. The concept is important in the U.S. largely because the Constitution expressly provides that direct taxes "shall be apportioned among the several states . . . according to their respective numbers." Since the Constitution does not define the concept, however, the definition has been left to the courts. The constitutionality of the Federal income tax was first questioned during the Civil War, when the U.S. Supreme Court held that the Federal income tax was not a direct tax and was therefore legal; this decision was reversed in 1894, and the legality of the Federal income tax was not finally established until 1913, when passage of the Sixteenth Amendment permitted the collection of an income tax without apportionment among the states. See E. H. Plank, *Public Finance,* Richard D. Irwin, Inc., Homewood, Ill., 1953.

DISC   *See Domestic International Sales Corporation.*

Discontinuous Hypotheses   In econometrics, hypotheses that lead to "yes" or "no" solutions to assumed relationships. For example, where there is interdependence between two variables (or several variables), it is possible to determine which variable is the causal factor. For additional information, see Stefan Valavanis, *Econometrics,* McGraw-Hill Book Company, New York, 1959.

Discounted-Cash-Flow Method   A method of measuring the return on capital invested. The value of a project is expressed as an interest rate at which the project's total future earnings, discounted from the time that they occur to the present, equal the original investment. It is more precise than most of the other methods used to measure return on capital invested because it recognizes the effect of the time value of money. It may be used to determine whether a given project is acceptable or unacceptable by comparing each project's rate of return with the company's standard. For additional information, see Robert Beyer, *Profitability Accounting for Planning and Control,* The Ronald Press Company, New York, 1963; Ezra Solomon (ed.), *The Management of Corporate Capital,* University of Chicago Graduate School of Business, The Free Press of Glencoe, New York, 1961; M. G. Wright, *Discounted Cash Flow,* McGraw-Hill Book Company, New York, 1967.

Discount House   A retailing outlet that sells merchandise at low prices because it operates on low markups and offers minimal consumer services. Discount houses usually specialize in consumer durable goods, such as appliances, radios and television sets, and carpeting, but quite often they sell many other items, such as apparel and drugs. Sales of discount houses grew rapidly in the U.S. in the post-World War II period, but because of low markups, profits were very small. In the early 1960s, several discount houses failed because of overexpansion, inadequate financing, poor judgment, and increased price competition from department stores. A typical example of a chain of discount houses is Korvette's. See J. N. Wingate and A. Corbin, *Changing Patterns in Retailing: Readings on Current Trends,* Richard D. Irwin, Inc., Homewood, Ill., 1956.

Discounting   *See Accounts Receivable Financing.*

Discount Rate (Rediscount Rate)   The interest that a commercial bank pays when it borrows from a Federal Reserve bank, using a government bond or other eligible paper as security. The discount rate is one of the tools of monetary policy; when Federal Reserve authorities are trying to prevent inflation, they raise the discount rate. The opposite course is followed when business is lagging, although lowering the discount rate may be less effective in stimulating loans and investments if banks already possess ample reserves which they could lend. Over the years, the discount rate has ranged from 7%, in 1920–1921, to ½%, during World War II. Rates are set by the regional Federal Reserve banks with approval of the Board of Governors of the Federal Reserve System. The current levels of discount rates are given in *Federal Reserve Bulletin,* Washington, D.C.; their use is discussed in *Purposes and Functions of the Federal Reserve System,* Board of Governors of the Federal Reserve System, Washington, D.C., 1961.

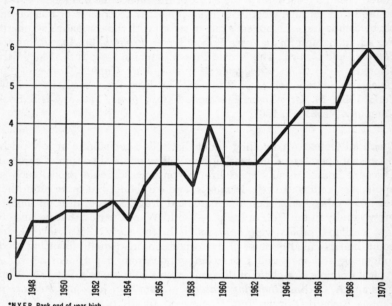

Discount Rate*   (Percent per annum)

*N.Y.F.R. Bank end of year high.

Source: Federal Reserve Bank of New York.

Discretionary Income   *See Discretionary Purchasing Power.*

Discretionary Purchasing Power   A measure, developed by the National Industrial Conference Board, of aggregate purchasing power (disposable personal income, net household credit, and credits from government insurance and other adjustments) less net contractual savings, imputed income and income in kind, fixed commitments, and essential expenditures. This concept is theoretically similar to discretionary income, but the latter measure had to be substantially modified to conform to revisions in the national income accounts. The series measures the growth in the ability of the American consumer to exercise some degree of discretion over the direction and manner of his spending and saving. For more details, see Morton Ehrlich, *Discretionary Spending,* National Industrial Conference Board, Inc., Technical Paper 17, New York, 1966.

Discretionary Purchasing Power (Billions of dollars)

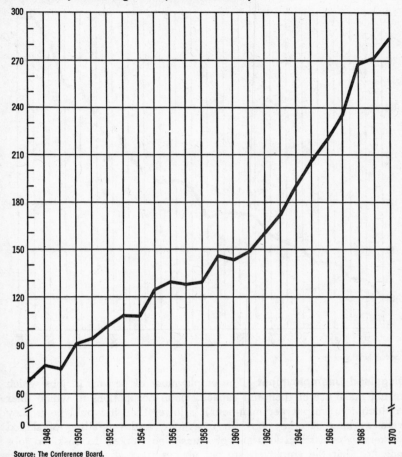

Source: The Conference Board.

Discretionary Spending   A measure, developed by the National Industrial Conference Board, which reflects the extent of consumer spending as the result of a decision relatively free of prior commitment, pressure of necessity, or force of habit. It includes all personal expenditures not accounted for specifically or in equivalent form in imputed income, fixed commitments, or essential outlays. The series measures the growth and the ability of the American consumer to exercise some degree of discretion over the direction and manner of his spending and saving. For more details, see Morton Ehrlich, *Discretionary Spending*, National Industrial Conference Board, Inc., New York, 1966.

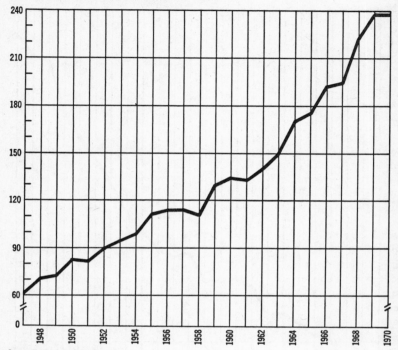

Discretionary Spending (Billions of dollars)

Source: The Conference Board.

Disguised Unemployment   The employment of persons in jobs which do not make use of their full capacity or in occupations in which their productivity (output per man-hour) is lower than it would be if they were working at other jobs. In recessions, a downgrading of skilled workers to semiskilled jobs and of semiskilled workers to unskilled jobs indicates that the employed are not always used effectively. Disguised unemployment is high even in prosperous times in service industries where workers earn relatively low wages and have a relatively low output per man-hour. It is also relatively important in underdeveloped areas where job opportunities for highly educated and skilled persons are limited. For additional details, see Lloyd G. Reynolds, *Labor Economics and Labor Relations*, Prentice-Hall, Inc., Englewood Cliffs, N.J., 1959.

Disinflation   The process of retarding the rate of price inflation. In the U.S. economy, some rate of inflation is expected to occur each year. Economists now generally claim that a rate of inflation of about 3 to

3.5% per year would be acceptable and would not cause much problem to the economy. But when the general rate of price increase goes much beyond this level, as has been true since the mid-1960s, many problems of income distribution emerge, especially for those on fixed incomes. State and municipal governments also face tremendous obstacles in meeting their financial obligations when inflation is galloping. A number of proposals have been advanced for disinflating the economy from the cost-push price spiral we have been experiencing. These range from "jawboning" (or mild reproach by government) to complete wage and price controls. The wage-price guideposts of the Kennedy-Johnson years were an attempt to hold price increases to the rate of increase in output per man-hour. The guideposts were unsuccessful in holding down wage demands, which soared in the late 1960s and into the 1970s. The Nixon administration attempted to disinflate by making direct attacks on wage demands and price increases which it considered to be excessive and extremely inflationary.

Disintermediation   The removal of funds from interest-bearing time accounts in savings institutions and commercial banks for the purpose of reinvesting the funds at higher rates in market instruments. This process occurs when rates on market instruments—for example, corporate bonds—are substantially higher than the rates being paid by financial intermediaries. Time accounts in financial institutions generally carry a maximum interest-rate ceiling set by state law regulatory bodies. When the demand for money becomes extremely heavy, relative to the supply, corporations can compete in the marketplace by offering much higher yields than financial institutions, which are subject to state interest-rate ceilings. The process of disintermediation generally continues until the supply of funds becomes more plentiful and/or the demand for funds slackens. Then yields on market instruments decline, and putting funds in savings institutions becomes more attractive. A 6% yield in time deposits would probably be more attractive than a 6% corporate bond because the risk is somewhat less, since banks' funds are insured by the Federal government. Disintermediation generally causes major problems for housing construction since savings and loan associations, mutual savings banks, and life insurance companies are the major source of mortgage loans for housing construction in the U.S. When disintermediation takes place, funds for housing shrink. A heavy demand for new housing cannot be met at such times, and housing shortages grow more severe. Between March and September, 1966, savings and loan associations were hard hit, actually experiencing a net outflow of savings shares in April and July and only relatively small inflows in the other months. Mutual savings banks were affected too, with the net inflow of deposits falling by more than 40% in the first ten months of 1966, as compared with the same period in 1965. Policyholders in life insurance companies increased their demand for loans at the contracted 5% interest rate and invested at higher rates. Thus the net flow of funds available to life insurance companies for purchasing other assets—primarily mortgages and corporate bonds—shrank about one-third below the 1965 level. The restrictions on mortgage lending resulted in a sharp drop in new housing starts in 1966. For additional information, see Lester V. Chandler, *The Economics of Money and Banking*, 5th ed., Harper & Row, Publishers, Incorporated, 1969, pp. 535–538.

Dismal Science   The name given by Thomas Carlyle to the social science known as political economy or economics. The economic theories of Thomas Malthus, which engendered an impression of futility, prompted Carlyle to coin this term. In *An Essay on the Principle of Population as It Affects the Future Improvement of Society*, Malthus said that there is a tendency in nature for population to outstrip all means of subsistence production. Society, instead of improving and moving upward, is caught in a hopeless trap between ever-increasing population and the insufficient supply of food. For Carlyle's original statement, see Thomas Carlyle (ed.), "Occasional Discourses on the Nigger Question," *Latter Day Pamphlets*, Chapman & Hall, Ltd., London, 1858; J. A. Schumpeter, *History of Economic Analysis*, Oxford University Press, Fair Lawn, N.J., 1954.

Disposable Personal Income   The income that individuals retain after they have deducted personal taxes—including income taxes, estate and gift taxes, personal property taxes, poll taxes, and automobile use taxes—and have paid to government other noncommercial fees, such as state-college tuition, traffic fines, and public hospital fees. It is the concept closest to what is commonly known as take-home pay. It is the amount which individuals can use either to make personal outlays or to save. Considered the single most important determinant of consumption expenditures, U.S. disposable personal income since World War II has grown far more steadily than any other measure of economic activity. After adjustment for changes in population and prices, disposable income is frequently used to measure changes in the nation's standard of living. Monthly data are published in U.S. Department of Commerce, *Survey of Current Business*.

Dissaving   The expenditure of more than one's income, either from past savings or from loans. The subtraction of total dissaving from gross saving gives net saving, the figure used in national income statistics. Studies of empirical data made during the 1940s and 1950s showed that dissaving

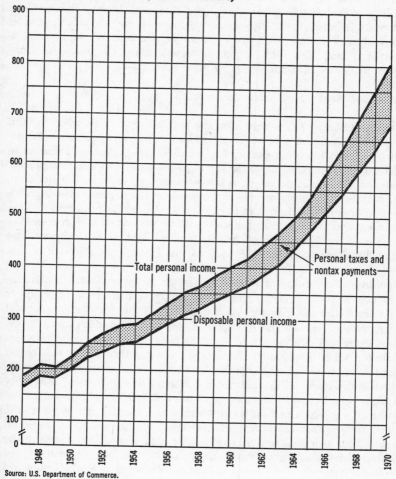

Disposable Personal Income (Billions of dollars)

Source: U.S. Department of Commerce.

was not directly related to income but to other factors. For example, George Garvy explained that dissaving occurred in relatively the same proportion of spending units in all income classes except the very highest. According to Garvy, dissaving seemed to depend on such factors as high unexpected expenses, unemployment or retirement of the head of the spending unit, purchases of consumer durable goods, or a recent decline in income. See George Garvy, "The Role of Dissaving in Economic Analysis," *Journal of Political Economy,* The University of Chicago Press, Chicago, October, 1948; see also James S. Duesenberry, "Income-Consumption Relations and Their Implications," *Income, Employment, and Public Policy: Essays in Honor of Alvin H. Hansen,* W. W. Norton & Company, Inc., New York, 1958; George Katona, *The Powerful Consumer,* McGraw-Hill Book Company, New York, 1960.

Distressed Area   *See Depressed Area.*

Distributed Lag   In econometrics, the problem that arises when the full response to some form of economic stimulus or change spans several established data reporting periods—specifically, the pattern of response in affected areas immediately after the stimulus and in subsequent periods until the stimulus is no longer a factor generating change. For example, the pattern of changes in private business capital expenditures immediately after liberalization of rules governing depreciation charges for tax purposes and in subsequent data-reporting periods would represent a distributed lag. For additional information, see Karl A. Fox, *Intermediate Economic Statistics,* John Wiley & Sons, Inc., New York, 1968.

Disutility   The ability of a good or service to cause discomfort, inconvenience, or pain. It is the opposite of utility. Whereas short periods of exposure to the sun may feel good and provide the skin with a pleasant color, too great an amount of exposure will cause pain and skin damage. Thus, each added increment of exposure beyond a certain point provides disutility rather than utility. In classical economic theory, it was believed that the utility of the wage when a given volume of labor is employed is equal to the marginal disutility of the amount of employment. Disutility of labor is understood to mean any reason that would cause a worker not to accept a job at a certain wage which was under his minimum utility. Thus, the wage serves to overcome the disutility of working. As wages increase, their marginal utility is no longer high enough to overcome the disutility of the additional work required. For further information, see W. Stanley Jevons, *The Theory of Political Economy,* 5th ed., Kelley and Millman, Inc., New York, 1957, chap. 3; J. M. Keynes, *The General Theory of Employment, Interest, and Money,* Harcourt, Brace & World, Inc., New York, 1936, p. 6.

Diversification   The participation by a single firm in the production or sale of widely divergent kinds of goods and services. In diversifying its output, a firm seeks to avoid the sharp changes in revenue that might accompany the fluctuations of business in a single market or in closely related markets. To stabilize revenues, a firm with substantial income from the production of consumer durable goods, which tend to undergo sharp fluctuations, might choose to diversify its operations by undertaking the production of food products, whose sales tend to grow at a fairly regular, albeit moderate, pace as population increases. See Michael Gort, *Diversification and Integration in American Industry*, Princeton University Press, Princeton, N.J., 1962.

Dividend   A payment, usually in cash, that a corporation makes to its stockholders. It represents the stockholders' share of that part of the profits of the business which the board of directors decides to distribute. In some cases, to maintain a consistent record of dividend payments, a corporation will pay a dividend even though a loss was incurred in its last accounting period. Preferred stockholders receive a fixed amount of dollars in dividends, provided that the company earns enough to pay them and the board of directors declares the dividend. They must, however, be paid their dividends before the common stockholders are paid. The amount of the dividend declared on a common stock is determined mainly by the company's earnings and the portion of its earnings that the company retains to finance expansion, modernization, and operations. The total amount of dividends paid by corporations is published in U.S. Department of Commerce, *Survey of Current Business;* for individual companies, see their annual reports; for further information on dividends, see George L. Leffler, *The Stock Market,* The Ronald Press Company, New York, 1957.

Corporate Dividends (Billions of dollars)

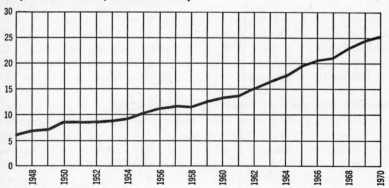

Source: U.S. Department of Commerce.

Dividend Yield   The rate of return on investments in corporate stocks. The dividend yield, or yield on stocks, is determined by dividing the annual dividend payment by the purchase price of the stock. Changes in the market price after the stock has been bought do not affect the rate of return to existing holders, but they alter the dividend yield available to new buyers. Since stock investment is a form of business ownership, the dividend yield is related to profit rates on business assets. For a number of reasons, however, the yield may not follow the rate of profit exactly; the dividends received by stockholders do not represent all corporate earnings, since some funds are retained and since the yield depends on the price of the stock as well as on the dividend paid. The rate of return on stocks is usually higher than the yield on bonds because stocks are generally more speculative than bonds. Although the dividend yield may be important for securities on which dividends are regular, it may not be a significant factor for others. Yield reflects the general quality of bonds, but it may not reflect that of common stocks, whose investors may be more interested in growth and capital gains than in dividend income. For further information, see Benjamin Graham et al., *Security Analysis,* 4th ed., McGraw-Hill Book Company, New York, 1962.

Division of Labor A method of production in which each worker specializes in some aspect or step of the production process. Division of labor is characteristic of a modern industrial economy; it increases a nation's productivity. In a chronological division of labor, one man carries out one step in production, another man does his part, and a third then adds his share, until the finished product emerges. The advantages of specialization have been recognized since the late eighteenth century. They include the greater skill acquired in specialization, the avoidance of wasted time in shifting from one task to another, and the employment of persons best suited to particular types of work. For Adam Smith's classic example of the division of labor, see *The Wealth of Nations,* Random House, Inc., New York, 1937, pp. 7–8; for further information, see Armen A. Alchian and William R. Allen, *University Economics,* 2d ed., Wadsworth Publishing Company, Inc., Belmont, Calif., 1967.

Domestic International Sales Corporation (DISC) A new form of corporation, proposed by the U.S. Treasury, the purpose of which is to reduce the tax differential between export sales by U.S. corporations or their domestic subsidiaries and sales abroad of goods produced by foreign subsidiaries. A DISC would have to secure virtually all its income, directly or indirectly, from export sales from the U.S., but for tax purposes it would be treated as a foreign subsidiary not engaged in business or trade in the U.S. At present the income derived from export sales is subject immediately to U.S. tax, whereas the income derived from the sales by a foreign subsidiary generally is not subject to U.S. tax until it is paid to the U.S. parent company as dividends. The adoption of the DISC proposal would result in deferring taxes that would otherwise be paid by corporations already exporting their product. Those who object to the DISC proposal indicate that it does not reduce the bias in the present tax law against the returns to capital, nor does it simplify the law with reference to both its compliance and administration aspects. For more details, see "The Report of the President's Task Force on Business Taxation," *Business Taxation,* Washington, 1970, pp. 42–44, 57–59.

Dominant Firm   A company so powerful that smaller firms in the industry hesitate to take independent action in trade policy. For example, U. S. Steel was for a long time considered the dominant firm in the steel industry. Nevertheless, it was Wheeling Steel that was the first steel company to increase steel prices selectively in April, 1963.

Doolittle Method   A computational technique used in solving a set of simultaneous, symmetrical linear equations. Similar methods were worked out by both Gauss and Doolittle. The technique enables the statistician immediately to detect arithmetic errors made while solving simultaneous equations. Its use is recommended whenever more than two variables are involved in computations. The same technique can be extended to include computation of the standard errors of partial regression coefficients. For additional information, see Mordecai Ezekiel, *Methods of Correlation Analysis,* 2d ed., John Wiley & Sons, Inc., New York, 1941; Lawrence R. Klein, *A Textbook on Econometrics,* Row, Peterson & Company, Evanston, Ill., 1953.

Double Taxation   The application of two distinct taxes to the same tax base. Double taxation may occur because the same base is assessed twice by the same tax jurisdiction or because it is assessed by two competing tax jurisdictions. A common case of the first kind of double taxation in the U.S. is the taxation of dividends, in which a corporate income tax is levied against all corporation profits and a personal income tax is then levied against the same profits distributed as dividends to stockholders. Double taxation of the second kind often arises through the imposition of taxes on the same base by different levels of government, as in the case of Federal and state taxation of personal incomes and inheritances. Another example of the second kind is territorial multiple taxation, in which the same levels of government in several different areas all claim jurisdiction in taxing the same base. The double taxation of the property owner who owns property in one state and resides in another is a common instance of this type. Cases of double taxation in which all sources of income are treated equally, such as that of Federal and state income taxes, result not in inequality but only in higher taxes, since the actual burden of this double taxation is the same as if one tax equal in amount to the other two taxes were imposed. Inequality does arise when double taxation treats income received from different sources in a discriminatory manner, as is the case in the taxation of dividends. For further information on the nature and effects of double taxation, see Daniel Holland, *The Income Tax Burden of Stockholders*, Princeton University Press, Princeton, N.J., 1958; ———, *Dividends under the Income Tax*, Princeton University Press, Princeton, N.J., 1962; C. W. Guillebaud, "Income Tax and Double Taxation," *Economic Journal*, vol. XLV, no. 179, pp. 484–492, Royal Economic Society, London, September, 1935. For a historical treatment of double taxation, see Edwin R. A. Seligman, *Essays in Taxation*, Augustus M. Kelley, Publishers, New York, 1969; John F. Due, *Government Finance: Economics of the Public Sector*, 4th ed., Richard D. Irwin, Inc., Homewood, Ill., 1963, provides a modern textbook treatment of the subject.

Dow-Jones Averages Four stock price averages computed and published by Dow Jones & Co., publishers of the *Wall Street Journal*. They comprise the Dow-Jones industrial average of thirty industrial stocks, the oldest and most popular average; an average of twenty transportation stocks; an average of fifteen utility stocks; and a composite average of these sixty-five stocks. All stocks in the Dow-Jones averages are listed on the New York Stock Exchange. Originally, the Dow-Jones averages represented the average (arithmetic-mean) price of a share of stock in the group. As stock splits, the substitution of issues in the averages, and other factors occurred, however, a formula was devised to compensate for these changes. Although the Dow-Jones averages no longer represent the actual average prices of the stocks in the groups, they still represent the levels and changes in the stock prices reasonably well. Hourly Dow-Jones averages are published in each edition of the *Wall Street Journal*. Many other newspapers publish the high, low, and closing Dow-Jones averages each day. For further information and criticism, see D. K. Eiteman, C. A. Dice, and W. J. Eiteman, *The Stock Market*, 4th ed., McGraw-Hill Book Company, New York, 1966, chap. 9.

Downtime Any brief period in which machinery is idle because of necessary adjustments, maintenance, or repairs. Downtime, also known as dead time, is time lost to workers because of factors beyond their control.

Dow Theory A theory that purports to predict future stock price movements solely on the basis of the past actions of the Dow-Jones industrial and railroad averages. Originally promulgated by Charles H. Dow, founder of the Dow-Jones financial news service (publishers of the *Wall*

Dow-Jones Industrial Stock Average (Price)

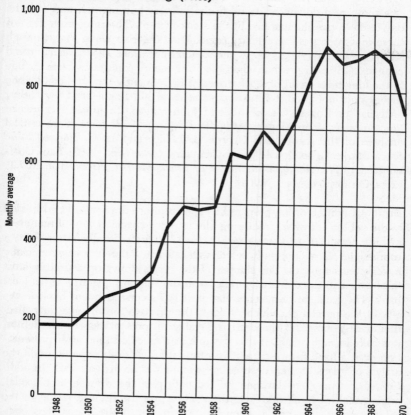

Source: Dow-Jones, U.S. Department of Commerce.

Street Journal), as a technique of forecasting business activity, the Dow theory was refined and formulated by William P. Hamilton, who succeeded Dow as editor of the *Wall Street Journal*. The basic rationale of the Dow theory, as of all technical analyses of the stock market or of individual stocks, is that past price and volume movements of the averages or of individual stocks discount everything except acts of God; that is, the careful interpretation of these patterns gives the best picture of the supply and demand for stocks or for a given stock because the combined actions of all investors are reflected. The Dow theory is based on three basic stock-market movements: (1) the primary trend, which is either a long-term upward (bull) or downward (bear) trend in prices; (2) the secondary trend, which is a short-term upward trend in a primary bear market or a short-term downward-trend in the primary bull market; and (3) the day-to-day price fluctuations in the stock market. The most important of these movements is the primary trend. Dow theorists claim that, through study of the averages, they can determine when the primary trend changes. Critics argue that when the Dow theory confirms a basic change in the long-term trend of stock prices, it is frequently too late, or that the theory does not predict future movements at all. For a pro-Dow theory analysis, see Robert J. Edwards and John Magee, *Technical Analysis of Stock Trends*, John Magee, Springfield, Mass., 1958; for a more critical analysis of the theory, see George L. Leffler and L. C. Farwell, *The Stock Market*, The Ronald Press Company, New York, 1963; Paul Coofner (ed.), *The Random Character of Stock Market Prices*, The M.I.T. Press, Cambridge, Mass., 1964.

Draft   A written order, prepared by the creditor (drawer) and addressed to the debtor (drawee), requiring him to pay a specified sum of money to a third person or to the bearer (payee). A draft usually arises from a commercial transaction between firms located in different areas, especially in different countries. The shipper of the goods draws up a draft against the buyer and discounts the draft (with the shipping papers) at his local bank. The bank, in turn, sends the draft to its correspondent bank in the city of the purchaser, which presents the draft to the drawee for collection or acceptance. If the draft is payable on presentation to the debtor, it is called a sight draft. If it is payable at a specified time after presentation or at a fixed future date, it is a time draft. A draft payable upon the arrival of goods at their destination is known as an arrival draft. In addition, drafts may be classified by the nature of the drawee as personal, commercial, or bank drafts. If the drawer and the drawee reside in the same country, the draft is known as a domestic draft; if not, it is commonly called a foreign draft or bill of exchange. For additional details, see William J. Schultz and Hedwig Reinhardt, *Credit and Collection Management*, 3d ed., Prentice-Hall, Inc., Englewood Cliffs, N.J., 1962.

Dummy Variable   A constructed variable used as a means of including factors that are not naturally quantifiable in an econometric model. It may assume two and only two values (usually 1 and 0) used to represent the presence of a factor and its opposite or its absence. For example, if an economic model builder knows or suspects that a worker's sex influences income levels, he may introduce a dummy variable in which the number 1 is paired with data for male workers and 0 is paired with data for female workers in a single-equation model. Dummy variables that assume values of 1 and 0 can be used like any other numerical variables in correlations.

The dummy variable may also represent a composite of many factors, such as those associated with "wartime" in contrast to "peacetime." An alternative to the use of dummy variables is that of splitting the sample into two parts for the purposes of analysis. For additional information, see Lawrence R. Klein, *An Introduction to Econometrics,* Prentice-Hall, Inc., Englewood Cliffs, N.J., 1962; Stefan Valavanis, *Econometrics,* McGraw-Hill Book Company, New York, 1959.

Dumping   The sale of a product in another country for less than in the home market in order to gain an advantage in competition with other foreign suppliers. The General Agreement on Tariffs and Trade, which almost all the world's major trading nations have signed, prohibits the practice and provides for a defense against it through higher tariffs. Charges of dumping are difficult to prove, however, and this is especially true when the exporter's government shares the blame because it offers an export subsidy or facilitates the export through foreign aid or discriminatory currency arrangements. Whereas an individual firm dumps its product abroad mostly for competitive reasons, a government may have political reasons or a balance-of-payments incentive to encourage such sales, making prosecution all the more difficult. In the U.S., the Antidumping Act of 1921 gives the Tariff Commission power to recommend retaliatory action when it finds that foreign goods are being dumped in the country. The theoretical aspects of dumping are discussed in Gottfried Haberler, *The Theory of International Trade,* The Macmillan Company, New York, 1936; see also Stephen Enke and Virgil Salera, *International Economics,* Prentice-Hall, Inc., Englewood Cliffs, N.J., 1957; Charles E. Staley, *International Economics,* Prentice-Hall, Inc., Englewood Cliffs, N.J., 1970. For examples of dumping see Irving B. Kravis and Robert E. Lipsey, *Price Competitiveness in World Trade,* National Bureau of Economic Research, Inc., New York, 1971.

Duopoly   A market structure in which there are only two sellers of a commodity. The important feature of duopoly is that each producer generally must consider the other firm's reaction to any changes that he may make in price or output. Since there are only two competing firms, their interdependence is great. There is a strong tendency for duopolists to reach a tacit agreement to set a common price, limit output, or divide markets. In actual practice, genuine duopolies are rare. The air-brake industry is one example of the existence of only two manufacturers of a commodity in the U.S., Westinghouse Air Brake and New York Air Brake. For many years, two companies, Texas Gulf Sulphur and Freeport Sulphur Company, produced about 90% of all the sulphur sold in the U.S. For further information, see Alfred W. Stonier and Douglas C.

Hague, *A Textbook on Economic Theory*, 3d ed., John Wiley & Sons, Inc., New York, 1964; James M. Henderson and Richard E. Quandt, *Microeconomic Theory: A Mathematical Approach*, 2d ed., McGraw-Hill Book Company, New York, 1971, pp. 223–235.

Durable Good   A piece of equipment, for either consumers or producers, that in normal use is likely to last longer than three years. Consumer durable goods include automobiles, appliances, furniture, jewelry, and books. Producer durable goods include a wide range of machinery and equipment. Buildings, roads, airports, etc., are excluded. In 1970 expenditures for consumer durables in the U.S. totaled more than $89 billion; expenditures for producer durable goods, more than $67 billion. The purchase of many durable goods is postponable, and in periods of declinable earnings both consumers and producers tend to put off buying new durables and continue to use existing equipment. As a result, spending for durable goods fluctuates widely. During the 1960–1961 recession the rate of durable-goods spending in the U.S. declined from $74 billion to $63 billion. Quarterly data on durable-goods expenditures appear in U.S. Department of Commerce, *Survey of Current Business;* for a discussion of factors influencing the purchase of consumer durable goods, see George Katona, *The Powerful Consumer*, McGraw-Hill Book Company, New York, 1960; for a discussion of factors affecting purchases of producer durable goods, see National Bureau of Economic Research, Inc., *Regularization of Business Investment*, Princeton University Press, Princeton, N.J., 1954.

Durbin-Watson Statistic   A measure d that tests for the presence (or absence) of autocorrelation in least-squares relationships. It is computed by dividing the sum of the squared first differences of residuals by the sum of the squared residuals. Exact significance levels for d are not available, but Durbin and Watson have tabulated lower and upper bounds for various values of n (the number of paired observations) and k (the number of explanatory variables). If the derived statistic d falls below the lower limit d_L, autocorrelation is present. If it falls above the upper limit d_U, the residual is random. And if it falls between the upper and lower limits, the test is inconclusive. For additional information, see J. Durbin and G. S. Watson, "Testing for Serial Correlation in Least Squares Regression," parts I and II, *Biometrica*, 1950 and 1951.

Dynamics   The study of movement and change in economic systems. In contrast to static analysis, dynamics is concerned mainly with the changes in given conditions over time and the dynamic processes of adjustment and not with the determinants of equilibrium. The dynamic emphasis is achieved by introducing the element of time, so that the values of the economic variables at a given instant depend partly on their values of past moments of time. Economic processes are traced over a time path made up of a sequence of periods with the use of appropriate time lags. An economic model is characterized as dynamic if at least one observable variable in the equations has values taken at various points of time or at least one equation contains a function of time, such as trend or seasonal fluctuations. Complex problems in economics, especially when they involve movement toward a constantly changing equilibrium, may be analyzed by dynamics. For example, economic dynamic analysis has played an essential role in studies of economic growth. For further information, see Herman O. A. Wold, *Econometric Model Building*, North-Holland Publishing Company, Amsterdam, 1964; Frank Knight, *On the History and Method of Economics*, The University of Chicago Press, Chicago, 1956, chap. 8; T. C. Koopmans (ed.), *Statistical Inference in Dynamic Economic Models*, John Wiley & Sons, Inc., New York, 1950; William Fellner, *Modern Economic Analysis*, McGraw-Hill Book Company, New York, 1960, chap. 23; Paul A. Samuelson, "Dynamic Process Analysis," in Howard S. Ellis (ed.), *A Survey of Contemporary Economics*, Richard D. Irwin, Inc., Homewood, Ill., 1948, vol. I, chap. 10; Kenneth F. Wallis, "Some Applied Developments in Applied Econometrics," *Journal of Economic Literature*, vol. 7, no. 3, pp. 771–796, September, 1969; William J. Baumol, *Economic Dynamics*, 3d ed., The Macmillan Company, New York, 1970.

E

Earmarking of Taxes (Dedicating of Revenues)   The practice of designating specific revenues for the financing of specific public services or projects. Generally, it refers to a single tax source, for example, a state tax on gasoline for a single public project, such as the building and maintenance of roads. In the overall U.S. tax system, earmarking is relatively important; it is particularly important at the local-government level, at which such special projects as schools claim a preponderant share of tax revenues. A Tax Foundation study indicated that 50% of the state collections in 1954 were earmarked. Earmarking of funds at the Federal level appears to be growing more important each year. For additional information, see *Earmarked State Taxes*, Tax Foundation, New York, 1955; James M. Buchanan, *The Economics of Earmarked Taxes*, The Brookings Institution, Washington, D.C., 1963.

Earned Revenue   An accounting term which refers to the income that results when goods are disposed of or when services are rendered. In distinction to the situation with regard to unearned revenue, a company or business enterprise renders service and receives payment in the same accounting period. For example, in wholesale and manufacturing businesses the point of sale is generally regarded as the point at which income is earned. In service industries, revenue is earned as services are performed. The term is often referred to as earned income. For a brief discussion of earned revenue and its related expenses in the determination of income, see H. A. Finney and H. E. Miller, *Principles of Accounting*, 6th ed., Prentice-Hall, Inc., Englewood Cliffs, N.J., 1965; Harold Bierman, Jr., and Allen R. Drebin, *Managerial Accounting*, The Macmillan Company, New York, 1969.

Easy Money (Cheap Money)   The term used to designate a condition in which a combination of relatively low interest rates and great credit availability exists. When the term is used, it means that interest rates are lower than they were earlier, that many qualified borrowers who previously were denied loans are now granted them, and that capital is somewhat easier to raise. Since the term indicates a relative condition, no specific interest rate or degree of credit availability signals easy money. In the U.S., the Federal Reserve System can help create easy-money conditions by providing commercial banks with free reserves (reserves above those that they are legally required to hold minus their borrowings from the Federal Reserve), thereby making it easier for them to extend loans. Even if the Federal Reserve System supplies banks with as much as $500 million in free reserves (a sign of ample lending ability in the post-World War II period), however, banks may not respond immediately with more liberal lending policies. One reason may be that banks believe that they have already extended too great a volume of loans in relation to their capital. Moreover, even during easy-money periods no single individual or organization can borrow indefinitely without encountering increased resistance from lenders. For further information, see James M. Buchanan, *The Public Finances*, Richard D. Irwin, Inc., Homewood, Ill., 1960, pp. 111–113.

Econometrics The branch of economics which expresses economic theories in mathematical terms in order to verify them by statistical methods. It is concerned with the empirical measurement of economic relations that are expressible in mathematical form. Econometrics seeks to measure the impact of one economic variable on another in order to be able to predict future events or advise the choice for economic policy to produce desired results. Economic theory can supply qualitative information concerning an economic problem, but it is the task of econometrics to provide the quantitative content for these qualitative statements. Econometrics can be divided into four major divisions: specification, estimation, verification, and prediction. Specification is the process of building a mathematical model of an economic theory, i.e., of expressing the economic theory in mathematical terms. Through estimation, the parameters of the equation are filled in. Then, by verification certain criteria of success are used to accept or reject the economic theory under investigation. Finally, through prediction the model can be rearranged and fed new data about autonomous variables, and their effect on the endogenous variable can be predicted. The ability of the econometric model to make accurate predictions is a crucial test of the theoretical relationships that the model expresses. The use of econometrics has been confined largely to problems of the type included in partial-equilibrium theory and in the theory of income and employment. In partial-equilibrium theory, an estimation of the functions of supply and demand, a forecast of price in a single market, and an estimation of cost curves are included. In income theory, forecasts of consumer demand at various levels of income and estimations of the demand for money have been made. Attempts at large-scale econometric models of a whole economy have not been entirely successful. For further information, see Lawrence R. Klein, *A Textbook of Econometrics,* Harper & Row, Publishers, Incorporated, New York, 1953; for an econometric model of the United States, see Lawrence R. Klein and A. S. Goldberger, *An Econometric Model of the United States 1929–1952,* North-Holland Publishing Company, Amsterdam, 1955.

Economic Determinism   *See Economic Interpretation of History.*

Economic Efficiency The use of resources in the most efficient manner. Economic efficiency is concerned with the utilization of scarce resources employed in turning out products and with the resulting output itself. An economy is considered 100% efficient if it is producing at 100% of capacity, employing all methods of production and resources as effectively as present technology allows. An economy that has achieved full employment has attained economic efficiency, but full employment has not necessarily been reached when all workers are employed. A worker harvesting wheat by hand or using a horse-drawn plow may have a job, but in terms of economic efficiency he is unemployed. In this case, the worker is underemployed; he is doing a job, but not efficiently. If he were replaced by more efficient production methods, output could still be maintained at the same level. Unutilized resources, both human and capital, mean waste and inefficiency. For a study of particular aspects of the problem of economic efficiency, see Armen A. Alchian and William R. Allen, *University Economics,* Wadsworth Publishing Company, Inc., Belmont, Calif., 1967.

Economic Good   A desired good or service which is scarce and thus requires effort or sacrifice to obtain. The fact that an economic good is scarce does not mean that it is rare, but only that it is not freely available for the taking. To obtain an economic good, one must either produce it or offer other economic goods in exchange. Economic goods are transferable, and because they command other goods in exchange, they have a market value. The best criterion for determining whether or not an article is an economic good is to see whether it can be bought and sold; in other words, anything which has a market price can be called an economic good. Nearly all material articles, from apples to zinc, are economic goods. The term also includes services, such as the labor of a factory worker. Goods such as air and sunshine, which are abundant and thus are not economic goods, are called free goods. See Campbell R. McConnell, *Economics,* 4th ed., McGraw-Hill Book Company, New York, 1969.

Economic Growth   An increase in a nation's or an area's capacity to produce goods and services coupled with an increase in production of these goods and services. Usually, economic growth is measured by the annual rate of increase in a nation's gross national product, as adjusted for price changes. A better measure, however, is the increase in the real gross national product per capita; in some underdeveloped countries yearly gains in output are surpassed by gains in population, leaving the average person with a lowered standard of living. Even when population changes are taken into account, however, growth rates do not always accurately measure changes in the standard of living. U.S. workers, for instance, have gained about 30 hours of additional leisure per week since 1900, but the value of this commodity, the freedom from work, is nowhere included in U.S. growth rates. Comparative growth rates are usually deceptive. One reason is that, because of business fluctuations, output does not rise smoothly and evenly from one year to another. As a result,

Annual Average Growth Rates of the U.S. Economy, 1953–1971 *

(Percentage increases, from starting year to terminal year, of GNP in 1970 dollars)

Starting Year	Terminal Year 1953	1954	1955	1956	1957	1958	1959	1960	1961	1962	1963	1964	1965	1966	1967	1968	1969	1970	1971
1953	...	−1.4	3.0	2.6	2.3	1.6	2.4	2.4	2.3	2.8	2.9	3.2	3.4	3.7	3.6	3.7	3.6	3.4	3.3
1954	...	...	7.6	4.7	3.6	2.4	3.2	3.1	2.9	3.4	3.4	3.6	3.9	4.1	4.0	4.0	3.9	3.7	3.6
1955	...	...	...	1.8	1.6	0.7	2.1	2.2	2.1	2.8	2.9	2.9	3.5	3.8	3.7	3.8	3.7	3.4	3.4
1956	...	...	...	...	1.4	0.2	2.2	2.2	2.2	2.9	3.1	3.4	3.7	4.0	3.5	3.9	3.8	3.5	3.5
1957	...	...	...	...	...	−1.1	2.6	2.5	2.4	3.2	3.3	3.6	4.0	4.2	4.1	4.1	4.0	3.7	3.6
1958	...	...	...	...	...	...	6.4	4.4	3.6	4.3	4.3	4.5	4.7	4.9	4.7	4.7	4.5	4.1	4.0
1959	...	...	...	...	...	...	...	2.5	2.2	3.6	3.7	4.1	4.4	4.7	4.5	4.0	3.9	3.6	3.5
1960	...	...	...	...	...	...	...	...	1.9	4.2	4.2	4.5	4.8	5.1	4.8	4.8	4.5	4.0	3.9
1961	...	...	...	...	...	...	...	...	...	6.6	5.3	5.3	5.6	5.8	5.2	5.2	4.9	4.3	4.1
1962	...	...	...	...	...	...	...	...	...	...	4.0	4.7	5.3	5.6	5.0	4.9	4.6	4.0	3.9
1963	...	...	...	...	...	...	...	...	...	...	...	5.4	5.9	6.1	5.2	5.1	4.7	4.0	3.8
1964	...	...	...	...	...	...	...	...	...	...	...	...	6.3	6.4	5.1	5.0	4.6	3.7	3.6
1965	...	...	...	...	...	...	...	...	...	...	...	...	...	6.5	4.5	4.6	4.2	3.2	3.1
1966	...	...	...	...	...	...	...	...	...	...	...	...	...	...	2.6	3.7	3.4	2.4	2.4
1967	...	...	...	...	...	...	...	...	...	...	...	...	...	...	...	4.7	3.8	2.3	2.4
1968	...	...	...	...	...	...	...	...	...	...	...	...	...	...	...	...	2.8	1.2	1.6
1969	...	...	...	...	...	...	...	...	...	...	...	...	...	...	...	...	...	−0.4	1.0
1970	...	...	...	...	...	...	...	...	...	...	...	...	...	...	...	...	...	...	2.5
1971	...	...	...	...	...	...	...	...	...	...	...	...	...	...	...	...	...	...	...

* Compound rates of growth.

by a careful selection of beginning and terminal years, it is possible to make economic growth over a period of time appear either bad or good in relation to another period. Comparisons of international growth rates are even more complicated because of differences in national income definitions and accounting methods. Moreover, in some cases statistics may be used deceptively for propaganda purposes. Annual growth rates for some major industrialized countries during the 1960s were as follows: Federal Republic of Germany, 5%; Italy, 6.5%; Japan, 11%; United Kingdom, 2.5%; and U.S.S.R., 7%. These may be compared with a U.S. growth rate of about 4% in the same period. Current growth rates for foreign countries may be computed from the national income figures reported in Statistical Office of the United Nations, *Monthly Bulletin of Statistics*, New York; see also Evsey Domar, *Essays in the Theory of Economic Growth*, Oxford University Press, Fair Lawn, N.J., 1957; W. A. Lester, *The Theory of Economic Growth*, George Allen & Unwin Ltd., London, 1955; Paul Baran, *The Political Economy of Growth*, Monthly Review Press, New York, 1957.

Economic Indicator A statistical series that has been found to represent fairly accurately changes in business conditions. There are three major groups of economic indicators that demonstrate a consistent relationship to the timing of general business fluctuations: (1) Leading indicators, such as new orders and profits, usually rise and fall in advance of turns in general business activity. (2) Coincident indicators, such as the unemployment rate and bank debits, generally rise and fall with the changes in overall business activity. (3) Lagging indicators, such as capital expenditures and consumer installment debt, usually move up or down after general business activity has altered its course. Although economic indicators constitute a valuble tool in forecasting business conditions, they are not infallible, and relationships among the indicators and business activity on the whole do not always hold fast. Hence, changes in key indicators cannot automatically be taken as evidence of impending changes in general business conditions. For a fuller discussion of the indicators, see Geoffrey H. Moore (ed.), *Business Cycle Indicators*, Princeton University Press, Princeton, N.J., 1961, vol. 1.; for current indicator data, see U.S. Bureau of the Census, *Business Cycle Developments*, monthly. Also see J. Shiskin, "Business Cycle Indicators: The Known and The Unknown," *Business Cycle Developments*, U.S. Department of Commerce, Washington, D.C., September, 1963.

Economic Interpretation of History (Economic Determinism; Materialistic Concept of History) The thesis, advanced by Karl Marx in *A Contribution to the Critique of Political Economy* (1859), that the events of any historical epoch are determined by the economic institutions prevailing at the time rather than by the wishes and will of the individuals of the period; in short, that the manner in which men make their living practically dictates their worldly outlook and actions. In Marx's words, "The mode of production in material life determines the general character of the social, political and spiritual process of life. It is not the consciousness of men that determines their existence, but, on the contrary, their social existence that determines their consciousness." To Marx, the systems of production and distribution of goods in any society established the society's class structure. In order to change undesirable features of an existing class structure, it was necessary to alter the means of production and the distribution of wealth. There is a close relationship between Marx's interpretation of history and his thesis of class struggles, which held that antagonisms between social classes are the driving forces on history. These two doctrines provide the basis for the Communists' firm belief in inevitable success for their economic system. Scholars have criticized Marx's insistence on the overriding importance of economic organization in history. See J. A. LeRossignol, *From Marx to Stalin: A Critique of Communism,* Thomas Y. Crowell Company, New York, 1940, chap. 9: Benedetto Croce, *Historical Materialism and the Economics of Karl Marx,* The Macmillan Company, New York, 1914; Joseph A. Schumpeter, *Capitalism, Socialism, and Democracy,* Harper & Row, Publishers, Incorporated, New York, 1950, chap. 11; ———, *History of Economic Analysis,* Oxford University Press, Fair Lawn, N.J., 1954, pp. 440ff.

Economic Law A generalization concerning the relationship between various economic phenomena, such as that between price and total sales. The most important purpose of an economic law is to permit prediction, and prediction, in turn, permits control over phenomena. Economic laws are generalizations, containing no precise quantitative results. Thus, they are stated in ordinal terms, such as *increasing* and *greater than,* rather than in cardinal terms, such as *increase by 20%.* An example of an economic law is the law of variable proportions, which holds that if the quantity of one productive service is increased while the quantities of other services are held constant, the resulting increments of product will decrease after a certain point. See George J. Stigler, *The Theory of Price,* 3d ed., The Macmillan Company, New York, 1966.

Economic Man The concept of man motivated solely by economic reasons, created by the economists of the classical school. Economic man was considered representative of the average man, with all the characteristics of the human race, but average only in an economic sense.

All his characteristics were economic. It was on this generalized concept of man that economists of the classical school based their theory. By use of the deductive method, they tried to fashion economics into an exact science known as pure economy. They failed to realize, however, that besides profit and other pecuniary interests, man desires leisure, independence, security, and other nonmonetary benefits. It was these contradictions that led to the development of a rival view of man, the so-called historical or realist school, which studied men (not man) at different ages and under different conditions. For a study of past economic theories, see Frank Amandus Neff, *Economic Doctrines,* 2d ed., McGraw-Hill Book Company, New York, 1950; Charles R. Noyes, *Economic Man in Relation to His Natural Environment,* Columbia University Press, New York, 1948.

Economic Model   A mathematical statement of economic theory. An economic model is a method of analysis which presents an oversimplified picture of the real world. The situation in the real world is composed of a bewildering variety of major and minor variables, and unless the less important factors are eliminated, rigorous analysis is either hopelessly complicated or impossible. By making certain assumptions, many minor elements can be eliminated and a model can be set up. The model permits analysis of the specific situation defined by the assumptions. Economic models themselves can be set out in equation form with diagrams or with words. A complete mathematical model must have as many equations as there are unknowns. For further information, see David Gale, *The Theory of Linear Economic Models,* McGraw-Hill Book Company, New York, 1960; Earl F. Beach, *Economic Models,* John Wiley & Sons, Inc., New York, 1957; Lawrence R. Klein and A. S. Goldberger, *An Econometric Model of the United States 1929–1952,* North-Holland Publishing Company, Amsterdam, 1955.

Economic Planning   Governmental direction of the economy. There are two types of modern economic planning. One is the partial economic planning that has evolved under the private-enterprise system, and the other is total control, or overall planning, by Communist and Socialist governments. Under a partial economic-planning system, government direction may be applied through economic policy that is designed to smooth economic fluctuations experienced in a free-enterprise economy. It may take the form of actions to offset a recession, the institution of public works projects to provide employment, the reduction of taxes to increase purchasing power, or the lowering of interest rates to encourage investment. Governmental policies to prevent inflation and to encourage economic growth are also examples of limited economic planning. Total economic planning implies the determination by a supreme governmental authority of the quality, kind, and quantity of goods to be produced by a nation. Although economic planning is quite broad in scope, it always involves some specific forecasts of the results of economic operations. For further information see Louis J. Zimmerman (ed.), *Economic Planning*, Humanities Press, New York, 1963; Seymour E. Harris, *Economic Planning*, Alfred A. Knopf, Inc., New York, 1949; see also Henry Grayson, *Economic Planning under Free Enterprise*, Public Affairs Press, Washington, D.C., 1954.

Economics The social study of the production, distribution, and consumption of wealth. With the expansion of the tools used by modern economists in their analyses and the discarding of out-of-date theories, economics is becoming more a science and less an art. Despite this trend, however, economists still interpret the same economic data differently. Like scientific research, economics can be divided into two major categories, basic economics and applied economics. Basic economics is the study of economic principles, which for the most part is carried out by academic economists, while applied economics puts the basic principles to work in developing economic programs and policies with economic progress as the overall goal.

Economic Sanction A coercive but nonforceful measure that calls for the complete or partial interruption of economic relations with an unruly and perverse nation in an attempt to make it conform to international law. Such a sanction is usually adopted by an international organization in dealing with the affairs of an uncooperative nation. In 1935 the League of Nations imposed sanctions against Italy in an attempt to prevent its aggression against Ethiopia. These sanctions included an arms embargo, a financial embargo, and trade restrictions against materials that were essential to Italy's war machine. The Charter of the UN provides the groundwork for such action by that organization. A more recent example of the use of economic sanctions was the imposition of sanctions on the Dominican Republic by the members of the Organization of American States. For examples of such provisions, see Covenant of the League of Nations, art. 16; UN Charter, art. 41; see also P. W. Bonsal, "O.A.S. Recommends Further Economic Action Regarding Dominican Republic," *Department of State Bulletin*, Feb. 20, 1961, pp. 273–276.

Economic Theory The study of relationships in the economy. Its purpose is to analyze and explain the behavior of the various economic elements. The relationships established by economic analyses, which are called economic principles, may be analytical generalizations, following

logically from certain assumptions, or empirical statements, defining
relationship between observed data. The body of economic theory ca
be divided into two broad categories, positive theory and welfare theor\
Positive theory is an attempt to analyze the operation of the econom
without considering the desirability of its results in terms of ultimat
goals. Its major subdivisions are price and distribution theory, which :
concerned with the behavior of individuals and firms and with the deter
mination of the prices, output, and distribution of goods, and nation;
income theory, which focuses on the level of national income and em
ployment. Welfare theory is concerned primarily with an evaluation c
the economic system in terms of ethical goals which are not themselve
derived from economic analysis. For further information, see T. V\
Hutchison, *The Significance and Basic Postulates of Economic Theor*
Macmillan & Co., Ltd., London, 1938; William Fellner, *Modern Economi*
Analysis, McGraw-Hill Book Company, New York, 1960; Kenneth F
Boulding, *Economic Analysis,* 4th ed., Harper & Row, Publishers, Incor
porated, New York, 1966; William Baumol, *Economic Theory and Oper*
ations Analysis, 2d ed., Prentice-Hall, Inc., Englewood Cliffs, N.J., 196£

Economic Trend   *See Secular Trend.*

Economies of Mass Production   *See Benefits of Large-Scale*
Production.

Economies of Scale   *See Benefits of Large-Scale Production.*

Economist   An individual with a knowledge of economic theory wh
can apply the theory to the real world. An economist must, therefore
understand the behavior of consumers and businessmen. His problem
generally concern numerical magnitudes which vary from time to time
from place to place, and from case to case.

Effective Interest Rate   The true rate of interest paid on an installmen
loan. The problem of effective interest rates arises in the case of consume
loans, in which the principal is paid back in periodic installments. The rat
of interest quoted by the lender on consumer installment loans is usuall\
the simple nominal rate of interest; e.g., on $120 borrowed for a yea\
with an interest charge of $6, repayable in twelve monthly installments o
$10, the nominal rate of interest is 5% per annum. This is not the effectiv\
rate of interest, or that actually paid by the borrower, however, since th\
credit in use is reduced as each payment is made. Thus, in the exampl\
given above, $120 is not borrowed for twelve months; rather, $10 i\

borrowed for one month, $10 is borrowed for two months, etc. The effective rate of interest must be calculated only on the basis of the unpaid balance and not on the total amount of the original loan. The effective rate, which is about twice as high as the nominal rate, can be calculated according to the following formula:

$$\text{Effective rate} = \frac{2 \times \text{(nominal rate of interest)} \times \text{(number of payments)}}{\text{(number of payment plus one)}}$$

Thus, in the example given above, the effective rate of interest would not be 5%, but rather $2(.05)(12)/13$, or 9.23%. Another convenient method for calculating the annual effective rate of interest is as follows:

$$\text{Effective rate} = \frac{2 \times \text{(number of payments in one year)} \times \text{(total amount of finance charges)}}{\text{(original unpaid balance)} \times \text{(number of payments plus one)}}$$

For additional information, see Hillel Black, *Buy Now, Pay Later*, William Morrow & Company, Inc., New York, 1961; Robert W. Johnson, *Methods of Stating Consumer Finance Charges*, Columbia University, Graduate School of Business, New York, 1961; see also National Bureau of Economic Research, Inc., Conference on Population, *Consumer Installment Credit*, vol. I, part 1, Board of Governors of the Federal Reserve System, Washington, D.C., 1957, pp. 49–65.

Efficiency In statistics and econometrics, an estimating criterion or objective evaluation of the relative merits of possible estimators (parameters) attributed to Fisher. Thus if c_1 and c_2 are two estimators from a sample of observations, the one with the smaller variance is the more efficient. Efficiency implies also sufficiency, i.e., that no other estimator from the same sample can add to information about the parameter. For additional information, see Stefan Valavanis, *Econometrics*, McGraw-Hill Book Company, New York, 1959.

Elastic Demand The percentage change induced in one factor of demand divided by a given percentage change in the factor that caused the change. For example, if the price of a commodity is raised, purchasers tend to reduce their buying rate. The relationship between price and purchasing rate, which is known as the elasticity of demand, expresses the percentage change in the buying rate divided by the percentage change in price. The concept of elasticity for a given point on a line or curve is simple, but in practice elasticities may have to be calculated over given finite ranges of price and quantity changes. In such cases, there is a great difference if the percentage change is computed from the beginning of the change, from the midpoint of the change, or from the end of the change. To illustrate the difference in percentage change in quantities, let us assume that the amount of wheat purchased per day changes from 1,000 bushels to 1,200 bushels. The change, therefore, is 200 bushels, and the percentage change (200 divided by 1,000) is 20%. If we move from 1,200 bushels to 1,000 bushels, the change is the same, 200 bushels, but the percentage change (decrease) is only 16.67% (200 divided by 1,200). One formula designed to eliminate this asymmetry is as follows, with Q_1 representing the initial purchase rate, Q_2 the second purchase rate, and similarly for prices:

$$\text{Elasticity of demand} = \frac{(Q_2 - Q_1)}{(P_1 - P_2)} \frac{(P_1 + P_2)}{(Q_1 + Q_2)}$$

The elasticity concept is extremely useful because it applies independently of the units in which prices and quantities are measured. The concept may be used to express the relationship between any two variables, such as price and amount supplied or income and purchase rate. The rudiments of the concept are treated in Paul A. Samuelson, *Economics*, McGraw-Hill Book Company, New York, 1961; for a more advanced treatment, see George J. Stigler, *The Theory of Price*, 3d ed., The Macmillan Company, New York, 1966; for the mathematics of the topic, see James M. Henderson and Richard E. Quandt, *Microeconomic Theory: A Mathematical Approach*, 2d ed., McGraw-Hill Book Company, New York, 1971.

Elasticity   The relative response of one variable to a small percentage change in another variable. The general formula for elasticity is $\frac{\Delta y/y}{\Delta x/x}$, which can be written $\frac{dy}{dx} \cdot \frac{x}{y}$ if the changes are extremely small. The concept of elasticity is dimensionless; that is, it is totally independent of units of measurement. This allows one to compare, for example, the price elasticity of demand for land with that of automobiles, ball-point pens, or any other good or service. Perhaps the most common specific examples of the concept of elasticity are price elasticity of demand $\frac{q/q}{\Delta P/P}$ and income elasticity of demand $\frac{\Delta q/q}{\Delta y/y}$, where q is quantity demanded, p is price, and y is disposable income. For additional information, see George Stigler, *Theory of Price*, 3d ed., The Macmillan Company, New York, 1966; Campbell R. McConnell, *Economics*, 4th ed., McGraw-Hill Book Company, New York, 1969, pp. 417–422.

Elasticity Coefficient Many problems in economics involve relationships between one factor and another. If the percentage change in one factor is related to the percentage change in the other, the units in which the items are measured become irrelevant, and one percentage divided by the other will yield a pure signed number. For example, it is well known that the purchase rate of a commodity or service tends to decline as the price rises, and elasticity of demand is defined as the percentage change in the purchase rate divided by the causative factor, the percentage change in the price. Since price and purchase rate move in opposite directions, the number will have a negative sign, although descriptive material concerning the elasticity of demand often neglects the sign because it is understood to be negative. The percentage response of price may be greater than, the same as, or less than the percentage change in price (*see Elastic Demand and Inelastic Demand*). The elasticity concept may be applied to any pair of relevant statistics, such as income and purchase rate. Unfortunately, the question of calculating the correct percentage changes is often troublesome. Strictly speaking, the elasticity coefficient applies to an infinitesimally small point on a function, but the calculation of percentage changes is necessarily over some finite distance. If the distance appears to be relatively small, the distinction is sometimes ignored. If the distance is deemed to be of some significance, an arc-elasticity coefficient may be calculated. This procedure calculates an elasticity at the midpoint of a straight-line segment connecting the initial and terminal points on the function. The arc elasticity is calculated as follows:

$$\text{Arc elasticity} = \frac{(Q_2 - Q_1)}{(Q_2 + Q_1)} \frac{(P_2 + P_1)}{(P_2 - P_1)}$$

where the subscripts 1 and 2 indicate the initial and terminal periods, respectively. If the exact formula of the demand function is known, as it often will be in empirical estimation of demand functions, calculus may be used to yield a more precise measure of elasticity at a point:

$$\text{Elasticity} = \frac{dq}{dp} \frac{p}{q}$$

The above formula will be seen to be the slope of the function at the point, multiplied by the quotient of the price (independent variable) over the purchase rate (the dependent variable). A general description of elasticity calculations will be found in D. S. Watson, *Price Theory and Its Uses*, 2d ed., Houghton Mifflin Company, Boston, 1968, and the mathematical applications will be found in the Mathematical Notes to the various sections of the work.

Elasticity of Substitution   A measure of the ease with which one input can be substituted for another input when responding to a change in the ratio of the prices of the inputs. For instance, given a production function suppose that the ratio of the return to capital to wages declined 1% making labor relatively more expensive than capital. If the ratio of the amount of capital input to labor input used increases more than 1%, the elasticity of substitution is elastic, which implies that it is relatively easy to substitute capital for labor. Formally the elasticity of substitution i defined as follows:

$$\frac{\Delta(K/L/CK/L)}{\Delta(MPK/MPL)/(MPK/MPL)}$$

where K is capital input, MP_K is marginal product of capital, L is labor input, and MP_L is marginal product of labor. Originally introduced by J. R. Hicks in 1932, the concept of the elasticity of substitution has played an important role in economic theory, particularly production and growth theory. The Cobb-Douglas production function, which is frequently used in economic growth models, has an elasticity of substitution equal to 1. Unitary elasticity of substitution means that the relative shares of income going to capital and labor remain unchanged even if the ratio of the prices of these inputs changes. For additional information, see J. R. Hicks, *The Theory of Wages*, The Macmillan Company, New York, 1932; Joan Robinson, *The Economics of Imperfect Competition*, 2d ed., St. Martin's Press, Inc., New York, 1969; Kenneth J. Arrow, Hollis B. Chenery, Bagicha S. Minhas, and Robert M. Solow, "Capital-Labor Substitution and Economic Efficiency," *Review of Economics and Statistics*, vol. XLIII, pp. 225–250, August, 1961.

Elastic Money Supply   The situation occurring in a monetary system in which the volume of currency in circulation can be varied to meet different needs. In the U.S., for example, the amount of currency needed by the public increases on such holidays as July 4, Labor Day, and Christmas. The demand for currency varies for different days of the week, and in agricultural regions the need is heavy at harvest time. There is also a long-term aspect of monetary growth: a rising level of business requires a greater amount of currency. The Federal Reserve System was established in 1914 to provide the U.S. with an elastic currency supply, which had not been available under earlier banking systems. It provides elasticity by increasing bank reserves at times when currency is in greatest demand. Technically, the term elastic money supply is erroneous, because elasticity refers to the conversion of checking accounts into currency and vice versa. Normally, money is considered to be the sum of currency and demand deposits (except for demand deposits owned by banks). The seasonal pattern of the demand for currency is discussed in detail in *The Federal Reserve System: Purposes and Functions,* Board of Governors of the Federal Reserve System, Washington, D.C., 1964; John J. Klein, *Money and the Economy,* Harcourt, Brace & World, Inc., New York, 1970.

Elastic Supply   A measure of a relative responsiveness of a producer in supplying quantities of a good when the market price of the good changes. When a producer is responsive to price changes, supply is elastic; when he is relatively insensitive to price changes, supply is inelastic. The elasticity of supply is measured by the elasticity coefficient E_s:

$$E_s = \frac{\text{percentage change in quantity supplied}}{\text{percentage change in price}}$$

The main determinant of the elasticity of supply is the time during which a producer must respond to a given change in the price of a product. A given change in price will have a greater effect on the quantity supplied over the long run. A supply schedule is perfectly elastic if an unlimited amount is offered at all prices and perfectly inelastic if the quantity supplied is the same regardless of price. Supply elasticity is considered less useful as an economic concept than demand elasticity because the latter provides some indication of what is happening to the producer's revenue. For additional information, see George J. Stigler, *The Theory of Price,* 3d ed., The Macmillan Company, New York, 1966; Donald S. Watson, *Price Theory and Its Uses,* 2d ed., Houghton Mifflin Company, Boston, 1968, pp. 48–51.

Eminent Domain   The right of a government to take private property for public use even against the owner's will, provided that just compensation is paid. The right of eminent domain, considered a right of every sovereign state, is provided for in the Fifth Amendment to the U.S. Constitution, which states: "nor shall private property be taken for public use without just compensation." Nearly all states have similar provisions in their constitutions. The major problems connected with government's exercise of its right of eminent domain are the nature of the public uses for which the private property is needed, the nature of the property rights for which compensation must be paid, and the size of just compensation. The doctrine of eminent domain does not mean that the government must make compensation for acts adversely affecting the value of property if such action is part of the exercise of lawful power. Thus, such government acts as the lowering of tariffs or the declaration of war are not considered grounds for compensation for those who suffer losses.

For additional details, see C. Herman Pritchett, *The American Constitution*, McGraw-Hill Book Company, New York, 1959, chap. 36.

Employment The state of being employed. According to the concept of the U.S. Department of Labor, all persons who work for pay or profit or for fifteen hours or more without pay in a family business or farm are employed. Total employment is measured each month by the U.S. Bureau of the Census for the Department. During the week containing the twelfth of the month, census interviewers visit 50,000 households in 449 different areas, asking questions designed to learn who was employed and who was unemployed during the survey week. The Bureau also compiles from

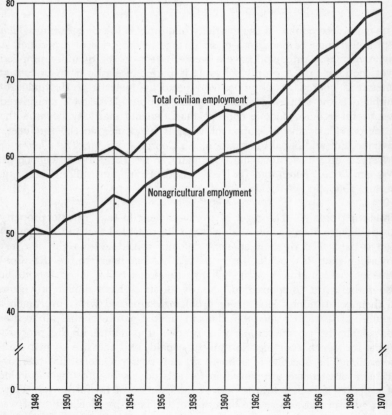

Total Employment vs. Nonagricultural Employment (Millions of people)

Total civilian employment

Nonagricultural employment

Source: U.S. Bureau of Labor Statistics.

payroll data civilian employment figures for all nonagricultural establishments. Its figures exclude proprietors, self-employed persons, and domestic servants. For a study of economic theory and its relationship in
determining the level of employment, see Abba P. Lerner, *Economics of
Employment*, McGraw-Hill Book Company, New York, 1951.

Employment Act of 1946   An act of Congress which placed the official
responsibility for promoting stable prosperity in the hands of the Federal
government. An essential objective of the act is the maximum utilization
of available resources, which means a low unemployment rate and a high
rate of utilization of industrial facilities. The act created little new authority for the management of the national economic program, but it did
establish additional machinery to achieve a better understanding and
focusing of attention on the important problems of the economy. It required that the President make an annual economic report to Congress on
current economic trends and prospects and that he recommend a program
designed to promote high levels of employment, production, and purchasing power. The Employment Act also established the Council of Economic Advisers and a Joint Committee on the Economic Report. For
further information, see Paul Strayer, "The Council of Economic Advisers: Political Economy on Trial," *American Economic Review*, vol. 40,
American Economic Association, Evanston, Ill., May, 1950, pp. 144–154;
Alvin H. Hansen, *Economic Policy and Full Employment*, McGraw-Hill
Book Company, New York, 1947; "The Employment Act in the Economic
Thinking of Our Times: A Symposium," *American Economic Review*,
American Economic Association, Evanston, Ill., May, 1957.

Enclosure   A process of fencing off agricultural land. The development
of enclosures was an important factor in the growth of English agriculture.
In the sixteenth century, the high price of wool induced many landowners
to undertake sheep raising on a large scale. For this, it was necessary to
have large pastures enclosed by fences or hedges and to remove the
peasants who were working small plots on the landowners' property.
Many peasants were unable to find other employment and had to go
onto the public rolls, with the result that laws were passed to limit the size
of flocks and to prevent the conversion of arable land to pasture. During
the second enclosure movement, from 1700 to 1845, 14 million acres of
farm land, or one-fourth of all the arable land in England, were enclosed
in this manner. Once again, many peasants were uprooted from their
land and forced to seek employment either on consolidated farms or in
the growing manufacturing industries. Some historians think that these
peasants, forced off their land by the enclosures, provided the large labor
force that was needed for the Industrial Revolution to be successful. For

additional details, see N. S. B. Gras, *A History of Agriculture in Europ and America*, Appleton-Century-Crofts, Inc., New York, 1940; see als Lord Ernle, *English Farming, Past and Present*, Longmans, Green & Co. Inc., New York, 1936; J. D. Chambers, "Enclosures and Labor Supply i the Industrial Revolution," *Economic History Review*, ser. 2, vol. 5, no. 3 pp. 319ff, Kraus Reprint Corp., New York, 1953.

Endogenous Business-Cycle Theory A business-cycle theory base on the self-generating cyclical process. Proponents of theories of th type recognize that the variation of business activity is influenced by out side shocks. Among endogenous theories are the profit-motive, overcapi talization-of-profits, psychological, monetary and credit, monetary-over investment, nonmonetary-overinvestment, and underconsumption theories For further discussion, see Elmer C. Bratt, *Business Cycles and Fore casting*, Richard D. Irwin, Inc., Homewood, Ill., 1961, chap. 4.

Endogenous Variables In econometrics, any economic time series tha influences a set of economic relationships that is being studied and is als itself influenced by changes in the same relationship—hence, a variabl that is determined within the system itself. For example, private wag payments, consumption, savings, investment, and profit are generall treated as endogenous variables in studies of a nation's aggregate eco nomic activity. For additional information, see Lawrence R. Klein, *A Introduction to Econometrics*, Prentice-Hall, Inc., Englewood Cliffs, N.J 1962.

Energy Source A material found in nature or in a manufactured prod uct that provides the power required for the manifold physical tasks per formed in the economy. In addition to coal, familiar energy sources ar crude petroleum, water, natural gas, and, far less important, wood. Th storage battery is a common example of a man-made energy source. I 1900 coal was by far the leading energy source in the U.S. More recently petroleum has assumed the primary role. The post-World War II perio has witnessed the appearance of new energy sources, including fissionabl materials, the source of nuclear energy. A new man-made energy sourc is the fuel cell, which produces electrical energy by means of chemica reactions among its components. For a detailed discussion of energy an its role in the U.S. economy, see Sam H. Schurr and Bruce C. Netschett *Energy and the American Economy, 1850–1975*. The Johns Hopkin Press, Baltimore, 1960; *Resources for Freedom*, a report of the President' Materials Policy Commission, Government Printing Office, Washington D.C., 1952; for a briefer account of the nation's current and future energy sources, see "Energy Sources to the Year 2000," *Chemical Week*, May 14, 1960.

Engel's Law The law which states that, as a family's income increases, a smaller and smaller proportion of the income is spent for food. It was named for Ernst Engel, a nineteenth-century German administrator and statistician who was the first to call attention to the different proportions of income spent for various categories of goods and services by different income groups in Saxony. More recently, it has become clear that other basic necessities of life, such as clothing and housing, similarly claim a declining share of a family's growing income. Thus, higher-income groups spend relatively and absolutely larger sums for luxury goods and services than do lower-income groups. Among modern offshoots of Engel's law is the concept of optional consumption, which states that a considerable proportion of consumer expenditures in relatively wealthy nations is devoted to goods and services not essential to physical well-being and that the consumer consequently has the option of spending or refraining from spending money for these items. A related concept is that of discretionary income, a measure of the share of consumer income that remains after consumers have made essential purchases and hence can be used for luxuries and less pressing expenditures. For a discussion of Engel's law, see Joseph A. Schumpeter, *History of Economic Analysis,* Oxford University Press, Fair Lawn, N.J., 1954, p. 961; see also *Discretionary Income,* National Industrial Conference Board, Technical Paper 6, New York, 1958; for a related discussion, see Dexter M. Keezer and Associates, *New Forces in American Business,* McGraw-Hill Book Company, New York, 1959, chaps. 4 and 5; see also J. K. Galbraith, *The Affluent Society,* Houghton Mifflin Company, Boston, 1958; for a discussion of consumer spending patterns, see Willard W. Cochrane and Carolyn S. Bell, *The Economics of Consumption,* McGraw-Hill Book Company, New York, 1956, chap. 11.

Engrossment The buying of commodities in large quantities in order to create a monopoly and sell them at a higher price. Engrossing, or the purchase of goods wholesale to sell them again wholesale, was a criminal offense in England from 1552 to 1844. The practice of engrossing is now more commonly known as cornering the market.

Entrepreneur A proprietor of a business enterprise who recognizes opportunities to introduce a new product, a new productive process, or an improved organization. He raises the necessary money, assembles the factors of production, and organizes the management. The entrepreneur may or may not be a capitalist, in that he may or may not provide funds of his own. He does not, however, function simply as a routine manager. Many economists of all schools, including Karl Marx, have emphasized the contribution of the entrepreneur to the development of capitalist economies, but Joseph A. Schumpeter, who argued that the rate of growth in an economy depends in large measure on the activities of entrepreneurs, has probably put greater emphasis on the entrepreneurial function than any other economist. For a classic statement of the entrepreneur's role, see Joseph A. Schumpeter, *The Theory of Economic Development*, Harvard University Press, Cambridge, Mass., 1934.

Equal Pay for Equal Work   The principle that the pay rate should apply to the job and not to the worker. Employees doing identical jobs should be paid at the same rate. Thus, women should be paid at the same rate as men, and Negroes at the same rate as whites for substantially identical operations.

Equilibrium   The state of an economic system in which all forces for change are balanced, so that the net tendency to change is zero. An economic system is considered to be in equilibrium when all the significant variables show no change over a period of time. For example, at an equilibrium price for a given good, the buyers in the market are just willing to purchase the entire amount of the good which the sellers are willing to offer. The equilibrium price is the only one at which both buyers and sellers will be satisfied, so that while given supply-and-demand conditions remain unchanged, the price remains the same. The concept of equilibrium is used in economics not only as a description of a final set of conditions but also as an indication of the direction in which economic variables are headed. Often, the external conditions defining the equilibrium position are constantly changing, so that equilibrium is never attained. It is still useful to know the direction in which the economic variables are changing, however, whether or not they are expected to reach the equilibrium value. There are two general types of economic equilibriums, stable and unstable. In a stable equilibrium, any movement away from the equilibrium level automatically generates forces tending to bring the variables back to the equilibrium level. On the other hand, any movement away from an unstable equilibrium generates forces tending to move the variables even farther away from the equilibrium level, even though at the equilibrium position itself there is no set pressure for change. For example, when the slope of the supply curve for a given good is steeper than the slope of its demand curve, a stable-equilibrium position is determined, whereas if the slope of the supply curve is less steep than that of the demand curve, an unstable equilibrium results. For additional details, see Frank Knight, *On the History and Method of Economics*,

The University of Chicago Press, Chicago, 1956, chap. 8; V. Dubey, "Equilibrium: Static and Dynamic," *Indian Journal of Economics,* vol. XXXV, pp. 131–149, Indian Economic Association, University of Allahabad, Allahabad, India, October, 1954; Paul A. Samuelson, "The Stability of Equilibrium: Comparative Statics and Dynamics," *Econometrica,* vol. 9, pp. 97–120, Econometric Society, Menasha, Wis., April, 1941; Edward Shapiro, *Macroeconomic Analysis,* Harcourt, Brace & World, Inc., New York, 1966.

Equity The excess of a firm's assets over its liabilities. In a proprietorship or partnership, equity is the claim or stake of the owner or owners. In a corporation, it is measured by the capital stock and surplus. For further information, see J. Fred Weston and Eugene F. Brigham, *Managerial Finance,* 2d ed., Holt, Rinehart and Winston, Inc., New York, 1966, pp. 397–408.

Equity Capital The total investment in a business by all its owners. Investors supply equity capital to a corporation when they buy newly issued shares of its stock. They are not promised a fixed rate of interest but participate in the profits. Firms can raise additional money by accepting a greater amount of equity capital and by admitting the persons who furnish it into the enterprise as stockholders or owners. Equity capital is usually associated with the development of a new business and with business expansion. For further information, see D. Durand, "The Cost of Debt and Equity Funds for Business: Trends and Problems of Measurement," in Ezra Solomon (ed.), *The Management of Corporate Capital,* The Free Press of Glencoe, New York, 1959; J. Fred Weston and Eugene F. Brigham, *Managerial Finance,* 2d ed., Holt, Rinehart and Winston, Inc., New York, 1966, pp. 397–408.

Error Term The error term in an econometric model is a special variable (usually designated by U) to allow for the facts that economic theory is necessarily incomplete, that the analyst may not have specified the correct relationship, and that some variables affecting the model have almost certainly been omitted. The error term can be included as an additive, multiplicative, or exponential factor. It is always assumed to be a random real variable, and it can be either discrete or continuous. The error term is never observed, but its existence is established by the known imperfections of econometric technique. After estimates of a model's parameters (for example, the familiar $\hat{a}$ and $\hat{b}$ of a linear equation) have been derived, it is possible to compute residuals $\hat{u}$ as estimates of the error u. For additional information, see Stefan Valavanis, *Econometrics,* McGraw-Hill Book Company, New York, 1959.

Escalator Clause   A contractual provision in the financial terms of an agreement that requires the payment of automatic increases or decreases in the event of certain price changes. One of the most familiar forms of the escalator clause is that found in wage agreements, in which the clause provides for adjustments in wage rates on the basis of increases or decreases in consumer prices. The path-making agreement was between General Motors and the Auto Workers in 1948. In periods of relative price stability, escalator clauses lose some of their attraction for labor unions, but in periods of inflation interest increases. The number of workers covered by an escalator clause rose from about 500,000 in the late 1940s to 2.5 million in September, 1952. During the 1954 recession, the number declined and then rose to 4 million in 1958. The number was down to 2 million in 1966, after a long period of price stability. Interest in escalator clauses rose tremendously in the late 1960s and early 1970s with the inflationary wave. A typical clause provides for a 1-cent hourly wage change for a half-point change in the U.S. Bureau of Labor Statistics' consumer price index. There is always a specified floor to the downward movement of wage escalators. Other price and cost indices, such as the Bureau of Labor Statistics' wholesale price index and *Engineering News-Record's* construction cost index, are used in escalation agreements to adjust costs of plant and equipment. For a discussion of escalator clauses in labor contracts, see U.S. Department of Labor, *Prices, Escalation and Economic Stability*, Washington, D.C., 1971, chap. 3.

Escape Clause   A provision in U.S. trade agreements that enables the U.S. to terminate or modify a specific trade concession if the concession threatens serious injury to a domestic industry. First suggested by President Franklin D. Roosevelt in 1934, it became applicable to agreements concluded under the National Trade Agreements Act by means of an executive order of February, 1947, and was written into the act in 1948. The Trade Agreements Extension Act of 1951 made the inclusion of an escape clause in all new trade agreements a statutory requirement. Recommendations to the President for use of the escape clause originate in the Tariff Commission, which, at its own motion or at the request of an interested party, is required to investigate whether or not a proposed or actual tariff reduction has injured or is likely to injure an American industry. The Commission has recommended action for only one-fourth of the relief applicants, and the President has followed their recommendations only about one-half of the time. Where tariffs have been reinstated, the imports affected have been of little economic significance to the U.S. Escape-clause action does not give an American industry indefinite protection, because a review of each case of tariff relief is required two years

Typical Cost-of-Living Escalator Increases in Selected Industries, 1957–1969

Industry	Increases (in Cents per Hour) in Allowances Effective in										
	1969	1968	1967	1966	1965	1964	1963	1962	1961	1960	1959
Automobile	5	5	2 or 5	11	4	3	3	3	2	4	3
Farm and construction equipment	5	5	5	11	4	3	3 or 4	3	1 or 2	4	3
Aerospace	8–17	3–13	3–8	5–10	4	4	3 or 4	3	3	1 or 2	2 or 3
Trucking	4	3	11	3	.....	.....	4	1	.....	4	2
Meatpacking	16	12	5	8	4	4	3	2	2	3	3
Steel	.....	.....	.....	.....	.....	.....	.....	.....	3	3	1
Aluminum	.....	.....	.....	.....	.....	.....	.....	.....	3	3	1
Containers (cans)	.....	.....	.....	.....	.....	.....	.....	.....	3	3	3
Railroads	.....	.....	.....	.....	.....	.....	.....	.....	.....	.....	3
Mean increase	5.5	4.9	5.8	8.3	4.0	3.3	3.3	2.4	2.5	3.4	2.3

SOURCE: "Collective Bargaining Calendar for 1970," *Monthly Labor Review*, January, 1970, p. 13.

after the granting of relief and in each year thereafter. Although many factors are used to determine injury to an industry, production trends and profit levels are employed most often. Since 1955 injury to one product of a multiproduct industry is considered acceptable as serious injury, although previously injury was applicable only to the overall operations of an industry. See I. B. Kravis, "The Trade Agreement Escape Clause," *American Economic Review*, American Economic Association, Evanston, Ill., 1954, p. 319; Stephen Enke and Virgil Salera, *International Economics*, Prentice-Hall, Inc., Englewood Cliffs, N.J., 1957; Thomas B. Curtis and John Robert Vastine, Jr., *The Kennedy Round and the Future of American Trade*, Frederick A. Praeger, Inc., New York, 1971.

Escrow A deed, bond, or other written document adopted by two parties and deposited with a third party for safekeeping, to be surrendered by the latter to the grantee only upon fulfillment of some condition. For example, the buyer of a factory may place funds in escrow in a bank, and the bank official will release the funds when the seller of the factory provides the deed.

Establishment A statistical concept of the U.S. Bureau of the Census, that covers plants, stores, or offices at specific locations with one or more employees. The number, location, and other data on establishments are used primarily in market analysis. Tabulations of establishments differ from those of firms in two important respects. First, establishments include each store, office, or plant as a separate entity, while firms combine those under a single ownership or under a single corporate charter. Second, breakdowns of other statistical information on establishments are more narrowly defined than those for firms. For example, capital investment for manufacturing establishments covers only investment going into manufacturing plants, whereas capital investment for manufacturing firms covers all the investment of these firms, including that spent for offices or wholesale and retail outlets. For a detailed discussion of the concept, see U.S. Bureau of the Budget, *Standard Industrial Classification Manual*, 1958; for industry and regional data, see U.S. Department of Commerce, U.S. censuses of 1958 and 1963.

Estate Tax A levy on the entire estate left by a decedent. Whereas an inheritance tax is based on the amount of the estate received by each beneficiary, the estate tax is levied on the value of the entire estate before it has been divided. The estate tax is simpler and more productive than the inheritance tax, because it avoids the sometimes difficult task of determining the value of each beneficiary's share. On the other hand, the inheritance tax is considered to be more equitable than the estate tax, because it is more closely linked to the heirs' ability to pay. There is often little or no difference between the effects of estate and inheritance taxes, since in most cases the estate is passed on to the survivor's spouse. The estate tax is usually based on a steeply progressive rate schedule, so that it involves a sizable redistribution of wealth. Avoidance of estate taxes is attempted principally through gifts and the creation of limited interests in an estate. For additional details, see Boris Bittker, *Federal Income, Estate, and Gift Taxation*, 3d ed., Little, Brown and Company, Boston, 1964; Richard B. Stephens and Thomas L. Marr, *Federal Estate and Gift Tax*, Tax Club Press, Tucson, Ariz., 1959.

Euler's Theorem   The proposition that, if a production function involves constant returns to scale, the sum of the marginal products will equal the total product. Euler's theorem played an important role in the development of the marginal-productivity theory of distribution. The theorem involves the partial differentiation of homogeneous equations. It states that if $f(x,y)$ is homogeneous to degree n, then:

$$x \frac{\partial f}{\partial x} + y \frac{\partial f}{\partial y} = nf(x,y)$$

To prove the theorem, let $P = f(L,C)$ be the production function involving labor (L) and capital (C) for a given good. Since it is assumed that the production has constant returns to scale, the production function is linearly homogeneous, and Euler's theorem can be applied, with $n = 1$ as such:

$$L \frac{\partial F}{\partial L} + C \frac{\partial f}{\partial c} = f(L,C) = P$$

Since $\partial F/\partial L$ and $\partial F/\partial C$ are the marginal products of a single unit of labor and capital respectively, the equation states that the marginal product of labor $\partial f/\partial L$, multiplied by the number of laborers (L), plus the marginal product of capital $\partial F/\partial C$, multiplied by the number of capital units (C), equals the total product, P. For additional details, see James M. Henderson and Richard E. Quandt, *Microeconomic Theory*, 2d ed., McGraw-Hill Book Company, New York, 1971; see also Joan Robinson, "Euler's Theorem and the Problem of Distribution," *Economic Journal*, Royal Economic Society, London, vol. 44, pp. 398–414, September, 1934.

Euro-Dollars   Dollar deposits with U.S. banks that are acquired by foreigners and are redeposited in banks outside the U.S., mainly in Europe. The trading center for Euro-dollars is London, where merchant bankers lend these dollars to local or foreign banks or to commercial borrowers. This form of financing is playing an increasingly important role in world trade, providing the nucleus of a trade international money market. In theory, a typical Euro-dollar transaction works as follows: A West German commercial bank with a surplus of marks may exchange them with the West German central bank for dollars, which the central bank has accumulated because of the persistent surplus in the German balance of payments. The German bank then puts its newly acquired dollars to work in London at an interest rate of 3 or 4%. The London banker relends the dollars, perhaps to a Japanese banker at 6 or 7%, and the Japanese can now finance imports calling for payment in dollars. The Euro-dollar market provides incentives for both borrowers and lenders. Short-term holders of dollars can put their money to work at interest rates above those available in New York, and short-term borrowers generally can obtain credit at rates below those in the United States and abroad. For a recent report, see Herber V. Prochnow (ed.), *The Eurodollar*, Rand McNally & Company, Chicago, 1970; for two studies, see International Monetary Fund, *International Monetary Fund Staff Papers*, Washington, D.C., December, 1961; Alan R. Holmes and Fred Klopstock, "Market for Dollar Deposits in Europe," *Monthly Review*, Federal Reserve Bank of New York, November, 1960.

Ever-Normal Granary A plan for agricultural price stabilization based on the Biblical concept of seven lean and seven fat years. In essence, it attempts to stabilize supplies by removing crops from the market in periods of surplus production and returning them to the market in periods of relative scarcity. The concept of an ever-normal granary has been proposed at various times as the basis for international commodity agreements, and it is the basis for U.S. agricultural support programs. For long-run successful operation, the ever-normal granary plan requires the disposal of surpluses. Two powerful forces operate against such disposal: First, the initial effect of government purchases, whether they are made directly or through nonrecourse loans, is to increase effective demand, which stimulates further production, rather than to reduce the supply. Second, farmers and farm lobbies have a stronger voice in Congress than the consumers who benefit from reduced prices. In the end, it appears that the ever-normal granary becomes an ever-growing granary. See Rainer Schickele, *Agricultural Policy, Farm Policy and National Welfare*, McGraw-Hill Book Company, New York, 1954; see also Charles P. Kindleberger, *International Economics*, Richard D. Irwin, Inc., Homewood, Ill., 1958.

Ex Ante A Latin phrase meaning "beforehand" and "as applied." In business-cycle theory, it refers to quantities of investment, savings, or consumption defined in terms of action planned at the beginning of the period in question. It alludes to the anticipations, calculations, and plans driving the dynamic economic machinery forward. Recognition of the time period under discussion is important in dynamic economic theory. In this context, the concepts of ex ante and ex post were originated by Gunnar Myrdal in his discussion of monetary theory. Myrdal pointed out that there is an important distinction between prospective (ex ante) and retrospective (ex post) methods of calculating economic quantities. The ex ante method is based on discounted anticipations or forecasts of expected profitability, which is a decisive element in business decisions. For further discussion, see Gunnar Myrdal, *Monetary Equilibrium*, William Hodges Co., Ltd., London, 1939.

Excess Profits Tax A tax on profits above a specified level that is defined as normal. Excess profits taxes are usually applied only in periods of wars or high defense spending. Their purpose is to capture those additional profits which grow out of the high government spending in wartime. The U.S. had excess profits taxes in the periods 1917–1921, 1940–1945, and 1950–1953. The most important of the three taxes, the World War II excess profits tax, was set at 95% of all income in excess of the income that was determined to be a normal profit. Normal profit for the individual firm could be based either on a 5 to 8% return on investment or on the average rate of earnings during the period 1936–1939. Administration of the excess profits tax resulted in many problems, especially in the measurement of invested capital, the treatment of borrowed capital and accumulated deficits, the readjustment of firm size, and the treatment of new businesses. For further information, see C. J. Curran, *Excess Profits Taxation*, American Council on Public Affairs, Washington, 1943; Marion Gillim, *The Incidence of Excess Profits Taxation*, Columbia University Press, New York, 1945; "Symposium on Excess Profits Tax," *National Tax Journal*, vol. IV, National Tax Association, Boston, September, 1951.

Excess Reserves The surplus of cash and deposits owned by commercial member banks of the Federal Reserve System over what they are legally required to hold at reserve banks or in their own vaults. The excess-reserve position of a bank is an indication of its ability to invest in government bonds or to make loans to customers. Therefore, if the Federal Reserve System is trying to stimulate business in periods of economic sluggishness, it buys government bonds from private sellers, thus increasing bank reserves; it takes the opposite course when inflation is a problem. At any given time, however, reserves do not give a complete picture of the potential of commercial-bank lending, since commercial banks can borrow at the local Federal Reserve bank to obtain reserves. A better indication of the banking system's lending potential consists of free reserves, that is, excess reserves minus borrowing at the reserve banks. The concept of excess reserves is theoretically applicable to banks that are not members of the Federal Reserve System, but since reserve rules in each state differ, no statistics are available on a current basis for nonmembers' excess reserves. The dollar volume of free and excess reserves is reported monthly in *Federal Reserve Bulletin,* Washington, D.C.; for a criticism of the use of excess reserves as a reflection of monetary policy and the behavior of excess reserves in the business cycle, see E. M. Lerner, "Criticism of Free Reserves," *Review of Economics and Statistics,* pp. 225–228, Harvard University Press, Cambridge, Mass., May, 1962.

Exchange Control   A system of governmental regulation of foreign exchange. Under this system, all purchases and sales of foreign exchange are handled by the government, which allocates or rations the supply of foreign currencies to its citizens. In this way, a country facing balance-of-payment difficulties may restrict imports to the amount earned through the accumulation of foreign exchange by its nationals. The government can force a balance-of-payments equilibrium on the nation by restricting imports to the value of exports. Exchange control can also be used to discriminate against importers so that only desired goods are imported. For example, in order to encourage imports of more essential goods, foreign exchange may be denied for the importation of luxury or nonessential goods. For further information, see Armen A. Alchian and William R. Allen, *University Economics,* Wadsworth Publishing Company, Inc., Belmont, Calif., 1967, chap. 37; David B. Zenoff and Jack Zwick, *International Financial Management,* Prentice-Hall, Inc., Englewood Cliffs, N.J., 1969.

Excise Tax   A levy imposed on the sale of a particular commodity. An excise tax is usually levied on the manufacturers of consumer goods, but it can be shifted to the consumers of the product by including the amount of the tax in the selling price. The tax is frequently paid by the purchase of tax stamps, which must be affixed to the product before it enters distribution channels. In the U.S., excise taxes are part of both Federal and state taxation systems. Commodities subject to excise taxation usually are widely consumed, have a relatively inelastic demand, and generally are not among the necessities of life. Among the more common excise taxes are those levied on cigarettes, alcohol, and gasoline. Excise taxes may be specific, amounting to a fixed sum per unit of the product (e.g., 5 cents per pound of tobacco), or they may be ad valorem, amounting to a fixed percentage of the selling price of the product (e.g., 4% of the selling price). Although excise taxes are considered regressive, placing a larger burden on the poor than on the rich, they offer the advantages of stable revenues, a low cost of collection, and the ability to produce revenue immediately. They also can be used to regulate consumption (e.g., of luxuries). For additional details, see Roy G. Blakely and Gladys C. Blakely, *Sales Taxes and Other Excises,* Public Administration Service, Chicago, 1945; J. K. Hall, "Excise Tax Incidence and the Postwar Economy," *American Economic Review Supplement,* American Economic Association, Evanston, Ill., March, 1942.

Exogenous Business-Cycle Theory A business-cycle theory based on the observation of the variable which exerts an influence on, but is not itself influenced by, the economy. Proponents of theories of this type explain expansions and recessions in terms of these external factors. Among exogenous theories are the sunspot, weather, war, innovation, population, and episodic theories. For further discussion, see Elmer C. Bratt, *Business Cycles and Forecasting,* Richard D. Irwin, Inc., Homewood, Ill., 1961, chap. 4.

Exogenous Variable In econometrics, any economic time series that influences a set of economic relationships that is being studied but is not itself influenced by changes in those relationships—hence, a variable that is determined outside the system. For example, export statistics are usually considered an exogenous variable in a study of a nation's aggregate economic activity. For additional information, see Lawrence R. Klein, *An Introduction to Econometrics,* Prentice-Hall, Inc., Englewood Cliffs, N.J., 1962; ———, *Textbook of Econometrics,* Row, Peterson & Company, Evanston, Ill., 1953.

Expansion, Business-Cycle The phase of the business cycle during which general business activity is rising from the trough to the next peak. The amplitude of expansion may be expected to show a high degree of consistency with the rate of growth during the previous expansion. Expansion rates are usually higher when the expansion follows a severe contraction than when it follows a mild contraction. The severity of the previous recession also affects the length of time required to return from the trough to the prerecession level of business activity. Moreover, there is a tendency toward slower growth after the initial expansion. For a detailed discussion of expansion in the business cycle, see Geoffrey H. Moore (ed.), *Business Cycle Indicators,* Princeton University Press, Princeton, N.J., 1961, vol. I.

Expansion, Capital-Expenditure The increase in plant and equipment installed to raise output. Since 1968 about two-thirds of capital expenditures in the U.S. have been devoted to the expansion of manufacturing facilities. Manufacturers emphasized the modernization of facilities rather than the expansion of new capacity in the period 1969–1971 because of the excessive industrial capacity built up between 1965 and 1968. For statistical data on expenditures for expansionary purposes, see *Annual Surveys of Business' Plans for New Plants and Equipment*, McGraw-Hill Department of Economics, New York.

Expected Value   The mean value of single observations drawn from a finite or infinite universe in repeated sampling. Valavanis has described the expected value as a statistical or combinatorial concept in contrast to the arithmetic mean, an algebraic concept. The expected value is not necessarily the most frequently encountered value, and it need not be a possible value. For additional information, see Stefan Valavanis, *Econometrics*, McGraw-Hill Book Company, New York, 1959.

Exploitation   Payment of a wage less than the worker's marginal-revenue product (his contribution to production). If a worker's pay is $1.75 per hour but his contribution to production is worth $2.00 per hour, he is being exploited at 25 cents per hour. It has been found that exploitation is more likely to exist in high-wage industries than in low-wage ones. In the past, other definitions have not been so precise. According to Karl Marx, the amount by which a worker was being exploited was the difference between his wage for a given period of time and the amount that he added to the value of production in that time. Since this amount was also equal to the capitalist's profit, exploitation would always exist under capitalism. Joan Robinson also provided a definition: payment to a worker of a wage less than the value of his marginal physical product. See Karl Marx, *Capital*, Charles Kerr and Company, Chciago, Ill., 1906; for a discussion of the current meaning, see Gordon F. Bloom, "A Reconsideration of the Theory of Exploitation," *Quarterly Journal of Economics*, Harvard University Press, Cambridge, Mass., May, 1941; see also Joan Robinson, *The Economics of Imperfect Competition*, St. Martin's Press, Inc., New York, 1945.

Export   A good or commodity that is shipped from one country or area to another in the conduct of foreign trade. The country that ships the good is the exporter. In the U.S., exports usually are higher than imports, so that the U.S. has generally enjoyed a trade surplus. For example, U.S. exports averaged $84 billion higher than exports for the years 1955 to 1970. However, exports were lower than imports for the first time in 1971. This was one of the reasons for the devaluation of the dollar at the end of that year. For further information, see *An Introduction to Doing*

Import and Export Business, Chamber of Commerce of the United States, Washington, D.C., 1964; Edward Ewing Pratt, *Modern International Commerce,* Allyn and Bacon, Inc., Boston, 1956; Morton Ehrlich and John Hein, *The Competitive Position of United States Exports,* National Industrial Conference Board, Inc., Studies in Business Economics, no. 101, New York, 1968.

Merchandise Exports (Billions of dollars)

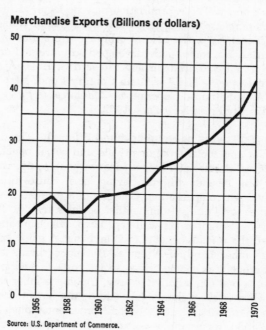

Source: U.S. Department of Commerce.

Export Trade Act   *See Webb-Pomerene Act.*

Ex Post   A Latin phrase meaning "afterward" and "as applied." In business cycle theory, it refers to quantities of investment, savings, or consumption defined in terms of measurement made at the end of the period in question. Thus, it refers to realized investment, savings, or consumption. Recognition of the time period under discussion is important in dynamic economic theory. In this context, the concepts of ex post and ex ante were originated by Gunnar Myrdal in his discussion of monetary theory. Myrdal pointed out that there is an important distinction between retrospective (ex post) and prospective (ex ante) methods of calculating economic quantities. The ex post method is based on actual bookkeeping results and represents past experience. Ex post profitability is used only indirectly as evidence of the possibility of future profitability. For further discussion, see Gunnar Myrdal, *Monetary Equilibrium*, William Hodges Co., Ltd., London, 1939.

Expropriation The forceful removal of an individual's property. Usually, the term refers to the acquisition of private property by the state or some other public authority. The expropriation may be legal, as in the case of a government's purchase of property under the rights of eminent domain, or it may be illegal, as in the case of arbitrary expropriation of foreign-owned industries by some underdeveloped countries. For additional details, see Norman S. Buchanan and Howard S. Ellis, *Approaches to Economic Development*, The Twentieth Century Fund, New York, 1955, pp. 356–358; A. A. Fatouros, *Government Guarantees to Foreign Investors*, Columbia University Press, New York, 1962.

Externalities (Spillovers or Neighborhood Effects) The discrepancies between private and social costs or private and social benefits. The key aspect of externalities is interdependence without compensation. Some individual or firm benefits without paying, or it causes others to have higher costs without compensation. Consumption externalities exist when someone gains or loses utility from another person's activity. For instance, neighbor A enjoys neighbor B's well-kept lawn, which means that social benefits exceed the private benefits to B and that A gains external economies. On the other hand, if A envies B's higher living standard, he suffers an external diseconomy, since social costs exceed private costs. In production, if one firm's activities—say, training a labor force—benefit other firms (when workers change jobs and do not have to be retrained), external economies exist. Conversely, and prevalent today, if one firm's activities—pollution, for example—cost other firms and society more than is recorded on the firm's private accounting statements, external diseconomies exist. The concept of externalities is important for economic theory and policy. In the former case, the existence of externalities makes it impossible to reach a Pareto optimum unless external economies are exactly offset by external diseconomies. In the latter case, the existence of externalities provides a strong argument for government intervention in the private economy. See A. C. Pigou, *The Economics of Welfare*, The Macmillan Company, New York, 1932; James Meade, "External Economies and Diseconomies in a Competitive Situation," reprinted in *American Economic Association Readings in Welfare Economics*, Richard D. Irwin, Inc., Homewood, Ill., 1969; Francis Bator, "The Anatomy of Market Failure," *Quarterly Journal of Economics*, vol. LXXII, pp. 351–379, August, 1958; Donald Watson, *Price Theory and Its Uses*, Houghton Mifflin Company, Boston, 1968, pp. 291–292.

Extractive Industry   An industry which obtains products directly from the land or water. The extractive industries, such as forestry, mining, and oil and natural gas production, are responsible for the production of all natural resources. In 1969 the extractive industries of the U.S. produced $16 billion worth of output and employed about 650,000 workers. For additional details, see John G. Glover and Rudolph Lagai, *The Development of American Industries*, 4th ed., Simmons-Boardman Publishing Corporation, New York, 1958; H. Landsberg et al., *Resources in America's Future*, The Johns Hopkins Press, Baltimore, 1963; D. Tyler, *From the Ground Up*, McGraw-Hill Book Company, New York, 1948.

Extraneous Estimates (A Priori Estimates)   Estimates of parameters that do not emerge in final form from computations but instead involve the use of related economic information not obtained from the available sample of data being studied. For example, a priori information can be used to overcome barriers caused by multicollinearity in multiple correlation. For additional information, see Karl A. Fox, *Intermediate Economic Statistics*, John Wiley & Sons, Inc., New York, 1968.

Extremes (Outliers)   Values in the irregular component of economic time series which are so far from the mean of the distribution of irregulars that they tend to distort the estimates of season and trend-cycle components. These values are usually caused by sudden, pronounced occurrences, such as strikes. They must be identified and modified or removed before a final estimation of seasonal and trend-cycle components can be made.

F

Fabian Socialism   The theory that socialism can be introduced gradually and through parliamentary procedures without violence and revolution. It was originally espoused by the Fabian Society in Great Britain, which took its name from Fabius Cunctator, the Roman general who in the war against Hannibal avoided decisive battles and restricted himself to delaying tactics because he knew that time was on his side. Characteristically, the Fabian Society believes that, in the name of individual freedom and social welfare, most measures to which Socialists aspire will gradually but inevitably be introduced and that this will be accomplished by democratic processes. This view played a major role in the establishment of the British Labor Party in 1900. Members of the Fabian Society, among them Sidney and Beatrice Webb and George Bernard Shaw, published hundreds of tracts, some of which are reprinted in *Fabian Essays,* Jubilee Editions, George Allen & Unwin, Ltd., London, 1948; for Fabian economic theory, especially as it differs from Marxism, see Paul M. Sweezy, "Fabian Political Economy," *Journal of Political Economy,* The University of Chicago Press, Chicago, Ill., June, 1949.

Face-Amount Certificate Company An investment company that promises to pay a fixed amount of money at a specified maturity date to holders of its certificates. It requires the holder to pay a specified amount periodically for ten to twenty years. The purchaser of a face-amount certificate gains compound interest on the money that he invests, but the interest rate is low because the guaranteed payment at maturity forces the company to make conservative investments. The similarity of face-amount certificates to endowment insurance policies (although they lack the insurance feature of these policies) and their low interest rate compared with the rates of savings banks and savings bonds explain why only six certificate companies were registered with the U.S. Securities and Exchange Commission on June 30, 1967. See U.S. Securities and Exchange Commission, *Annual Reports;* Investment Company Act of 1940; Commission on Interstate and Foreign Commerce, *Report of the Security and Exchange Commission on the Public Policy Implications of Investment Company Growth,* Dec. 2, 1966.

Factoring A type of business finance in which financial specialists called factors take responsibility for collection and the credit of their clients. Let us assume that an apparel manufacturer annually sells $100,000 worth of merchandise to various department stores, which are allowed sixty days to pay their accounts. The manufacturer transfers these accounts to his factor who accepts the responsibility for making collections and absorbs any credit losses. The factor pays the manufacturer $90,000 and retains about 10% of the total amount to cover various charges, which include the factoring commission of about 2% and the interest on the money advanced, normally computed at 6% per annum on the basis of the daily net debit balance. Factoring differs from other types of accounts receivables financing in two essential respects. First, the factor assumes the seller's credit functions, including credit investigation and record keeping. Second, he buys the receivables outright, that is, without recourse to the seller for credit losses. In 1970, U.S. businesses received about $6 billion worth of financing through factoring. For a discussion of the advantages and disadvantages of factoring, see Clyde William Phelps, *The Role of Factoring in Modern Business Finance,* Commercial Credit Company, Baltimore, 1956.

Factor of Production An economic resource which goes into the production of a good. The three major productive factors are property resources, including land; capital; and human resources, or labor. Land includes all natural resources: land itself, mineral deposits, forests, etc. Capital includes all man-made aids to production, such as buildings, machinery, and transportation facilities. Labor includes all the human physical and mental talents employed in producing goods. Entrepreneurial ability is often considered a fourth factor of production; it includes the organization of the other three factors for productive purposes, innovation, and the bearing of the risks of the business operation. Since all economic resources are relatively scarce and limited in supply, they all receive some type of income for their services. Income for the use of land is rent, income for use of capital in interest, and the income of labor is wages. Income for entrepreneurial ability is profits. For further information, see William Fellner, *Modern Economic Analysis,* McGraw-Hill Book Company, New York, 1960; Donald S. Watson, *Price Theory and Its Uses,* 2d ed., Houghton Mifflin Company, Boston, 1968, pp. 400–417.

Fair Rate of Return The percentage of profitability which a public utility is entitled to earn in order to pay interest and dividends and purchase new plants and equipment. Establishment of a fair rate of return is an important part of the regulation of public utilities since it is largely on this basis that public-utility rates are set and adjusted. Factors considered by regulatory commissions in the U.S. in establishing a fair return include the rate necessary to attract capital to the given utility company, the rates earned by comparable but unregulated industries, and the historical cost of capital to the utility. There may be other important factors, such as the record of the public utility, the effects of taxation, and competition. In some states, the rate of return is increased or decreased according to the efficiency of the service. The fair rate of return for most public utilities usually varies from 6 to 7%. For further information, see Ellsworth Nichols, "Ruling Principles of Utility Regulation: Rate of Return," *Public Utilities Reports*, Washington, D.C., 1955; James Bonbright, *Principles of Public Utility Rates*, Columbia University Press, New York, 1961, chap. 15.

Fair-Trade Law   A state statute that permits resale price agreements by which manufacturers can set minimum retail prices for certain commodities. A fear of unbridled competition and a belief that the growth of chain stores would force independent retailers out of business led to the rise of fair-trade laws in the U.S. Such laws were aimed especially at the elimination of the practice of using a loss leader to attract customers. Loss leaders often caused hardship to specialized retailers, who could not afford to meet this competition. A fair-trade law allows the manufacturer of a brand-name good to fix a minimum resale price and, in some cases, to fix the final resale price, thus preventing the use of the good as a loss leader. Generally, a contract made between the manufacturer and one retailer becomes binding on all the sellers when they are notified. A sale below the fixed floor price is allowed in only a few cases, such as damage to goods or discontinuance of a line of products. The first fair-trade law was passed by California in 1931, and by 1955 only three states lacked a resale price-maintenance law. The U.S. Supreme Court upheld such laws in 1936, and the Miller-Tydings Act, passed by Congress in the following year, suspended the antitrust laws as they applied to resale price agreements. This act authorized the use of such voluntary agreements in interstate commerce, provided that they applied only to brand-name products and were legal in the state involved. In 1952, Congress passed the McGuire Act, which amended the antitrust laws to exempt resale price-fixing contracts that applied to all sellers, whether or not they were part of the original contract, as long as such contracts were permitted under state law. For additional information, see E. T. Grether, *Price Control under Fair Trade Legislation*, Oxford University Press, Fair Lawn, N.J., 1939; U.S. Federal Trade Commission, *Report on Resale Price Maintenance*, Washington, D.C., 1945; E. H. Gault, *Fair Trade*, Michigan Business Studies, The University of Michigan Press, Ann Arbor, Mich., 1939, vol. IX, no. 2.

Family   A statistical concept that attempts to measure the number of households composed of individuals related by blood, marriage, or adoption and residing together. All such persons are considered members of one family. The average family size in the U.S. is about 3.7 persons. In March, 1970, there were 51.2 million families in the U.S., or only about 625,000 more than in 1960. Because of the age distribution of the population in the years 1955 to 1967, in which there were fewer persons in marriageable-age groups because of the relatively low birthrates of the

1930s, the absolute increase in the number of families was lower than in earlier years. The number of families was expected to increase more rapidly after 1967, when there would be many more persons of marriageable age in the population because of the higher birthrates of the 1940s. The number and characteristics of families are used to determine market potentials for consumer durable goods, such as passenger cars and house furnishings. For definitions, historical statistics, and forecasts of the number of families in the U.S. population, see U.S. Bureau of the Census, *Current Population Reports: Population Characteristics,* ser. P–20.

Number of Families in the U.S. (Millions)

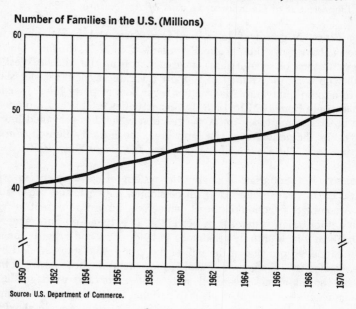

Source: U.S. Department of Commerce.

Family-sized Farm   A farm where the farm operator and his family provide a major portion of the labor and management. On farms of this type, capital investment is relatively lower than on commercial farms. Most farm operators, however, derive from their farms a level of living approximately equal to that received in comparable occupations off the farm.

Farm   A tract of land devoted to the raising of animals or the growing of crops that is usually operated by an owner or a tenant. According to the 1964 *Census of Agriculture* in the U.S., agricultural operations existed if (1) any livestock was kept on the place; (2) a total of twenty or more chickens, turkeys, or ducks were kept on the place; (3) any grain, hay, tobacco, or field crops were grown; (4) a total of twenty or more fruit trees, grapevines, or nut trees were on the place; or (5) any vegetables, berries, or nursery or greenhouse products were grown on the place for sale. Places of less than 10 acres were counted as farms if sales of agricultural products in 1964 amounted to at least $250. Farms of 10 acres or more were counted as farms if sales of agricultural products in 1964 amounted to at least $50. In addition, places having sales of less than the $50 and $250 minimums in 1964 were classified as farms if they could normally be expected to produce farm products in sufficient quantity to meet the requirements. For a detailed definition and farm statistics, see U.S. Department of Commerce, *Census of Agriculture,* 1964.

Farm Bloc A group of legislators from farm states who place farm interests above party lines. Formally organized in 1921, the farm bloc was an organization of senators and congressmen from the Middle West and South who were determined to support favorable agricultural legislation and to oppose unfavorable legislation regardless of party lines. It existed formally only from 1921 to 1923, but its activities established a precedent for a bipartisan approach to farm legislation which has prevailed into the 1960s. For the activities of the farm bloc, see Ezra T. Benson, *Farmers at Crossroads,* The Devin-Adair Company, Inc., New York, 1956.

Fascism A totalitarian, collectivistic system of government in which central control is exercised over all economic, political, and social activities. A complete rejection ol liberal democracy, fascism represents a return to an authoritarian system of power elites. It is based on an exaggerated nationalism which entirely eliminates individualism and regards the state as the highest expression of the will of the group. The state is ruled by an elite, headed by a leader whose will is supreme and whose power is based on the control of an organized system of terror and propaganda. All economic activities are subservient to national ends, which are determined by the ruling elite. Private ownership of production is maintained, but extreme restrictions are imposed on private economic freedoms. Decisions on production, investment, prices, and wages are all subject to arbitrary government control. There is no concentrated program for progressive economic development; instead the economic system is subordinated to the political and military ends of the state. Fascism is similar to communism, in that both are totalitarian systems that accept the principle of terror and submerge the individual, but fascism relies on the private ownership of industry, whereas communism abandons private ownership. Fascism denies the equality of man and emphasizes class and racial distinctions, whereas communism pursues absolute equality and the elimination of all elites. Moreover, in a fascist system the state is regarded as a necessary and permanent form of control, whereas Communists see the totalitarian state as only a temporary phase which will eventually disappear. Fascism arose in Italy after World War I under the leadership of Benito Mussolini and was later adopted in Germany in the similar form of national socialism (Nazism). For additional information, see William G. Welk, *Fascist Economic Policy*, Harvard University Press, Cambridge, Mass., 1938; Robert A. Brady, *The Spirit and Structure of German Fascism*, The Viking Press, Inc., New York, 1937; G. L. Field, *The Syndical and Corporative Institutions of Fascism*, Columbia University Press, New York, 1938.

Featherbedding A term applied to union rules or practices designed to increase artificially the number of persons employed. Unions can attempt to regulate the number of workers employed in a crew, such as dock workers on the waterfront or musicians in an orchestra, or they can require the employment of unnecessary workers, such as the use of two operators for each projection machine in a motion picture theater or a fireman on a diesel-powered locomotive. See Neil W. Chamberlain, *Sourcebook on Labor*, rev. ed., McGraw-Hill Book Company, New York, 1966, pp. 320–323; Robert D. Leiter, *Featherbedding and Job Security*, T. Wayne Publishers, New York, 1964.

Federal Budget: National-Income-Accounts Basis (Federal Sector Account) A measure of the direct impact of Federal fiscal activity on the current flow of income and output in the U.S. The Federal sector account, like the Federal cash budget, is more comprehensive than the Federal administrative budget, for it includes most trust-fund transactions. Differing from both the administrative and the cash budgets, it records only receipts and expenditures which directly affect the flows of current income and output. The Federal budget on the national-income-accounts basis records the purchase of goods and services when delivery is made, whereas the other two budgets generally count expenditures at the time of payment. Moreover, the Federal sector account records some business tax receipts, particularly corporate income taxes, as they accrue, whereas in the administrative and cash budgets business tax receipts are counted as they are collected. For additional details on the size and description of the Federal budget on the national-income-account basis, see *Special Analyses, the Budget of the United States Government Fiscal Year 1972*, Government Printing Office, Washington, D.C., 1971, pp. 7–21.

Federal Debt Subject to Limitation *See Administrative Budget.*

Federal-Funds Market An informal market for the trading of reserves among member banks of the Federal Reserve System. A bank with deposits at the regional Federal Reserve bank in excess of its legal require-

Federal Budget: National-Income-Accounts Basis, Receipts and Expenditures for the Calendar Years, 1947-1970 (Billions of dollars)

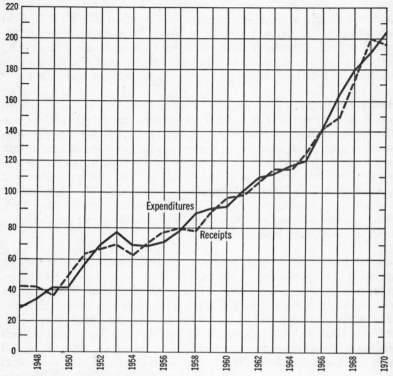

Source: U.S. Department of Commerce; Bureau of the Budget.

ments can sell (lend) some of these deposits (in multiples of $1,000,000), usually for one day at a time, to another bank that is deficient in reserves. The money lent by one bank to another is called Federal funds because it is legally in the hands of the Federal Reserve System and is merely transferred from the account of one commercial bank to that of another. Most large New York City banks have an officer who acts as a Federal-funds broker for correspondent banks in other large cities and purchases and sells reserves for his own bank. In addition to the major banks, one commercial finance house in New York City acts as a broker for Federal funds, mainly for banks that do not trade in the market regularly. The net effect of trading reserves among banks is to enable each bank to hold only the legal minimum in non-interest-earning reserves. Normally, the interest rate on Federal funds does not rise above the Federal Reserve discount rate, since a bank can borrow from the Federal Reserve System at the low rate rather than from private sources at the high rate. However, in periods of tight credit some banks pay a premium in order to avoid facing Federal Reserve lending officers. The System takes no part in the Federal-funds market other than to transfer reserves on its books as dictated by the bank that owns them. The Federal-funds market becomes more active in tight-money periods, but no instruments of monetary policy are brought to bear in this market. The daily volume of Federal-funds transactions usually varies between $2 billion and $3 billion. For further information, see Wesley Lindow, "The Federal Funds Market," *Bankers Monthly*, New York, September, 1960; Marcus Nadler et al., *The Money Market and Its Institutions*, The Ronald Press Company, New York, 1955; Eli Shapiro, Ezra Solomon, and William L. White, *Money and Banking*, Holt, Rinehart and Winston, Inc., New York, 1968, pp. 324–325; "The Federal Funds Market Revisited," *Economic Review*, pp. 3–13, Federal Reserve Bank of Cleveland, February, 1970.

Federal Funds, Receipts, and Outlays   *See Administrative Budget.*

Federal Reserve Note   Currency in denominations of $1 and more that is issued by the Federal Reserve System. Federal Reserve notes are direct obligations of the Federal government. They constitute about seven-eighths of the currency circulating in the U.S., the remaining one-eighth consisting of treasury currency in the form of $1 bills and coin. The Federal Reserve System limits the amount of notes in circulation in relation to the goods available for purchase. The Federal Reserve note differs from the now-unimportant Federal Reserve bank note, which is being withdrawn from circulation. The latter had to be secured dollar for dollar by U.S. bonds. For monthly statistics on the amount of Federal Reserve notes in circulation, see *Federal Reserve Bulletin*, Washington, D.C.

Federal Sector Account   *See Federal Budget: National-Income-Accounts Basis.*

Fertility Rate   The ratio of births to each 1,000 females of childbearing age (generally from fifteen to forty-four years). It is more refined than the crude birthrate, which takes into account the whole population. Additional breakdowns are available, such as ratio of births for various age groups within the fifteen- to forty-four-year category. As of February, 1971, the fertility rate of the U.S. was 88.5 births per 1,000 females between the ages of fifteen and forty-four. Between 1957 and 1968, the rate declined steadily, but since 1968 it has been increasing moderately. For additional details, see Robert P. Kuczynski, *Fertility and Reproduction*,

Falcon Press, New York, 1932; for current and historical statistics on fertility rates in the U.S., see U.S. Department of Health, Education, and Welfare, *Health, Education, and Welfare Indicators,* monthly.

Fertility Rate (Births per 1,000 females aged 15-44 years)

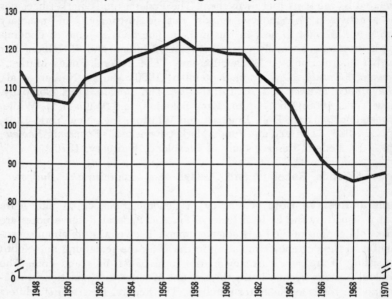

Source: U.S. Department of Health, Education, and Welfare, Public Health Service, National Vital Statistics Division.

Fiat Money Legal tender which has value only because the issuing authority declares that it is money and the public at large accepts it as such. Paper currency is the usual form of fiat money. Unlike full-bodied money (gold or silver coins), it is readily printed in large denominations and thus is easy to carry. Furthermore, its quantity does not depend on the amount of metal that a country possesses. If a government issues too great a quantity of money and the public loses confidence in it, fiat money loses much of its value. Examples of fiat money are the greenbacks issued by the U.S. government during the Civil War. See Paul B. Trescott, *Money, Banking, and Economic Welfare,* 2d ed., McGraw-Hill Book Company, New York, 1965.

Fidelity Bond An insurance agreement guaranteeing an employer against loss caused by the dishonesty of his employees in positions of trust. The issuing insurance company usually investigates the background of the employees named in the bond. Two important differences distinguish a fidelity bond from a surety bond: there must be an employer-employee relationship, and the dishonesty of the employee is the hazard insured against. Generally, fidelity bonds are issued for three classes of risks: larceny or embezzlement, culpable negligence, and the unfaithful discharge of duty. For further information, see G. W. Crist, Jr., *Corporate Suretyship*, 2d ed., McGraw-Hill Book Company, New York, 1950; James L. Athearn, *Risk and Insurance*, 2d ed., Appleton Century Crofts, New York, 1969, pp. 399–406.

Fiduciary Money   Money that embodies a credit element, in the sense that its face value is greater than the gold or silver by which it is supported. Paper money issued by a bank or a government is an example of fiduciary money. Theoretically, since 1933 all currency in the U.S., including all Federal notes and all coins, is fiduciary money because no currency is redeemable into gold. For further information, see Walter W. Haines, *Money, Prices and Policy*, 2d ed., McGraw-Hill Book Company, New York, 1966.

Field Warehousing   A technique of securing business loans against inventories. Using this technique, the warehouseman ordinarily leases part of the borrower's establishment and assigns a custodian to care for the goods. He is in exclusive possession of the merchandise until it has been released to the borrower on the lender's order. Charges for this service average from 0.5 to 2% of the value of the goods, the most common charge being about 1%.

Final Goods and Services   Goods and services which are purchased for final use or consumption and not for resale or for further processing or manufacturing. In order to eliminate double counting, only the value of final goods and services is included in the national income and product accounts. The following example shows that if all the transactions involved in the selling of a suit of clothing were included in the U.S. national accounts, the estimate of the national product would be affected by double counting (in this case, quintuple counting). Wool comes from a sheep rancher, who sells it for $20 to a wool processor. The processor, in turn, sells the processed wool for $30 to a suit manufacturer, who, in turn, sells the suit to a wholesaler for $50. The wholesaler sells the suit for $70 to a retail store which sells it to a consumer for $80. Thus, the final value of $80 is included in the U.S. national income accounts and not the $250 total of the five values. Clearly, the level of the gross national product could be increased by merely increasing the number and frequency of intermediate transactions, but this procedure would not give much information about the actual output of goods and services in the nation. For a detailed definition, see Richard Ruggles and Nancy D. Ruggles, *National Income Accounts and Income Analysis,* 2d ed., McGraw-Hill Book Company, New York, 1956; for a criticism of the concept, see National Bureau of Economic Research, Inc., *A Critique of the U.S. Income and Product Accounts,* Studies in Income and Wealth, vol. XXII, Princeton University Press, Princeton, N.J., 1958.

Financial Intermediary A financial institution that receive funds from savers and lends them to borrowers. In a broad sense, the term financial intermediary is applicable to all financial institutions, including commercial banks, mutual savings banks, savings and loan associations, insurance companies, finance companies, pension trusts, and investment trusts. In a narrower sense, however, it excludes commercial banks. In this sense, financial intermediaries constitute a large and growing part of the U.S. financial system. Between 1952 and 1957 the assets of financial intermediaries grew by 47%, compared with a 7% gain in demand deposits at commercial banks. For statistical data, see Raymond W. Goldsmith, *Financial Intermediaries in the American Economy since 1900,* Princeton University Press, Princeton, N.J., 1958; for further information, see Raymond W. Goldsmith, *Financial Institutions,* Random House, Inc., New York, 1968.

Firm A business unit producing goods and services. It consists of capital facilities and other resources combined under entrepreneurial control for the purpose of making a profit. The firm buys labor and other resource materials, transforms these materials through a productive process, adding value, and sells the goods or services in another market. The firm is distinguished from other social organizations, such as households and government, by its relatively great emphasis on profit seeking. Ownership and control of the firm may take various forms, such as proprietorship, partnership, and corporation. In 1963 there were approximately 4.8 million firms in operation in the U.S. For additional details, see Joseph D. Coppock, *Economics of the Business Firm,* McGraw-Hill Book Company, New York, 1959; Neil W. Chamberlain, *The Firm,* McGraw-Hill Book Company, New York, 1962; Edith Penrose, *The Theory of the Growth of the Firm,* John Wiley & Sons, Inc., New York, 1959.

First In First Out (fifo) An accounting method of valuing inventory which assumes that the first goods purchased are the first goods used up during an accounting period. It is the opposite of last in first out (lifo). As an example for an accounting period of one month, the fifo method of valuing inventory is illustrated below for the XYZ Company.

Inventory as of December 31, 1962	1,000 units	@ $10	$10,000
Purchased during January, 1963	500 units	@ 7	3,500
Total	1,500 units		$13,500
Used up during January, 1963	400 units	@ $10	4,000
Left in inventory as of January 31, 1963	1,100 units		$ 9,500

The aim of fifo is to measure the cost of goods used up by the cost of original items. This method may, however, undervalue inventory when prices are falling and overvalue it when prices are rising. Since fifo yields higher taxable income when prices are rising, many firms stopped using this method during the inflationary period 1955–1957. See Harold Bierman, *Managerial Accounting*, The Macmillan Company, New York, 1959.

Fiscal Dividend The money available for discretionary use by the President and the Congress to expand existing federal programs, to create new ones, to reduce Federal taxes, or to hold as a surplus for economic stabilization purposes. The revenue-raising power of the Federal tax system produces a built-in average increase of about $10 billion a year in Federal revenues. Unless it is offset by such fiscal dividends as tax cuts or expanded Federal programs, this increase in revenues will act as a fiscal drag, siphoning off too much from the private economy and thus checking expansion. This is part of the basic philosophy of the New Economics. For additional information, see Walter Heller, *New Dimensions of Political Economy*, Harvard University Press, Cambridge, Mass., 1966, chap. 11; for a specific projection of the budget and fiscal dividend, see Charles L. Schultze et al., *Setting National Priorities: The 1972 Budget*, The Brookings Institution, Washington, D.C., 1971, chap. 17.

Fiscal Drag The retarding effects on economic activity produced when automatic growth in Federal revenues siphons off increasing amounts of funds from the private sector. The concept of fiscal drag is important to the understanding of the New Economics. Growth of the national economy brings forth an increase in Federal revenues each year. In times of severe inflation, an appropriate course for fiscal policy might be to allow the increment to become absorbed into a government surplus, thus slowing down inflation. But when economic activity is slack, the New Economics holds that the added revenues received by government should be turned back to the private sector in the form of fiscal dividends. These dividends could take a number of forms, including tax cuts, increased government spending, and revenue sharing with state and municipal governments. See Walter Heller, *New Dimensions of Political Economy*, Harvard University Press, Cambridge, Mass., 1966; Herbert Stein, *The*

Fiscal Revolution in America, The University of Chicago Press, Chicago, 1969; George Terborgh, *The New Economics,* Machinery and Allied Products Institute, Washington, D.C., 1968.

Fiscal-Monetary Mix   The mix of fiscal and monetary policy consistent with full employment. For example, one mix could consist of tight money and a large Federal deficit; another, of easy money and a large budget surplus. Another example would be to adopt the mix to the balance-of-payments situation—a mix that would yield higher or lower interest rates relative to the desire to increase or decrease capital outflows. For additional information, see Herbert Stein, *The Fiscal Revolution in America,* The University of Chicago Press, Chicago, 1969.

Fiscal Policy   The use of a government's spending and revenue-producing activities to achieve specific objectives. In the U.S. since the 1940s, the objectives of the Federal government's fiscal policy have been largely the achievement of full employment with price stability. To realize these objectives, the government may alter its decisions on the amount and source of its revenues. When the government taxes to a greater extent than it spends, it causes a net reduction in the flow of income, thereby reducing aggregate demand. When it spends a greater amount of money than it receives in taxes, it stimulates the flow of national income and aggregate demand. Fiscal policy uses budget deficits or surpluses to regulate economic stability and growth. Some tools of fiscal policy work automatically, without specific action by the President or Congress. The progressive income tax, for example, is a built-in stabilizer that tends to reduce the government's revenue collections when personal and business incomes are declining and hence helps offset the cutbacks in consumer and business spending that accompany such declines. During business expansions, on the other hand, Federal tax collections tend to rise fairly rapidly and hence tend to reduce inflationary pressures. In postwar business declines, Congress has legislated emergency spending measures, such as temporary increases in public works expenditures, as additional means of offsetting cutbacks in private spending and preventing unemployment. See Wilfred Lewis, Jr., *Federal Fiscal Policy in the Postwar Recessions,* The Brookings Institution, Washington, D.C., 1962; Edward Shapiro, *Macroeconomic Analysis,* Harcourt, Brace & World, Inc., New York, 1966; Herbert Stein, *The Fiscal Revolution in America,* The University of Chicago Press, Chicago, 1969.

Fiscal Year   An annual period established for accounting purposes by business or government. It may start at any time in the calendar year. The U.S. government's fiscal year, for example, runs from July 1 through

June 30; thus, its fiscal year 1972 began on July 1, 1971, and ended on June 30, 1972. As of 1971, only a relatively small proportion of U.S. corporations were on a fiscal-year rather than a calendar-year basis.

Fixed Asset   An asset of a relatively permanent nature, such as land, buildings, and machinery. A fixed asset is used in the regular operation of a business and cannot be sold for cash without disrupting normal operations. Usually, any asset with a life greater than one year is classified as fixed. Most fixed assets except land have a limited life, and their cost is distributed over their productive life by permitting periodic depreciation. For further information, see Roy A. Foulke, *Practical Financial Statement Analysis*, 6th ed., McGraw-Hill Book Company, New York, 1968; Harold Bierman, *Managerial Accounting*, The Macmillan Company, New York, 1956.

Fixed Cost   A cost which does not vary with changes in a firm's output over the short run. Fixed costs, or overhead, would remain even if there were no output, since they are associated with the existence and maintenance of the firm's facilities. Rent, interest payments, depreciation of plants and equipment, property taxes, and the salaries of top management are commonly classed as fixed costs. Such costs are fixed because they cannot be avoided; the firm has no choice with respect to them. While these costs are fixed in the short run, in the long run there are no fixed costs, since the firm can change its scale of operations as well as its products. For further information, see George J. Stigler, *The Theory of Price*, 3d ed., The Macmillan Company, New York, 1966; *Cost Behavior and Price Policy*, National Bureau of Economic Research, Inc., New York, 1943.

Fixed Input   A productive resource employed by a firm in set amounts. Generally, the term fixed input refers to a factor whose quantity is invariable over the short run, such as land, buildings, and machinery. The longer the time period considered, the less clear is the dividing line between fixed and variable inputs. Over the long run, no inputs are fixed, since a firm can vary the scale of its operations as well as its output.

Flag of Convenience   The national flag flown by a merchant ship that has been registered in a country other than that of its owners in order to escape high domestic wages and taxes. At the end of 1969, more than 433 vessels owned by foreign affiliates of U.S. companies were registered under eight foreign flags, mainly Panamanian and Liberian. Shipowners contend that they must engage in this practice because they cannot pay high American maritime wages and compete with foreign shipowners.

Labor unions argue that flags of convenience constitute an unfair violation of collective bargaining. For a full discussion of the subject, see Boleslaw Adam Boczek, *Flags of Convenience: An International Legal Study*, Harvard University Press, Cambridge, Mass., 1962.

Flation The absence of both inflation and deflation. Thus, flation generally mean a period of stable prices. Price stability does not, however, preclude some fluctuations in the price indices. Thus, the period 1958–1964, when the wholesale price index ranged narrowly between 94.5 and 94.9 (1967 = 100), may be characterized as a period of flation in the U.S. See J. P. Wernett, *Growth and Prosperity Without Inflation*, The Ronald Press Company, New York, 1961.

Flexible Price A price that is not rigid. It can move downward to as great an extent as it can move upward. For the most part, flexible prices are limited to the prices for agricultural products and other basic raw materials, especially those purchased on organized exchanges, but they also apply to a few manufactured products of which the dominant cost component is a flexibly priced material. For example, leather is a flexibly priced item because its dominant cost component is the price paid for hides. Among other flexibly priced products are those, such as apparel, in which a large number of sellers actively compete in market areas in which the particular prices are determined. See Gardiner C. Means, *Administrative Inflation and Pricing Policy*, Anderson Kramer Associates, Washington, D.C., 1959.

Flexible Tariff A duty on foreign-made products which can be raised or lowered quickly. In the U.S., the President can order a flexible-tariff program without the ratification of Congress. Introduced into the U.S. tariff system in 1922, the first flexible-tariff law empowered the President to raise by 50% the duty levied on any and all products of a country found to be discriminating against U.S. exports. This flexibility to raise tariffs, both for the purpose of preventing discrimination and for the protection of U.S. industries, has since been included in all tariff agreements. The first authorization for downward tariff flexibility was included in the Reciprocal Trade Agreements Act of 1934, which permitted the President to lower existing duties by 50%. This downward flexibility has also been included in all subsequent tariff acts. For further information, see Don D. Humphrey, *American Imports*, The Twentieth Century Fund, New York, 1955.

Flight from the Dollar A widespread movement by foreigners to convert their holdings of U.S. money into currencies of other nations. A flight from the dollar arises from fears that the value of the dollar is declining in terms of other currencies. Such a decline in value might be caused by rapid inflation in the U.S. or by an official devaluation of the U.S. monetary unit in terms of other currencies. In either case, the buying power of the U.S. dollar in foreign lands is substantially reduced, providing a motive for a flight from the dollar into other currencies. For further information, see Arthur I. Bloomfield, *Speculative and Flight Movements in Postwar International Finance,* Princeton University Press, Princeton, N.J., 1954.

Float   The amount of money outstanding at any specific time in checks which have been issued but not collected. The float arises from the time differential between the crediting and collection of payments. If, for example, the Federal Reserve Bank of New York credits a New York City member bank on its reserve account for a check drawn on a California bank in advance of the actual collection of the check, total reserve balances temporarily increase, since the New York bank has been given a credit while the California bank has not yet been charged. This type of credit extension is necessary because of the huge task of check collection and the large volume of checks that are handled each year. Instead of keeping track of each check and crediting the proper account only at the time of collection, the reserve banks grant credit according to a specified time schedule, based primarily on the location of the drawee bank in relation to its Federal Reserve bank office. Under present time schedules, credit is granted in two business days for checks dawn on banks in areas where no Federal Reserve banks or branches are located, even if it takes three days to make the collection. The inability of the system to make the collection within a specific time schedule is due to the impossibility of meeting time requirements even though no unusual delays have occurred, to bad weather, and to strikes or similar factors which delay the delivery or payment of checks. Figures for the float appear in the Federal Reserve report and are published weekly in most national newspapers. See "Forecasting Float," *Monthly Review,* Federal Reserve Bank of New York, 1963, pp. 30–35; John J. Klein, *Money and the Economy,* Harcourt, Brace & World, Inc., New York; 1970.

Floating Exchange Rate   A technique to allow exchange rates in a single country and for a certain time period to float freely in order for the currency to find its own level in a free market. This method of flexibility was chosen by West Germany and the Netherlands in May, 1971, outside the Articles of Agreement of the International Monetary Fund. This device anticipates exchange-rate adjustments and thus prevents a long period of speculation. For additional information, see Paul A. Samuelson, *Economics*, 8th ed., McGraw-Hill Book Company, New York, 1970.

Floating Prime Rate of Interest   A base rate on commercial loans, relative to the ninety-day commercial-paper rate. A shift to a floating prime rate was first introduced by the First National City Bank of New York on October 21, 1971. Initially, the base rate was set by the FNCB at one-half of one percentage point above the ninety-day commercial-paper rate. The base rate is reviewed each week and adjusted on a weekly basis as needed. Alternative methods of achieving flexible and market-related bank charges have been introduced by other banks. For further discussion, see Dwight B. Crane and William L. White, "Who Benefits from a Floating Price Rate?" *Harvard Business Review*, January–February, 1972, pp. 121–129.

Flow-of-Funds Analysis (Money-Flow Analysis)   A method of social accounting which focuses attention on the sources and uses of funds not only for goods and services, but also for instruments of ownership and debt. Since the expenditures of one economic unit are the receipts of others and every financial liability is someone else's asset, the flow-of-funds analysis is used to give an overall picture of financial relationships between the various sectors of the economy, tracing the use made by the various sectors of their savings and the sources of investors' funds. The flow-of-funds analysis is more comprehensive than the national product accounts, since it includes transactions of existing capital assets, borrowing, etc. It also shows how the saving of one sector is used to finance the investment of another sector. The major sectors used in the flow-of-funds accounting system are consumers, corporations, nonfarm, noncorporate businesses, farms, the Federal government, state and local governments, commercial banks, savings banks, insurance companies, other investors, and the rest of the world. The flow-of-funds approach is useful in analyzing the effect that different monetary policies have on the general functioning of the economy. For quarterly figures on the flow-of-funds account in the U.S. see *Federal Reserve Bulletin*, Washington, D.C.; see also Morris Copeland, *A Study of Moneyflows in the U.S.*, National Bureau of Economic Research, Inc., New York, 1952; *The Flow of Funds in the United States*, Board of Governors of the Federal Reserve System, Washington, D.C., 1955; John P. Powelson, *National Income and Flow-of-Funds Analysis*, McGraw-Hill Book Company, New York, 1960, part 3. See the accompanying flow-of-funds table on pp. 234–235.

Forced Saving   Involuntary saving by individuals. Forced saving may take place in a full-employment economy during inflation. When new investment is undertaken, fewer consumer goods are available. Consumers then push up the prices of the remaining goods until they reach a level at which consumers withdraw from the market an amount of funds equal to the funds invested. As long as the prices of goods increase faster than money wages, the inflation results in a drop in real consumption and a rise in real (forced) saving. When a corporation retains most of its earnings, it is forcing stockholders to save. The individual stockholder cannot spend his share of the income of the corporation and is thus forced to save, the saving being reflected in an increase in his assets. When a government taxes its citizens and makes the funds available for investment, this, too, is a form of forced saving because it prevents consumers from spending part of their income. Some countries, such as the Soviet Union and many underdeveloped nations, achieve a large part of their saving in this way. Consumption is kept artificially low to allow capital formation to take place. For further information, see F. A. von Hayek, "The Development of the Doctrine of Forced Saving," *Quarterly Journal of Economics,* vol. XLVII, pp. 123–133, Harvard University Press, Cambridge, Mass., November, 1932; Fritz Machlup, "Forced or Induced Savings: An Exploration of Its Synonyms and Homonyms," *Review of Economics and Statistics,* vol. XXV, pp. 26–39, Harvard University Press, Cambridge, Mass., February, 1943; Armen A. Alchian and William R. Allen, *University Economics,* Wadsworth Publishing Company, Inc., Belmont, Calif., 1967, pp. 660–661.

Foreclosure   A legal proceeding by which the lender on a mortgage takes title to the property involved because the borrower has failed to repay the loan. When a person who has borrowed money on a mortgage (mortgagor) does not pay back the loan at the time appointed and certain conditions, differing from state to state, have not been fulfilled, the lender (mortgagee) brings foreclosure proceedings to gain the property or the proceeds from the sale of the property which has been mortgaged. In states which adhere to the title theory of mortgage, the mortgaged property is turned directly over to the lender by the judgment of the court; this is called strict foreclosure. In states which adhere to the lien theory of mortgage, the mortgaged property is sold at a foreclosure sale; this is called statutory foreclosure. If the proceeds of the foreclosure sale do not fully repay the debt, the borrower is still responsible. When a bank holds a mortgage, the two methods of foreclosure do not differ essentially because the bank sells the property in any case. For more specific information regarding an individual state, see that state's law code; for statistics on nonfarm real estate foreclosures, see Federal Home Loan Bank Board reports. (See illustration on page 236.)

Summary of Flow-of-Funds Accounts for Second Quarter, 1970
(Seasonally adjusted annual rates; in billions of dollars)

| Transaction Category | Private Domestic Nonfinancial Sectors | | | | | | | | U.S. Govt. | |
| | House-holds | | Busi-ness | | State and Local Govts. | | Total | | | |
	U	S	U	S	U	S	U	S	U	S
1 Gross saving	....	163.4	....	81.8	....	−.6	....	244.6	....	−17.8
2 Capital consumption	....	90.4	....	71.3	....	....	....	161.7	....	....
3 Net saving (1–2)	....	73.0	....	10.6	....	−.6	....	82.9	....	−17.8
4 Gross investment (5+10)	153.8	....	76.6	....	−2.1	....	228.3	....	−18.0	....
5 Private capital expenditures	115.8	....	108.8	....	....	....	224.6	....	....	....
6 Consumer durables	91.9	....	....	....	....	....	91.9	....	....	....
7 Residential construction	18.5	....	9.9	....	....	....	28.4	....	....	....
8 Plant and equipment	5.5	....	95.8	....	....	....	101.3	....	....	....
9 Inventory change	....	....	3.1	....	....	....	3.1	....	....	....
10 Net financial investment (11–12)	37.9	....	−32.2	....	−2.1	....	3.6	....	−18.0	....
11 Financial uses	56.3	....	28.7	....	9.7	....	94.6	....	1.4	....
12 Financial sources	....	18.3	....	60.9	....	11.8	....	91.0	....	19.3
13 Gold and official foreign exchange	....	....	....	....	....	....	....	....	−2.2	....
14 Treasury currency	....	....	....	....	....	....	....	....	....	.1
15 Demand deposits and currency	....	....	....	....	....	....	....	....	....	....
16 Private domestic	−.7	....	−1.8	....	−.3	....	−2.8	....	....	....
17 U.S. Government	....	....	....	....	....	....	....	....	.9	....
18 Foreign	....	....	....	....	....	....	....	....	....	....
19 Time and savings accounts	24.8	....	....	....	....	....	44.3	....	....	....
20 At commercial banks	9.5	....	11.4	....	8.1	....	29.0	....	.1	....
21 At savings institutions	15.3	....	....	....	....	....	15.3	....	....	....
22 Life insurance reserves	4.6	....	....	....	....	....	4.6	....	....	.1
23 Pension-fund reserves	15.5	....	....	....	....	....	15.5	....	....	3.5
24 Interbank items	....	....	....	....	....	....	....	....	....	....
25 Credit market instruments	15.2	22.1	.9	49.2	2.0	11.3	18.0	82.5	2.8	17.2
26 Corporate shares	1.3	....	....	6.2	....	....	1.3	6.2	....	....
27 U.S. government securities	−1.0	....	−1.1	....	−2.1	....	−4.2	....	*	17.3
28 State and local obligations	1.6	....	−2.1	....	.2	11.0	−.4	11.0	....	....
29 Corporate and foreign bonds	10.4	....	....	22.7	3.7	....	14.1	22.7	....	....
30 Home mortgages	.7	12.6	....	−.8	.2	....	.9	11.8	.1	−.1
31 Other mortgages	2.2	1.0	....	10.8	....	....	2.2	11.8	.4	....
32 Consumer credit	....	6.2	1.8	....	....	....	1.8	6.2	....	....
33 Bank loans n.e.c.	....	−.6	....	5.5	....	....	....	4.9	....	....
34 Other loans	....	2.7	2.2	4.9	....	.3	2.2	7.9	2.3	....
35 Security credit	−1.8	−4.5	....	....	....	....	−1.8	−4.5	....	....
36 To brokers and dealers	−1.8	....	....	....	....	....	−1.8	....	....	....
37 To others	....	−4.5	....	....	....	....	....	−4.5	....	....
38 Taxes payable	....	....	....	−1.2	*	....	*	−1.2	.1	....
39 Trade credit	....	.4	12.8	7.7	....	.5	12.8	8.6	−.8	−1.1
40 Equity in noncorporate business	−3.6	....	....	−3.6	....	....	−3.6	−3.6	....	....
41 Miscellaneous claims	2.3	.3	5.4	8.8	....	....	7.7	9.1	.4	−.4
42 Sector discrepancies (1–4)	9.6	....	5.2	....	1.5	....	16.3	....	.1	....

* Commercial banks and unconsolidated affiliates.

| Financial Sectors | | | | | | | | | | Rest of the World | | All Sectors | | Discrepancy | Natl. Savings and Investment |
| Total | | Sponsored Credit Agencies | | Monetary Auth. | | Coml. Banks * | | Pvt. Nonbank Finance | | | | | | | |
U	S	U	S	U	S	U	S	U	S	U	S	U	S	U	
....	3.6	....	.1	....	.1	....	3.0	....	.4	....	−1.1	....	229.2	....	230.4
....	1.6	....	....	....	....	....	.9	....	.7	....	....	....	163.3	....	163.3
....	2.0	....	.1	....	.1	....	2.1	....	−.3	....	−1.1	....	65.9	....	67.0
4.5	....	.7	....	*	....	2.6	....	1.1	....	−.2	....	214.6	....	14.6.....	226.4
1.5	....	....	....	....	....	.6	....	.9	....	....	....	226.2	....	3.1.....	226.2
....	....	....	....	....	....	....	....	....	....	....	....	91.9	....	....	91.9
....	....	....	....	....	....	....	....	....	....	....	....	28.4	....	....	28.4
1.5	....	....	....	....	....	.6	....	.9	....	....	....	102.8	....	....	102.8
....	....	....	....	....	....	....	....	....	....	....	....	3.1	....	....	3.1
3.0	....	.7	....	*	....	2.0	....	.2	....	−.2	....	−11.6	....	11.6.....	.2
77.9	....	6.6	....	1.3	....	30.3	....	39.6	....	3.9	....	177.8	....	....	4.1
....	74.9	....	5.9	....	1.2	....	28.3	....	39.4	....	4.1	....	189.4	....	3.9
−2.0	....	....	....	−2.0	....	....	....	....	....	−.1	−4.2	−4.2	−4.2		
.3	....	....	....	.3	....	....	....	....	....	....	....	.3	.1	−.2	
....	*	....	....	....	1.9	....	−1.9	....	....	....	....	−2.2	*		
.3	−1.8	*	....	....	5.3	....	−7.1	.3	....	....	....	−2.6	−1.8	.8	
....	2.4	....	....	....	−3.2	....	5.6	....	....	....	....	.9	2.4	1.5	
....	−.6	....	....	....	−.2	....	−.4	....	....	−.6	....	....	−.6		
.4	42.3							.4	....			....	42.3		
....	26.6							....	26.6	−2.4	....	....	26.6		
.4	15.7							.4	15.7			....	15.7		
....	4.5							....	4.5			....	4.6		
....	12.0							....	12.0			....	15.5		
−4.4	−4.4			−2.9	−1.3	−1.4	−3.0					−4.4	−4.4		
86.7	15.6	6.6	4.7	5.9	....	33.8	4.1	40.5	6.8	9.4	1.6	116.9	116.9		
8.7	3.3					....	*	8.7	3.3	−.5	....	....	9.5		
17.6	4.7	−.8	4.7	5.7	....	9.2	....	3.5	....	8.5	....	....	21.9		
11.4	....					11.6	....	−.2	....			....	11.0		
10.0	2.3					....	*	10.0	2.3	.6	−.4	....	24.6		
10.8	....	4.9	....			1.3	....	4.7	....			....	11.7		
9.2	....	.9	....			.8	....	7.5	....			....	11.8		
4.4	....					2.2	....	2.2	....			....	6.2		
4.5	−.1			.2	....	4.3	....	....	−.1			....	4.5		
10.3	5.4	1.7	....	−.1	....	4.4	4.1	4.3	1.2	.8	2.4	....	15.6		
−10.6	−7.9	....	....	....	....	−5.7	....	−4.9	−7.9	−.1	−.2	....	−12.5		
−6.0	−7.9					−5.8	....	−.2	−7.9	−.1	....	....	−7.9		
−4.6	....					.1	....	−4.7	....	....	−.2	....	−4.6		
....	*			*		....	.1	....	−.1			.1	−1.2	−1.3	
.3	....							.3	....	1.6	.4	14.0	7.9	−6.0	
....	....											....	−3.6		
6.8	12.8	.1	.4	....	.7	3.7	2.3	3.1	8.5	−3.8	6.5	11.1	28.0	16.9	
−.9	....			*		.4	....	−.7	....	−.9	....	14.6	....	14.6	4.0

Nonfarm Real Estate Foreclosures (Thousands)

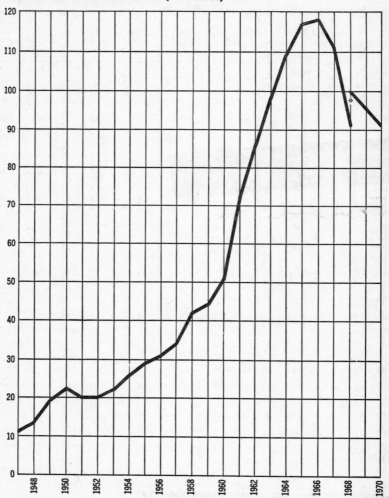

*Old series discontinued in 1968; 1968 and on includes Alaska and Hawaii.

Source: Federal Home Loan Bank Board.

Foreign Aid Program A governmental program of financial and technical assistance to foreign countries. Since World War II, the U.S. has
continuously pursued programs of foreign aid. Immediately after the war,
it undertook an emergency program of relief and rehabilitation for the
war-devastated European countries. These temporary measures were in-

adequate, however, and in 1948 the U.S. embarked on the Marshall Plan, a $13-billion program to rebuild the economy of Western Europe. Since 1949, with the introduction of the Point Four program of technical assistance, the U.S. has shifted its attention to the problems of aiding the underdeveloped nations of the world. This approach concentrates on long-run development, and its main purposes are to promote economic growth in underdeveloped areas and to bring about freer trade and payments policies. With the passage of the Mutual Security Act of 1951, combining economic and military assistance programs, the U.S. added the defense of the free world against communism as another major aim of its foreign aid program. In the period from 1948 to 1961, the U.S. distributed more than $86 billion worth of assistance to about 130 nations and territories. Of the total, $39 billion was in the form of military aid, the remaining $47 billion being extended as economic assistance, 17% of which was in loans. Of the total foreign aid, Europe received more than $15 billion; the Near East and South Asia, about $11 billion; East Asia, including Vietnam, about $11 billion; Latin America, $5 billion; and Africa, $2 billion. The aid has taken the form of direct assistance between governments, Export-Import Bank hard loans, technical assistance grants, long-term soft loans by the Development Loan Fund, and sales of agricultural surpluses under the Food-for-Peace program. The greater part of the U.S. aid program is now administered by the Agency for International Development (AID). There has been a growing tendency in the U.S. foreign aid program to rely on loans to a greater extent than on grants, to concentrate on economic rather than on military assistance, and to extend aid for flexible development programs rather than for specific individual projects. For additional information, see *Foreign Aid Program: Compilation of Studies and Surveys,* Senate Document 52, 85th Cong., 1st Sess., July, 1957; Max F. Millikan and Walt W. Rostow, *A Proposal: Key to an Effective Foreign Policy,* Harper & Row, Publishers, Incorporated, New York, 1957; Robert Asher, *Grants, Loans and Local Currencies,* The Brookings Institution, Washington, D.C., 1961.

Foreign Exchange   All monetary instruments which give residents of one country a financial claim on another country. The use of foreign exchange is a country's principal means of settling its transactions with other countries. Thus, a country's demand for foreign exchange depends on the amount of goods that it wants to import, while the supply of foreign exchange available to it depends on the amount of goods that it can export. When a nation imports a greater amount of goods than it exports, so that foreign-exchange expenditures exceed foreign-exchange receipts, the nation has a balance-of-payments deficit, which it must finance from reserves of foreign exchange accumulated in the past. The balancing out of the supply and demand for foreign exchange occurs in the foreign-exchange markets. The most common forms of foreign exchange are foreign currencies and gold. Since August 15, 1971, the buying and selling of gold in transactions with foreign central banks has been suspended. Thus foreign central banks acquiring dollars are not able to convert them into gold or any other monetary reserve asset. For additional information, see Fritz Machlup, "The Theory of Foreign Exchanges," in Howard S. Ellis and Lloyd A. Metzler, *Readings in the Theory of International Trade*, McGraw-Hill Book Company, New York, 1959, chap. 5; Raymond F. Mikesell, *Foreign Exchange in the Postwar World*, The Twentieth Century Fund, New York, 1954; Frank Southard, Jr., *Foreign Exchange Practice and Policy*, McGraw-Hill Book Company, New York, 1940.

Foreign-Exchange Rate   The price of a foreign nation's unit of money in terms of that of another nation. Thus on a given day, in U.S. dollars

Foreign-Exchange Rates
(National currency units per U.S. dollar)

Currency Unit	October 30, 1970	June 30, 1962
Canada (dollar)	1.018	1.082
Mexico (peso)	12.48	12.48
Brazil (cruzeiro)	4.673 *	359.48 *
Belgium (franc)	49.60	49.75
West Germany (Deutsche mark)	3.63	3.991
Venezuela (bolivar)	4.48 †	3.33–3.35 ‡
Austria (schilling)	25.77	25.85
Italy (lira)	621.89	620.60
Netherlands (guilder)	3.597	3.592
Australia (pound)	0.8961	0.0074
Denmark (krone)	7.496 *	6.899
Norway (krone)	7.14	7.14
India (rupee)	7.55	4.768
Japan (yen)	357.8	361.8
Sweden (krona)	5.18 *	5.15
France (new franc)	5.516	4.900
United Kingdom (pound)	0.4183	0.3561
Argentina (peso)	396.83 *	135.00

* Free rate.
† Selling rate.
‡ Controlled rate.
SOURCE: Statistical Office of the United Nations, *Statistical Yearbook 1970*, New York.

the Japanese yen may be worth $0.003, the English pound $2.61, and the French franc $0.195. A knowledge of foreign-exchange rates helps Americans buy some foreign goods directly, since dollars can easily be converted into the proper currencies and payment be made. For example, if an American wishes to purchase an English automobile the price of which is £1,000, $2,610 is required to buy the necessary pounds to purchase the car. There are two types of exchange rates, the freely fluctuating rate based on supply and demand and the stable exchange rate based on government adherence to the gold standard. A free exchange rate is determined by the freely competitive forces of supply and demand; in the case of the U.S., the demand is composed of the desires of the nationals of a particular country to import U.S. goods, while the supply of dollars is determined by the desires of Americans for the goods of the other country. Under a stable exchange rate, the government offers to buy gold at a fixed price and to sell gold at about the same price. By fixing each currency in terms of gold, each currency is then in a fixed exchange rate with every other one. For further information, see Raymond F. Mikesell, *Foreign Exchange in the Postwar World,* The Twentieth Century Fund, New York, 1954.

Foreign Trade   The exchange of goods and services of all types between different countries. Business firms in industrial countries sell machinery and equipment to developing countries, which, in turn, sell raw materials to firms in industrial countries. The growth of international trade has been greatly helped by modern techniques of transportation and communications. These relatively new developments have brought countries closer together than they had ever been in the past and have made the conduct of trade much easier. More up-to-date and complete international economic information has made the buyer and the seller more knowledgeable regarding available products and markets. For further information, see J. B. Condliffe, *The Commerce of Nations,* W. W. Norton & Company, Inc., New York, 1950; Harold Heck, *Foreign Commerce,* McGraw-Hill Book Company, New York, 1953.

Fourier Analysis   A technique for analyzing periodic movements in composite time series—hence, a form of harmonic analysis. It treats the variable under study as the sum of a series of sine and cosine terms where the unknown periods of component series are not necessarily identical. Variances of deviations from a fitted Fourier series provide estimates of the variance of the error term. For additional information, see Lawrence R. Klein, *A Textbook of Econometrics,* Row, Peterson & Company, Evanston, Ill., 1953.

Fractional-Reserve Banking   A system in which banks hold less than 100% of their depositors' money idle. Usually, the government specifies that not less than a certain percentage (20%, for example) of total deposits must be held in reserve as cash in the bank or placed on deposit with the government. Since all banks want to earn as much money as possible, they lend and invest the portion of deposits that they are not legally required to hold idle. Thus, the banking system creates money, because demand deposits (checking-account balances) are money, and the bank lends a major proportion of its deposits, which are subsequently deposited at another bank in the system and thus are counted as money again. If the reserve ratio is 20%, the banking system may create $400 of additional deposits for each new deposit of $100. Only a banking system with a reserve ratio of less than 100% can create money, and the ability to do so has been criticized on two major counts. First, it is often said that no special group in the economy should have the power to create money to earn interest. Second, it is often observed that banks extend their loans greatly during booms, thereby promoting inflation, and contract their loans sharply when business slackens, thus deepening recessions. For additional details, see Paul A. Samuelson, *Economics*, 7th ed., McGraw-Hill Book Company, New York, 1967; Harold Barger, *Money, Banking and Public Policy*, Rand McNally & Company, Chicago, 1962.

Franchise   A special privilege usually granted by a government to an individual or a corporation by which the grantee is permitted to operate a business under certain conditions. For example, the operation of public transportation facilities within a city is awarded under a franchise. Sometimes, the term is used when a private organization grants an exclusive right to another corporation, as when a soft-drink manufacturer grants certain corporations the privilege of bottling and distributing the drink in a given area. Most governments that issue franchises provide for their regulation through a public service commission. Private corporations also set standards under which a franchise is issued. Among the principal features of a franchise are (1) the duration of issue, (2) the rates charged for services, (3) the services to be conducted, and (4) capitalization. For more information, see Harry Kursh, *The Franchise Boom*, Prentice-Hall, Inc., Englewood Cliffs, N.J., 1968.

Free Banking   A liberalization of the granting of bank charters. Until the early nineteenth century, bank charters in the U.S. were granted only by special legislative acts. Often political corruption was involved in securing charters, and the monopoly power which the chartered banks enjoyed was sometimes abused. In 1838, in an attempt to reform this system, New York adopted the first free banking law, which was based on the principle that banking should not be the privilege of the few but, like other businesses, be open to all. Under the free-banking law, any individual or group of individuals who met a few minimum requirements could receive a state charter for a bank. To safeguard the public, the law required that the bank's note issues could be secured only by depositing with the state approved bonds or mortgages equal in value to the note issue. The New York law was copied by many states. However, while the New York system worked relatively efficiency, the application of free banking in other states led to the introduction of unsound banks, since the authorities granted charters too liberally, and deposit requirements to back issues of notes were sometimes very lenient. In the West, the practice of free banking degenerated into wildcat banking. Issue requirements were gradually tightened, however, and in 1863 Congress adopted the National Bank Act, patterned after the provisions of the New York Free Banking Act. For additional details, see Bray Hammond, *Banks and Politics in America: From the Revolution to the Civil War,* Princeton University Press, Princeton, N.J., 1957; Paul Studenski and Herman E. Krooss, *The Financial History of the United States,* 3d ed., McGraw-Hill Book Company, New York, 1963.

Free Coinage   The unrestricted right of the individual to bring bullion to the mint and have it coined. Under a system of free coinage, any citizen is entitled to bring unlimited amounts of the standard monetary metal to be minted. The term free does not mean that no charge is made for mintage, but rather that everyone has the right to have bullion coined freely. The charge made for the actual minting is called brassage, while the premium sometimes charged by the government for coinage is called seigniorage. A system under which the government does not charge the individual for the minting at all is called gratuitous coinage. The United States had a system of free coinage of silver from 1792 until 1873 and a system of free coinage of gold from 1792 until 1933. For further information on the U.S. experience with free coinage, see Paul Studenski and Herman E. Krooss, *The Financial History of the United States,* 3d ed., McGraw-Hill Book Company, New York, 1963.

Freedom of Contract   The freedom of the individual to make any legal contract regarding his personal services or property. The U.S. Constitution guarantees freedom of contract by forbidding any state to pass "any law impairing the obligation of contracts." There are, however, some traditional limitations on the right to make a contract. For instance, contracts made under force, in opposition to public policy, or in violation of legitimate statutes are not valid. The concept of freedom of contract became important in the nineteenth century, when it was used by the courts to invalidate statutes limiting the conduct of business in its relations with labor. Laws restricting child labor and setting maximum hours of work were enacted in an attempt to equalize the bargaining power of the worker in relation to the employer. Although equality of bargaining power is an implicit requirement in the concept of freedom of contract, the courts held that such state restrictions violated a firm's freedom of contract and were an undue deprivation of liberty and property, thus violating the Fourteenth Amendment. For further information, see Roscoe Pound, "Liberty of Contract," *Yale Law Journal*, vol. xviii, New Haven, Conn., 1908–1909, pp. 454–487.

Freedom of Entry   The ease with which new sellers may enter a market. The term refers to the advantages which established firms in an industry have over new entrants. Barriers to entry, factors which make it hard for additional firms to enter the market, may arise for a number of reasons. There may be economies of large scale which place the new, small-scale firms at a cost disadvantage; the buyers of the industry's goods may have preferences for the products of the established firms; or certain firms may have absolute cost advantages, such as patent rights and ownership of essential raw materials. When freedom of entry is restricted, established firms are able to raise their selling prices above the minimal competitive costs without attracting new firms into the industry. Strong barriers to entry give rise to industries characterized by an oligopolistic market structure; weaker barriers permit a greater number of firms, often resulting in monopolistic competition. One statistical measure of freedom of entry into an industry is the degree to which established firms can raise their prices above minimal average costs without attracting new firms. A very high barrier exists if prices can be raised by 10% or more, a substantial barrier exists if they can be raised by 5 to 8%, and a moderate barrier exists if they can be raised by 3 or 4%. In the U.S., entry into agriculture, wholesale and retail distribution, construction, and service industries is easy, whereas entry into the finance industry is of medium difficulty, and entry into public utilities, such as transportation and communications, is very difficult. Freedom of entry into manufacturing industries is mixed. Barriers in the automobile, cigarette, and liquor industries are very high; in steel, copper, and petroleum, they are substantial; and in rubber tire manufacturing, meat packing, and cement, they are low. See Joe Bain, *Industrial Organization*, John Wiley & Sons, Inc., New York, 1959; ———, *Barriers to New Competition*, Harvard University Press, Cambridge, Mass., 1956; Richard Caves, *American Industry: Structure, Conduct, Performance*, 2d ed., Prentice-Hall, Inc., Englewood Cliffs, N.J., 1967.

Free-Enterprise System (Capitalism)   An economic system characterized by private ownership and initiative. Basic to a free-enterprise, or
capitalist, system is the concept of private property, the right of ownership and use of wealth to earn income. From private property comes the
institution of private enterprise or production by privately owned businesses. Firms are free to hire, produce, and price as they see fit. Furthermore, there is private initiative to carry on production. The motive for
this private initiative is the desire of the owners of business firms to earn
profits. Because of private ownership and initiative, a free-enterprise
system is characterized by the very large number of decisions reached
independently by producers and consumers. The function of controlling
the economy and coordinating the many independent decisions is
achieved through the operation of a free-price system. The force of competition is expected to be an important factor in assuring the smooth and
efficient functioning of the price system. Finally, a free-enterprise system
implies a relative absence of governmental control of the economy. Governmental activity is limited to a few spheres, such as national defense
and police protection, but in questions of production and pricing the
government is expected to take a laissez-faire position and exert little or
no control. For further information, see Louis Kelso and Mortimer J.
Adler, *The Capitalist Manifesto*, Random House, Inc., New York, 1958;
National Association of Manufacturers, Economic Principles Commission,
The American Individual Enterprise System, McGraw-Hill Book Company, New York, 1946; Marshall Dimock, *Free Enterprise and the Administrative State*, University of Alabama Press, University, Ala., 1951;
Paolo Leon, *Structural Change and Growth in Capitalism*, The Johns
Hopkins Press, Baltimore, 1967.

Free Good   A good that exists in such abundant supply that everyone
can have all he wants without effort or cost. Water, air, and sunshine are
frequently cited as examples of free goods. In most modern economies,
however, these do not always meet all the requirements of the concept
free good. Pure water is not freely available in most communities, since
the existing water supply is often contaminated and requires chemical
treatment. Air and sunshine come closer to being free goods, but in many
large cities, because of smog, smoke, and general air pollution, even
these canont be had without the economic cost involved in smoke control
and other regulations. For the distinction between free and economic
goods, see Armen A. Alchian and William R. Allen, *University Economics*,
2d ed., Wadsworth Publishing Company, Inc., Belmont, Calif., 1967, pp.
15–16.

Free List   The list of all the commodities on which no import duties are levied. Although once commodities have been placed on the free list, they are not generally removed, the importance of free imports has fluctuated widely. In 1909, with the enactment of the Payne-Aldrich Law, free imports accounted for 49% of all imports, By 1917 the percentage was 74%, but it fell to 59% in 1935, rose again during World War II to reach 70% in 1944, and then fell once again, so that by 1950 goods on the free list accounted for only 55% of total imports into the U.S. It is likely, however, that because of the Trade Expansion Act of 1962, which gave the President new power to reduce tariffs and the right to put goods on the free list, the importance of free imports in U.S. trade will rise again. For additional details, see Don D. Humphrey, *American Imports,* The Twentieth Century Fund, New York, 1955.

Freely Flexible Exchange Rates   Rates of foreign exchange which would be determined by the supply-and-demand mechanism, not by the balance of international payments. Thus all exchange rates would be determined in the free market, avoiding all official interventions. Under this system gold would be completely demonetized and a nation would be free to do anything it desired domestically, allowing the exchange rate to adjust to economic conditions. Flexible exchange rates can make the effects of inflation and price rigidities less intolerable. For additional information, see Paul A. Samuelson, *Economics,* 8th ed., McGraw-Hill Book Company, New York, 1970, pp. 625–628, 700–702.

Free Reserves   The margin by which excess reserves exceed borrowings at Federal Reserve banks. They are a better indicator of the banking system's ability to expand loans and investments than excess reserves. Manipulation of the net free-reserve position of member banks is an indication of the monetary policy which the Federal Reserve wishes to pursue. If the policy is one of aggressive ease, the Federal Reserve pumps reserves into the banking system with the intention of stimulating sluggish business activity. Free reserves act as high-power money, each dollar being capable of supporting more than a dollar's worth of loans and investments. Thus, with an average legal reserve requirement of 15%, the banking system may expand its loans and investments by as much as six and two-thirds times per dollar of free reserves. On the other hand, to halt a business upswing that is exerting inflationary pressures, it adopts a policy of aggressive tightness, contracting free reserves by the appropriate methods. The net free-reserve position of the banking system is published weekly in the Federal Reserve reports and appears in the Friday newspapers. For a criticism of the use of free reserves as a reflection of Federal Reserve policy, see E. M. Lerner, "Criticism of Free Reserves," *Review of Economics and Statistics,* Harvard University Press, Cambridge, Mass., May, 1962, pp. 225–228; see also "Significance and Limitations of Free Reserves," *Bulletin of the Federal Reserve Bank of New York,* November, 1958, pp. 162–167; Charles R. Whittlesey, Arthur M. Freedman, and Edward S. Herman, *Money and Banking: Analysis and Policy,* 2d ed., The Macmillan Company, New York, 1968, chap. 7; Beryl W. Sprinkel, *Money and Markets,* Richard D. Irwin, Inc., Homewood, Ill., 1971, pp. 85–93; Robert E. Knight and Paul S. Anderson, "Free Reserves in Monetary Policy Formulation," *New England Economic Review,* pp. 1–17, Federal Reserve Bank of Boston, November–December, 1969.

Free Reserves (Millions of dollars)

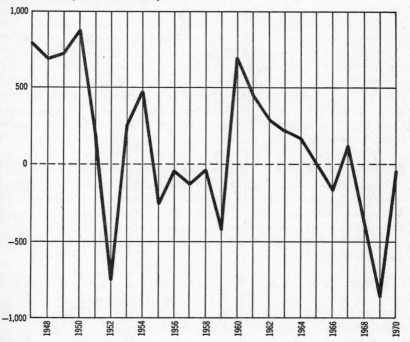

Source: Board of Governors, Federal Reserve System.

Free Trade A situation in which there are no restriction on the international exchange of goods. In such a situation, there would be no import duties, quotas and import licenses, import embargoes, exchange controls, government-purchasing preferences, subsidies to domestic producers, compulsory marks of origin, copyright and trademark enforcement, excessive valuations, unnecessary inconvenience in clearing customs, dumping duties, and escape clauses. In a free-trade economy, each country would be free to specialize in those products in which it had a comparative advantage, i.e., a relatively plentiful supply of the necessary resources of production. The prices at which goods would be traded would be determined by the reciprocal demand schedules of the respective countries involved, which, in turn, would be determined by the price structures existing in these countries. Rates of exchange would be determined by the demand and supply for the various currencies, which, in turn, would depend on the demand for goods purchasable with these currencies. Each country would specialize in the goods which it produced most efficiently, so that the production of all goods in the economy as a whole would be maximized and goods would be plentiful and inexpensive. On balance, academic economists favor a freer trade than now exists among the industrial nations of the world, but they would not demand the utopian state of complete free trade, since they would support some restrictions for the protection of health and welfare, the furthering of national security, and, possibly, the economic development of underdeveloped countries. See Jacob Viner, *International Trade and Economic Development*, Oxford University Press, Fair Lawn, N.J., 1953; W. R. Allen and Clark Lee Allen, *Foreign Trade and Finance*, The Macmillan Company, New York 1959; Imanuel Wexler, *Fundamentals of International Economics*, Random House, Inc., New York, 1968.

Frequency Distribution　A statistical method of condensing large masses of economic data by arranging them into various classes. This simple classification makes analyses of the data much easier, as the frequency distribution table (opposite) illustrates. For further information on the organization of data into frequency distribution tables, see W. A. Spurr et al., *Business and Economic Statstics*, Richard D. Irwin, Inc., Homewood, Ill., 1954.

Frictional Unemployment　Temporary unemployment caused by functional imperfections in the labor market. It arises because of the dynamic structure of the U.S. economic system, in which changing consumer tastes cause old jobs to disappear and new jobs to replace them. Frictional unemployment is due to the time required in changing jobs, and its magnitude depends on the structural difficulty encountered in getting the unemployed worker and the job together. The main structural difficulties in finding a new job are lack of information about work opportunities and inability to reach the job. Frictional unemployment is also associated with the freedom of workers to seek new jobs and to change jobs at will, since

Family Income	Number of Primary Families (Thousands)
Under $1,000	767
$ 1,000–$ 1,499	664
$ 1,500–$ 1,999	920
$ 2,000–$ 2,499	1,227
$ 2,500–$ 2,999	1,124
$ 3,000–$ 3,499	1,329
$ 3,500–$ 3,999	1,380
$ 4,000–$ 4,999	2,760
$ 5,000–$ 5,999	3,015
$ 6,000–$ 6,999	3,271
$ 7,000–$ 7,999	3,731
$ 8,000–$ 9,999	7,360
$10,000–$14,999	13,647
$15,000–$24,999	8,024
$25,000 and over	1,891

SOURCE: U.S. Bureau of the Census, *Current Population Reports: Consumer Income*, ser. P-60, no. 75, Dec. 14, 1970.

such voluntary work changes also require the time to find new employment. Since frictional unemployment is noncyclical and is only indirectly connected with the state of the national economy, it cannot be reduced merely by increasing public spending. It can, however, be decreased by increasing labor mobility and information about employment opportunities so that the time required for job hunting can be reduced. For further information, see Herbert S. Parnes, *Research in Labor Mobility*, Social Science Research Council, New York, 1954; Lloyd G. Reynolds, *Labor Economics and Labor Relations*, 5th ed., Prentice-Hall, Inc., Englewood Cliffs, N.J., 1970, pp. 124–125.

Fringe Benefit Any nonwage benefits or payment received by workers in addition to their wages, for example, supplemental unemployment benefits, pensions, travel pay, vacation and holiday pay, and health insurance. Fringe benefits include benefits provided by law, those introduced unilaterally by employers, and those obtained by unions through collective bargaining. Although fringe benefits antedate World War II, it was the war that stimulated their growth because wages were frozen. In 1971 fringe benefits totaled $140 billion in the U.S., as compared with $65 billion a decade earlier. Fringe benefits have accounted for a greatly increasing percentage of worker income and labor costs, particularly in firms in which unions are active, although they have also been popular with employers, who realize that some fringe benefits (those that accumulate over the period of the worker's service and cannot be transferred to another firm) reduce the costs of labor turnover. For the economy at large, however, diminished labor mobility may impede efficiency and a smooth adjustment to changing conditions. Another incentive to fringe benefits is the high level of income taxes, since some of the benefits are either not taxed at all or taxed at a preferential rate. For a more detailed discussion, see Lloyd G. Reynolds, *Labor Economics and Labor Relations,* 5th ed., Prentice-Hall, Inc., Englewood Cliffs, N.J., 1970; Albert Rees, *The Economics of Trade Unions,* The University of Chicago Press, Chicago, 1962; Jack Barbash, *The Practice of Unionism,* Harper & Row, Publishers, Incorporated, New York, 1956.

Fringe Benefits as a Percentage of Payroll, 1969

Industry	Percentage
All industries	27.9
All manufacturing	27.0
Food, beverages, and tobacco	30.3
Textile products and apparel	22.2
Pulp, paper, lumber, and furniture	23.9
Printing and publishing	25.6
Chemicals and allied products	32.2
Petroleum industry	32.4
Rubber, leather, and plastic products	27.1
Stone, clay, and glass products	27.4
Primary metal industries	29.9
Fabricated metal products	24.6
Machinery, except electrical	26.8
Electrical machinery and equipment	26.5
Transportation equipment	28.5
Instruments and miscellaneous manufacturing industries	25.9
Nonmanufacturing	29.3
Public utilities	30.3
Department stores	23.1
Other retail and wholesale	21.7
Banks, finance and trust companies	33.9
Insurance companies	30.3
Other industries	25.1

SOURCE: U.S. Chamber of Commerce.

Frozen Asset   An asset that is not readily convertible into cash or one which can be sold only with great loss in value. It is the opposite of a liquid asset. If money is invested in a foreign country and cannot be withdrawn before a certain time period has elapsed, the asset is considered frozen until the end of the period.

Full Employment A state of the economy in which all persons who want to work can find employment without much difficulty at prevailing rates of pay. Some unemployment, both voluntary and involuntary, is not incompatible with full employment, since allowances must be made for frictional and seasonal factors which are always present to some degree. In the U.S., a figure of 4% is generally taken as the normal rate of such temporary unemployment, and this figure is thus also considered the maximum permissible unemployment level for a full-employment situation. The achievement and maintenance of full employment constitute an important factor in economic growth. Also important is the raising of the standard of living, since total demand must increase at a rate equal to the expansion of the economy's productive capacity if maximum growth is to be realized. Periods of less than full employment depress investment and capital accumulation and thus hamper future growth. The U.S. government set full employment as a major goal with the introduction of the New Deal, relying on the use of monetary and fiscal policy to achieve this aim, but it was not until passage of the Employment Act of 1946 that detailed objectives were formalized. For further information on full employment, see Alvin H. Hansen, *Economic Policy and Full Employment*, McGraw-Hill Book Company, New York, 1947; Sir William Beveridge, *Full Employment in a Free Society*, W. W. Norton & Company, Inc., New York, 1945; *Financing American Prosperity*, The Twentieth Century Fund, New York, 1945; U.S. Joint Economic Committee, *State of the Economy and Policies for Full Employment*, hearings, Aug. 7–10, 13–17, 20–21, and 22, 1962, Government Printing Office, Washington, D.C., 1962.

Full-Employment Budget A budget concept which indicates for any point in time what the budget position would be if the economy were operating at full employment (96% of the civilian labor force) given actual Federal expenditure programs and tax rates. The concept was originally developed by the Committee for Economic Development in 1947. Under this system there is no effort to raise taxes or cut Federal expenditures in order to offset deficits caused by the shortfall in revenues that is due to economic slack. The absolute level of the full-employment budget does not tell much about its impact on the economy. Instead, it is the change in the full-employment surplus or deficit as measured on the national-income-account basis that indicates whether a proposed new budget is likely to be expansive, neutral, or depressing. For more detail, see Herbert Stein, *The Fiscal Revolution in America*, The University of Chicago Press, Chicago, 1969, chap. 9; see also Frank Schiff, "Control of Inflation and

Recession," *The Annals*, American Academy of Political and Social Science, Philadelphia, July, 1971.

Full-Employment Output *See Potential Gross National Product.*

Functional Finance A system in which the Federal government's fiscal policy not only would concern itself with raising or borrowing enough money to meet expenses, but also would consider the state of the national economy: the level of income and employment, price stability, and a satisfactory rate of economic growth. The proponents of functional finance would suggest a deficit in the Federal budget in times of lagging economic activity whether or not higher government expenditures were then needed; they might also suggest a budget surplus to withdraw liquid funds from the public in times of inflationary pressures. Furthermore, they would countenance the printing of additional amounts of money, without raising taxes or the Federal debt, in periods when the government needed greater funds but could not raise them from the public. In short, they would advocate much greater flexibility for both the tools and the objectives of governmental fiscal policy. Their position has been attacked by those who believe that such flexibility is ill-advised when no clear standards of behavior have been set up and no policy goals have been defined. For varying views of functional finance, see Abba P. Lerner, *Functional Finance and the Federal Debt*, reprinted in Arthur Smithies and J. Keith Butters (eds.), *Readings in Fiscal Policy*, Richard D. Irwin, Inc., Homewood, Ill., 1955; ———, *Economics of Employment*, McGraw-Hill Book Company, New York, 1951; Harley Lutz, "Debt, Taxation, and Functional Finance," *Tax Review*, Tax Foundation, Inc., New York, January, 1944; also Owen Brownlee's review of *Economics of Employment* in *Journal of Political Economy*, The University of Chicago Press, Chicago, February, 1952; for the argument that the concept of functional finance ignores the banking system and the scope of monetary policy, see Lawrence S. Ritter, "Functional Finance and the Banking System," *American Journal of Economics and Sociology*, New York, July, 1956; John G. Ranlett, *Money and Banking: An Introduction to Analysis and Policy*, John Wiley & Sons, Inc., New York, 1965, chap. 25.

Funded Debt The long-term indebtedness of a corporation or a government, generally in the form of long-term, interest-bearing bonds. Payment on this type of debt is generally due more than one year after the debt has been incurred. In public finance, funded debt usually refers to the debt incurred from the sale of long-term securities whose proceeds have been used to retire one or more issues of short-term bills. For more detailed information, see Roy A. Foulke, *Practical Financial Statement Analysis*,

5th ed., McGraw-Hill Book Company, New York, 1961; Charles W. Gerstenberg, *Financial Organization and Management of Business*, 4th ed., Prentice-Hall, Inc., Englewood Cliffs, N.J., 1959.

Futures Market   A market in which contracts for the future delivery of commodities or foreign exchange are bought and sold. The commodities themselves are not brought to the futures market; it is only the promises of future delivery, commonly called futures, that are traded. The futures market for a commodity is often incorporated in an organized commodity exchange, which offers a continuous and stable market on which the futures may always be bought and sold. The primary service of the futures market lies in its provision of a means of insurance against the risk of adverse price fluctuations between the time of the production of the commodity and its final utilization. This insurance function is carried out by hedging, or taking an opposite position on the futures market from that held in the spot market. A commodity market without a futures market usually does not have a large enough number of risk-bearing dealers and a sufficient amount of risk capital to carry out this hedging function adequately. The continuous existence of a stable and liquid futures market also makes the formal financing of commodities much easier. For further information on the operation of the futures market, see Julius Baer and E. Olin Saxon, *Commodity Exchanges and Futures Trading*, Harper & Row, Publishers, Incorporated, New York, 1949; Gerald Gold, *Modern Commodity Futures Trading*, Commodity Research Bureau, Inc., New York, 1959; G. Wright Hoffman, *Futures Trading*, University of Pennsylvania Press, Philadelphia, 1932.

Galloping Inflation   *See Hyperinflation.*

Garnishment   A court order requiring an employer to pay part or all of the wages of a debtor employee to a court officer for the benefit of a creditor. In practice, the garnished wages or salaries may be sent directly from the employer to the creditor. In this manner, the debtor's account is settled.

Gauss-Markoff Theorem   The variance of an unbiased linear estimate of a population parameter is minimized when the estimator is obtained by the method of least squares. This theorem can be expanded to include the simultaneous estimation of several parameters or their linear functions. It is subject to the conditions that the function to be estimated be linear in the unknown parameters and that the errors or deviations (actual minus calculated) be independent random variables. For additional information, see Gerhard Tintner and Charles B. Millham, *Mathematics and Statistics for Economists,* Holt, Rinehart and Winston, Inc., New York, 1970.

General Agreement on Tariffs and Trade (GATT)   An international code of tariffs and trade rules, signed in 1947 by twenty-three countries, including the U.S. It became effective on January 1, 1948. The agreement was the culmination of an American-led drive for freer trade after World War II. GATT was originally intended to be a temporary provision to handle tariff and trade questions along multilateral lines until the charter of the International Trade Organization (ITO) was established, but in 1950 the U.S. Senate rejected the ITO charter and GATT became effective. Since then, it has been renewed and amended many times. GATT is dedicated to three basic principles: (1) equal, nondiscriminatory treatment for all trading nations, (2) reduction of tariffs by negotiations, and (3) elimination of import quotas. GATT has eliminated and negotiated reductions in binding tariffs, quantitative restrictions, and discriminations, permitting the freer movement of international trade. About 55,000 tariff concessions were involved in the first three major

Year	Tariff Law	Duties Collected (Percentage of Value of Dutiable Imports)
1913–1921	Underwood law	27.0
1922–1929	Fordney-McCumber law	38.5
1930–1933	Hawley-Smoot law	52.8
1939	Reciprocal Trade Agreements Act	37.3
1947	GATT	15.3
1960	GATT	12.2
1970	GATT	10.0

rounds of tariff reductions concluded in the agreement. On August 15, 1971, the Nixon administration unilaterally set a 10% surcharge on imported goods other than those items covered by quotas, thus setting a barrier to trade and voiding the intent of GATT. The surcharge was revoked on November 13, 1971. The latest problem facing GATT is the reaching of an arrangement with the European Common Market. GATT would like to make sure that the Common Market does not result in higher barriers to trade than had existed previously. See the table (opposite) for the impact of GATT on import duties collected in the U.S. For further information, see Contracting Parties to the General Agreement on Tariffs and Trade, *International Trade 1960*, Geneva, 1961; *Operation of the Trade Agreements Program: 13th Report, July 1959–June 1960*, Government Printing Office, Washington, D.C., 1962; Thomas B. Curtis and John R. Vastine, Jr., *The Kennedy Round and the Future of American Trade*, Frederick A. Praeger, Inc., New York, 1971.

General-Equilibrium Theory   That part of economic theory concerned with the structure of prices and output of the economy as a whole. Developed by Leon Walras at the end of the nineteenth century, general-equilibrium theory takes into account the interrelationship of prices and outputs of goods and resources in different markets. Once resource supply schedules, consumer preferences, and production functions have been given, general-equilibrium theory can demonstrate mathematically that resources and commodity prices can adjust themselves to levels which are mutually consistent with each other. Thus any given set of basic determinants defines a unique stable equilibrium state for the economy as a whole. Any shift in the determinants affecting one good may have widespread repercussions on the equilibrium prices and outputs of the other goods. Although general-equilibrium analysis is very useful as a theoretical tool for stressing the interdependence of the various sectors of the economic system, it is essentially static and thus of limited value in studying trends in economic development. Furthermore, the tremendous complexity of the economic system makes it very hard to use general-equilibrium theory to determine the actual equilibrium values for the real world. For a fuller discussion of general-equilibrium analysis, see Leon Walras, *Elements of Pure Economics*, Eng. tr. by W. Jaffe, Richard D. Irwin, Inc., Homewood, Ill., 1954; J. R. Hicks, *Value and Capital*, Oxford University Press, Fair Lawn, N.J., 1938, chaps. 4–8; Don Patinkin, *Money, Interest and Prices*, 3d ed., Harper & Row, Publishers, Incorporated, New York, 1964.

General Sales Tax   *See Turnover Tax.*

General Strike   A cessation of labor by the majority of workers in all the vital industries of any locality or region. A general strike differs from a generalized strike in a single industry. The vital element in a general strike, whether it involves the entire economy or is restricted to a single locality, is the more or less complete paralysis of the economic life of the community in order to bring about the desired ends. The general strike may be aimed at the redress of special injustices in industrial relations, or it may be invoked as a weapon to wrest some new constitutional right for the working class. The general strike achieved some popularity in the U.S. as a weapon of labor during the earliest and most frustrating periods of unionism, but as organized labor became more successful and employers met some of its demands, the general strike lost its popularity. Such attempts at general strikes as took place in the U.S. were short-lived because of a lack of support among the working class, whereas in Europe these strikes were made in response to very popular causes, giving them popular support and enabling the strikers to bring the entire economy to a standstill. See W. H. Crook, *The General Strike: A Study of Labor's Tragic Weapon in Theory and Practice*, The University of North Carolina Press, Chapel Hill, N.C., 1931.

Giffen Paradox   A famous exception to demand theory in which an increase in the price of bread in Ireland was followed by an increase in the consumption of bread—hence, any instances in which demands for a product increases in response to price increases. Also known as the Giffen effect. For additional information, see Alfred Marshall, *Principles of Economics*, 9th ed., The Macmillan Company, New York, 1961; Oskar Lange, *Introduction to Econometrics*, The Macmillan Company, New York, 1963.

Gift Tax   A levy on the value of donated property. It is paid by the donor. The gift tax was first used in the U.S. in 1924 as a supplement to estate and inheritance taxes, which were avoided by giving away property before death. Except for specified exemptions, all gifts are taxable at progressive rates, and the rate on gifts made in a single year is based on the cumulative sum of all gifts made during the donor's lifetime. There is a cumulative lifetime exemption of $30,000 and, in addition, a yearly exemption of $3,000 per recipient. Gift taxes constitute only a minor part of Federal and state revenues and are not levied at the local level. See Boris Bittker, *Federal Income, Estate and Gift Taxation*, 3d ed., Little, Brown and Company, Boston, 1964; Philip E. Taylor, *The Economics of Public Finance*, The Macmillan Company, New York, 1953; H. S. Block, "Economic Objectives of Gratuitous Transfer Taxation," *National Tax*

Journal, National Tax Association, Boston, Mass., June, 1951; for statistics on Federal revenues from death and gift taxes (combined), see U.S. Internal Revenue Service, *Statistics of Income, Estate and Gift Tax Returns Filed during Calendar Year* . . . ; for statistics on state revenues, see U.S. Department of Commerce, *Compendium of State Government Finances.*

Gini Coefficient   A measure that shows how close a given distribution of income is to absolute equality or inequality. Named for Corrado Gini, the Gini coefficient is a ratio of the area between the 45-degree line and the Lorenz curve and the area of the entire triangle. As the coefficient approaches zero, the distribution of income approaches absolute equality. Conversely, as the coefficient approaches 1, the distribution of income approaches absolute inequality. The Gini coefficient can be used to determine the impact of a change in taxes on income distribution. For example, if a given tax change would decrease the Gini coefficient, that tax would be progressive in its overall effects since it would lead to an income distribution closer to absolute equality. See Richard Musgrave, *The Theory of Public Finance,* McGraw-Hill Book Company, New York, 1959, pp. 224–225.

Gold Certificate   Paper currency issued by the U.S. Treasury Department for which there is a 100% reserve of gold bullion. From the end of the Civil War until 1933, gold certificates which were freely convertible into gold circulated as part of the U.S. money supply. In 1933 the convertibility of gold certificates ended, and they were withdrawn from circulation. Since then, only Federal Reserve banks have been permitted to hold gold certificates, but they have no control over the number that they wish to hold, since they must buy all that the Treasury offers and turn in all that the Treasury demands. As of April 28, 1971, Federal Reserve banks held more than $10 billion worth of gold certificates outstanding, amounting to about 13% of their total deposits and outstanding notes. See Lester V. Chandler, *Economics of Money and Banking,* 5th ed., Harper & Row, Publishers, Incorporated, New York, 1969; for statistics on the number of gold certificates, see *Federal Reserve Bulletin,* Washington, D.C., monthly.

Gold Crisis   A situation created when a nation, in order to meet its international financial obligations, must export a quantity of gold so great that its remaining gold supply is brought close to the quantity required by law as a backing for its money supply. In the U.S., prior to 1968, the Federal Reserve System was required to hold in reserve a quantity of gold equal to 25% of all Federal Reserve notes outstanding plus its deposit liabilities to commercial banks. Any loss that reduced gold reserves below that margin would precipitate a financial crisis, since the Federal Reserve could be required to make a corresponding cut in its circulating currency and deposits, thereby drastically reducing the nation's money supply. In 1968, after our supply of gold had been cut sharply, the gold-reserve requirement was suspended by Congress. For more information, see Robert Triffin, *Gold and the Dollar Crisis,* Yale University Press, New Haven, Conn., 1966.

Gold Exchange Standard   An elaboration of the pure gold standard under which some countries keep their monetary reserves in currency other than gold that is convertible into gold at a fixed rate of exchange. The gold exchange standard owes its existence to the facts that requirements for reserves to back rising national money supplies outstripped the rate of gold production and that convertible foreign currencies were the next-best reserve available. Before 1931 the world's major reserve currency was the British pound sterling, and the gold exchange standard collapsed when this currency was devalued by 18%. After World War II, the U.S. dollar, one of the few convertible currencies of the time, became the most popular reserve currency. With the spread of convertibility in succeeding years, it was joined by British sterling, Belgian francs, Swiss francs, Deutsche marks, and others. The major prerequisite for a reserve currency is a stable rate of exchange, a requirement which may, however, limit the freedom of the currency's issuing authorities to tailor their monetary policy to domestic requirements. For example, interest rates in the U.S. may have to be kept higher than the domestic situation warrants to forestall excessive liquidation of foreigners' dollar holdings and a run on the dollar. Since August 15, 1971, the buying and selling of gold in transactions with foreign central banks has been suspended. Thus foreign central banks acquiring dollars are not able to convert them into gold or any other monetary reserve asset. For a critical analysis of the gold exchange standard, see Rober Triffin, *Gold and the Dollar Crisis: The Future of Convertibility,* Yale University Press, New Haven, Conn., 1960; for the history of the gold exchange standard in the interwar period, see *International Currency Experience,* League of Nations, Geneva, 1944. For additional information, see Eli Shapiro, Ezra Solomon, and William L. White, *Money and Banking,* 5th ed., Holt, Rinehart and Winston, Inc., New York, 1968, pp. 615–619.

Gold Points   Rates of exchange at which, under the gold standard, the import or export of gold became profitable. The gold points have not operated in the U.S. since 1933, when the gold standard was abandoned and it became illegal for private citizens to buy or sell gold. Under the gold standard, an exchange rate (e.g., the dollar price of pounds sterling) could not rise above a certain point, because if it had done so, a U.S. importer, instead of buying pounds for dollars, could buy gold at the Treasury. He could then export the gold to England and sell it for pounds, paying fewer dollars than it would have cost him on the regular exchange market. The upper rate at which the supply of pounds became perfectly elastic was called the upper gold point or gold export point. It was the ceiling price for pounds in terms of dollars, the point at which the importer found it cheaper to buy gold and export it in payment for his imports than to buy foreign exchange directly. The reverse situation worked in the same way. The rate at which the demand for pounds became perfectly inelastic was called the lower gold point or the import point for pounds. It was the lowest price at which pounds would sell in terms of dollars, since gold could always be imported at a lower rate. The distance between the export and import points depended on the costs of shipping the gold and the interest charges on the value of the gold while it was in transit. Any increase in transportation costs increased the spread of the gold points, while any decrease in the interest charges narrowed the gap between the gold points. The operation of the gold points under the gold standard provided a high degree of exchange stability, since the range in which the exchange rate could fluctuate was limited. For additional details, see Fritz Machlup, "The Theory of Foreign Exchanges," in Howard S. Ellis and Lloyd A. Metzler (eds.), *Readings in the Theory of International Trade*, McGraw-Hill Book Company, New York, 1949; Imanuel Wexler, *Fundamentals of International Economics*, Random House, Inc., New York, 1968, pp. 126–127; Charles R. Whittlesey, Arthur M. Freed-

Gold Points

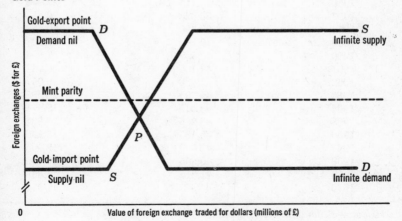

man, and Edward S. Herman, *Money and Banking: Analysis and Policy,* 2d ed., The Macmillan Company, New York, 1968, pp. 496–499.

Gold Reserve The monetary stock of gold held by a country. Gold is held by the government to cover issued domestic currency, provide a reserve for future domestic credit expansion, and effect international payments. In the U.S. gold was nationalized in 1933, and since then all gold produced domestically or imported is purchased automatically by the Treasury, which pays for the gold with a check on its own bank account with the Federal Reserve System. Under the Gold Reserve Act of 1934, Federal Reserve banks had to maintain gold certificates as a gold reserve cover, equivalent to at least a 25% minimum against Federal Reserve notes and deposits. In 1968, Congress eliminated the gold reserve cover. The U.S. gold reserve has been declining since 1953. The gold reserves of the central banks and governments of the free world totaled $41.3 billion in the spring of 1971. Since August 15, 1971, the buying and selling of gold in transactions with foreign central banks has been suspended. Thus foreign central banks acquiring dollars are not able to convert them into gold or any other monetary reserve asset. For addi-

Reported Gold Reserves of Central Banks and Governments (In millions of dollars)

End of Period	Estimated Free-World Total	U.S.
1953	36,680	22,091
1954	37,340	21,793
1955	37,620	21,753
1956	38,115	22,058
1957	38,820	22,857
1958	39,490	20,582
1959	40,190	19,507
1960	40,525	17,804
1961	41,105	16,947
1962	41,430	16,057
1963	42,305	15,596
1964	43,015	15,471
1965	43,230	13,806
1966	43,185	13,235
1967	41,600	12,065
1968	40,905	10,892
1969	41,015	11,859
1970	41,285	11,072

SOURCE: *Federal Reserve Bulletin.*

tional information, see Robert Triffin, *Gold and the Dollar Crisis,* Yale University Press, New Haven, Conn., 1960; O. L. Altman, "A Note on Gold Production and Additions to International Gold Reserves," *International Monetary Fund Staff Papers,* Washington, D.C., April, 1958; Raymond P. Kent, *Money and Banking,* 5th ed., Holt, Rinehart and Winston, Inc., New York, 1966.

Gold Standard   A monetary standard under which the basic unit of currency of a country is a fixed quantity of gold and the currency is freely convertible at home or abroad into the fixed amount of gold per unit of currency. Whenever the gold value of the monetary unit of a country is divorced from the market value of gold in free world markets, the country is not on a true gold standard. Advantages of the gold standard include simplicity, public confidence, automatic operation requiring little political management, an international character, and stability of value. The basis of the gold standard is the fact that the value of a monetary unit is tied to the value of gold by fixing the gold price. Inasmuch as gold is a commodity in the world market, it has a world value, and the gold standard therefore gives a world value to the monetary unit itself. When the gold standard was predominant, the market for gold was simply the market for gold-standard currencies. The task of a central bank was to keep the value of the monetary unit in the international market as near as possible to par with other gold-standard currencies. Any failure would mean a gain or loss of gold, which was liable to be both larger and more sudden than any movement to and from internal circulation. These international movements were the main consideration in settling the amount of gold reserves. When currency demands outstripped the supply of gold for reserves, however, the gold exchange standard was developed. In using the gold standard, it is essential to guard against exhaustion of the reserve of gold. See R. G. Hawtrey, *The Gold Standard in Theory and Practice,* 5th ed., Longmans, Green & Co., Ltd., London, 1947; Wendell Gordon, *International Trade,* Alfred A. Knopf, Inc., New York, 1965, chap. 18.

Goodwill   An accounting term used to explain the difference between what a company pays when it buys another company and what it gets in the form of tangible assets. The term can also be used as an expression in money value of the reputation of a company. Goodwill is an intangible asset, represented on the asset side of the balance sheet. It comes into existence only when a company is purchased or transferred and cannot exist when a new company is founded. In more technical terms, goodwill is the capitalized value of excess profits over and above the normal rate of return on the investment, discounted at some rate in excess of the current rate of interest. Goodwill does not always mean payment for excess profits: it can also mean payment for a good competitive situation, a good location, and a monopoly position. For the method of dealing with goodwill in accounting theory, see John P. Powelson, *Economic Accounting*, McGraw-Hill Book Company, New York, 1955.

Government Expenditure Spending by Federal, state, and local governments. In 1970 the manifold governments of the U.S. spent nearly $221 billion in terms of the gross national product, the Federal government accounting for about $100 billion, and state and local governments

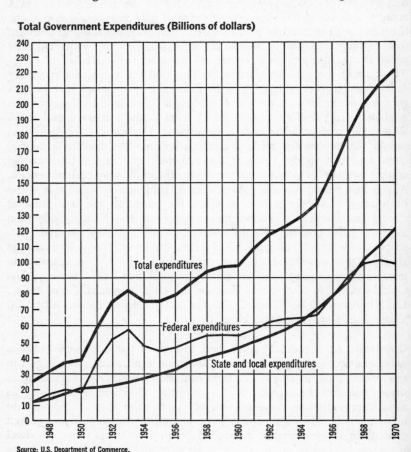

Total Government Expenditures (Billions of dollars)

Source: U.S. Department of Commerce.

for about $121 billion. Total U.S. expenditures by governments have increased over the years (exclusive of war years), so that by 1970 they accounted for about 23% of the gross national product, whereas in 1929 they accounted for only 8%. Most Federal expenditures pay for national defense, and national security accounts for about 75% of all Federal spending. Natural resources, agriculture and agricultural services, social security, welfare and health, and commerce and housing are the other major areas of Federal government expenditures. Among state and local government expenditures, education is the largest item. For statistics on government expenditures in gross-national-product form, see U.S. Department of Commerce, *Survey of Current Business: National Income Supplement;* for statistics on government budget bases, see *The Budget of the United States Government* for fiscal years, Government Printing Office, Washington, D.C.

Government Sector   *See Public Sector.*

Grant-in-Aid   A payment by a central government to assist smaller governmental units. In the U.S., for example, the Federal government makes grants to both state and local governments (but primarily to the states), and the states make grants to municipalities, counties, school districts, and other governmental units. The common characteristic of all grants-in-aid is that the larger governmental units provide financial assistance without supplanting the smaller units that actually provide the public service. Grants-in-aid have been used primarily to achieve specific objectives rather than to offer general financial assistance. Such objectives have included the building of roads, lunches for schoolchildren, old-age assistance, and cancer research. In 1929, Federal grants amounted to less than 2% of total state spending; by 1969 they had grown to 23%. During the same year, state grants accounted for about 30% of local government spending. Grants are lauded primarily because they serve as an effective device for cooperative government and stimulate state and local governments to launch and expand services for which these governments should have responsibility. They are sometimes criticized because they lessen the democratic dispersal of political power and add to the cost of public services by placing two levels of administration on a single program. For a detailed discussion of grants-in-aid, their uses, advantages, and disadvantages, see Robert Asher, *Grants, Loans and Local Currency,* The Brookings Institution, Washington, D.C., 1961. See also Commission on Intergovernmental Relations, *Report to the President,* Washington, D.C., June, 1955; for current data on Federal grants, see U.S. Treasury Department, *Annual Report of the Secretary of the Treasury.*

Graveyard Shift   A work shift beginning at or about 12 P.M. and continuing until 8 A.M. Graveyard shifts are worked when an enterprise is operating twenty-four hours a day, with three shifts each working eight hours.

Gray Market   A market in which scarce commodities are sold for immediate delivery at exorbitant prices, taking unfair advantage of market demand. The gray market existed after World War II, when suppliers were unable to meet the latent demand that built up during the war. Although price controls had been removed, many producers continued to allocate their goods to their regular customers and did not take advantage of the situation by permitting prices to rise. On the other hand, some manufacturers and brokers who were allocated materials resold them at three and four times the prices that they had paid for them. Thus, a true gray market is characterized by a two-price system, one price paid by favored customers, who have been allocated a certain amount by the supplier, and a much higher price paid by less-favored customers, who must scout the gray market in order to fulfill their demands. The difference between gray-market operations and black-market selling is that, although gray-market transactions may be unethical, they are not illegal. For an expanded study of this type of market and its operations, see "That Daffy Gray Market," *Fortune*, May, 1948, pp. 94–97.

Gresham's Law   A law usually stated simply as follows: "Bad money drives out good." It was named for Sir Thomas Gresham, a sixteenth-century English financier, merchant, and adviser to Queen Elizabeth I. Gresham pointed out to the Queen that because of the debasement of English coin by her predecessor, England's foreign trade, which was being financed by coins of cheaper metallic content, was suffering while the valuable metals were being hoarded and kept out of circulation. Gresham's law also holds that when metals of differing value are endowed with equal powers of legal tender, the cheaper metal will become the chief circulating medium, while more costly metals are hoarded or exported and hence disappear from circulation. The principles embodied in Gresham's law remain an important part of economic theory and practice. They enter, for example, into foreigners' decisions to accept gold as opposed to dollars in payment for goods imported by the U.S. See Joseph A. Schumpeter, *History of Economic Analysis,* Oxford University Press, Fair Lawn, N.J., 1954, p. 342, note 4; for a full discussion of Gresham's law and its implications, see Irving Fisher, *The Purchasing Power of Money,* The Macmillan Company, New York, 1912, chap. 7; for a discussion of Gresham's law and American monetary history, see Charles R. Whittlesey, Arthur M. Freedman, and Edward S. Herman,

Money and Banking: Analysis and Policy, The Macmillan Company, New York, 1968, pp. 31–40.

Gross Cash Flow   *See Cash Flow.*

Gross Income Tax   *See Turnover Tax.*

Gross National Product (GNP)   The most comprehensive measure of a nation's total output of goods and services. In the U.S., the GNP represents the dollar value in current prices of all goods and services produced for sale plus the estimated value of certain imputed outputs, that is, goods and services that are neither bought nor sold. The rental value of owner-occupied dwellings and the value of farm products consumed on the farm are the most important imputed outputs included; the

Gross National Product (Billions of dollars)

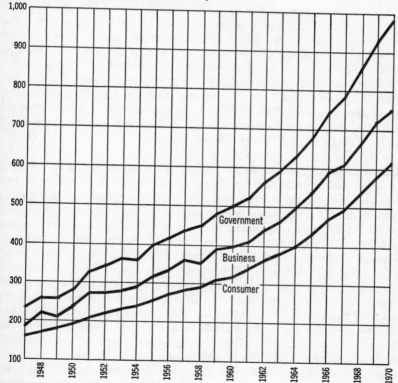

Source: U.S. Department of Commerce.

services of housewives are among the most important nonmarket values excluded. The GNP includes only final goods and services; for example, a pair of shoes that costs the manufacturer $2.50, the retailer $4.50, and the consumer $6.00 adds to the GNP only $6.00, the amount of the final sale, and not $13.00, the sum of all the transactions. The GNP may be calculated by adding either all expenditures on currently produced goods and services or all incomes earned in producing these goods and services. Calculated from the expenditure side, it is the sum of (1) consumption expenditures by both individuals and nonprofit organizations, plus certain imputed values; (2) business investment in equipment, inventories, and new construction (residential as well as business construction is counted as an investment); (3) Federal, state, and local government purchases of goods and services; and (4) the sale of goods and services abroad minus purchases from abroad. From the income side, the GNP is the sum of all wages, interest, and profits before taxes and depreciation earned in the current production of goods and services. The GNP is a key measure of the overall performance of the economy and a gauge of the health of important sectors. Historically, the U.S. gross national product has fluctuated to a much smaller extent than measures of industrial activity. For a detailed discussion of the concept, coverage, and sources of data, see U.S. Department of Commerce, *National Income Supplement*, 1954; see also Richard Ruggles and Nancy D. Ruggles, *National Income Accounts and Income Analysis*, 2d ed., McGraw-Hill Book Company, New York, 1956; for quarterly and annual data, adjusted for price changes as well as in current dollars, see U.S. Department of Commerce, *Survey of Current Business*, monthly.

Gross-National-Product Gap   The gap between the economy's output of goods and services and its potential output at full employment (4% unemployment rate) without inflation. The magnitude of the gap is imprecise, and there have been arguments among economists about the possibility of measuring potential GNP at all. Without an estimate of potential GNP, the gap cannot be estimated. At the end of 1961, the Council of Economic Advisers attempted to measure the gap, and found that it was $32 billion (in 1960 prices) for the year 1960. The council used mid-1955, when a 4% unemployment rate was prevalent, as the bench mark and a growth rate of 3.5% to measure potential GNP. In refuting the notion of a gap or the size of the gap, Arthur F. Burns showed that the gap could be $20 billion, or even −$2 billion, if the second quarter of 1957 and the second quarter of 1947 were used as respective bench marks (an unemployment rate of about 4% was prevalent at both times). Arthur M. Okun has estimated the GNP gap by measuring the extent to which output is depressed by unemployment in excess of 4%, a relationship that can be expressed as follows: "On the average, each extra percentage point in the unemployment rate above 4% has been associated with an approximate 3% decrease in real GNP." For further discussion of the GNP gap, see *Economic Report of the President,* Government Printing Office, Washington, D.C., 1962, pp. 49–53; for Arthur F. Burns' position, see *The Morgan Guaranty Survey,* Morgan Guaranty Trust Company, New York, May, 1961; for the Council of Economic Advisers' reply to Burns and for Burns' comments on the council's reply, see *The Morgan Guaranty Survey,* Morgan Guaranty Trust Company, New York, August, 1961; see also Arthur M. Okun, "Potential GNP: Its Measurement and Significance," *American Statistical Association: 1962 Proceedings of the Business and Economic Section,* American Statistical Association, Washington, D.C., 1962, pp. 98–104.

Gross National Product, Actual and Potential [Billions of dollars (ratio scale)] *

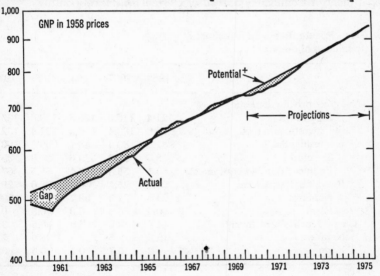

*Seasonally adjusted annual rates.

+Trend line of 3.5 percent from middle of 1955 to 1962 IV, 3.75 percent from 1962 IV to 1965 IV, 4 percent from 1965 IV to 1969 IV, 4.3 percent from 1969 IV to 1970 IV, 4.4 percent from 1970 IV to 1971 IV, and 4.3 percent from 1971 IV to 1975 IV.

Source: U.S. Department of Commerce and Council of Economic Advisers.

Gross Private Domestic Investment   Expenditures by private businesses and individuals for new buildings, machinery, vehicles, and inventories. Gross private domestic investment includes all agricultural and business spending on new plants and equipment, all new private housing and construction, and the net change in privately held inventories. As calculated by the U.S. Department of Commerce, it also includes a small amount of outlays for equipment and construction that some firms carry on their books as current expenditures rather than as investment (for example, jigs and dies used in the automobile industry). It is the most comprehensive measure of nongovernmental investment. The term gross indicates that no allowance is made for depreciation or for the retirement of existing plants and equipment. Gross private domestic investment differs from capital formation, which is gross investment minus the loss of value that plants and equipment suffer in use. The use of the concept in economic analysis is described in Richard Ruggles and Nancy D. Ruggles, *National Income Accounts and Income Analysis*, 2d ed., McGraw-Hill Book Company, New York, 1956; for a detailed explanation of technical concepts, see U.S. Department of Commerce, *Survey of Current Business: National Income Supplement*, 1954; for recent quarterly data, see U.S. Department of Commerce, *Survey of Current Business*, monthly.

Gross Private Domestic Investment
(In billions of dollars)

	1966	1967	1968	1969	1970
Total gross private domestic investment	121.4	116.6	126.5	139.8	135.7
Fixed investment, total	106.6	108.4	118.9	131.4	132.3
Nonresidential	81.6	83.3	88.7	99.3	102.6
Structures	28.5	28.0	29.6	33.8	35.2
Producer durable equipment	53.1	55.3	59.1	65.5	67.4
Residential structures	25.0	25.1	30.3	32.0	29.7
Nonfarm	24.5	24.5	29.7	31.5	29.1
Farm	0.5	0.6	0.6	0.5	0.6
Change in business inventories	14.8	8.2	7.6	8.5	3.5
Nonfarm	15.0	7.5	7.5	8.0	2.9
Farm	−0.2	0.7	0.1	0.5	0.6

Gross Private Fixed Investment Expenditures by private businesses and individuals for new buildings, machinery, and vehicles. It is a measure of additions and replacements of private capital brought about through purchases of durable equipment and structures for business and residential purposes. This is a major component of the gross national product and has accounted for about 15% of U.S. GNP over the past decade. It does not take account of that portion of the stock of capital used up in the course of producing the current period's output. There is no direct measure of net private fixed investment. For a detailed discussion of the concept, coverage, and sources of data, see U.S. Department of Commerce, *National Income Supplement,* 1954; see also Richard Ruggles and Nancy D. Ruggles, *National Income Accounts and Income Analysis,* 2d ed., McGraw-Hill Book Company, New York, 1956; for quarterly and annual data, see U.S. Department of Commerce, *Survey of Current Business,* monthly.

Gross Profits *See Profits.*

Group Banking An arrangement whereby two or more separately incorporated banks are brought under the control of a single corporation known as a holding company. The holding company may have as its principal business the control of banks, or it may itself be a bank or business trust. At the end of 1969, group banks represented 10% of the banking offices in the U.S. and held 15% of the total deposits. For further information on this type of banking, see C. E. Coyle, *Branch, Group and Chain Banking,* Banking Studies, Board of Governors of the Federal Reserve System, Washington, D.C., 1941; Gerald C. Fischer, *American Banking Structure,* Columbia University Press, New York, 1968, pp. 72–121; for statistics on the number of group banking organizations, their members, and deposits by state, see *Federal Reserve Bulletin,* Washington, D.C., usually the July issue.

Group Insurance A master insurance policy under which individual members of a group are able to obtain insurance protection. In general, the group must consist of at least twenty-five persons. Group-insurance plans cover accidents, life insurance, hospital expenses, medical expenses, and pensions and annuities. With few exceptions, group insurance is issued without medical examination or other evidence of individual insurability. Another characteristic feature of group insurance is that it provides insurance under a single blanket policy. Thus, individuals entitled to benefits under the policy are not actually parties to the contract, since the contract is made between the insurance company and the group policyholder. A third feature of this type of insurance is its low-cost, wholesale protection. Mass distribution and administration methods afford the insurance company many important economies of scale that are not available on an ordinary, individual basis. Since its first use in 1911, the number of group-insurance plans and the number of persons covered have grown tremendously, and most large corporations and large unincorporated businesses now have group-insurance plans for their employees. Under these plans, payment may be made entirely by the company, the company and the employees may share the cost on a predetermined basis, or the employees may pay the entire cost of the program but enjoy the benefits of lower costs available under the plan. For further information, see Louise Wolters Ilse, *Group Insurance and Employee Retirement Plans*, Prentice-Hall, Inc., Englewood Cliffs, N.J., 1953; see also David W. Gregg, *Group Life Insurance*, Richard D. Irwin, Inc., Homewood, Ill., 1957.

Guaranteed Annual Wage A type of wage payment that would assure minimum earnings for employees over a year. In most guaranteed-annual-wage plans, employees with a degree of seniority (usually one to three years of steady employment) are assured a specified number of hours or weeks of work each year. If work is not available, the company must provide the employees with income to supplement unemployment benefits. By means of such programs, labor unions hope to stabilize employment throughout the year, eliminating the seasonal ups and downs of some industries. The agreement made between the Ford Motor Company and the UAW-CIO in June, 1955, is the best-known guaranteed-annual-wage plan, although many plans antedated it. For a history and discussion of guaranteed-annual-wage plans, see A. D. H. Kaplan, *The Guarantee of Annual Wages*, The Brookings Institution, Washington, D.C., 1947.

Guidelines for Noninflationary Wage Increases *See Annual Improvement Factor.*

Guild A group of merchants or artisans formed in medieval times to reserve for its members the practice of a particular occupation or profession. It limited the number of persons working at an occupation in order to protect the livelihood of members and to safeguard consumers from fraud and falsification. By this means, guild members gained a monopoly position in their occupations and professions. Although guilds set certain specifications for workmanship, thus measuring a certain level of proficiency, at the same time they freed themselves from all competition. In modern usage, a guild is the name applied to any group organized for common interest, mutual aid, and benefit.

H

Haavelmo's Proposition When the two variables in a two-equation economic model are both influenced by a third variable (as, for example, consumption and income are influenced by investment), any assumption of an exact linear relationship is likely to be wrong and unrealistic, even in the simplest cases where one of the equations is an identity. A least-squares solution to the model tends to result in an overstatement of the slope (b) and an understatement of the intercept (a). This problem can usually be overcome by the use of a simultaneous-equation-estimation technique. For additional information, see Trygve Haavelmo, "The Statistical Implications of a System of Simultaneous Equations," *Econometrica,* vol. 11, pp. 1–12, January, 1943; Stefan Valavanis, *Econometrics,* McGraw-Hill Book Company, New York, 1959.

Hard Currency A national currency that is freely convertible into gold or into the currencies of other countries. A nation allows its currency to become freely convertible when it has no fear of depreciation that might force devaluation. Convertibility develops when the currency's official exchange rate as set by the government either values correctly or undervalues the currency and when the currency is relatively stable, so that the nation need not consider quick changes in its value. Hard currency therefore differs from soft currency, which is regulated by exchange controls and is thus not freely convertible. Nations are willing to export a greater amount of goods to a country paying in hard currency than to a country paying in soft currency, because hard currency can be exchanged for their own currency. Hard currencies thus serve as international currency. See Raymond F. Mikesell, *Foreign Exchange in the Postwar World,* The Twentieth Century Fund, New York, 1954.

Hard Loan A foreign loan repayable in a hard currency, usually U.S. dollars. This type of loan typically has a high interest rate. Hard loans are difficult to repay, because countries receiving them usually have soft currencies which are not freely convertible into dollars and therefore must obtain most of their dollars through trade. The theory behind the extension of foreign aid in the form of hard loans is that the difficulty of repayment makes the receiving country use the money more wisely than if the aid took the form of a grant. Nevertheless, the difficulty involved in accumulating dollars means that some of the countries most in need of foreign aid are unable to receive much money through hard loans. In an attempt to arrive at a compromise between hard loans and grants, soft loans (loans repayable in the receiving countries' own soft currency) formerly were made. Soft loans proved unsatisfactory, however, and most lending agencies now make foreign loans repayable in dollars. See Benjamin Higgins, *Economic Development*, W. W. Norton & Company, Inc., New York, 1968; Raymond F. Mikesell and Robert Allen, *Economic Research Toward Less Developed Countries*, a study prepared for the Subcommittee on Economic Policy of the U.S. Joint Economic Committee, Government Printing Office, Washington, D.C., 1961.

Head Tax *See Poll Tax.*

Health Insurance Insurance that provides relatively quick compensation for the loss of time due to illness or for medical expenses incurred because of accident or illness. It does not cover total or permanent disability. Health insurance is underwritten by (1) casualty and life insurance companies; (2) fraternal societies; (3) hospital and medical service organizations, of which the Blue Cross and Blue Shield are typical; (4) labor unions; (5) some state governments; and (6) employee and mutual-benefit associations. Before the 1930s, most health-insurance plans provided for a cash payment to reimburse the worker for wages lost during his illness. Since then, hospital confinement, surgery, various kinds of medical care, and diagnostic examinations have been included in the various plans. In the 1950s and 1960s, great controversy arose over the question of the institution of a compulsory health-insurance program by the U.S. government. For further information, see Edwin J. Faulkner, *Health Insurance*, McGraw-Hill Book Company, New York, 1960; see also George W. Bachman and Lewis Meriam, *The Issue of Compulsory Health Insurance*, The Brookings Institution, Washington, D.C., 1948

Hedge Fund A limited partnership set up to invest in securities. Pioneered by Alfred W. Jones, who established the first one in 1952, hedge funds grew rapidly in number from 1966 to 1970, when it was estimated that roughly 150 existed. Hedge funds work like this: A small group of investors (less than 100) acting as limited partners put a large sum of money (averaging more than $300,000) into an investment fund.

The fund is managed by general partners who can share in the profits earned on the limited partners' investment. Unlike investment companies, hedge funds can gain leverage by borrowing money from a bank, and they can take short positions in securities. Originally the hallmark of a hedge fund was always having part of the portfolio in a short position as a "hedge" against declining security prices. See "Hard Times Come to the Hedge Funds," *Fortune*, January, 1970, pp. 100–103, 134–140.

Hedging A technique of buying and selling that minimizes the risk of loss due to price fluctuations. It is commonly used by commodity dealers and by a variety of manufacturers, including flour millers, shortening processors, and textile producers. The technique can best be explained by an example. A grain-storage operator who makes his profit through the storage and distribution of grain rather than through speculation buys corn at current market prices (spot prices) but does not ordinarily resell it until some months later, when prices may be lower. In order to protect himself against such price declines, the dealer can hedge his purchases. At the same time as he purchases corn in the spot market, he sells an equal amount in the futures market—that is, he contracts to deliver an equivalent amount of corn at a later date for a price that is set now. If prices fall, he loses on his corn inventories but gains an equal sum on his futures sales because the corn called for in the contract can be purchased at a lower price. If prices rise, he loses on his futures sales but gains on his inventories. In either case, he ensures himself against loss caused by price declines, although he also relinquishes the possibility of gain through rising prices. And he is then free to devote all his attention to the provision of his particular service, which is the storage and distribution of corn. Hedging is also used to a considerable extent in the foreign-exchange market. For a discussion of hedging in the commodity markets, its advantages, and its limitations, see Gerald Gold, *Modern Commodity Futures Trading*, 2d ed., Commodity Research Bureau, Inc., New York, 1961; for a discussion of hedging in the foreign-exchange markets, see Imanuel Wexler, *Fundamentals of International Economics*, Random House, Inc., New York, 1968, pp. 130–134; David B. Zenoff and Jack Zwick, *International Financial Management*, Prentice-Hall, Inc., Englewood Cliffs, N.J., 1969, pp. 242–247.

Hedonism The principle which states that individuals, through their pursuit of pleasure, will try to improve their way of life. It is based on the philosophical and psychological doctrine that man's behavior is guided solely by the pursuit of pleasure and the avoidance of pain. Jeremy Bentham set forth the principle as follows: "Nature has placed mankind under the governance of two sovereign masters, pain and pleasure. It is for them alone to point out what we ought to do, as well as to determine what we should do." This theory of behavior was later developed by economists who reconstructed their science on the basis of this "utility" concept. Bentham himself did not apply his theories to economics along these lines. He conceived an economic theory based on rational or most useful behavior. Bentham believed that businessmen, through their pursuit of the higher pleasures, rationally seeking greater wealth and happiness, would cooperate in building and operating a democratic state, a rational legal order, and a free-market economy. Recognizing and accepting most men's simple, selfish, worldly aims and propensities, he advocated education that would cope with these realities and stress the need for higher pleasures conducive to the common welfare. For further study, see W. Stark (ed.), *Jeremy Bentham's Economic Writings,* 3 vols., published for the Royal Economic Society by George Allen & Unwin, Ltd., London, 1952–1954.

Hidden Persuader   Any of various motivational research tools used by advertising organizations in their campaigns. The term was originated by Vance Packard in 1957. In his book, *The Hidden Persuaders,* Packard presented examples of the successful manipulation of consumer images and opinions which consequently directed consumer spending. See Vance Packard, *The Hidden Persuaders,* David McKay Company, Inc., New York, 1957.

Hidden Tax   An indirect tax which is paid by the consumer without his knowledge. Certain taxes, such as import duties, some excise taxes, and taxes on the gross income of businesses, are classified as hidden because they often can be shifted to the consumer by increasing the price of the goods sold and because the consumer often does not know how much of the price is due to the tax. In fact, he may not even be aware of the existence of the tax that has caused an increase in price. Thus, the excise tax on gasoline, which has received wide publicity, cannot be considered a hidden tax, whereas a duty on imported petroleum can be so classified.

Hiring Rate   *See Accession Rate.*

Historical School   A school of economic thought which advocated a departure from the abstract, deductive approach of the classical economists toward a more inductive historical study of economic systems. Its major leaders were primarily Germans of the mid-nineteenth century, among them Wilhelm Roscher, Bruno Hildebrand, and Gustav Schmoller. The historical school developed because the classical and neoclassical approaches were considered too theoretical, too atomistic, and too materialistic. Greater emphasis was placed on dynamic elements and on the history and the observation of actual economic institutions and phenomena as the basis for economic analysis. Members of the historical school argued that the earlier writers had underestimated nonmaterialistic human motivations and neglected activities which people follow as members of groups rather than as single individuals. For this reason, they placed great emphasis on nationalism. They also stressed the continuous evolution of economic societies and the constantly changing nature of economic and social institutions. For further information, see Joseph A. Schumpeter, *History of Economic Analysis,* Oxford University Press, Fair Lawn, N.J., 1954; J. Dorfman, "The Role of the German Historical School in American Economic Thought," *American Economic Review Supplement,* American Economic Association, Evanston, Ill., May, 1955, vol. XLV, pp. 17–28; Howard D. Marshall, *The Great Economists,* Pitman Publishing Corporation, New York, 1967, pp. 183–200.

Historic Stage   Any of the various stages of society which, according to Karl Marx, were based on a distinct pattern of property ownership. Marx advanced an economic interpretation of history for which the economic relationships of each period were the main factor in controlling all human motivations and activity. In his view, the historical progression of society is basically an evolution of the techniques, methods, and organization of production. Every stage of social organization, with the exception of the final stage of communism, generates forces within itself which eventually overthrow it, according to the mechanism of the dialectic: thesis, antithesis, and synthesis. An institution or a given state of society, called the thesis, becomes overdeveloped and gives way to something opposed, called the antithesis. The antithesis expands, but eventually it also becomes unstable and collapses into a third, more moderate form, the synthesis. The synthesis is adequate for a while, but soon it, too, is ready to collapse and start the cycle over again. The driving force in this constant evolution of social organization is the class struggle between the bourgeois class, which owns the means of production, and the proletarian class, which does not. According to Marx, the first historical stage was the common ownership of land by primitive peoples. As production increased, division of labor arose, and the distribution of material shares became increasingly unequal. Finally, the institution of private property emerged, and with it the stage of chattel slavery. In time, chattel slavery brought about its antithesis, the stage of empire. Growing empires eventually led to increasing decentralization and to the next stage, feudalism. Feudalism, in turn, caused the growth of towns and industry and the accumulation of capital, ushering in the stage of full-fledged capitalism. In Marx's opinion, the inadequacies of capitalism would result in the proletarian revolution and the achievement of the final stage, pure communism. For further information, see Karl Marx, *Capital*, Charles Kerr & Co., Chicago, 1906; Paul M. Sweezy, *The Theory of Capitalist Development*, Oxford University Press, Fair Lawn, N.J., 1942.

Hoarding   The accumulation of money or goods in excess of immediate needs. Reasons for hoarding include fear of a future shortage and expectation of a future rise in the price of the goods or in the money hoarded. In monetary theory, hoarding is considered to be any part of savings which is not used for investment. Thus, hoarding is a leakage in the income stream, taking money out of circulation and reducing total income. The larger the proportion of income hoarded in the form of money, the more slowly money turns over. The velocity of money in circulation varies inversely with the rate of hoarding. For additional details, see Walter W. Haines, *Money, Prices and Policy*, 2d ed., McGraw-Hill Book Company, New York, 1966.

Holding Company   A corporation that owns the majority of stock or securities of one or more other corporations for purposes of control rather than of investment. A corporation which exists only for this purpose is a pure holding company. One which also carries on a business of its own is called a mixed holding company or a holding-operating company. A holding company can acquire a subsidiary either by purchasing the stock of an existing corporation or by forming a new corporation and retaining all or a controlling share of the stock of the new corporation. The advantages of forming a holding company are as follows: (1) The company is a legally simpler and less expensive way of acquiring control over another corporation than consolidation, merger, or purchase of assets. (2) The parent company retains the goodwill and reputation of the subsidiary without necessarily becoming responsible for its liabilities. (3) A corporation can gain legal advantages by purchasing or forming a subsidiary that is incorporated in states or countries that have laws directed against corporations from other states or countries. There are also a number of disadvantages to the formation of a holding company: (1) The relations between a holding company and its subsidiaries can become so complex that they result in inefficiency. (2) Taxes imposed because of the maintenance of separate subsidiaries often are greater than if the companies were united. (3) A holding company may encounter legal difficulties because of the laws specifically regulating holding companies. See Charles W. Gerstenberg, *Financial Organization and Management of Business*, 4th ed., Prentice-Hall, Inc., Englewood Cliffs, N.J., 1959.

Holiday Variation   A fluctuation in monthly economic time series attributable to major national holidays. Since some holidays, such as Easter, do not occur at the same time each year, it may be necessary to estimate and remove this variation from retail sales of apparel, for example, in order to prevent it from distorting the estimate of the seasonal variation.

Horizontal Integration   The situation existing in a firm whose products or services are competitive with each other. The term also applies to the expansion of a firm into the production of new products that are competitive with older ones. Horizontal integration may be the result of a merger of competing firms in the same market, or involve expansion of a firm from its original base to a wider area, as is the case in the growth of retail chains. The advantages of horizontal integration stem primarily from economies of large-scale management, large-scale buying from suppliers, and large-scale distribution. Horizontal integration may result in a monopoly in a particular market. For additional details, see Joe S. Bain, *Industrial Organization*, 2d ed., John Wiley & Sons, Inc., New York, 1968.

Horizontal Labor Mobility   *See Labor Mobility.*

Hot Money   A term used to describe speculative and flight movements of capital which are generally motivated by the anticipation of a change in exchange rates, a desire to escape losses associated with war, high taxation, capital levies, internal economic difficulties, or inflation. These movements accentuate instability because they aggravate balance-of-payments difficulties rather than moderate them. This is so because hot money leaves countries with balance-of-payment deficits and goes to countries with surpluses. For an examination of movements of hot money in postwar international economics, see Arthur I. Bloomfield, *Speculative and Flight Movements in Postwar International Finance*, Princeton University Press, Princeton, N.J., 1954.

Hourly Earnings, Average   Average pay per hour worked. Average hourly earnings are computed by dividing the total wages of an industry or economy by the number of man-hours worked. They include sick pay and holiday and vacation pay and are computed before deductions for taxes and social security. Thus, statistics on hourly earnings reflect changes in basic hourly rates and also take account of pay for overtime and late-shift work at premium rates. Average hourly earnings should not be confused with wage rates, which represent the basic rate for a given unit of work. National, state, and industry data are published in U.S. Bureau of Labor Statistics, *Employment and Earnings*.

Average Hourly Earnings of Production Workers

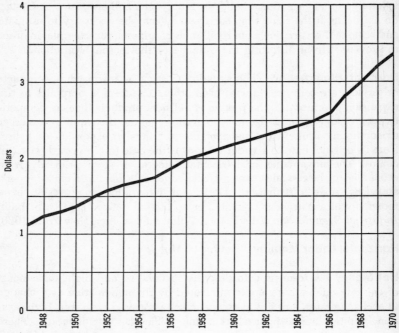

Source: U.S. Department of Labor.

Household A housing unit in which people live. It is a statistical concept used to measure the number of occupied housing units in a nation. A household may consist of a single individual living alone or of more than one family living together. In March, 1970, there were 63.3 million households in the U.S., averaging about 3.4 persons each. This was nearly 12.1 million more than the number of families. Between 1947 and 1951 the number of households increased by about 1.4 million per year, whereas in the period 1952–1967, the annual average increase was about 900,000. After 1952, the rate of family formation and therefore of household formation declined, partly because of the age distribution of the U.S. population. The number of households increased more rapidly after 1968, when there were many more persons of marriageable age in the U.S. population. Furthermore, a greater amount of housing was likely to be available than was the case in the mid-1960s, and this in turn would encourage household formation. The number and characteristics of households are important statistics in establishing market potentials for consumer durable goods, such as stoves and refrigerators. For a detailed discussion of the concept, historical statistics, and forecasts of number of households, see U.S. Bureau of the Census, *Current Population Reports: Population Characteristics,* ser. P-20.

Number of Households in U.S. (Millions)

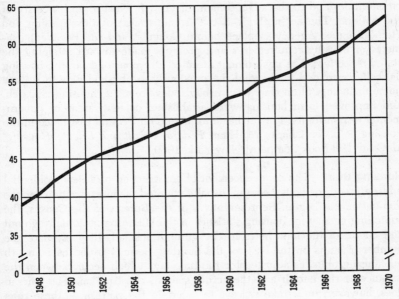

Source: U.S. Department of Commerce.

Household Formation The net annual increase in the number of households. Estimates of future household formation are used to forecast the demand for new homes as well as the sales potential for many types of consumer durable goods. Forward estimates of this statistical series prepared by the U.S. Bureau of the Census have not, however, proved particularly useful because of the wide range of the projections. In the Bureau's interim report for 1965, for example, the range of estimates for average household formations in that year runs from 860,000 under one set of assumptions to 1,130,000 under another set. For projections of household formation to 1985, see U.S. Bureau of the Census, *Current Population Reports: Population Characteristics,* ser. P-25.

Housing Act of 1949 The law which established a national housing policy to be followed by the U.S. Federal government. It stated: "The general welfare and security of the nation and the health and living standards of its people require housing production and related community development sufficient to remedy the serious housing shortage, the elimination of substandard and other inadequate housing through the clearance of slums and blighted areas, and the realization as soon as feasible of the goal of a decent home and a suitable living environment for every American family, thus contributing to the development and redevelopment of communities and to the advancement of growth, wealth, and security of the nation." The act authorized the Administrator of the Housing and Home Finance Agency to place before Congress and the President estimates of housing requirements and progress made toward attaining the stated objectives. The government assumed a responsibility in the housing field that extended far beyond the previously established aids to private home financing. Slum clearance, urban redevelopment, housing research, and improved farm housing were established as new areas of governmental responsibility. For further information on Federal assistance in the housing field, see Charles M. Haar, *Federal Credit and Private Housing,* McGraw-Hill Book Company, New York, 1960.

Housing Start   The commencement of construction of a new residential unit designed for housekeeping, usually counted when excavation for the foundation has begun. Representatives of the Bureau of the Census, the compiling agency for housing statistics in the U.S., do not actually go out and count all the new holes in the ground; instead, they estimate the number of starts on the basis of the building permits issued each month for housing units, as adjusted for the time lags which occur between the issuance of the permit and the actual start of construction. The Bureau does, however, undertake surveys to ascertain the pattern of these time

Housing Starts, Public and Private (Thousand units)

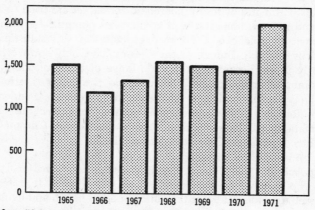

Source: U.S. Census Bureau; McGraw-Hill Department of Economics.

lags and the number of construction projects that are canceled after permits have been issued. Monthly data on housing-start statistics may be found in U.S. Department of Commerce, *Construction Reports: Housing Starts;* for a detailed discussion of housing-start statistics, see U.S. Department of Commerce, *Construction Review,* June, 1960.

Human Capital   The investment in the education and skills of a nation's population. The development of human capital is one of the most distinctive features of the U.S. economic system. The growth of human capital, particularly investment in education, is one of the largest sources of past and future economic growth. According to some authorities, the gains in human capital have made greater contributions to the growth of the U.S. than the growth of its physical plants and equipment. For further information on the contribution of human capital to growth, see Edward F. Denison, *The Source of Economic Growth in the United States and the Alternatives Before Us,* Committee for Economic Development, New York, 1962; Gary S. Becker, *Human Capital,* Columbia University Press, New York, 1964.

Hyperinflation   The rapid rise of prices without limit. Hyperinflation, also known as runaway inflation or galloping inflation, consists of continuously rising prices, which result in the disruption of normal economic relations, an astronomical depreciation of the currency, and the eventual breakdown of the entire monetary system. Hyperinflation has been rare, usually occurring during or after wars or revolutions, and is often the product of a social and economic breakdown. It is frequently caused by the large-scale creation of new money by the government, which leads to rising prices and a flight from money to goods. During the hyperinflation in Germany in 1923, prices rose 2500% in one month, and the value of the mark fell so far during the hyperinflation period that it was worth only one trillionth of its earlier value. A similar kind of inflation occurred in Greece, China, and Hungary after World War II. For example, in Hungary in 1946, 828 octillion (828 with 27 zeros after it) depreciated pengös equaled the value of one prewar pengö. For additional details, see Harold G. Moulton, *Can Inflation Be Controlled?* Anderson Kramer Associates, Washington, D.C., 1958; C. Bresciani-Turroni, *The Economics of Inflation,* George Allen & Unwin, Ltd., London, 1931; see also P. Cagen, "The Economics of Hyperinflation," in Milton Friedman (ed.), *Studies in the Quantity Theory of Money,* The University of Chicago Press, Chicago, 1956.

Identification In simplest form, the problem of distinguishing, for example, between a supply function and a demand function when a single set of paired prices and quantities, for a single time interval, is available for analysis. Usually such limited data do not permit a good estimate of either function. When two endogenous or logically dependent variables appear in a single equation, there is one equation with which to determine the values of two variables. Thus, in general, the identification problem arises in systems of stochastic equations where it is not possible to estimate all parameters without bias, no matter how extensive the information and even when the number of equations is equal to the number of endogenous variables. Haavelmo generalized the problem of identification and developed the method of reduced forms for solving it in many instances. The problem also gave rise to the limited-information–maximum-likelihood method, two- and three-stage least-squares techniques, and k-class estimators. For additional information, see Karl A. Fox, *Intermediate Economic Statistics*, John Wiley & Sons, Inc., New York, 1968; T. C. Koopmans (ed.), *Statistical Inference in Dynamic Economic Models*, Cowles Commission Monograph no. 10, John Wiley & Sons, Inc., New York, 1950; Stefan Valavanis, *Econometrics*, McGraw-Hill Book Company, New York, 1959.

Identity Equation In econometrics, the regression of a variable upon itself; hence, $y = 0 + 1.0\,y$. Thus the term identity is used here in a restricted sense and should not be confused with the term identity used in a purely algebraic sense and meaning identical equations. For additional information, see Karl A. Fox, *Intermediate Economic Statistics*, John Wiley & Sons, Inc., New York, 1968.

Import A good or commodity that is received from a foreign country or area in the conduct of foreign trade. The country that receives the good is the importer. In the U.S., imports have usually been considerably lower than exports, so that the U.S. has enjoyed a trade surplus. For example, imports averaged $4 billion less than exports in the years 1955 to 1970. However, imports in 1971 were higher than exports, so that 1971 was the first year in which the U.S. experienced a trade deficit. This was one of the reasons for the devaluation of the dollar at the end of that year. For further information, see *An Introduction to Doing Import and Export Business,* Chamber of Commerce of the United States, Washington, D.C., 1962; Don D. Humphrey, *American Imports,* The Twentieth Century Fund, New York, 1955; Morton Ehrlich and John Hein, *The Competitive Position of United States Exports,* National Industrial Conference Board, Inc., Studies in Business Economics, no. 101, New York, 1968.

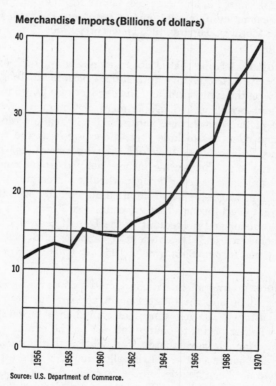

Merchandise Imports (Billions of dollars)

Source: U.S. Department of Commerce.

Import Duty   A tax on goods imported. Most nations now levy some import tariffs. There are two main purposes of import duties, protection and revenue. In the U.S., import tariffs are not considered important as a method of raising Federal revenues, but in smaller countries in which imports account for a sizable share of the national product, revenue import tariffs may be significant. In the free world, many protective import tariffs are being reduced or eliminated. For an analysis of the effects of import duties, see Hugh B. Kellough and Lucy M. Kellough, *Economics of International Trade*, McGraw-Hill Book Company, New York, 1948; for a schedule of U.S. import tariffs, see U.S. Tariff Commission, *United States Import Duties*.

Impulse Buying   The act of purchasing without previous intention, performed by a consumer who happens to see a product in a display at the point of purchase. According to one authority, imaginative packaging of products has resulted in an increase of one-third in impulse buying over a decade. For examples of impulse buying, see Vance Packard, *The Wastemakers*, David McKay Company, Inc., New York, 1960.

Imputed Income   Income that is not in money form, such as free food or lodging received in exchange for services performed, food produced and consumed on the same farm, and the services of a house in which the owner lives rent-free. The U.S. Department of Commerce estimates the market value of imputed income and includes it in the national income accounts. Some countries include other items, such as the income that housewives would receive if they did their housework for hire. Other forms of income—e.g., the psychic income derived from living in a particularly pleasant spot or from doing particularly pleasant work despite a somewhat lesser wage—are never imputed numerically even though they resemble the imputed incomes that are estimated. For a thorough discussion of the problems and procedures of the Department of Commerce in imputing income, see U.S. Department of Commerce, *Survey of Current Business: National Income Supplement*, 1954.

Imputed Interest   Interest that is considered a cost even though no cash outlay is ever made and the interest never appears on the financial records of the business. The investment of capital in a business raises the question of whether or not to charge interest on the capital and count it as a manufacturing overhead charge. The belief is that this capital has an opportunity alternative cost which is called imputed interest; that is, if the capital had not been invested in the business, it would have provided the firm with some other income. This income creates an opportunity cost, resulting in an imputed-interest charge. Although very few firms enter imputed interest in their accounts, many use it in the solution of problems of alternative choice. For a presentation of reasons for inclusion and noninclusion of imputed interest as a manufacturing overhead charge, see

W. B. Lawrence, *Cost Accounting*, 4th ed., rev. by J. W. Ruswinckel, Prentice-Hall, Inc., Englewood Cliffs, N.J., 1954.

Income   The gain derived from capital or labor or from both combined. Because of the broad interpretations of income made by economists, it is difficult to draw lines between the various income classifications. This difficulty has led many economic writers to urge a more precise use of the concept of income. Generally, income is applied to a family of concepts all of which are related in some way to wealth and value. Such categories as personal income, business income, gross income, net income, national income, and taxable income are used. For further information, see James N. Morgan et al., *Income and Welfare in the United States*, McGraw-Hill Book Company, New York, 1962.

Income Distribution   The manner in which personal income is distributed among the various income classes in a nation. Generally, inequality in income is attributable to differences in (1) educational and training opportunities; (2) native ability; (3) property ownership; (4) ability to exert market power; and (5) such arbitrary factors as illness, accident, and other misfortunes. It is believed that the distribution of personal income in the U.S. is tending toward greater equality and that the upper-income groups are losing ground to the rest of the income classes. Arthur F. Burns characterized this development as a revolution. Studies by the National Bureau of Economic Research and the U.S. Bureau of the Census seem to indicate that a revolution in income distribution has taken place. Since 1929 the share of income of the upper 5% of income receivers has decreased from about one-third of total income to about one-fourth. Part of the explanation for this trend can be found in

Families by Total Money Income in Constant Dollars			Percentage Share of Aggregate Income Received by Each Fifth of Families		
	Percent, 1968	Percent, 1947		Percent, 1968	Percent, 1947
Under $3,000	10	26	Lowest fifth	6	5
$3,000–$4,999	12	28	Second fifth	13	12
$5,000–$6,999	15	22	Middle fifth	18	17
$7,000–$9,999	23	14	Fourth fifth	23	23
$10,000 and over	40	10	Highest fifth	40	43

SOURCE: U.S. Department of Commerce, *Current Population Reports: Consumer Income*, ser. P-60, no. 66, Dec. 23, 1969.

the progressive tax system and the development of welfare policies. For the historical development of income-distribution theory, see John Bates Clark, *The Distribution of Wealth,* The Macmillan Company, New York, 1899; see also Simon Kuznets, *Shares of Upper Income Groups in Income and Savings,* National Bureau of Economic Research, Inc., New York, 1953.

Income Effect   A term used in demand analysis to indicate the increase or decrease in the amount of a good that is purchased because of a price-induced change in the purchasing power of a fixed income. When the price of a commodity declines, the income effect enables a person to buy more of this or other commodities with a given income. The opposite occurs when the price rises. By using indifference curves, it is possible to separate the income effect from the so-called substitution effect, in which the demand for a price-reduced good rises as it is substituted for other goods whose price has remained constant. See George J. Stigler, *Theory of Price,* 3d ed., The Macmillan Company, New York, 1966; Donald S. Watson, *Price Theory and Its Uses,* 2d ed., Houghton Mifflin Company, Boston, 1968.

Incomes Policy   Any attempt by a government to affect the level of money incomes or prices, usually in an effort to slow down or reduce the rate of price inflation. Great Britain, following the Netherlands and Sweden, tried to develop an incomes policy in the 1960s that would make full employment and price stability compatible. Incomes policies can take various forms. Wage-price guideposts are one type. During the Kennedy administration norms were established for "noninflationary" price and wage increases. These norms were based on the average increase in productivity during the period 1945–1960. The guideposts called for an average increase in prices and wages of 3.2% per year, the long-term rate of productivity gain. Jawboning, or government pressure in specific wage or price situations, is another form of incomes policy. Wage-price control, where the government sets and enforces criteria for wages and prices throughout the economy, is a third type of incomes policy, employed in the U.S. during World War II and the last phase of the Vietnam War. In recent years, as inflation had worked its way through our economy, many public leaders called for wage and price controls, as a solution to the wage-price spiral. Others opposed such controls, claiming that controls would distort the supply-and-demand mechanism of a market economy and lead to extreme shortages of some goods and services and large surpluses of others. However, wages and prices were frozen in August, 1971 and after the freeze was lifted, wages and prices were controlled. For additional information, see Paul A. Samuelson, *Economics,*

8th ed., McGraw-Hill Book Company, New York, 1970, pp. 814–815; Andrew Shonfield, *Modern Capitalism,* Oxford University Press, New York, 1965.

Income Tax   A tax levied on individual and corporate incomes. The basic purpose of the tax is to finance governmental operations. The base of the U.S. income tax is net income, which is calculated by subtracting the amount of specific items from gross income of a given period (generally one year). Gross income is defined as all accretion to wealth plus any increase in net worth during the period. From this total are subtracted income not taxable (e.g., interest from state and municipal bonds), credits (e.g., credits for the taxpayer and his dependents), and other deductions. Such deductions can take the form of business and professional expenses or of certain personal expenses (e.g., contributions to charity and specified medical expenses). Once the tax base of net income has been determined, the tax is calculated by applying graduated rates to the income brackets. The progressive nature of both personal and corporate income taxes is based on the ability-to-pay principle of taxation, whereby a larger tax burden is placed on individuals or firms whose capacity to pay the tax is greater. The first Federal income tax in the U.S. appeared temporarily during the Civil War. Reenacted in 1894, it was declared unconstitutional by the Supreme Court, and not until the passage of the Sixteenth Amendment in 1913 did the U.S. have a permanent income tax. The tax rate in 1913 was 1% of both net personal and net corporate income. Since then, the tax has grown in size and importance, so that in 1963 the rate on net personal income ranged from a minimum of 20% to a maximum of 91% of all income over $400,000, and the normal tax on net corporate income was 30%, with a surtax of 22% on income in excess of $25,000. However, in March, 1964, lower personal and corporate income tax rates became effective for 1964 and subsequent years. For 1964, the personal income tax rates ranged from 16 to 77% of all income over $200,000, and for 1965 and later, the range was set at 14 to 70% of all income over $200,000. For 1964 and later, the normal corporate income tax rate was set at 22%, while the surtax became 28% of income in excess of $25,000 for 1964 and 26% for 1965 and later. A 10% surcharge on personal income tax became effective April 1, 1968, with the effect of increasing by 7.5% the tax due for 1968 and 10% for 1969. The surcharge on personal income tax was cut to 5% for the period January 1, 1970, to June 30, 1970, with the effect of increasing by 2.5% the personal income tax due for 1970. A 10% surcharge on normal corporate tax and surtax became effective January 1, 1968. The tax reform act of 1969 extended the surcharge on corporate tax liabilities at a 5% annual rate for the period January 1, 1970, to June 30, 1970. In 1970, Federal receipts from individual income taxes totaled about $90 billion, and receipts from corporate income taxes nearly $33 billion. These two income taxes provided the bulk of Federal revenues, together accounting for about 85% of all Federal taxes collected in 1970. Many states have turned to income taxation as a source of revenue, collecting a total of about $13 billion in income tax receipts in 1970. Some municipalities have also adopted taxation of income in one form or another. For further information, see Harold Groves, *Financing Government*, 6th ed., Holt, Rinehart and Winston, Inc., New York, 1964; Henry C. Simons, *Personal Income Taxation*, The University of Chicago Press, Chicago, 1938; Richard Goode, *The Corporation Income Tax*, John Wiley & Sons, Inc., New York, 1951; Harold Groves, *Postwar Taxation and Economic Progress*, McGraw-Hill Book Company, New York, 1946.

Income Velocity   *See Velocity of Money.*

Incorporation Procedure   The action which must be taken to form a corporation. Nearly all U.S. corporations are chartered by the individual states. To form a corporation, a group of adult citizens (usually three or more), at least one of whom is a citizen of the state of incorporation, must file an application for a charter. In the application, the name, purpose, duration, location, authorized capital stock, and number of shares of the proposed corporation must be specified, as well as the names and addresses of the incorporators and the subscribers of the capital stock. This application must be sent with the required fees to a state official for approval. If everything is in order, the state issues a charter setting forth the powers, rights, and privileges of the corporation under state law. Usually, the charter must be filed with the state recording office in the city in which the corporation is located. Once the charter has been received and filed, the corporation is legally in existence and has authority to operate. The actual requirements for incorporation vary from state to state and for different kinds of businesses within a state. For additional details on incorporation procedure, see the individual state constitutions; see also C. Rohrlich, *Organizing Corporate and Other Business Enterprises*, 3d ed., Matthew Bender & Company, Inc., Albany, N.Y., 1958.

Increasing Costs   Increases in the average costs of unit production that take place as the volume of output rises. In any type of business, because of the operation of the law of diminishing returns, increasing output (in the short run) leads eventually to increasing costs. A plant is designed for a certain level of efficient output. When production increases beyond that level, average costs rise because of such factors as overcrowding, the use of obsolete equipment, and the overuse of machinery. While the concept of increasing average costs is a short-run phenomenon, an increasing-cost industry is one in which the long-run cost schedules of individual firms rise as the number of firms in the industry increases and the total output of the industry rises. Such long-run increasing-cost conditions result from external diseconomies of large-scale production. Usually, the diseconomies are due to increases in factor prices as a larger number of factors is employed by the industry. Increasing-cost industries are most likely to be those which use a large portion of a resource, the supply of which cannot be increased very easily. For example, wheat farming is an increasing-cost industry. As wheat production rises, the demand for wheat-growing land increases, and thus the rental and sale prices for all wheat land rise. Long-run increasing costs may also be due to a reduced efficiency that occurs as output increases. For example, the greater the number of oil wells in a certain area, the more costly it is for each well to pump up the oil because of the reduced pressure in each well. For further information, see John F. Due and Robert W. Clower, *Intermediate Economic Analysis,* 5th ed., Richard D. Irwin, Inc., Homewood, Ill., 1966; Howard S. Ellis and William Fellner, "External Economies and Diseconomies," *American Economic Review,* vol. XXXIII, p. 493, American Economic Association, Evanston, Ill., September, 1943; Milton H. Spencer, *Managerial Economics,* Richard D. Irwin, Inc., Homewood, Ill., 1968.

Increasing Returns, Theory of   *See Returns to Scale.*

Indenture (Trust Indenture; Deed of Trust)   An agreement between a corporation and a trustee (or trustees) that governs the conditions under which bonds are issued and names and empowers the trustee to act for all the bondholders. Bonds are basically debts of corporations. To avoid the hopelessly complicated situation that would exist if each bondholder had to deal individually with the corporation, the indenture sets the rights and privileges of the bondholders and the rights, privileges, and liabilities of the debtor corporation. The trustee, usually a bank or a trust company, enforces the terms of the indenture, protects the bondholders, and carries out some mechanical duties, such as handling interest payments. Because issuing corporations sometimes had failed to name an independent trustee, the Trust Indenture Act was passed in 1939. This act stipulates that institutions must meet certain requirements before they can be named trustees and protects bondholders by requiring that indentures contain standard provisions. For further information, see Charles W. Gerstenberg, *Financial Organization and Management of Business,* 4th ed., Prentice-Hall, Inc., Englewood Cliffs, N.J., 1959.

Index Number A measure of the relative changes occurring in a series of values compared with a base period. The base period usually equals 100, and any changes from it represent percentages. For example, if an index of machinery prices with the year 1967 = 100 as a base rises to 110, the price of machinery has increased by 10% since 1967. Comparisons are usually made over periods of time, but indices may also be used for comparisons between places or categories. For example, an index of consumption expenditures in Philadelphia and San Francisco could be computed in relation to an index in New York, or an index of the relative efficiency of the voltage output of different machines in different types of generating equipment could be calculated. By use of an index number, large or unwieldy business data, such as sales in thousands of dollars or costs in dollars and cents, are reduced to a form in which they can be more readily used and more easily understood. An Italian, Giovanni R. Carli, is generally credited with inventing index numbers. For a detailed explanation of index-number construction, theory, and practice, see Frederick E. Croxton and Dudley J. Cowden, *Applied General Statistics,* Prentice-Hall, Inc., Englewood Cliffs, N.J., 1955.

Indifference Curve A graphic curve which represents the various combinations of two goods that will yield the consumer the same total satisfaction. For example, a household may receive the same satisfaction from consuming 4 pounds of steak and 3 pounds of chicken as from consuming 5 pounds of steak and 1 pound of chicken. By assuming that the two commodities can be substituted for each other, it is possible to draw an indifference schedule that contains all of the possible combinations of the commodities which will yield the same satisfaction. When the schedule is plotted on a graph, with one commodity along the vertical axis and another along the horizontal axis, the curve which connects the points is called an indifference curve. The curve tells nothing about the absolute level of satisfaction, but only that each point represents a combination that is equal to any other combination in total satisfaction. For each level of total satisfaction, there is another indifference curve. Most indifference curves slope downward to the right, indicating that as more of one good is added, less of the other good is required to maintain the level of satisfaction. The slope of the curve is the marginal rate of substitution between the two commodities: the amount of one commodity necessary to replace one unit of the other commodity while maintaining the same level of satisfaction. Because of the diminishing rate of marginal substitution, indifference curves are usually convex to the point of origin; that is, as additional units of one commodity are added, progressively less of the other commodity will be necessary to replace units of the first commodity to maintain the same level of satisfaction. For further information, see John R. Hicks, *Value and Capital,* 2d ed., Oxford University Press, Fair Lawn, N.J., 1946; W. Harrison Carter and William P. Snavely, *Intermediate Economic Analysis,* McGraw-Hill Book Company, New York, 1961; John F. Due and Robert W. Clower, *Intermediate Economic Analysis,* 5th ed., Richard D. Irwin, Inc., Homewood, Ill., 1966; Donald S. Watson, *Price Theory and Its Uses,* Houghton Mifflin Company, Boston, 1968.

Indirect Cost   Any cost which cannot be consistently identified with a specific product unit. Indirect costs, which include all fixed costs, are joint in nature and can be apportioned to different products only by a rough approximation. They are related to the quantity of output only in an indirect way, if at all. As a whole, indirect costs are often called burden, overhead, or indirect manufacturing expense. Such factors as the wages of supervisors, power, maintenance, and taxes are classified as indirect costs. For further information, see "Report of the Committee on Cost Concepts and Standards," *Accounting Review,* vol. XXVII, American Accounting Association, Menasha, Wis., April, 1952.

Indirect Labor   Labor which is not applied specifically to the direct production of goods or services but which is part of the general productive process. Indirect labor includes the labor of certain auxiliary groups, such as maintenance men, storeroom and clerical workers, and salesmen, and also supervisory, control, and engineering groups, such as plant managers, foremen, and product engineers. Indirect-labor costs are not directly identifiable with specific product costs but are usually included in overhead expenses. For further information, see *Accounting for Labor Costs and Labor Related Costs,* National Association of Accountants, Research Series, no. 32, New York, 1957.

Indirect Production   The production of capital goods that will later be used to produce consumer goods. The indirect-production method is undertaken not to satisfy human wants immediately but to provide the capital with which to facilitate an increased production of consumer goods, thus achieving greater satisfaction at a later date. Indirect or roundabout production is given great importance by Eugen von Böhm-Bawerk in his theory of interest. Böhm-Bawerk believed that "every lengthening of a roundabout process is accompanied by a further increase in the technical results." The fact that an increase in the length of the productive process (an increase of its indirectness) increased final output was the major factor which he cited to account for a positive rate of interest. See Eugen von Böhm-Bawerk, *Capital and Interest*, Libertarian Press, South Holland, Ill., 1959.

Indirect Tax A tax that can be shifted from the original payer to the ultimate consumer of the good or service taxed. Sales taxes, excise taxes, and import duties are generally regarded as indirect taxes, although some economists believe that sales and excise taxes, or some part of such taxes, are actually borne by the factors of production. See E. H. Plank, *Public Finance*, Richard D. Irwin, Inc., Homewood, Ill., 1953.

Indivisibility The qualification that certain factors of production (the work force and equipment) cannot be divided into smaller units. For example, a single big machine is indivisible in that it cannot be divided in half and produce half its maximum output at half its previous costs. It can, however, operate at 50% of its capacity, although unit costs are then higher than when it operates at 90% of capacity. Indivisibility is a prime factor in producing economies of large-scale production. Indivisible factors can be most efficiently employed when output is large; they work less efficiently at lower production levels because they cannot be divided into smaller units. For the relation of indivisibility to cost, see William Fellner, *Modern Economic Analysis*, McGraw-Hill Book Company, New York, 1960, pp. 236–237; Milton H. Spencer, *Managerial Economics*, 3d ed., Richard D. Irwin, Inc., Homewood, Ill., 1968, pp. 203–204.

Induced Investment Investment that occurs in response to actual or anticipated increases in outlays for specific existing products or throughout an economy. Among the causes of induced investment are income gains and population growth, which result in a greater demand for goods and services. In general, therefore, induced investment is an expenditure for additional equipment in order to produce greater quantities of a given good or service. Autonomous investment, in contrast, occurs independently of rising economic activity, as a result, for example, of the introduction of new products or processes. Through the additional economic activity that it produces, autonomous investment in a given industry may generate induced investment in the economy generally. In economic theory, the acceleration thesis holds that there is a fixed relationship between income or output changes and the investment that they induce. In fact, however, such a rigid relationship has not been confirmed. For a classical statement of the acceleration thesis, see John M. Clark, "Business Acceleration and the Law of Demand: The Technical Factor in Economic Cycles"; reprinted in *Readings in Business Cycle Theory*, McGraw-Hill Book Company, New York, 1944; for a more recent discussion of induced investment, see D.

Hamburg and Charles L. Schultze, "Autonomous Investment vs Induced Investment," *Economic Journal,* Royal Economic Society, London, March, 1961; Gardner Ackley, *Macroeconomic Theory,* The Macmillan Company, New York, 1961, pp. 485–493, 518–529; John P. Lewis and Robert C. Turner, *Business Conditions Analysis,* 2d ed., McGraw-Hill Book Company, New York, 1967, pp. 191–214.

Induced Variable   In statistics and econometrics, a variable that depends wholly on economic factors. Its movement can be predicted from correlation relationships with business activity. An induced variable changes freely in structure over the short run. Consumption expenditures for soft goods and for services are generally considered induced variables. See Elmer C. Bratt, *Business Cycles and Forecasting,* Richard D. Irwin, Inc., Homewood, Ill., 1948.

Inductive Method   A method of analyzing an economic problem. An alternative to the deductive method, the inductive method proceeds from the particular to the general, stressing the observation of facts from the empirical world as the basis for its generalizations. Induction bases its conclusions on the collection and observation of many particular and illustrative cases in actual life. Thus, it stresses variation and allows for a changeable theory. The major fault of the inductive method is that its use makes it impossible to reach a degree of finality in economic thinking. The system is always open to new observations that might yield a different conclusion. The validity of a system depends on the observable facts used in making the generalizations. For additional history, explanation, and examples, see William Fellner, *Modern Economic Analysis,* McGraw-Hill Book Company, New York, 1960, chap. 2.

Industrial Migration   The movement of industries from one region to another within a country. The basis for the migration of individual industries may be found in the demand for the firm's product, in the supply of resources which it needs, or in wage differentials or tax benefits. In the early history of the U.S., manufacturing plants were located as close as possible to sources of raw materials, since transportation was slow and expensive. Transportation is now much less of a problem, however, and the importance of raw materials has therefore declined. For this reason, the consumer market exerts a much stronger influence on plant location, and the areas of fastest population growth are becoming the areas of fastest industrial development. In the U.S., this trend has meant that industries have migrated from east to west and from north to south. For example, a major portion of New England's textile industry moved southward to North and South Carolina, while its shoe industry moved westward to St. Louis, Mo. Similarly, a significant share of Pittsburgh's steel industry moved to the south and the west. For a detailed study of industrial migration, see Victor Fuchs, *Changes in the Location of Manufacturing in the United States since 1929*, Yale University Press, New Haven, Conn., 1962.

Industrial Production Index A measure of the physical output of U.S. manufacturing, mining, and utility industries compiled monthly by the Board of Governors of the Federal Reserve System. Covering about 35% of the total U.S. output of goods and services, the index includes a representative group of products, ranging from pig iron and cotton yarn to machine tools and electricity. It excludes agriculture, construction, and service industries. The relative importance assigned to individual products is based on quantity and value data determined from recent government censuses. Manufacturing accounts for 88.55% of the index, mineral production for 6.37%, and utilities for 5.08%. Current output is expressed as a percentage of annual production levels during 1967; by November, 1971, the index had risen to 107 from its 1967 base of 100.

Industrial Production Index (1967 = 100)

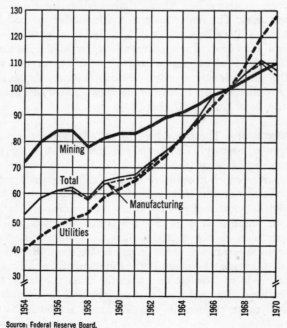

Source: Federal Reserve Board.

Historically, the industrial production index has fluctuated to a greater extent than most other measures of economic activity. In addition to the total index, indices are prepared for individual items, product classes, industries, and industry groups. All indices are published monthly in *Business Indexes,* Board of Governors of the Federal Reserve System, Washington, D.C.; for detailed information, see *Industrial Production,* Board of Governors of the Federal Reserve System, Washington, D.C., February, 1972; for industrial production data of other countries, see Statistical Office of the United Nations, *Monthly Bulletin of Statistics,* New York.

Industrial Union   A labor union which represents all the workers, skilled and unskilled, in a plant, industry, or group of industries. The industrial union evolved as a consequence of the development of mass production, since skilled and unskilled workers worked together in large production plants. Many traditional craft unions have become industrialized in certain industries without abandoning their craft ties in others. An outstanding example is the Machinists Union, which is, in effect, an industrial union in the aircraft industry. Pure industrial unions which limit themselves to one identifiable industry are rare. Virtually all industrial unions function in more than one industry, and often the concept of industry is not precise. The industrial union differs from the semi-industrial union and the multi-industry union. The International Ladies Garment Workers, a semi-industrial union, does not typically cover maintenance employees. The Automobile Workers, a multi-industry union, has members in the automobile, aircraft, and farm-implement industries. Industrial unions often adopt a policy of reducing relative price differentials among occupations, principally by bargaining for across-the-board wage increases. See Jack Barbash, *The Practice of Unionism,* Harper & Row, Publishers, Incorporated, New York, 1956; Albert Rees, *The Economics of Trade Unions,* The University of Chicago Press, Chicago, 1962.

Inelastic Demand (Inelasticity)   A term used to describe a proportionately smaller change in the purchase rate of a good than the proportional change in price that caused the change in amount bought. When the demand for a product is inelastic, a relatively large price change is necessary to cause a relatively small increase in purchases. To calculate the elasticity of demand, the percentage change in buying rate (the quantity bought per period of time) is divided by the percentage change in price. Theoretically, the numerical value of the elasticity can vary from zero to infinity, and the sign of the number is negative, denoting the fact that price and quantity move in opposite directions. When the number is less than 1, demand is said to be inelastic; when it is exactly 1, demand is called unitary; and when elasticity is greater than 1, it is simply called elastic. The following table summarizes the relationship between various elasticities and the behavior of total receipts (price times purchase rate):

	Elastic Demand (−1 or More)	Unitary Demand (−1)	Inelastic Demand (Less than −1, e.g., −½)
Price fall	Receipts rise	Receipts unchanged	Receipts fall
Price rise	Receipts fall	Receipts unchanged	Receipts rise

For further information, see Campbell R. McConnell, *Economics*, 4th ed., McGraw-Hill Book Company, New York, 1969; Donald S. Watson, *Price Theory and Its Uses*, 2d ed., Houghton Mifflin Company, Boston, 1968.

Inelastic Supply   The relative insensitiveness of a producer to supply a good when the market price of the good changes. A supply schedule is perfectly inelastic when the quantity supplied by the producer remains the same regardless of price. It is perfectly elastic if an unlimited quantity is offered by the producer at all prices. For further information, see George J. Stigler, *Theory of Price*, 3d ed., The Macmillan Company, New York, 1966.

Infant Industry   An undeveloped industry which may not be able to weather the initial period of experimentation and financial stress because of strong foreign competition. In the *Report of Manufacturers,* Alexander Hamilton stated that such industries should be protected by tariffs until they had a chance to grow out of the infantile stage. It was believed that, given such a grace period, they could be expected to develop economies of scale and technological efficiency so that prices would be reduced and they would be more competitive with foreign industries. Essentially, the argument says, "We can produce it cheaper if you give us the chance." For an example of such an industry and its eventual development, see Frank W. Taussig, *Some Aspects of the Tariff Question,* Harvard University Press, Cambridge, Mass., 1931.

Inferior Good (Giffen Good)   A good whose demand curve rises. That is, the higher the price, the larger the quantity demanded, all other things remaining equal. In the case of any inferior good, the income effect of a price change always outweighs the price effect. The idea of an inferior good is attributed to Sir Robert Giffen, a Victorian economist who witnessed one of the very few examples of this kind of good. The 1845 Irish potato famine raised the price of potatoes. Since potatoes constituted a large part of the food budgets of lower-income Irish families, their real incomes declined, forcing them to purchase more potatoes (at higher prices) and less of more expensive foods, such as meat. See Paul A. Samuelson, *Economics,* 7th ed., McGraw-Hill Book Company, New York, 1967, p. 423; J. R. Hicks, *Value and Capital,* Oxford University Press, New York, 1946, pp. 28–29; James M. Henderson and Richard E. Quandt, *Microeconomic Theory: A Mathematical Approach,* 2d ed., McGraw-Hill Book Company, New York, 1971, p. 27.

Inflation   A persistent upward movement in the general price level. It results in a decline of purchasing power. According to most economists, inflation does not occur until price increases average more than 2.5% per year for a sustained period. Price increases of less than 2.5% per year need not cause concern for the U.S. economic system, although an increase of 1.5% per year over a decade would reduce the purchasing power of a dollar by 16 cents. Price inflation is most likely to occur when demand increases while the labor supply is tight and industrial capacity is fully utilized, when increases in wage rates are out of step with gains in productivity, when sources of supply dry up, or when the money supply rises faster than output increases. The greater part of inflation in U.S. history is associated with wars or their aftermath. Some economists use the term inflation to designate the forces or pressures that cause a general increase in prices rather than the increase itself. For a comprehensive discussion of inflation, see Willard L. Thorp and Richard E. Quandt, *The New Inflation,* McGraw-Hill Book Company, New York, 1959; *Staff Report on Employment, Growth and Price Levels,* prepared for the U.S. Joint Economic Committee, Government Printing Office, Washington, D.C., Dec. 24, 1959.

Inflationary Gap   A term used to describe the excess of investment over savings in a full-employment economy. The inflationary gap is the value of excess demand for goods and services over the goods and services that can be produced with full employment. For example, the demand for goods and services in the U.S. totals $850 billion, but actual output at full employment is $780 billion. The $70-billion excess in purchasing power can result only in price increases because only through price changes can national income increase above the maximum full-employment output level. The upward movement in price continues as long as there is an inflationary gap, that is, while demand is greater than supply. For a brief explanation of the inflationary gap, see Paul A. Samuelson,

Economics, 8th ed., McGraw-Hill Book Company, New York, 1970, pp. 227–228; for a more advanced analysis, see Gardner Ackley, *Macroeconomic Theory*, The Macmillan Company, New York, 1961, pp. 424–439.

Inflationary Gap, New The excess of the increase in average hourly earnings of employees over the increase in output per man-hour. The term was first used by Sumner H. Slichter in his argument that wage increases are the major causes of inflation. There are only two means of closing the gap, a reduction in the rate of wage increases or an increase in the rate of productivity gains. For additional details on the new inflationary gap, see Sumner H. Slichter, *Reconciling Expansion with a Stable Price Level: Problems of United States Economic Development*, Committee for Economic Development, New York, 1958, vol. I.

Inflation, Cost-Push A rise in prices believed to occur because wages increase to a greater extent than productivity. Frequently cited examples of cost-push inflation are the U.S. inflationary periods 1957–1958 and 1969–1971, when prices rose while economic activity declined well below capacity operations. Employers frequently take the view that cost-push inflation is spurred by strong labor unions that force wage increases. Union leaders, on the other hand, charge large corporations with raising prices independently of increases in costs. A U.S. economist, Harold G. Moulton, provides an argument for the cost-push theory based on the view that sellers' prices are determined by their costs and that wage costs are the most important factor in total costs. The Chicago school of economists, led by Milton Friedman, is opposed to the cost-push theory. Adhering to the quantity theory of money as the basic reason for inflation, this group argues that there is no conclusive evidence that prices behave differently than they probably would behave if strong labor unions and administered prices were not in existence. Many U.S. economists believe that during an inflationary period some cost-push, some demand-pull, and some structural inflation take place at the same time. For a comprehensive discussion of cost-push inflation, see Harold G. Moulton, *Can Inflation Be Controlled?* Anderson Kramer Associates, Washington, D.C., 1958; see also Willard L. Thorp and Richard E. Quandt, *The New Inflation*, McGraw-Hill Book Company, New York, 1959.

Inflation, Demand-Pull A rise in prices believed to occur because consumers and investors with rising incomes increase their wants and compete for a relatively limited supply of available goods. Goods are in short supply either because resources (labor and industrial capacity) are being fully utilized or because production cannot be increased on very short notice. When purchasing power exceeds the total value of capacity output, the excess can cause a rise in the price level in an unregulated economy. The example of demand-pull inflation usually cited for the U.S. is the inflationary period 1955–1956. Most U.S. economists believe that during a period of inflation some demand-pull, some cost-push, and some structural inflation take place at the same time. For a comprehensive discussion of demand-pull inflation, see Harold G. Moulton, *Can Inflation Be Controlled?* Anderson Kramer Associates, Washington, D.C., 1958; Willard L. Thorp and Richard E. Quandt, *The New Inflation,* McGraw-Hill Book Company, New York, 1959.

Inflation, Structural A rise in prices believed to be caused by excess demand for the output of particular industries even when overall economic demand is not excessive. Initially, prices and wages increase because of pressures in specific sectors of the economy. As a result, general inflation occurs because the floor under prices and wages in those sectors in which demand has not kept pace tends to be inflexible. For example, in the 1950s the demand for services and the prices of services and wages of service workers rose substantially while there was a relative decline in the demand for consumer durable goods and capital goods. Wages of workers in the consumer-durable-goods industries and capital goods industries rose, however, while prices did not decline significantly, resulting in general inflation. Most U.S. economists believe that during an inflationary period some structural, some demand-pull, and some cost-push inflation take place at the same time. For a comprehensive discussion of structural inflation, see Charles L. Schultze, "Recent Inflation in the United States," Study Paper 1, a report prepared in connection with the study of *Employment, Growth and Price Levels,* U.S. Joint Economic Committee, Government Printing Office, Washington, D.C., Sept. 21, 1959.

Infrastructure (Social Overhead Capital) The foundation underlying a nation's economy (transportation and communications systems, power facilities, and other public services) upon which the degree of economic activity (industry, trade, etc.) depends. It may include such intangible assets as the population's educational level and social attitudes, industrial skills, and administrative experience. The better and more complete a nation's infrastructure, the better and more effectively its economic activity can be carried on. Because of its essential nature, the infrastructure is discussed most often in connection with the economic development of underdeveloped nations. The building up of a country's infrastructure, which generally involves projects with a high initial cost and a very long payoff period, is frequently carried out either by the government or with its aid. Private investment alone cannot finance such development. Most underdeveloped countries are well aware of the importance of social overhead capital, but some economists warn that the building of the infrastructure can be overemphasized and that perhaps, after a minimum amount of infrastructure has been constructed, investment funds could be better utilized in productive activities. See Ragnar Nurkse, *Problems of Capital Formation in Underdeveloped Countries,* Oxford University Press, Fair Lawn, N.J., 1958; Albert O. Hirschman, *The Strategy of Economic Development,* Yale University Press, New Haven, Conn., 1958; Walter W. Rostow, *The Stages of Economic Growth: A Non-Communist Manifesto,* Harvard University Press, Cambridge, Mass., 1960.

Inheritance Tax A tax on individuals who receive property upon the death of a benefactor. It differs from an estate tax, which is levied on the deceased's estate before the estate is divided among the heirs. Inheritance tax rates are generally progressive, and they also increase as the relationship of the heir to the decedent grows more remote. There are usually fairly high exemptions to the tax. The main theoretical justification for an inheritance tax is the ability-to-pay principle. It is reasoned that a bequest of property creates an ability on the part of the heir to contribute to the support of the government. Another argument in favor of the tax is that it can help prevent the formation of a permanent moneyed group that can live on property handed down from one generation to another. See Philip E. Taylor, *The Economics of Public Finance,* The Macmillan Company, New York, 1953.

Initial Claim for Unemployment Insurance An application made for the first time for unemployment-insurance benefits. The initial claim may be the first claim in a benefit year or the first claim at the beginning of a second or additional unemployment period in the same benefit year. The initial claim establishes the first date for any insured unemployment, but it does not guarantee that any benefit payment will be made, since some claimants may not meet eligibility requirements. The initial-claims series is a significant indicator of overall business activity, which the National Bureau of Economic Research classifies as one of its thirty leading indicators. A rise in initial claims takes place when gains in business activity begin to slow down, and a decline occurs when business prospects appear bright. The statistical series is compiled by the U.S. Bureau of Employment Security and released weekly in *Unemployment Insurance Claims;* for monthly figures, see U.S. Department of Labor, *The Labor Market and Employment Security.*

Injunction A court order that requires a person (or a company, union, etc.) to do or to refrain from doing a certain thing. Its purpose is to protect property rights and not to punish violations of the law, and it is often

Initial Claims for Unemployment Insurance (Millions)

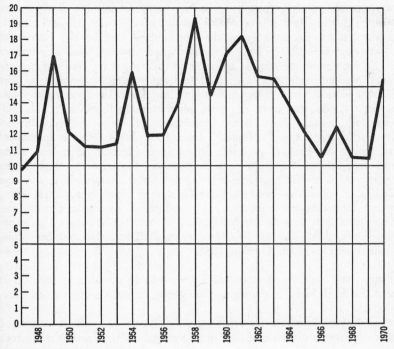

Source: Board of Employment Security.

invoked on a temporary basis, without hearing or notice, when one party to a dispute appeals to the courts for rapid action to protect its threatened property rights. A court injunction was a very popular device with which to thwart the aspirations of labor until 1932, when passage of the Norris-La Guardia Act severely limited its application in labor disputes. Under the Labor-Management Relations Act of 1947 (Taft-Hartley Act), however, the President retains the right to seek injunctions in labor disputes when national health or safety are in danger. For a thorough discussion of these issues, see Wayne L. McNaughton and Joseph Lazar, *Industrial Relations and the Government,* McGraw-Hill Book Company, New York, 1954.

Innovation   The introduction of something new—either new goods and services or new ways of producing them. Innovation differs from invention in one essential respect; an invention is the discovery of something new, whereas an innovation is the actual introduction or application of something new. Usually a means of increasing productivity or of providing a superior product, innovation has long been recognized as a vital ingredient of economic growth. Joseph A. Schumpeter, a twentieth-century U.S. economist who cited the economic impact of the railroads and electric power, called inovation ". . . the outstanding fact in the history of capitalist societies." The hope of increasing profits or of maintaining them in the face of competition is an important incentive for business innovations. Major innovations often lead to large capital investment in new plants and equipment, thus providing an important stimulant to economic activity. Among the more dramatic innovations in the U.S. in the mid-twentieth century have been jet airliners, nuclear-powered electric-generating stations, and automated automobile plants. Other examples are transistors, the packaging of soft drinks in cans, credit cards, and wash-and-wear fabrics. For a classical discussion of the impact of innovations on the level of business activity, see Joseph A. Schumpeter, *Business Cycles*, 2 vols., McGraw-Hill Book Company, New York, 1939; for a recent treatment of innovation as a source of economic growth, see Leonard S. Silk, *The Research Revolution*, McGraw-Hill Book Company, New York, 1960; see also John Jewkes et al., *The Sources of Invention*, Macmillan & Co., Ltd., London, 1958.

Input   Any good or service that a firm uses to produce an output. It could be land, labor, materials, capital goods, or management skills.

Input-Output Analysis (Interindustry Analysis)   A systematic method of analyzing in great detail the interrelationships between an industry's or an economy's output of goods and services and the volume of goods and services needed to achieve a given volume of production. For example, the steel industry, in increasing its output of steel ingots, needs additional quantities of coal, iron ore, flatcars, electricity, and many other items. To satisfy the additional demands from the steel industry, coal and iron-ore mines, railroad-equipment makers, and electric-generating stations similarly need additional quantities of the goods and services that they consume in turning out their final products. Input-output analysis is usually conducted with the aid of a numerical grid showing in detail the interrelationships among industries along vertical and horizontal axes. U.S. economists agree that the introduction of the input-output technique has greatly aided the historical analysis of the economy's performance. Some, however, doubt its usefulness as a means of predicting future interindustry requirements. For further discussion and a sample input-output table, see Richard Ruggles and Nancy D. Ruggles, *National Income Accounts and Income Analysis*, 2d ed., McGraw-Hill Book Company, New York, 1956, chap. 9; National Bureau of Economic Research, Inc., *Input-Output Analysis: An Appraisal*, Princeton University Press, Princeton, N.J., 1956;

Wassily Leontief, *The Structure of the American Economy,* Harvard University Press, Cambridge, Mass., 1951, a pioneering work in the field; see also Wassily Leontief and Marvin Hoffenberg, "Economic Consequences of Disarmament," *Scientific American,* Apr. 1, 1961; Wassily W. Leontief, *Input-Output Economics,* Oxford University Press, Fair Lawn, N.J., 1966; "Divining the Future," *The Wall Street Journal,* Feb. 17, 1970, p. 1; updated statistics for input-output work are provided by the U.S. Department of Commerce in the monthly *Survey of Current Business.*

Insider Information   Information about a company's financial or business condition available to certain parties prior to its general public release. The use of such information for personal profit is prohibited by the Securities and Exchange Act of 1934. Another provision of the act prohibits owners of more than 10% of a company's stock from making short-term profits on the company's stock. Short-term in this sense is defined as six months or less. The insider provisions were enacted to prevent those who have access to material and pertinent facts about a company because of their special relationship to that company from reaping advantage from this knowledge.

Insolvency   The inability of a business firm to meet its debts. There are two senses in which the term insolvency is used: actual insolvency, in which a firm's liabilities exceed its assets, and technical insolvency, in which a firm cannot meet its current debts as they come due. In technical insolvency, assets may be greater than liabilities but not liquid enough to meet current debts. The Federal Bankruptcy Act defines insolvency in the first sense, while equity courts have defined insolvency in the second sense. When insolvency seems imminent, there are a number of steps which a firm may take to avoid defaulting: negotiating an extension of its debts; securing an emergency loan from its owner, officers, etc.; artificially accelerating its inventory turnover (e.g., through closeout sales); selling receivables to a bank or finance company; reducing or postponing managers' salaries and workers' wages; or selling the entire business. For additional details, see Bion B. Howard and Miller Upton, *Introduction to Business Finance,* McGraw-Hill Book Company, New York, 1953.

Installment Credit   Credit granted in which repayment, including interest charges, is made by regular payments at specified intervals. The origin of installment credit is uncertain, but it is believed that it began in the U.S. in a New York City furniture store in the mid-nineteenth century. The rapid growth of installment credit did not take place until after World War I. For a long time, installment credit was used by only relatively poor people, but subsequently all income classes came to use it as a convenient means of making purchases although it is a relatively expensive type of credit. Installment credit is also used in the business field for the purchase of industrial machinery and equipment as well as for goods and services. Automobile purchases constitute the largest single item of installment credit. For further information, see Clyde William Phelps, *Using Installment Credit,* Commercial Credit Company, Baltimore, 1955; for the role of consumer installment credit in a growing

Installment Credit (Millions of dollars)

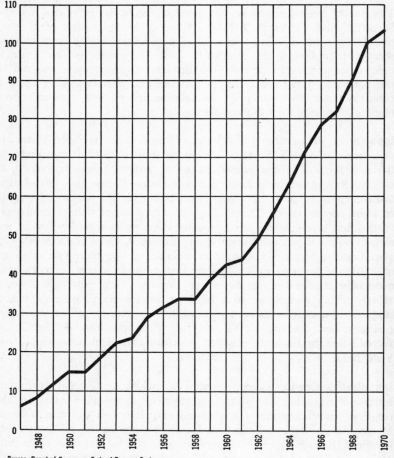

Source: Board of Governors, Federal Reserve System.

economy, see National Bureau of Economic Research, Inc., Conference on Regulation, *Consumer Installment Credit,* 4 parts, Board of Governors of the Federal Reserve System, Washington, D.C., 1957.

Institutional Economics A school of economic thought that holds that most economic activities are determined by institutions which are largely psychological and are composed of customs and existing economic arrangements. The leader of this school was Thorstein Veblen. Institutionalists used the elements of economic theory as tools for measuring and modifying the economic institutions which they studied. According to this school of thought, competition was an important feature of economic behavior, but it was competition for property and power rather than competition in the marketplace. According to the institutionalists, the classicists erred in basing economic behavior largely on rational motives instead of instincts and customs. For further discussion of institutional economics and institutionalists, see Frank Amandus Neff, *Economic Doctrines,* Mc-Graw-Hill Book Company, New York, 1950; Allen G. Gruchy, *Modern Economic Thought: The American Contribution,* Prentice-Hall, Inc., Englewood Cliffs, N.J., 1947; Howard D. Marshall, *The Great Economists,* Pitman Publishing Corporation, New York, 1967, pp. 284–309.

Instrumental Variable In econometrics, a predetermined variable that is used to derive consistent estimators of the parameters of a system of equations. A predetermined variable is one whose values are known at any point in time; hence it may be an exogenous variable or a lagged endogenous variable. Use of an instrumental variable may be applied to incomplete systems, and it is efficient in relation to a complete set of equations in the sense that only a limited portion of information is employed. The instrumental variable is one of several limited-information methods for estimating an exactly identified or overidentified equation. For additional information, see Stefan Valavanis, *Econometrics,* McGraw-Hill Book Company, New York, 1959.

Integer Programming A mathematical technique designed to choose the "best" course of action from among various alternatives. Integer programming is similar to linear programming, the chief distinction between the two methods being that integer programming requires that the answer consist only of integers, that is, whole numbers. Integer programming can be a useful tool in those situations where inputs or outputs are indivisible. For example, suppose a firm were trying to determine the optimum number of trucks to acquire. Because you cannot buy a fractional part of a truck, nor can you hire, say, three-quarters of a driver, the optimum answers must be whole numbers, and integer programming might be helpful. For additional information, see William J. Baumol, *Economic Theory and Operations Research,* Prentice-Hall, Inc., Englewood Cliffs, N.J., 1965.

Interest The price paid for the use of money over a period of time. Individuals, businessmen, and governments buy the use of money. Businessmen pay interest for the use of money to purchase capital goods because they can increase production and productivity through the introduction of new plants and new machines. Individuals pay interest for the use of money because they wish to make purchases of goods and services in excess of their current income. Governments pay interest for the use of money because their expenditures usually exceed their receipts. According to the loanable-funds theory of interest, the price of money equals the price paid for the use of loanable funds. The intersection of the supply and demand curves of loanable funds designates the rate of interest. In medieval canon law, interest was prohibited because money was considered barren, that is, incapable of producing goods and services. For further information, see J. M. Keynes, *The General Theory of Employment, Interest, and Money,* Harcourt, Brace & World, Inc., New York, 1936; Irving Fisher, *The Theory of Interest,* Kelley and Millman, Inc., New York, 1954; John J. Klein, *Money and the Economy,* Harcourt, Brace & World, Inc., New York, 1970.

Interindustry Analysis *See Input-Output Analysis.*

Interindustry Competition Competition between firms in different industries. It may cut across industry lines when different industries produce products which are substitutes for each other. For example, companies in the aluminum and steel industries or in the plastics and glass industries must compete for sales not only with other firms in their own industry, but also with manufacturers of close substitutes for their products. Another form of interindustry competition arises in the struggle for consumers' discretionary income, or optional expenditures. Thus, while luxury, recreational, and educational industries might compete to induce the customer to spend his discretionary income in their industries, banks, insurance companies, and security firms try to induce the consumer to save or invest some of these funds. Furthermore, the essential consumer goods industries, such as food, housing, and clothing, also compete with the others, trying to get the consumer to increase the share of income spent on their goods. Interindustry competition is growing in importance as a result of continuing research into new methods of satisfying consumer wants and into different uses of various materials. For a general discussion and examples, see Simon N. Whitney, *Antitrust Policies,* The Twentieth Century Fund, New York, 1958, vol. II.

Interlocking Directorate   The term used to describe the presence on the boards of directors of competing enterprises of one or more directors in common. Under the Clayton Antitrust Act of 1914, this arrangement is illegal in the U.S. In a few antitrust cases, most notably those against the Aluminum Corporation of America and Sears, Roebuck, individuals were obliged to resign their multiple directorships. One reason why there has been little litigation on this point is that the threat of court action has sufficed to correct malpractices. Another is that the law is easily avoided; for example, an officer or a major stockholder of one company is not prohibited from serving as a director of a competing firm. See Victor H. Kramer, "Interlocking Directorship and the Clayton Act," *Yale Law Review,* vol. LIX, New Haven, Conn., 1959; Simon N. Whitney, *Antitrust Policies,* The Twentieth Century Fund, New York, 1958, vol. II.

Intermediate Goods   Goods that enter into the production of other goods. In the manufacturing process, goods and materials pass through various stages of production, frequently requiring transfer from one plant to another or sale by one firm to another. For example, a steel ingot made in a blast furnace may be processed into a steel sheet in a rolling mill and then into an automobile chassis at a stamping mill before being made into a car at an assembly plant. In this case, the steel ingot, the steel sheet, and the chassis are intermediate goods even though each may be the final good of a particular plant or firm. According to the analysis of Eugen von Böhm-Bawerk, it is normal for a mature economy to devote most of its resources to the production of intermediate goods. In principle, the value of intermediate goods does not enter into the calculation of the gross national product, which counts only the value of the final product (in the example cited above, the automobile) that embodies the intermediate goods. Since some intermediate goods, such as flour that a bakery buys, can also be final goods (if a housewife buys flour), national income statistics class as intermediate goods only those products which another firm buys and charges off as a current cost during a particular accounting period. This means that capital goods, an integral factor in roundabout production, are counted in the gross national product because they are depreciated over a long period of time. For a detailed definition, see Richard Ruggles and Nancy D. Ruggles, *National Income Accounts and Income Analysis,* McGraw-Hill Book Company, New York, 1956; for a criticism of the concept, see Conference on Research in Income and Wealth, *A Critique of the United States Income and Product Accounts,* Studies in Income and Wealth, vol. XXII, Princeton University Press,

Princeton, N.J., 1958; for a discussion of the relationship between production of intermediate goods and mature and less advanced economics, see Eugen von Böhm-Bawerk, *Capital and Interest*, Libertarian Press, South Holland, Ill., 1959.

International Commodity Agreement A pact between the countries exporting and importing a particular commodity that specifies, sometimes in fixed amounts and sometimes in ranges of maximum to minimum, the volume and price at which the commodity shall be traded while the agreement is in force. International commodity agreements seek to replace individual, uncoordinated national policies that have frequently led to international price wars and to chaos in the commodity markets, but they generally have encountered problems because of the enormous difficulty of accurately forecasting demand, supply, and trading channels. For example, the International Wheat Agreement of 1949 suffered from unexpected price rises after the outbreak of the Korean conflict, and the International Sugar Agreement of 1958 disintegrated with the severing of commercial relations between Cuba, the world's major exporter of sugar, and the U.S., its principal customer. Droughts, currency devaluations, and many other developments can render international commodity agreements useless and even detrimental to their signatories. Economists generally oppose commodity pacts because they rigidify the structure of commodity trade instead of allowing flexible adjustments to changing conditions. On the other hand, commodity producers, who hope for stable export prices for their product; commodity importers, whose domestic producers press for protection against increasing foreign competition; and internationally oriented agencies, which seek to promote not only economic, but also social and political stability in underdeveloped countries, remain firm advocates of such agreements. For the U.S. attitude toward them, see Percy W. Bidwell, *Raw Materials: A Study of American Policy*, Council on Foreign Relations, Inc., New York, 1958; for a theoretical discussion of their effects by a panel of experts, see *Trends in International Trade*, General Agreement on Tariffs and Trade, Geneva, October, 1958; see also UN Department of Economic and Social Affairs, *International Compensation for Fluctuations in Commodity Trade*, New York, 1961; see also A. W. Hanson, *America's Role in the World Economy*, W. W. Norton & Company, Inc., New York, 1945.

Interstate Commerce Commerce between any place in one state of the U.S. and any place in another state or between places in the same state through another state. Interstate commerce may move wholly by motor vehicle or partly by motor vehicle and partly by rail, express, or water. It is regulated by the Interstate Commerce Commission. For statistics on interstate commerce, see U.S. Interstate Commerce Commission, *Annual Report*.

Invention   The active combination of presently known elements into a new form. The term is closely associated with discovery, since discoveries often lead to invention and since the process is often reversed. For example, the invention of the steam engine led to the discovery of the theories that led, in turn, to the development of thermodynamics, while the discovery that liquids expand and contract when temperature changes led to the invention of the thermometer. Many believe that the important inventions which contributed to the technical and social changes in Western Europe and the U.S. during and after the Industrial Revolution were momentous. These innovations provided the seeds of capitalism, thus increasing production and opening ever-widening markets. The leading inventions of this period took place in the textile trades, metallurgy, and chemistry. For further information, see Alf K. Berle and L. Sprague de Camp, *Inventions, Patents and Their Management*, D. Van Nostrand Company, Inc., Princeton, N.J., 1959; Roger Burlingame, *Machines That Built America*, Harcourt, Brace & World, Inc., New York, 1953; John W. Oliver, *The History of American Technology*, The Ronald Press Company, New York, 1956.

Inventory   The supply of various goods kept on hand by a firm in order to meet needs promptly as they arise and thus assure uninterrupted operation of the business. In manufacturing, for example, inventories include not only finished products awaiting shipment to selling outlets, but also raw materials, nuts and bolts, paper and pencils, and countless other major and minor items required for the production and distribution of the products. Occasionally, because of sudden changes in demand or unanticipated changes in output, excessive inventories accumulate, and deliberate efforts are then made to reduce new purchases until the excessive supplies have been eliminated. When widespread, such inventory-cutting endeavors have been a chief ingredient of U.S. business recessions since World War II. Because inventories are a costly form of investment, firms strive to keep them at the lowest level consistent with good business practice, and sophisticated techniques, such as linear programming and operations research, have been developed for achieving that goal. Detailed data on business inventories are published regularly in U.S. Department of Commerce, *Survey of Current Business;* see also Moses Abramowitz, *Inventories and Business Cycles*, Princeton University Press, Princeton, N.J., 1950; John F. Magee, *Industrial Logistics*, McGraw-Hill Book Company, New York, 1968.

Inventory Change   The increase or decrease in the level of total business
inventories in a given period. As a form of business investment, inventory
change, like investment in new plants and equipment, can have a sharp
impact on a nation's economic activity. Since World War II, inventory
changes have played a major role in business fluctuations in the U.S., and

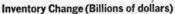

Inventory Change (Billions of dollars)

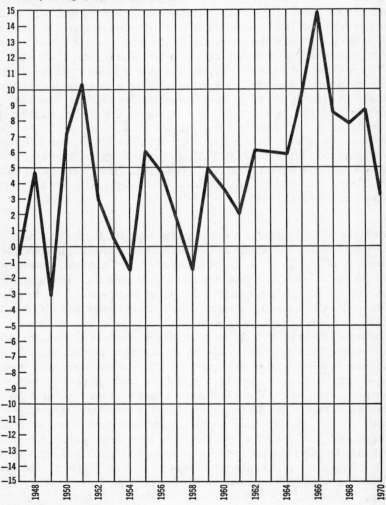

Source: U.S. Department of Commerce.

in four postwar recessions (1953–1954, 1957–1958, 1960–1961, and 1969–1970) declines in the gross national product and industrial production were largely the result of inventory reductions. Inventory changes are included in the calculation of the gross national product in annual-rate terms. Quarterly data on inventory changes as a segment of gross private domestic investment may be found in *Economic Indicators*, prepared by the Council of Economic Advisers for the U.S. Joint Economic Committee, Government Printing Office, Washington, D.C., monthly; for details of calculations on inventory change, see U.S. Department of Commerce, *Survey of Current Business: National Income Supplement*, 1954; for a discussion of inventories and their role in business fluctuations, see Moses Abramowitz, *Inventories and Business Cycles*, Princeton University Press, Princeton, N.J., 1950.

Inventory-Sales Ratio The ratio between a company's or an industry's stock of goods and its sales or shipments in a given period. One objective of inventory control is to maintain inventory-sales ratios at the lowest level possible under existing business conditions. The rapid introduction of effective inventory control in the late 1950s permitted many U.S. firms

Total Manufacturing and Trade Inventories to Sales Ratio (Ratio scale)

Source: U.S. Department of Commerce.

to reduce permanently the inventories required to service their customers. As a result, inventory-sales ratios in many industries have tended to decline, although short-term fluctuations still occur. Inventory-sales ratios are a useful forecasting tool. Relatively sharp increases in the ratios suggest that inventories are growing at a faster pace than an industry's sales; hence, it may be necessary to cut back production in the immediate future. A declining inventory-sales ratio, on the other hand, indicates that sales are growing in relation to an industry's inventory of goods; hence, it may be necessary to increase production in the immediate future to meet customers' demands. Historical data on inventory-sales ratios for major industry groups appear in U.S. Department of Commerce, *Survey of Current Business,* June, 1961, p. 20; current data are printed in this publication monthly.

Inventory-Valuation Adjustment   A measure of the profit or loss which takes place as a result of increases or decreases in prices affecting the values of inventories held by corporations. Total business profits include profits or losses made on inventory as well as profits from operations. Since corporations generally value the materials that they consume in production at the original cost and not at the cost of replacement, profits tend to be overstated when the costs of materials are rising and understated when their costs are falling. The inventory-valuation adjustment is used by the U.S. Department of Commerce in its computations of national income to correct the overstatement or understatement of profits. For example, in 1950, when industrial prices rose substantially because of the Korean conflict, the inventory-valuation adjustment accounted for $5 billion of the $40.6 billion in corporate profits before taxes. During the 1949 recession, when industrial prices fell substantially, there was a loss of inventory value of nearly $2 billion. For a detailed discussion of the inventory-valuation adjustment, see U.S. Department of Commerce, *Survey of Current Business: National Income Supplement,* 1954.

Inverted Economic Series   A series of key business-cycle indicators which conform negatively to the business cycle; that is, they decline when general business activity rises and rise when general business activity declines. Examples of negatively conforming indicators are the unemployment rate, initial claims for unemployment insurance, and liabilities of business failures. A rise in one of these series indicates deterioration in business activity, and a decline indicates improvement. In business-cycle analysis, it is convenient to invert these indicators so that their behavior may be compared more easily with that of the other indicators. Depending on the type of analysis to be made, there are several methods of inverting indicators. Two of the simplest: (1) invert the

Inventory-Valuation Adjustment, 1947–1970
(In billions of dollars)

Year	Inventory-Valuation Adjustment
1947	−5.9
1948	−2.2
1949	1.9
1950	−5.0
1951	−1.2
1952	1.0
1953	−1.0
1954	−0.3
1955	−1.7
1956	−2.7
1957	−1.5
1958	−0.3
1959	−0.5
1960	0.2
1961	−0.1
1962	0.3
1963	−0.5
1964	−0.5
1965	−1.7
1966	−1.8
1967	−1.1
1968	−3.3
1969	−5.4
1970	−4.8

SOURCE: U.S. Department of Commerce.

scale in graphic presentation, that is, show numbers of the scale in increasing magnitude from top to bottom; and (2) take period-to-period percentage changes in the actual data and invert the signs, that is, show declines as positive (+) and rises as negative (−) changes. For further discussion on inverted series, see Geoffrey H. Moore (ed.), *Business Cycle Indicators,* Princeton University Press, Princeton, N.J., 1961, vol. I.

Invested Capital (Capital Structure)   The sum of bonds and owner-contributed capital (stock accounts and surplus) in a corporation. Thus, invested capital is the total of a corporation's net worth and its long-term debt. The rate of return on invested capital is an important measure of the profitability of a corporation. For further information, see J. Fred Weston and Eugene F. Brigham, *Managerial Finance,* 2d ed., Holt, Rinehart and Winston, Inc., New York, 1966, pp. 253–274.

Investment Bank   *See Investment Banking.*

Investment Banking   The marketing of new corporate securities. The investment-banking firm purchases large blocks of new corporate issues of stocks and bonds and resells them in smaller amounts to individual or institutional investors. The investment bank acts as the middleman between the issuer of securities and the investing public, facilitating the flow of available savings into investment. Most investment banking takes the form of the purchase, or underwriting, of entire new issues of securities. Since the capital involved in such underwriting is often so large that no one investment bank can handle it alone, it is common practice for several firms to form a purchasing syndicate to buy and distribute the securities jointly. The purchase group assures the issuing corporation a definite price for the securities and then bears the risk of selling the securities to the public at a price high enough to realize a profit. Besides purchase and sale of entire issues, investment-banking syndicates may participate in standby underwriting, under which the group underwrites the offering (usually of stockholders' rights) by agreeing in advance to buy at a specified price all securities which are not sold by the corporation itself. Another aspect of investment banking is best-efforts selling, or agency marketing, in which the investment banker merely markets a new security as the agent of the issuing corporation, but makes no agreement to underwrite the issue and assumes none of the risk of selling it. For additional details, see Irwin Friend et al., *Investment Banking and the New Issues Market*, The World Publishing Company, Cleveland, 1967; Investment Bankers Association of America, *Fundamentals of Investment Banking*, Prentice-Hall, Inc., Englewood Cliffs, N.J., 1949.

Investment Company (Investment Trust)   An organization that combines the funds of many persons and invests them in a wide selection of securities. Although a few earlier companies resembled modern investment companies, the first real investment trust was the Foreign and Colonial Trust, which was established in London in 1868. Its purpose was to give small investors the same advantage—diversification—that large capitalists had. Today, along with diversification, investment companies give shareholders the advantage of professional management. In the U.S., the Securities and Exchange Commission (SEC) regulates investment companies under the Investment Company Act of 1940. Any company that falls within the act's definition of an investment company must register with the SEC. The SEC classifies investment companies under four types: management open-end (mutual funds), management closed-end, unit investment trusts, and face-amount certificate companies. As of June 30, 1967, there were 435 open-end investment companies, 161 closed-end investment companies, 141 unit investment trusts, and 6 face-amount certificate companies registered with the SEC. Their total assets were estimated at $58.2 billion. See Investment Company Act of 1940; U.S. Securities and Exchange Commission, *Annual Reports;* Charles W. Gerstenberg, *Financial Organization and Management of Business,* 4th ed., Prentice-Hall, Inc., Englewood Cliffs, N.J., 1959; George L. Leffler and L. C. Farwell, *The Stock Market,* The Ronald Press Company, New York, 1963; *Report of the Securities and Exchange Commission on the Public Policy Implications of Investment Company Growth,* Commission on Interstate and Foreign Commerce, Dec. 2, 1966.

Investment Guarantee   Government insurance against the risks of inconvertibility or expropriation of foreign investments. The investment-guarantee program was initiated by the U.S. government to encourage the flow of private capital to less developed areas. Private individuals making approved foreign investments in less developed countries may purchase protection against the risk of being unable to convert foreign currencies into dollars and the risk of expropriation or confiscation by the foreign government. In the U.S., the Agency for International Development can provide this type of insurance to U.S. firms or subsidiaries that are contemplating new or additional investments in those countries which have concluded special bilateral agreements with the U.S. Investment guarantees do not protect the investor against ordinary business risks but only against adverse actions of foreign governments. For additional details, see David B. Zenoff and Jack Zwick, *International Financial Management,* Prentice-Hall, Inc., Englewood Cliffs, N.J., 1969, pp. 108–111; Lawrence A. Collins and Aaron Etra, "Policy, Politics, International Law and the United States Investment Guaranty Program," *The Columbia Journal of Transnational Law,* vol. 4, no. 2, pp. 240–296, 1966; Marina V. N. Whitman, *Government Risk Sharing in Foreign Investment,* Princeton University Press, Princeton, N.J., 1965.

Investment Plan   The expectation of a business firm for investment in new plants and equipment. Most business firms have a program of investment projects which are expected to be carried out over the short or the long run. Since anticipatory investment information is valuable in forecasting business conditions, both company planners and government planners pay close attention to surveys of investment plans, such as the quarterly survey of the U.S. Department of Commerce and the Securities and Exchange Commission and the annual surveys of the McGraw-Hill Department of Economics. The dollar value of investment plans for a specific time period often differs from the dollar value of actual investment in the same period. The difference arises because of the addition of new programs, the deferral of other programs, and the cancellation of still others. At the company level, the difference between planned investment and actual investment is very large, but as the data of individual companies are aggregated into industry totals and then into a total for all business, the differences tend to offset each other, with the result that total investment plans are very close to actual investment. For additional information on surveys of investment plans and the accuracy of investment plans, see National Bureau of Economic Research, Inc., *The Quality and Economic Significance of Anticipations Data,* Princeton University Press, Princeton, N.J., 1960, part IV.

Investment Trust   *See Investment Company.*

Invisible Exports and Imports   Exports and imports of services. Services that are rendered for foreigners or those that foreigners render for Americans belong to this category. Shipping charges, banking services, royalties, insurance income, rents, interest, profits, dividends, and tourist expenditures are included. Invisible exports and imports are items in the balance of international payments.

Invisible-Hand Doctrine   The doctrine, introduced by Adam Smith in 1776, that individuals, all seeking to further their self-interest, will be led, as if by an invisible hand, to achieve the best good for all. The purpose of introducing the invisible hand was to demonstrate that any government interference with free competition would be harmful to society, since such competition by itself was able to channel the selfish motives of individuals so that they automatically, though unintentionally, furthered the best interests of society. Since self-interest guides man as if he were "led by an invisible hand to promote an end which was no part of his intention," *laissez faire* was considered the best policy for the government to pursue in economic matters. A major limitation of the invisible-hand doctrine is that it works well only under conditions of perfect competition, which is an unrealistic assumption to make about the real world. For additional details, see Adam Smith, *The Wealth of Nations,* Random House, Inc., New York, 1937, p. 423.

Isocost Curve   A graphic line showing the various possible combinations of resources that can be purchased with a given quantity of money, on the assumption that the prices of the factors are in some fixed proportion. For example, let us assume that we wish to know the various combinations of steel at $80 per ton and of aluminum at $40 per ton with a given outlay of \$320. The isocost line in the accompanying illustration indicates the possibilities of all purchase combinations (4 tons of steel, 8 tons of aluminum, or any combination between these two extremes). The isocost line, which represents the ratio of the prices of the two items, is used to determine minimum cost for a given level of output by choosing that combination of factor inputs which is cheaper than any alternative combination which could be used to produce the given output. This is done by using the isoquant, which represents the marginal rate of substitution between the factors, and its tangency to the lowest isocost line (the one farthest left). For a further explanation, see William Fellner, *Modern Economic Analysis,* McGraw-Hill Book Company, New York, 1960, pp. 266–274; Donald S. Watson, *Price Theory and Its Uses,* 2d ed., Houghton Mifflin Company, Boston, 1968.

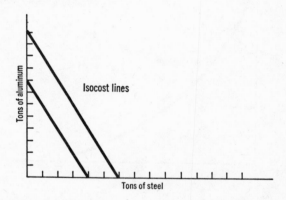

Isoquant   A graphic line showing the various possible combinations of factors which will yield a given quantity of output. For example, let us assume that we wish to know the various combinations of steel and aluminum needed to build ten automobiles. The isoquant in the illustration (page 316) indicates the possibilities. The slope of the isoquant represents the marginal rate of substitution between the two factors at that particular point. Because of a diminishing rate of marginal substitution, the isoquant will usually be convex to the point of origin. This means that the greater the amount of one factor used, the less of the other factor is needed to replace a unit of the first factor. Thus, each additional unit of steel, past some point, replaces less than a unit of aluminum, and, correspondingly in the same area, less than a unit of aluminum can be substituted for more than a unit of steel. If the two factors are perfect substitutes, however, the isoquant will be a straight line, since the marginal rate of substitution will be constant. The more easily the two factors can be substituted, the less will be the curvature of the line. If, at the other extreme, the factors cannot be substituted, the isoquant will show a right-angle bend at the point of required output. For further information, see John M. Cassels, "On the Law of Variable Proportions," in William Fellner and Bernard F. Haley (eds.), *Readings in the Theory of Income Distribution,* McGraw-Hill Book Company, New York, 1946, pp. 103–118; see also William Fellner, *Modern Economic Analysis,* McGraw-Hill Book Company, New York, 1960, pp. 266–274; Donald S. Watson, *Price Theory and Its Uses,* 2d ed., Houghton Mifflin Company, Boston, 1968.

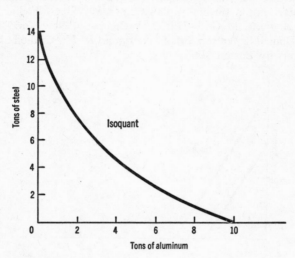

Issued Stock   *See Capital Stock.*

Iteration (Iterative Method)   Several successive applications of a given statistical technique to a given single sample of raw data with a view to eliminating extreme observations and/or deriving estimates of parameters whose estimating equations are essentially nonlinear and of a type not suited for direct solution. In the case of estimating parameters, iteration refers to a sequence of approximations to the solution for a parameter that is obtained in such a way that the essential step in determining each approximation constitutes a linear function. For additional information, see Lawrence R. Klein, *A Textbook of Econometrics,* Row, Peterson & Company, Evanston, Ill., 1953; Tjalling C. Koopmans (ed.), *Statistical Inference in Dynamic Economic Models,* Cowles Commission Monograph no. 10, John Wiley & Sons, Inc., New York, 1950.

Iterative Method   *See Iteration.*

J

Jawbone Economics An oral statement by a political leader on the economic health of the nation as he sees it, together with a series of suggestions on economic action which should be carried out in order to improve the situation. For example, it has been suggested at various times by "experts" of this type that business is entering a deep recession when it has already started rising from the bottom of a very mild recession. Such an amateur economist would also suggest that the way to cut the high unemployment rate to the so-called full-employment unemployment rate is to reduce taxes, which obviously may not provide a complete solution of the unemployment problem. He might also suggest that the only cure for a rapid rate of inflation is wage-price controls. For additional information, see Mark H. Willes, "The Fight Against Inflation: Barebone, Jawbone or Lawbone?" *Business Review,* Federal Reserve Bank of Philadelphia, Philadelphia, February, 1971.

Jobber A wholesaler acting as a middleman, generally in soft-goods industries, such as apparel or shoes. A jobber buys products from a producer and sells to retailers. Although he is not limited to any specific sales territory, in most cases he is unable to buy large enough quantities of merchandise made to his own specifications to qualify him as a manufacturing wholesaler. For general information on wholesaling and types of wholesalers, see David A. Revzan, *Wholesaling in Marketing Operations,* John Wiley & Sons, Inc., New York, 1961.

Job Evaluation A systematic method of classifying different jobs in one plant or firm. It involves a rating by certain criteria: physical effort, skill, education, degree of responsibility for materials and products, and so on. Once each factor has been assigned a value, each job in the plant or firm can be analyzed and given a point rating which may be converted into cents per hour to create a wage-rate schedule. Management likes the definite standards of job evaluation because they provide uniformity and simplicity in the handling of wage matters and of complaints by workers and unions. Unions, on the other hand, are critical of job evaluation, for it tends to remove the determination of wage rates from collective bargaining and place it wholly under management's control. As a result, unions are generally unwilling to accept job-evaluation systems whose structure and implementation have not been negotiated. Even with union cooperation, job-evaluation plans have proved difficult to administer—for instance, in times of labor shortage or of continual changes in a job because of technical advances. For an authoritative source, see Helen Baker and John M. True, *The Operation of Job Evaluation Plans*, Princeton University Press, Princeton, N.J., 1947; see also Lloyd G. Reynolds, *Labor Economics and Labor Relations*, 5th ed., Prentice-Hall, Inc., Englewood Cliffs, N.J., 1970, pp. 627–632.

Job Vacancy Rate The ratio of the number of job vacancies to the sum of employment plus vacancies. Job vacancy data are collected monthly by state employment security agencies from a representative sample of employers. A job vacancy is a vacant job that is available for filling and for which firms are actively trying to find or recruit a worker from outside the firm. The firm must be engaged in efforts to fill the job vacancies by means of orders listed with public or private employment agencies and school placement offices, notification to labor unions and professional organizations, "help wanted" advertising, recruitment programs, and interview and selection of applicants. Vacancy data are broken down into long-term and current rates, by industry and by occupation. Job vacancy data are intended to help manpower programs be more responsive to current needs of both job seekers and employers in planning training programs and identifying imbalances between demand and supply. The job vacancy rate for the manufacturing industry in May, 1970, was 0.8, as compared with 1.4 in May, 1969. The U.S. Department of Labor is responsible for releasing job vacancy data. For additional information, see Daniel Creamer, *Measuring Job Vacancies*, National Industrial Conference Board, Inc., Studies in Business Economics, no. 97, New York, 1967.

Joint Costs Expenses involved in the simultaneous production of two or more commodities or services. Joint costs are usually found in basic industries in which one raw material is the source of several different products. Since the various products must be produced together from a single input-cost factor, part of the cost of the several different products is incurred together as a joint sum and not separately for the individual products. For example, the expenses entailed in the refining of petroleum into gasoline, kerosine, and other products can be regarded as joint costs, since all these refined petroleum products come from a single input factor

Job Vacancies in Manufacturing

Industry	1970										1971		
	Mar.	Apr.	May	June	July	Aug.	Sept.	Oct.	Nov.	Dec.	Jan.	Feb.	Mar.
Job vacancies in manufacturing (number, in thousands)	165	158	151	123	126	137	118	93	76	77	81	80	83
Job vacancy rates:													
Manufacturing	0.8	0.8	0.8	0.6	0.6	0.7	0.6	0.5	0.4	0.4	0.4	0.4	0.4
Durable goods industries	0.8	0.7	0.7	0.6	0.6	0.6	0.5	0.4	0.3	0.3	0.4	0.4	0.4
Nondurable goods industries	0.9	0.9	0.9	0.7	0.7	0.8	0.7	0.6	0.5	0.5	0.5	0.5	0.5
Selected durable goods industries:													
Primary metal industries	0.6	0.7	0.6	0.5	0.4	0.6	0.4	0.3	0.2	0.2	0.3	0.3	0.3
Machinery, except electrical	1.0	0.9	0.8	0.6	0.5	0.6	0.5	0.4	0.4	0.4	0.4	0.4	0.4
Electrical equipment and supplies	0.9	0.8	0.8	0.6	0.6	0.7	0.6	0.4	0.3	0.4	0.4	0.4	0.4
Transportation equipment	0.7	0.5	0.6	0.5	0.5	0.6	0.4	0.4	0.4	0.4	0.4	0.3	0.4
Instruments and related products	1.7	1.4	1.1	0.7	0.6	0.7	0.7	0.6	0.4	0.5	0.6	0.5	0.6
Selected nondurable goods industries:													
Textile mill products	1.0	1.1	1.1	0.8	0.9	1.0	1.0	0.8	0.6	0.6	0.7	0.6	0.8
Apparel and other textile products	1.6	1.5	1.5	1.4	1.4	1.5	1.4	1.1	1.1	1.1	1.2	1.2	1.3
Printing and publishing	0.7	0.7	0.6	0.5	0.5	0.6	0.5	0.4	0.4	0.3	0.4	0.4	0.4
Chemicals and allied products	1.0	0.8	0.8	0.7	0.6	0.6	0.6	0.4	0.4	0.4	0.4	0.4	0.5

SOURCE: U.S. Department of Labor.

and are all affected similarly by certain basic cost changes (e.g., a change in the price of crude oil). The cost of producing gasoline cannot be regarded as completely separate from the production cost of kerosine; rather, the two are joint costs. See Albert E. Waugh, *Principles of Economics*, McGraw-Hill Book Company, New York, 1947; Milton H. Spencer, *Managerial Economics*, Richard D. Irwin, Inc., Homewood, Ill., 1968, p. 215.

Joint Demand Demand for two or more products which are generally used together, sometimes because of necessity and sometimes because of preference. Joint demand is demonstrated when the purchase of a greater quantity of one good leads to the purchase of a greater quantity of another. This concept, which was originated by Alfred Marshall, is used in the analysis of both demand for factors of production and consumer demand. In the case of factors of production, the joint demand for inputs, such as graphite and wood, is derived from the demand for pencils, the good which they combine to produce. Because there is a demand for pencils, there is a joint demand for wood and graphite. In the case of consumer demands, the joint demand results from the combinations, such as record players and records and automobiles and tires, in which consumers wish to use their goods. The theory of joint demand is used to help explain the course of demand for one good when the demand for another changes, as for example, through a price change. A discussion of consumer joint demand can be found in J. R. Hicks, *Value and Capital*, Oxford University Press, Fair Lawn, N.J., 1946; for the classical presentation of joint factor demand, see Alfred Marshall, *Principles of Economics*, Macmillan & Co., Ltd., London, 1920; for a more modern analysis, see Joan Robinson, *The Economics of Imperfect Competition*, Macmillan & Co., Ltd., London, 1945; for a presentation of both types of analysis, see Paul A. Samuelson, *Economics*, 7th ed., McGraw-Hill Book Company, New York, 1967.

Joint Products Two or more commodities produced by a single process or from a single raw material in such a manner that it is impossible to produce one good without turning out the other or others. Such goods are produced under conditions of joint cost and joint supply. The refining of petroleum into gasoline, kerosine, and other products is an example of the production of two or more commodities by a single process. For further information, see Albert E. Waugh, *Principles of Economics*, McGraw-Hill Book Company, New York, 1947.

Joint-Stock Bank The name given to an incorporated commercial bank in Great Britain. Unlike the United States, Britain has not enacted special legislation regulating the management and organization of its banks, which are therefore incorporated under the Companies (Consolidation) Act of 1908. The British joint-stock banks are typical deposit banks. About 60% of their deposits are deposits on current account, draw no interest, and are subject to withdrawal on demand. Such deposits may be transferred by check, banker's order, or credit clearing. The remaining 40% of deposits are accounted for by balances on deposit account, which cannot be withdrawn on less than seven days' notice. Interest on these deposits is usually paid at a rate 2% below the Bank of England discount rate. Joint-stock banks are highly concentrated, operating many branches; by the end of 1962, the 11 London clearing banks, 5 banks in Scotland, and 3 in Northern Ireland operated more than 13,000 branches. Of the 11 clearing banks, Barclay, Lloyds, Midland, National Provincial, and Westminster are commonly known as the Big Five. For further information on joint-stock banking and its development, see Kenneth Mackenzie, *The Banking Systems of Great Britain, France, Germany and the United States of America*, St. Martin's Press, Inc., New York, 1945; Raymond P. Kent, *Money and Banking*, Holt, Rinehart and Winston, Inc., New York, 1966, pp. 392–393.

Joint Venture An association of individuals or firms formed to carry out a specific business project. Although a joint venture is very similar to a partnership, it differs in that it is limited to the success or failure of the specific project for which it was formed. As in the case of the partnership, a joint venture is formed by a contract agreement in which each partner assumes unlimited liability for the organization's debts. For a more detailed discussion of joint venture, see Joseph H. Bonneville et al., *Organizing and Financing Business*, Prentice-Hall, Inc., Englewood Cliffs, N.J., 1959; for joint ventures in developing countries, see W. G. Friedman and G. Kalmanoff, *Joint International Business Ventures*, Columbia University Press, New York, 1961.

Juglar Cycle A business cycle of intermediate duration. Named for Clement Juglar, who was the first to isolate the major industrial business cycle, Juglar cycles are fluctuations of prices, production, employment, etc., over a period of nine to ten years. They are classified as major nonseasonal cycles. Juglar cycles, used by Joseph A. Schumpeter in his three-cycle analysis of business cycles, were explained by the mechanism of capitalist development innovations. They are superimposed on the Kondratieff cycles of fifty to sixty years, so that each Kondratieff cycle contains six Juglar cycles. For additional details, see Joseph A. Schumpeter, *Business Cycles*, 2 vols., McGraw-Hill Book Company, New York, 1939.

Jurisdictional Disputes A controversy over the choice of the union whose members are entitled to work on a job. A jurisdictional dispute differs from a representation controversy, which is a dispute over the choice of the union to represent a group of workers. Jurisdiction is a property right of the national union. The enforcement and administration of jurisdictional rights must be adapted to a wide variety of local situations with differences in degree of specialization, custom, employer preference and relationships, and the relative power of different local unions. In the building industry, there is a tendency for jurisdictional disputes to become jurisdictional strikes because, unless the job is shut down immediately, there will be no work to do after the dispute has been settled. Jurisdictional disputes among AFL–CIO unions must be brought for arbitration before the AFL–CIO Internal Disputes Committee. Jurisdictional strikes are considered an unfair labor practice, subject to injunction under the Taft-Hartley Act. See Jack Barbash, *The Practice of Unionism*, Harper & Row, Publishers, Incorporated, New York, 1956; see also *How Collective Bargaining Works*, The Twentieth Century Fund, New York, 1942; U.S. Code, title 29, section 158(b), paragraph 4(D).

Jury-of-Executive-Opinion Method A type of sales forecasting that combines the views of top executives. This method facilitates forecasting without elaborate statistics and is said to yield more accurate results than methods using a single forecaster. It is criticized on the grounds that it is based on opinion alone, requires the use of costly executive time, and disperses the responsibility for forecasting. See *Forecasting Sales*, National Industrial Conference Board, Inc., Studies in Business Policy, no. 106, New York, 1963.

Just Price The price of a good which approximates the general opinion of society of the worth of the good. Thus, a seller who receives a just price for his good is able to buy another good equivalent in value to the one that he has sold. Associated with St. Thomas Aquinas, the concept is based on the scholastic idea that justice requires that exchange involve equivalent values. In the Middle Ages, this concept was used to judge the morality of economic activity, only those trading activities in which a just price was charged being considered moral. In most instances it was considered morally wrong to charge interest on a loan, since the repayment and the loan should be equivalent. Because the concept of just price involves a moral judgment, it has been abandoned by most economists, but references are made to it with regard to some forms of price control and economic exploitation. For the scholastic position, see St. Thomas Aquinas, *Summa Theologica*, Benziger Bros. Inc., New York, 1947; for the history of the concept, see Bernard W. Dempsey, "Just Price in a

Functional Economy," *The American Economic Review,* American Economic Association, Evanston, Ill., September, 1935; for a longer study, see R. Kaulla, *The Theory of Just Price,* W. W. Norton & Company, Inc., New York, 1941; Howard D. Marshall, *The Great Economists,* Pitman Publishing Corporation, New York, 1967.

Kennedy Round   The 1964 round of global tariff negotiations. It was named for President John F. Kennedy's 1962 trade legislation, which gave the U.S. government greater authority to negotiate and reduce tariffs than it had ever enjoyed before. The negotiations were begun under the auspices of the General Agreement on Tariffs and Trade (GATT), but many more than the 58 countries in the GATT community were involved. The big powers concerned in the Kennedy round were the U.S., the European Common Market countries, Great Britain and its six partners in the European Free Trade Association, Japan, and Canada. For additional details, see Thomas B. Curtis and John R. Vastine, Jr., *The Kennedy Round and the Future of American Trade,* Frederick A. Praeger, Inc., New York, 1971.

Key Industry   An industrial field which has an important bearing on a nation's economic activity. Although a key industry is not necessarily one of the biggest industries in a country, it generally is. In the U.S., capital goods manufacturing, construction, automobiles, and steel have long been considered bellwethers of the economy. In developing countries, food and textiles may be key industries.

Keynes-Effect Theory   The theory that a reduction in the overall price level leads to lower interest rates and to increased investment. It is based on the following line of reasoning: (1) Individuals establish a desired relationship between the money balances that they hold and their expenditures on goods and services. (2) Price reductions raise the real value of their money holdings; that is, the quantity of goods and services that can be bought with a given amount of money rises. (3) Thus, the desired relationship between real balances and expenditures is disturbed, and individuals have an excess supply of liquid assets. (4) Individuals are willing to lend part of this excess supply. (5) An increase in the supply of funds in the loan market lowers the rate of interest. (6) With a lower rate of interest, greater investment takes place. The Keynes effect operates only in the market for bonds; in this respect, it differs from the Pigou effect, which operates only in the market for goods and services, and from the real-balance effect, which operates in both the bond market and the market for goods and services. For the original statement of the Keynes effect, see J. M. Keynes, *The General Theory of Employment, Interest, and Money,* Harcourt, Brace & World, Inc., New York, 1936, p. 257; for a further analysis, see Don Patinkin, *Money, Interest and Prices,* Harper & Row, Publishers, Incorporated, New York, 1964.

Keynesian Economics The body of economic thought developed by John Maynard Keynes and his followers. The central theme of Keynesian economics is an analysis of the causes and results of variations in aggregate spending and income. Total income equals total consumption plus investment. If every increase in savings is not offset by increased investment, income will fall and unemployment will rise. The level of consumption (and saving) is said to depend on the individual's propensity to consume, which is a function of income. The amount of business investment is set largely through the marginal efficiency of capital or businessmen's expectations as to future returns on capital investment. The interest rate is seen not as a factor tending to equalize the supply of savings and the demand for investment but rather as an independent element, depending on the extent of the individual's desire to hold savings in cash (his liquidity preference). Thus, savings and investment will not necessarily tend toward equilibrium; instead, the level of savings will generally be higher than investment, and the result will be frequent unemployment and stagnation. Keynes therefore proposed, for the first time in economic theory, the possibility of an underemployment equilibrium. To prevent mass unemployment in the depression phase of the business cycle, he argued that the central government should compensate for the deficiency in aggregate demand by using deficit financing to stimulate spending and to create investments which would raise income to the full-employment level, aided by the operation of the investment multiplier. The basic elements of the Keynesian theory of economics were introduced in 1936 by Keynes in his major work, *The General Theory of Employment, Interest, and Money,* and were further developed by his disciples, such as Alvin H.

Hansen in the U.S. Soon accepted in most academic circles, this "new economics" remains the most significant force on modern economic theory. For a fuller exposition of Keynesian economics, see J. M. Keynes, *The General Theory of Employment, Interest, and Money*, Harcourt, Brace & World, Inc., New York, 1936; Alvin H. Hansen, *A Guide to Keynes*, McGraw-Hill Book Company, New York, 1953; Seymour E. Harris (ed.), *The New Economics: Keynes' Influence in Theory and Public Policy*, Alfred A. Knopf, Inc., New York, 1947; Lawrence R. Klein, *The Keynesian Revolution*, The Macmillan Company, New York, 1947.

Keynes Plan   A proposal, put forward by John Maynard Keynes, for an international clearing union. The Keynes Plan, presented in 1943 as the British plan for the proposed United Nations monetary agency, was an attempt to ease the flow of international payments and promote trade. All international payments were to be handled through a central clearinghouse (clearing union), which would balance the trade credits and debits of the individual member countries. The unique aspect of this plan was that the credits of the clearing union, called bancor, would replace gold as the international medium of exchange. Instead of gold payments, the members would have to accept bancor transfers to their accounts on the books of the clearing union. Thus, the clearing union would provide debtor nations with a means of making payments to their creditors. In effect, the clearing union would be a central bank for nations, lending the reserves of the creditor countries (in bancor) to countries which needed them. The Keynes Plan was not accepted for the United Nations agency; instead, the U.S. plan for an International Monetary Fund (White Plan) was finally approved. For additional details on the Keynes Plan, see "Proposals by British Experts for an International Clearing Union," *Proceedings and Documents of the U.N. Monetary and Financial Conference*, vol. II, pp. 1548–1573, Government Printing Office, Washington, D.C., 1948; Robert Triffin, *Europe and the Money Muddle*, Yale University Press, New Haven, Conn., 1957, pp. 93–109.

Kickback   The return of a portion of a worker's wages to his employer or supervisor as a condition of his obtaining and keeping a job. In 1934 the Congress of the U.S. enacted the Kickback Racket Act, which outlawed this practice. The law, which was designed to cover employers coming under fair-wage and minimum-wage legislation, immediately put an end to the widespread practice of kickbacks.

Kitchin Cycle   A short, rhythmic fluctuation in business activity. Named for Joseph Kitchin, who was the first analyst to study it in detail, the Kitchin cycle is a regular, forty-month fluctuation of prices, production, employment, etc. Kitchin cycles, used by Joseph A. Schumpeter in his three-cycle analysis of business cycles, are explained largely by changes in inventory investment and by small waves of innovations, especially in equipment which can be produced fairly quickly. They are superimposed on the longer Juglar and Kondratieff cycles, so that there are three Kitchin cycles to every Juglar cycle and eighteen Kitchin cycles in every Kondratieff cycle. For additional information, see Joseph A. Schumpeter, *Business Cycles*, 2 vols., McGraw-Hill Book Company, New York, 1939. For a brief criticism of the Kitchin cycle, see Carl A. Dauten and Lloyd M. Valentine, *Business Cycles and Forecasting*, South-Western Publishing Company, Incorporated, Cincinnati, 1968, pp. 347–350.

Kondratieff Cycle   A series of long waves of economic fluctuation. Named for N. D. Kondratieff, a Russian economist, Kondratieff cycles consist of waves in prices, production, and trade lasting from fifty to sixty years. According to Kondratieff, these cycles are due to processes inherent in the nature of capitalism, especially that of capital accumulation. He argued that changes in techniques of production, wars and revolutions, the opening of new markets, etc., are not random occurrences affecting the cycle, but rather are part of the rhythm of the long waves. For example, the expansion into new markets does not start a long-term upswing; instead, the upswing makes the expansion into new markets possible and necessary. Similarly, the declining phase of the long wave leads to important discoveries which are utilized on a large scale only at the beginning of the next major upswing. The upward phase of the wave, producing high tension in the expansion of economic forces, is a major factor in provoking wars and revolutions. Joseph A. Schumpeter, in adopting the Kondratieff cycle as part of his three-cycle analysis of business fluctuations, considered that the long cycle was closely linked to the waves of innovations, predominantly of a definite type, by which the long wave in question was characterized. Thus, the Kondratieff wave from about 1780 to 1840 was that of the Industrial Revolution; the next, from 1840 to 1890, was that of steel and steam; and the one from 1890 to 1950 was that of electricity, chemistry, and motors. For additional details, see N. D. Kondratieff, "The Long Waves in Economic Life," *Review of Economics and Statistics*, Harvard University Press, Cambridge, Mass., November, 1935; George Garvy, "Kondratieff's Theory of Long Cycles," *Review of Economics and Statistics*, Harvard University Press, Cambridge, Mass., November, 1943; Joseph A. Schumpeter, *Business Cycles*, 2 vols., McGraw-Hill Book Company, New York, 1939; Carl A. Dauten and Lloyd M. Valentine, *Business Cycles and Forecasting*, South-Western Publishing Company, Incorporated, Cincinnati, 1968, pp. 347–350.

L

Labor In economic theory, the human effort or activity that is directed toward production. As a factor of production, labor is distinct from raw materials, capital, and management and includes only the efforts of hired workers. In another sense, labor comprises all persons who work for a living. This definition refers to the labor force of a nation, which includes all the employable population over a certain age. In a somewhat more restricted sense, labor signifies the whole working class or organized employees as opposed to employers; it thus includes all nonsupervisory workers (workers below the rank of foreman) in all kinds of public and private employment. The term has also come to mean the organized labor movement. For a consideration of labor economics, see Alfred Kuhn, *Labor: Institutions and Economics,* Harcourt, Brace & World, Inc., New York, 1967.

Labor Agreement A written contract between an employer and a freely chosen representative of his workers, setting forth the terms and conditions of employment. Since the employer is the sole buyer of labor for a particular plant, the typical employee is in a relatively weak position when he deals individually with his employer. So that they, too, can gain a degree of monopoly power, employees are therefore organized into strong unions. When agreement has been reached through collective bargaining and the approval of the workers has been obtained, the contract is signed. Such a contract covers the terms of agreement and lasts for a specified period of time. If agreement cannot be reached, labor can use its chief weapon, the strike, to induce the employer to agree to the union's terms. See Elias Lieberman, *The Collective Labor Agreement,* Harper & Row, Publishers, Incorporated, New York, 1939.

Labor Force According to the concept of the U.S. Department of Labor and the U.S. Bureau of the Census, the noninstitutionalized population, sixteen years of age or older, that either is employed or is not working but is looking for work. The labor force of the U.S., which totaled nearly 86 million in 1970, includes members of the armed forces as well as civilians. Most persons in the civilian labor force are employed in business or in industrial establishments working for wages and salaries, but self-employed persons, unpaid family workers on farms or in stores, and the unemployed are also included. The labor force is measured monthly by the Bureau of the Census for the Department of Labor. In a survey conducted in the week containing the twelfth day of the month, census interviewers ask questions of 50,000 households in 449 areas to learn which persons are in the labor force in that week. For further information, see Stanley Lebergott, *Manpower in Economic Growth: The United States Record since 1800,* McGraw-Hill Book Company, New York, 1964; Louis Ducoff and Margaret Jarman Hagood, *Labor Force Definition and Measurement: Recent Experience in the United States,* prepared for the Subcommittee on Labor Force Statistics of the Committee on Labor Market Research, Social Science Research Council, New York, 1947; current statistics are found in U.S. Department of Labor, *Employment and Earnings,* monthly.

Status of the Labor Force (Millions of people)

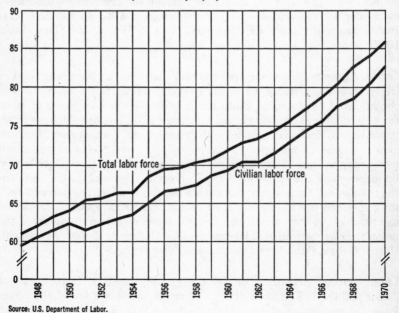

Source: U.S. Department of Labor.

Labor-Management Relations Act of 1947   *See Taft-Hartley Act.*

Labor-Market Area   A geographical unit consisting of a central city or cities and the surrounding territory within a reasonable commuting distance. It is an economically and socially integrated, primarily urban unit within which workers may readily change jobs without changing their residence. In most cases, the boundaries of major labor-market areas coincide with those of standard metropolitan areas, such as the New York metropolitan area and the Chicago metropolitan area. The Bureau of Employment Security of the U.S. Department of Labor rates 150 major labor-market areas and a number of smaller areas according to the adequacy of their labor supply. For a listing of labor-market areas and their classification, see U.S. Bureau of Employment Security, *Area Labor Market Trends*, monthly.

Labor Mobility   The ease with which workers are able to change jobs and occupations. There are two types of mobility, horizontal and vertical. Horizontal mobility refers to the degree to which workers shift from job to job at the same level of skill. This type of movement, which may occur between geographical areas or within a single location, is due primarily to differences in the terms of employment, such as wages, hours, and working conditions. The main barriers to this type of mobility are certain characteristics of the workers themselves, such as lack of information concerning job opportunities and the psychological and financial difficulties of moving into a new area, and the characteristics of certain jobs which prevent workers from moving even though they desire to do so, such as restrictive union practices and preferential hiring. Vertical mobility refers to the degree to which workers are able to acquire education and new skills which permit them to move up (or down) the occupational ladder. This type of mobility is an index of the relative openness of a social structure, representing the mobility within income, prestige, and other structures. For further information on labor mobility, see Lloyd G. Reynolds, *Labor Economics and Labor Relations*, Prentice-Hall, Inc., Englewood Cliffs, N.J., 1970, chap. 3; Natale Rogoff, *Recent Trends in Occupational Mobility*, The Free Press of Glencoe, New York, 1953; Herbert S. Parnes, *Research in Labor Mobility*, Social Science Research Council, New York, 1954; W. Warner and J. Abergglen, *Occupational Mobility*, The University of Minnesota Press, Minneapolis, 1955.

Labor Monopoly   The ability of strong labor unions to exert monopoly power through their ability to regulate the supply of labor and thus significantly affect the price of labor (wage rates). There is considerable disagreement over the extent and effect of this power and whether or not it is in need of additional public control. See Dexter M. Keezer and Associates, *Making Capitalism Work,* McGraw-Hill Book Company, New York, 1950, pp. 234–236.

Labor-Shortage Area (Surplus-Labor Market)   A U.S. labor-market area in which unemployment usually amounts to less than 1.5% of an area's labor force. This labor-market classification is assigned by the Bureau of Employment Security on the basis of information submitted by affiliated state employment-security agencies, which draw upon the information available in local public employment offices. A low unemployment rate is not the sole criterion used to classify labor-market areas. Consideration also is given to the outlook for the area as reflected in employers' estimates of future labor needs and other developments. Areas falling in Group A, the grouping of the Bureau of Employment Security in which unemployment is less than 1.5% of the labor force, are regarded as areas of labor shortages. For monthly area classifications, see U.S. Bureau of Employment Security, *Area Labor Market Trends.*

Labor Slowdown   A temporary slackening in the normal pace of work. Workers stay on the job, but reduce their output in order to gain some particular objective, such as improved washroom facilities, from management. The slowdown is a very effective pressure tactic. The term slowdown differs from restriction of output, which is usually an effort to prolong a job. For further discussion of the slowdown, see Sumner H. Slichter, James J. Healy, and E. Robert Livernash, *The Impact of Collective Bargaining on Management,* The Brookings Institution, Washington, D.C., 1960, chap. 22; R. S. Hammett et al., "The Slowdown as a Union Tactic," *Journal of Political Economy,* vol. LXV, pp. 126–134, The University of Chicago Press, Chicago, April, 1957.

Labor Theory of Value   The theory that the entire value of all reproducible commodities stems from the labor that produces them, whether this labor is applied directly or is used to improve the land and build the machines that contribute to the productive process. Developed by the classical economists of the late eighteenth and early nineteenth centuries, the theory was soon modified to take account of the relative scarcity of goods and services that also determines market value. Karl Marx adopted the labor theory of value in full and used it to explain why he thought that workers were being exploited whenever capitalists sold products for more than their labor costs. His argument, the touchstone of Communist economic theory, has frequently led the managers of the Soviet economy

to place too low a value on capital, an error which many Western economists believe has resulted in a considerable misuse of resources within
the Soviet Union. There are a number of shortcomings to the labor theory
of value. Among them are the facts that it does not incorporate interest
and that it does not take into account the length of the productive process.
For a general discussion of the labor theory of value, see Alexander Gray,
The Development of Economic Doctrine, David McKay Company, Inc.,
New York, 1948; for an explanation of the Marxist view, see Paul M.
Sweezy, *The Theory of Capitalist Development,* Oxford University Press,
Fair Lawn, N.J., 1942; for a description of the application of the theory
in Soviet planning, see Gregory Grossman, *Value and Plan: Economic
Calculation and Organization in Eastern Europe,* University of California
Press, Berkeley, Calif., 1960.

Labor Turnover, Firm The frequency of hirings and layoffs in an
individual firm. Labor turnover rates among firms provide indications of
labor mobility. Since World War II, the amount of a U.S. worker's fringe
benefits has resulted in lower rates of labor turnover in firms and in lower
labor mobility as well.

Labor Turnover, National The movement of wage and salary workers
into and out of employment on the national level. This movement is divided into two major categories, hirings and layoffs. These two categories
of labor turnover are generally considered leading indicators of national
economic activity, since they provide early indications of turning points
in business cycles. For U.S. industry statistics on labor turnover, see U.S.
Department of Labor, *Employment and Earnings,* monthly.

Lagging Indicator A measure of economic activity that usually reaches
a turning point of the business cycle after the overall economy has turned.
The use of statistical indicators of this type was developed by Wesley
Mitchell, Warren Persons, and Arthur F. Burns, members of the staff of
the National Bureau of Economic Research, to indicate historical changes
in the general course of business. Geoffrey H. Moore and Julius Shiskin,
also staff members of the bureau, have carried forward the indicator
method of business-cycle analysis, and they consider the timing of the
laggards necessary to round out the picture of the changing business
scene. Increases in lagging series, such as unit labor costs, interest rates, or
finished goods inventories, can help bring about declines in leading series,
such as profit margins, capital investment commitments, or additions to
materials inventories. Some economists pay little attention to the lagging
indicators, suggesting that they do not represent a significant contribution
to business forecasting. *Business Conditions Digest,* a report of the Bureau

of Economic Analysis, lists seven lagging indicators, but there is n
special division into related groups. For the development and analysis o
lagging indicators, see Geoffrey H. Moore (ed.), *Business Cycle Indi
cators,* Princeton University Press, Princeton, N.J., 1961; for curren
statistics of the indicators, see Bureau of Economic Analysis, *Busines
Conditions Digest,* monthly; J. Shiskin, "Business Cycle Indicators: Th
Known and the Unknown," *Business Cycle Developments,* U.S. Depart
ment of Commerce, Washington, September, 1963.

Laissez Faire   The doctrine that government should limit itself to th
maintenance of law and order and remove all legal restraints on trade an
prices. It was developed in the atmosphere of the highly regulative mon
archies of France and England in the late seventeenth and early eighteentl
centuries, when there were many local and national barriers to busines
activity. The first use of the phrase is attributed to a French manufacture
named Legendre, who, in reply to a question by the minister Jean Bap
tiste Colbert on how government could help business, said *"laissez nou
faire"* (leave us alone). Adam Smith, the great eighteenth-century Eng
lish economist, and his followers argued that a laissez faire policy woul
promote individual freedom, the best use of economic resources, an
economic growth. The doctrine reached its popular height in the lat
nineteenth century, but it lost influence thereafter as demands for gov
ernment regulation grew. Nevertheless, some economists have continue
to advocate positive programs of laissez faire in which government woul
avoid direct interference with prices and trade, but would be charge
with the heavy responsibilities of (1) the maintenance of competitiv
conditions in industry, (2) the control of the money supply, and (3
certain social welfare activities. The classic statement in favor of laisse
faire is Adam Smith, *The Wealth of Nations,* Random House, Inc., Nev
York, 1937; for a discussion of the doctrine's decline in popularity, se
J. M. Keynes, *The End of Laissez Faire,* L. & V. Woolf, London, 1926
for a modern restatement of the doctrine, see Henry C. Simons, "A Posi
tive Program for Laissez Faire," *Economic Policy for a Free Society,* Th
University of Chicago Press, Chicago, 1948; F. A. von Hayek, *The Roa
to Serfdom,* The University of Chicago Press, Chicago, 1944.

Large-Scale Production   *See Mass Production.*

Laspeyers Index   A statistical method for computing weighted aggre
gative index numbers, named after its originator and most frequently use
in the construction of price indices. The formula assigns to each curren
price relative a quantity weight that is appropriate for the base year
The quantity weight for each commodity is held constant for a numbe

of years' computations. Therefore, the index allows for no changes in tastes or environment. Price indices derived by this means are said to have an upward bias because they cannot allow for shifts in quantity in response to price increases. A modified form of the Laspeyers index is used in computing the U.S. Bureau of Labor Statistics' wholesale and consumer price indices:

$$P = \frac{\Sigma p_n q_o}{\Sigma p_o q_o}$$

For additional information, see Karl A. Fox, *Intermediate Economic Statistics*, John Wiley & Sons, Inc., New York, 1968; Lawrence R. Klein, *A Textbook of Econometrics*, Row, Peterson & Company, Evanston, Ill., 1953.

Last In First Out (lifo)   An accounting method of valuing inventory which assumes that the latest goods purchased are the first goods used up during an accounting period. It is the opposite of first in first out (fifo). As an example, for an accounting period of one month, the lifo method of valuing inventory as illustrated below for XYZ Company.

Inventory as of December 31, 1962	1,000 units @ $10		$10,000
Purchased during January, 1963	500 units @ 7		3,500
Total	1,500 units		$13,500
Used up during January, 1963	400 units @ 7		2,800
Left in inventory as of January 31, 1963	1,100 units		$10,700

The aim of lifo is to measure the cost of goods used up by the cost of replacing them. Many accountants feel that this is the best way to arrive at a meaningful income statement in times of rising prices. This method may, however, overvalue inventory when prices are falling and undervalue it when prices are rising. Since lifo yields lower taxable income when prices are rising, many firms adopted it during the inflationary period of 1955–1957. See Harold Bierman, *Managerial Accounting*, The Macmillan Company, New York, 1959.

Layoff Rate   *See Separation Rate.*

Leading Indicator   A measure of economic activity that usually reaches peaks or troughs of business activity before total business does. The use of statistical indicators of this type was developed before World War II by Wesley Mitchell, Warren Persons, and Arthur F. Burns, members of the staff of the National Bureau of Economic Research, to indicate historical changes in the general course of business. Geoffrey H. Moore and Julius Shiskin, also staff members of the bureau, have carried forward the indicator method of business-cycle analysis so that many business and academic economists consider that the leading indicators provide significant clues in making early judgments about future shifts in the general course of business. Many economists use the leading indicators as merely one tool in a large kit of forecasting devices. *Business Conditions Digest*, a report of the Bureau of Economic Analysis, lists thirty leading indicators and divides them into five major groups for analysis: (1) sensitive employment and unemployment indicators, (2) new investment commitments, (3) new business incorporations and business failures, (4) profits and stock prices, and (5) inventory investment, buying policy, and sensitive prices. For the development and analysis of leading indicators, see Geoffrey H. Moore (ed.), *Business Cycle Indicators*, National Bureau of Economic Research, Inc., Princeton University Press, Princeton, N.J., 1961, vol. I; for current statistics of the leading indicators, see Bureau of Economic Analysis, *Business Conditions Digest*, monthly; J. Shiskin, "Business Cycle Indicators: The Known and the Unknown," *Business Cycle Developments*, U.S. Department of Commerce, Washington, D.C., September, 1963.

Lead-Lag Relationship A term which describes the timing of changes in one statistical series in relation to changes in another series. It is frequently used in sales forecasting, which makes use of the timing pattern between a company's sales and a particular economic indicator. The economic indicator must consistently lead the company's business in order to make it useful as a forecasting device. This relationship can be determined by plotting the historical movements of a particular indicator and the company's sales on the same graph. For example, the sales of construction-material companies follow the fluctuations of the F. W. Dodge Company's data on contracts awarded, which are found to lead such sales by six months. Thus, by use of a mathematical relationship, a prediction of sales six months ahead can be made with a fairly high degree of accuracy. For further information on sales forecasting and the use of lead-lag relationships, see Vernon G. Lippitt, *Statistical Sales Forecasting*, Financial Executives Research Foundation, New York, 1969; *Sales Forecasting: Uses, Techniques and Trends*, American Management Association, Special Report 16, New York, 1956; T. G. MacGowan, "Forecasting Sales," *Harvard Business Review*, Harvard Graduate School of Business Administration, Boston, November, 1949.

Lead Time The amount of time which elapses between the day on which goods are ordered and the day on which they are delivered. Since 1955, with the buildup of spare manufacturing capacity and the emphasis on standardization of many types of goods, lead times have generally shortened for most goods. This is particularly true of industrial goods, such as machinery. A McGraw-Hill Department of Economics survey carried out in 1971 showed that the average lead time for nonelectrical machinery had decreased from about six months during World War II to less than four months in 1971. Because of the increasing complexity of office machines, the office-equipment industry was the only one in which lead time ran counter to the overall trend. See *Delivery Time for Machinery*, McGraw-Hill Department of Economics, New York, May 24, 1971.

Leaseback   A business deal in which a company owning land, buildings, and equipment sells all or part of its property to another company or to a private investor and simultaneously leases the property back under a long-term lease. The purposes of such a deal are to obtain funds for working capital or investment and to convert occupancy costs to rent, which is tax deductible as a business expense. The advantage to the investor is a relatively safe investment at a good rate of return. For a detailed discussion of sale and leaseback, see J. Fred Weston and Eugene F. Brigham, *Managerial Finance*, 2d ed., Holt, Rinehart and Winston, Inc., New York, 1966.

Least Squares   In statistics and econometrics, a method of estimation that involves the choice of an estimate such that the sum of the squares of the deviations of the data from the estimate is a minimum. A least-squares estimate has a smaller variance than any other linear estimate and is unbiased: the average of many least-squares estimates is likely to differ only slightly from the true value. For additional information, see Karl A. Fox, *Intermediate Economic Statistics*, John Wiley & Sons, Inc., New York, 1968; Gerhard Tintner and Charles B. Millham, *Mathematics and Statistics for Economists*, Holt, Rinehart and Winston, Inc., New York, 1970.

Legal Tender   Money that the law states must be accepted in payment of all public and private debts. Money is made legal tender in order to clarify the government's position on the enforcement of contracts drawn in monetary terms and to promote public acceptance of fiat and fiduciary money. In most countries, all types of lawful money have been automatically considered legal tender. In the U.S., however, this has not always been the case. In colonial times, coins were so scarce that individual colonies occasionally declared commodities legal tender. In 1631, for example, Massachusetts declared corn legal tender unless the contract specifically called for payment in money or in beaver hides. From this practice evolved the American doctrine that nothing was legal tender unless the government declared it to be so. A law passed in 1933 made all U.S. coins and paper currency legal tender. Bank checks not legal tender. For a comprehensive history of legal tender, see S. P. Breckinridge, *Legal Tender*, The University of Chicago Press, Chicago, 1903; for a later discussion, see Paul B. Trescott, *Money, Banking and Economic Welfare*, 2d ed., McGraw-Hill Book Company, New York, 1965.

Letter of Credit   A letter issued by a bank, instructing a correspondent bank to advance a specified sum of money to a third person. The issuing bank guarantees the reimbursement of the money advanced by the correspondent bank. This instrument of credit permits the conduct of foreign and domestic commerce on a safer and more expedient basis than if individual transactions were made. For further information, see J. L. O'Halloran, *The ABC of Commercial Letters of Credit*, Manufacturers Hanover Trust Company, New York, 1962; for information concerning the use of letters of credit in financing foreign trade, see Major B. Foster et al., *Money and Banking*, Prentice-Hall, Inc., Englewood Cliffs, N.J., 1953, pp. 436–441; Richard P. Ettinger and David E. Golieb, *Credits and Collections*, 5th ed., Prentice-Hall, Inc., Englewood Cliffs, N.J., 1962.

Level of Aspiration   The objectives which the individual worker hopes to reach. These hopes, mainly for promotion and salary increases, tend to be limited by the worker's realistic evaluation of the situation. Generally, an individual of relatively higher family status and educational level will tend to have relatively greater aspirations within the organizational structure. The level of aspiration is also closely related to the individual's previous successes and failures and to his rate of progress in the organization. Raising the aspiration level of workers may result in more efficient production, but if these higher expectations are not subsequently fulfilled, the overall result may be frustration and greater inefficiency. For further information, see William Foote Whyte, *Men at Work*, Richard D. Irwin, Inc., Homewood, Ill., 1961.

Leverage   The effect of the use of senior capital (bonds and preferred stocks) over junior capital (common stock) in capitalizations. Leverage enables a relatively small issue of common stock to benefit from the earnings of a much larger capital fund, since the total capital fund will usually earn more than the cost of the borrowed capital. Thus, the rate of return on the equity capital will be higher than the rate on the entire capital stock. As the rate of earnings on total capital increases, leverage will produce a magnified increase in the earnings of common stock. On the other hand, as the rate of earnings on capital decreases, leverage will cause a proportionately larger fall in the common-stock earnings than would have been the case without capital investment. The earning power of highly leveraged stocks can disappear entirely even if the capital fund is earning profits as a whole. Leverage is thus a speculative factor, increasing possibilities for both gain and loss. For more details, see Benjamin Graham et al., *Security Analysis*, 4th ed., McGraw-Hill Book Company, New York, 1962, chaps. 40 and 48; Pearson Hunt, "A Proposal for Precise Definitions of 'Trading on the Equity' and 'Leverage,'" *Journal of Finance*, American Finance Association, New York, September, 1961; J. Fred Weston and Eugene F. Brigham, *Managerial Finance*, 2d ed., Holt, Rinehart and Winston, Inc., New York, 1966, pp. 253–270.

Liabilities   The debts or amounts of money owed by an individual, partnership, or corporation to others. Considered from another point of view, liabilities are the claims or rights, expressed in monetary terms, of an individual's or a corporation's creditors. In accounting, liabilities are classified as either short-term or long-term liabilities or as secured or unsecured liabilities. Short-term liabilities are those which will be satisfied, or paid, within one year's time. Examples are payroll obligations, accounts payable, taxes due, accrued interest, and short-term notes (maturing within one year). Long-term liabilities are those which will not be satisfied within one year, such as mortgages, long-term notes, and bonds. Secured liabilities are claims that have specific assets pledged to ensure satisfaction; unsecured liabilities are debts which depend on the general resources of the firm for satisfaction. See William A. Paton and Robert L. Dixon, *Essentials of Accounting*, The Macmillan Company, New York, 1958.

Lien   The right of one person, usually a creditor, to keep possession of the property of someone else to satisfy a debt. A lien gives the creditor the right to hold the property as security until his claim for payment has been met. Applicable to personal and real property, a lien consists of the right of retention only until the debt is paid. In most cases, the person exercising the lien does not have the right to sell the property. Among the many different types of liens are (1) a mortgage, which is a lien on real property to secure a debt; (2) a mechanic's lien, which is the right of a person performing services on real property to claim a lien against the property to which he has added value; (3) a hotelkeeper's lien, which is a claim on the baggage and other property of guests; (4) a judgment, which is the lien against the property of the defendant in a civil suit; and (5) taxes and assessments, which, if unpaid, are liens on the property or income taxed. Taxes take priority over all other liens. For additional details, see William H. Schrampfer, *Law in Its Application to Business*, Holt, Rinehart and Winston, Inc., New York, 1952.

Life Insurance A contract between an individual and an insurance company to protect the family of the insured individual against the risk of his death and loss of income. The policy, or contract, provides that if premiums are paid in accordance with the policy, the insuring company will make a cash payment or the equivalent, in the event of the death of the insured, to a designated beneficiary or beneficiaries. Payments are also provided for if the insured reaches a certain age. Life insurance is available in many different forms, the principal ones being term insurance and straight life insurance. In term insurance, each year stands by itself. Each person in a group, for example, of persons aged 40, is charged a certain premium, which is determined by the mortality statistics for that group. The premiums increase as age increases. In addition, the insurance is payable at death provided death occurs within a specified period. Straight life insurance sets a constant yearly premium to be paid until death, the size of the premium varying with the age at which the person became insured. The premiums are payable until death. For further information on life insurance, see Joseph B. Maclean, *Life Insurance*, McGraw-Hill Book Company, New York, 1962; Dan M. McGill, *Life Insurance*, Richard D. Irwin, Inc., Homewood, Ill., 1959.

Likelihood Function The mathematical statement (formula or measure) of the probability of drawing (observing) a particular sample. The formula says that the probability of the particular sample is equal to the probability that the error term of the estimating equation will have taken the particular values associated with the particular sample multiplied by a factor det J. The term det J equals 1 in all single-equation cases. Assuming that the particular sample drawn *is* the most probable, precise estimates of unknown parameters can be obtained by manipulating the likelihood function. Maximizing the likelihood function generates maximum likelihood estimates of the unknown parameters. For additional information, see T. C. Koopmans (ed.), *Statistical Inference in Dynamic Economic Models*, Cowles Commission Monograph no. 10, John Wiley & Sons, Inc., New York, 1950; Stefan Valavanis, *Econometrics*, McGraw-Hill Book Company, New York, 1959.

Limited-Coinage System A system under which the right of the individual to bring bullion to the mint and have it coined is restricted. Under a system of limited coinage, the government accepts only a specified amount of bullion for minting during a given period. For example, the Bland-Allison Act of 1878 provided that the U.S. Treasury Department buy between $2 million and $4 million worth of silver to be minted each month. This act was amended in 1890 by the Sherman Silver Purchase

Act, which directed the Treasury to buy 4,250,000 ounces of silver each month. The repeal of this act in 1893 marked the end of the limited coinage of silver in the U.S. For further information on the U.S. experience with limited coinage, see Paul Studenski and Herman E. Krooss, *The Financial History of the United States,* 3d ed., McGraw-Hill Book Company, New York, 1963.

Limited-Information Methods Econometric methods for estimating parameters that do not use all the available information. Such methods include, for example, using instrumental variables, reduced forms, and limited-information–maximum-likelihood. They make it possible to avoid the formidable computations of the maximum-likelihood method. The term is usually used in reference to methods that yield consistent estimates, that is, estimates that tend to approach the population value as sample size increases. For additional information, see Lawrence R. Klein, *Econometrics,* Row, Peterson & Company, Evanston, Ill., 1953; Stefan Valavanis, *Econometrics,* McGraw-Hill Book Company, New York, 1959.

Limited Liability The restriction of an owner's loss in a business to the amount of capital that he has invested in it. Limited liability applies to the stockholder's position in a corporation: he is liable only for the amount of money that he has invested. This fact distinguishes him from a partner or a single proprietor, both of whom are liable not only for their invested capital but for their personal assets as well. The concept of limited liability began with the joint-stock companies in Great Britain (corporations in U.S. usage) as a device to encourage the accumulation of large amounts of capital to finance big business endeavors. If there were no limited liability, it would be difficult to induce people to invest money in a business in which they would have virtually no voice while their personal assets were vulnerable to legal action. Limited liability was a key factor in the rise of large corporations. See Charles W. Gerstenberg, *Financial Organization and Management of Business,* 4th ed., Prentice-Hall, Inc., Englewood Cliffs, N.J., 1959.

Limit Order (Limited Order) An order that a customer gives to his broker to buy or sell a certain amount of stock at a stated price or better. For instance, if a customer places a limit order to buy 100 shares of ABC Corporation at $50, his broker can buy ABC only at $50 or at a price below $50; he cannot pay more than $50 no matter what happens. Limit orders to buy must always be at a price lower than the current market price; limit orders to sell must always be at a price higher than the current market price. An example shows why customers place limit orders. Let us suppose that a customer believes that a stock's true value is $40, but the stock is currently trading at $45. This customer can place a limit order to buy at $40. If the price of the stock declines to the level that the customer thinks it is worth, the broker will buy it; if it does not, no trade will occur. The disadvantages of limit orders are that a person can miss the market (that is, never buy a stock that is rising because his limit price is too far below the market price) and that he will have difficulty in deciding at what price to set the limit. See George L. Leffler and L. C. Farwell, *The Stock Market*, The Ronald Press Company, New York, 1963.

Linear Programming   A mathematical technique of optimizing (maximizing or minimizing) linear objective functions subject to constraints in the form of linear inequalities. It is designed to select from among alternative courses of action the one most likely to achieve a desired goal, such as producing a product or group of products at the lowest possible cost. A decision-making tool of business management, linear programming has been employed on a variety of problems, ranging from the selection of the ingredients appropriate to producing the cheapest cattle feed of a given nutritional value to the determination of profitable sites for plant location. See Robert O. Ferguson and Lauren F. Sargent, *Linear Programming: Fundament ls and Applications*, McGraw-Hill Book Company, New York, 1958; Robert Dorfman et al., *Linear Programming and Economic Analysis*, McGraw-Hill Book Company, New York, 1958; Saul I. Gass, *Linear Programming*, 3d ed., McGraw-Hill Book Company, New York, 1969; William J. Baumol, *Economic Theory and Operations Analysis*, 2d ed., Prentice-Hall, Inc., Englewood Cliffs, N.J., 1965.

Line of Credit   An arrangement by which a bank agrees to provide funds up to a certain limit for a business firm. The credit line is the upper limit which the bank sets on a firm's borrowing. Once the line has been established, the firm merely informs the bank that it wants to make use of some of the credit and signs notes for the amounts advanced. A line of credit is often employed when a firm needs bank credit only during certain seasons of the year, e.g., when the purchase of raw materials is concentrated in the few months of a crop season or when sales are concentrated because of seasonal demand. Usually, banks have a compensating-balance requirement, by which the borrower is required to keep in his account a minimum balance equal to a specified percentage of his credit line, e.g., 15 or 20%. Some banks also require an annual clearance, or complete payment of all debts at least once a year. This requirement ensures that the line of credit is being used only to fulfill its seasonal purpose. The amount of the credit line is usually based on the credit standing of the borrower and his legitimate needs. For additional details, see Charles L. Prother, *Financing Business Firms,* 3d ed., Richard D. Irwin, Inc., Homewood, Ill., 1966.

Linkage The ability of one industry to induce the establishment and growth of other industries. It develops through the interdependence of inputs (raw materials) and outputs (semifinished or finished goods). The first industry buys inputs that can be made by other domestic industries instead of being imported (the effect that this inducement has on other domestic industries is called backward linkage). It can sell some or all of its output to other domestic industries for use in production instead of exporting it or selling it as a finished product (the effect that this inducement has on other domestic industries is called forward linkage). An example of an industry with both backward and forward linkage is the iron and steel industry. It creates a market for such raw materials as iron ore and coal for other industries, such as machinery and power, and the iron and steel which it makes can be used by other domestic industries in their production. See Albert O. Hirschman, *The Strategy of Economic Development,* Yale University Press, New Haven, Conn., 1958; Benjamin Higgins, *Economic Development,* W. W. Norton & Company, Inc., New York, 1968.

Liquid Asset Currency plus any holding quickly convertible into cash without great loss. Among assets which may be easily converted into currency are bank demand deposits, savings and loan shares, and U.S. government savings bonds. Liquid assets held by individuals in the U.S. at the end of 1970 were estimated at $786 billion. For data on total liquid assets, see U.S. Securities and Exchange Commission, *Statistical Series.*

Liquidation The process of selling assets, such as inventories or securities, in order to achieve a better cash position. The term also refers to the termination of a business by converting its assets to cash, paying its liabilities, and distributing the residue among the partners or stockholders.

Liquidity The ability of an individual, group, business, or any organization to meet its financial obligations. Liquidity is usually measured by examining the organization's balance sheet and relating some or all of its current assets to some or all of its current liabilities. For example, the current ratio (current assets to current liability) is a measure of a firm's liquidity. Or, in the case of a commercial bank, the ratio of loans to deposits is the most commonly used measure of bank liquidity. Liquidity is, however, a nebulous concept. Fundamentally, a firm's liquidity rests not so much on its balance sheet as on whether or not it is doing well and earning money. A strong balance sheet with a large current ratio simply postpones liquidity problems for a short while if the firm is losing money. Moreover, liquidity is a relative concept because there is no specific level of any balance-sheet ratio that indicates that the firm is no longer liquid. For instance, what is considered a dangerous loan-deposit ratio has changed over time, varies in different countries in the world, and ultimately depends on what bank managers and the monetary authorities *think* is too high. For additional information, see J. R. Hicks, "Liquidity," *The Economic Journal*, vol. LXXII, pp. 787–802, December, 1962; Lester V. Chandler, *The Economics of Money and Banking*, 5th ed., Harper & Row Publishers, Incorporated, New York, 1969, pp. 151–153; Louis B. Lundborg, "Where Did Our Liquidity Go?" *Conference Board Record*, New York, March, 1968, pp. 17–21.

Liquidity Preference The desire to hold cash or checking accounts rather than assets, such as stocks and bonds, that earn a return and are less easy to convert to cash. There are three motives for liquidity preference: the transactions motive, or the common desire to have a supply of money available to carry out everyday transactions; the precautionary motive, or the need to keep a cash reserve for emergencies; and the speculative motive, or the belief that interest rates may rise, thereby reducing the value of earning assets. If only the last motive is affected by public policy, it may be futile for the monetary authorities to raise interest rates in times of a business recession in order to reduce liquidity preference and bring a larger amount of funds into the capital markets. Instead, John Maynard Keynes suggested a policy of low interest rates, which, by encouraging capital investments and quickened business activity, would support the general level of demand for production and output of goods, thus reducing the danger of falling prices and countering the speculative motive. The notion of liquidity preference is important at times when people decide to hold liquid assets rather than make investments because it is then that investment funds are likely to shrink and capital investment to decline. In the inflationary atmosphere of the post-World War II years, liquidity preference has not been a problem. The American public has proved to be very conscious of interest-rate levels: it has shifted large sums of savings to California savings institutions that offer a higher return than their Eastern counterparts, and it has given unprecedented support to individual government-security issues that have promised a high return. For a more detailed discussion, see Paul A. Samuelson, *Economics*, 7th ed., McGraw-Hill Book Company, New York, 1967; J. M. Keynes, *The General Theory of Employment, Interest, and Money*, Harcourt, Brace &

World, Inc., New York, 1963; Alvin Hansen, *A Guide to Keynes*, McGraw-Hill Book Company, New York, 1953.

Liquidity Trap In liquidity-preference theory, the idea that at some low interest rate, the speculative demand for money becomes infinitely elastic. John Maynard Keynes argued that it is possible that if the interest rate declined to, say, 2%, people would be on the margin, indifferent between holding bonds or money. Thus, interest rates could fall no lower because no one would purchase bonds at the implied higher prices. If the economy were caught in the liquidity trap, monetary policy would be effective. The monetary authorities could expand the money supply during a depression, which tends to lower interest rates and therefore encourages investment and consumer spending. But if interest rates dropped low enough to reach the liquidity-trap level, further increases in the money supply would not lower rates any further and would simply pile up as idle bank balances. For additional information, see John Maynard Keynes, *The General Theory of Employment, Interest, and Money*, The Macmil-

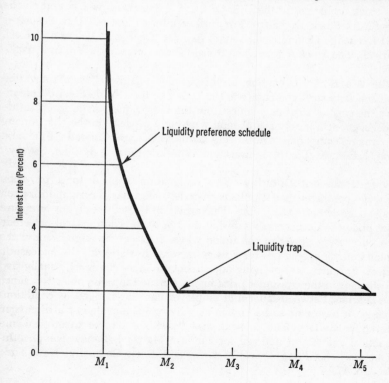

lan Company, New York, 1936; Gardner Ackley, *Macroeconomic Theory,* The Macmillan Company, New York, 1961.

Listed Security A stock or bond that has been registered with a stock exchange and is eligible for trading on that exchange. Corporations that want to list their securities on an exchange must meet its listing requirements and comply with all its rules and regulations. Of the sixteen stock exchanges in the U.S., the New York Stock Exchange has the most stringent listing requirements. Its requirements are such that only large corporations, the stock of which is widely held and which have demonstrated earning power, are eligible for listing. The other exchanges have similar but less stringent listing requirements. Corporations list their securities on stock exchanges because (1) they want to broaden the market for their securities, (2) capital might be raised more cheaply if the company were more widely known, and (3) corporations like the prestige attached to having their stock traded on a national exchange. As of December 31, 1970, about 3,400 issues of preferred and common stock were listed on the stock exchanges of the U.S. Of these, 1,840 issues were listed on the New York Stock Exchange. For further information, see U.S. Securities and Exchange Commission, *Annual Reports;* George L. Leffler and L. C. Farwell, *The Stock Market,* The Ronald Press Company, New York, 1963.

Little Steel A designation of the smaller integrated, semi-integrated and specialty steel companies in the U.S. The term Little Steel differentiates the smaller steel companies from the bigger ones. As a group, Little Steel accounts for only 20% of total steel-ingot capacity in the U.S. Among the many companies constituting Little Steel are Colorado Fuel and Iron, Kaiser, McLouth, Sharon, and Wheeling-Pittsburgh Steel.

Living-Document Doctrine The designation applied to a provision of wage contracts that stipulates that the union has the right to reopen wage negotiations at any time. This provision is used by unions to ensure that price changes occurring during the life of the contract will not erode the purchasing power of the union wage. If prices rise significantly, the union enters negotiations for a wage increase in step with the increase in prices. Frequent cost-of-living adjustments in labor contracts, usually tied to changes in the consumer price index, pursue the same objective. Since the contract between labor and employer can be changed as conditions change, it has come to be known as a living document. For a discussion of the living-document doctrine and its effects on the theoretical and practical analysis of national income, see Martin J. Bailey, *National Income and the Price Level,* McGraw-Hill Book Company, New York, 1962, p. 47.

Loanable Funds The supply of funds available to the money market. It consists of three parts: current savings; dishoarding, i.e., a decrease in cash balances; and any increase in the money supply. The demand for such funds is made up of dissavings by consumers, representing the financing of consumption expenditures from idle balances previously accumulated and from newly created bank credit; hoarding, representing the increase in idle balances; and investment demand. The loanable-funds theory of interest is based on the relationship between the demand and the supply of these funds. According to this theory, the interest rate fluctuates with the relative supply of, and demand for, funds available for lending. For a brief description of the loanable-funds analysis, see W. Harrison Carter and William P. Snavely, *Intermediate Economic Analysis*, McGraw-Hill Book Company, New York, 1961, pp. 343–347; J. Conard, *An Introduction to the Theory of Interest*, University of California Press, Berkeley, Calif., 1959; for major criticisms of the theory and for a treatment of loanable funds as opposed to liquidity-preference theories, see W. W. Smith, "Monetary Theories of the Rate of Interest: A Dynamic Analysis," *Review of Economics and Statistics*, vol. XL, pp. 15–21, Harvard University Press, Cambridge, Mass., 1958.

Loanable-Funds Theory of Interest *See Loanable Funds.*

Loan Shark An unlicensed lender who lends small sums of money at interest rates which are higher than are permitted by law. The loan shark lends money primarily to low-income wage earners and relies for payment on the borrower's prospective income rather than on any material collateral. Sums lent by loan sharks generally are small, ranging from $10 to $100, with interest charges running from 5 to 40% a month. The loans are usually made for short periods of time, e.g., one month. The loan-shark problem is being combated in many states of the U.S. by means of small-loan laws, which authorize interest rates on small loans high enough to induce legitimate lenders to enter the small-loan business, thus driving out the loan sharks. For further information, see "Combatting the Loan Shark," *Law and Contemporary Problems*, Duke University School of Law, Durham, N.C., Winter, 1941; "The Loan Shark Problem Today," *Law and Contemporary Problems*, Duke University School of Law, Durham, N.C., Winter, 1954.

Lobby A person or a group of persons seeking to influence the proceedings of legislative bodies through personal intervention. Lobbies are maintained by most employers' associations, by most large unions, and by innumerable groups with specific legislative interests. Lobbying in the

U.S. involves both formal and informal activity, the former generally taking place on Capitol Hill and the latter frequently at social events. In pursuance of the Lobbying Act of 1946, all lobbyists practicing in the halls of Congress must register with the clerk of the House of Representatives and make an affidavit of their receipts and expenditures during each quarter of the year. As of 1964, there were some 520 organizations registered as maintaining lobbies in Washington, D.C. Lobbying is found at all levels of government. Generally, lobbyists are well versed in the procedures followed in getting legislation enacted and are often acquainted with key members of the legislature toward whom they direct their activities. There are firms of lobbyists that handle more than one client. The primary function of the lobbyist is to keep his employer informed about legislative activity that affects him directly or indirectly. The lobbyist notes all bills related to his employer's interest and watches the reactions of the legislators. If it seems probable that a harmful bill will be passed, he prepares arguments against it, which are circulated among the members of his employer's organization. He induces people to testify before congressional committees and organizes campaigns to deluge legislative offices with mail in order to prevent passage of the prejudicial bill or to expedite passage of a bill which favors his employer's organization. See Wayne L. McNaughton and Joseph Lazar, *Industrial Relations and the Government*, McGraw-Hill Book Company, New York, 1954; Paul W. Cherrington and Ralph L. Gillen, "The Company Representative in Washington," *Harvard Business Review*, vol. XXXIX, no. 3, Harvard Graduate School of Business Administration, Cambridge, Mass., May–June, 1961.

Location Theory   An economic theory of the factors influencing the location of firms. According to the analysis of location theory, firms will locate at the point at which their total transportation costs are minimized, all other things being equal. A firm's transportation costs include the procurement costs of materials and the distribution costs of finished products. Whereas procurement costs can be reduced by moving the plant closer to supplies, distribution costs are lowered by moving the plant closer to a point with good access to markets. Since these two considerations are likely to point in different directions, the producer must balance the relative advantages of each cost factor in deciding on the location for his plant. In some instances, the problem is simple; for example, the location of agriculture and mining is determined by the location of the relevant resources. Similarly, selling and many other services must be located near purchasers. In manufacturing, however, the determination of the optimum location is more complex. If the manufacturing process results in a considerable loss of weight or some other lowering of distribution costs in relation to procurement costs (e.g., smelting or cotton ginning), it is cheaper to locate the plant near the source of the raw material. On the other hand, if the finished product may spoil or if transportation costs for the product are relatively high (e.g., bread or compressed gases), the firm will locate its plant closer to the market. For a more complete exposition of location theory, see E. M. Hoover, *The Location of Economic Activity*, McGraw-Hill Book Company, New York, 1948; Melvin Greenhut, *Plant Location: In Theory and Practice*, The University of North Carolina Press, Chapel Hill, N.C., 1956; Royall Brandis, *Principles of Economics*, Richard D. Irwin, Inc., Homewood, Ill., 1968, pp. 581–594; Hugh O. Nourse, *Regional Economics*, McGraw-Hill Book Company, New York, 1968; August Losch, *The Economics of Location*, Yale University Press, New Haven, Conn., 1954.

Locked-in Capital   Securities which the owner has held for six months or more and continues to hold because they have greatly appreciated in value and because, if they were sold, the realized capital gain would be subject to tax. In seeking reductions in the U.S. capital gains tax, the New York Stock Exchange argues that the rate of the tax deters many investors who have unrealized capital gains from selling their securities. This factor immobilizes capital movements (particularly after periods of rising prices) and accentuates stock price movements, both of which are detrimental to the public interest. Critics argue that many investors retain securities for investment and not for tax reasons; that there is no evidence that price movements are accentuated because of the capital gains tax and available data indicate that the opposite might be true; and that, even though some persons are "locked in," they are actually insulated from the tax because the gain will never be taxed unless they sell before they die. See Jonathan A. Brown, *The Locked-in Problem: Federal Tax Policy for Economic Growth and Stability*, Joint Committee on the Economic Report, 84th Cong., 1st Sess., 1955, pp. 367–381; *Factors Affecting the Stock Market*, staff report of the Committee on Banking and Currency, U.S. Senate, July 30, 1955, pp. 79–81; Harold Somers, "An Economic Analysis of the Capital Gains Tax," *National Tax Journal*, National Tax Association, Harrisburg, Pa., September, 1948; Harold Groves, *Taxation of Capital Gains: Tax Revision Compendium*, submitted to the Committee on Ways and Means, U.S. House of Representatives, Nov. 16, 1959, vol. II, pp. 1193–1201.

Lockout   A device by which an employer refuses to admit workers to their jobs. The antithesis of a strike, the lockout is used primarily to avert a threatened strike. An employer rarely resorts to a lockout. At the expiration of an agreement, he can always announce his terms unilaterally and give the union the choices of striking, reaching an agreement, or working without an agreement during further negotiations. Almost the only occasion for a true lockout arises when a union calls for a strike against a member of an employers' association; the other employers may then close down their plants to support the struck employer. The term lockout and others referring to various forms of work stoppages are grouped under the heading strike. See Robert D. Leiter, *Labor Economics and Industrial Relations*, Barnes & Noble, Inc., New York, 1958; Albert Rees, *The Economics of Trade Unions*, The University of Chicago Press, Chicago, 1962; Neil W. Chamberlain and James W. Kuhn, *Collective Bargaining*, 2d ed., McGraw-Hill Book Company, New York, 1965, p. 179.

Logarithmic Chart   A graph in which one or both axes are scaled in terms of logarithms. Where only the vertical scale is so scaled, the graph is known as semilogarithmic. Where both axes are scaled in terms of logarithms, the graph is known as double-logarithmic. In both cases, natural numbers are plotted on the logarithmic grids. This method of plotting is used to depict relative changes in statistical variables since equal slopes mean equal rates of change. For additional information, see Frederick E. Croxton and Dudley J. Cowden, *Applied General Statistics*, Prentice-Hall, Inc., Englewood Cliffs, N.J., 1967.

Logarithmic Transformation   The conversion of a statistical variable stated in natural numbers into the logarithms of those numbers. This transformation is frequently used in statistics to reduce a curvilinear relationship to a linear relationship in regression analysis. For additional information, see Gerhard Tintner and Charles B. Millham, *Mathematics and Statistics for Economists*, Holt, Rinehart and Winston, Inc., New York, 1970.

Long-and-Short-Haul Clause   The clause of section 4 of the Interstate Commerce Act which makes it unlawful for a common carrier to charge a higher rate for carrying passengers or freight a shorter distance than it charges to carry them a longer distance by the same route, in the same direction, and under basically the same conditions. For the conditions that gave rise to the long-and-short-haul clause, see *The Annual Report of the Interstate Commerce Commission*, 1887; see also C. Bigham and M. J. Roberts, *Transportation*, McGraw-Hill Book Company, New York, 1952.

Long Run   A period of time that is long enough for a firm to vary all factors of production. In the short run, a producer can vary his output only by using his existing plant and equipment more or less intensively;

he cannot adjust the size, or scale, of the plant and equipment. In the long run, however, a firm can change its output not only by using existing plant and equipment more or less intensively, but also by altering the scale of the plant. For example, a firm plans to build a new plant and purchase new equipment. This is a long-run situation because the firm can vary the scale of the plant and other factors of production to achieve the optimum size for anticipated output. Once the plant has been finished, costs of building and equipping it are fixed, and variation in output is limited by the plant scale. The concept of the long run is important to microeconomic theory because the "equilibrium" in much of the analysis occurs only in the long run. See Alfred Marshall, *Principles of Economics*, St. Martin's Press, Inc., New York, 1956; Jacob Viner, "Cost Curves and Supply Curves," *Zeitschrift für Nationalökonomie*, vol. III, 1931; reprinted in American Economic Association, *Readings in Price Theory*, Richard D. Irwin, Inc., Homewood, Ill., 1952; William Fellner, *Modern Economic Analysis*, McGraw-Hill Book Company, New York, 1960; Donald S. Watson, *Price Theory and Its Uses*, 2d ed., Houghton Mifflin Company, Boston, 1968.

Long-Term Forecast   A business forecast which extends at least five years ahead of the current period, although such a forecast is often made for a period extending as far ahead as fifteen years. Thus, a forecast using 1963 data as the starting point could extend to 1978. Long-term forecasts are not as popular with business economists as those for the short-term outlook, but they are more popular than medium-term forecasts. A 1962 survey of the membership of the National Association of Business Economists showed that 72% of those who made forecasts projected long-term prospects, 66% prepared medium-term forecasts, and 95% assessed the short-term outlook. One reason why fewer economists prepare long-term projections than short-term outlooks is that the former are of less immediate importance to their companies. Moreover, in long-term projections a small error accumulated over five, ten, or fifteen years can seriously affect the estimate. In the 1962 survey of business economists, most used the historical trend for long-term forecasts. Judgment is the second-ranking method, and the full-employment approach is the third-ranking method in terms of usefulness for long-term forecasting. For a discussion of the length of business forecasts and long-term forecasting techniques and tools, see McGraw-Hill Department of Economics, report, New York, Feb. 5, 1962; see also Elmer C. Bratt, *Business Forecasting*, McGraw-Hill Book Company, New York, 1958.

Lorenz Curve   A curve used in depicting the nature of any distribution—wealth, for example. It is, however, usually used in depicting the income distribution of a country. As shown in the accompanying illustration, the Lorenz curve is derived by plotting the cumulative proportion of people (ranked from the poorest up) against the cumulative share of total income which they receive. Thus, in the U.S. in 1967, the poorest 20% of the population earned only 5.4% of the total national income, and the poorest 80% earned 59% of the total income. This means that the top 20% of the population earned 41% of the national income. If there were perfect equality in the distribution of income, with everyone receiving the same amount of money, the Lorenz curve would be a 45° straight line. On the other hand, for the hypothetical case of absolute inequality, with one person earning all the income, the Lorenz curve would form the bottom and right side of the square. Any actual income distribution falls between these two hypothetical extremes and is thus represented by a sagging line. The greater the sag of the Lorenz curve, the greater the inequality of the income distribution. A statistical method of stating the degree of inequality shown by the Lorenx curve is to divide the area between the curve and the diagonal (*A* in the illustration) by the total area under the diagonal (*A* plus *B*). This measure, the proportion of the triangular area which is

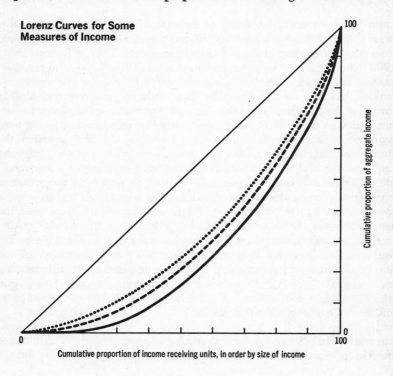

Lorenz Curves for Some Measures of Income

Cumulative proportion of aggregate income

Cumulative proportion of income receiving units, in order by size of income between the curve and the diagonal, is known as the Lorenz coefficient or the Gini index. In 1959 the Lorenz coefficient for the U.S. was about 0.39. For annual data on income distribution in the U.S., see *Survey of Consumer Finances,* University of Michigan Survey Research Center, Ann Arbor, Mich., annually; see also James N. Morgan et al., *Income and Welfare in the United States,* McGraw-Hill Book Company, New York, 1962, chap. 20; James N. Morgan, "The Anatomy of Income Distribution," *Review of Economics and Statistics,* p. 270, Harvard University Press, Cambridge, Mass., August, 1962; U.S. Bureau of the Census, *Statistical Abstract of the United States,* Washington, D.C., annually.

Loss Leader   *See Fair-Trade Law.*

Luddite   One of a group of English rioters who, between 1811 and 1816, attacked and destroyed much of the machinery introduced by manufacturers on the ground that it was causing economic distress and unemployment. The term is now sometimes used in an invidious sense to characterize a person who opposes the introduction of automated or other advanced types of machinery.

Lump-Sum Appropriation   A budgetary appropriation that specifies an allowance for a particular department and does not outline in detail the method by which the department shall dispose of its allotment. The principal argument for use of a lump-sum appropriation is that it puts the administrator in a more advantageous position to determine proper use of the funds. Since general or lump-sum appropriations inevitably grant a degree of legislative power to the administrator, legislators often prefer specific appropriations. Lump-sum appropriations are sometimes made in what is known as a performance budget.

Luxury Tax   A levy on goods or services which are considered unnecessary for the maintenance of a minimum standard of living. The theory is that since luxuries are, by definition, not a necessary part of poor persons' spending, a tax on such goods and services is not regressive. In practice, it is sometimes difficult to adhere to the definition and, at the same time, raise an appreciable amount of revenue. When luxury taxes are levied on mink coats, French perfume, and expensive jewelry, there is no question that these goods are luxuries, but taxes on such items do not raise much revenue. When luxury taxes are extended to cosmetics and tickets for sporting events to increase revenues, the poor will continue to buy such items despite the tax. Thus, the luxury tax, contrary to its purpose, could be regressive. See E. H. Plank, *Public Finance,* Richard D. Irwin, Inc., Homewood, Ill., 1953.

McGuire Act *See Fair-Trade Law.*

Macroeconomics Modern economic analysis that is concerned with data in aggregate as opposed to individual form. It concerns itself with an overall view of economic life, considering the total size, shape, and functioning of economic experience rather than the workings of individual parts. More specifically, macroeconomics involves the analysis of the general price level rather than the prices of individual commodities, national output or income rather than the income of the individual firm, and total employment rather than employment in an individual firm. For further information on macroeconomics, see Gardner Ackley, *Macroeconomic Theory*, The Macmillan Company, New York, 1961; Thomas F. Dernburg and Duncan M. McDougall, *Macroeconomics*, 3d ed., McGraw-Hill Book Company, New York, 1968.

Mail-Order House An establishment engaged primarily in selling merchandise through the mail as a result of mail orders received. Sears, Roebuck and Montgomery Ward are two examples of mail-order houses in the U.S., although both companies also have retail outlets. Over the years, mail-order houses have lost relative importance in terms of the share of total retail sales, and the number of companies doing a mail-order business exclusively has declined significantly. Meanwhile, however, department stores have increased their own mail-order business substantially. For general information concerning trends in retailing, see J. N. Wingate and A. Corbin, *Changing Patterns in Retailing: Readings on Current Trends*, Richard D. Irwin, Inc., Homewood, Ill., 1956.

Maintenance-of-Membership Clause A part of a collective bargaining agreement that requires workers who were union members at the time that the contract was signed to remain members for the life of the contract. Usually, an escape period of fifteen to thirty days is provided so that workers may leave the union before the contract goes into effect. Frequently, the clause provides that all new employees be required to sign a union membership application which automatically goes into effect if the new employee does not withdraw his application within fifteen days. Forgetfulness and inertia usually capture some new union members under this arrangement, but the maintenance-of-membership clause technically does not require new employees to join the union. In 1946 one-fourth of the union members in the U.S. had this clause in their contracts, but by 1960 less than 7% had such a clause in their collective bargaining agreements. For a discussion, see Joseph Shister, *Economics of the Labor Market*, 2d ed., J. B. Lippincott Company, Philadelphia, 1956.

Make-Work Activities   Various ways of reducing or limiting average output per man-hour in a plant or an industry so that more labor must be employed. Among such arrangements are (1) a limitation of the daily or weekly output per worker, (2) a limitation of output through the control of the quality of work and the use of time-consuming methods, (3) a requirement that unnecessary work be done or that work be done more than once, (4) a regulation of the number of men in a crew or a requirement that unnecessary workers be employed, and (5) a requirement that work be done by members of a particular craft. Labor urges the adoption of make-work rules because of the threat of unemployment. Make-work activities might be justified if they were only temporary expedients in times of high unemployment, but, once adopted, restrictive work rules and practices are hardly ever discarded even in periods of full employment. Nor is it evident that make-work activities actually benefit the group that puts them into effect, for they generally cause a rise in labor costs, which eventually results in lower wages or in fewer employees. See Lloyd G. Reynolds, *Labor Economics and Labor Relations*, 5th ed., Prentice-Hall, Inc., Englewood Cliffs, N.J., 1970; Sumner H. Slichter, *Union Policies and Industrial Management*, The Brookings Institution, Washington, D.C., 1941.

Malthusian Doctrine   The theory, developed by Thomas Robert Malthus, a British economist and clergyman, that the world's population tends to increase faster than its means of subsistence. In *An Essay on the Principles of Population*, published in 1798, Malthus said that population tends to grow at a geometric rate (for example, 1, 2, 4, 8, 16), while the food supply grows only in arithmetic progression (1, 2, 3, 4, 5). He argued that only the positive checks of vice, pestilence, famine, and wars could curb the tendency of population to outstrip the food supply. In a later edition of his essay, however, he placed less emphasis on precise growth ratios and suggested that preventive checks (continence and late marriage) could help alleviate the problem. Malthus's gloomy prediction has not come to pass in the industrial nations of the world because of rapid increases in agricultural productivity and the tendency of upper-income groups voluntarily to limit the size of their families. Many Asian, African, and Latin-American countries, however, still have difficulty in expanding agricultural production as fast as their population grows. Malthus has been attacked from many sides, but the post-World War II population explosion has revived interest in his ideas even in advanced industrial countries. For recent discussions of population prospects and problems, see Harrison Brown, *The Next Hundred Years,* Viking Press, Inc., New York, 1957; *Population Control,* Duke University School of Law, Durham, N.C., 1960; Nathan Keyfity and Wilhelm Flieger, *World Population: An Analysis of Vital Data,* The University of Chicago Press, Chicago, 1968.

Manchester School A school of classical economic thought which emphasized free trade. It arose in England in the middle of the nineteenth century because of the Corn Laws. The primary interest of its leaders, Richard Cobden and John Bright, was the repeal of the Corn Laws and eventual free trade for England. Because Manchester was the center of opposition to these laws, the English economists who believed in this reform were called the Manchester school. This group advocated laissez faire, or completely unhampered private initiative and competition, as the best means of achieving prosperity and growth. They opposed the commercial policy of protection, public care of the poor, the Factory Acts, compulsory education, and similar measures. For additional details, see Frank Amandus Neff, *Economic Doctrines,* 2d ed., McGraw-Hill Book Company, New York, 1950, chap. 16; Francis W. Hirst (ed.), *Free Trade and Other Fundamental Doctrines of the Manchester School,* 1903, reprinted by Augustus M. Kelley, Publishers, New York, 1968.

Man-Days of Strike Idleness A measure of the amount of time lost by members of the labor force in the U.S. economy because of work stoppages. The measurement is calculated by the U.S. Bureau of Labor Statistics (BLS) from a tabulation of every major work stoppage in the country, the number of workers involved, the number of days' duration, and other pertinent information. For the purposes of this tabulation, the BLS does not differentiate between work stoppages initiated by workers and those initiated by employers. The number of employees idled, together with the number of days' duration, are converted into man-days of strike idleness. An estimate is also made of strike idleness as a percentage of total working time. Sixty-two million man-days of work were lost in

1970, representing 0.34% of total estimated working time. Data on work stoppages and man-days of idleness are published monthly by the BLS.

Man-Days Idle (Percent of estimated working time)

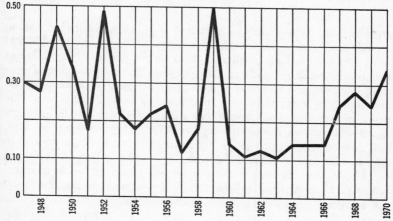

Source: U.S. Department of Labor.

Manufacturers' Sales Branches Establishments owned by manufacturers and maintained apart from their producing plants, primarily for the purpose of selling or marketing their products at wholesale. Manufacturers' sales branches usually carry inventories of goods, whereas manufacturers' sales offices do not. According to the 1967 *Census of Business*, there were more than 30,000 manufacturers' sales branches and sales offices out of a total of 311,000 wholesale establishments in 1967. Their sales, which aggregated $157 billion out of a total of $460 billion, registered the biggest increase from 1958 to 1967 of any major type of wholesale operation. Recent statistics of manufacturers' sales branches and sales offices are included in U.S. Bureau of the Census, *Census of Wholesale Trade*, 1967.

Manufacturing Industry A general term encompassing all plants, companies, and industries which produce or assemble manufactured goods. Manufacturing industry is generally broken down into two major categories, durable goods and nondurable goods. The single most important industry in the U.S., manufacturing ranks first in number of employees, capital investment, and contributions to the national income. Nevertheless, it has been declining in relative importance. Although total employment was at an all-time high in 1971, manufacturing employment was lower than it had been in 1966. The contribution of manufacturing to national income was also lower in 1971 than in earlier years. For a detailed study of the manufacturing industry and its individual industries, see E. B. Alderfer and H. E. Michl, *Economics of American Industry*, 3d ed., McGraw-Hill Book Company, New York, 1957.

Marginal Cost The additional cost that a producer incurs by making one additional unit of output. If, for example, total costs were $13,000 when a firm was producing two machine tools per day and $18,000 when it was producing three machine tools per day, the marginal cost of producing one machine tool was $5,000. The marginal cost may be the same, higher, or lower in moving from three to four machine tools. The concept of marginal cost plays a key role in determining the quantity of goods that a firm chooses to produce. The purely competitive firm, which faces a given price set in the market, increases its output until marginal cost equals price. That point is the firm's best-profit output point. The imperfectly competitive firm equates marginal cost to marginal revenue (additional revenue) to obtain the highest profits. For most firms, marginal costs decline for a while and then begin to rise. The pattern of the marginal-cost graph depends on the nature of the firm's production function and the prices of the goods that it buys. Understandably, if a firm grows to a relatively very large size in its industry, its purchasing decisions may strongly influence the prices of the goods that it buys. The emphasis placed in the U.S. on maintaining competition is due in large part to the efficiency of a firm that equates marginal costs to price. Only when a firm so equates marginal cost is it producing as much as possible for society from the relatively scarce resources of labor and capital that are available. Paul A. Samuelson, *Economics*, 7th ed., McGraw-Hill Book Company, New York, 1967, gives an elementary treatment of marginal costs; George J. Stigler, *The Theory of Price*, 3d ed., The Macmillan Company, New York, 1966, presents a more complete explanation of the way in which marginal costs depend on the production function.

Marginal Cost of Acquisition (Marginal-Factor Cost) The additional cost to a purchaser when he buys one more productive factor. When a buyer purchases a good in a highly competitive market (one with many small buyers and sellers, each of whom is too insignificant to influence the price), the additional cost of purchasing one more unit of the product remains constant. For example, if bolts are selling at $1.73 per gross, the additional cost of purchasing an additional gross will remain $1.73. If, on the other hand, the market is not characterized by many small buyers and sellers, sellers may demand a higher price as they sell additional items. In this case, the additional cost of buying a unit rises. Since perfect competition is a relatively rare phenomenon, it is not surprising that price increases as demand rises over the course of a business cycle and, conversely, that the prices of many items tend to decline as the quantity sold decreases. The theoretical concept of the rising marginal cost of acquisition is usually associated with monopsony (a market structure with a single buyer of a commodity or service). Obviously, if there is only one buyer of a good or service, his influence in the market is considerable, and he will tend to restrict the amount that he buys in order to keep his costs down. The monopsonist will equate the marginal cost of acquisition of goods with his marginal revenue. For an elementary treatment of the concept, see Campbell R. McConnell, *Economics,* 4th ed., McGraw-Hill Book Company, New York, 1969; Donald S. Watson, *Price Theory and Its Uses,* 2d ed., Houghton Mifflin Company, Boston, 1968, pp. 407–409.

Marginal-Factor Cost   *See Marginal Cost of Acquisition.*

Marginal-Productivity Theory of Wages   A theory that explains the overall level of wages and wages in different industries with reference to (1) the additional output that can be produced by adding one more worker (the marginal productivity of labor) and (2) the number of workers. It is based on the assumption that employers, in order to make the greatest possible profit, will hire additional workers at any given wage as long as the value added to the total product by the additional worker is at least equal to his wage. In this theory, wages can rise through (1) reductions in the number of workers or (2) increases in the marginal productivity of labor, which may arise through higher worker skills, increases in the quantity of capital used in production, or technological improvements. Thus, unlike the earlier subsistence and wages-fund theories, the marginal-productivity theory allows for short- and long-run increases in both wages and the number of workers. The theory has been subject to two widespread criticisms: (1) It assumes perfect competition in the labor and product markets. (2) It is a partial-equilibrium analysis. Adherents of the theory, however, argue that both the theory and the analytical techniques used in conjunction with it are fully capable of dealing with monopoly and unemployment. For the classical statement of the theory, see John Bates Clark, *The Distribution of Wealth,* Kelley and Millman, Inc., New York, 1956; for another discussion, see Paul H. Douglas, *The Theory of Wages,* The Macmillan Company, New York, 1934; J. R. Hicks, *The Theory of Wages,* Macmillan & Co., Ltd., London,

1932; for detailed description of the analytical techniques employed in the theory, see Tibor Scitovsky, *Welfare and Competition,* Richard D. Irwin, Inc., Homewood, Ill., 1951; Donald S. Watson, *Price Theory and Its Uses,* 2d ed., Houghton Mifflin Company, Boston, 1968, pp. 419–432.

Marginal Revenue   The additional revenue that a seller receives from putting one more unit of output on the market. The price, obviously, is the average revenue that the seller receives. The following table indicates the manner in which marginal, or additional, revenue is calculated:

Price	Number Sold	Total Receipts	Marginal Revenue (Additional Receipts)
$3	2	$ 6	
4	3	12	6
5	4	20	8
6	5	30	10

The marginal-revenue concept is important because producers maximize profits (and minimize losses) when they continue to produce until their marginal revenue equals the additional cost of producing an additional unit of output. This is the profit-maximization point for any firm in any type of industry structure. The logic is obvious: if it costs $5 more to produce a good and only an additional $3 will be received, no producer who is intent on making a profit will produce the additional unit. See Campbell R. McConnell, *Economics,* 4th ed., McGraw-Hill Book Company, New York, 1969; Donald S. Watson, *Price Theory and Its Uses,* 2d ed., Houghton Mifflin Company, Boston, 1968.

Marginal-Revenue Product (Marginal-Value Product)   The additional amount of revenue produced by using one additional unit of a productive resource while holding other productive inputs at the same level. The additional amount of receipts depends on two factors (1) the amount of additional output that the additional resource helps produce and (2) the selling price. If the selling firm is not in a perfectly competitive industry, it faces a downward-sloping demand curve, which means that as it sells additional output, the price that it receives will fall. To maximize profits, a firm will hire additional productive resources (human and material) as long as the amount added to receipts is greater than the amount added to cost. See Campbell R. McConnell, *Economics,* 4th ed., McGraw-Hill Book Company, New York, 1969; Donald S. Watson, *Price Theory and Its Uses,* 2d ed., Houghton Mifflin Company, Boston, 1968, pp. 406–409.

Marginal Utility   The additional satisfaction that a purchaser derives from buying an additional unit of a commodity or service. Since the unit of measurement is different for each individual (as different as the various moods of a single individual), marginal utility is a psychological phenomenon rather than an objectively measurable concept. To induce consumers to buy larger quantities of a good, the price must be lowered, other things remaining the same. The notion of diminishing marginal utility is an often-cited explanation (among others) for the downward-sloping demand curve. The hypothesis is that consumers receive less and less additional satisfaction from buying more and more of a particular commodity. The observed necessity for lower prices to induce buyers to make additional purchases would be expected if consumers received less and less additional satisfaction from additional purchases. Relatively little use is now made of the marginal-utility concept in economic theory. Another approach, in which it is assumed that any consumer can recognize the combinations of various goods that render the same satisfaction (the indifference-curve approach), now finds favor in advanced price theory. For further information, see Alfred Marshall, *Principles of Economics,* St. Martin's Press, Inc., New York, 1956; see also Kenneth E. Boulding, *Economic Analysis,* 4th ed., Harper & Row, Publishers, Incorporated, New York, 1966; Campbell R. McConnell, *Economics,* 4th ed., McGraw-Hill Book Company, New York, 1969; for a more advanced treatment, see George J. Stigler, *The Theory of Price,* 3d ed., The Macmillan Company, New York, 1966.

Marginal-Value Product   *See Marginal-Revenue Product.*

Margin Requirement   That part of the total purchase price of securities which must be put up in cash. Because excessive use of credit was one of the factors that led to the stock-market crash in 1929, the Congress of the U.S. empowered the Federal Reserve Board to limit the amount of borrowed funds that can be used to purchase and carry securities. The Board prescribes the maximum-loan value (the amount of money that can be borrowed as a percentage of the purchase price of the security) of securities registered with the Securities and Exchange Commission (SEC). Obviously, this amount also sets the minimum amount of cash that must be put up when buying securities. The Board changes the maximum-loan value as conditions warrant. For example, if borrowings to purchase securities are increasing, the Board may lower the loan value (raise margins) of securities; conversely, if borrowings are decreasing, it may raise the loan value (reduce magins) of securities. At the beginning of 1970 the margin requirement for stocks was 80%, and the margin for convertible bonds was 60%. These margins were implemented in June, 1968. Although the Federal Reserve Board does not set margins on securities exempted from registration with the SEC (municipal bonds and U.S. government securities), the New York Stock Exchange sets a margin of 5% on U.S. government securities and 15% on municipal bonds. In addition to this official and semiofficial regulation of credit, many brokerage houses set higher margin requirements on some securities. For further information, see Jules I. Bogen and Herman E. Krooss, *Security Credit: Its Economic Role and Regulation*, Prentice-Hall, Inc., Englewood Cliffs, N.J., 1960; George L. Leffler and L. C. Farwell, *The Stock Market*, 3d ed., The Ronald Press Company, New York, 1963.

Market-Directed Economy   A mode of economic organization in which the forces of supply and demand are relied upon to solve the problems of the selection of which goods to produce, the method of producing them, and the persons who will receive them once they have been produced. For example, in the U.S. supply and demand, supported by individual initiative, self-interest, and the state of technology, determine how many automobiles will be produced in relation to the number of refrigerators, the production techniques that will be employed, and the relative incomes of the people and capital used in production. The U.S. is thus primarily a market-directed economy. Nevertheless, there are in the U.S. many elements of non-market-directed activity, such as the output of numerous agricultural products, which is determined by government-decreed acreage allotments and price supports. See Robert L. Heilbroner, *The Making of Economic Society*, Prentice-Hall, Inc., Englewood Cliffs, N.J., 1962; Paul A. Samuelson, *Economics*, 7th ed., McGraw-Hill Book Company, New York, 1967.

Marketing   A related group of business activities whose purpose is to satisfy the demands for goods and services of consumers, businesses, and government. The marketing process includes estimating the demand, producing the product, pricing the product to satisfy profit criteria, and promoting and distributing the product. In addition, fulfilling warranty and service obligations, both explicit and implicit, is considered by many to be part of the marketing process. Underlying the basic philosophy of marketing is the concept that a customer should have a choice in most types of buying situations. Under these conditions, the individual or business firm involved in any stage of marketing a product must seek to make its product more attractive to customers than products of competing firms. Marketing is generally concerned with activities taking place in the private business sector of the economy. The government, in general, is not considered to be marketing goods and services, but rather to be providing services that cannot be economically fulfilled by the private sector. Over the long run, the goal of the elaborate structure of modern marketing is the maximization of consumer satisfaction and profitable sales. For additional information, see William J. Stanton, *Fundamentals of Marketing*, 2d ed., McGraw-Hill Book Company, New York, 1967; Marketing Staff of Ohio State University, "A Statement of Marketing Philosophy," *Journal of Marketing*, January, 1965, pp. 43–44.

Marketing Research (Market Research) The systematic gathering, recording, computing, and analyzing of data about problems relating to the sale and distribution of goods and services for certain time periods. It includes various types of research, such as the size of the potential market and potential sales volume, the selection of the consumers most apt to purchase the products, and the advertising media most likely to stimulate their purchases. Marketing research has been developed as a tool to aid management in solving its increasingly difficult and complex problems. Research may be carried out by business firms, consultants to business firms, or impartial agencies. Nearly every medium-sized and large corporation in the U.S. has a market research department or an individual who is responsible for market research. For problems of marketing research and the processes by which they are solved, see Richard D. Crisp, *Marketing Research*, McGraw-Hill Book Company, New York, 1967; for an explanation of the basic methods of marketing research, see James H. Lorie and Harry V. Roberts, *Basic Methods of Marketing Research*, McGraw-Hill Book Company, New York, 1951; David J. Luck, Hugh G. Wales, and Donald A. Taylor, *Marketing Research*, 3d ed., Prentice-Hall, Inc., Englewood Cliffs, N.J., 1970.

Market Order An order that a customer gives to his broker to buy or sell a certain amount of stock at the best price available when the order reaches the floor of a stock exchange. The most common type of stock-market order, the market order, is used mainly because it is the fastest way of buying or selling stock. In virtually every case, the customer knows in a few minutes that he has bought or sold the stock and how much he paid or received for it. See George L. Leffler and L. C. Farwell, *The Stock Market*, The Ronald Press Company, New York, 1963.

Market Share The ratio of a company's sales, in units or dollars, to total industry sales, in units or dollars, on either an actual basis or a potential basis for a specific time period. For example, General Motors' share of the U.S. passenger-car market, in units, was 45% in 1970. In order to increase their market shares, companies often carry out sustained advertising campaigns or expand their sales forces.

Obviously, if General Motors planned to increase its 1970 share of 45% to a potential share of 65% by 1976, it would have to devote a greater amount of time and money to selling and advertising than it did before, or it would have to introduce new products which would have an extraordinarily high consumer acceptance in relation to its competitors' new products. See Francis E. Hummel, *Market and Sales Potential*, The Ronald Press Company, New York, 1961; John B. Matthews, Jr., et al., *Marketing: An Introductory Analysis*, McGraw-Hill Book Company, New York, 1964; Vernon G. Lippitt, *Statistical Sales Forecasting*, Financial Executives Research Foundation, New York, 1969, pp. 50–52.

Market Structure   The organizational characteristics of an economic market. The most important organizational aspects are those which influence the nature of competition and pricing within the market. Perhaps the key element in the structure of a market is the degree of seller concentration, or the number and size distribution of the sellers. The number of sellers may be one (monopoly), few (oligopoly), or many (atomism), and the sellers may be relatively equal in size or unequal, with a few large firms and many small ones. Just as the degree of seller concentration affects the intensity and effectiveness of competition among the sellers, another important factor, the degree of buyer concentration, influences the nature of buyer competition. The degree of product differentiation, or the degree to which buyers can distinguish the quality, design, reputation, etc., of the products of different sellers, is another important element in market structure. The more homogeneous the products of different sellers, the more vigorous the price competition can be expected to be. The barriers to entry, characterizing the advantage that established producers have over potential entrants, also play a role in determining the effect of potential competition on the market conduct of sellers. For additional details on the actual market structures of American industry, see Stanley Vance, *Industrial Structure and Policy*, Prentice-Hall, Inc., Englewood Cliffs, N.J., 1961; see also Walter Adams (ed.), *The Structure of American Industry*, The Macmillan Company, New York, 1950.

Markup   The difference between the cost and the selling price of an article. It may be expressed as a dollar amount or as a percentage of cost or retail price. In retailing, the markup is usually based on the retail price. Thus, if an article sold for $8 and the cost was $5, the markup would be ⅜, or 37.5%. Based on cost, the markup would be ⅗, or 60%. For further discussion of markup, see Glenn A. Welsch, *Budgeting, Profit–Planning and Control*, Prentice-Hall, Inc., Englewood Cliffs, N.J., 1959.

Marshall Plan A post-World War II program of U.S. aid to Western European countries, designed to accelerate their economic growth and thus stop the spread of communism. The program was first proposed by Secretary of State George C. Marshall in 1947. He said that aid to Europe should not be "on a piecemeal basis as various crises develop" but "should provide a cure rather than a mere palliative." A new program was required which would involve the active participation of the recipients. These ideas were translated into the European Recovery Program (ERP), enacted in the Economic Cooperation Act of 1948. The new plan was devised to increase the production of the countries involved by supporting needed imports of equipment and supplies, encouraging internal measures to promote financial stability, and furthering closer economic cooperation among European countries. Through this program, the dependence of European countries on U.S. trade would be reduced. Sixteen European countries formed the Organization for European Economic Cooperation (OEEC), which was to integrate the recovery plans of the participants. Each country was to formulate a plan for the four-year period 1948–1951, proposing measures to increase production and reduce balance-of-payments deficits. The plans were to be reviewed and coordinated by the OEEC and screened by the Economic Cooperation Administration. This screening ensured that the U.S. would provide only necessary assistance and gave it a measure of control over the monetary and fiscal policies of the participating countries. Over the four-year period of operation of the ERP, the U.S. extended $11.4 billion of aid to Europe, almost 90% of which was in the form of outright grants. The major recipient countries were the United Kingdom (24%), France (20%), the Federal Republic of Germany (11%), and Italy (10%). By its conclusion, Marshall Plan aid had resulted in a substantial expansion of European production. In 1951 industrial production in Western Europe was about 40% greater than in 1938. Moreover, the westward movement of communism had been halted. Balance-of-payments problems persisted, however, and U.S. foreign aid was continued after the completion of the Marshall Plan in order to alleviate the dollar shortage. For further information, see Seymour E. Harris, *The European Recovery Program*, Harvard University Press, Cambridge, Mass., 1948; Howard S. Ellis, *The Economics of Freedom*, Harper & Row, Publishers, Incorporated, New York, 1950; William Diebold, Jr., *Trade and Payments in Western Europe*, Harper & Row, Publishers, Incorporated, New York, 1952; Harry B. Price, *The Marshall Plan and Its Meaning*, Cornell University Press, Ithaca, N.Y., 1955.

Mass Production (Large-Scale Production) The use of technology and mechanization to turn out a large volume of standardized products.

A large volume of production permits the efficient application of modern technology and the division of the productive process into a number of steps that can be mechanized. The economies of mass production are realized by substituting cost-cutting machinery for high-priced labor. Mass-production methods are used in industries in which the product and production process can be standardized and the market is large enough to absorb the high volume of output. Mass-production techniques were first applied in the automobile industry in the early twentieth century. Since then, nearly every large-output industry has adopted mass-production methods in one form or another. Postwar advances in mass-production technology include transfer machines, which automatically move parts from one machine to another, and automatic-control and feedback devices for the self-regulating control of the production process. For further information, see John Shubur, *Managerial and Industrial Economics*, The Ronald Press Company, New York, 1961.

Materialistic Concept of History *See Economic Interpretation of History.*

Matrix A rectangular array of economic data written in columns and rows, in which the rows represent the distribution on an economic variable, such as output, and the columns represent the distribution of another economic variable, such as input. A column vector is a matrix with one column, and a row vector is a matrix with only one row. The matrix is simply a device to facilitate the study and solution of problems, such as the investigation of the importance of steel in the production of machinery.

Mature Economy An economy that has reached the final stage of growth, in which the rate of population increase begins to decline, a greater-than-average proportion of the national income is devoted to consumer expenditure, and a smaller-than-average proportion is devoted to business investment. Specifically, three things happen when a nation moves toward maturity: (1) The working force changes its composition. In the underdeveloped stage of an economy, about 80% of a nation's population is engaged in agriculture, living at a near-subsistence level; by the mature stage, this proportion has fallen below 20%. Along with a shift to an industrial, urban population in a mature economy, there is an increase in the level of skill and education of the workers. (2) The nation's leaders change from rugged individualists to an efficient managerial class and a bureaucratic machine. (3) The outlook of society changes from one of a man's love of his tools to one of complacency toward industrial and scientific advances. The chief question that faces the mature economy is the use of its wealth. For further information, see Walt W. Rostow,

The Stages of Economic Growth: A Non-Communist Manifesto, Cambridge University Press, New York, 1960.

Mature-Economy Thesis   *See Secular-Stagnation Thesis.*

Maturity   The date at which a loan, bond, note, etc., comes due and must be repaid in full by the borrower. Most securities have a definite maturity date (e.g., ninety days, one year, ten years), but common stocks (equities) have no maturity date, since they represent ownership rather than indebtedness. Securities which have only a short time before maturing are considered more liquid than those with longer maturities, and short-term interest rates are thus lower than long-term rates. Securities maturing in the near future also present less risk, since a change in interest rates will cause a smaller price change than in longer-term securities, and they will thus be less affected by future contingencies. For these reasons, the shorter the maturity of a bill or bond, the less it will fluctuate in market value. As a bond approaches maturity, however, its value approaches its original face value. At redemption, the maturity value of a security equals its face value plus any unpaid interest. For additional details, see Benjamin Graham et al., *Security Analysis,* 4th ed., McGraw-Hill Book Company, New York, 1962.

Maximum-Likelihood Method   A method of estimating a parameter of a population that maximizes the probability of a sample. The maximum-likelihood criterion is based on the assumptions that the most likely factor or factors have generated the most probable sample and that the parameters of a relationship are unknown constants. The likelihood function reveals what values of the parameter (or parameters) attach the greatest probability to an observed event and the degree of reliability of such values. For additional information, see Karl A. Fox, *Intermediate Economic Statistics,* John Wiley & Sons, Inc., New York, 1968; Stefan Valavanis, *Econometrics,* McGraw-Hill Book Company, New York 1959.

Means Test   The requirement that applicants for public assistance must prove their need before they become eligible to receive benefits. The needy must present adequate proof that they are unable to provide even a meager living for themselves and their families. The purpose of the means test is to establish the existence of need as defined by law and to determine the amount of benefit necessary to relieve that need. It is argued that the means test, used in many states of the U.S. for the distribution of public relief, is degrading to the individual in that it treats him as a second-class citizen. There has, however, been a trend toward administering the means test in a more humane way; individual circumstances are investigated, and the applicant is not required to exhaust all his savings or to sell his home before becoming eligible for assistance. The means test is not used in programs of social insurance, such as the social security program in the U.S., the benefits of which are considered a right of the individual whether he is shown to be in need or not. For further information, see Charlotte Towle, *Common Human Needs,* 2d ed., American Association of Social Workers, New York, 1952; Eveline M. Burns, *Social Security and Public Policy,* McGraw-Hill Book Company, New York, 1956; J. Henry Richardson, *Economic and Financial Aspects of Social Security,* University of Toronto Press, Toronto, Canada, 1960.

Median The middle value in a group of values that are arrayed from low to high or from high to low. The median is one of several types of averages, and its principal advantage is that it is not unduly influenced by unusually high or low values. It is often used in describing the typical income of a group of people. See Frederick E. Croxton and Dudley J. Cowden, *Applied General Statistics,* Prentice-Hall, Inc., Englewood Cliffs, N.J., 1955.

Income Class	Percentage of Families in the Class in 1962
Under $3,000	10
$ 3,000–$4,999	12
$ 5,000–$6,999	15
$ 7,000–$9,999	23
$10,000–$14,999	25
$15,000 and over	15
Median income, $8,632	

SOURCE: U.S. Department of Commerce.

Mediation (Conciliation) The intervention of a third party in collective bargaining. Usually, mediation is performed by a governmental agency whose purpose is to keep discussion moving constructively, to achieve a resumption of discussion if it has broken down, to search for areas of agreement, or to devise compromises and induce both sides to accept them. This is the weakest form of intervention, for the mediator has no power to force a settlement. The U.S. government provides most of its mediation services through an independent agency, the Federal Mediation and Conciliation Service, which was established in 1947 under the Taft-Hartley Act. This agency can intervene at the request of either party or on its own motion, although its intervention is mandatory under the emergency provision of the act. The Railway Labor Act provides for a three-man national mediation board to handle disputes over new contract terms. Most states and even some larger municipalities provide analogous services on the local level. For further information, see Gordon F. Bloom and Herbert R. Northrup, *The Economics of Labor Relations*, 6th ed., McGraw-Hill Book Company, New York, 1969; Wayne L. McNaughton and Joseph Lazar, *Industrial Relations and the Government*, McGraw-Hill Book Company, New York, 1954.

Medium-Term Forecast   A business forecast which extends from seven quarters to four years ahead of the current period. For example, a medium-term forecast made in July, 1970, could cover the period from January, 1972, through 1974. Forecasts for this time span are not as popular with business economists as those for short or long terms. A 1962 survey of the membership of the National Association of Business Economists showed that 66% of those who made forecasts prepared one for medium-term prospects, 72% projected long-term prospects, and 95% assessed the short-term outlook. One reason for the lack of popularity of the medium-term business forecast is that in times of rising business activity economists must pinpoint the next recession, and in times of declining business activity they must pinpoint the beginning of recovery. The principal guide for medium-term forecasters is the indicator technique developed by the National Bureau of Economic Research, with particular emphasis on the duration and amplitude of business cycles. Judgment is given about as much importance among medium-term forecasters as the indicator method. For a discussion of the length of business forecasts and medium-term forecasting techniques and tools, see McGraw-Hill Department of Economics, report, New York, Feb. 5, 1962; see also Elmer C. Bratt, *Business Forecasting*, McGraw-Hill Book Company, New York, 1958.

Member Bank   A bank which is a member of the Federal Reserve System. All banks with national charters must belong to the Federal Reserve System, and banks with state charters may join if they are qualified for membership and are accepted by the System. In 1971 there were more than 5,700 member banks, or somewhat more than 40% of all U.S. banks. Of these, four-fifths were national banks, and one-fifth were state banks; together, they held four-fifths of the country's total bank deposits and 82% of the demand deposits of all banks. To become a member bank, an individual bank must subscribe a fixed percentage of its capital and surplus to the capital stock of its district reserve bank, must maintain legal reserves on deposit at its reserve bank, honor checks drawn against it when presented for payment at the reserve bank, comply with Federal banking laws, and, if it is a state bank, be subject to general supervision and examination by the Federal Reserve System. The privileges of a member bank include the right to borrow from Federal Reserve banks, to use Federal Reserve check-clearing facilities, to obtain currency when required, and to participate in the election of six out of nine of the regional Federal Reserve directors. For additional details, see Raymond P. Kent, *Money and Banking,* 5th ed., Holt, Rinehart and Winston, Inc., New York, 1966; Rollin Thomas, *Our Modern Banking and Monetary System,* Prentice-Hall, Inc., Englewood Cliffs, N.J., 1946.

Mercantilism An economic policy, pursued by almost all the trading nations in the seventeenth and early eighteenth centuries, which aimed at increasing a nation's wealth and power by encouraging the export of goods in return for gold. As part of the program, individual governments promoted large investment in export industries, built high tariff walls to encourage import-competing industries, and, in several cases, prohibited the sales of precious metals to foreigners. Since one country's gold gain almost always meant a gold loss to one of its trading partners, not all nations could succeed at the same time in their ambition—a fact that sharpened trade rivalries. When successful, mercantilist policies generally resulted in the full employment of a country's resources and led to rapid economic growth. As the later classical economists pointed out, however, these policies also produced inflation and a low level of consumption. For an early statement of mercantilist doctrines, see Thomas Mun, *England's Treasure by Foreign Trade,* Doubleday & Company, Inc., Garden City, N.Y., 1953; for Adam Smith's criticism of the mercantilists, see *The Wealth of Nations,* Random House, Inc., New York, 1937; see also Eli Heckscher, *Mercantilism,* The Macmillan Company, New York, 1955; Joseph A. Schumpeter, *History of Economic Analysis,* Oxford University Press, Fair Lawn, N.J., 1954; Howard D. Marshall, *The Great Economists,* Pitman Publishing Corporation, New York, 1967.

Merchandise Balance *See Balance of Trade.*

Merchant Wholesaler A merchant middleman engaged primarily in buying from manufacturers and selling to retailers and other merchants, to industrial, institutional, and commercial users, or to both types of customers. A merchant wholesaler does not sell in significant amounts to the ultimate consumer. Wholesalers generally carry inventories of goods and provide various services to their customers. Sales of merchant wholesalers in the U.S. reached a record high of $247 billion in 1970. For general information concerning wholesalers, see David A. Revzan, *Wholesaling in Marketing Organization,* John Wiley & Sons, Inc., New York, 1961; for current monthly sales and inventory statistics, see U.S. Bureau of the Census, *Monthly Wholesale Trade Report.*

Merger The acquisition of one corporation by another, in which the one survives while the other loses its corporate existence. Basically, there are three methods by which a merger occurs: (1) One company, A, may buy the assets of another company, B, with payment being made either in cash or in securities issued by the purchasing company. (2) The purchasing company, A, may buy B's stock, becoming a holding company for B, which continues to operate as a separate company. (3) The stock of A may be issued to the owners of B rather than to the corporation, with A acquiring the assets and liabilities of B and B dropping out of existence; this arrangement is called a statutory merger. A merger differs from a consolidation, in which a new company is formed and the consolidating

Mergers and Acquisitions, Manufacturing and Mining Companies

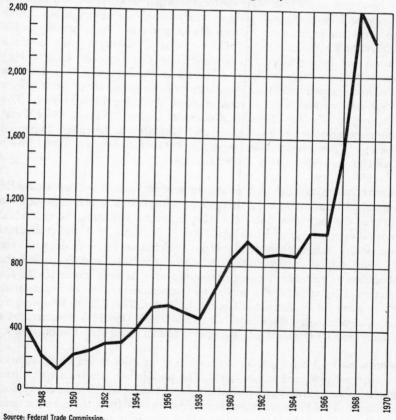

Source: Federal Trade Commission.

corporations lose their separate identities. For further information, see Betty Bock, *Mergers and Markets: 7,* National Industrial Conference Board, Inc., Studies in Business Economics, no. 105, New York, 1969; *Corporate Mergers and Acquisitions,* American Management Association, New York, 1958; *Corporate Growth through Merger and Acquisition,* American Management Association, New York, 1963; Ralph L. Nelson, *Merger Movements in American Industry, 1895–1956,* a study by the National Bureau of Economic Research, Inc., Princeton University Press, Princeton, N.J., 1959; J. Fred Weston and Eugene F. Brigham, *Managerial Finance,* Holt, Rinehart and Winston, Inc., New York, 1966, pp. 631–711.

Metrocorporation A large business corporation that emphasizes civic, social, and economic goals. Its objectives go beyond company operations to the nation as a whole. The metrocorporation is concerned with specific groups and individuals directly connected with the organization. There are pressures which tend to turn the corporation into a broadly based cultural and social institution. The business of making a profit is still a central but by no means an all-controlling consideration. One striking manifestation of this tendency is found in the fact that U.S. business firms and company-controlled foundations contributed about $400 million to educational and welfare enterprises in 1960. See Richard Eells, *The Meaning of Modern Business,* Columbia University Press, New York, 1960; see also Dexter M. Keezer and Margaret K. Matulis, "Industrial Giants of Tomorrow," *Challenge,* Institute of Economic Affairs, New York University, New York, December, 1961.

Microeconomics Modern economic analysis concerned with data in individual form as opposed to aggregate form. It is concerned with the study of the individual firm rather than aggregates of firms, the individual consuming unit rather than the total population, and the individual commodity rather than total output. Microeconomics deals with the division of total output among industries, products, and firms and the allocation of resources among competing uses. It is concerned with the relative prices of particular goods and the problem of income distribution. For further information, see George J. Stigler, *The Theory of Price,* 3d ed., The Macmillan Company, New York, 1966; Donald S. Watson, *Price Theory and Its Uses,* 2d ed., Houghton Mifflin Company, Boston, 1968.

Middleman A businessman or firm that is involved in the distribution of goods from producer to consumer. The middleman performs specialized functions and renders specialized services. Automobile dealers are typical examples of middlemen, since they purchase cars from the manufacturer and, in turn, sell them to consumers. For general information on middlemen, see David A. Revzan, *Wholesaling in Marketing Organization,* John Wiley & Sons, Inc., New York, 1961.

Miller-Tydings Act   *See Fair-Trade Law.*

Minimax Principle   The notion that when a choice must be made among several possible actions, the decision maker should look only at the worst possible consequence of each action and choose the action for which the worst consequence is least injurious. In this manner, he minimizes the maximum harm which can be done to him through his actions. In many cases, this principle would lead to actions which a businessman would reject because they would make him violate good business judgment. For further discussion, see Robert Schlaifer, *Introduction to Statistics for Business Decisions,* McGraw-Hill Book Company, New York, 1961; T. R. Dyckman, S. Smidt, and A. K. McAdams, *Management Decision Making under Uncertainty: An Introduction to Probability and Statistical Decision Theory,* Macmillan & Co., Ltd., London, 1969, pp. 251–254.

Minimum Standard of Living   The level of consumption at which only those goods and services which a person regards as absolutely necessary are purchased. For large groups, it is approximated by calculating their budgetary breakeven point, or the income at which no saving occurs. Any reduction in the level of living below the minimum standard is strongly resisted, and this factor is important in the depression phase of a business cycle. Thus, consumption will not drop as fast as incomes but will be maintained at the minimum level even if it involves reduced savings or dissavings. Each society has a different minimum standard of living, and as a society grows more affluent, this minimum standard rises. The minimum standard for an American therefore differs from that of an African. See J. S. Davis, "Standards and Content of Living," *American Economic Review,* vol. XXXV, no. 1, pp. 1–15, American Economic Association, Evanston, Ill., March, 1945.

Minimum Wage   The lowest wage rate allowed in the U.S. by either Federal, state or local law. It was instituted on the Federal level by the Fair Labor Standards Act of 1938, commonly known as the Wage and Hour Act, which set the minimum wage at 25 cents per hour for workers in industry engaged in interstate commerce, exclusive of agriculture and a few other types of industry. By 1971 the minimum wage had reached $1.80 per hour. As of 1970, thirty-eight states, including the major industrial states, and the District of Columbia had minimum-wage laws applying to intrastate industries; these were generally lower than Federal minimums. Minimum-wage rates are set to eliminate extremely low wages without unduly disrupting the general wage and price level of the economy. The immediate effect of a minmum-wage law is to raise labor costs in industries employing labor paid below the minimum. In an effort to maintain wage differentials, however, this is eventually followed by an increase in all wages. If higher wages induce management to substitute machinery for labor, some technological unemployment may result. See Lloyd G. Reynolds et al., *The Evolution of Wage Structure*, Yale University Press, New Haven, Conn., 1956; Lloyd G. Reynolds, *Labor Economics and Labor Relations*, 5th ed., Prentice-Hall, Inc., Englewood Cliffs, N.J., 1970.

Minor Coin A coin made of a base metal, a metal that is of comparatively low value but is especially resistant to corrosion. Pennies and nickels are examples of minor U.S. coins.

Mixed Economy An economic system in which characteristics of both capitalism and socialism can be found. In a mixed economic system, both public and private institutions exercise a degree of economic control. In most free-world industrial economies, a mixture of governmental industries and private industries exists in varying degrees. Even in the U.S., where free enterprise dominates the economic system, many forms of government enterprise and direct control can be found. The Post Office and the Tennessee Valley Authority are both operated by the Federal government, and public transportation facilities are owned and operated by state and local governments. Federal, state, and local regulatory agencies exercise direct controls over the operation of much of private enterprise, substantially restricting its freedom of action. For further information, see Alvin H. Hansen, *The American Economy*, McGraw-Hill Book Company, New York, 1957; Paul A. Samuelson, *Economics*, 7th ed., McGraw-Hill Book Company, New York, 1967.

Mode The most frequently occurring value in a group of values. Like the median, the mode is not influenced by extreme values in the group, but it is used less often in statistical analysis than either the median or the mean. An example of the mode is found in most men's clothing stores, where the biggest proportion of the stock will be accounted for by the current mode in both size and color. The reason is that most men follow the prevailing custom or style. See Frederick E. Croxton and Dudley J. Cowden, *Applied General Statistics*, Prentice-Hall, Inc., Englewood Cliffs, N.J., 1955.

Model In econometrics, an equation or set of equations depicting the causal relationships that are believed to generate observed data. Also, the expression of a theory by means of mathematical symbols or diagrams.

For detailed discussions and formulas of various specific economic models, consult Stefan Valavanis, *Econometrics,* McGraw-Hill Book Company, New York, 1959.

Model-Year Variation A variation in economic time series attributable to the annual introduction of new models, particularly in the automobile industry. Since the date of model introductions may vary from year to year, a special model-year adjustment is necessary to estimate and remove this variation from the time series.

Modernization The installation of technologically advanced machinery in place of old machinery. Modernization differs from the substitution of a new machine for a similar machine because the modern equipment's superiority is attributable to technical improvements rather than to mere newness. Large amounts of outmoded plants and equipment are still being used by American industry. A McGraw-Hill survey made in the fall of 1970 indicated that it would cost $145 billion to replace all the technologically outmoded facilities in the U.S. with the most up-to-date facilities. Moreover, the development of new technological improvements is making production techniques introduced only a short time ago obsolete. See Dexter M. Keezer and Associates, *New Forces in American Business,* McGraw-Hill Book Company, New York, 1959; for industry's expenditures on modernization, see *Annual Surveys of Business' Plans for New Plants and Equipment,* McGraw-Hill Department of Economics, New York.

Moment Matrix A matrix consisting of second-order moments; a matrix whose ith row and jth column are the product moment of x_i and x_j. A moment matrix need not be square. The notation and form of matrix algebra in this and many other instances are extremely convenient in computations. For additional information, see Lawrence R. Klein, *Econometrics,* Row, Peterson & Company, Evanston, Ill., 1953.

Monetary Base A monetary aggregate consisting of currency held by banks and by the public plus member-bank deposits at Federal Reserve banks. The base may also be viewed as Federal Reserve credit (security holdings, loans to member banks, and float) plus Treasury accounts, the gold stock, and miscellaneous Federal Reserve accounts. The expansion of the monetary base determines the potential growth rate of the money stock. For additional information, see Beryl W. Sprinkel, *Money and Markets,* Richard D. Irwin, Inc., Homewood, Ill., 1971, pp. 65–67, 80–84.

Monetary Policy Management by a central bank of a nation's money supply to ensure the availability of credit in quantities and at prices consistent with specific national objectives. In the U.S. in the mid-twentieth century, monetary policy, which is under the direction of the Board of Governors of the Federal Reserve System, has, like fiscal policy, been directed toward achieving the twin goals of price stability and full employment. Frequently, however, measures adopted to achieve one of these objectives have hampered the efforts to achieve the other. In addition, the task of monetary policy has been complicated by the nation's balance-of-payments difficulties. Among the tools of monetary policy directly available to the Board of Governors are the authority to alter the level of currency reserves that commercial banks must keep on deposit at Federal Reserve banks against their own deposits and the authority to alter the discount rate which is the payment that commercial banks make for borrowing from the Federal Reserve System. See Max F. Millikan (ed.), *Income Stabilization for a Developing Democracy*, Yale University Press, New Haven, Conn., 1953; Lester V. Chandler, *The Economics of Money and Banking*, 5th ed., Harper & Row, Publishers, Incorporated, New York, 1969; Arthur I. Bloomfield, *Monetary Policy under the International Gold Standard: 1880–1914*, Federal Reserve Bank of New York, New York, 1959; Arthur F. Burns, *Prosperity without Inflation*, Fordham University Press, New York, 1958; Milton Friedman and Walter W. Heller, *Monetary vs. Fiscal Policy: A Dialogue*, W. W. Norton & Company, Inc., New York, 1969.

Monetization of the Debt   The process of increasing currency in circulation by increasing the public debt. The debt becomes monetized when new securities issued by the government are purchased by the banking system to expand reserves. The debt can also be monetized to create a greater amount of credit in the economy by using the newly created bank reserves to support additional demand deposits. Whereas the first method of monetization permits an increase in the money supply equal to the size of the new debt, the expansion of bank credit permits a much greater increase in the money supply (five times as much with a reserve requirement of 20%). For additional details, see R. I. Robinson, "Monetary Aspects of National Debt Policy," *Public Finance and Full Employment*, Board of Governors of the Federal Reserve System, Washington, D.C., 1945, p. 69; John F. Due, *Government Finance: Economics of the Public Sector*, 4th ed., Richard D. Irwin, Inc., Homewood, Ill., 1968, pp. 293–315.

Money   Anything which serves as a medium of exchange and is generally acceptable for this purpose, or as a unit of value in terms of which the price of everything else is stated. Because of these uses, money makes possible the complex economic relationships necessary for an advanced economy, but since money tends to fluctuate in value, it has never performed these functions perfectly. Historically, many different commodities have served as money. Precious metals and paper notes were long the most important forms of money, since their quantity can be limited and they are durable, portable, and easily divided into different amounts. Today, however, they take second place to a system of bookkeeping debits and credits represented by demand deposits. See Lester V. Chandler, *The Economics of Money and Banking*, 5th ed., Harper & Row, Publishers, Incorporated, New York, 1969; for a comprehensive study of money and its role, see J. M. Keynes, *A Treatise on Money*, Macmillan & Co., Ltd., London, 1930.

Money-Flow Analysis   *See Flow-of-Funds Analysis.*

Money Illusion   The psychological valuation of currency without regard to its purchasing power. The money illusion arises when an individual associates money directly with its face value without considering its purchasing power. Thus, an individual subject to the money illusion feels better when his wages double even though prices also double and his real wage remains constant. Some economists believe that the effects of the money illusion are very strong, and that a worker bases his actions to a much greater extent on the level of his money wages than on the level of his real wage. Thus, a worker may refuse to work when his money wages drop even if prices fall so that his real wage remains the same, but he will not stop working when his money wages remain constant even if prices rise so that his real wage is lower. The effect of the money illusion is to make the supply schedule of labor elastic to changes in the money wage (at a constant real wage) and particularly inelastic to changes in real wages caused by shifts in the price level. The money illusion also has an impact on consumption, an equal rise in wages and prices (leaving the real wage unchanged) having the effect of raising the real consumption level (at least in the short run). For additional details, see Irving Fisher, *The Money Illusion*, Adelphi Co., New York, 1928.

Money Market   The term designating the financial institutions which handle the purchase, sale, and transfer of short-term credit instruments. The money market includes the entire machinery for the channeling of short-term funds. Concerned primarily with small business's needs for working capital, individuals' borrowings, and government short-term obligations, it differs from the long-term, or capital, market, which devotes its attention to dealings in bonds, corporate stocks, and mortgage credit. The money market is not a single, homogeneous market but consists of a number of distinct markets, each of which deals in a different type of credit. The most important of these markets are the commercial-paper market, which handles the short-term promissory notes of businesses; the collateral-loan market, which deals in loans granted on the security of bonds and other forms of property (also called broker's loans); the acceptance market, in which bankers' acceptances are traded; and the Treasury bills market, which handles short-term government securities. The major institutions operating in the money market are commercial banks, insurance companies, dealers in government bonds, commercial-paper dealers, finance companies, and factors. The money market may also be divided into customers' and organized markets. Most private short-term borrowing, especially by businesses, is carried out in the customers' markets, in which commercial banks and finance companies play the largest roles. The organized short-term markets include those dealing in government obligations, commercial paper, acceptances, and Federal funds. Most organized markets, such as the securities exchanges, investment banks, and the mortgage market, operate to a greater extent in the area of long-term financing. The New York money market is the largest and most important center for short-term financing in the U.S., absorbing the surplus funds of the entire country. It plays a major role in financing the short-term needs of the Federal government as well as the requirements of the entire business community. For additional information on the workings of the money market, see Marcus Nadler et al., *The Money Market and Its Institutions,* The Ronald Press Company, New York, 1955; S. M. Robbins et al., *Money Metropolis,* Harvard University Press, Cambridge, Mass., 1960; see also Robert V. Roosa, *Federal Reserve Operations in the Money and Government Securities Markets,* Federal Reserve Bank of New York, New York, 1956; Carl Madden, *The Money Side of "The Street,"* Federal Reserve Bank of New York, New York 1959; George W. Woodworth, *The Money Market and Monetary Management,* Harper & Row, Publishers, Incorporated, New York, 1964.

Money Stock   *See Money Supply.*

Money Supply (Money Stock)   The amount of money in an economy. Narrowly defined, the money supply (M_1) consists of currency and demand deposits. Currency includes all coin and paper money issued by the government and the banks. Since the monetary authorities hold some stocks of currency, only circulating currency is included in the money supply. Bank deposits, which are payable on demand, are also regarded as part of the supply of money; in fact, they constitute three-fourths of the total money supply in the U.S. Some economists also include near money, or cash liquid assets as commercial bank time deposits and deposits at savings and loan associations and mutual savings banks, in the money supply. The amount of currency in circulation is determined by the public. If individuals want a greater amount of cash, they withdraw it from their bank accounts; if they want to hold a smaller amount of cash, they deposit surplus cash in their accounts. The volume of demand deposits is determined primarily by the commercial banks. By increasing their loans and demand deposits, the banks are able to expand the money supply within the limits of the reserve requirements set by the Federal Reserve. They cannot expand loans, however, unless businessmen, consumers, and the government are willing to borrow. Thus, the total money supply is determined by the banks, the Federal Reserve, businessmen, the government, and consumers. At the end of 1970, the money supply (M_1) in the U.S. was approximately $210 billion. For further information, see Walter W. Haines, *Money, Prices and Policy,* 2d ed., McGraw-Hill Book Company, New York, 1966; "A New Measure of the Money Supply," *Federal Reserve Bulletin,* Washington, D.C., October, 1960; William J. Frazer, Jr., *The Demand for Money,* The World Publishing Company, Cleveland, 1967.

Money Supply (M_1)(Billions of dollars)

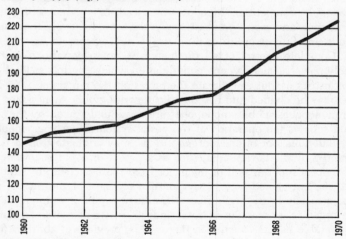

Source: Board of Governors, Federal Reserve System.

Money Wage   The amount of money received per hour, day, week, etc., in payment for services rendered or work done. It differs from real wages, which represent the purchasing power of the money wage, or the quantity of goods and services that can be purchased with the money wage. At times, the movements of money wages and real wages may be diverse; for example, average weekly earnings (money wages) in U.S.

manufacturing industries rose from $129.51 or $133.73 between 1969 and 1970, but the average price of consumer goods rose so much faster in the same period that real wages actually declined from $129.51 to $122.26. In times of recession, money wages sometimes fall less rapidly than the prices of consumer goods, so that real wages rise. Current statistics on money wages (average hourly or weekly earnings) are given in U.S. Department of Labor, *Monthly Labor Review;* for further information, see Paul H. Douglas, *The Theory of Wages,* The Macmillan Company, New York, 1934; J. M. Keynes, *The General Theory of Employment, Interest, and Money,* Harcourt, Brace & World, Inc., New York, 1936.

Monopolistic Competition   *See Competition, Imperfect.*

Monopoly   A market structure with only one seller of a commodity. In pure monopoly, the single seller exercises absolute control over the market price at which he sells, since there is no competitive supply of goods on the market. He can choose the most profitable price and does so by raising his price and restricting his output below that which would be achieved under competition. Monopoly thus leads to a higher selling price, a lower output, and excess profits. Usually, the term monopoly is extended to include any firm or group of firms which act together to fix prices or output. Complete control of all production is not necessary to exercise monopoly power; generally, any consolidation which controls at least 80% of an industry's output can dictate the prices on the remaining 20%. Monopolies may be divided into two broad categories, public monopolies and private monopolies. Public monopolies are those undertaken by the government, such as the operation of the postal system. Private monopolies, held by individuals or business organizations, may originate from a privilege granted by the government, such as a patent or copyright, from the possession of a superior skill or talent, or from the ownership of strategic capital. The last-named factor is responsible for most of the private monopolies associated with big business. The huge capital investment necessary to organize a company in some industries, which raises an almost insurmountable barrier to entry in these fields, provides established firms in these industries with the potential of monopoly power. The use of such monopoly power may, however, lead to the development of substitute products, an attempt at entry into the field by new firms (if the profits seem high enough), or the possibility of public prosecution or regulation. Monopoly power is not widespread in American industry, partly because of the antitrust policies of the Federal government, which have prevented the domination of an industry by one firm or even by a few firms. The

U.S. Supreme Court, in the 1937 Alcoa case, ruled that the antitrust laws were intended not only to regulate business practices, but also "to perpetuate and preserve for its own sake, and in spite of possible costs, an organization of industry into small units which can effectively compete with each other." For further information, see Joan Robinson, *The Economics of Imperfect Competition,* St. Martin's Press, Inc., New York, 1950; George W. Stocking and Myron R. Watkins, *Monopoly and Free Enterprise,* The Twentieth Century Fund, New York, 1951; Mark S. Massel, *Competition and Monopoly,* The Brookings Institution, Washington, D.C., 1962; Clair Wilcox, *Public Policies toward Business,* Richard D. Irwin, Inc., Homewood, Ill., 1966.

Monopsony A market structure with a single buyer of a commodity. Pure monopsony, or buyer's monopoly, is characterized by the ability of the single buyer to set the buying price. In the case of a monopsonist who maximizes profits, both his buying price and the quantity bought are lower than they would be in a competitive situation. Pure monopsony is not very common, but it may occur, as in the case of the demand for labor in a company town. Monopsonistic elements can arise in the market for a homogeneous product, in which a large number of competitive sellers offer their goods to a few large buyers. In such a case, no seller can influence price, but the price can be determined by the monopsonistic buyers. Such a situation arises in the wholesale markets for crude petroleum, tobacco, and sugar beets. For additional details, see Joan Robinson, *The Economics of Imperfect Competition,* St. Martin's Press, Inc., New York, 1950; Donald S. Watson, *Price Theory and Its Uses,* 2d ed., Houghton Mifflin Company, Boston, 1968.

Moonlighting The holding of more than one job by an individual. After working for a full day on one job, workers called moonlighters turn to a second job in the evening hours. In a survey made in May, 1969, the U.S. Bureau of Labor Statistics reported that 4 million persons, or 5.2% of all persons employed in the U.S., held more than one job. Moonlighting has been attacked by both labor unions and management. Unions believe that it is a significant cause of unemployment. (This argument was largely refuted by the Bureau of Labor Statistics survey.) Management fears that moonlighting results in lower productivity. For an appraisal of some of the commonly held views on dual jobholders, together with information on their characteristics, the occupations in which they are employed, and trends in the number of such workers, see Vera C. Perrella, "Moonlighters: Their Motivations and Characteristics," *Monthly Labor Review,* pp. 57–64, Washington, D.C., August, 1970.

Moral Suasion   Pressure exerted by the Federal Reserve System on the U.S. banking system without an attempt to compel compliance with the suggested action. The Federal Reserve exercises moral suasion when it suggests action instead of requiring it. Moral suasion has been important as an instrument for achieving voluntary credit restraint during periods of inflation, such as the period of the Korean conflict. At that time, instead of using its direct credit controls, the Federal Reserve resorted to oral and written statements and appeals to induce bankers voluntarily to restrict the expansion of credit. During the 1930s, moral suasion was used in another way, to stimulate the expansion of credit by encouraging banks to be more liberal in their lending policies. The Federal Reserve also exercises moral suasion in its day-to-day activities of advising individual member banks in matters of ordinary loan policy. For further information, see Walter W. Haines, *Money, Prices and Policy,* 2d ed., McGraw-Hill Book Company, New York, 1966.

Mortgage   A legal transfer of ownership but not possession of property from a debtor to a creditor. The transfer becomes void upon payment of the debt for which the property has been put up for security. Thus, certain property is conditionally transferred when a debt is incurred, but ownership is regained upon completion of all obligations. In legal terms, there are two types of mortgages: (1) the common-law mortgage, which gives the creditor title to the property serving as security for the debt, subject to the conditions of subsequent payment; and (2) the legal-lien mortgage, which entitles the mortgagee merely to a legal lien upon the property. The advantage of a mortgage arrangement is that the debtor retains possession of the property and is thus able to operate it. The advantage to the creditor is that he is protected against nonpayment by retaining ownership until the debt has been repaid. See Willis R. Bryant, *Mortgage Lending: Fundamentals and Practices,* McGraw-Hill Book Company, New York, 1962.

Mortgage Debt   The amount of long-term debt of individuals, businesses, institutions, and nonprofit organizations that place mortgages on their property in order to buy or repair it. Mortgage debt represents the amount of interest and principal to be paid. In 1963 it became apparent that individuals in the U.S. were taking out mortgages to obtain funds for the purchase of goods and services other than homes and home repair. These individuals were taking advantage of the relatively low interest rate of mortgages instead of using installment credit. A statistical series on mortgage debt outstanding on nonfarm properties housing one to four families is prepared by the Federal Home Loan Bank Board with the cooperation of the Federal Reserve Board. For a discussion of mortgage debt and mortgage interest rates, see Saul B. Klaman, *The Postwar Residential Mortgage Market*, Princeton University Press, Princeton, N.J., 1961; for current statistics, see Federal Home Loan Bank Board, *Estimated Home Mortgage Debt and Financing Activity*, Washington, D.C., quarterly.

Mortgage Debt Outstanding, 1-4 Family Houses, Nonfarm (Billions of dollars)

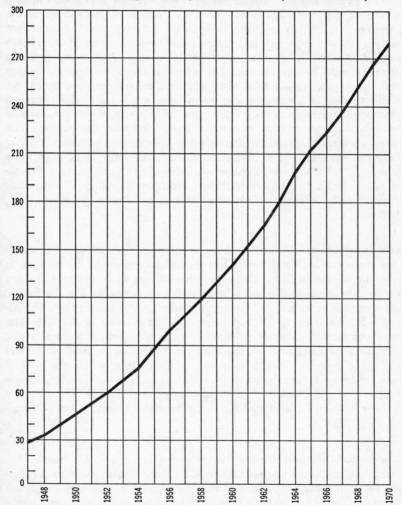

Source: Federal Home Loan Bank Board.

Mortgage Market A term comprising all financial institutions associated with the marketing of mortgages. The market in which the actual mortgage transactions are negotiated between the borrowers and the initial lenders is called the primary mortgage market. The purpose of this market is to bring together the seekers of mortgage funds and those willing to invest. The market in which the previously created mortgage securities are traded between investors is known as the secondary mortgage market. It provides a means for holders of mortgages who need funds to dispose of their holdings before maturity. The chief institutions of the mortgage market, participating in both the primary and the secondary markets, are the mortgage originators, construction lenders, interim lenders, brokers, and ultimate investors. The major suppliers of mortgage credit are savings and loan associations, life insurance companies, mutual savings banks, and commercial banks. Although there are no organized exchanges for the trading of mortgages, the large brokerage houses, which arrange transactions for most of the major types of institutions and transactions between these institutions, provide a bridge between the primary and secondary markets and offer the nearest approach to an organized trading place for mortgages. For additional details, see Saul B. Klaman, *The Postwar Residential Mortgage Market*, Princeton University Press, Princeton, N.J., 1961; J. E. Morton, *Urban Mortgage Lending: Comparative Markets and Experience*, Princeton University Press, Princeton, N.J., 1956.

Mortgage Money Funds for home construction. The amount of mortgage money available to home buyers varies because of fluctuations in general economic activity. There have been times when mortgage money was hard to secure and others when it was easy to obtain. For the future, however, it is expected that mortgage money should be adequate to support a high and rising level of home-building activity in the U.S. The numerous savings institutions, commercial banks, mutual savings banks, savings and loan associations, life insurance companies, mutual funds, and pension funds are all sources of mortgage funds. In addition, the Federal government provides funds through the Federal National Mortgage Association. For a discussion of mortgage money, see Saul B. Klaman, *The Postwar Residential Mortgage Market*, Princeton University Press, Princeton, N.J., 1961.

Most-Favored-Nation Clause A provision in commercial treaties between two or more countries that protects them against tariff discrimination by each other. It guarantees that all partners to the agreement will automatically extend to each other any tariff reductions that they might offer to nonmember countries. For example, if a trade agreement between the U.S. and the Netherlands contained a most-favored-nation clause, any reduction of the import duty on bicycles that the U.S. might offer to Great Britain (perhaps in exchange for a reduction of the British tariff on American automobiles) would automatically be extended to the Netherlands. Since 1948, when the General Agreement on Tariffs and Trade (GATT) provided for multilateral tariff negotiations under international auspices, all signatories to this convention (42 countries, which together account for more than 80% of world trade) have agreed to adhere to the most-favored-nation principle. Consequently, the problem of tariff discrimination, formerly a burning international issue, has been much reduced although it still exists. Furthermore, GATT specifically exempts from most-favored-nation obligations those countries, such as members of the Common Market, that plan to complete a customs union (without tariffs at all) among themselves. See Jacob Viner, *International Economics: Studies,* The Free Press of Glencoe, New York, 1951.

Motivation Research   A group of techniques developed by behavioral scientists (psychologists and sociologists) which are utilized by marketing researchers to discover the factors influencing marketing behavior, such as consumer attitudes, reactions, and preferences. A few motivation-research studies were carried out in the U.S. soon after World War II, but since 1950 there has been a marked increase of interest in learning why people buy. For general information on motivation research and surveys, see Joseph Newman, *Motivation Research and Marketing Management,* Harvard Business School, Division of Research, Boston, 1957; for a different view of the importance of motivation research in marketing research, see Robert Ferber and Hugh G. Wales, *Motivation and Market Behavior,* Richard D. Irwin, Inc., Homewood, Ill., 1958; Charles N. Cofer and M. H. Appley, *Motivation: Theory and Research,* John Wiley & Sons, Inc., New York, 1964.

Muckraker   One of a group of U.S. writers, including Lincoln Steffens, Ida M. Tarbell, and Upton Sinclair, whose work was directed at exposing graft and corruption in government, business, labor unions, and other social institutions. The group achieved its greatest prominence between 1902 and 1912. For the most part, its writings were published in monthly magazines, such as *McClure's, Cosmopolitan,* and *Collier's.* The term muckraker was first applied to members of the group by President Theodore Roosevelt, who in 1906 likened them to the man with the muckrake in John Bunyan's *Pilgrim's Progress* who ignored a proffered celestial crown and continued "to rake to himself the filth of the floor." For examples of muckraking writing and a discussion of the group's significance in U.S. life, see Arthur Weinberg and Lila Weinberg, *The Muckrakers,* Simon and Schuster, Inc., New York, 1961.

Multicollinearity The tendency of many economic time series (theoretically, independent variables) to expand or contract simultaneously over time as a result of a common cause. When this condition prevails, the statistician is not able to isolate each series' separate contribution to simple and multiple correlation. If multicollinearity is serious, the sampling errors of the individual coefficients become large in a linear correlation, and the coefficients will not be precisely estimated even though the correlation for the entire equation is high. Thus the presence of multicollinearity may seriously impair the significance of the overall correlation. For additional information, see Lawrence R. Klein, *An Introduction to Econometrics,* Prentice-Hall, Inc., Englewood Cliffs, N.J., 1962; Stefan Valavanis, *Econometrics,* McGraw-Hill Book Company, New York, 1959.

Multiforecasting A forecast of the upper and lower limits that are expected for sales in a given period. Forecasting a precise value of sales for a period extending six months or a year ahead is extremely difficult. Multiforecasting provides the maximum range because it pinpoints the upper and lower limits within which sales may reasonably be expected to move. Naturally, the distance between the upper and lower limits is greater for periods further in the future than for the near term. If the multiforecast is revised regularly, the area between the optimistic and the pessimistic forecasts becomes smaller, and management may gear production, inventory, and other policies to a particular value of sales within the narrow range of expected sales for specific planning purposes. See *American Machinist/Metalworking Manufacturing,* New York, Sept. 17, 1962, p. 148.

Multi-industry Company A company that operates in more than one industry, such as a major producer of military and space systems that also sells cement, drugs, and chemicals. Such diversification is precipitated by the desire of a company to participate in a greater number of markets. The so-called battle of materials, in which a product competes against all possible substitutes as well as against the same commodity, has been responsible for much of the diversification. Thus, the U.S. tin-can industry, which has come under pressure from other metals and paper products, has been diversified to the extent that, in 1958, 29.1% of its 107,300 employees were used in the production and sale of products other than tin. Security against fluctuations in the demand for one product and new technology are other factors contributing to the growth of the multi-industry company. For additional information, see Michael Gort, *Diversification and Integration in American Industry*, Princeton University Press, Princeton, N.J., 1962.

Multilateral Compensation The settling of debts and credits among a number of participants in a clearing. For example, a clearinghouse settles claims that individual banks have on each other. Let us assume that bank A owes bank B $100, that bank A owes bank C $50, and that bank B owes bank C $35. A clearing would establish that bank A owes $150 to the other banks, that bank B has a net credit of $65 due from its partners, and that bank C is owed $85. To consolidate all debits and credits of the participants into net balances and to settle them by a single payment is much more convenient and economical than individual transactions, especially when the compensation involves a large number of participants. A clearing is more convenient because each member either makes or receives one payment. A New York Clearing House operation in which ten banks participate involves a maximum of nine checks, as opposed to the forty-five checks that would have to be written if the banks settled their daily balances bilaterally. A clearing is more economical because a smaller amount of money is needed to make settlements. In the example cited above, $185 of total debts are settled by net payments of $150. John Maynard Keynes, the British economist, proposed multilateral compensation on an international scale in 1943; beginning in 1948, a limited version of his proposal was embodied in the operation of intra-European payments agreements. For a full discussion of the actual operation of multilateral compensations, see New York Clearing House, *Annual Reports*, New York; European Payments Union, *Annual Reports*, Organization of European Economic Cooperation, Paris, 1950–1956.

Multilateral Negotiations and Agreements Negotiations and agreements between more than two parties. The term is generally used to refer to the intricate trading relationships developed by many countries. Since trade between any two countries normally is not balanced, a typical trading country usually deals with a number of countries, developing a crisscross network of trading relationships in the world economy. The General Agreement on Tariffs and Trade (GATT) is an example of an agreement which seeks to establish multilateral trade. For further information, see Raymond F. Mikesell, *Foreign Exchange in the Postwar World*, The Twentieth Century Fund, New York, 1954; Henry Chalmers, *World Trade Policies*, University of California Press, Berkeley, Calif., 1953.

Multinational Company A company that has (1) a manufacturing base or other form of direct investment that gives it roots in at least one foreign country and (2) a global perspective. A global perspective means that its management makes fundamental decisions on marketing, production, and research in terms of alternatives available to it anywhere in the world. For further information, see "Multinational Companies: How U.S. Business Goes Worldwide," *Business Week*, Apr. 20, 1963, pp. 62–86; for a more recent analysis, see Sidney E. Rolfe and Walter Damm (eds.), *Multinational Corporation in the World Economy: Direct Investment in Perspective*, Praeger Publishers, Inc., New York, 1970.

Multiplier A conceptual tool employed in the study of business fluctuations. Introduced by R. F. Kahn in 1931 and used a few years later by John Maynard Keynes, it deals with the magnified impact that changes in investment spending have on total income. The money spent in building a new plant, for instance, sets off a chain reaction. It increases the incomes of the workers directly engaged in its construction, the incomes of the merchants with whom the workers trade, the incomes of the merchants' suppliers, and so on. The dollars do not multiply indefinitely, however, for people do not ordinarily spend all their new income; instead, they spend part and save part. Theoretically, the multiplier's final effect, or value, can be calculated by dividing the numeral 1 by the percentage of new income saved. For example, if people on the average save 20% of their additional income, a $1 billion increase in investment will ultimately raise total income by $5 billion ($1/0.20 = 5; 5 \times 1 billion = $5 billion). This basic idea has been developed into many specialized multipliers, such as the foreign-trade multiplier, which deals with the effects of changing imports, and the successive-period multiplier, which deals with the timing of the multiplier effects. There are so many unknowns at work in the economy, however, that it is virtually impossible to discover the precise impact of any multiplier. See J. M. Keynes, *The General Theory of Employment, Interest, and Money*, Harcourt, Brace & World, Inc., New York, 1936; Alvin H. Hansen, *A Guide to Keynes*, McGraw-Hill Book Company, New York, 1953; Gardner Ackley, *Macroeconomic Theory*, The Macmillan Company, New York, 1961; Thomas F. Dernburg and Duncan M. McDougall, *Macroeconomics*, 3d ed., McGraw-Hill Book Company, New York, 1968.

Multishift Operation The practice of an industry or a company of operating its facilities on more than one shift. An industry or a company may operate on a two-shift or a three-shift day, depending on the type of industry (continuous-processing industries generally operate their facilities on three shifts per day) and on the volume of demand (companies may pass from one to two shifts when demand is high).

Mutatis Mutandis A Latin term meaning "with the necessary changes having been made." In economic analysis, it is generally assumed that all variables except those being studied are kept constant. A change in a variable might result in a change in some of the conditions which are outside the particular area being studied.

Mutual Company A corporation without capital stock in which profits, after deductions for reserves, are divided among the members in proportion to the business that each of them did with the company. Examples of this type of company are mutual savings banks and mutual insurance companies.

Mutual Fund (Open-End Investment Company) An investment company that has a flexible capital structure. Because in virtually all cases open-end investment companies continuously sell shares in mutual funds and because they will redeem any outstanding shares, their capital structures are almost constantly changing. Their capital increases when sales exceed redemptions and decreases when redemptions exceed sales. The price at which mutual funds will sell or redeem their shares is usually the net asset value of the fund per share. (Total assets minus total liabilities divided by number of shares equals net asset value per share.) A distribution fee or commission is added when the mutual fund sells shares. Mutual-fund share prices are determined solely by the prices of the securities held by the fund. Unlike the prices of the shares of closed-end investment companies, the prices of the shares of open-end investment companies are not directly evaluated by the market. Like closed-end investment companies, however, mutual funds can be classified by investment objectives. Common-stock funds invest money primarily in common stocks, although they reserve the right to hold cash or to invest in defensive securities, such as bonds. Some common-stock funds invest money in specialized fields, such as growth stocks, electronics issues, or blue chips. Others diversify their investments over a wide range of common stocks. Balanced funds invest in common and preferred stocks and bonds and generally try to hold the proportions of each type of security close to stated policies. Because they diversify not only the companies they hold, but also the kinds of securities, they are more conservative than common-stock funds. Fully managed funds are funds that invest money at the discretion of the management. They have no stated investment objectives. See *Fact Book*, Investment Company Institute, New York, periodically; U.S. Securities and Exchange Commission, *Annual Reports;* Wharton School of Finance and Commerce, *A Study of Mutual Funds*, prepared for the Securities and Exchange Commission, Government Printing Office, Washington, D.C., Aug. 28, 1962.

Mutual Savings Bank   A savings bank which is owned and operated wholly for the benefit of its depositors, who must all be individuals. Banks of this type differ from cooperative banks in that they are directed by a self-perpetuating board of directors. Depositors have no voice in their policies. As of December, 1968, the U.S. had 501 mutual savings banks (90% of them in New England and New York) with $71 billion in total assets. Only one of these banks was a member of the Federal Reserve System and subject to its regulations; for all the others, the distribution of investments, the maximum insurance on deposits, and the amount of interest they might pay on deposits were governed by state law. The first mutual savings bank was established in Scotland in 1810; the first one in the U.S., in 1816. For further historical information, see Walter W. Haines, *Money, Prices and Policy*, 2d ed., McGraw-Hill Book Company, New York, 1966; statistics are presented monthly in *Federal Reserve Bulletin*, Washington, D.C., and in greater detail in U.S. Comptroller of the Currency, *Annual Reports*.

Naïve Model   Not a formal mathematical model but rather an assumption that whatever the forces were that produced an economic event, or a change in a time series, in the immediate past, the same forces will be present in the immediate future and will act in such a way as to produce a similar or identical event or change. The application of this assumption implies complete ignorance of all causal factors and other related information. Its use in econometrics cannot be justified under other circumstances. For comparisons of naïve models with economic forecasts, see Victor Zarnowitz, *An Appraisal of Short-Term Economic Forecasts*, National Bureau of Economic Research, Occasional Paper 104, Columbia University Press, New York, 1967.

National Bank   A commercial bank chartered by the Federal government. Established under the National Banking Acts of 1863–1864, national banks were authorized to issue bank notes on a large reserve of U.S. government securities. Since it was believed that national banks would provide a stable national paper currency, the Federal government, in 1866, placed a 10% tax on state bank notes to drive them out of existence. With the passage of the Federal Reserve Act in 1913, all national banks were required to join the Federal Reserve System, but no bank was required to be a national bank. Since 1935, when national banks lost their note-issuing privilege, the main reason for a national bank's existence has been prestige. As of June 30, 1970, there were 4,637 national banks out of 13,671 commercial banks in the U.S., and they controlled 59% of the assets and deposits of all commercial banks. See Lester V. Chandler, *The Economics of Money and Banking,* Harper & Row, Publishers, Incorporated, New York, 1959; for statistics on national banks, see *Federal Reserve Bulletin,* Washington, D.C., monthly.

National Debt The total indebtedness of a national government. It is generally smaller than the public debt, which includes the debt of local governments as well as that of the national government, and it is usually larger than the net national debt, which omits the portion of the debt that is owed to government agencies and trust funds. In the U.S., the national debt, after rising rapidly during World War II, reached an all-time high of nearly $383 billion at the end of fiscal 1970, or nearly eight times greater than it had been in 1940. Interest payments rose from $1 billion to almost $21 billion per year over the same period. Although the U.S. debt increased in dollar terms in the postwar period, it actually declined in relation to the nation's total production: in 1970 it was 40% of the gross national product, compared with more than 100% in 1947. Many persons who worry about the increasing size of the Federal debt are concerned (1) that an increasing burden is being passed on to future generations or (2) that a big debt will eventually bankrupt the government. Those who deny the first problem readily concede that the national debt redistributes income, but they do not believe that the burden is passed on to future generations as a whole. With regard to the bankruptcy problem, they argue that the government can never become bankrupt because it can either increase taxes or create additional sums of money to pay the debt. A more real concern regarding a mounting national debt is the threat of inflation. Detailed statistics on the U.S. national debt are published monthly in U.S. Treasury Department, *Treasury Bulletin;* for a discussion of the national debt's structure and economic impact, see Charles C. Abbott, *United States Public Debt,* The Twentieth Century Fund, New York, 1953; for a discussion of the particular problems of financing World War II, see Henry C. Murphy, *The National Debt in War and Transition,* McGraw-Hill Book Company, New York, 1950; for a discussion of national debt management, see Tilford C. Gaines, *Techniques of Treasury Debt Management,* The Macmillan Company, New York, 1962.

National Debt (Billions of dollars)

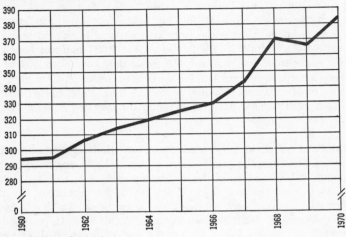

Source: U.S. Treasury Department.

National Income   The total compensation of the elements used in production (land, labor, capital, and entrepreneurship) which comes from the current production of goods and services by the national economy. It is the income earned—but not necessarily received—by all persons in the country in a specified period. It consists of wages, interest, rent, profits, and the net income of the self-employed. National income can be classified according to the industry in which it originates, such as mining, construction, or manufacturing. The difference between national income and net national product (gross national product minus capital consumption allowances) is accounted for mainly by indirect business tax and nontax payments: Federal excise taxes, customs duties, state taxes and fees, local property taxes. National income generally is considered a better series for income-distribution analyses than the gross national product, but national income data have been criticized because they include some items for which there are no formal records, such as the amount of food consumed by a farmer which he has produced himself. For a detailed discussion of national income data, see Richard Ruggles and Nancy D. Ruggles, *National Income Accounts and Income Analysis,* 2d ed., McGraw-Hill Book Company, New York, 1956; for detailed definitions of the techniques and terminology of national income accounting, see U.S. Department of

Commerce, *Survey of Current Business: National Income Supplement,* 1954; for current quarterly data on national income, see U.S. Department of Commerce, *Survey of Current Business.*

National Income by Industry

	1950		1970	
	$ Billion	% of Total	$ Billion	% of Total
All industries	241.1	100.0	795.9	100.0
Agriculture, forestry, and fisheries	17.6	7.3	24.5	3.1
Mining and construction	17.2	7.1	49.4	6.2
Manufacturing	76.2	31.6	217.7	27.4
Transportation	13.4	5.6	29.5	3.7
Communication	3.3	1.4	16.9	2.1
Electric, gas, and sanitary services	3.9	1.6	14.4	1.8
Wholesale and retail trade	40.9	17.0	122.1	15.3
Finance, insurance, and real estate	22.0	9.1	87.0	10.9
Services	21.8	9.0	103.2	13.0
Government and government enterprises	23.6	9.8	126.5	15.9
Rest of world	1.2	0.5	4.6	0.6

SOURCE: U.S. Department of Commerce.

National Income and Product Accounts A statistical statement of national output or receipts, such as gross national product, net national product, personal income, and disposable income. The national income and product accounts consist of the following individual accounts: consolidated business income and product account; personal income and expenditure account; consolidated government receipts and expenditures account; rest of the world account; and gross savings and investment account. The early work in developing national income and product accounts was done by the National Bureau of Economic Research. In 1932, Congress directed the preparation of national income accounts, and a few years later the Department of Commerce began publishing its estimates. The monthly personal income series was initiated in the late 1930s. During World War II, the development of the gross-national-product series was greatly accelerated because of its value in planning the war effort and in instituting controls. In the postwar period, the accounts have gone beyond the scope of measuring the size and composition of national output. Through the use of income and expenditure accounts, an understanding of the factors that determine the output can be gained. For further information, see U.S. Department of Commerce, *Survey of Current Business: National Income Supplement,* 1954; Richard Ruggles and Nancy D. Ruggles, *National Income Accounts and Income Analysis,* 2d ed., McGraw-Hill Book Company, New York, 1956; John P. Powelson, *National Income and Flow-of-Funds Analysis,* McGraw-Hill Book Company, New York, 1960; Simon Kuznets, *National Income: A Summary of Findings,* National Bureau of Economic Research, Inc., New York, 1946.

Nationalization   An act by which a government takes over the ownership and operation of an industry or a business previously in the hands of private citizens. It has been argued that nationalization increases productive efficiency by permitting the direct investment of public funds, by enlarging the scale of operations, and by coordinating operations more effectively. On the other hand, opponents of nationalization state that the record of private enterprise is such that governmental take-over and control are unnecessary, and that government ownership is usually characterized by excessive costs because of elaborate, overcentralized organization. Nationalization has been used by some countries purely as a means of eliminating foreign ownership of their basic industries. For a study of Great Britain's experience with nationalization, see Ben W. Lewis, *British Planning and Nationalization,* The Twentieth Century Fund, New York, 1952; see also "The Nationalization of British Industries," *Law and Contemporary Problems,* Duke University School of Law, Durham, N.C., Autumn, 1951.

National Labor Relations Act (Wagner Act)   The principal labor relations law of the U.S. It applies to all interstate commerce except airlines and railroads, which are covered by the Railway Labor Act. The National Labor Relations Act, which was passed in 1935 and subsequently amended, guarantees employees the right of full freedom in self-organization and in the choice of representatives for collective bargaining; it also prohibits specific unfair labor practices by employers or by unions. In 1947 it was amended by the Labor-Management Relations Act (Taft-Hartley Act). One of the amendments changed the composition of the National Labor Relations Board to include five members instead of three and provided for a general counsel. In addition, the Board's judicial functions were separated from its prosecuting duties by delegating to its general counsel final authority to issue complaints of unfair labor practices and to prosecute the complaints before the Board. Major amendments in the law banned the closed shop and defined certain union actions as unfair labor practices. The Landrum-Griffin Act of 1959 also substantially amended the basic act. Among other things, it authorized the Board to delegate to its regional directors power to determine representation questions, subject to review by the Board. For further discussion of the National Labor Relations Act, see W. S. Woytinski and Associates, *Employment and Wages in the United States*, The Twentieth Century Fund, New York, 1953, chap. 10.

National Wealth   The aggregate value of all the tangible nonmilitary assets of a country. National wealth statistics are a measure of the economic stocks of an area. Whereas the common concept of national income stems from an income-statement approach to social accounting, the measurement of national wealth is derived from a balance-sheet approach. The simplest calculation of national wealth is gross wealth, summing the value of all of a country's assets on an undepreciated basis and ignoring their age, usefulness, etc. A more realistic measure is net wealth, for which assets are valued on a depreciated basis. National wealth includes both reproducible tangible assets (capital stock) and nonreproducible assets, such as land and natural resources. The value of reproducible assets is estimated by the perpetual-inventory method of accumulating past capital expenditures, depreciated in accordance with the life of the asset. The value of nonreproducible assets is estimated independently, often from census or tax data. In 1967 net national wealth of the U.S., which had been growing at an average annual rate of 3.6% since World War II, totaled about $2,800 billion. As a measure of economic growth, reproducible tangible wealth, excluding land and other natural resources, is more appropriate than total wealth. In the postwar period, the real value of reproducible wealth in the U.S. has been growing at an annual rate of about 4%. For additional details on the concept and measurement of national wealth, see Raymond W. Goldsmith, *The National Wealth of the United States in the Postwar Period*, National Bureau of Economic Research, Inc., Princeton University Press, Princeton, N.J., 1962; see also *Studies in Income and Wealth*, vols. 12 and 14, National Bureau of Economic Research, Inc., New York, 1950–1952; for a recent study of the problems and possibilities of a meaningful national wealth inventory, see John W. Kendrick (ed.), *Guidelines for the Improvement of Wealth Data and Estimates*, Report of the Wealth Inventory Planning Study, George Washington University, Washington, D.C., June, 1964; for annual data on national wealth, see U.S. Bureau of the Census, *Statistical Abstract of the United States*, Washington, D.C., annually.

Nation's Economic Budget   A rearrangement of national-income-accounts data so that each of the accounts of the four sectors, government, business, consumers, and international accounts, balances in terms of receipts and expenditures. Users of this budget format ordinarily do not consider it a planning or programming device but rather a useful tool for economic analysis. The nation's economic budget was devised by Gerhard Colm and Grover Ensley in the 1940s. Data on the form of the nation's economic budget may be found in *Economic Indicators*, prepared by the Council of Economic Advisers for the U.S. Joint Economic Committee, Government Printing Office, Washington, D.C., monthly; for additional discussion of this format, see Gerhard Colm, *The American Economy in 1960*, National Planning Association, Washington, D.C., 1952, pp. 26–29; see also John P. Lewis and Robert C. Turner, *Business Conditions Analysis*, 2d ed., McGraw-Hill Book Company, New York, 1967, pp. 562–566.

Natural Monopoly A natural condition that makes the optimum size of the firm so large in relation to the market that there is room for only one firm. The crucial criterion for the existence of a natural monopoly is that the market demand must be sufficiently small so that it can be satisfied by a single firm which is operating in an area of decreasing costs. It is not feasible for a second firm to enter the industry because one firm alone could produce the potential output of both firms at a lower total cost than the two firms would incur. Therefore, an entering firm must seek to capture the entire market through price-cutting techniques, and thus only one of the two firms would survive. A typical situation exists in the railroad industry, in which costs decrease as additional passengers and freight are carried. This is a direct result of the indivisibilities in the production function for railroad services. Once service is established with the necessary tracks and terminals, additional freight or passenger traffic serves to reduce average costs. If the demand for such service is limited to a particular run with declining costs, a natural monopoly exists, and it is unprofitable for other firms to enter the field. In the U.S. in the 1880s such situations resulted in price wars between railroads that operated parallel tracks. The lost revenue was made up in areas in which there was no competition. Economic growth can destroy natural monopolies, because demand also grows, and the natural monopoly is broken when the monopolist no longer operates in the limited area of decreasing costs. Public utilities are now given monopoly positions under the guise of the theory of natural monopoly. For a discussion of monopoly in this industry, see Walter Adams and Horace M. Gray, *Monopoly in America: The Government as Promoter*, The Macmillan Company, New York, 1955, chap. 3; see also C. L. Allen et al., *Prices, Income, and Public Policy*, McGraw-Hill Book Company, New York, 1959, pp. 368–382; Clair Wilcox, *Public Policies toward Business*, 3d ed., Richard D. Irwin, Inc., Homewood, Ill., 1966.

Natural Order A concept held by the eighteenth-century physiocrats that economic life was governed by laws that were universally applicable, and that in most respects the government should not interfere with the actions of individuals. The principle of laissez faire developed from this concept. Influenced by the physiocrats, Adam Smith believed that the natural order was a state of nature, contrasting with an order that was artificially created. Thus, the essence of the natural order was the fact that the particular interest of the individual coincided with the common interest. Since the pursuit of self-interest was instinctive, the removal of restrictions and the elimination of coercion provided a common advantage in all affairs. For a study of economic thought, see Frank Amandus Neff, *Economic Doctrines,* McGraw-Hill Book Company, New York, 1950; see also William Fellner, *Modern Economic Analysis,* McGraw-Hill Book Company, New York, 1960, chap. 4; Howard D. Marshall, *The Great Economists,* Pitman Publishing Corporation, New York, 1967, pp. 30–36.

Natural Resource   Any of the manifold raw materials and wildlife available in nature for man's use, including minerals, forests, water, fish, and fowl. Although natural resources are still an important factor in economic activity in the U.S. and the rest of the world, many synthetics (fibers, rubber, detergents, oils) and substitutes (plastics, plywood) have been developed in industrialized nations since the 1940s. For a discussion of the resources available in the U.S., see H. H. Landsberg et al., *Resources in America's Future,* Johns Hopkins University, Baltimore, 1963; J. Frederic Dewhurst and Associates, *America's Needs and Resources,* The Twentieth Century Fund, New York, 1955.

Natural Rights   Essential rights of individuals for the enjoyment of the fullest possible prosperity and happiness. According to François Quesnay, one of the eighteenth-century physiocrats, natural rights were determined by observation of the facts concerning actual human situations and relations. Quesnay observed the situation of particular individuals, the services that they needed from each other and were in a position to render each other, and the reciprocal rights and duties that they must recognize. He called attention to the rights and duties of parents and children as an example. Young children are unable to care for themselves and thus require various parental services. Parents are best situated to provide these services; hence, children have natural rights to the service in question while the parents have a natural duty toward their children. In later years, the situation is reversed. Grown-up children are in the best position to aid their aging parents and thus have the natural duty to do so while the parents retain the natural rights to such aid. It was believed that it was the business of government to make and enforce a system of positive laws to protect these natural rights. When such natural rights existed in economic dealings, the government was not to interfere with these rights but to endeavor to protect them. Quesnay's essay *Droit naturel* can be found in Auguste Oncken (ed.), *Oeuvres de Quesnay*, Jules Peelman and Company, Paris, 1888, pp. 359–377.

Near Money An asset whose value is fixed in terms of money and which can easily be converted into money, yet which cannot be spent directly. The most important forms of near money are time deposits and U.S. government bonds, both of which can readily be converted into a specific amount of money but which are excluded from the definition of money because they do not function directly as a medium of exchange. Near moneys often have an important effect on the consumption habits of individuals, since the greater the amount of wealth held in the form of near money, the greater is the willingness of consumers to make purchases from their money incomes. Furthermore, highly liquid near money can be converted very quickly into actual money, adding significantly to the money supply. Thus, it can pose serious problems in inflationary periods. For further details, see Walter W. Haines, *Money, Prices and Policy*, 2d ed., McGraw-Hill Book Company, New York, 1966.

Negative-Tax Plan A scheme in which all family units with incomes above the amount necessary for a subsistence level of living would pay a progressive income tax, while all other family units would receive a government subsidy sufficient to raise their incomes to subsistence level. The subsidy in this case would be the negative tax. Under this system, existing welfare programs would be abolished. Critics of this scheme point out that it would be impractical, reducing incentives to work and to save. For further discussion, see Margaret S. Gordon, *The Economics of Welfare Policies*, Columbia University Press, New York, 1963, pp. 117–118; Michael J. Boskin. "The Negative Income Tax and the Supply of Work Effort," *National Tax Journal*, vol. XX, no. 4, December, 1967; Christopher Green, "Negative Taxes and Monetary Incentives to Work: The Static Theory," *The Journal of Human Resources*, vol. III, no. 3, pp. 280–288, Summer, 1968.

Neoclassical School A school of economists which existed between 1870 and World War I. Members of the school reconstructed classical economic theory to take into account the changes that had occurred since the early nineteenth century. The founders of the neoclassical school were William S. Jevons in England, Carl Menger in Austria, and Léon Walras in France. Subsequent leaders were Alfred Marshall in Cambridge, Eugen von Böhm-Bawerk in Vienna, Vilfredo Pareto in Lausanne, and John Bates Clark and Irving Fisher in the U.S. Neoclassicists believed that the power of competition was the regulating force of economic activity which would establish equilibrium between production and consumption. Their theory was mainly a theory of price and the allocation of resources to specific uses under the incentives of utility maximization for the consumer and profit maximization for the producer. The innovations of the neoclassical school as compared with the doctrines of the classical school were mostly mathematical. Neoclassical theorists applied logical concepts of integral and differential calculus to the analysis of relationships between inputs and outputs. Their emphasis on mathematical economics resulted in economics becoming technical and, at the time, less acceptable to the general public and to government. This school of economic thought did not continue the work of classical theorists in developing the aggregative approach to the measurement of total economic output or income. John Maynard Keynes broke with orthodox neoclassical theory in the early 1930s, when he developed his anti-neoclassical point of view, which emphasized liquidity preference and the notion of an underemployment equilibrium. For further discussion of the neoclassicists, see William Fellner, *Modern Economic Analysis*, McGraw-Hill Book Company, New York, 1960; Overton Taylor, *A History of Economic Thought*, McGraw-Hill Book Company, New York, 1960; for theories of the neoclassicists, see Léon Walras, *Elements of Pure Economics*, Eng. tr. by W. Jaffe, Richard D. Irwin, Inc., Homewood, Ill., 1954; Alfred Marshall, *Principles of Economics*, 8th ed., The Macmillan Company, New York, 1948; Howard D. Marshall, *The Great Economists*, Pitman Publishing Corporation, New York, 1967, pp. 247–283.

Neoliberalism An economic philosophy which holds that, on the whole, the market mechanism works well in satisfying human wants and in allocating productive resources to alternative uses. An economy composed of small units (one as close as possible to pure competition) is essential to ensure that the price mechanism works well. In general, neoliberalists prefer as little governmental intervention in the economy as possible. Neoliberalism is the modern adaptation of the laissez faire doctrine of the 1800s. Among its current proponents, Ludwig von Mises advocates a return to the economic doctrines of laissez faire espoused by the nineteenth-century liberals. F. A. von Hayek, believing that the gradual growth of government leads to socialism and that freedom and democracy cannot exist under socialism, considers that the drift toward further governmental control should stop and that competition should be strengthened. Henry C. Simons advocates increased competition, dissolution of monopolies, and a minimum role for government. Milton Friedman favors a return to a rather extreme version of laissez faire in which market prices would determine a great many things now in government hands. For further discussion, see D. S. Watson, *Economic*

Policy, Houghton Mifflin Company, Boston, 1961; for individual points of view, see Ludwig von Mises, *Human Action,* Yale University Press, New Haven, Conn., 1949; F. A. von Hayek, *The Road to Serfdom,* The University of Chicago Press, Chicago, 1944; Henry C. Simons, *Economic Policy for a Free Society,* The University of Chicago Press, Chicago, 1948; Milton Friedman, *Capitalism and Freedom,* The University of Chicago Press, Chicago, 1962.

Net Cash Flow   *See Cash Flow.*

Net National Product   The market value of a country's output of goods and services after deducting the capital that has been used up in the production process. Among the deductions to be made are depreciation charges, accidental damage to fixed capital assets, and outlays charged to current account. Net national product differs from gross national product because it excludes all business products used by business during the specific accounting period. For a detailed explanation of net national product, see U.S. Department of Commerce, *Survey of Current Business: National Income Supplement,* 1954; Richard Ruggles and Nancy D. Ruggles, *National Income Accounts and Income Analysis,* 2d ed., McGraw-Hill Book Company, New York, 1956.

Net Profits   *See Profits.*

Net Worth   The excess of assets over liabilities. The net worth of a business represents the equity of the owners (proprietors or stockholders) in it. Thus, a statement of net worth shows the total investment of the owners in the business (capital) and the profits which have been allowed to remain in the business and increase the proprietors' equity (surplus). Net worth is affected by the owners' original investment, additional investments, subsequent profits and losses of the business, and withdrawals from accumulated profits or investments. Only tangible assets are included when net worth is calculated for the purpose of judging credit risks, but intangible assets, such as goodwill and patents, are included for an accounting computation.

New Economic Program, Phase 1   A Nixon administration economic program geared to help solve the problems of slow economic growth, inflation, and a serious balance-of-payments deficit by (1) freezing wages, prices, and rents for ninety days; (2) introducing a 10% import surcharge on items other than those coming under the quota system; and (3) halting the convertibility of dollars into gold. The program was announced on August 15, 1971, and was altered significantly with the introduction of

Phase 2 on November 13, 1971. For further discussion, see *The Annual Economic Report of the President,* Government Printing Office, Washington, D.C., 1972.

New Economic Program, Phase 2   The introduction on November 13, 1971, of (1) flexible controls on wages, prices, and rents instead of the freeze; (2) a continuation of the inconvertibility of dollars into gold; (3) a removal of the 10% import surcharge; and (4) a 7.9% devaluation of the dollar, or an 8.5% increase in the price of gold, which must be acted on by Congress. For further discussion, see *The Annual Economic Report of the President,* Government Printing Office, Washington, D.C., 1972.

New Economics   The use of aggressive Federal government intervention to bring about economic growth through manipulation of the Federal budget position. The correct policy moves in any given economic situation will depend on how the economy is performing in relation to its potential performance at the theoretical full-employment level. The proponents of the New Economics have held that a full-employment economy, under present conditions, occurs when unemployment is at about the 4% level. Lower levels of unemployment would yield less real growth and higher rates of inflation. The difference between the actual gross national product and the potential GNP at full employment is called the GNP or performance gap. Economic policy under the New Economics would consist of attempting to close this performance gap by taking appropriate actions to influence the government's budget position. For example, in a slack economy, Federal government policy would generally require running a budget deficit to stimulate economic activity. The New Economics depends to a great extent on the abilities of government economists to forecast accurately the trends in economic activity and the likely responses to various policy measures. Actions taken under accurate assessments of future activity are often the cause of as much difficulty as the problems the actions were designed to eliminate. In addition to accurate forecasting, the New Economics requires pinpoint timing of policy actions to achieve desired objectives. For additional information, see Walter Heller, *New Dimensions of Political Economy,* Harvard University Press, Cambridge, Mass., 1966; Herbert Stein, *The Fiscal Revolution in America,* The University of Chicago Press, Chicago, 1969, chaps. 15, 16, and 17. For a different view see, George Terborgh, *The New Economics,* Machinery and Allied Products Institute, Washington, D.C., 1968.

New Incorporation   A new business issued a charter under the general business corporation laws of the 50 states of the U.S. The number of

New Business Incorporations (Thousands)

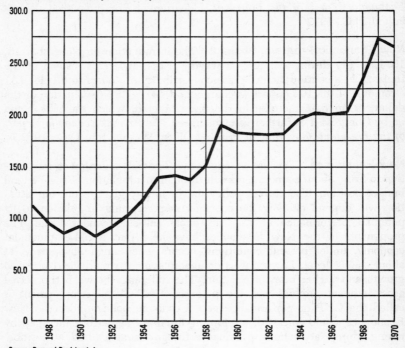

Source: Dun and Bradstreet, Inc.

new incorporations includes both completely new businesses that are incorporated and existing businesses that have changed from noncorporate to corporate status. The number of incorporations is much smaller than the number of new businesses. The number of new incorporations is a significant indicator of overall business activity, which the National Bureau of Economic Research classifies as one of its thirty leading indicators. The number generally increases when business expands and decreases when it declines. New incorporations in the U.S. declined to 266,075 in 1970. For current statistics, see *Business Trends News* and *Monthly New Incorporations,* Dun and Bradstreet, Inc., New York; for cyclical aspects of new incorporations, see Victor Zarnowitz, "Cyclical Aspects of Incorporations and the Formation of New Business Enterprises," in Geoffrey H. Moore (ed.), *Business Cycle Indicators,* vol. I, National Bureau of Economic Research, Inc., Princeton University Press, Princeton, N.J., chap. 13.

New Order   A commitment to buy goods, received and accepted by a company, for present or future delivery. Since a lag normally exists between receipt and shipment of an order, new orders usually serve as a leading indicator of future business conditions. An increase in new orders generally means that production will increase in the future, thus providing a greater number of jobs and higher incomes. Because data on new orders provide significant information to the business and industry forecaster, many trade associations collect and compile such data. For example, the National Machine Tool Builders Association collects data on new orders for machine tools, the National Electrical Machinery Association collects industry information on new orders for various types of electrical equipment, and the McGraw-Hill Department of Economics collects data on new orders for nonelectrical machinery. The U.S. Department of Commerce provides a monthly series of new orders in manufacturing industries. For monthly data on new orders, see U.S. Department of Commerce, *Survey of Current Business;* see also Victor Zarnowitz, "The Timing of Manufacturers' Orders during Business Cycles," in Geoffrey H. Moore (ed.), *Business Cycle Indicators,* vol. I, National Bureau of Economic Research, Inc., Princeton University Press, Princeton, N.J., 1961, chap. 14.

Nineteenth-Century Liberalism   *See Classical Liberalism.*

Nominal Price   A term used to describe a price that is estimated because no actual price exists. Nominal price refers to a price quotation that is given by a commodity or security specialist because a particular commodity or security is not traded often enough to establish a definite market price.

Nonborrowed Reserves   A reserve aggregate consisting of total bank reserves (deposits of the Federal Reserve and vault cash) minus borrowings by member banks from the Federal Reserve. For additional information on reserve aggregates, see "Monetary Aggregates and Money Market Conditions in Open Market Policy," *Federal Reserve Bulletin,* February, 1971. For statistics on nonborrowed reserves, see *Federal Reserve Bulletin,* monthly.

Noncompeting Groups   Groups of workers that do not compete with each other for employment. Noncompeting groups arise when certain jobs require skills possessed by a relatively small number of workers. For example, brain surgeons and electricians do not compete with unskilled workers or with each other for jobs. Thus, brain surgeons would be classified as a noncompeting group of workers, competing only with other brain surgeons for employment. On the other hand, a large number of unskilled and semiskilled workers may fall into a single noncompeting group. For example, store clerks, farmhands, and elevator operators may be considered part of a single noncompeting group, since each is capable of doing the others' jobs. Yet none of them offers any competition to the brain surgeon or even to the electrician. For additional details, see Orme W. Phelps, *Introduction to Labor Economics,* 3d ed., McGraw-Hill Book Company, New York, 1961.

Nondurable Goods   *See Soft Goods.*

Nonflexible Price   A price that is less flexible on the down side than on the up side. When demand increases for a product with a nonflexible price, the price rises to a smaller extent than the price of a flexibly priced product in the same situation. Nonflexible prices occur in the case of manufactured products turned out by an industry that is highly concentrated, such as steel and automobiles. They also occur in the case of products turned out by a few producers that dominate a local market, such as beer. See Gardiner C. Means, *Administrativ Inflation and Pricing Policy,* Anderson Kramer Associates, Washington, D.C., 1959.

Noninstallment Credit   Credit granted in which future repayment is made in a lump sum. The term is used in contradistinction to installment credit, which is repayable in separate installments. An example of noninstallment consumer credit is the department store charge account, which requires one payment by a specified date for all purchases made within a certain period. In 1970 noninstallment credit in the U.S. totaled

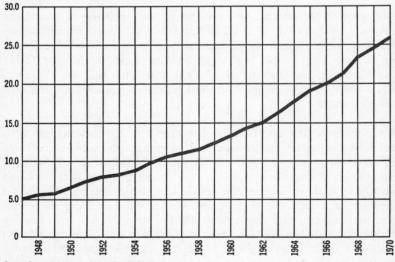

Noninstallment Credit (Billions of dollars)

Source: Board of Governors, Federal Reserve System.

$25.6 billion. For current statistics on noninstallment credit, see *Federal Reserve Bulletin,* Washington, D.C., monthly.

Nonmanufacturing Industry An industry that is not involved in the production of finished goods from raw materials. The major types of nonmanufacturing industries are trade, services, agriculture, construction, transportation, finance, communications, mining, and government. In 1970 these industries accounted for about 70% of the national product and total employment in the U.S.

Nonmember Bank In the U.S., a bank that does not belong to the Federal Reserve System. Since all national banks are required to be member banks, the nonmember banks are either state banks or private banks. State banks choose to be nonmember banks either (1) because they do not meet the minimum requirements for membership in the Federal Reserve System or (2) because they prefer the generally less strict regulations of state laws to Federal Reserve regulations. For instance, nonmember banks can charge a fee for clearing checks, and state reserve requirements are frequently more lenient than those set by the Board of Governors of the Federal Reserve System. As of June 30, 1970, out of 13,671 commercial banks, 7,868 were nonmember banks, but the nonmember banks controlled only about 17% of total commercial bank assets. See Walter W. Haines, *Money, Prices and Policy,* 2d ed., McGraw-Hill Book Company, New York, 1966; for an article on the reasons why banks do not join the Federal Reserve System, see B. Magruder Wingfield, "Deterrents to Membership in the Federal Reserve System," *Banking Studies,* Board of Governors of the Federal Reserve System, Washington, D.C., 1941; for statistics on nonmember banks, see *Federal Reserve Bulletin,* Washington, D.C., monthly.

Nonprice Competition Methods of competition which do not involve changes in the selling price. The main types of nonprice competition are product differentiation and advertising. Through product differentiation, a firm tries to distinguish its product from that of its rivals. This may be achieved by improving the product's quality, efficiency, etc., and by periodic restyling. Besides changing its product to suit consumer demand, a firm may try to increase its share of the market by attracting consumers by means of advertising and sales promotion. Less important types of nonprice competition include favorable terms of sale and customer services. The result of nonprice competition, especially product differentiation, is that the consumer is given a wide variety of types, styles, and qualities of a given product from which to choose. Furthermore, such competition serves to accelerate technological innovation and product improvement.

Nonprice competition is most prevalent in oligopolistic industries, such as automobile and cigarette manufacturing, in which the possibility of increasing a firm's market share through price competition is small. For additional details, see E. H. Chamberlain, "The Product as an Economic Variable," *Quarterly Journal of Economics*, pp. 1–29, Harvard University Press, Cambridge, Mass., February, 1953; L. Abbot, "Vertical Equilibrium under Pure Quality Competition," *American Economic Review*, pp. 826–845, American Economic Association, Evanston, Ill., December, 1953; N. Kaldor, "The Economic Aspects of Advertising," *Review of Economic Studies*, vol. XVIII, no. 1, pp. 1–27, Oliver & Boyd Ltd., Edinburgh, 1950; E. Jerome McCarthy, *Basic Marketing: A Managerial Approach*, 3d ed., Richard D. Irwin, Inc., Homewood, Ill., 1968, pp. 593–594.

Nonresidential Fixed Investment Expenditures by private business and nonprofit organizations and institutions for new and replacement construction (buildings, stores, warehouses) and producer durable equipment (machinery, office equipment, motor vehicles). The basic purpose of nonresidential fixed investment is to increase and modernize the capacity to produce goods and services for future consumption. With residential investment it adds up to gross private fixed investment. The difference between the nonresidential-fixed-investment expenditures series and the series on business expenditures for new plants and equipment (capital expenditures) is that the former includes investment by farmers, private institutions (such as hospitals and colleges), nonprofit organizations, professionals (such as doctors and dentists), and real estate operators, while the latter series does not. Also included in the nonresidential series but excluded from the capital spending series are oil-well drilling costs charged to current expense and expenditures for passenger cars for business purposes by salaried workers who receive reimbursement for the use of the cars. For a detailed discussion of the concept, coverage, and sources of data for the major components, see U.S. Department of Commerce, *National Income Supplement*, 1954; see also Richard Ruggles and Nancy D. Ruggles, *National Income Accounts and Income Analysis*, 2d ed., McGraw-Hill Book Company, New York, 1956; for quarterly and annual data, see U.S. Department of Commerce, *Survey of Current Business*, monthly.

Nonresidential Structures Investment New and replacement business expenditures on buildings such as factories, warehouses, and retail stores; on farm structures; on all private nonprofit institutions; on churches, schools, and hospitals; and on public utility expenditures for such items as railroad tracks and stations and telephone, electric, and gas distribution systems. It also includes petroleum and gas-well drilling and exploration expenditures. This series differs conceptually from the construction activity series compiled by the U.S. Census Bureau in that it includes the cost of petroleum and natural-gas-well drilling, brokers' commissions on the sale of structures, and net purchases of used structures from government and excludes farm dwellings. Nonresidential structures investment accounted for 35% of private nonresidential fixed investment over the past decade. For a detailed discussion of the concept, coverage, and sources of data, see U.S. Department of Commerce, *National Income Supplement*, 1954; see also Richard Ruggles and Nancy D. Ruggles, *National Income Accounts and Income Analysis*, 2d ed., McGraw-Hill Book Company, New York, 1956; for quarterly and annual data, see U.S. Department of Commerce, *Survey of Current Business*, monthly.

Nonsingularity Within the general econometric problem of identification, a condition that exists for an econometric model involving several equations each of which represents a sector of the economy that is economically different from all the others. The equations may respond to exogenous stimuli identically or in any other manner. However, each equation must respond to endogenous stimuli in a different or unique way. When this condition is met, it follows that none of the involved equations is a linear combination of other equations in the model, and the model is complete. For additional information, see Stefan Valavanis, *Econometrics*, McGraw-Hill Book Company, New York, 1959.

Normal Year A year in which the physical volume of goods and services and industrial production in the U.S. increase by between 3.5 and 4.5%, prices rise from 2 to 2.5%, consumer money incomes rise from 5 to 6%, and unemployment ranges between 4.5 and 5% of the labor force. No single year in the post-World War II period meets all these requirements, but the postwar average for each of these key economic gauges falls about midway between the limits. The criteria given above are used by many business economists in describing a normal business year.

Nuisance Tax A tax whose revenue value is negligible but which acts as an inconvenience to the taxpayers. For instance, a tariff with a very low rate of duty may be considered a nuisance tax, since importers become involved in a great deal of clerical work and other red tape.

Obligational Authority, New The total amount of grants enacted by the Congress of the U.S. to cover appropriations and other financial authorizations made available to Federal agencies for a given fiscal year. New obligational authority is a direct measure of congressional action on the budget recommendations of the President. In a few cases, such as interest on the national debt, there is permanent authority under which additional sums of money are made available automatically from year to year without new congressional action. New obligational authority does not include the unspent balances of prior years which are still available for current obligations. The granting of new obligational authority is a key control over Federal expenditures. For the fiscal year 1970, new obligational authority totaled more than $141 billion. For details of the process by which the Federal government reaches decisions on expenditures, see Arthur Smithies, *The Budgetary Process in the United States,* McGraw-Hill Book Company, New York, 1955; see also Murray L. Weidenbaum, "The Federal Government Spending Process," in U.S. Joint Economic Committee, *Federal Expenditure Policy for Economic Growth and Stability,* Washington, D.C., 1957; for current statistics, see U.S. Bureau of the Budget, *The Federal Budget* and *The Budget Review,* annual reports.

Obsolescence The shortening of the life of a capital asset, such as a plant, machine, or piece of equipment, because of technological progress, such as an invention, improvement in processes, changed economic conditions, or legislation. Obsolescence differs from depreciation, which is the actual wearing out of plants and equipment because of use. In 1970 the McGraw-Hill Department of Economics carried out a survey of a large sample of industrial companies to establish the magnitude of obsolescence. The results indicated that it would cost industry $144.5 billion to replace all obsolete facilities with the best new plants and equipment. See Dexter M. Keezer and Associates, *New Forces in American*

Business, McGraw-Hill Book Company, New York, 1959; How Modern Is American Industry? McGraw-Hill Department of Economics, New York, 1970.

Obsolescence in Business
(In billions of dollars)

Industry	Cost of New Facilities
Manufacturing	80.0
Mining	2.0
Transportation	15.3
Communications	9.6
Utilities	13.2
Finance, trade, and services	24.4
All business	144.5

Occam's Razor (Ockham's Razor) The principle that the primary assumptions of a logical system should be as few as possible. It was first formulated by William of Occam in the fourteenth century. The principle of Occam's razor, now also known as the principle of economy or the law of parsimony, asserts that in any system (e.g., an economic model) the number of unconnected propositions and those for which there are no proof should be at a minimum. Thus, in deciding between two explanations for the same phenomenon, the one which requires fewer simplifying assumptions should be chosen. For further information, see Columbia Associates in Philosophy, Introduction to Reflective Thinking, Houghton Mifflin Company, Boston, 1951; G. N. Bueschen, Eucharistic Teachings of William Ockham, The Catholic University of America Press, Washington, D.C., 1950.

Odd Lot An amount of stock that is less than the unit of trading established by a stock exchange. For example, the unit of trading, or round lot, is 100 shares for most stocks listed on the New York Stock Exchange, and any number of shares from 1 to 99 is therefore an odd lot. Because only round lots are traded on exchanges, brokers who want to buy or sell an odd lot for a customer must execute the order with an odd-lot dealer, a member of the exchange who stands ready to buy or sell odd lots. Odd-lot dealers charge a differential on orders that they execute. For instance, on the New York Stock Exchange the odd-lot dealer's price is based on the first round-lot transaction that occurs after the odd-lot order reaches the trading post. If that price were under $40, the odd-lot dealer would charge a differential of 12.5 cents per share; if the price were more than $40, he would charge a differential of 25 cents per share. See George L. Leffler and L. C. Farwell, *The Stock Market,* The Ronald Press Company, New York, 1963; Charles O. Hardy, *Odd-Lot Trading on the New York Stock Exchange,* The Brookings Institution, Washington, D.C., 1939; *Report of Special Study of the Securities and Exchange Commission,* part 2, July 17, 1963.

Old Age and Survivors Insurance (OASI)   A Federal program of retirement pensions in the U.S., financed equally by contributions from employees and their employers. In 1971, employers deducted 5.2% from wages up to $7,800 per year for each employee and matched this contribution. The 5.2% rate is broken down into 4.6% for retirement survivors and disability and 0.6% for hospital insurance. The self-employed are subject to a 7.5% tax. The program, which was established by the Social Security Act of 1935, is administered by both the Treasury Department and the Bureau of Old Age and Survivors Insurance of the Social Security Administration. Various basic types of benefits are paid either monthly or in a lump sum: (1) The primary insurance benefit, a percentage of the worker's average monthly wage, is payable to the fully insured retired worker at the age of sixty-five. (2) The wife's benefit is one-half of the primary insurance benefit, payable at the age of sixty-five to a retired worker's wife. (3) The widow's benefit is three-fourths of the primary insurance benefit, payable at the age of sixty-two to the widow of a fully insured worker. The same percentage is paid if the widow is under the age of sixty-two but has a child of an insured worker in her care. (4) The child's benefit is one-half of the primary insurance benefit, payable to a retired or deceased worker's unmarried children under the age of eighteen. (5) The parents' benefit is one-half of the primary benefit, payable at the age of sixty-five to the surviving dependent parents of a deceased fully insured worker if no other relatives are eligible to receive benefits. (6) The lump-sum death payment is three times the primary benefit, payable on the death of an insured worker if no other monthly benefits are immediately payable. Payments are also made in the case of total and permanent disability, subject to certain conditions and limitations. In mid-1970, the Social Security Administration paid old-age benefits to more than 23 million persons. The original coverage of the program, which was quite limited, has been expanded. The only exclusions now are a few types of professional workers, part-time farm and domestic laborers, government employees, and workers in nonprofit organizations. See James A. Hamilton and Dorrance C. Bronson, *Pensions,* McGraw-Hill Book Company, New York, 1958; Eveline M. Burns, *Social Security and Public Policy,* McGraw-Hill Book Company, New York, 1956; for monthly statistics, see U.S. Social Security Administration, *Social Security Bulletin.*

Oligopoly A type of market structure in which a small number of firms supplies the major portion of an industry's output. The best-known examples in the U.S. economy are the automobile industry, in which three firms account for 92% of the output of passenger cars; the gypsum industry, in which four firms supply 90% of the industry's output; and the aluminum industry, in which three firms provide nearly all the supply of aluminum ingots. Although oligopolies are most likely to develop in industries whose production methods require large capital investments, they also cover such diverse items as cigarettes, light bulbs, chewing gum, detergents, and razor blades. In economic theory, the term oligopoly means a mixture of competition and monopoly, and the benefit or harm done to the economy at large by oligopolies remains in dispute. Prices in oligopolistic industries generally fluctuate less widely than those in more competitive industries; each seller hesitates to lower prices because he knows that his few competitors will immediately match the cuts, leaving him with essentially the same share of the total market and lower profits. Nevertheless, other forms of competition, such as styling, quality, new features, marketing, and advertising, may be very keen. Moreover, the large size of oligopolists may permit greater investment in an industry than if the industry were composed of more competitive sellers. Although there is no way to measure the extent of oligopolies statistically, the prevailing view is that the number of oligopolies in the U.S. has grown since 1900, if only because the monopolies and near monopolies that once characterized many basic industries have become oligopolies (for example, the steel and petroleum industries). Furthermore, new processes and products have created new oligopolies in the computer, airline, synthetic-fiber, and other industries. For case studies of oligopolies, see Walter Adams, *The Structure of American Industry*, The Macmillan Company, New York, 1961; for an extensive theoretical discussion of the effects of oligopolies, see Corwin Edwards, *Maintaining Competition*, McGraw-Hill Book Company, New York, 1949; for the legal aspects, see Clair Wilcox, *Public Policies toward Business*, 3d ed., Richard D. Irwin, Inc., Homewood, Ill., 1966; see also William Fellner, *Competition among the Few*, Alfred A. Knopf, Inc., New York, 1949; for a discussion of classical and modern oligopoly models, see Donald S. Watson, *Price Theory and Its Uses*, 2d ed., Houghton Mifflin Company, Boston, 1968, pp. 361–396.

Oligopsony A market structure with relatively few buyers. The high degree of buyer concentration results in a significant amount of interdependence, since the purchasing patterns of any one firm affect all the others. An oligopsonistic situation may lead to express or tacit collusion among the buyers to depress their buying prices, generally at the expense of the sellers who supply them. Often it is possible for a single large buyer, even without collusion, to exercise his bargaining power to negotiate lower prices. An oligopsonistic market may face either an atomistic, competitive selling market or one with a significant degree of seller concentration. The first case, that of concentrated buying from a large number of small sellers, occurs in the U.S. mainly in some agricultural and mining markets, such as the leaf-tobacco market, the fluid-milk market, and the crude petroleum market. The second case, that of concentrated buying from concentrated selling, or bilateral oligopoly, occurs in some markets for manufactured goods in which manufacturers sell to other manufacturers or to large distributive firms. The markets for sheet steel, rails, and primary copper are examples of this type of oligopoly. For additional information, see Joe Bain, *Price Distribution and Employment,* Holt, Rinehart and Winston, Inc., New York, 1953; Joel Dean, *Managerial Economics,* Prentice-Hall, Inc., Englewood Cliffs, N.J., 1951, chaps. 7–9; H. Speight, *Economics,* 3d ed., Methuen & Co., Ltd., London, 1968, chaps. 14 and 15.

Open Account   The name given to a method of extending commercial credit in which the only evidence of the debt is an entry in the seller's books. Also known as the book account, the open account is the simplest credit instrument and is widely used in the extension of mercantile credit. The seller keeps a record of the credit which has been advanced to the buyer and sends him a bill when payment is due, usually from thirty to ninety days after the sale. The main advantage of the open account is its flexibility, since the terms of the original agreement can be modified very easily, e.g., to provide for an extension. Furthermore, the open account is relatively simple and inexpensive to maintain. This flexibility, plus the fact that the buyer never sees the ledger entry, may, however, result in disagreements concerning the terms of the sale. The entry on the ledger is not considered conclusive evidence that the debt exists; further proof, such as invoices or shipping papers, is needed. For further information, see William J. Shultz and Hedwig Reinhardt, *Credit and Collection Management,* 3d ed., Prentice-Hall, Inc., Englewood Cliffs, N.J., 1962.

Open Economy   The economy of an area in which trade is unrestricted. In an open economy, any individual may have unhindered business and trade relationships with anyone outside the area. The term open economy usually refers to an economy in which there are no restrictions on imports, exports, or the movement of factors across boundaries.

Open-End Investment Company   *See Mutual Fund.*

Open-Market Operations   The buying and selling of government bonds by Federal Reserve banks in the open market for the purpose of implementing Federal Reserve monetary policies. The Federal Reserve, through private securities dealers, buys and sells marketable securities of the U.S. government. The purposes of open-market operations are (1) to contract or expand the supply of reserves of member banks, thus affecting the power of these banks to expand credit; (2) to influence interest rates through the quantitative effect on reserves; (3) to provide an orderly market for government securities; and (4) to exert an effect on exchange rates and international gold movements through the effect on interest rates. Open-market operations are considered the most flexible instrument of monetary policy. For example, to expand reserves the Federal Reserve buys government bonds from the public or other institutions. The commercial banks thus relinquish part of their security holdings to the Federal Reserve, which pays for the securities by increasing the reserves of the commercial banks by the amount of the purchase. If the bonds are purchased from a private individual, the seller's demand deposit is increased, and bank reserves also are increased. A contraction of reserves may be brought about by selling bonds to commercial banks. Open-market policy is decided upon by the Federal Open Market Committee and is carried out by the manager of the open-market account, a senior officer of the New York Federal Reserve Bank. For further information, see W. W. Riefler, "Open Market Operations in Long Term Securities," *Federal Reserve Bulletin*, Washington, D.C., November, 1958; Robert V. Roosa, *Federal Reserve Operations in Money and Government Securities Markets*, Federal Reserve Bank of New York, New York, 1956; *Monetary Policy, Decision Making, Tools and Objectives*, Federal Reserve Bank of Philadelphia, Philadelphia, 1960.

Open Shop   A business enterprise that is open equally to members and nonmembers of unions. The employer is free to hire anyone he desires. After the employee has been hired, there is no contractual requirement or contractual pressure on the worker to join a union. The open shop was long referred to as the closed nonunion shop because of the policy followed by many employers of refusing to hire union members. The National Labor Relations Act of 1935 rendered this policy illegal in industries engaging in interstate commerce. For arguments for and against open and closed shops, see Julia E. Johnsen (ed.), *The Closed Shop*, The H. W. Wilson Company, New York, 1942.

Operating Profits   *See Profits.*

Operating Rate (Capacity Utilization Rate) The ratio of physical output to physical capacity. The operating rate is a key factor in evaluating the short-run business outlook, specially with regard to investment in facilities for expansion. It correlates fairly well with profits, so that forward estimates of the operating rate provide a rough gauge of the future level of profits. Moreover, the direction of the operating rate, whether up or down, may have an impact on industrial prices. The operating rate is a rather difficult concept because it depends on the definition of capacity, which varies widely from industry to industry and from company to company. Data on operating rates in the U.S. are available for manufacturing industries and for the industrial sector of the economy. End-of-year operating rates for manufacturing and for major manufacturing industries since 1954 are found in *Annual Surveys of Business' Plans for New Plants and Equipment*, McGraw-Hill Department of Economics, New York; for various measures of the operating rate and evaluations, see *Measures of Productive Capacity*, Hearings before the Subcommittee on Economic Statistics of the U.S. Joint Economic Committee, May 14, 22, 23, and 24, 1962, Government Printing Office, Washington, D.C., 1962.

Operating Statement *See Profit and Loss Statement.*

Operation Nudge *See Operation Twist.*

Operations Research The use of certain mathematical techniques in analyzing particular activities in order to provide a more or less scientific basis for a choice among alternative means of accomplishing a given goal. In carrying out an operations research (O.R.) project, a team of experts is organized, each member of which is familiar with one aspect of the problem and, generally, with advanced mathematical techniques. The introduction of electronic computers has made it possible to apply O.R. to problem solving. O.R. was first used widely during World War II, when it was employed to analyze complex logistical and other military problems. More recently, it has received considerable attention as a business-management tool. Among the business problems to which it has been applied are production and inventory control, transportation planning, and plant location. For a technical treatment of the subject, see Thomas L. Saaty, *Mathematical Methods of Operations Research*, McGraw-Hill Book Company, New York, 1959; for a more general treatment, see Russell L. Ackoff and Maurice W. Sasieni, *Fundamentals of Operations Research*, John Wiley & Sons, Inc., New York, 1968; see also *Operations Research: A Basic Approach*, American Management Association, New York, 1956; *Operations Research Reconsidered*, American Management Association,

New York, 1958; for a discussion of operations research as a general tool of economic analysis, see "Economic and Operations Research: A Symposium," *Review of Economics and Statistics,* Harvard University Press, Cambridge, Mass., August, 1958; see also Robert Dorfman, "Operations Research," *American Economic Review,* American Economic Association, Evanston, Ill., September, 1960; George Odiorne, "Some Limitations on Operations Research," *Michigan Business Review,* University of Michigan, School of Business Administration, Ann Arbor, Mich., January, 1959.

Operation Twist (Operation Nudge)   The attempt by the Federal Reserve and the Treasury in 1961 to raise short-term interest rates relative to long-term rates in order to reconcile international and domestic objectives. Federal Reserve and Treasury officials believed that short-term rates should be raised to minimize the outflows of speculative funds to other countries while holding down the costs of long-term funds to expand business's capital investment. Through Treasury debt management operations and Federal Reserve open-market operations, the supply of treasury bills and other short-term issues was increased relative to the supply of long-term government bonds. The end result was that the interest rate paid by commercial banks on time deposits was increased several times, and funds were redirected from short- to long-term objectives. For additional information, see Lester V. Chandler, *The Economics of Money and Banking,* 5th ed., Harper & Row, Publishers, Incorporated, New York, 1969.

Opportunity Costs (Alternative Costs)   The value of the productive resources used in producing one good, such as an automobile, instead of another good, such as a machine tool. With a relatively fixed supply of labor and capital at any given time, the economy cannot produce all it wants of everything. Thus, the real cost to society of producing an automobile is the value of the other things that cannot be produced because the same resources are not available to build them. The fact of alternative costs is most clearly demonstrated in wartime, when a nation can have guns and tanks or new automobiles and appliances but not both weapons and consumer durable goods. The principle of opportunity costs, which was developed by the neoclassicists in the nineteenth century, is based on notions of Jean Baptiste Say and Nassau William Senior of the classical school of political economy. The concept of alternative costs covers more than the conventional accounting costs encountered in a profit and loss statement. For example, a production worker in a plant earns $5,000 per year and saves his money to buy a machine shop for $3,000, but he takes home only $4,500 per year in profits from the shop. According to the principle of opportunity costs, the machine-shop owner has made no profit because he has not even covered the alternative cost of $5,000 that he could have earned at the plant, to say nothing of the loss of interest on his savings. For further discussion of opportunity costs, see William Fellner, *Modern Economic Analysis,* McGraw-Hill Book Company, New York, 1960, pp. 104–106; Milton H. Spencer, *Managerial Economics,* 3d ed., Richard D. Irwin, Inc., Homewood, Ill., 1968, pp. 214–215.

Optimist   An economist of a mid-nineteenth-century school that rejected the foundations and pessimistic conclusions of contemporary economic dogma. On the basis of the writings of Thomas Robert Malthus and David Ricardo, economic opinion of the early decades of the nineteenth century maintained that rising population combined with diminishing returns in agriculture would ultimately reduce mankind to a mere subsistence level of existence. The optimists refused to accept this interpretation of the economic outlook. One of them, Henry C. Carey, an American, maintained that increasing rather than decreasing returns were the rule in agriculture. He denied, also, the validity of the Malthusian population doctrine. Among Carey's works are *The Past, the Present and the Future* and *The Princ:ples of Social Science,* H. C. Baird, Philadelphia, 1869; for a further discussion of Carey and other optimists, see Frank Amandus Neff, *Economic Doctrines,* McGraw-Hill Book Company, New York, 1950, chap. 21.

Option   A contract permitting the purchaser, at his discretion, to require the seller to perform his part of an agreement within a stipulated period. If the buyer of the contract does not choose to exercise his option, he loses only the amount of money paid for it. Options are used in many businesses: in real estate, when, for example, a tenant is given the temporary right to purchase the property that he is renting at a given price; or in the theater or films, when a producer buys an option to a particular actor's services for a certain time. In the securites industry, options take many forms, including puts, calls, spreads, straddles, stock options, and warrants, but they all have one feature in common: the option buyer has the right to buy or sell a specified amount of securities, at a stated price, for a certain length of time. For further discussion, see John C. Clendenin; *Introduction to Investments,* 4th ed., McGraw-Hill Book Company, New York, 1964; D. K. Eiteman, C. A. Dice, and W. J. Eiteman, *The Stock Market,* 4th ed., McGraw-Hill Book Company, New York, 1966.

Optional Consumption   The purchase of goods and services that are not essential for comfort and well-being. The standards of measuring optional consumption, or comfort and well-being, are arbitrary; they generally vary from place to place, from group to group, and from decade to decade. When income reaches a certain level, an individual or a family is able to choose between adequate or expensive housing, food, clothing, and other goods and services. It has been estimated that as much as one-third of all consumer spending in the U.S. is optional in this sense. In another sense, all buying of luxuries is optional. In either case, when a significant portion of the market decides to use its option to buy fewer goods and services or less expensive items (compact cars, for example), this decision can have a pronounced effect on the economy. When a country reaches a certain level of prosperity, optional consumption becomes widespread and introduces an element of business instability. Salesmanship and advertising are not required to induce purchases for subsistence, but they are essential in stimulating optional consumption. For the impact on the U.S. economy of a decision by consumers to forgo optional consumption, see Dexter M. Keezer and Associates, *New Forces in American Business,* McGraw-Hill Book Company, New York, 1959.

Organized Labor   The association of workers for the purpose of improving their economic position by bargaining with employers. The sheer weight of numbers in organized labor places it in a better position than that of individual workers to bargain with employers. The activities of organized labor in the past, and especially in countries outside the U.S., have often been political rather than economic, ranging from lobbying and the exertion of unified pressure through established political channels to occasional successful attempts to overthrow the established order. Organized labor came into existence almost immediately after the development of the factory system, under which wage earners worked with tools provided by employers. It became necessary for an individual to join with other laborers in order to improve his bargaining power and maximize the fraction of the total value of the product which went to him in the form of wages. As of 1966, union membership in the U.S. was estimated at 17.5 million, the AFL-CIO having the largest membership. The extent of labor organization varies with the sector of the economy. In the construction, coal and metal mining, and transportation and public utility industries the great majority of wage earners are union members. A large majority of the wage earners in manufacturing also are union members, although in some manufacturing industries only a minority of the workers are organized. These four sectors—manufacturing, construction, mining, and transportation and public utilities—account for less than 80% of all union membership in the U.S. In service and distributing industries unionism is generally weak, but certain skilled workers, such as musicians, bartenders, barbers, and meatcutters, have fairly strong unions in large cities. In government, union membership is growing rapidly. In the early 1960s, there was a slight decrease in the number of organized workers from the 1956 peak. See Leo Troy, "Trade Union Growth in a Changing Economy," *Monthly Labor Review*, U.S. Department of Labor, Washington, D.C., September, 1969; Harry P. Cohany, "The Membership of American Trade Unions, 1960," *Monthly Labor Review*, U.S. Department of Labor, Washington, D.C., December, 1961; see also Leo Wolman, *Ebb and Flow of Trade Unionism*, National Bureau of Economic Research, Inc., New York, 1936.

Orthogonal   In a strict mathematical sense this term means perpendicular, or right-angled, as, for example, orthogonal coordinate axes. The term is used in the same sense in connection with orthogonal regression, where vertical deviations from the regression line are minimized. The term has also been extended to describe certain techniques of matrix algebra, e.g., linear orthogonal factor analysis. Occasionally in the literature of statistics, two variables are said to be orthogonal if they are statistically independent of each other. For additional information, see Lawrence R. Klein, *A Textbook of Econometrics*, Row, Peterson & Company, Evanston, Ill., 1953; Stefan Valavanis, *Econometrics*, McGraw-Hill Book Company, New York, 1959.

Outliers   *See Extremes.*

Out-of-Pocket Cost   A cost that requires the utilization of current resources, usually cash or near cash, as opposed to a sunk cost, which does not require the utilization of current resources and may at times be avoidable. Out-of-pocket costs may be fixed (the president's salary) or variable (material or labor). See Harold Bierman, *Managerial Accounting: An Introduction*, The Macmillan Company, New York, 1959.

Output   Any commodity or service that a firm produces for sale. It could be a steel ingot, an automobile, a machine, or a financial service.

Overhead Cost   A cost that a firm incurs irrespective of the level of its production: the salary of a night watchman, for instance, or the rent of the plants and buildings that it uses, or the interest on outstanding bonds. Costs of this type, which are also called fixed costs, enter significantly into management's decision to continue production at a loss or to close down a firm. Frequently, it pays to continue output at a loss if the firm's revenue is high enough to cover variable costs (raw materials, labor, and other costs that are directly related to the scale of the firm's output) and only part of the overhead costs; if the firm shut down, it would not earn even a portion of its overhead costs and its current losses would be greater. In the long run, of course, all overhead costs become variable. After a lease expires, the rent may be raised or lowered; after a loan becomes due, it may be renegotiated on different terms; and even the night watchman can eventually be replaced by closed-circuit television. The accountant uses the term overhead cost somewhat differently, to denote a cost that he cannot attribute to any particular department or operation of the firm. He may charge the rent for a particular factory building to the cost of producing the item that is made inside and an executive's salary to the division of the firm in which the executive is active, but he finds great difficulty in apportioning interest on general bank loans or the cost of institutional advertising. These unapportioned expenses he calls overhead costs even if some of them—for example, the water bill for a plant producing many different products—appear to the economist to be variable costs. For the accountant's definition, see Harold Bierman, *Managerial Accounting: An Introduction,* The Macmillan Company, New York, 1959.

Overidentification   A condition that exists when more relations are given by a system of stochastic equations than are necessary to derive unbiased estimates of all parameters. This condition can be removed by abandoning reduced-form methods and resorting to longer computations. For additional information, see Karl A. Fox, *Intermediate Economic Statistics,* John Wiley & Sons, Inc., New York, 1968; Stefan Valavanis, *Econometrics,* McGraw-Hill Book Company, New York, 1959.

Overpopulation   A condition of excess population. Overpopulation is the existence of too many persons in a given area, with the result that their standard of living is at a subsistence or near-subsistence level. According to the theory of population formulated by Thomas Robert Malthus, overpopulation develops because population increases faster than the means of subsistence. Malthus claimed that population increased by geometrical progression (1, 2, 4, 8, 16), while the means of food production increased by arithmetical progression (1, 2, 3, 4, 5). He therefore believed that unless population growth could be changed, human beings were destined to misery and poverty. According to Malthus, there are preventive checks (moral restraint, late marriage, celibacy) as well as positive checks (famine, war, plague) which serve to keep population at least at subsistence levels. For a discussion of Malthus' theory in contemporary terms, see M. K. Bennett, *The World's Food,* Harper & Row, Publishers, Incorporated, New York, 1954, chap. 3; see also Roy G. Francis (ed.), *The Population Ahead,* The University of Minnesota Press, Minneapolis, 1958.

Overproduction   *See Underconsumption.*

Oversaving Theory   The theory that when planned saving is greater than planned investment the result is oversaving. When oversaving occurs, the amount of money removed from the income flow is greater than the amount returned to it; income must therefore fall. Oversaving has long been used by such economists as Thomas Robert Malthus and John Atkinson Hobson to explain low or falling national income. The lack of a theoretical base led some economists to believe that the oversaving theory was also an overinvestment theory, reasoning that oversaving caused overinvestment. John Maynard Keynes pointed out, however, that the level of planned investment does not depend on the level of planned saving. He maintained that, in maturing economies, people desire to save a larger amount of money at full employment than can be profitably invested because of diminishing investment opportunities. Keynes expected that, in mature economies, unless oversaving was prevented or compensated for by the government, there would be high unemployment. See William Fellner, *Modern Economic Analysis,* McGraw-Hill Book Company, New York, 1960; see also J. M. Keynes, *The General Theory of Employment, Interest, and Money,* Harcourt, Brace & World, Inc., New York, 1936; Royall Brandis, *Principles of Economics,* Richard D. Irwin, Inc., Homewood, Ill., 1968, chap. 10.

Over-the-Counter Market   A market for securities which includes all transactions in securities that are not made on organized stock exchanges. Unlike a stock exchange, which is an auction market located in one place, the over-the-counter market comprises thousands of stock and bond dealers who negotiate transactions primarily by telephone. Trading takes place when a potential buyer or seller of a particular security (or his broker) canvasses securities dealers who trade in that security and is quoted an acceptable price. By most measures, the over-the-counter market is the largest securities market in the U.S. In addition to common and preferred stocks, almost all U.S. government securities and municipal and corporate bonds are traded over the counter. Stocks that are traded over the counter range from those of smaller and usually more speculative companies to those of large, high-quality corporations, such as, for example, most U.S. commercial banks and insurance companies. Although the over-the-counter market is virtually unregulated by the Federal government, the National Association of Securities Dealers, which was established in 1939, provides self-regulation of over-the-counter securities dealers and their trading practices. The amorphous nature of the over-the-counter market makes statistical data difficult to obtain, but some information is given in U.S. Securities and Exchange Commission, *Annual Reports;* for a brief description of the over-the-counter market, see George L. Leffler and L. C. Farwell, *The Stock Market,* The Ronald Press Company, New

York, 1963; see also Irwin Friend et al., *Over-the-Counter Securities Markets*, McGraw-Hill Book Company, New York, 1958.

Overtime   Hours worked above and beyond the standard workweek, as defined by a labor-management agreement or by statute, for which the laborer must receive a higher rate of pay. Most unionized industries are subject to the Fair Labor Standards Act of 1938, which accords certain workers engaged in interstate commerce time and a half pay for work beyond forty hours per week, a standard that is usually adopted also in industries not covered by the act. Collective bargaining often imposes additional requirements, such as double pay for work on holidays and Sundays, and some unions have negotiated shorter standard work-weeks than are required by law: workweeks of thirty-five or thirty-six hours are not uncommon, especially in the printing, garment, building, and rubber industries. Since premium-pay rates put overtime in great demand, it is usually allocated according to seniority. Management,

Average Weekly Overtime Hours in Manufacturing

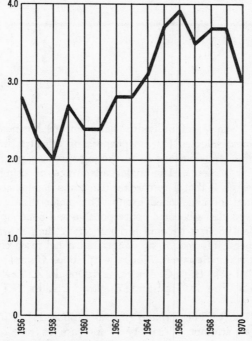

Source: U.S. Bureau of Labor Statistics.

however, generally prefers to avoid overtime altogether, since it is an expensive way of obtaining production: it raises labor costs for work time when an employee, already tired from a full workday or workweek, is likely to work less efficiently. According to the U.S. Bureau of Labor Statistics, an average of two and eight-tenths hours of overtime was worked in U.S. manufacturing industries in May, 1971. See Lloyd G. Reynolds, *Labor Economics and Labor Relations,* 5th ed., Prentice-Hall, Inc., Englewood Cliffs, N.J., 1970, p. 587; Albert Rees, *The Economics of Trade Unions,* The University of Chicago Press, Chicago, 1962; see also Dale Yoder et al., *Handbook of Personnel Management and Labor Relations,* McGraw-Hill Book Company, New York, 1958; for statistics on the number of overtime hours worked in manufacturing, see U.S. Department of Labor, *Employment and Earnings,* monthly.

P

Panel   A fixed sample of individuals at home or businessmen at their places of business selected for the purpose of repeated interviewing or reporting by the same persons in marketing research projects or in the testing of advertisements. The major advantage of using a panel for marketing research is that a researcher can trace changes occurring over a period of time for a matched group. The major disadvantage is that after a time respondents become nonresponsive and noncooperative. Panel research in the U.S. has become less important than it was during the 1950s. For general information on panels and panel research, see Richard D. Crisp, *Marketing Research,* McGraw-Hill Book Company, New York, 1957; David J. Luck, High G. Wates, and Donald A. Taylor, *Marketing Research,* 3d ed., Prentice-Hall, Inc., Englewood Cliffs, N.J., 1970, p. 98.

Paradox of Thrift   The principle, first proposed by John Maynard Keynes, that an attempt by society to increase its rate of saving may result in a reduction in the amount which it actually can save. This ironic conclusion is arrived at through the Keynesian savings-investment approach to the determination of national income, according to which the attempt to save (consume less) results in a reduced national income and in the inability of individuals, because of their smaller incomes, to save as much. The paradox, that saving is a vice and spending a virtue, is an illustration of a contradiction in incentives; while thrift may be desirable from the point of view of the individual, it may have disastrous effects on total output and employment from the point of view of society. For further information, see J. M. Keynes, *The General Theory of Employment, Interest, and Money,* Harcourt, Brace & World, Inc., New York, 1936; Gardner Ackley, *Macroeconomic Theory,* The Macmillan Company, New York, 1961; Armen A. Alchian and William R. Allen, *University Economics,* 2d ed., Wadsworth Publishing Company, Inc., Belmont, Calif., 1967, pp. 545–546.

Parameter   In economics, a constant which is assigned a value or a set of values at the outset of a problem. A parameter thus differs from a variable, which can take on any value. The values of a parameter are restricted by the particular problem under study, and a parameter can vary only when there is a change in the entire system being studied. In statistics, a parameter is a summary measure, such as a mean, median, or proportion of a characteristic of members of a population.

Parametric (Regression) Method, Seasonal-Adjustment   A method of seasonal adjustment. In the parametric method, the systematic (trend-cycle and seasonal) components of the series are estimated by regression techniques, using explicit mathematical expressions in the form of the general linear model.

Parent Company   A controlling company that actively owns or operates business properties. It thus differs from a holding company, which does not engage in a business operation. Most parent companies own all or more than half of the voting stock of their subsidiaries. An outstanding example of a parent company is American Telephone and Telegraph, which owns about 98% of the stock of Western Electric. For additional information on the difference between a parent company and a holding company, see J. F. Bradley, *Fundamentals of Corporation Finance,* Holt, Rinehart and Winston, Inc., New York, 1955.

Paretian Optimum   A situation that exists when no one in a society can move into a position that he prefers without causing someone else to move into a position which that person prefers less. In other words, a situation is not a Paretian or social optimum if it is possible, by changing the way in which commodities are produced or exchanged, to make one person better off without making another person (or persons) worse off. The term is named for Vilfredo Pareto, who first defined the social optimum, or the standard by which an economy can be judged. Although N. Kaldor, J. R. Hicks, and T. Scitovsky have attempted to refine the Paretian optimum, it still sets the conditions that maximize the economic wealth of any given society and therefore remains one of the cornerstones of welfare economics. See Vilfredo Pareto, *Manuale di economia politica*, Società Editrice Libraria, Milan, 1906; Kenneth E. Boulding, "Welfare Economics," in Bernard F. Haley (ed.), *A Survey of Contemporary Economics*, Richard D. Irwin, Inc., Homewood, Ill., 1952, vol. II; C. Tisdell, "Uncertainty and Pareto Optimality," *Economic Record*, December, 1963, pp. 405–412; Tibor Scitovsky, "A Note on Welfare Propositions in Economics," *Review of Economic Studies*, 1941, reprinted in American Economic Association, *Readings in Welfare Economics*, Richard D. Irwin, Inc., Homewood, Ill., 1969; for a mathematical interpretation of this condition see Gerard Debreu, "Valuation Equilibrium and Pareto Optimum," in The American Economic Association, *Readings in Welfare Economics*, Richard D. Irwin, Inc., Homewood, Ill., 1969, vol. XII, pp. 39–45.

Pareto's Law A law that states that the distribution of income is the same everywhere. Formulated by Vilfredo Pareto after wide-ranging statistical investigations, it states that if A equals a given income and B equals the number of persons with incomes greater than A, then if the logarithms of A and B are plotted on the y-axis and x-axis, respectively, or if A and B are plotted on log paper, the resulting curve, no matter which country is examined, will always be inclined by roughly 56° from the y-axis. This law, which Pareto induced from statistical evidence, describes the fact that incomes are not distributed equally. More important, because of the rigidity that Pareto thought existed (the curve is always within 3 to 4° of a 56° incline from the y-axis), the distribution of income is always the same no matter what the average income level of a nation may be. The implication is that the only way in which the income of the poorer segment of a country can be increased is by raising the income of the whole nation; in short, it is impossible to redistribute income. For the original statement of the law, see Vilfredo Pareto, *Cours d'economie politique*, F. Rouge, Lausanne, 1897; for a refutation of the law, see Arthur C. Pigou, *The Economics of Welfare*, Macmillan & Co., Ltd., London, 1932.

Pari Passu A Latin phrase meaning "with equal progress." The term pari passu is used in economics to indicate a simultaneous and equal hange. For example, the quantity theory of money holds that if the tock of money in an economy is increased by 5%, there will be a pari assu increase in the price level.

Parity Price A price received by U.S. farmers for many commodities vhich are adjusted to provide the same relative purchasing power that arm prices had in the base period (1909–1914). At the beginning of each marketing year, the U.S. Department of Agriculture announces the evels at which farmers' prices for basic commodities will be supported, provided the marketing quotas are accepted by two-thirds of the eligible armers voting in a referendum. If production is greater than can be sold at these prices, prices are supported by nonrecourse loans or purchase agreements with farmers. In the process, the Commodity Credit Corporation may purchase many commodities. Prices have been supported at 60 to 90% of parity. Parity prices for a selected list of commodities are published in U.S. Department of Agriculture, Statistical Reporting Service, *Agricultural Prices*, monthly; for further information on parity, see *Possible Methods of Improving the Parity Formula*, report of the Secretary of Agriculture, Government Printing Office, Washington, D.C., 1957.

Parity Ratio, Agricultural A measure that shows whether the prices received by farmers are higher or lower in relation to the prices that they paid in a base period. In the U.S., this period is August, 1909–July, 1914, when the prices that farmers received and the prices that they paid for goods, services, farm wages, interest, and taxes were considered in good balance. The parity ratio is calculated by dividing the index of prices received by farmers into the index of prices paid by them. Thus, if the prices received by farmers had doubled since 1909–1914 and the prices paid had quadrupled, current farm prices would be at 50% of parity (200/400 = 0.50). Occasionally, as in 1951, U.S. farm prices have exceeded 100% of parity, but usually they have been below parity, and in mid-1971 they were at 74%. Changes in the parity ratio actuate several government price-support programs. Price-support programs, which were begun in 1929 to protect farmers against violent price fluctuations, are criticized primarily because they discourage the most efficient use of productive resources. Monthly data on the ratio of current farm prices to parity prices are reported in U.S. Department of Agriculture, *Agricultural Prices*.

Partial-Equilibrium Theory The theory that individual sectors of the economy are not related to other sectors in terms of price or production. It ignores the mutual interrelationships between the prices and outputs

Parity Ratio (1910-1914 = 100)

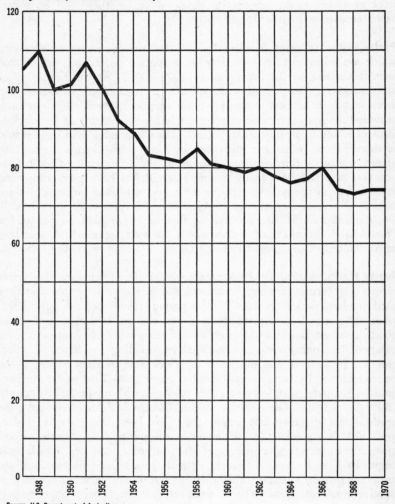

Source: U.S. Department of Agriculture.

of various goods and factors, assuming that repercussions from one market
to another will be slight enough to be disregarded. All partial-equilibrium
analyses are based on the assumptions of *ceteris paribus*. The familiar
supply-and-demand analysis is an example of partial-equilibrium analysis.
Although its basic assumptions are quite restrictive, partial-equilibrium

analysis is valid for the study of a wide range of problems. For example, in studying the effects of an excise tax on a particular commodity, e.g., tobacco, it is not very unrealistic to assume that prices are as given in all markets other than the tobacco market. Similarly, partial-equilibrium theory can be used to analyze the effect of a lower price of steel on the automobile industry. The total effect on the economy of the lower steel price cannot, however, be regarded simply as the sum of the effects on each individual market. For such an analysis, partial-equilibrium theory is inadequate, and general-equilibrium theory must be used. For an exposition of the major aspects of partial-equilibrium theory, see George J. Stigler, *The Theory of Price*, 3d ed., The Macmillan Company, New York, 1966; Kenneth E. Boulding, *Economic Analysis*, 4th ed., Harper & Row, Publishers, Incorporated, New York, 1966; for a discussion of the distinction between partial and general equilibrium, see Richard G. Lipsey and Peter O. Steiner, *Economics*, Harper & Row, Publishers, Incorporated, New York, 1966, chap. 42.

Participation Loan A loan in which two or more banks take part. Such participation agreements are usually made between a country bank and a large city bank. In this way, smaller country banks can take better advantage of investment opportunities in the larger money markets of cities and thus have a ready outlet for available short-term funds. Actual loans are made and terminated by the larger bank at its convenience, the smaller bank merely turning funds over to the larger one. The larger bank also holds the collateral for the joint protection of the two banks. The term participation loan may also refer to a large loan in which several large banks participate jointly. Such a loan is sometimes referred to as a syndicate loan.

Partnership A type of business organization in which two or more persons agree on the amount of their contribution (capital and effort) and on the distribution of profits, if any. Partnerships are common in retail trade, accounting, and law. Since the partners pool their capital, partnerships, in general, are larger than proprietorships, but they still are relatively small when compared with corporations. In many respects, however, partnerships are similar to proprietorships. They are subject to little government regulation and taxation. In addition, the partnership ends if any one of the partners dies, becomes insane, or goes bankrupt. A partnership is characterized by unlimited liability, which means that all the personal assets of the partners are available as security for their creditors. For a more detailed discussion of partnership, see Lyman A. Keith and Carlo E. Gubellini, *Introduction to Business Enterprise*, 2d ed., McGraw-Hill Book Company, New York, 1967.

Par Value   The value which is printed on the face of common and preferred stocks and bonds. In the case of common stocks, par value originally purported to represent the initial investment of cash, property, or services behind each share of stock that was issued. After the company was operating for a while, however, par value usually bore little relation to market value or even to book value. Over the years, the par value of common stocks has become a meaningless number. Recognizing this fact, many corporations now either issue no-par stock or issue stock with low par values because Federal transfer taxes are based on par value. Par value is more important in the case of preferred stocks and bonds because dividend and interest rates are calculated on par value. For example, with a 4% preferred stock the company will pay $4 a year on each share with a par value of $100 (the usual par value for preferred stocks). Although the par value of preferred stocks and bonds is normally closer to market value than is true of common stocks, they rarely are equal, and they can differ widely. See Charles W. Gerstenberg, *Financial Organization and Management of Business*, 4th ed., Prentice-Hall, Inc., Englewood Cliffs, N.J., 1959.

Patent   A contract between the government and an inventor providing that, in return for full disclosure of his invention, the government grants him an exclusive right to practice the invention for a period of seventeen years from the date of the grant. At the end of this period, the patent expires and becomes public property available to all. Patents are granted to encourage inventors to disclose their inventions to the public and thereby to "promote the progress of science and the useful arts." In 1623 patent laws were first enacted in England, where patents on inventions or new trades brought into the kingdom were limited to fourteen years. The first U.S. Patent Act became law on April 10, 1790, and the present statute dates from July 4, 1836. For a discussion of the American patent system, see Floyd L. Vaughan, *The United States Patent System*, University of Oklahoma Press, Norman, Okla., 1956.

Paternalism   A term applied to the extensive government welfare services of the modern welfare state. These government benefits, such as social security, make-work projects, and protection against unfair business practices, are viewed in the U.S. as the gracious protection of a doting and paternal Uncle Sam. At times, the term paternalism is used to describe the extreme regulation by the government of certain areas of individual activity, and in this sense it is employed in a derogatory manner. Industrial paternalism refers to an employer's excessive interest in providing for the comfort and welfare of his employees, usually in order to stimulate favorable labor-management relations.

Pattern Bargaining The technique of a union whereby it completes labor negotiations with one leading company in an industry and offers the same terms subsequently to all other companies in the industry, with the threat of a strike if the terms are not accepted. The International Union of Electrical, Radio and Machine Workers attempts to set a pattern for the electrical-machinery industry by selecting General Electric or Westinghouse as the primary target of its negotiations. After the settlement, the union proceeds to bargain with other electrical-machinery manufacturers on the same terms. For additional details, see Lloyd G. Reynolds, *Labor Economics and Labor Relations*, 5th ed., Prentice-Hall, Inc., Englewood Cliffs, N.J., 1970.

Payoff Period (Payout Period) A popular means of determining how quickly a company can get its money back from a capital investment. For example, if a new $1,000 machine increases revenue by $500 annually or permits savings in costs of $500 annually, its payoff period is two years. The average payout in U.S. manufacturing is about four years, but for an individual company the period ranges from less than one year to more than nine years. The major limitations of this method of assessing capital investments are that it gives no indication of the total return that a machine brings in over its entire life span, ignores the cost of making the investment, and does not tell whether investment in other assets (for instance, in inventory) might not produce a higher return. For various methods of evaluating the profitability of proposed equipment purchases, see C. Aubrey Smith and Jim Ashburne, *Financial and Administrative Accounting*, McGraw-Hill Book Company, New York, 1960; see also George Terborgh, *Business Investment Policy*, Machinery and Allied Products Institute, Washington, D.C., 1958.

Payroll Tax A tax levied on the payroll of a firm. It is based on the amount of wages and salaries of the firm and is paid by the employer. Payroll taxes are used in the U.S. to finance the employer's part of the social security programs. Whereas all employers pay the same rate of payroll tax for the old age, survivors, and disability insurance programs, different firms may pay different rates of payroll tax for their unemployment insurance. Although the social security payroll tax cannot be deducted from wages, the final burden of the tax is generally believed to be borne largely by the employee and by the consumer. For further information on payroll taxes in the U.S., see J. E. Hughes, *Federal Payroll Tax*, Flood Co., Chicago, 1946; J. K. Hall, "Incidence of Federal Social

Security Payroll Taxes," *Quarterly Journal of Economics, Harvard* University Press, Cambridge, Mass., 1938; Ralph Compton, *The Social Security Payroll Taxes,* Commerce Clearing House, Inc., New York, 1940.

Peak   The high mark of the expansionary phase of economic activity. It is usually a short interval lasting for one or two months. According to the National Bureau of Economic Research, in the five recoveries from recessions, the peaks were November, 1948; July, 1953; July, 1957; May, 1960; and November, 1969. For more detailed information on peaks, see Geoffrey H. Moore (ed.), *Business Cycle Indicators,* Princeton University Press, Princeton, N.J., 1961.

Pegging   In finance, the fixing of the price of a security or securities. The most recent example of pegging in the U.S. occurred during World War II. To finance the war, the Treasury, over the Federal Reserve System's protests, decided to adopt a cheap-money policy. Forced to carry out this plan, the Federal Reserve announced in April, 1942, that it would buy or sell unlimited amounts of treasury bills at ⅜ of 1%. This effectively pegged the short-term government securities market because no one would pay more or take less for bills, which they could always buy or sell at a member bank of the System for a fixed price. The Treasury was assured of obtaining all the funds that it needed at low interest rates. The Federal Reserve authorities went further and pegged the entire government securities market (2.5% of government bonds) for the duration of the war. In July, 1947, the System began to remove the peg by ceasing to maintain the treasury bill rate. At first, the Treasury and Federal Reserve authorities agreed on policy, but eventually a conflict arose because the Federal Reserve, fearing inflation, wanted to tighten money while the Treasury wanted to maintain an easy-money policy. The conflict was finally resolved in the accord of March, 1951. See Henry C. Murphy, *The National Debt in War and Transition,* McGraw-Hill Book Company, New York, 1950; Paul Studenski and Herman E. Krooss, *The Financial History of the United States,* 3d ed., McGraw-Hill Book Company, New York, 1963.

Penny Stock   A common stock that is traded at prices of less than $1. Because virtually all such stocks are highly speculative, the term penny stock is often used to disparage any stock that is speculative or of dubious investment value.

People's Capitalism   A type of capitalism in which the ownership of industry is shared by a large part of the population, including middle- and lower-income groups. The phrase is frequently used to describe the

U.S. of the mid-twentieth century, in which stock ownership is widespread, and to contrast it with the U.S. of the late nineteenth century, when most big businesses were owned by a few wealthy individuals. For a discussion of people's capitalism in the U.S., see Marcus Nadler, *People's Capitalism*, Manufacturers Hanover Trust Company, New York, 1956; for a critique of the view that stock ownership has become more widespread in the U.S., see Victor Perlo, "People's Capitalism and Stock Ownership," *American Economic Review*, p. 333, American Economic Association, Evanston, Ill., June, 1958.

Percentage Depletion   *See Depletion Allowance.*

Performance Budgeting   A method of preparing a governmental budget in which items appearing in the budget represent functions to be performed or activities to be undertaken. Under other budgeting methods, proposed expenditures for particular functions tend to become scattered under various titles, making it difficult to control expenditures. The performance budget seeks to reach a reasonable compromise between general appropriations, which give an agency freedom to allocate funds to specific projects, and appropriations that are so specific as to prevent adjustment to changing conditions. The performance-budgeting method was recommended by the Hoover Commission. See *Budgeting and Accounting*, a report to the Congress by the Commission on Organization of the Executive Branch of Government, February, 1949, pp. 7–13 and annex I.

Peril Point   The maximum cut in a U.S. import duty which could be made for a given commodity without causing serious injury to domestic producers or to a similar commodity. First included in the Trade Agreements Extension Act of 1948, the peril-point mechanism was in effect almost continuously until it was eliminated in the Trade Expansion Act of 1962. The peril-point provision stated that, before entering into any tariff discussions with other countries, the President must submit to the Tariff Commission a list of the commodities to be negotiated. The Commission would then conduct an investigation on the effect of tariff reduction on these commodities, determine the respective peril points, and present a list of recommendations to the President. If in the subsequent trade agreement, the President did not follow the Tariff Commission's peril-point recommendations, he was obligated to send Congress a message stating the reasons for his action. The threat of a congressional investigation usually was effective in inducing the negotiators to follow the advice of the Tariff Commission on peril points. The inclusion of the peril-point provision in tariff legislation was a victory for protectionist interests because it sought to prevent concessions which would really liberalize trade. For additional details, see Don D. Humphrey, *American Imports,* The Twentieth Century Fund, New York, 1955.

Periodogram A chart with time on the horizontal axis and a composite series on the vertical axis. This chart is expected to reveal turning points in a time series that can be related to one or more statistically consistent causal factors or sources of variation. The technique works fairly well if the series under study consists of periodic, trigonometric terms and a random component. It works poorly or not at all for economic time series that are autoregressive and stochastic and where little or nothing is known about the time cycles of the causal factors or sources of variation. For a detailed discussion and the necessary formulas, consult Stefan Valavanis, *Econometrics,* McGraw-Hill Book Company, New York, 1959.

Permanent Consumption *See Permanent-Income Hypothesis.*

Permanent Income *See Permanent-Income Hypothesis.*

Permanent-Income Hypothesis A theory of the income concept most relevant for determining consumption. The permanent-income hypothesis has been highly regarded by economists because it helps explain apparent inconsistencies of empirical data on the relationship of saving to income. Cross-section data for a single year show that as income rises, savings account for an increasing share of income, while data for a long period of years show that even though total income rises over the years, total savings account for a fairly stable share of total income. Milton Friedman states that this occurs because a study of measured income and consumption involves inaccurate concepts of what income and consumption really are. For example, there are actually two types of income—permanent and transitory. Permanent income is the amount which a consumer unit expects to receive over a long period of time and to which it adjusts its permanent consumption—a certain fraction of permanent income which does not depend on the permanent-income level but on factors affecting the unit's desire for current consumption versus the accumulation of assets. Transitory income is that amount which a consumer unit receives unexpectedly. When transitory income differs from permanent income, the consumer unit saves or dissaves the difference between the two concepts (consumer durables, according to Friedman, are savings and not consumption). Thus planned or permanent savings differ from measured savings, and increases and decreases in transitory consumption cause permanent consumption to differ from measured consumption. For this reason, annual data give a distorted picture of consumer behavior. Friedman indicates that the factors affecting the ratio of permanent consumption to permanent income are more significant than levels of income in analyzing consumer behavior. See Milton Friedman, *A Theory of the Consumption Function,* National Bureau of Economic Research, Inc., New York, Princeton University Press, Princeton, N.J., 1957, for a detailed discussion of the permanent-income and permanent-consumption hypothesis. The role of permanent consumption and permanent income among the many other theories affecting consumption is placed in perspective by Robert Ferber, "Research on Household Behavior," *American Economic Review,* vol. LII, no. 1, pp. 19–63, American Economic Association, Evanston, Ill., March, 1962.

Permanent Saving   *See Permanent-Income Hypothesis.*

Personal Finance Company   *See Consumer Finance Company.*

Personal Income   According to the concept of the U.S. Department of Commerce, the amount of current income received by persons from all sources, including transfer payments from government and business but excluding transfer payments from other sources. Personal income also includes the net incomes of unincorporated businesses and nonprofit institutions and nonmonetary income, such as the estimate of the value of food consumed on farms and the estimated rental value of homes occupied by their owners. The major monetary components of personal income are labor income, proprietors' income, rental income, dividends, interest, and transfer payments. Personal income is a measure of income before taxes have been deducted. The statistical series on personal income is a useful indicator of general trends, although the inclusion of nonmonetary income and of the income of unincorporated businesses and nonprofit institutions makes it difficult to tell how much income actually is received by consumers only. The personal income figures are the only U.S. income and product data currently estimated on a monthly basis. For monthly estimates of personal income, see U.S. Department of Commerce, *Survey of Current Business;* for further information, see Daniel Creamer, *Personal Income during Business Cycles,* National Bureau of Economic Research, Inc., Princeton University Press, Princeton, N.J., 1956; U.S. Department of Commerce, *Personal Income by States Since 1929,* A Supplement to the Survey of Current Business, U.S. Government Printing Office, Washington, D.C.

Personal Outlays   The disbursements made by individuals of that portion of personal income available after payment of personal taxes. It is composed of personal consumption expenses for goods and services,

Total Personal Income (Billions of dollars)

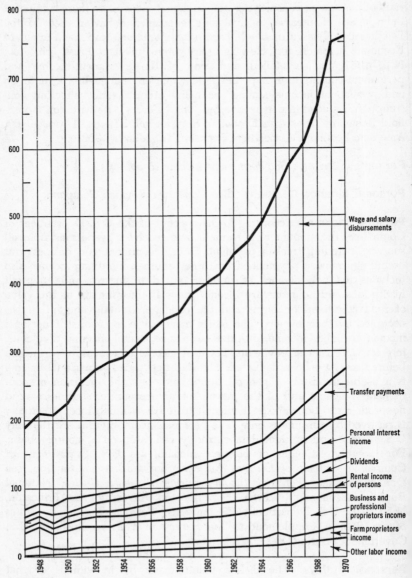

Source: U.S. Department of Commerce.

interest paid by consumers, and personal transfer payments. For quarterly and annual data, see U.S. Department of Commerce, *Survey of Current Business*, monthly.

Personal Property Tax   A levy on the personal property of an individual. Personal property should not be confused with real property, or real estate, which consists of land and improvements. It includes all other possessions of an individual or firm and can be divided into two categories: tangible personal property, which consists of furniture, jewelry, merchandise, etc.; and intangibles, such as stocks, bonds, and money. A few states of the U.S. tax both tangible and intangible personal property, while many tax only tangible property. Some states, such as New York, do not tax personal property at all. Numerous municipalities also resort to personal property taxation, which supplies a substantial part of the tax base (sometimes as much as 15 to 20%). A personal property tax involves many problems of administration, especially those of valuation and evasion. Furthermore, as applied to businesses, the personal property tax discriminates against the merchant with a slow turnover and favors the chain store over the independent retailer. For additional details, see "Interim Report of the Committee on Personal Property Taxation in the Taxation of Tangible Personal Property Used in Business," *Proceedings of the National Tax Association Conference*, National Tax Association, Boston, 1952, pp. 76–106; "Improvements in Personal Property Tax Administration," *Property Taxes: A Symposium*, Tax Policy League, New York, 1940, chap. 16.

PERT/CPM   A method of planning and scheduling the interrelated activities of a major project to meet optimum cost and time criteria. It involves the use of network diagrams which indicate the relationship between the various component activities of the overall project. These relationships include the time each phase of the project is expected to take, the costs involved with these time factors, and the resultant time and cost expected for the entire project. A simple PERT network is shown below. The network shows that events 2 and 3 are independent, but that event 4 depends on the completion of both events 2 and 3. The times shown between each event are the most likely times for these activities as evaluated by the project planner. A more sophisticated analysis assigns probabilities to the most likely time, the earliest time, and the longest time possible for each phase of the project. The longest path network, i.e., that path identified with the longest time period for completion, defines the expected time for the entire project. This longest path is called the critical path. In the network below, path 1-3-4-5 defines the critical path, and its time is seven weeks. PERT/CPM scheduling allows planners and project managers to identify "slack times" within the network. Slack time is the amount of time which any phase of the project can be delayed without delaying the overall completion schedule. For example, path 1-2-4 yields one week of slack time since path 1-3-4 is expected to take five weeks, while 1-2-4 should take four weeks. Since both paths must be completed before the final activity 4-5 is started, one week of slack is available. The identification of slack allows project managers to delay the activities associated with slack times and shift resources to other phases of the entire project. The use of PERT programs allows planners and managers to quantify their schedule times and costs at each stage of a project and to adjust to contingencies that may arise.

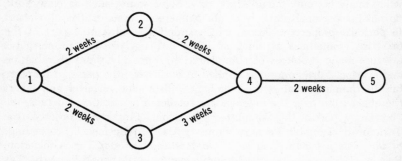

Phase 1   *See New Economic Program, Phase 1.*

Phase 2   *See New Economic Program, Phase 2.*

Phillips Curve   A hypothesis advanced by A. W. Phillips stating originally that, assuming a given annual increase in productivity, the percentage rate of the change of money wage rates in the United Kingdom can be explained to a very large extent by (1) the percentage of the labor force that is unemployed and (2) the rate of change of unemployment. He further concluded that not only is there a clearly observable relationship between these variables, but also the form of the relationship has been remarkably stable over a period of almost one hundred years (1861 to 1957). Samuelson and Solow conducted a similar study using U.S. data. The results, while not contradictory, are not as clear-cut as those obtained by Phillips. Richard J. Lipsey has also questioned the findings of Phillips and has suggested that the relationship does not hold over the entire period in question, but can be relevant for shorter periods of time. For further details, see A. W. Phillips, "The Relationship between Unemployment and the Rate of Change of Money Wage Rates in the United Kingdom, 1861–1957," *Economica*, vol. 25, pp. 283–299, November, 1958; Paul A. Samuelson and R. M. Solow, "Analytical Aspects of Anti-inflationary Policy," *American Economic Review, Papers and Proceedings,* vol. 50, no. 2, pp. 177–194, May, 1960; Richard J. Lipsey, "The Relations between Unemployment and the Rate of Change of Money Wage Rates in the United Kingdom, 1862–1957: A Further Analysis," *Economica,* vol. 27, pp. 1–31, February, 1960. For a summary analysis, see Michael K. Evans, *Macroeconomic Activity,* Harper & Row, Publishers, Incorporated, New York, 1969. The use of the Phillips curve in national decision making is indicated in "GOP Is Thrown a Price Job Curve," *Business Week,* March 22, 1969, p. 60.

Physical Market   *See Spot Market.*

Physiocrat   A member of a school of French economists of the mid-eighteenth century. Based largely on the idea of François Quesnay and Anne Robert Jacques Turgot, the physiocratic philosophy had as its central tenet an overriding belief in land as the single source of income and wealth. Land alone, the physiocrats held, has the power to produce an output in excess of the materials used up in the productive process. In contrast to the working of the land, which produces this *produit net* (net product), manufacturing and commercial activities, the physiocrats thought, are sterile, yielding no excess over the quantity of materials that they receive as inputs. Physiocratic doctrines thus contrasted sharply with those of the mercantilists, who stressed the importance of trade and commerce as the source of a nation's wealth. In addition, the physiocrats adhered to a firm belief in natural law (laissez faire, or freedom from government regulation) as the best possible means of regulating human affairs. The physiocrats classified society into four groups: (1) the "productive" class, or agriculturists; (2) the proprietors, or landowners; (3) the nonproductive class (*la classe sterile*), which included merchants, artisans, and professional men; and (4) wage earners or laborers. In their opinion, the first three classes are independent and play an active part in the national economy since they are in possession of some capital and also exercise some enterprise. The fourth class is dependent and passive and only a minor factor in their classification. Adam Smith, during a journey to France, came under the influence of physiocratic doctrines in the course of discussions with Quesnay and other members of the school. Among the leading spokesmen of the school was a member of the French government, Pierre Samuel du Pont de Nemours, who later went to the U.S. and laid the foundations for the vast E. I. du Pont de Nemours interests. For further discussion of the physiocrats, see Alexander Gray, *The Development of Economic Doctrine,* John Wiley & Sons, Inc., New York, 1931; Joseph A. Schumpeter, *History of Economic Analysis,*

Oxford University Press, Fair Lawn, N.J., 1954, chap. 4; see also Frank Amandus Neff, *Economic Doctrines*, McGraw-Hill Book Company, New York, 1950, chap. 5; G. R. Madan and H. S. Dhooria, *The History and Development of Economic Thought*, S. Chand & Company, Ram Nagar, New Delhi, 1963, chap. 4.

Piece Wage Rate   Compensation of an employee that is based on his productive output. Under a piece wage rate, a worker is not paid a fixed sum per hour or per week, as is the case for a time wage rate, but is compensated by a varying amount, depending on the quantity of goods that he produces. Also known as an incentive wage structure, piece wage rates are usually stated in terms of money per unit produced. They utilize definite production standards, determined by time and motion studies, and correlate earnings with productive performance in terms of such standards. While piece rates usually include a floor below which the hourly earnings of a worker may not fall, a ceiling is never imposed on the earnings of employees. Production above the established standard may be compensated by a bonus rate, providing additional incentives for efficient production on the part of individual employees. For additional details, see J. K. Louden, *Wage Incentives*, John Wiley & Sons, Inc., New York, 1944; C. W. Lytle, *Wage Incentives Methods*, The Ronald Press Company, New York, 1942.

Pigou-Effect Theory   The theory that a reduction in the overall price level leads to increased spending on goods and services. It is based on the following line of reasoning: (1) Individuals establish a desired relationship between the money balances that they hold and their expenditures on goods and services. (2) Price reductions raise the real value of their money holdings; that is, the quantity of goods and services that can be bought with a given amount of money is increased. (3) Thus, the desired relationship between real balances and expenditures is disturbed, and individuals have an excess supply of liquid assets. (4) They spend part of this excess supply on goods and services. The Pigou effect operates only in the market for goods and services; in this respect, it differs from the Keynes effect, which operates only in the market for bonds, and from the real-balance effect, which operates in both the bond market and the market for goods and services. For the original statement of the Pigou effect, see Arthur C. Pigou, *Lapses from Full Employment*, St. Martin's Press, Inc., New York, 1945; see also Gottfried Haberler, "The Pigou Effect Once More," *Journal of Political Economy*, p. 240, The University of Chicago Press, Chicago, June, 1952; Don Patinkin, *Money, Interest and Prices*, 2d ed., Harper & Row, Publishers, Incorporated, New York, 1961; for a critique of the Pigou effect, see M.

Kalecki, "Professor Pigou on the 'Classical Stationary State,'" *Economic Journal,* Royal Economic Society, London, 1952.

Pit (Trading Ring) One of the many designated places on the floor of a commodity exchange in which buy and sell orders are executed. At the Chicago Board of Trade, the oldest and largest commodity exchange in the U.S., the pits are octagonal in shape and consist of a series of steps. The traders and brokers stand on the steps facing one another as they buy and sell commodity futures.

Planned Economy An economic system in which some or all of the decisions on allocation, production, investment, and distribution are made by a central governmental agency. The collective economic planning used in a planned economy is based on the assumption that social welfare can be recognized and pursued more ably under centralized control. The assumption denies the advantages of private enterprise, which is said to lead to chaotic disharmony between production and consumption. In a planned economy, the initiative for economic activities and decisions concerning them does not originate with the entrepreneur. Rather, the government starts with an overall plan of major objectives and then attempts to achieve the fullest possible utilization of available resources in line with the stated objectives. In a completely planned economy, the market mechanism in price formation is eliminated, and the government undertakes to replace the market functions. The planning agency sets all the goals for production, allocates scarce resources among competing uses, makes decisions on production and investment, and distributes the output to consumers. Because of this, the planned economy claims to achieve maximum social welfare. Examples of planned economies are those found in the U.S.S.R., France, Yugoslavia, and Poland. For further information, see C. Landauer, *The Theory of National Economic Planning,* 2d ed., University of California Press, Berkeley, Calif., 1947; Seymour E. Harris, *Economic Planning,* Alfred A. Knopf, Inc., New York, 1949; J. E. Meade, *Planning and the Price Mechanism: The Liberal-Socialist Solution,* The Macmillan Company, New York, 1948; for a description and analysis of planned economies in operation, see Malcolm Maclennan, Murray Forsyth, and Geoffrey Denton, *Economic Planning and Policies in Britain, France and Germany,* Frederick A. Praeger, Inc., New York, 1968.

Planned Obsolescence Yearly or other periodic changes in the styling or design of products that induce consumers to buy new items before old ones have been worn out. In the U.S., there are many examples of planned obsolescence. Among the most clear-cut are annual changes in automobile models that involve little more than adding or subtracting decorative chromium and changes in clothing fashions, such as the raising and lowering of hemlines. Critics of planned obsolescence state that it is wasteful, particularly of natural resources (see, for example, Vance Packard, *The Waste Makers*, David McKay Company, Inc., New York, 1960). Others state that it satisfies the demand of consumers for newness and helps maintain prosperity in free-enterprise economies (see, for example, Steuart H. Britt, *The Spenders*, McGraw-Hill Book Company, New York, 1960). The phrase planned obsolescence is used occasionally to include so-called built-in obsolescence, which involves deliberately shoddy workmanship intended to produce an unnecessarily short life span and premature replacement.

Planning, Programming, and Budgetary System (PPB) A system to achieve long-term goals or objectives by means of analysis and evaluation of the alternatives. PPB is designed to solve problems by finding the most effective and most efficient solution on the basis of objective criteria. In the 1950s the RAND Corporation and others applied PPB to defense problems. In 1961 it was first used by the Department of Defense. In 1965 all major civilian agencies of the Federal government were directed to install PPB. For additional information, see Allen Schick, "The Road to PPB: The Stages of Budget Reform," *Public Administration Review*, vol. XXVI, no. 4, December, 1966; Charles L. Schultz, *The Politics and Economics of Public Spending*, The Brookings Institution, Washington, D.C., 1968.

Plant Capital asset units, such as factory buildings, warehouses, stores, and other commercial buildings. Spending for plants accounted for roughly 25% of total capital expenditures by U.S. manufacturers in the 1950s. In the 1960s, the percentage was lower because of a lack of emphasis on the expansion of capacity. For estimates of annual expenditures on plants, see *Annual Surveys of Business' Plans for New Plants and Equipment*, McGraw-Hill Department of Economics, New York.

Point Four Program A U.S. program of technical assistance to underdeveloped countries. It was launched by President Harry S Truman in his inaugural address of January 20, 1949, when he said, "Fourth, we must embark on a bold new program for making the benefits of our scientific advances and industrial progress available for the improvement and growth of underdeveloped areas." The Point Four program (so named because it was the fourth point in Truman's speech) was enacted into law as part of the Foreign Economic Assistance Act of 1950. Its major objective was to raise the average standard of living in the underdeveloped countries by providing U.S. technical assistance and know-how. Technical assistance involved studying the economic development problems of the individual countries, furnishing advisers and technicians to both public and private organizations for development projects, cooperating financially and administratively in government development programs, and sending teachers to provide technical training. The Point Four program was far less costly to the U.S. than the Marshall Plan. For further information, see U.S. Department of State, *Point Four*, 1950; see also William Adams Brown, Jr., and Redverse Opie, *American Foreign Assistance*, The Brookings Institution, Washington, D.C., 1953.

Poll Tax (Head Tax)   A direct tax of a fixed sum that is levied on individuals. Exemptions are sometimes made because of sex or age, as, for example, when women or persons over the age of 65 are exempted. Because the amount of the poll tax is fixed and is generally the same for all persons, there are no problems of computation, and the tax can thus be used in underdeveloped countries to tax a largely illiterate population whose income may be mostly nonmonetary. Since a poll tax taxes a larger percentage of the income of poor persons than of rich persons, it is considered regressive. Developed countries occasionally use the poll tax for nonrevenue purposes. An outstanding example of this is found in some Southern states of the U.S., where, since payment of the tax is required before one can vote, it has been used to prevent poor Negroes from voting. As of 1962, however, only five Southern states—Alabama, Arkansas, Mississippi, Texas, and Virginia—still levied poll taxes as a prerequisite to voting. In only two of these states, Alabama and Mississippi, was the poll tax generally considered a major deterrent to Negro voting. In 1962 the Congress of the U.S. approved a constitutional amendment that outlawed the poll tax as a requirement for voting in Federal elections. The amendment became effective on February 4, 1964, after it had been approved by the legislature of three-fourths of the states.

Pool   A temporary association of two or more persons who act as a group to manipulate the stock market. Because securities trading is regulated, the pool has become virtually extinct. In the U.S., pools enjoyed their heyday in the 1920s. Pool agreements ranged from simple, oral understandings to detailed, written contracts. Two basic types of pools were used—option pools and trading pools. In an option pool, the operators secured options, or calls to buy stock; then, by various techniques, they pushed the price of the stock upward as far as they could. When they thought that the price was high enough, they exercised their options, sold the stock, and frequently made huge profits. Most trading pools proceeded through four stages to the goal of profits: accumulation, shake-out, markup, and distribution. By secret and discreet purchases that would not force the price up, the pool accumulated as much stock as it could. Usually, some persons detected the operation of the pool and bought stock so that they also could profit. Fearing that this development might damage the operation, the pool got rid of these traders by shaking them out; that is, they violently knocked the stock's price down by selling, which forced "weak" holders to sell because they lacked adequate margin. The pool could then reaccumulate the stock that it had sold. Next, it marked up the stock's price, that is, forced the price up sharply and quickly. There were many types of markup. The pool might recklessly bid up the price, perhaps by buying additional stock, or it might tout the stock by various means, such as hiring journalists, radio announcers, or market-letter writers to spread rumors and tips. If the markup worked, the pool began to distribute its holdings (sell the stock slowly so that it would not drive the price down too quickly) when the price was as high as the pool thought it would go. Since the pool's manipulations had pushed the price up to an untenable level, the price invariably plummeted when the distribution phase was over. The public, which had bought the stock at high prices, was the loser. The term also refers to a group of firms acting together to set or fix the price of a product. In this case, a separate selling agency may be established for the purpose of acting as a representative of the pool. See George L. Leffler and L. C. Farwell, *The Stock Market*, The Ronald Press Company, New York, 1963; Alfred L. Bernheim, *The Security Markets*, The Twentieth Century Fund, New York, 1935.

Population Explosion A rapid upsurge in population. Discoveries which have reduced mortality rates are the main contributors to the population explosion. As more of these discoveries combat disease and death, population growth will accelerate. Formerly, the population trend was determined wholly by the balance between the forces of fertility and mortality, but since the forces of mortality are being greatly reduced, it appears that, in the long run, control of fertility alone can prevent disaster in the shape of famine. The problem is particularly acute in underdeveloped areas in which new medical discoveries are just being introduced. For further information, see J. O. Hertzler, *The Crisis in World Population*, University of Nebraska Press, Lincoln, Nebr., 1956; Warren S. Thompson, *Population Problems*, 8th ed., McGraw-Hill Book Company, New York, 1961.

Populism A socialistic movement to improve the living conditions of peasants. Populism was a type of agrarian utopian socialism founded in Russia by Aleksander Herzen and Nikolai Chernyshevski in the mid-

World Population (Billions)

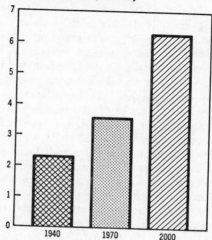

Source: Population Reference Bureau, Inc.

nineteenth century. The Populist program, which was strong in Russia until the rise of the Bolsheviks, encompassed a demand for more land and liberty for the peasants and a plea for the equal distribution of land among them. The Populists rejected the Marxist belief that capitalism is an inevitable stage on the road to a socialistic society. They held that utilization of the peasant commune made capitalism necessary to agrarian Russia. For further information, see Carl Landauer, *Contemporary Economic Systems*, J. B. Lippincott Company, Philadelphia, 1964.

Pork-Barrel Legislation   The appropriation of money by a legislature for local projects that are not critically needed. Pork-barrel projects, such as local highways, hospitals, and river and harbor construction projects, are sought by individual legislators for their districts as a means of demonstrating their service to the voters in their constituencies and of thus improving their chances of reelection. Much of the pork-barrel legislation is enacted through a system of logrolling under which the legislators do not question each other's pet local projects in order to ensure that their own projects will be approved. For additional details on the causes and mechanics of pork-barrel legislation, see W. Riker, *Democracy in the United States*, The Macmillan Company, New York, 1953.

Portal-to-Portal Pay   Payment of wages from the time that certain workers enter the door of an establishment to begin work until they pass through the door after they stop work. In mining and in certain other industries, substantial periods of time are devoted to the preliminary and subsequent activities connected with a job, such as the putting on and taking off of protective clothing or the traveling down and up a mine shaft to and from the vein being worked. Proponents of portal-to-portal pay insist that the worker should be paid for the time involved in necessary activities before or after actual on-the-job time on the ground that otherwise the work could not be done, but it is questionable if time so spent should be considered part of regular working time in the computation of wages. Section 3(o) of the Fair Labor Standards Act of 1938 excludes from working time the time spent at the beginning or end of the day in washing up or changing clothes, provided that these activities are not covered in the provisions of a contract or by custom and practice under a bona fide collective bargaining agreement. The Portal to Portal Act of 1947 also excludes from working time traveling time and other preliminary and subsequent activities, provided that these activities are not compensable by contract, custom, or practice. A statement of the meaning of the term can be found in U.S. Code, title 29; see also Fair Labor Standards Act of 1938.

Port of Entry   Any place at which imported merchandise or individuals can enter a country. Hence, in the U.S., customs officers, who are authorized to collect duties, taxes, or fees, are stationed at all ports of entry. New York, Baltimore, Boston, Los Angeles, and San Francisco are leading ports of entry into the U.S.

Port of Exit   Any place from which exported merchandise or individuals can leave a country. New York, Baltimore, Boston, Los Angeles, and San Francisco are leading ports of exit from the U.S.

Potential Gross National Product (Full-Employment Output)   The output that the economy can produce under full-employment conditions. Potential GNP is maximum production without inflationary pressures. It is an imprecise measure of productive capacity, using a 4% unemployment rate as the criterion for full employment. Some economists doubt that potential GNP can be measured at all. When the Council of Economic Advisers prepared estimates of potential GNP at the end of 1961, using a 3.5% growth rate and mid-1955 as the bench mark (the unemployment rate was then about 4%), the potential GNP for 1960 (in 1961 prices) was placed at $543 billion, compared with an actual GNP of $511 billion. In refuting the notion of a gap or the size of the gap, Arthur F. Burns obtained quite different results by using as bench marks the second quarter of 1957 and the second quarter of 1947 (the unemployment rate was then also about 4%). He showed that potential GNP would be about $531 billion when he used the second quarter of 1957 as the bench mark and a 3.5% growth rate, but when he used the second quarter of 1947 as the bench mark and a 3.5% growth rate, he found that the gap vanished and that potential output in 1960 would have been $509 billion, or $2 billion less than the actual GNP. Another method of computing potential GNP is offered by Arthur M. Okun, a former chairman of the Council of Eco-

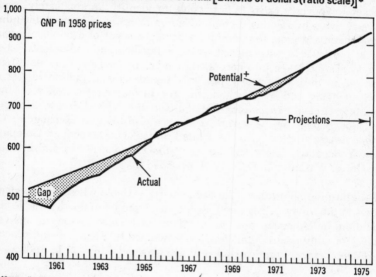

Gross National Product, Actual and Potential [Billions of dollars(ratio scale)]*

*Seasonally adjusted annual rates.

+Trend line of 3.5 percent from middle of 1955 to 1962 IV, 3.75 percent from 1962 IV to 1965 IV, 4 percent from 1965 IV to 1969 IV, 4.3 percent from 1969 IV to 1970 IV, 4.4 percent from 1970 IV to 1971 IV, and 4.3 percent from 1971 IV to 1975 IV.

Source: U.S. Department of Commerce and Council of Economic Advisers.

nomic Advisers, who measures the extent to which output is depressed by unemployment in excess of 4%. This relationship can be stated as follows: "On the average, each extra percentage point in the unemployment rate above 4% has been associated with about a 3% decrease in real GNP." For further discussion of the potential GNP, see *Economic Report of the President,* Government Printing Office, Washington, D.C., 1962, pp. 49–53; for Arthur F. Burns's position, see *The Morgan Guaranty Survey,* Morgan Guaranty Trust Company, New York, May, 1961; for the Council of Economic Advisers' reply to Burns and Burns's comments on the council's reply, see *The Morgan Guaranty Survey,* Morgan Guaranty Trust Company, New York, August, 1961; see also Arthur M. Okun, "Potential GNP: Its Measurement and Significance," *Proceedings of the Business and Economic Statistics Section,* American Statistical Association, Washington, D.C., 1962, pp. 98–104.

Poverty   A condition in which income is insufficient to meet subsistence needs. Thus, levels of living may be considerably lower than those that are deemed adequate standards of living. Despite gains in levels of living in the U.S. since World War I, there is still considerable inequality in the distribution of income and wealth, particularly in some areas, in which pockets of poverty exist. It is possible to identify approximately where poverty exists by relating a comprehensive measure of income, including nonmonetary income, to the estimated budget needs of a family. In some cases, particularly with regard to older families and individuals, assets should also be taken into account in studies of poverty. It is almost impossible to measure poverty precisely because the definition hinges on varying living and social standards. For further information see James N. Morgan et al., *Income and Welfare in the United States,* McGraw-Hill Book Company, New York, 1962; see also Michael Harrington, *The Other America: Poverty in the United States,* The Macmillan Company, New York, 1962; *Economic Report of the President,* Government Printing Office, Washington, D.C., 1964, pp. 55–84.

Predetermined Variable   An econometric variable whose values at any point in time may be regarded as known. A predetermined variable may therefore be either an exogenous variable or a lagged endogeneous variable. For additional information, see Lawrence R. Klein, *An Introduction to Econometrics,* Prentice-Hall, Inc., Englewood Cliffs, N.J., 1962.

Preemptive Right   The right of stockholders, under common law, to maintain their proportionate control of and equity in a corporation if and when the corporation issues additional stock. In practice, this usually means that a corporation must give its shareholders rights to subscribe to a new stock issue in proportion to their previous holdings. Thus, if a stockholder owned 10% of a corporation's outstanding stock, he would be entitled to subscribe to 10% of a new issue. In the U.S., many state corporation laws prescribe the nature of preemptive rights, and most states allow corporate charters to deny these rights to stockholders. For further information, see Jules I. Bogen (ed.), *Financial Handbook,* 4th ed., The Ronald Press Company, New York, 1968; Charles W. Gerstenberg, *Financial Organization and Management of Business,* 4th ed., Prentice-Hall, Inc., Englewood Cliffs, N.J., 1959.

Preferential Shop   A plant or establishment in which the employer must give preference to union members in hiring workers. Some contracts provide that if no union members are available within a specified period, usually twenty-four hours, the employer may hire nonunion workers. This provision was developed in the garment industry to protect manufacturers against shortages of union labor at peak seasonal periods. The preferential shop never achieved a dominant place in union-security arrangements and is now used infrequently. See Joseph Shister, *Economics of the Labor Market*, 2d ed., J. B. Lippincott Company, Philadelphia, 1956; Melvin W. Reder, *Labor in a Growing Economy*, John Wiley & Sons, Inc., New York, 1957.

Preferred Operating Rate   The percentage of its productive capacity that a firm or an industry believes to be most profitable. The industrial rate preferred, on the average, in the U.S. in 1970 was 93%. If a company

Preferred Operating Rate, December, 1969

Industry	Preferred Rate, %
Iron and steel	NA *
Nonferrous metals	98
Electrical machinery	91
Machinery	94
Autos, trucks, and parts	87
Aerospace	93
Other transportation equipment	91
Fabricated metals	87
Instruments	92
Stone, clay, and glass	92
Other durables	92
Total durables	92
Chemicals	91
Paper and pulp	98
Rubber	95
Petroleum	98
Food and beverages	94
Textiles	95
Other nondurables	97
Total nondurables	96
All manufacturing	93
Mining	99
Electric utilities	89
Gas utilities	93
All industry	93

* Not available.
SOURCE: *23rd Annual Survey of Business' Plans for New Plant and Equipment*, McGraw-Hill Department of Economics, New York.

operates above its preferred rate, it may be using obsolete facilities and incurring excessive costs. If it operates below its preferred rate, some efficient capacity remains idle. Statistics on preferred operating rates are collected by the McGraw-Hill Departmen of Economics. See *Annual Surveys of Business' Plans fo New Plants nd Equipment,* McGraw-Hill Department of Economics, New York.

Preferred Stock Capital stock issued by a corporation which has preference over the common stock of the corporation in respect to the payment of dividends. This preference means that before any dividends can be paid to the common shareholders, the preferred shareholders must be paid a stipulated amount of money. Furthermore, in the event of dissolution, reorganization, or bankruptcy, the preferred stockholders usually have priority over the common stockholders in the distribution of the corporation's assets. Since the preferred stockholder is an owner and not a creditor of the corporation, however, his claim to assets must wait until the claims of the bondholders and other creditors have been met. Preferred stock is less speculative than common stock of the same corporation, but it is more speculative than the corporation's bonds; typically, this fact is reflected in its yield. Preferred stock can be cumulative, which means that all dividends due preferred stockholders from past years must be paid in full before a dividend can be declared to the common stockholders. Noncumulative stock does not offer this provision. For further information, see Jules I. Bogen (ed.), *Financial Handbook,* 4th ed., The Ronald Press Company, New York, 1968; Joseph H. Bonneville et al., *Organizing and Financing Business,* Prentice-Hall, Inc., Englewood Cliffs, N.J., 1959.

Price Control Government regulation of the prices of goods and services designed to prevent the cost of living from spiraling upward. Price controls are usually imposed during a war, but they have been imposed in peacetime in countries in which inflationary pressures have accumulated. The prices of goods and services at all distribution levels are fixed generally at the highest levels prevailing for some stated period, usually immediately before the date of the announced control. Transactions at prices higher than those that have been established are prohibited by law unless they have been demonstrated to be necessary. Prices were frozen for ninety days on August 15, 1971, in order to halt inflation. After November 13, 1971, the Price Commission attempted to hold price increases to no more than 2½% per year. During World War I, the U.S. price-control program was less general than during World War II. The General Maximum Price Regulation of April 28, 1942, froze the prices of goods and services at the highest price prevailing during March, 1942, at the specific selling unit. Thus, different stores of the same chain could charge different prices if they had done so in March, 1942. See Julius Hirsch, *Price Control in the War Economy,* Harper & Row, Publishers, Incorporated, New York, 1943.

Price Discrimination   The charging of different prices to different buyers for the same good. Price discrimination can occur only when the seller has a degree of monopoly power and when his market is divided into segments with which he can deal separately. Customers are charged as much as they are willing to pay. Price discrimination generally produces greater profits for the monopolistic seller, but it can also have some beneficial value if it results in a reduction of costs. The Clayton Antitrust Act of 1914 made it illegal in the U.S. "to discriminate in price between different purchasers of commodities . . . where the effect of such discrimination may be to substantially lessen competition or tend to create a monopoly in any line of commerce." This provision was strengthened in 1936 by the Robinson-Patman Act, which authorized additional controls on price discrimination resulting from large market power. For additional details, see Corwin Edwards, *The Price Discrimination Law,* The Brookings Institution, Washington, D.C., 1959; Joel Dean, *Managerial Economics,* Prentice-Hall, Inc., Englewood Cliffs, N.J., 1951; Joel Dirlam and Alfred Kahn, *Fair Competition,* Cornell University Press, Ithaca, N.Y., 1954.

Price-Earnings Ratio   The current market price of a company's stock expressed as a multiple of the company's per-share earnings. It is computed by dividing the annual per-share earnings of a company into the market value of its stock. For example, if company A's stock is selling at $100 per share and the company earned $5 per share, the price-earnings ratio is 20. The price-earnings ratio is a highly regarded measure of stock value because it gives a good indication of corporate success as measured against the price of the stock. Stockholders buy stocks with high price-earnings ratios (generally growth stocks) because they anticipate higher earnings and dividends in the future. Investors interested in stable income are more apt to invest in stocks with lower price-earnings ratios and steady dividend records. For further information, see Benjamin Graham et al., *Security Analysis,* 4th ed., McGraw-Hill Book Company, New York, 1962.

Price-Fixing Agreement   An agreement among competing firms to avoid competitive pricing by charging identical prices or by raising or lowering prices at the same time. An agreement of this type is usually based on direct consultation and exchange of promises, although the actual agreement may be oral rather than written. Price fixing may be carried out effectively when the number of sellers is small, but it is difficult to keep a large number of sellers in line and to preserve the secrecy of the agreement. Price-fixing agreements are acceptable in several European countries, but in the U.S., no matter how reasonable the fixed prices may be, they constitute a violation of the Sherman Antitrust Act. For additional details, see John J. Galgay, *Antitrust Considerations in the Exchange of Price Information among Competitors,* Current Business Studies, no. 45, The Society of Business Advisory Professions, Inc., in cooperation with the New York University Graduate School of Business Administration, New York, 1963.

Prices-Paid-by-Farmers Index   A measure of the change from month to month in the average prices of goods and services bought by American farmers for family living and farm production. The index is based on a price series for 235 commodities and services in family living and 244 items used in farm production. It includes interest, taxes, and wage rates. Information on commodity prices is collected at chain and independent stores, while costs of electricity and telephone service are based on an annual survey of some 20,000 farmers. The base period is set by law at 1910–1914. The index is published at the end of each month by the

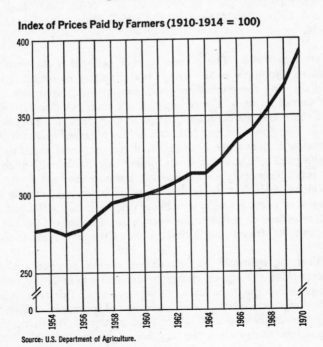

Index of Prices Paid by Farmers (1910-1914 = 100)

Source: U.S. Department of Agriculture.

Bureau of Agricultural Economics. When the index of prices received by farmers is divided by the index of prices paid by farmers, the result is the parity ratio. For further information concerning the history of the index, see U.S. Department of Agriculture, *Major Statistical Series of the United States Department of Agriculture: Agricultural Prices and Parity*, vol. I, 1957; see also *1962 Supplement to Economic Indicators: Historical and Descriptive Bcakground*, prepared for the U.S. Joint Economic Committee, Government Printing Office, Washington, D.C., 1962.

Prices-Received-by-Farmers Index A measure of the change from month to month in the average prices received by American farmers for their products. The index is based on the prices of 55 important commodities that accounted for 93% of total cash receipts from the sale of farm products in the years 1953–1957. The prices quoted are those received at points of first sale, local markets or other centers to which farmers deliver their products. No specifications are made as to grades; instead, average prices for all grades and qualities are used. Most of the data are gathered from price reporters, who are scattered throughout the U.S. The reporters are usually buyers of agricultural commodities and other persons well informed regarding the local price situation. For the official index, conversion is made from 1953–1957 to the 1910–1914 = 100 base, which is the base period prescribed by law. The index is published at the end of each month by the Bureau of Agricultural Economics. When this index is divided by the index of prices paid by farmers, the result is the parity ratio. For further information concerning the history of the index, see U.S. Department of Agriculture, *Major Statistical Series of the United States Department of Agriculture: Agricultural Prices and Parity*, vol. I, 1957; see also *1962 Supplement to Economic Indicators: Historical and Descriptive Background*, prepared for the U.S. Joint Economic Committee, Government Printing Office, Washington, D.C., 1962.

Price Stability Maintenance of the purchasing power of a currency at a level which encourages investment, production, and employment without inflationary or deflationary price movements. Together with full employment and balanced international payments, it is one of the major objectives of U.S. economic policy. During the eight-year period from 1958 through 1965, the U.S. experienced a period of relative price stability. For further information on price stability, see *Defense against Inflation: Policies for Price Stability in a Growing Economy*, Committee for Economic Development, Research and Policy Committee, New York, July, 1958.

Price-Support Program A government program designed to keep market prices from falling below a minimum level. U.S. agriculture has been

Index of Prices Received by Farmers (1910-1914 = 100)

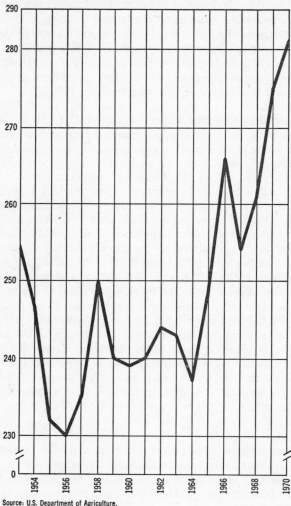

Source: U.S. Department of Agriculture.

the object of such a program because farming is a fluctuating industry, the products of which are sold in a highly competitive market subject to rapidly changing prices. The farmer has little control over his prices or his production, which is subject to such factors as weather and crop diseases. Because of these conditions, a feeling developed that the U.S.

government should guarantee farmers a standard of living favorable to some period in history. The years 1909–1914 were chosen as a period when the farmer enjoyed a favorable purchasing power for his commodities. By the 1960s almost every commodity was supported at some level of parity. This complex system of price supports had been accomplished by three basic programs: (1) crop limitation designed to cut supply and raise prices, (2) purchase-loan storage programs that guarantee to support prices, and (3) a purchase-and-resale differential-subsidy plan known as the Benson-Brannan Plan. For a discussion of these price-support plans, see Paul A. Samuelson, *Economics*, 6th ed., McGraw-Hill Book Company, New York, 1964, pp. 411–412; U.S. Joint Economic Committee, *Economic Policies for Agriculture in 1960's*, Government Printing Office, Washington, D.C., 1960; ———, *Subsidy and Subsidylike Programs of the United States Government*, Government Printing Office, Washington, D.C., 1960.

Primary Boycott   An organized campaign undertaken by a union to bring an employer to terms by exerting pressure directly on him. A primary boycott attempts to restrict the market of the employer by dissuading consumers from purchasing his products. It differs from other forms of boycott because the workers carry it out against an employer with whom they are in dispute for the purpose of modifying the terms of their own employment. In practice, it is not an effective weapon against management, and its use has greatly diminished. The primary boycott is legal, whereas most types of secondary boycott are considered illegal under the Taft-Hartley Act of 1947. For a discussion of the primary boycott, see Leo Wolman, *Boycott in American Trade Unions*, Studies in Historical and Political Science, vol. XXXIV, no. 1, Johns Hopkins Press, Baltimore, 1916.

Primary Demand Deposit   *See Demand Deposit.*

Primary Mortgage Market   *See Mortgage Market.*

Prime Rate of Interest   The rate charged by commercial banks for short-term loans extended to their best customers, the fifty or sixty corporations in the U.S. with the highest credit ratings. Thus the prime rate is generally low in relation to other commercial rates. It provides the base on which other commercial interest rates rest. The differential between the prime rate and any other rate of interest charged for a commercial loan is an approximate measure of the premium for the additional risk involved. Prior to 1971, bankers considered the prime rate the best index of conditions in the bank loan market, since variations in the interest rate on all types of business loans are closely related to variations in the prime rate. More changes in the prime rate took place in the first half of 1971 than in any other single year. On October 21, 1971, First National City Bank of New York shifted from an administratively determined rate to a flexible rate. A list of prime rates is shown in the accompanying table. For further discussion of the nature of the prime rate, see Albert Wojnilower and Richard Speagle, "The Prime Rate," *Monthly Review,* Federal Reserve Bank of New York, New York, April and May, 1962; for reasons why a flexible prime rate was introduced, see Dwight B. Crane and William L. White, "Who Benefits from a Floating Prime Rate," *Harvard Business Review,* Graduate School of Business Administration, Harvard University, January–February, 1972.

Prime Rate, %	Effective Date	Prime Rate, %	Effective Date
5	Dec. 6, 1965	7½	Mar. 17, 1969
5½	Mar. 10, 1966	8½	June 9, 1969
5¾	June 29, 1966	8	Mar. 25, 1970
6	Aug. 16, 1966	7½	Sept. 21, 1970
5½–5¾	Jan. 26–27, 1967	7¼	Nov. 12, 1970
5½	Mar. 27, 1967	7	Nov. 12, 1970
6	Nov. 20, 1967	6¾	Dec. 22, 1970
6½	Apr. 19, 1968	6½	Jan. 6, 1971
6–6¼	Sep. 25, 1968	6¼	Jan. 15, 1971
6¼	Nov. 13, 1968	6	Jan. 18, 1971
6½	Dec. 2, 1968	5¾	Feb. 16, 1971
6¾	Dec. 18, 1968	5¼–5½	Mar. 11, 1971
7	Jan. 7, 1969	5¼	Mar. 19, 1971
		5¼–5½	Apr. 23, 1971

Private Bank   An unincorporated bank. Private banks formerly constituted a very important part of the U.S. banking system. There were about 5,000 unincorporated banks in the country in 1900, but they declined very greatly in number and volume of business thereafter, and by 1940 there were only about 60 private banks with aggregate deposits of $146 million. Before the passage of the Banking Act of 1933, many important U.S. banks, such as J. P. Morgan and Co., engaged in both commercial banking operations and the underwriting of securities. The act forced private banks to relinquish either their deposit services or their investment services and to submit to periodic examination by Federal or state authorities. The supervision and regulation of private banks are now left to the states. In some states, private banks are prohibited; in others, regulations are very liberal; and in a few states, such as New York, private banks are regulated as strictly as incorporated banks.

Private Corporation   *See Closed Corporation.*

Private Debt, Net   The net debt of private individuals, noncorporate business, and corporations. At the end of 1970 net private debt in the U.S. totaled $1,357 billion, or nearly three-fourths of the aggregate net public and private debt. The debt of private individuals is usually in the form of mortgages, consumer credit, and bank loans. In 1970 individual and noncorporate net debt amounted to $583 billion, about three-fifths of this indebtedness being in the form of mortgages. Total corporation debt in 1970 was $774 billion, of which about 56% was in short-term debt. For statistics on private debt, see U.S. Department of Commerce, *Survey of Current Business,* May, 1971.

Private Debt at Year's end, 1947–1970
(In billions of dollars)

Year	Total	Corporate Debt	Total, Individual and Noncorporate Debt
1947	178.3	108.9	69.4
1948	198.4	117.8	80.6
1949	208.4	118.0	90.4
1950	246.4	142.1	104.3
1951	276.8	162.5	114.3
1952	300.4	171.0	129.4
1953	322.7	179.5	143.2
1954	340.0	182.8	157.2
1955	392.2	212.1	180.1
1956	427.2	231.7	195.5
1957	454.3	246.7	207.6
1958	482.4	259.5	222.9
1959	528.3	283.3	245.0
1960	566.1	302.8	263.3
1961	609.1	324.3	284.8
1962	660.1	348.2	311.9
1963	722.3	376.4	345.8
1964	789.7	409.6	380.1
1965	870.4	454.3	416.1
1966	953.5	506.6	446.9
1967	1,034.3	553.7	480.6
1968	1,148.4	618.1	520.3
1969	1,271.6	715.5	556.0
1970	1,356.9	774.1	582.8

SOURCE: U.S. Department of Commerce.

Private Sector That part of the economy composed of consumer expenditures for goods and services and business expenditures for plants, equipment, and inventories. The private sector excludes all government purchases of goods and services. When government employees act as consumers by purchasing consumer goods and services, however, these expenditures become part of the private sector. In 1971 the private sector accounted for nearly 78% of the U.S. economy. For a breakdown of items of goods and services in the private sector, see U.S. Department of Commerce, *Survey of Current Business: National Income Supplements*, July issues.

Producer Goods (Producer Durable Equipment) The machinery and equipment (newly produced) that are acquired by private business and nonprofit institutions. Producer goods include such items as machine tools, generators, blast furnaces, freight cars, and passenger cars purchased for business use. The three largest components of this category are electrical machinery; trucks, buses, and truck trailers; and office, computing, and accounting machinery. Not all producer goods are capital goods, for some items, such as jigs and dies used up in one year in the automobile industry, are not charged to capital accounts but to current expenses, in accordance with conventional accounting procedures. In the U.S., sales of producer goods accounted for about $70.0 billion in 1971. For historical statistics and methods of estimating producer goods in the national accounts, see U.S. Department of Commerce, *United States Income and Output: Supplement to the Survey of Current Business*, 1958; for the latest quarterly estimates, see *Survey of Current Business*, monthly.

Production Function The various combinations of land, labor, materials, and equipment that are needed to produce a given quantity of output. The production function expresses the maximum possible output which can be produced with any specified quantities of the various necessary inputs. Every production function assumes a given level of technology; once technological innovations have been introduced, the production function changes. The quantities of the particular factors necessary to produce a unit of output may be fixed or variable, in which case one factor may be substituted for another in the production process. All production functions whose technological coefficients are variable are subject to the law of diminishing returns: The marginal productivity of a factor must eventually decline if the rate of its use is increased while the use of the other factors is held constant. Another characteristic of a production function is the nature of its returns to scale. If a proportional increase in the input rate of each factor increases output by the same proportion, the production function is subject to constant returns to scale; that is, it is linearly homogeneous. On the other hand, if a proportional increase in all inputs increases output more than proportionately, increasing returns to scale are present, whereas if output is increased less than proportionately, the production function is characterized by decreasing returns to scale. An example of a linearly homogeneous production function is the Cobb-Douglas production function, which is $Y = kL^aC^bN^{1-a-b}$, where Y is output, L is quantity of labor input, C is quantity of capital input, N is quantity of natural resources input, and k, a, and b are positive constants. For additional details, see Sune Carlson, *A Study of the Pure Theory of Production*, P. S. King & Staples, Ltd., London, 1939; James M. Henderson and Richard E. Quandt, *Microeconomic Theory: A Mathematical Approach*, 2d ed., McGraw-Hill Book Company, New York, 1971; Diran Bodenhorn, *Intermediate Price Theory*, McGraw-Hill Book Company, New York, 1961; Michael K. Evans, *Macroeconomic Activity*, Harper & Row Publishers, Incorporated, New York, 1969.

Production Worker An employee who is engaged in all phases of production, such as fabricating, processing, and assembling, and in the various services associated with production operations, such as receiving, packing, shipping, and maintenance. The jobs covered range from floor sweeper to foreman. Supervisors above the level of foreman are excluded. In 1953, the number of production workers in U.S. manufacturing industries totaled 14,055,000, the postwar high mark for this category of workers until 1966. Between 1953 and 1966, the number of production workers ran well below that figure, and in 1958 it totaled less than 12 million. For industry statistics and a more detailed definition of production workers, see U.S. Department of Labor, *Employment and Earnings*, monthly.

Productivity The goods and services produced per unit of labor, capital, or both; for example, the output of automobiles per man-hour. The ratio of output to all labor and capital is a total productivity measure; the ratio of output to either labor or capital, a partial measure. Anything that raises output in relation to labor and capital leads to an increase in productivity. For the U.S. private economy, the ratio of total output to total labor and capital grew by 2.1% per year from 1919 to 1960. What caused the rise? Economists disagree. Some point to improvements in technology, mainly in the form of more efficient machines, as the important factor. Others state that investment in education and improvements in the quality of the labor force are the major causes. The most commonly used measure of productivity is the ratio of output to man-hours worked, called labor

**Manufacturing Production Workers as a
Percent of Total Employees in Manufacturing**

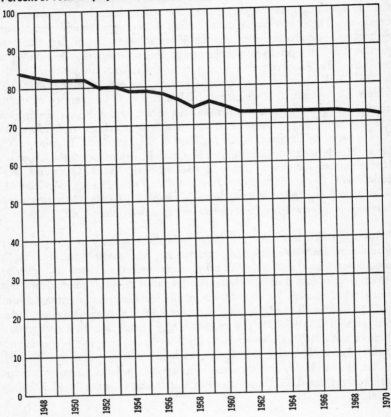

Source: U.S. Department of Labor.

productivity. This does not measure the gains due to labor alone, however, because a man working with a more efficient machine can produce a greater amount of goods even though he works no harder and no better than he did before. For the U.S. private economy, the ratio of total output to total labor grew by about 3% per year between 1950 and 1970. For historical data and a detailed discussion of concepts and methods, see John W. Kendrick, *Productivity Trends: Capital and Labor*, National Bureau of Economic Research, Occasional Paper 53, New York, 1956; Solomon Fabricant, *Basic Facts on Productivity Change*, National Bureau of Economic Research, Occasional Paper 63, New York, 1959; for statistics on labor productivity see U.S. Department of Labor, *Index of Output per Man-Hour for Selected Industries*, annually; see also John W. Kendrick, *Productivity Trends in the United States*, National Bureau of Economic Research, Inc., Princeton University Press, Princeton, N.J., 1961; Bela Gold, *Foundations of Productivity Analysis*, The University of Pittsburgh Press, Pittsburgh, Pa., 1955.

Output per Man-Hour (1957–1959 = 100)

Year	Total, Private Economy	Farm	Nonfarm	Manufacturing
1947	69.0	49.8	74.1	72.3
1948	72.0	58.0	76.5	76.4
1949	74.2	56.5	79.5	79.3
1950	80.3	64.4	84.4	85.0
1951	82.7	64.7	86.3	86.9
1952	84.3	70.3	87.0	87.3
1953	87.8	79.6	89.6	90.2
1954	89.9	83.7	91.6	91.8
1955	93.9	84.4	95.7	97.2
1956	94.1	88.0	95.2	96.2
1957	96.9	93.3	97.2	98.2
1958	99.8	103.0	99.7	98.1
1959	103.4	104.8	103.1	103.7
1960	105.0	110.7	104.4	105.5
1961	108.6	119.4	107.4	107.9
1962	113.8	122.2	112.3	114.3
1963	117.9	133.1	115.7	118.9
1964	122.5	135.5	120.0	124.7
1965	126.6	148.1	123.6	129.8
1966	131.7	153.8	127.9	131.8
1967	134.3	168.5	129.9	132.1
1968	138.7	168.5	134.2	139.2
1969	139.9	182.7	134.7	142.6

SOURCE: U.S. Department of Labor.

Productivity Clause   *See Annual Improvement Factor.*

Productivity of Capital Stock   Output per unit of capital input. The productivity of capital stock is the ratio of the physical productive capacity (output) to the current real value of the stock of capital facilities and equipment. It depends on the level of technology, the size and nature of the capital stock, organization and management, etc. The major sources of changes in the productivity of capital stock are changes in the quality of capital inputs, changes in the effectiveness with which capital goods are utilized, and technological improvements which increase the productive capacity of current investment in capital facilities. Increases in the apparent productivity of capital stock may not be due to the enhanced contribution of the capital factor, however, but may result from greater contributions by other input factors, such as labor. For a detailed study of the changes in the productivity of capital stock of the U.S., see John W. Kendrick, *Postwar Productivity Trends in the United States, 1948–1969*, National Bureau of Economic Research, Inc., Columbia University Press, New York, 1972; see also National Bureau of Economic Research, Inc., *Output, Input, and Productivity Measurement*, Princeton University Press, Princeton, N.J., 1961; Bela Gold, *Foundations of Productivity Analysis*, The University of Pittsburgh Press, Pittsburgh, 1955.

Output Per Unit of Capital Input in Private Domestic Economy (1958 = 100)

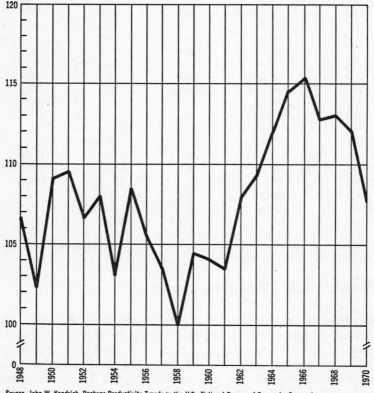

Source: John W. Kendrick, Postwar Productivity Trends in the U.S., National Bureau of Economic Research.

Profit and Loss Statement (Operating Statement)   A summary statement of the revenues and expenses of an enterprise for a given period. It sets forth the dollar value and sources of revenue, the types and amount of expenses, and the resulting net income (profit) or net loss for the accounting period. One of the objectives of running a business is to make a profit and this statement shows the degree to which this objective has been realized. The profit and loss statement provides operating facts and figures, a study of which may indicate ways of increasing profits. Prospective sellers, buyers creditors, and stockholders are interested in the profit and loss statement because, to some extent, operations in the past provide clues to future potential. For further information, see Morton Backer (ed.), *Handbook of Modern Accounting Theory*, Prentice-Hall, Inc., Englewood Cliffs, N.J., 1955, pp. 437–440, 443–446.

Profiteering   The making of unreasonably large profits on the sale of goods and services. The charging of excessively high prices becomes possible in periods of emergency, such as panics and wars, when competition declines and people are willing to pay exorbitant prices for the commodities they want. Profiteering may also arise in industries which sell strategic goods to the government. The U.S. attempted to eliminate profiteering during World War II by means of price control, limiting the prices that producers could charge, and by excess profits taxation, attempting to tax away excessive profits.

Profit Margin   The percentage that net profit from operations is of net sales or of capital invested. These percentages measure the efficiency of a company or an industry. Nevertheless, profit margins vary widely among industries and among companies within the same industry. Although the absolute level of profits may reach new peaks every year, profit margins do not. As a matter of record, profit margins were generally lower in the early 1960s than they were in former periods of prosperity. However, 1970 was the low point for the postwar period. For statistics on profit margins of manufacturing corporations classified by industry and by size, see U.S. Federal Trade Commission and Securities and Exchange Commission, *Quarterly Financial Report for Manufacturing Corporations*.

Profit Maximization   The level of output which will yield the largest total profit. A business firm that has as its sole objective the maximization of profits will seek the level of production that is most profitable. This can be accomplished by constructing a table on the costs at each level of output and the total revenue that the sale of this output will yield.

Profit Margin of Manufacturing Corporations (Profits per dollar of sales, in cents)

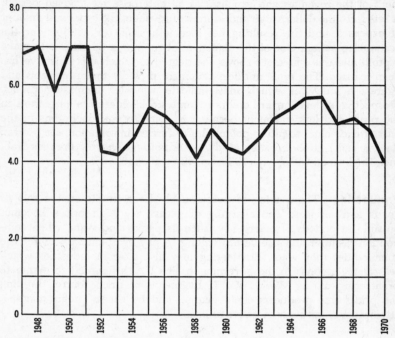

Source: Federal Trade Commission; Securities and Exchange Commission.

The optimal, or profit-maximization, output will be located where the difference between total revenue and total cost is greatest. Another method of determining profit maximization is to learn whether the marginal revenue received from the sale of an additional unit of output is greater than the marginal cost of the same unit. If marginal revenue is greater than marginal cost, the additional unit will be produced and production will continue as long as the same conditions prevail. On the other hand, if marginal cost exceeds marginal revenue, output will be contracted. The best profit position is the point at which marginal cost and marginal revenue are equal. This is the optimal situation of maximum profits. For further information, see Diran Bodenhorn, *Intermediate Price Theory*, McGraw-Hill Book Company, New York, 1961, chap. 9; W. M. Corden, "The Maximization of Profit by a Newspaper," *Review of Economic Studies*, vol. XX, no. 3, pp. 181–190, Oliver & Boyd Ltd., Edinburgh, 1953; Robert L. Heilbroner, *The Economic Problem*, Prentice-Hall, Inc., Englewood Cliffs, N.J., 1968.

Profits The amount left over after a business enterprise has paid all its bills. In accounting, profits may be expressed as gross (the difference between sales and the cost of goods sold), operating (the difference between the gross profit and the operating expenses), and net (the difference between the operating profit and income taxes). Not all companies make profits every year. Even during the prosperous 1950s, more than 40% of the active corporations in the U.S. either failed to earn a profit or went into the red. Profits vary from time to time, from company to company, and from industry to industry. In high-profit industries, workers receive high pay. By means of research and modern tools, high-

Corporate Profits After Taxes (Billions of dollars)

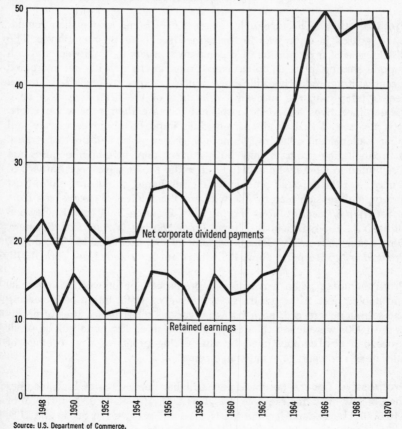

Net corporate dividend payments

Retained earnings

Source: U.S. Department of Commerce.

profit industries provide consumers with a greater number of goods, of better quality, and in greater variety. Profits lead the economy. After profits begin to rise, employment and income generally rise as well; when profits fall, employment and income follow closely behind them. The National Bureau of Economic Research classifies corporate profits among its leading indicators. Profits motivate private citizens to put their savings into useful enterprise, and they provide the largest single source of funds for economic growth. In the first quarter of 1971, corporate profits after taxes ran at an annual rate of $47.5 billion in the U.S. For further discussion, see Claude Robinson, *Understanding Profits,* D. Van Nostrand Company, Inc., Princeton, N.J., 1961; see also Edmund A. Mennis, "Different Measures of Corporate Profits," *Financial Analysts Journal,* The Financial Analysts Federation, New York, September–October, 1962.

Profit Sharing The receipt by workers of a bonus above their regular wage, geared in some way to the earned profits of their employer. The distribution of a proportion of a company's profits to employees through a profit-sharing plan is undertaken primarily to provide an increased incentive for productive efficiency. Since workers so rewarded have a keener interest in the successful operation of the firm, they will have greater incentives to reduce costs and increase their productive effort. It is also stated that profit-sharing plans improve employee morale and labor-management relations, promote wage flexibility, and prevent strikes. A profit-sharing program may be a current one, in which bonuses are distributed to workers immediately after the profits have been earned, or it may be of the deferred type, in which the shared profits are held in trust in a type of pension plan for the workers. For additional details, see *How to Set Up a Successful Profit Sharing Plan,* Prentice-Hall, Inc., Englewood Cliffs, N.J., 1954; Edwin B. Flippo, *Profit Sharing in American Business,* Ohio State University, Columbus, Ohio, 1954; Kenneth M. Thompson, *Profit Sharing,* Harper & Row, Publishers, Incorporated, New York, 1949.

Profit Squeeze The narrowing of profits caught between rising costs and stable prices. Although the absolute level of profits might be increasing and setting new records each year, the various relative measures of profits in the 1960s were lower than they had been in earlier periods. The profit squeeze is best demonstrated by considering profits as a percentage of sales or as a percentage of national income.

Progressive Tax A tax that takes a higher percentage of high incomes than of low ones, for example, 5% of $1,000, 10% of $5,000, and 25% of $10,000. The Federal income tax is the most progressive tax in the U.S. In 1969 rates ranged from 20% of the first $2,000 of taxable income to 91%

of incomes over $200,000. This did not mean that the individual who earned $250,000 of taxable income paid 91% on all his earnings. The rates are marginal; that is, they apply only to the additional dollars (in this case, only the taxable income over $200,000). Taken as a whole, the U.S. tax system is progressive but not as progressive as Federal income tax rates make it appear. The system contains many regressive taxes, and there are numerous ways of escaping high rates, such as tax-free municipal bonds; capital gains, which bear a maximum rate of 25%; and marriage, which provides income-splitting privileges. Those who favor progressive taxes state that they are more equitable than regressive or proportional taxes in that they are levied according to the ability to pay. Those opposed to progressive taxes argue that too great a degree of progression discourages effort and risk taking. The rates for all Federal taxes are set forth in *United States Internal Revenue Code*, Government Printing Office, Washington, D.C.; see also F. Shehab, *Progressive Taxation*, Oxford University Press, Fair Lawn, N.J., 1953; W. Blum and H. Kalven, Jr., *The Uneasy Case for Progressive Taxation*, The University of Chicago Press, Chicago, 1953.

Prohibitive Duty   A tariff whose rate is so high that importation of a commodity is decreased to a very low level. A duty becomes prohibitive when it increases the selling price of an imported good so much above the price of a similar domestically produced good that it offers little competition to the home industry. Prohibitive duties are most often imposed to protect domestic producers against ruinous foreign competition or to retaliate against similar action by another country. The U.S. has had few prohibitive duties, but the protection of textiles and china, for example, has at times been excessive enough to call it prohibitive. For additional details, see Don D. Humphrey, *American Imports*, The Twentieth Century Fund, New York, 1955.

Proletariat   The working class. The term proletariat does not apply to persons in supervisory or executive positions, who are able to accumulate a significant amount of capital from their earnings, but only to those whose subsistence depends on their daily labor for others. Karl Marx saw the proletariat as a class of near slaves, exploited by the capitalists and receiving wages which were much lower than the value of the goods that they produced. He said that, as a result of increasingly severe capitalist economic crises, the workers would finally rise to break the chains of their labor and overthrow the exploiting capitalist classes. First, the workers would rule as a dictatorship of the proletariat, which would remain in existence until all remnants of the propertied classes had been destroyed. Then, the dictatorship of the proletariat would disappear, and a completely classless society would evolve. For further information on Marx's view of the role of the proletariat, see Karl Marx, *Capital,* Charles Kerr & Co., Chicago, 1906; Paul M. Sweezy, *The Theory of Capitalist Development,* Oxford University Press, Fair Lawn, N.J., 1942.

Promissory Note A written promise of one person to pay another a specified sum of money at a given date. Promissory notes offer several advantages to creditors: they serve as excellent evidences of debt, they eliminate misunderstanding with reference to the amount and time of payment, and they are usually negotiable, so that they may be transferred by endorsement. Whereas promissory notes are often used as evidence of bank loans and consumer installment credit, their use in other commercial transactions is limited. Mercantile credit is usually extended through an open account; only inferior credit risks are asked to give promissory notes. For additional details, see Theodore Beckman, *Credits and Collections,* 7th ed., McGraw-Hill Book Company, New York, 1962; Albert R. Chapin and George H. Hassett, *Credit and Collection Principles and Practice,* 7th ed., McGraw-Hill Book Company, New York, 1960.

Propensity to Consume, Average (APC) The ratio of consumption to income at any given income level. It differs from marginal propensity to consume, which refers to the ratio of changes in consumption to changes in income. For further discussion of the average propensity to consume, see J. M. Keynes, *The General Theory of Employment, Interest, and Money,* Harcourt, Brace & World, Inc., New York, 1936, chaps, 8 and 9; Edward Shapiro, *Macroeconomic Analysis,* Harcourt, Brace & World, Inc., New York, 1966.

Propensity to Consume, Marginal (MPC) The ratio of the additional amount that people will spend for consumption from an additional amount of income. Graphically, the marginal propensity to consume is represented by the slope of the consumption function at any particular income level. It may be calculated simply as follows:

$$\text{MPC} = \frac{\text{change in consumption}}{\text{change in income}}$$

The theory has sparked a great deal of controversy. For many years it was believed that the marginal propensity to consume declines as income increases, but numerous economists now believe that it may be constant for the economy as a whole. For further information, see Alvin Hansen, *A Guide to Keynes,* McGraw-Hill Book Company, New York, 1953, chaps. 3 and 4; J. M. Keynes, *The General Theory of Employment, Interest, and Money,* Harcourt, Brace & World, Inc., New York, 1936, chaps. 8 and 9; see also James S. Duesenberry, *Income, Savings, and the Theory of*

Consumer Behavior, Harvard University Press, Cambridge, Mass., 1949; John P. Lewis and Robert C. Turner, *Business Conditions Analysis,* 2d ed., McGraw-Hill Book Company, New York, 1967.

Propensity to Save, Average (APS)   The ratio of saving to income at any given income level. For any particular consumption function, the average propensity to save is equal to 1 minus the average propensity to consume. It differs from marginal propensity to save, which refers to the ratio of the changes in saving to changes in income. For further discussion of the average propensity to save, see J. M. Keynes, *The General Theory of Employment, Interest, and Money,* Harcourt, Brace & World, Inc., New York, 1936, chaps. 8 and 9; Edward Shapiro, *Macroeconomic Analysis,* Harcourt, Brace & World, Inc., New York, 1966.

Propensity to Save, Marginal (MPS)   The additional saving generated by additional income. It is the ratio of change in saving to change in income:

$$MPS = \frac{\text{change in saving}}{\text{change in income}}$$

For any particular consumption function, the marginal propensity to save is equal to 1 minus the marginal propensity to consume, or

$$MPS = 1 - MPC$$

The theory has engendered considerable argument. For many years it was thought that the MPS increases as income increases, but numerous economists now believe that it may be constant for the economy as a whole. For further information, see Alvin Hansen, *A Guide to Keynes,* McGraw-Hill Book Company, New York, 1953, chaps. 3 and 4; J. M. Keynes, *The General Theory of Employment, Interest, and Money,* Harcourt, Brace & World, Inc., New York, 1936, chaps. 8 and 9; James S. Duesenberry, *Income, Savings, and the Theory of Consumer Behavior,* Harvard University Press, Cambridge, Mass., 1949; John P. Lewis and Robert C. Turner, *Business Conditions Analysis,* 2d ed., McGraw-Hill Book Company, New York, 1967.

Property Tax   A tax on the value of real estate, that is, on land and on such improvements on land as residential, commercial, and industrial buildings. The use of this tax is limited to state and local governments in the U.S., and it is particularly important as a source of revenue for local governments. Nevertheless, revenue from property taxes has declined as a percentage of all U.S. state and local revenues. On a local-government basis, the property tax accounted for 56% of all tax revenue in 1970, whereas in 1929 it represented 98% of the total. On a state basis, the tax percentage dwindled from 59% in 1915 to 2% in 1970. The property tax has been criticized on the ground that property, such as a home or a vacant lot, which does not provide income is a poor measure of tax-paying ability. Some economists believe that a property tax in underdeveloped countries, where property is owned mainly by the wealthy, may be progressive. It may also be beneficial, for use of a property tax could result in the conversion of unproductive property to productive property. For property taxes in the U.S., see Philip E. Taylor, *The Economics of Public Finance,* The Macmillan Company, New York, 1953; for statistics, see U.S. Department of Commerce, *Compendium of State Government Finance;* for property taxes in underdeveloped countries, see John H. Adler, "The Fiscal and Monetary Implementation of Development Programs," *American Economic Review,* Papers and Proceedings, American Economic Association, Evanston, Ill., May, 1952; for Henry George's views on a land-value tax, see Henry George, *Progress and Prosperity,* Random House, Inc., New York, 1938.

Proportional Tax   A tax whose rate remains constant as the size of the base increases. A proportional tax rate is usually stated as a flat percentage of the base regardless of its size. For example, the property tax usually operates with proportional rates, and the tax might be expressed as 1% of assessed property value. Sales and excise taxes, payroll taxes, and most customs duties are also levied on the basis of proportional rates. For additional details on types of taxes, see Harold Groves, *Financing Government,* 6th ed., Holt, Rinehart and Winston, Inc., New York, 1964; Hugh Dalton, *Principles of Public Finance,* 10th ed., Routledge & Kegan Paul, Ltd., London, 1939.

Proprietorship   A type of business organization in which one individual owns the business. Legally, the owner is the business. Proprietorship is the commonest type of business organization in agriculture and retail trade. Generally, proprietorships are small businesses because of the limited capital available. Among the advantages of this type of operation are the simplicity of starting a business, the absence of much state regulation, and the direct acquisition of profits by the owner. Because the owner and the business are inseparable, there are certain disadvantages to proprietorships: The business stops if the proprietor dies, becomes insane, or is physically unable to continue it. Moreover, a proprietorship is characterized by unlimited liability, which means that all the proprietor's personal assets are available as security for his creditors. Because of the death or illness of the individual owner, proprietorships generally last for a relatively short time in comparison with partnerships or corporations.

For more detailed information concerning proprietorship, see Lyman A. Keith and Carlo E. Gubellini, *Introduction to Business Enterprise*, McGraw-Hill Book Company, New York, 1962.

Prospectus Any communication, either written or broadcast by radio or television, that offers a security for sale. The prospectus contains the most important parts of the registration statement, which must give all information revelant to the issue. The Securities Act of 1933, as amended, requires public offerings of more than $300,000 worth of securities, with a few exceptions, to be registered with the Securities and Exchange Commission (SEC). Actually, the prospectus is published information but is not easily obtainable. It is not timely enough to help the investor make a decision because it is unlawful to issue a prospectus before the SEC has declared the registration effective. (This declaration means only that the issue conforms to the Securities Act and that the securities can be sold.) Therefore, potential investors are provided with a preliminary prospectus, or red-herring prospectus, which usually contains all the information that will appear in the prospectus except the offering price and the underwriter's fee. The term red herring is derived from the statement in red print on every page, which says that the preliminary prospectus is not an offer to sell and that no offer to sell can be made until the registration is effective. For further information, see Securities Act of 1933, sec. 2(10); Jules I. Bogen (ed.), *Financial Handbook*, 4th ed., The Ronald Press Company, New York, 1968.

Prosperity A sustained period of high and rising business activity in which business and consumer optimism is high. Prosperity is characterized by increased production, high capital investment with an emphasis on new capacity, expansion of credit, rising prices, low unemployment, full employment, and a high rate of formation of new business enterprises. The longest sustained period of prosperity in the U.S. occurred between 1961 and 1969, with only a minor interruption in 1967. See Arthur F. Burns, *Prosperity without Inflation*, Fordham University Press, New York, 1957.

Proxy Statement A written power of attorney that stockholders give to another person (proxy) to vote corporate stock. Stockholders have the right to vote for the company's board of directors and to vote on other questions raised at the annual meeting. Because most of them find it difficult to attend the meeting, however, the proxy system is used extensively. Ordinarily, the current management of a corporation solicits proxies, which means that a director, an officer of the company, or some other person will vote the stock as the board wishes. When corporations whose stock is registered (listed) with a national securities exchange solicit proxies, the U.S. Securities and Exchange Commission requires (1) that certain information be included on the proxy statement, such as the remuneration of officers and directors and the number of shares held by them; and (2) that space be provided on the statement to permit stockholders to indicate that they want the proxy to vote contrary to the board's wishes. See U.S. Securities and Exchange Commission, *Rules Relating to the Solicitation of Proxies,* Regulation 240.14; Jules I. Bogen (ed.), *Financial Handbook,* 4th ed., The Ronald Press Company, New York, 1968.

Prudent-Man Rule   A rule that lends flexibility to a trustee in the handling of trust investments. The prudent-man rule states that when money is left in trust without specific directions for its investment, the trustees may use their own judgment in making whatever investments they feel right as long as they act in a prudent manner. The rule is derived from an 1830 court decision of Justice Samuel Putnam, in which he said, "All that can be required of a trustee to invest is that he conduct himself faithfully and exercise sound discretion. He is to observe how men of prudence, discretion, and intelligence manage their affairs. . . ." Legal prudence consists of care, skill, and caution. Although the prudent-man rule, adopted by most states of the U.S., gives trustees greater freedom in handling trust investments, they are generally held by the courts to very high standards in carrying out the three elements of prudence. For further information, see Mayo A. Shattuck and James F. Farr, *An Estate Planner's Handbook,* Little, Brown and Company, Boston, 1963; Harold B. Elsom, "The Law of Trust Investments: In Which the Prudent Man Theory Is Evaluated," *Financial Analysts Journal,* July, 1960, pp. 27–33; *Personal Trust Investment Management,* Proceedings, C.F.A. Research Seminar, 1967, Richard D. Irwin, Inc., Homewood, Ill. 1968, chap. 1.

Psychic Income   Income that is reckoned in terms of pleasure, satisfaction, or general feelings of euphoria. It is to be distinguished from income that is received in money or in the form of goods and services. Psychic income is commonly said to accrue to professional persons and creative artists who take pride in their accomplishments or gain satisfaction from their prestige and status. It may also frequently accrue to workingmen and housewives who enjoy their work surroundings and the company of their fellow workers and find pleasure in a job well done. There is no standard measurement of psychic income. See Albert E. Waugh, *Principles of Economics,* McGraw-Hill Book Company, New York, 1947, p. 41; Paul F. Gemmill, *Fundamentals of Economics,* 6th ed., Harper & Brothers, New York, 1960.

Public Debt, Net Total net government debt, including net Federal debt and net state and local government debt. In 1970 net public debt in the U.S. totaled about $483 billion, $339 billion of which consisted of Federal debt and $143 billion of state and local debt. The greater part of Federal borrowing has been undertaken for emergencies (wars and recessions), whereas state and local credit has been used primarily for capital construction, such as highways, schools, and other public works. Although the U.S. public debt has been increasing in absolute terms, its size in relation to the gross national product (GNP) has been decreasing. For example, the total net public debt declined from 72% of the GNP in 1952 to about 50% in 1970. The interest on the public debt in relation to national income has remained relatively stable, with interest charges on net public

Public Debt at Year's End, 1947–1970
(In billions of dollars)

Year	Total	Federal	Federal Financial Agencies	State and Local
1947	237.4	221.7	0.7	15.0
1948	232.9	215.3	0.6	17.0
1949	237.4	217.6	0.7	19.1
1950	239.8	217.4	0.7	21.7
1951	242.4	216.9	1.3	24.2
1952	249.8	221.5	1.3	27.0
1953	258.9	226.8	1.4	30.7
1954	265.9	229.1	1.3	35.5
1955	273.6	229.6	2.9	41.1
1956	271.2	224.3	2.4	44.5
1957	274.0	223.0	2.4	48.6
1958	287.2	231.0	2.5	53.7
1959	304.7	241.4	3.7	59.6
1960	308.1	239.8	3.5	64.9
1961	321.2	246.7	4.0	70.5
1962	335.9	253.6	5.3	77.0
1963	348.6	257.5	7.2	83.9
1964	361.9	264.0	7.5	90.4
1965	373.7	266.4	8.9	98.3
1966	387.9	271.8	11.2	104.8
1967	408.4	286.5	9.0	112.9
1968	436.1	291.9	21.4	122.8
1969	451.1	289.3	30.5	131.4
1970	482.8	301.1	38.3	143.3

SOURCE: U.S. Department of Commerce.

debt averaging about 1.7% of national income. For further discussion of the nature and significance of the debt, see Philip E. Taylor, *The Economics of Public Finance*, rev. ed., The Macmillan Company, New York, 1953; Charles E. Abbott, *United States Public Debt*, The Twentieth Century Fund, New York, 1953; for statistics on the public debt see U.S. Department of Commerce, *Survey of Current Business*, May, 1970.

Public Debt Transaction   *See Backdoor Financing.*

Public Domain   Land owned by the national government. As a result of U.S. expansion in the nineteenth century, the Federal government owned nearly 2 billion acres by 1867. Subsequently, through a variety of gifts and grants, more than 1 billion acres of the public domain were disposed of. With the growth of the conservation movement at the beginning of the twentieth century, however, there was increasing support for the view that the public lands should be retained by the government and reserved for public uses. Since then, the public domain has been increasingly closed to private ownership. In the early 1960s, the public domain consisted of more than 750 million acres, exclusive of 56 million acres held in trust for Indian tribes. The Federal government is concerned with conservation and public use of the lands for recreational purposes, but it also sells the rights to the operation of certain extractive industries, such as lumbering and mining, on public lands. The administration of the various aspects of the public domain is handled by the Department of Agriculture's Forest Service and the Department of the Interior's Fish and Wildlife Service, National Park Service, Office of Indian Affairs, Bureau of Reclamation, and Bureau of Land Management. For additional details, see E. Louise Piffer, *The Closing of the Public Domain*, Stanford University Press, Stanford, Calif., 1951; Marion Clawson and Burnell Held, *The Federal Lands: Their Use and Management*, The Johns Hopkins Press, Baltimore, 1957.

Public Finance   In common usage, the financing of government. More broadly defined, the term encompasses all activities of government, including not only the economics of finance but also the social effects and consequences of governmental policies. Modern public finance is concerned with adapting economic principles to areas of both economic and social concern, such as economic growth, counter-cyclical measures, and unemployment. Recent texts dealing with this subject are Richard A. Musgrave, *The Theory of Public Finance*, McGraw-Hill Book Company, New York, 1959; John F. Due, *Government Finance: An Economic Analysis*, 3d ed., Richard D. Irwin, Inc., Homewood, Ill., 1963; Leif Johansen, *Public Economics*, Rand McNally & Company, Chicago, 1965.

Public Housing   Low-rent housing authorized by the U.S. Housing Act of 1937. That act authorized Federal assistance to local communities "to remedy the unsafe and unsanitary housing conditions and the acute shortage of decent, safe and sanitary dwellings for families of low income." Local governments may establish local housing authorities to develop, own, and operate low-rent housing projects. The Public Housing Administration (PHA), which is the administrator of Federal aid to the local authorities, provides assistance in the form of loans and subsidies. Loan funds come from the U.S. Treasury, and subsidies are appropriated by Congress. The local housing authorities may receive temporary loans from the PHA to finance low-rent projects prior to permanent financing, or they may meet financing needs through the sale to the public of short-term notes which are guaranteed by PHA. Bonds covering the entire development cost are eventually sold to the public to repay the temporary loans. Nearly 1,200,000 dwelling units come under public housing in the U.S.

Public Ownership   Government ownership and operation of a business enterprise. Under public ownership, the government replaces the private owner as the capitalist. Thus, the government supplies the capital and determines the facilities to be provided. It chooses the management and assumes the responsibility of paying labor, purchasing supplies, setting the price for its goods and services, and reaping profits or meeting deficits if they are incurred. The governmental act of removing private ownership and assuming the operation of an enterprise is called nationalization. In the U.S., the most outstanding example of public ownership is the Tennessee Valley Authority, which is concerned with conservation and power production in the Tennessee Valley area. For an examination of public ownership of railroads, see Lewis C. Sorrell, *Government Ownership and Operation of Railways for the United States,* Prentice-Hall, Inc., Englewood Cliffs, N.J., 1939; for an examination of public ownership in Great Britain, see "The Nationalization of British Industries," *Law and Contemporary Problems,* vol. XVI, no. 4, Duke University School of Law, Durham, N.C., 1951; for a general discussion of public ownership, see R. Turvey (ed.), *Public Enterprise,* Penguin Books, Inc., Baltimore, 1968; A. H. Hanson (ed.), *Nationalization,* George Allen & Unwin, Ltd., London, 1963.

Public Sector (Government Sector)   That part of the economy which is composed of Federal, state, and local expenditures for goods and services. The public sector excludes spending by the private sector, but when government employees act as private consumers in purchasing consumer goods and services, these expenditures become part of the private sector. In 1970 the government sector accounted for about 22% of the U.S. economy. For a breakdown of items of goods and services in the government sector, see U.S. Department of Commerce, *Survey of Current Business: National Income Supplements,* July issues.

Public Service Commission A state commission regulating public utilities in the U.S. A semi-independent agency operating under general legislative power, it controls the rates and services of public utilities within the state. The commission method of utility regulation is said to have the advantages of expertness, flexibility, and practicality. A commission often involves much bureaucracy and red tape, however, and it may be subject to political and private influence. It is sometimes charged that many public service commissions are inadequately financed, understaffed, and limited in power, so that the proper regulation of public utilities is impaired. The first state regulatory commission was set up in Wisconsin in 1907. Subsequently, the idea was adopted by other states, and there are now public service commissions in every state (a few are still known as public utility commissions). Most public service commissions consist of three members who serve staggered terms. They have jurisdiction over motor carriers, telephone and telegraph companies, and electric power, water, and gas companies. The greater part of public service commissions' work originates in complaints brought by consumers and can be handled informally through negotiations between the commissioners and utility officials. For further information, see Emery Troxel, *Economics of Public Utilities,* Holt, Rinehart and Winston, Inc., New York, 1947; Eli W. Clemens, *Economics and Public Utilities,* Appleton-Century-Crofts, Inc., New York, 1950.

Public Welfare Payment A Federal, state, or local government payment to an individual who qualifies for assistance because he or she is either unemployed, retired, or a dependent, such as a senior citizen, a widow, an orphan, or a physically incapacitated or mentally defective person. Welfare payments were relatively unimportant in the U.S. before the depression of the early 1930s, but under the Social Security Act of 1935 the framework of a broad assistance program was established for the aged, dependent, and unemployed. At the same time, the states, spurred by the Federal government, set up unemployment-compensation and old-age assistance plans. The present system of welfare payments is supported on both humanitarian and economic grounds. Society generally recognizes the need to help those who, because of circumstances beyond their control, are unable to support themselves. Public welfare payments not only protect unfortunate individuals but help stabilize the economy during recession. For an analysis of the problems and objectives involved in the social insurance program, see Domenico Gagliardo, *American Social Insurance*, Harper & Row, Publishers, Incorporated, New York, 1949, pp. 3–27; for a discussion of the major economic issues associated with public welfare programs, see Margaret S. Gordon, *The Economics of Welfare Policies*, Columbia University Press, New York, 1963.

Public Welfare Program A government-sponsored social program designed to transfer income from earners to nonearners whose capacity for self-support has been damaged. Among programs of this type are social insurance, public aid, and such other welfare services as institutional care and school lunches, veterans' programs, and public housing. By the fiscal year 1971, public welfare expenditures in the U.S. totaled about $80 billion, or approximately 9.2% of national income. In European countries, public welfare expenditures account for a larger proportion of national income than in the U.S., partly because of the relative importance of U.S. private welfare programs. For further discussion of the economics of public welfare programs, see Margaret S. Gordon, *The Economics of Welfare Policies*, Columbia University Press, New York, 1963; James N. Morgan, Martin H. David, Wilbur J. Cohen, and Harvey E. Brazer, *Income and Welfare in the United States*, McGraw-Hill Book Company, New York, 1962.

Social Security Expenditures as a Percentage of National Income, Selected Countries

Country	Percentage
France	16.1
Germany, Federal Republic of	13.4
Italy	19.3
Netherlands	9.7
Norway	9.9
Sweden	7.3
Switzerland	14.4
United Kingdom	10.1
United States	9.2

SOURCE: United Nations.

Public Works Government-sponsored building or development projects. U.S. outlays for public works since the 1930s have been aimed at smoothing out cyclical declines in business activity. Under the title of public works, the government has adopted all projects that would not be undertaken by citizens or private corporations but that are essential to the development of the country. Under this heading are included such projects as the building of highways, slum clearance, public housing, rural electrification, and regional development. For information concerning public works and their use in economic stabilization policy, see Harold Groves, *Financing Government*, 6th ed., Holt, Rinehart and Winston, Inc., New York, 1965; see also Philip E. Taylor, *The Economics of Public Finance*, The Macmillan Company, New York, 1953, pp. 120–130.

Pump Priming Federal government expenditures in the U.S. that are designed to stimulate business recovery and achieve full employment. Such expenditures have taken the form of Federal public works, grants for state and local public works projects, and subsidies and grants to farmers. Pump priming is based on the notion that, when public funds in sufficient quantities are injected into the income stream before or during a business recession, the economy will be pulled out of the recession and full employment will be restored. The success of the operation implies the existence of a positive multiplier and accelerator and a change in the attitudes that influence decisions on both private consumption and business investment. The degree to which pump-priming techniques may be utilized successfully·as an economic stabilizer is in dispute. Much depends on the advance planning of projects and on the volume of work which can be crowded into recession years. Those who oppose pump priming point out that, by the time government expenditures have actually been made, the economy has usually begun to recover. Proponents of pump priming maintain that it induces recovery only when additional funds are put into circulation. If expenditures were to be financed by taxing persons or businesses, funds would merely be transferred from one group to another. Pump priming requires that expenditures for recovery be financed by borrowing or by incurring a budgetary deficit. For further information, see Harold Groves, *Financing Government*, 6th ed., Holt, Rinehart and Winston, Inc., New York, 1965; see also Philip E. Taylor, *The Economics of Public Finance*, The Macmillan Company, New York, 1953, pp. 106–107.

Purchasing Power The amount of goods and services that a monetary unit can buy. The purchasing power of the U.S. dollar is the reciprocal of a price index. Thus, if prices were to double in ten years, the purchasing power of the ten-year-old dollar would be cut in half. Since there are indices that measure prices at primary markets, at the retail level, and for the economy as a whole, different measures of purchasing power may be calculated. For example, by March, 1971, the primary-market dollar of 1967 was worth 88 cents, the consumer dollar was worth 83 cents, and the dollar for the overall economy also was worth 84 cents. For further

How Much Is the U.S. Consumer Dollar Worth?

	1913	1920	1929	1933	1939	1942	1948	1953	1958	1963	1965	1967	1970
1913 dollar	1.00	.50	.58	.76	.71	.61	.41	.37	.34	.32	.31	.30	.26
1920 dollar		1.00	1.16	1.54	1.45	1.23	.83	.75	.69	.65	.63	.60	.52
1929 dollar			1.00	1.32	1.23	1.05	.71	.64	.59	.56	.54	.51	.44
1933 dollar				1.00	.85	.79	.54	.49	.45	.42	.41	.39	.33
1939 dollar					1.00	.85	.58	.52	.48	.45	.44	.42	.36
1942 dollar						1.00	.68	.61	.56	.53	.52	.49	.42
1948 dollar							1.00	.90	.83	.79	.76	.72	.62
1953 dollar								1.00	.93	.88	.85	.80	.69
1958 dollar									1.00	.94	.92	.87	.75
1963 dollar										1.00	.97	.92	.79
1965 dollar											1.00	.94	.81
1967 dollar												1.00	.86
1970 dollar													1.00

information, see Irving Fisher, *The Purchasing Power of Money*, The Macmillan Company, New York, 1912.

Purchasing-Power-Parity Theory A theory used to explain the proper rate of exchange between two currencies. According to this doctrine, the exchange rate between two countries should be the same as the ratio of the price levels of the countries. For example, if a representative bundle of goods cost $2 in the U.S. and 10 francs in France, the exchange rate should be $1 equals 5 francs. Thus, the theory holds that an equilibrium rate is one which equates the respective domestic purchasing powers of any two currencies that are being compared. The underlying assumption is that the reason for desiring a foreign currency is to purchase goods and services in or from another country. Proponents of this notion hold that deviations from the rate which equates domestic purchasing powers cannot exist for a very long time. If goods in the U.S. cost one-fifth as many dollars as they cost in francs in France, while the exchange rate was $1 equals 1 franc, everyone who held francs would exchange them for an equal number of dollars and be able to purchase five times as many goods. The demand for dollars would raise the rate of exchange until it reached the level of $1 equals 5 francs, or the ratio of their purchasing power. At this rate, a franc spent in France would buy as much as it would if it were converted into a dollar and spent in the U.S. Unfortunately, the purchasing-power-parity theory does not explain the complete relationship between two currencies. If only commodities entered into international trade, the theory might come closer to the truth, but many services that influence exchange rates never enter into the price index. For example, unilateral capital transfers are not considered in the purchasing-power-parity theory, and yet they result in a large demand for foreign exchange. Thus, this theory applies to exchange rates in only a general way. For a discussion of the purchasing-power-parity theory, see P. T. Ellsworth, *The International Economy*, rev. ed., The Macmillan Company, New York, 1962; see also Imre De Vegh, *The Pound Sterling*, Scudder, Stevens & Clark, New York, 1939, pp. 74–80; Eli Shapiro, Ezra Solomon, and William L. White, *Money and Banking*, 5th ed., Holt, Rinehart and Winston, Inc., New York, 1968.

Pure Rate of Interest The interest rate on capital funds that would exist if all risk and administrative costs were eliminated. In effect, it represents the pure cost of being able to use someone else's funds instead of waiting to save one's own. The actual rate of interest paid by a borrower is higher than the pure rate, since it must include a risk premium large enough to cover possible default and the costs of processing the loan as well as the rate of interest for the use of the capital itself. The pure rate of interest is a conceptual tool in economic theory. An awareness of this concept assists the economist in isolating the factors that determine changes in interest rates as such from varying administrative cost or risk factors that are also inherent in every loan. For further discussion, see Irving Fisher, *The Theory of Interest*, Kelley & Millman, Inc., New York, 1954.

Put A contract which gives the holder the right to sell a certain amount of stock for a designated time period at a specified price. It is the reverse of a call. There are four parties to every put: the holder (buyer); the maker (seller); the broker who brought them together; and the endorser, a New York Stock Exchange member firm, which guarantees that the maker will comply with the agreement. Puts are usually written for thirty, sixty, or ninety days or for six months, but any time period longer than twenty-one days (which is a New York Stock Exchange rule) to which the parties agree is acceptable. For the right to sell the stock, the buyer pays a premium to the seller of the put. The seller, in turn, pays a small commission to the put and call broker. Four factors affect the price of a put: (1) the time period covered by the contract, (2) the price of the stock at the time the put is written, (3) the ability of the put to be exercised at that price or at a lower price, and (4) the volatility of past price movements of the stock. For further information, see George L. Leffler and L. C. Farwell, *The Stock Market*, The Ronald Press Company, New York, 1963; for an extensive study of puts and calls, see U.S. Securities and Exchange Commission, *Report on Put and Call Options*, August, 1961.

Pyramiding A trading technique which is used by stock-market speculators, usually in a rising market. Speculators employ the additional equity that arises in a margin account when the price of a stock increases in order to support additional stock purchases without further cash investment. The technique works as follows: If we assume margin requirements of 50% (i.e., cash equal to 50% of the purchase price must be put up), a trader buys $2,000 worth of stock, investing $1,000 in cash and borrowing $1,000. If the price of the stock increases by 10%, the trader's debit balance (debt) remains $1,000, but his equity (collateral value minus debit balance) increases to $1,200. Now he can buy an additional $200 worth of stock without putting up a larger amount of money. If he does purchase this stock, his account will be as follows:

Collateral value	$2,400
Debit balance	$1,200
Equity	$1,200
Equity/collateral value	50%

The trader can continue to buy stock until the equity-to-collateral-value ratio reaches a minimum of 50%, because the law states that no one can make a margin-account transaction that pushes the equity-to-collateral-value ratio below current margin requirements. If prices rose by an additional 10%, the trader could then buy an additional $240 worth of stock without further investment. As long as prices continue to rise, the trader can pyramid his holdings on a small original cash investment. Of course, caution is necessary because, if prices start to drop, the equity of a trader who has pyramided disappears very rapidly. For further information, see Charles A. Dice and Wilford J. Eiteman, *The Stock Market*, 3d ed., McGraw-Hill Book Company, New York, 1952, chap. 16.

Q

Qualitative Interview (Depth Interview)   A personal interview, used to explain consumer behavior, in which there is no fixed list of formal questions and little interruption on the part of a trained interviewer. Through the use of a general guide, the interviewer attempts to obtain a complete reaction to a product or an idea from a freely talking respondent. The qualitative interview differs from the quantitative interview, which follows a fixed list of questions, the answers to which can be tabulated and quantified. For general information on qualitative, or depth, interviews, see Robert Ferber and Hugh G. Wales, *Motivation and Market Behavior*, Richard D. Irwin, Inc., Homewood, Ill., 1958; for examples, see Joseph W. Newman, *Motivation Research and Marketing Management*, Harvard Business School, Division of Research, Boston, 1957.

Quantitative Trade Restriction (Quota)   A limitation on the number of units of a commodity that may enter a country during a specific period. There are five kinds of direct import quotas: (1) The tariff or customs quota allows a specified quantity of the commodity to enter the country under a special low tariff rate, but additional imports of the good are subject to a significantly higher duty. (2) The unilateral import quota sets an absolute limit on the importation of a commodity in any one period. (3) Import licensing prevents a rush of imports. (4) Bilateral quotas combat the monopolistic exploitation of importing countries by means of negotiation with foreign producers and administration by the exporting country. (5) Mixing quotas limit the amount of foreign-produced material that can be incorporated in domestically finished products. As in the case of a tariff, the effect is to reduce imports and to raise prices to consumers. Article XI of the General Agreement on Tariffs and Trade (GATT) contains an indictment against quotas, import restrictions, and licensing systems. The International Monetary Fund concurs. See J. B. Condliffe, *The Reconstruction of World Trade*, W. W. Norton & Company, Inc., New York, 1940; Charles P. Kindleberger, *International Economics*, 4th ed., Richard D. Irwin, Inc., Homewood, Ill., 1968; Stephen Enke and Virgil Salera, *International Economics*, Prentice-Hall, Inc., Englewood Cliffs, N.J., 1957.

Quantity Theory of Money The theory that the level of prices in an economic system is directly proportional to the quantity of its money supply. The quantity theory is based on the equation of exchange, which is simply $MV = PT$, where M is the quantity of money, V the velocity of its circulation, P the price level, and T the value of real output. The equation of exchange is a truism, stating that total demand (total money in circulation times its rate of circulation) equals total supply (price level times real output). The quantity theory of money assumes that V is determined by the spending habits of the population and tends to remain constant and that T is determined by the productive capacity of the economy. Thus, the equation of exchange for the quantity theory becomes $M = kP$, or, expressed in words, the price level depends only on the quantity of money and is directly proportional to it. For example, the quantity-of-money theorists, among them Irving Fisher, who popularized the theory in the U.S., would argue that if the quantity of money in circulation suddenly doubles, the price level would automatically double also. The quantity theory of money is related to the problem of income and employment, that is, the extent to which productive capacity is utilized. The quantity theory also considers money only in its role of a medium of exchange and not in its role as a store of value. For additional details, see Irving Fisher, *The Purchasing Power of Money*, The Macmillan Company, New York, 1926; Hugo Hegilang, *The Quantity Theory of Money*, Elenders Boktrycheri Aktiebolag, Göteborg, Sweden, 1957; Milton Friedman, *Studies in the Quantity Theory of Money*, The University of Chicago Press, Chicago, 1956; S. Sobajima, "The Rise and Fall of the Quantity Theory of Money," *Osaka Economic Papers*, Osaka, Japan, June, 1955, pp. 1–16.

Quasi Rent The return above the variable costs involved in using resources other than land. The concept of economic rent refers to the surplus which any factor of production earns above the income necessary to keep it at work. A factor will earn rent only if its supply is fixed; since supply of land is fixed even in the long run, the term rent is usually applied to payments for the use of land. The English economist Alfred Marshall realized, however, that in the short run the supply of the other factors, especially capital, is also fixed, and thus part of the return to these goods is a form of economic rent. Since such rent is temporary, Marshall called these payments quasi rents. Quasi rents for such productive factors as buildings and heavy machinery resemble land rents in that their size depends almost entirely on changes in demand and not in supply. For a fuller discussion of the concept of quasi rents, see K. C. Aggarwala, "Marshall's Concept of Quasi-Rent," *Indian Journal of Economics,* p. 555, Indian Economic Association, University of Allahabad, Allahabad, India, April, 1948; Sidney Weintraub, *An Approach to the Theory of Income Distribution,* Chilton Company-Book Division, Philadelphia, 1958, chap. 9; C. E. Bye, *Development and Issues in the Theory of Rent,* Columbia University Press, New York, 1940; Alfred Marshall, *Principles of Economics,* 9th ed., Macmillan & Co., Ltd., London, 1961.

Queuing Theory A theory of operations research which determines the amount of delay and the length of waiting lines that will occur when service has to be provided in sequence for customers arriving at a random rate. Queuing theory can be applied to any operation in which the objects to be dealt with arrive at irregular intervals and in which the operating facilities are of limited capacity. Check-out counters at supermarkets, the landing of aircraft at airports, highway toll booths, and the placing of telephone calls are practical examples in which queuing theory can be useful. By analyzing the frequency distribution of customer arrivals, queuing theory helps determine average waiting time, the expected length of waiting lines at different times of day, etc. The theory is used by management to determine the amount of customer-servicing facilities that should be available. For a fuller explanation of queuing theory, see Joseph McCloskey et al., *Operations Research for Management,* vols. I and II, The Johns Hopkins Press, Baltimore, 1954–1956; Charles Flagle et al., *Operations Research and Systems Engineering,* The Johns Hopkins Press, Baltimore, 1961, chap. 14; C. W. Churchman et al., *Introduction to Operations Research,* John Wiley & Sons, Inc., New York, 1957, part VI.

Quick Assets An accounting term used sometimes to refer to current assets but preferably to refer to current assets excluding inventories. Quick assets are convertible into cash immediately or in the due course of business. They tend to be converted into cash within a reasonably short time, the time limit usually being one year.

Quick Ratio   *See Acid-Test Ratio.*

Quota   The proportional share assigned to a particular division, group, or individual when a specific limit is desired. There are import quotas to control the influx of foreign goods, farm quotas to control farm production, etc. In international trade, there are two basic types of quotas: (1) a tariff quota that admits a certain amount of goods under a certain schedule of duties and additional goods at a higher-schedule rate and (2) an import quota that places a definite limit on the total quantity of an article that may be imported from a particular country within a specified time. Apparently first used by France in 1931, import quotas have since been adopted by many countries. The General Agreement on Tariffs and Trade (GATT) has sought to eliminate such restrictive quotas. For information on import quotas, see H. Austin Peck, *International Economics*, Thomas Y. Crowell Company, New York, 1957, chap. 11; Charles P. Kindleberger, *International Economics*, 4th ed., Richard D. Irwin, Inc., Homewood, Ill., 1968, pp. 130–134.

R

Random Variable   In statistics and econometrics, a variable that can take any of an infinite number of different values, regardless of their magnitude, each having a certain probability and provided there are at least two such values. Random variables are also called chance variables or stochastic variables. For additional information, see Gerhard Tintner and Charles B. Millham, *Mathematics and Statistics for Economists*, Holt, Rinehart and Winston, Inc., New York, 1970; Stefan Valavanis, *Econometrics*, McGraw-Hill Book Company, New York, 1959.

Ratchet-Effect Theory The notion that at the beginning of a recession consumers and investors try to maintain the previous high levels of consumption and investment, respectively. High consumption standards and high investment levels are not easily reversed. The term is used to describe this economic situation because a ratchet, when it takes hold of a mechanism, holds it in a fixed position. The ratchet keeps the economy from slipping back and losing all the income gains attained during the preceding expansion. It takes hold when economic activity has passed the peak and influences its course throughout the recession and subsequent recovery until the previous peak level has been surpassed. For further discussion, see Franco Modigliani, "Fluctuations in the Saving-Income Ratio: A Problem of Economic Forecasting," *Studies in Income and Wealth*, vol. XI, National Bureau of Economic Research, Inc., New York, 1949; James S. Duesenberry, *Income, Savings and the Theory of Consumer Behavior*, Harvard University Press, Cambridge, Mass., 1949, pp. 114–116; Arthur Smithies, "Economic Fluctuations and Growth," *Econometrica*, vol. XXV, no. 1, pp. 1–52, Econometric Society, Yale University Press, New Haven, Conn., January, 1957; John P. Lewis and Robert C. Turner, *Business Conditions Analysis*, 2d ed., McGraw-Hill Book Company, New York, 1967, chap. 6.

Rate of Change Month-to-month percentage changes, or differences, in statistical series. For example, the rate of change in the seasonally adjusted index of industrial production between February, 1971 (65.2 on a 1957–1959 base), and March, 1971 (65.5), was 0.2%, or 0.3 percentage point. For a discussion of the rate of change in diffusion indices, see Geoffrey H. Moore and Julius Shiskin, *Variable Span Diffusion Indexes and Economic Forecasting*, paper presented at the Sixth Annual Forecasting Conference, American Statistical Association, New York chapter, Apr. 17, 1964.

Rate of Return on Invested Capital The ratio of profits to capital or assets. The return on capital employed may be expressed as turnover times profit on sales. Manufacturing companies make their rate of return on invested capital with a low turnover and a high profit on sales, whereas merchandising companies produce their return on capital invested by means of a high turnover and a low profit on sales. This ratio is a measure of the effectiveness with which a company uses its existing assets. The rate of return on invested capital for manufacturing companies may be found in U.S. Federal Trade Commission and Securities and Exchange Commission, *Quarterly Financial Report for Manufacturing Corporations*.

Rate of Return on New Investment An evaluation of the profitability of proposed equipment purchases. The rate-of-return method of evaluation is the converse of the payoff or pay-out method. It assumes that an investment must earn something in addition to the recovery of the cost of the capital invested. Excess earnings (annual savings minus annual depreciation of the new facility) are measured against the investment to determine the rate of return. Rates of return vary for each company and for each product line. This popular method of determining the advisability of an investment does not help a businessman find the real cost of the capital used up by investment in a new machine. For further information, see "Corporate Profits and Rates of Return in the Fifties Adjusted for Comparison with Those of the Twenties," *Capital Goods Review*, Machinery and Allied Products Institute, Washington, D.C., May, 1959; for various methods of evaluating the profitability of proposed equipment purchases, see C. Aubrey Smith and Jim Ashburne, *Financial and Administrative Accounting*, McGraw-Hill Book Company, New York, 1960; see also George Terborgh, *Business Investment Policy*, Machinery and Allied Products Institute, Washington, D.C., 1958.

Rationalization The use of scientific management and industrial organization in production. Rationalization was based on the theory that a large, well-organized firm would achieve certain economies of scale and that the competition of small industrial units was wasteful. The use of more advanced technological methods of production was the most common form of rationalization. See Robert A. Brady, *The Rationalization Movement in German Industry: A Study in the Evolution of Economic Planning*, University of California Press, Berkeley, Calif., 1933.

Rationing of Exchange A means of controlling foreign exchange by requiring all holders of foreign exchange to surrender it for domestic currency at a specified rate. The government then allocates such exchange to importers whose activities it wishes to encourage and denies the exchange to those considered less essential to its national and foreign plans.

Rationing of Goods A policy of allocating a good or goods when supply and demand are not in balance at established price levels. Adoption of a rationing system helps distribute a product equally among the population and at the same time helps prevent inflation. During World War II, a rationing system based on points and coupons for various types of goods was adopted by the U.S. For further information, see M. McManus, "Points Rationing and the Consumer," *Metroeconomica*, pp. 118–134, Libreria L. Cappelli, Trieste, Italy, August, 1954.

Ratio-to-Moving-Average Method of Seasonal Adjustment   A method of computing seasonal adjustment. A preliminary trend cycle is estimated by taking a moving average of the original data after any prior adjustments. Seasonal-irregular (S–I) ratios are obtained by dividing the original series by the preliminary trend cycle. The S–I ratios for each month or quarter are smoothed out by a moving average to provide an estimate of the seasonal. Finally, the original series is divided by the seasonal to obtain the seasonally adjusted series. For further discussion, see Julius Shiskin, *Electronic Computers and Business Indicators,* National Bureau of Economic Research, Occasional Paper 57, New York, 1957.

Raw Material   A natural or semimanufactured material that is changed in the process of manufacturing. Thus, while iron ore is a raw material in the production of steel, steel is a raw material in the production of automobiles. Raw materials may be divided into three categories: those directly consumed, those indirectly adaptable to consumption, and those that can be converted into manufactured articles. See Percy W. Bidwell, *Raw Materials: A Study of American Policy,* Harper & Row, Publishers, Incorporated, New York, 1958.

Real-Balance-Effect Theory   The theory that a reduction in the overall price level leads to an increase in both consumption and investment. A generic term that covers both the Keynes effect and the Pigou effect, the real-balance effect is based on the following line of reasoning: (1) Individuals establish a desired relationship between the money balances that they hold and their expenditures on goods and services. (2) Price reductions raise the real value of their money holdings; that is, the quantity of goods and services that can be bought with a given amount of money rises. (3) Thus, the desired relationship between real balances and expenditures is disturbed, and individuals have an excess supply of liquid assets. (4) They spend part of this excess supply on goods and services. (5) They are also willing to lend part of this excess supply, which results in an increase in the supply of funds in the loan market and a lowering of the rate of interest. (6) With a lower rate of interest, additional investment takes place. Thus, the real-balance effect raises both consumption and investment. For a thorough discussion of the real-balance effect, see Don Patinkin, *Money, Interest and Prices,* 2d ed., Harper & Row, Publishers, Incorporated, New York, 1965.

Real-Bills Doctrine   A theory, held by members of the banking school, that all commercial bank loans should be short-term, self-liquidating loans so that the expansion and contraction of the money supply would be based mainly on the needs of business. Banks should issue credit only on the basis of real bills—self-liquidating, short-term notes based on goods in process. If this doctrine were followed, its proponents argued, the means of payment in an economy would expand or contract with the volume of goods produced. The real-bills doctrine was the basis of the Federal Reserve Act of 1913. For a study of the evolution of the real-bills doctrine through the nineteenth century, see L. W. Mints, *A History of Banking Theory*, The University of Chicago Press, Chicago, 1945; Herman E. Krooss (ed.), *Documentary History of Banking and Currency in the United States*, Chelsea House Publishers, New York, 1969, vol. I.

Real-Dollar Value *See Constant-Dollar Value.*

Real Income The purchasing power of the income of an individual or a nation. Real income is computed by adjusting money income to changes in consumer prices. Thus, if the price index rises by the same amount as money incomes, real incomes remain unchanged, for consumers can purchase neither more nor less with their money incomes. When prices rise more rapidly than money incomes, real incomes fall, and, conversely, when prices rise less rapidly than money incomes, real incomes rise. The table (page 486) gives a computation of real per capita income derived from income data of the U.S. Department of Commerce and price data of the U.S. Bureau of Labor Statistics. It can be readily seen that real income rose much more slowly over the five-year period 1964–1968 than money income because prices rose rapidly in that period. For further information, see J. S. Davis, "Standards and Content of Living," *American Economic Review*, American Economic Association, Evanston, Ill., March, 1945; John P. Powelson, *National Income and Flow-of-Funds Analysis*, McGraw-Hill Book Company, New York, 1960; for annual statistics of real income (real disposable income either on a national basis or on a per capita basis), see *The Annual Economic Report of the President*, Government Printing Office, Washington, D.C.

Real Wage The purchasing power of a worker's earnings. The real wage is computed by adjusting the money wage to changes in consumer prices. At times, the movements of money wages and real wages may diverge. For example, average weekly earnings (money wages) in the U.S. manufacturing industries rose from $129.51 to $133.73 between 1969 and 1970, but the average price of consumer goods rose so much more rapidly in the same period that real wages, i.e., the purchasing power of these earnings, fell from $129.51 to $122.26. Conversely, in times of recession, money wages sometimes fall less rapidly than the consumer price index, so that real wages actually rise. The possibility of

Calculation of Real Income

	1958	1959	1960	1961	1962	1963	1964	1965	1966	1967	1968	1969	1970
Money income (disposable income per capita)	$1,831	$1,905	$1,937	$1,983	$2,066	$2,139	$2,284	$2,436	$2,605	$2,751	$2,947	$3,117	$3,344
Consumer price index (1958 = 100)	100.0	101.3	102.9	103.9	104.9	106.2	107.4	108.8	111.5	114.4	118.5	123.4	129.3
Real income (disposable income per capita in 1958 dollars)	$1,831	$1,881	$1,883	$1,909	$1,969	$2,015	$2,126	$2,240	$2,336	$2,404	$2,487	$2,525	$2,587

such divergences over the course of business cycles was a major issue in John Maynard Keynes's *General Theory of Employment, Interest, and Money*, in which he disagreed with the view of the classical economists that a decline in money wages would result in a prompt solution of business recessions. Keynes believed that, if real wages were rising, a decrease in money wages might be ineffective in lowering costs and actually be very detrimental by lowering consumer demand. Omitting business-cycle changes, real wages in the U.S. are climbing slowly over the long run. Between 1939 and 1970, average weekly earnings in manu-

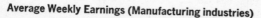

Average Weekly Earnings (Manufacturing industries)

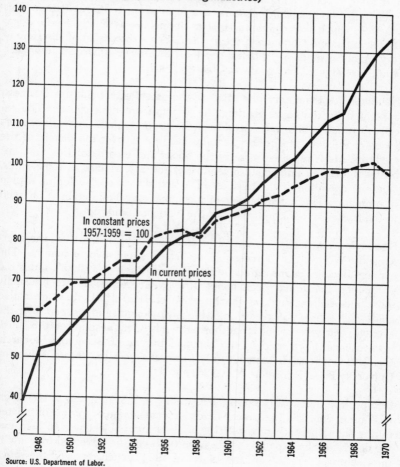

Source: U.S. Department of Labor.

facturing industries, adjusted for changes in the consumer price index, rose by an average of 2.3% annually. See J. M. Keynes, *The General Theory of Employment, Interest, and Money,* Harcourt, Brace & World, Inc., New York, 1936; for current statistics on real wages, see U.S. Department of Labor, *Monthly Labor Review;* for a discussion of the concept, see Lloyd G. Reynolds, *Labor Economics and Labor Relations,* 5th ed., Prentice-Hall, Inc., Englewood Cliffs, N.J., 1970.

Rebate   The return of part of a payment for goods or services. A rebate differs from a discount, which is deducted in advance. Rebates to large and more favored shippers were used extensively in the U.S. railroad industry in the nineteenth century as a form of price discrimination. This practice, which was unfair to smaller shippers, was finally made illegal by the Interstate Commerce Act of 1887. For a discussion of discriminatory practices involving rebates, see John F. Stover, *American Railroads,* The University of Chicago Press, Chicago, 1961.

Receiver   A temporary custodian of the assets of a bankrupt business, appointed by the court pending the appointment of a trustee. The receiver's function is to take custody of the property and, under the supervision of the court, to preserve the business's assets for the benefit of the creditors. He is required to seize the books and records of the bankrupt business, take an immediate inventory of the assets, and, in some cases, continue operation of the business. The actual task of developing a plan of reorganization, if feasible, or of recommending liquidation is charged to the trustee in bankruptcy under the National Bankruptcy Act.

Recession   A decline in overall business activity. In the U.S., the average post-World War II recession has lasted about twelve months. The average decline, as measured by the Federal Reserve System's industrial production index, has been about 10%. When recessions are unusually short and shallow, such as the recession of 1960–1961, they are called mild. The 1957–1958 recession, which was longer and deeper than the average, was severe. For an authoritative historical account of U.S. business recessions prepared by the National Bureau of Economic Research, Inc., see Geoffrey H. Moore (ed.), *Business Cycle Indicators,* Princeton University Press, Princeton, N.J., 1961.

Reciprocal Trade Agreements Program   A U.S. program of reciprocal tariff reduction. The Reciprocal Trade Agreements program was originated during the depression of the 1930s, and its main object was to help end the depression by expanding U.S. exports. It was first enacted into law in the Reciprocal Trade Agreements Act of 1934, which reversed the previous U.S. protectionist trade policy and empowered the President to negotiate treaties for the purpose of lowering or raising duties by as much as 50% of their 1934 levels. In 1945 this authorization was extended to permit reductions of 50% below the tariffs of that year, and in 1955 it was extended again to permit another 15% reduction. The President was to negotiate the treaties whereby duties might be lowered only if an equivalent tariff concession was made in return by another country. Once a tariff reduction had been concluded, the new rate is then applied non-discriminatively, according to the most-favored-nation principle, to all countries with which the U.S. has tariff agreements. To preserve its bargaining power, the U.S. generally follows the practice of making its most-favored-nation tariff reduction for a commodity only with the chief supplier of that good to the U.S. Although the Reciprocal Trade Agreements program was a significant step toward liberalizing trade, it was weakened by the addition of two provisions in later extension acts: the introduction in 1947 of the escape clause, permitting the U.S. to withdraw concessions on imports which had caused unforeseen serious injury to domestic producers; and the attachment in 1948 of the peril-point clause, whereby the Tariff Commission would recommend the maximum permissible tariff reduction which would not cause serious injury. For additional details on the history and results of the Reciprocal Trade Agreements program, see U.S. Tariff Commission, *Operation of the Trade Agreements Program*, periodically; Don D. Humphrey, *American Imports*, The Twentieth Century Fund, New York, 1955.

Reciprocity   The lowering of trade barriers by one country in return for similar concessions by other countries. The principle of reciprocity has been dominant in American tariff policy since 1934, when the Reciprocal Trade Agreements program was originated. Reciprocal agreements make it economically safe for each nation to reduce its tariffs, since mutual reduction eliminates the threat of a balance-of-payments deficit inherent in unilateral reduction. They also make it politically feasible, since the tariff reduction is viewed not as a surrender but as an exchange (in which the home country is always presumed to have gained the most). For further information on reciprocity and its beneficial effects on world trade, income, and production, see Don D. Humphrey, *American Imports*, The Twentieth Century Fund, New York, 1955.

Recourse Basis   A basis of purchasing consumer installment debt contracts by finance companies under which the dealer is not relieved of the credit risk. Contracts sold on a recourse basis are usually purchased by sales finance companies and arise from sales to consumers, mainly for automobiles, electrical appliances, and other consumer durables. On a nonrecourse basis, the finance company would assume the risk for the repayment.

Recovery   An increase in business activity after the low point of a recession or a depression has been reached. The recovery continues until business achieves approximately the same level that it had attained before the decline. After that point has been reached, the recovery moves into the expansionary stage. The rate of recovery is generally related directly to that of the preceding decline; that is, recoveries are more rapid after severe recessions than after mild ones. The average recovery rate, as measured by the index of industrial production, is faster during the period immediately following a recession than later on. Some sensitive barometers, such as new orders for durable goods, awards of industrial and commercial building contracts, the work week, and corporate profits, are early indicators of recovery. For an authoritative historical record of U.S. business recoveries, see Geoffrey H. Moore (ed.), *Business Cycle Indicators*, vol. I, National Bureau of Economic Research, Inc., Princeton University Press, Princeton, N.J., 1961.

Recursive System   A system of econometric equations having the property that when the values of the variables are fully determined up to time t minus 1, the equations yield the values of the variables for time t, one at a time. That is, the determination of the value of one variable at time t facilitates the determination of the value of another variable at time t, and so forth in some order or other. For additonal information, see Karl A. Fox, *Intermediate Economic Statistics*, John Wiley & Sons, Inc., New York, 1968.

Redemption   The exchange of bonds for cash. One of the three methods of extinguishing bonded indebtedness (the other two are refunding and conversion), redemption can take place at or before maturity. Corporations and the U.S. government (infrequently) redeem bonds at maturity by depositing the requisite funds with the trustee, who in turn pays the bondholders when they turn in their securities. Redemption occurs before maturity when the corporation has the necessary cash to reduce its fixed obligations and therefore to lower its interest costs. For the redemption of outstanding bonds before maturity, the indenture should contain a call provision; that is, the corporation is allowed to redeem the bonds prematurely, provided certain stipulations have been met. In some cases, however, corporations can negotiate a redemption by agreement with the bondholders even without the call feature. The term redemption also refers to the willingness and ability of monetary authorities to pay out standard money (the form of money with which the monetary authorities can meet their ultimate obligations) on a dollar-for-dollar basis in exchange for any other form of money whose circulation they wish to insure. As long as redemption facilities exist, all forms of money are on a parity with the standard and hence with one another. Thus the effects of Gresham's law are avoided. (See definition of Gresham's law.) For theory of bond redemption, see Charles W. Gerstenberg, *Financial Organization and Management of Business*, 4th ed., Prentice-Hall, Inc., Englewood Cliffs, N.J., 1959. For a discussion of monetary redemption, see Eli Shapiro, Ezra Solomon, and William L. White, *Money and Banking*, 5th ed., Holt, Rinehart and Winston, Inc., New York, 1968.

Rediscount Rate   *See Discount Rate.*

Reduced-Form Equation   A method of estimating the parameters in stochastic systems. It consists of expressing the endogenous variables individually in terms of predetermined variables, i.e., variables that are determined independently of, or before, the endogenous variables in a causal sense. Since each reduced-form equation contains a single endogenous variable, it is possible to estimate the coefficients of each such equation by the method of least squares. For additional information, see Karl A. Fox, *Intermediate Economic Statistics*, John Wiley & Sons, Inc., New York, 1968.

Reference Cycle   The succession of expansion and contraction in general business activity. The reference cycle is determined by the combined behavior of a group of economic indicators (roughly coincident indicators) which are regarded as defining general business activity: employment, income, production, prices, etc. The cycle for the individual indicators of general business activity need not coincide with the reference cycle. The term reference cycle is used synonymously with business cycle. For further discussion on reference-cycle patterns, see Geoffrey H. Moore (ed.), *Business Cycle Indicators*, National Bureau of Economic Research, Inc., Princeton University Press, Princeton, N.J., 1961, vol. I; Harry D. Wolfe, *Business Forecasting Methods*, Holt, Rinehart and Winston, Inc., New York, 1966; James A. Estey, *Business Cycles: Their Nature, Course, and Control*, 3d ed., Prentice-Hall, Inc., Englewood Cliffs, N.J., 1956.

Reflation   A type of inflation, occurring during a recovery from a depression or a recession, in which prices are restored to a so-called desirable level by decreasing the purchasing power of money. Reflation to a preexisting price structure is brought about through the use of governmental monetary powers. In periods of reflation, it is often difficult to distinguish the time at which reflation ends and inflation begins. The examples of reflation in the U.S. usually cited are for the periods 1917–1920 and 1933–1934. For details on the process of reflation, see G. F. Warren and F. A. Pearson, *Gold and Prices*, John Wiley & Sons, Inc., New York, 1935.

Reform Liberalism (Twentieth-Century Liberalism) An economic philosophy which embraces the idea that intervention by man in some markets will improve economic welfare. Contrary to classical liberalism, which held that there is a natural harmony in the economic system with benefits for all when each individual pursues his self-interest, reform liberalism holds that free markets permit maldistributions of resources and grossly unfair earnings for some workers. The general philosophy has been popularly termed the New Deal, the Fair Deal, the welfare state, or, most commonly, simply liberalism. The term liberal has come to mean almost exactly the opposite of what it meant at the turn of the twentieth century. Proponents of reform liberalism point to enormous monopoly profits, the rape of forests and other natural resources, polluted streams, booms and busts, and unequal distribution of incomes that may result from a hands-off policy on the part of government. The approach of reform liberals is pragmatic. They look at what is being achieved by the market. If it conforms to their general idea of what is best, they leave it alone, but if they find difficulties, they interfere. In some cases, the solution may be the improvement of competition by antitrust activity; in other cases, the solution may be government ownership. In combating business cycles, reform liberals are more likely to be concerned about the human misery caused by unemployment than by the burden of the Federal debt. When John Maynard Keynes suggested that the U.S. economy might suffer from a chronic lack of demand, many reform liberals seized upon this suggestion as additional proof that a larger role for government was required. See Eric F. Goldman, *Rendezvous with Destiny: A History of Modern American Reform*, Alfred A. Knopf, Inc., New York, 1952; D. S. Watson, *Economic Policy*, Houghton Mifflin Company, Boston, 1960; B. Hughel Wilkins and Charles B. Friday (eds.), *The Economists of the New Frontier*, Random House, Inc., New York, 1963.

Refunding The replacement of one bond issue by another whose maturity is deferred to a later date. Usually, refunding consists of retiring an outstanding issue with the proceeds of the sale of a new issue, but it may take the form of a direct exchange. The old issue may be fully or partly refunded, and refunding may be accomplished before maturity. The refunding process is used when market conditions are such that the new issue can be floated at a saving in fixed interest charges over the old issue. Refunding operations have also been undertaken to extend the length of existing debt by replacing short-term obligations with long-term obligations and to eliminate previous bond issues that contained unfavorable indenture provisions. For information on the refunding of the public debt, see Marcus Nadler et al., *The Money Market and Its Institutions,* The Ronald Press Company, New York, 1955, pp. 261–282; see also Charles W. Gerstenberg, *Financial Organization and Management of Business,* 4th ed., Prentice-Hall, Inc., Englewood Cliffs, N.J., 1959; Eli Schwartz, "The Refunding Decision," *Journal of Business,* vol. 40, no. 4, pp. 448–450, October, 1967; Oswald D. Bowlin, "The Refunding Decisions: Another Special Case in Capital Budgeting," *Journal of Finance,* vol. 21, pp. 55–68, March, 1966.

Region The term applied to an area which may vary in size from a small section within a metropolitan area to a huge subregion within a continent. In the U.S., for example, regional or subnational data are available for census tracts, metropolitan areas, counties, states, and groupings of states into major regions, such as New England and the Middle Atlantic states. For further information on regions, see Werner Hochwald (ed.), *Design of Regional Accounts,* papers presented at the Conference on Regional Accounts, 1960, sponsored by the Committee on Regional Accounts, published for Resources of the Future, The Johns Hopkins Press, Baltimore, 1961.

Regional Account An income and product account on a subnational basis. Limitations on data prevent the compilation of detailed regional accounts similar to the national income account. Nevertheless, accounts of this type offer a flexible framework for regional economic analysis by decision makers at all levels of government and business. For further information, see Werner Hochwald (ed.), *Design of Regional Accounts,* papers presented at the Conference on Regional Accounts, 1960, sponsored by the Committee on Regional Accounts, published for Resources of the Future, The Johns Hopkins Press, Baltimore, 1961.

Regional Analysis The study of comparative growth and development in a geographic area, emphasis being placed on the future role of the region in the national economy. Regional analysis requires data on the flow of regional products and the stock of regional resources. Since many data are lacking, comprehensive statements of the economics of regions are not available. Nevertheless, some regional data, such as personal income, population, employment, and industrial production, are available. For further information, see Werner Hochwald (ed.), *Design and Regional Accounts,* papers presented at the Conference on Regional Accounts,

1960, sponsored by the Committee on Regional Accounts, published for Resources of the Future, The Johns Hopkins Press, Baltimore, 1961.

Regional Stock Exchange   Any U.S. stock exchange except the New York Stock Exchange (NYSE) and the American Stock Exchange (ASE). As of 1970, there were fourteen regional stock exchanges in the U.S., eleven of which were registered with the Securities and Exchange Commission as national securities exchanges; the other three exchanges were exempted from registration because either they were too small or their trading activity was almost nonexistent. The regional stock exchanges registered as national securities exchanges were the Boston Stock Exchange, Chicago Board of Trade, Midwest Stock Exchange, Cincinnati Stock Exchange, Detroit Stock Exchange, Pacific Coast Stock Exchange, National Stock Exchange, Philadelphia-Baltimore-Washington Stock Exchange, Pittsburgh Stock Exchange, Salt Lake City Stock Exchange, and Spokane Stock Exchange. Those exempt from registration were the Colorado Springs Stock Exchange, Honolulu Stock Exchange, and Richmond Stock Exchange. All the regional stock exchanges are organized and governed in a way that closely resembles the structure of the NYSE. The major difference is that their rules and regulations are not as stringent as those of the NYSE, particularly regarding the requirements for listing stock. Most seats or memberships on regional exchanges are held by brokerage firms that are also members of the NYSE and the ASE. The basic purpose and function of the regional exchanges are to give small, regional, or local corporations, which cannot meet the listing requirements of the NYSE and the ASE, an opportunity to be listed on an organized stock exchange. See George L. Leffler and L. C. Farwell, *The Stock Market*, The Ronald Press Company, New York, 1963.

Regression Line   A statistical term that indicates a relationship between two or more variables. The regression line was first used by Sir Francis Galton to indicate certain relationships in his theory of heredity, but it is now employed to connote many functional relationships. A regression, or least-squares, line is derived from a mathematical equation relating one economic variable to another. The use of regression lines is important in determining the effect of one variable on another. For example, an increase in disposable income results in an increase in consumption, and a regression line can be used to show such a relationship. The regression technique is useful in forecasting general economic activity or individual fields. For further information, see R. Clay Sprowls, *Elementary Statistics*, McGraw-Hill Book Company, New York, 1955, chap. 10.

Regressive Tax   A tax whose rate decreases as the tax base increases. In this sense of the term, there are no actual regressive taxes in the U.S. Frequently, however, the rate structure of a tax is compared not with its actual base but with the net income of the taxpayer. When used in this way, the term regressive refers to a tax which takes a larger share of income from the low-income taxpayer than from the high-income taxpayer. A tax which is technically proportional in terms of the tax base can often be considered regressive in terms of the taxpayer's income. Common examples of such regressive taxes are sales taxes, excise taxes, and property taxes. For example, an excise tax on cigarettes is based on the number of cigarettes sold and thus by definition is proportional. Since the number of cigarettes consumed may rise as income rises, however, the rate of the tax decreases with increasing income and thus can be called regressive. The effect of a regressive tax is to increase inequalities of income, placing a larger burden on the poor man than on the rich. The accompanying chart illustrates the basic concepts. For additional details, see Hugh Dalton, *Principles of Public Finance*, 10th ed., Routledge & Kegan Paul, Ltd., London, 1939, chap. 9; William H. Anderson, *Taxation and the American Economy*, Prentice-Hall, Inc., Englewood Cliffs, N.J., 1951; John F. Due, *Government Finance*, 4th ed., Richard D. Irwin, Inc., Homewood, Ill., 1968.

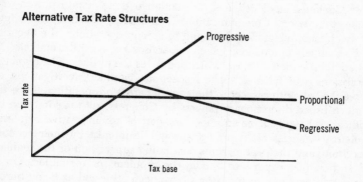

Alternative Tax Rate Structures

(y-axis: Tax rate; x-axis: Tax base; lines labeled Progressive, Proportional, Regressive)

Regulation Q   A banking regulation that determines the rates which the commercial banking system of the U.S. can pay on time deposits. First instituted in the Banking Act of 1933, it was amended in 1935. Because of the greater sensitivity in rates paid on time deposits in the 1960s, Regulation Q is playing a more important role in the Federal Reserve System's monetary policy. Between 1936 and 1957 only one change occurred in Regulation Q: in 1957 the maximum rate on savings was altered from 2½% to 3%. Effective January 1, 1962, the rate was raised to 4%. Rates were raised still further in the following years. In the 1960s and early 1970s, Regulation Q has been used as a tool of Federal Reserve policy, its effect being to shift the flow of money without altering the supply. It increases the flow of funds into commercial banks, over which the Federal Reserve Board has more direct control than it has over other financial intermediaries. To meet the higher rates, the commercial banks reinvest these funds, and this, in turn, has an important bearing on the interest costs of other investment media. For a discussion of the way in which a change in Regulation Q affected the flow of funds into the commercial banks, see "Time and Savings Deposits in the Second District since the Change in Regulation Q," *Monthly Review,* Federal Reserve Bank of New York, New York, April, 1963; for a historical review of Regulation Q, see Albert H. Cox, Jr., "Regulation of Interest on Deposits: An Historical Review," *Journal of Finance,* vol. XXII, no. 2, pp. 274–299, May, 1967.

Regulatory Commission, Federal   A U.S. governmental administrative agency which regulates the conduct of certain business activities. There are five Federal regulatory agencies with jurisdiction over the interstate operation of public utilities. These are the Interstate Commerce Commission, which supervises interstate transportation facilities; the Federal Power Commission, which has jurisdiction over interstate power transmission; the Federal Communications Commission, which regulates interstate telephone, telegraph, radio and television operations; the Securities and Exchange Commission, which supervises the security markets; and the Federal Aviation Agency, which regulates the airlines. The regulatory commissions issue licenses, make inspections, conduct investigations, and enforce the law with respect to their special areas of operation. Since they are given broad discretionary powers by Congress, rule making and rule adjudication have become an important part of administrative regulation. Regulatory agencies often protect the public interest by their economic supervision, and their use permits continuing supervision of the regulated field and enables experts to handle the problems of regulation. On the other hand, regulatory commissions have been criticized as being bureaucratic. Moreover, the combination of rule making, prosecution, and adjudication under the aegis of the same agency has led to charges of unfairness and bias, although the Administrative Procedures Act of 1946 undertook to separate these functions in order to ensure impartiality. The quasi-judicial hearings of the agencies, which usually are not limited by strict rules of evidence, etc., have been attacked as arbitrary and unfair and as subject to possible abuse. All the commission's decisions are, however, open to judicial review. For further information, see Emmette

S. Redford, *Administration of National Economic Control,* The Macmillan Company, New York, 1952; Robert Cushman, *The Independent Regulatory Commissions,* Oxford University Press, Fair Lawn, N.J., 1951; Commission on Organization of the Executive Branch of the Government, *Task Force Report on Regulatory Commissions,* Government Printing Office, Washington, D.C., 1949.

Relative-Income Hypothesis   The assumption that spending is related to a family's relative position in the income distribution of approximately similar families. Thus, for example, it would be expected that a Negro family earning $8,000 a year would save a greater amount than a white family earning the same sum, since the Negro family's position within its relevant income distribution would be considerably higher and more secure than the position of the white family. The relative-income hypothesis was conceived by James S. Duesenberry to help explain the differences found between consumption functions derived from data of families classified by groups and those derived from overall totals (time series). The accompanying three charts help illustrate the problem. Chart 1 shows how the consumption function looks when it is derived from time-series data. Chart 2 illustrates the consumption function estimated

Relative Income Hypothesis

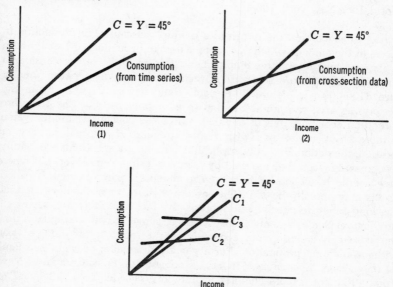

from family-group data. Obviously, in Chart 2 the dollars value of consumption exceeds the dollar value of income at low-income levels, whereas this is not true in Chart 1. Duesenberry hypothesized that, at any given moment in time, consumption is not particularly sensitive to current income. People spend in a manner consistent with their relative-income position. With incomes rising or falling over the course of years, their spending patterns change if their relative position changes. Chart 3 points this hypothesis up as a series of short-run consumption functions which trace the long-run equilibrium path uncovered in the time-series studies of the consumption function. James Tobin showed that other factors could cause the effects that Duesenberry explained by means of relative incomes. Discussion of the relative-income hypothesis greatly diminished after Milton Friedman conceived his consumption-function theory, which relies on the notion of permanent income. Friedman's theory was based on extensive mathematical exploration. See James S. Duesenberry, *Income Saving and the Theory of Consumer Behavior*, Harvard University Press, Cambridge, Mass., 1949; James Tobin, "Relative Income, Absolute Income, and Savings," *Money, Trade and Economic Growth*, The Macmillan Company, New York, 1951; Milton Friedman, *A Theory of the Consumption Function*, a study by the National Bureau of Economic Research, Inc., Princeton University Press, Princeton, N.J., 1957; Edward Shapiro, *Macroeconomic Analysis*, Harcourt, Brace & World, Inc., New York, 1966.

Rent In economics, the return to a unique factor used in production in excess of the amount which that factor (human or nonhuman) could earn in its next best alternative employment. For example, let us consider a female motion picture star with special attributes which permit her to earn $100,000 per picture. If the star could not earn her living in the performing arts, she might be able to earn only $4,000. She therefore earned an economic rent of $96,000. While the concept of unique value is more easily understood with respect to land of unusual fertility or location, the notion is equally applicable to human talent. Rents are readily recognizable when they are paid by a firm or a single employer, but when they accrue to owners of firms (entrepreneurs), part of what is called profits may actually be rent. One of the features of economic rent that has long interested social reformers is the fact that it is not a cost of production. Some, notably Henry George, suggested in a corollary that the state could expropriate economic rent through a tax (single tax) without affecting production. For a general discussion of rents, see Paul A. Samuelson, *Economics*, 7th ed., McGraw-Hill Book Company, New York, 1967; for a more complex exploration, see George J. Stigler, *The Theory of Price*, 3d ed., The Macmillan Company, New York, 1966; see also J. S. Keiper et al., *Theory and Measurement of Rent,* Chilton Company—Book Division, Philadelphia, 1951; for an antiquated expression of the economic doctrine of rent, see Francis A. Walker, *Land and Its Rent,* Macmillan & Co., Ltd., London, 1883.

Rentier An individual living primarily on the returns from fixed monetary investments. The rentier is a passive income receiver, his income depending on past rather than continuing economic activity. He thus differs from the finance capitalist, whose economic well-being is derived from production or from speculation in investment. The rentier is distinguished solely by the source and character of his income. In general, there are three type of rentiers: (1) the lifelong rentier who inherited his wealth; (2) the dependent rentier, the retired businessman, the widow, etc., each of whom has an annuity to carry him through the remainder of his life; and (3) the institutional rentier, a product mainly of the twentieth century, comprising foundations, endowments, educational institutions, cooperative societies, etc., which derives income from fixed investments and is independent of continuing productive activity but dependent on the stability of existing property relationships. The individual interest of the rentier group is generally focused on the preservation of monetary values. Rentiers thrive in periods of economic stagnation, when most income earners suffer, and they are often hard hit in times of growth, prosperity, and rising prices. Thus, this group is frequently pictured as personifying opposition to change of any kind, as feeling that its well-being depends on fixed property relationships, the sanctity of debts, and the stability of the currency. See J. M. Keynes, *The General Theory of Employment, Interest, and Money,* Harcourt, Brace & World, Inc., New York, 1936; for comments on Keynes's rentier concept, see R. G. Hawtrey, *Capital and Employment,* Longmans, Green & Co., Ltd., London, 1937.

Replacement The installation of new machinery for old. With the rapid pace of technological change in the mid-twentieth century, a machine is more likely to be displaced by a more efficient machine than replaced because of physical deterioration. Thus, the term replacement covers a large part of modernization. George Terborgh, of the Machinery and Allied Products Institute, comments on the economics of machinery replacement in *Capital Goods Review,* Machinery and Allied Products Institute, Washington, D.C., quarterly.

Repossession The retaking, without judicial process and without breach of the peace, of an article of personal property sold under a conditional bill of sale. The most outstanding example of repossession sometimes occurs in the sale of a durable good, such as an automobile. The purchaser agrees to pay for the automobile according to the terms of the conditional bill of sale but fails to do so. The holder of the conditional bill of sale may then seize the automobile, provided he can do so without breach of the peace. Delinquency rates on consumer loans can serve as an indication of the trend of repossession.

Representation Controversy   A dispute between rival unions over the choice of the one union to represent a certain group of workers. Representation rivalry may involve unorganized workers or organized workers. When the workers are unorganized, the union must court the votes of the majority of the workers in the unit appropriate for collective bargaining. The U.S. National Labor Relations Board (NLRB) decides whether an employer unit, a craft unit, or a subdivision is appropriate in each case. The action of a union to attract workers who are already represented by another union is known as raiding. Under NLRB representation proceedings, the raided union has a better than 3 to 1 chance of defeating the raider. The NLRB has made raiding easier because it has systematized the proceedings whereby one union can take away the representation rights of another union. See Jack Barbash, *The Practice of Unionism,* Harper & Row, Publishers, Incorporated, New York, 1956; see also Robert D. Leiter, *Labor Economics and Industrial Relations,* Barnes & Noble, Inc., New York, 1958.

Reproduction Rate   The number of daughters that 1,000 women entering their childbearing years will bear during their lives. The reproduction rate is a measure of the rapidity with which a population reproduces itself. There are two different measures of the reproduction rate: the gross rate and the net rate. The gross reproduction rate assumes that all female children born at a given time will live through their child-bearing period, whereas the net reproduction rate allows for deaths occurring among females before and during the childbearing age. Both reproduction rates assume that the childbearing rates will remain constant through each generation. The net rate gives a more accurate picture of changing population trends from one generation to the next. In 1967 the U.S. gross reproduction rate was 1,255, while the net rate was 1,213. Since a stationary population would have a net reproduction rate of 1,000, the U.S. population is growing. For further information, see Robert P. Kuczynski, *Fertility and Reproduction,* Falcon Press, New York, 1932; ———, *The Measurement of Population Growth,* Oxford University Press, Fair Lawn, N.J., 1936; Danold J. Bogue, *The Population of the United States,* The Free Press of Glencoe, New York, 1959, chap. 12; Paul A. Samuelson, *Economics,* 5th ed., McGraw-Hill Book Company, New York, 1961. p. 30.

Request for VA Appraisal The initial step in the process of obtaining the guarantee of the Veterans Administration (VA) for a prospective mortgage loan by a private institution to a U.S. service veteran who is buying a home. The request for VA appraisal is a formal application written by a veteran or a credit institution for an official VA appraisal of the value of a home or a planned home for which a veteran may be seeking a mortgage loan. The request is referred by the VA to a private property appraiser who, for a fee, reports his findings to the VA. On the basis of the appraiser's report, the VA issues a certificate of reasonable value, establishing the maximum price for which the home may be sold if it is purchased with a VA-guaranteed mortgage. In the case of new homes to be constructed, about three months elapse between the issue of the certificate and the beginning of construction, when the proposed home enters Census Bureau statistics as a new housing start. Hence, data on VA appraisal requests, which are reported monthly by the VA, serve as an advance indicator of new home construction activity. The VA appraisal request is analogous to the application for Federal Housing Administration (FHA) insurance. For a thorough discussion of the function of the appraisal request and its use as a housing indicator, see M. Wilkerson and D. K. Newman, "FHA and VA Statistics and the Housing Market," *Construction Review*, U.S. Department of Commerce, Washington, D.C.,

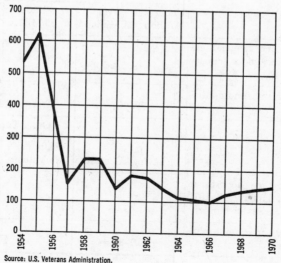

Requests for Veterans Administration Appraisals (Thousands)

Source: U.S. Veterans Administration.

June, 1957; see also Saul B. Klaman, *The Postwar Residential Mortgage Market*, National Bureau of Economic Research, Inc., Princeton University Press, Princeton, N.J., 1961; L. Grebler, *Housing Issues in Economic Stabilization Policy*, National Bureau of Economic Research, Occasional Paper 72, New York, 1960; for data on VA appraisal requests, see U.S. Department of Commerce, *Survey of Current Business*.

Required Reserves The percentage of their deposits that U.S. commercial banks are required to set aside as reserves at their regional Federal Reserve bank or as cash in their vaults. Reserve requirements vary according to the category of the bank. The purpose of required reserves is to give the central bank a method of controlling a member's behavior. Thus, Federal Reserve authorities are able to control the amount of bank money and demand deposits that the banking system can create. Banks that are not members of the Federal Reserve System have no such requirements. For further information, see American Bankers Association, Economic Policy Commission, *Member Bank Reserve Requirements*, New York, 1957; *Member Bank Reserve Requirements*, Federal Reserve Bank of New York, New York, 1957.

Member-Bank Reserve Requirements
(Percentage of Deposits)

	Reserve City Banks		Country Banks	
	Under $5 Million	Over $5 Million	Under $5 Million	Over $5 Million
Against net demand deposits in effect January 31, 1970	17	17½	12½	13
Statutory maximum-minimum	22–10		14–7	

			Other Time Deposits	
	Savings Deposits		Under $5 Million	Over $5 Million
Against time deposits in effect January 31, 1970 (all classes of banks)	3		3	6
Statutory maximum-minimum	10–3		10–3	

SOURCE: *Federal Reserve Bulletin.*

Research and Development According to the National Science Foundation, the basic and applied research and engineering, as well as the design and development of prototypes and processes, undertaken by business, governmental, and nonprofit organizations. The term research and development does not include quality control, routine product testing, market research, sales promotion, sales service, and geological or geophysical exploration. Many economists believe that research and development are the key to economic growth. Statistics on research and development expenditures are published in *Reviews of Data on Research and Development*, National Science Foundation, Washington, D.C., periodically; for a forecast of research and development expenditures, see Dexter M. Keezer et al., "The Outlook for Expenditures on Research and Development during the Next Decade," Papers and Proceedings, 72d annual meeting of the American Economic Association, *American Economic Review*, Evanston, Ill., May, 1960.

Reservation Demand In economic theory, the quantities of a commodity with a fixed supply which present holders wish to continue holding. Two important alternatives are open to holders of a commodity that has a fixed supply: (1) personal use or consumption and (2) sale at a future date. For example, a first edition of a book is a commodity that has a fixed supply. The owners at any given moment are seldom the only ones who desire the commodity for the next period. Population changes, changing income patterns, and changes in the prices of other goods lead to a continual redistribution of ownership. In an analysis of this type of demand, there are two classes of consumers: those who possess the commodity and those who do not. Let us suppose that, in the hypothetical case of a first-edition book, the consumer demand schedule for each of the two consuming groups look like this:

Price	Quantity Demanded by	
	Owners	Nonowners
$20	70	15
$19	80	20
$18	90	40

If the total supply is 100, a supply curve can be determined. If those persons who presently own the first edition wish to hold x books at a price y, then they wish to supply 100-x books at a price y. The supply schedule would look like this:

Price	Quantity Supplied	Quantity Held
$20	30	70
$19	20	80
$18	10	90

The equilibrium price is determined by equating the supply with the quantity demanded. In this case, the price would be $19. The quantities that present owners of the first edition wish to hold at each price is the reservation demand. The reservation demand is the willingness or reluctance of these potential sellers to sell their first editions or hold on to them. For a brief summary of this fixed-supply situation and how the reservation demand is transformed into the supply-and-demand analysis, see Alfred W. Stonier and Douglas C. Hague, *A Textbook of Economic Theory*, 3d ed., John Wiley & Sons, Inc., New York, 1964.

Reservation Price   The price below which a seller will refuse to sell some of his stock of goods. A seller cannot sell a greater quantity of goods than he has on hand, but he can sell a smaller quantity. The decision of whether to sell his entire stock or to hold some of it and wait for a more favorable price depends on the relationship between the market price and his reservation price. The seller's reservation price is controlled mainly by his estimate of future prices. If he believes that the price will rise, his reservation price will be high; if his expectations are for a price decline, his reservation price will be low. Reservation prices are also influenced by the costs of storage, including rental, interest, and depreciation of goods. The higher these costs, the lower the reservation price. Moreover, if the seller needs cash, his reservation price will be relatively low regardless of other considerations. If he does not need cash quickly, he can afford to take a chance that prices will rise. Reservation price thus plays an important role in determining the supply schedule of an individual seller with a fixed supply of goods on hand. For further information, see The Committee on Principles of Economics, *Principles of Economics*, Pitman Publishing Corporation, New York, 1969.

Residual   In econometrics, an estimate of the error involved in a hypothecated econometric relationship. For any given equation, the residual can be calculated after estimates of the parameters of a relationship have been settled upon. For additional information, see Lawrence R. Klein, *An Introduction to Econometrics*, Prentice-Hall, Inc., Englewood Cliffs, N.J., 1962; Stefan Valavanis, *Econometrics*, McGraw-Hill Book Company, New York, 1959.

Residual-Claimant Theory of Wages The notion that the shares of land, capital, and entrepreneurship in the total product are set by natural forces and are independent, leaving wages as the residual factor. This theory was first proposed by Francis A. Walker in the late nineteenth century. Profits and rent are determined by David Ricardo's differential principle of rent, while the rate of interest is the rate necessary to induce sufficient saving. Thus, the wage rate. is unlimited, and in a growing economy the workers will get an increasing share of the total product. For additional details on the residual theory of wages, see Francis A. Walker, *The Wages Question*, Henry Holt and Company, Inc., New York, 1876; G. R. Madan and H. S. Dhooria, *The History and Development of Economic Thought*, S. Chand & Company, Ram Nagar, New Delhi, 1963.

Restraint of Trade Any agreement, collusion, or action between two or more individuals or firms which has the effect of impairing free competition. Collusive agreements restraining trade can be horizontal (made by firms at the same stage of production) or vertical (made by firms at different levels of production). Common examples of horizontal restraint of trade include agreements of sellers to fix prices or output at specified levels, to follow the price leadership of the largest firm, or to divide markets. Exclusive supply or purchase agreements are forms of vertical restraint of trade. Restraint of trade can develop through the explicit agreement of the firms involved, as is often the case in price fixing, or it may be the result of a tacit but unwritten agreement, as may be the case in price leadership. In the U.S., the Sherman Antitrust Act of 1890 first prohibited collusive agreements among competitors which restrain or eliminate competition among them. While the Sherman Act applied to every contract or combination in restraint of trade, no matter how insignificant, this provision was modified in 1911 by the "rule of reason," developed by the U.S. Supreme Court in the Standard Oil and American Tobacco cases. These decisions considered only unreasonable restraint of trade a violation of the Sherman Act. No concrete criteria for determining unreasonable restraint were supplied by the Court, however, and since then it has been up to the courts to determine the boundaries of reasonable and unreasonable restraint. In general, the courts have viewed all agreements to restrain competition as per se unreasonable, regardless of the beneficial effects which may have ensued. For further information, see Vernon A. Mund, *Government and Business*, 3d ed., Harper & Row, Publishers, Incorporated, New York, 1960, pp. 151–153; Clair Wilcox, *Public Policies toward Business*, 3d ed., Richard D. Irwin, Inc., Homewood,

Ill., 1966; H. C. Purdy et al., *Corporate Concentration and Public Policy,* 2d ed., Prentice-Hall, Inc., Englewood Cliffs, N.J., 1950.

Restrictive Covenant   A contract made for the purpose of restraint of trade. Some of the most typical restrictive covenants provided for the collective determination of output and price by all companies in the market. The purposes of such agreements were to exclude competitors from markets, curtail production facilities, restrict output, fix prices, and allocate sales. Such agreements are prohibited in the U.S. by present antitrust laws. For further information, see George W. Stocking and Myron W. Watkins, *Monopoly and Free Enterpirse,* The Twentieth Century Fund, New York, 1957.

Retailer   A merchant or business establishment that sells mainly to the ultimate consumer. Among retailers are chain stores, mail-order houses, and department stores as well as independent grocery stores. Independent single-store retailers account for a greater number of individual retail outlets and a larger dollar volume of business than all other types of U.S. retailers combined. For general information on retailers and retailing, see Clare Wright Barker et al., *Principles of Retailing,* 3d ed., McGraw-Hill Book Company, New York, 1956; see also J. N. Wingate and A. Corbin, *Changing Patterns in Retailing: Readings on Current Trends,* Richard D. Irwin, Inc., Homewood, Ill., 1956.

Retail Sales   Sales of all establishments that sell directly to the ultimate consumer. Weekly and monthly retail-trade series reflect the trend of a major portion of consumer spending well in advance of the availability of more comprehensive data. Retail sales constitute a useful indicator of probable future economic activity at the manufacturing level and other earlier stages of production and distribution. Weekly and monthly sales estimates in the U.S. are based on the reports of a sample of respondents. In 1970 retail sales totaled $365 billion. For current statistics, see U.S. Department of Commerce, *Weekly and Monthly Retail Sales Report.*

Retained Earnings (Undistributed Profits)   The excess of a company's posttax income over all dividends distributed to stockholders. Retained earnings serve as an important internal source of funds for business expansion. In the decade 1961–1970, retained earnings of U.S. companies accounted for about $215 billion or an annual average of $21.5 billion. Many companies prefer to finance their growth with internal funds because this procedure makes it possible for them to avoid dilution of stock equity or fixed interest obligations. For many years, the term earned surplus was

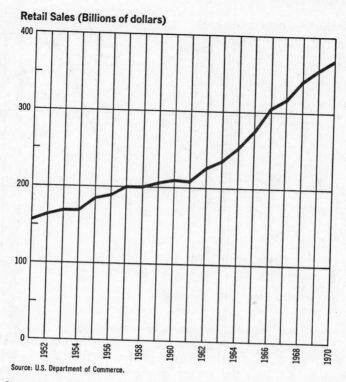

Retail Sales (Billions of dollars)

Source: U.S. Department of Commerce.

used, but today numerous accountants believe that the words retained earnings are more descriptive and less subject to misunderstanding.

Returns to Scale   The relationship between equal proportional increases in all productive inputs and the proportional change in output using the same type of technology. If, for example, a doubling of all productive inputs results in a doubling of the firm's output, it is said that the firm's production function is characterized by constant returns to scale in that range of output. Returns to scale involve the relationship between physical amounts of productive inputs and salable output, not prices or costs, although costs are affected by returns to scale. It is possible to construct various production functions which exhibit constant returns to scale, such as output = $(L \times C)^{1/2}$. If output were related to factor inputs by the formula output = $L^2 + C^2$, the firm would experience increasing returns to scale. When discussing returns to scale, we are concerned with a *given* production function—that is, one which does not involve better technology at some levels of output than at others. In practice, we know that firms

Retained Earnings (Billions of dollars)

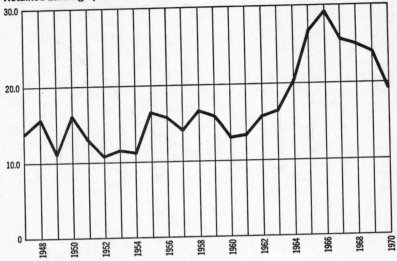

Source: Federal Trade Commission; Securities and Exchange Commission.

of very small size may not be able to take advantage of high levels of technology, but they will be able to do so as their output grows. Thus, most firms will actually have different production functions at different levels of output, and the various production functions may involve increasing, decreasing, or constant returns to scale. Returns to scale are not to be confused with the potential benefits of large-scale production, such as buying in carload lots, enjoying large size compared with suppliers, extensive division of labor with resultant economies, and other factors. A textbook treatment may be found in George J. Stigler, *The Theory of Price*, 3d ed., The Macmillan Company, New York, 1966; for an explicit application for business firms, see Milton H. Spencer, *Managerial Economics*, 3d ed., Richard D. Irwin, Inc., Homewood, Ill., 1968; empirical studies of returns to scale are presented in John R. Moroney, "Economics of Scale in Manufacturing," in D. S. Watson (ed.), *Price Theory in Action*, 2d ed., Houghton Mifflin Company, Boston, 1969, and in George J. Benston, "Economies of Scale and Marginal Costs in Banking Operations," in Kalman J. Cohen and Frederick S. Hammer (eds.), *Analytical Methods in Banking*, Richard D. Irwin, Inc., Homewood, Ill., 1966.

Revaluation   The upward or downward change in a currency's value relative to gold or other currencies. As of 1971, for example, £1 could be purchased for \$2.40, but the pound would appreciate relative to the dollar if its price rose to \$2.60, or depreciate if its price fell to \$2.20. When such changes in exchange rates are caused by the deliberate act of a government in buying and selling gold at a different price than it had previously, the currency is said to be revalued. The revaluation of a country's currency is an important tool in dealing with its balance of international payments. Chronic deficits may force a country to devalue its currency in order to return to equilibrium, while persistent surpluses may permit a country to let its currency appreciate and thus return its payments to equilibrium. For further information, see Raymond F. Mikesell, *Foreign Exchange in the Postwar World*, The Twentieth Century Fund, New York, 1954.

Revenue Sharing, General   The earmarking of a portion of Federal revenues for distribution to the states, in accordance with a formula. Local governments would get their share from their respective states. The Nixon administration's proposal as of July 1, 1971, would allocate an amount equal to 1.3% of taxable personal income for this purpose. These funds would be transferred automatically to the states to be used for any legitimate public purpose. They would not be subject to annual appropriation by the Congress. It is one method of strengthening the fiscal position of state and local governments. It would result in increased reliance on the Federal income tax as a source of funds for state and local governments, and it would allow them to have greater control over the ways these funds are spent. For additional information, see Charles L. Schultze et al., *Setting National Priorities: The 1972 Budget*, The Brookings Institution, Washington, D.C., 1971, chap. 6; Walter Heller, *New Dimensions of Political Economy*, Harvard University Press, Cambridge, Mass., 1966, chap. 3.

Revenue Sharing, Special   A proposal to restructure current Federal program funds by consolidating a large number of existing aid programs into a few major programs. Under the Nixon administration plan, 130 existing aid programs would be consolidated under six major grants covering urban community development, rural community development, education, manpower training, transportation, and law enforcement. Distribution of the funds to states and localities would be based on a formula or formulas established by law. They would be free to spend the funds on any type of activity falling within the broad purpose of the grant. Recipient governments would not be required to provide matching funds, nor would any state or locality in the first year of the program obtain less money from each of the new-formula grant programs than it previously received. This plan would result in less confusion and duplication than exist under the present system of grants. For more information, see Charles L. Schultze et al., *Setting National Priorities: The 1972 Budget,* The Brookings Institution, Washington, D.C., 1971, chap. 7.

Revisionism   The branch of modern Communist thought which wants to revise some of the traditional Marxist and Leninist doctrines. The revisionists believe that some of the old Communist theories must be altered to fit the present-day situation. They deny the historical necessity of a proletarian revolution and the dictatorship of the proletariat during the transition from capitalism to socialism, and they deemphasize the leading role of the Communist Party in this revolution and the importance of proletarian internationalism. Most important, they reject the Leninist principles of strict party organization and democratic centralism. Revisionists also believe that, in the nuclear age, peaceful coexistence rather than all-out war is the best policy for the Communist world to follow. For additional details, see Donald Zagoria, "The Spectre of Revisionism," *Problems of Communism,* U.S. Information Agency, Government Printing Office, Washington, D.C., July–August, 1958; Leopold Labedz (ed.), *Revisionism,* Frederick A. Praeger, Inc., New York, 1962.

Revolving-Credit Plan   A method of providing credit to consumers so that they can purchase each month an amount of goods equal to the monthly payment made against their previous debt. The credit limit for the customer is based on the amount of monthly payment that is best suited to his budget. In a twelve-month revolving-credit account, for example, a customer capable of paying $20 per month would have a limit on his account of $20 times 12, or $240. Thus, his monthly payment of $20 would permit him to charge up to $240 at any one time. The revolving-credit plan differs from the charge account, in which the customer is expected to liquidate his debt in a single payment. In revolving credit, the account is used almost as an open account for general shopping each month. The plan has many advantages over other methods of extending consumer credit. Unlike installment-credit contracts, which are usually limited to durable goods, revolving credit is extended to all goods in a store. It is a convenience for shoppers because it eliminates visits to credit departments in order to consolidate new balances with old balances. Because of the closer supervision by stores of this type of credit, it can be extended to somewhat poorer credit risks than is the usual practice. There is also a flexible revolving-credit account under which the customer does not pay a fixed monthly charge but rather a flexible amount which, when multiplied by 12 or some other figure, yields the present outstanding balance. Thus, the monthly payment changes with fluctuations in the unpaid balance.

Revolving Fund A fund that is continually replenished as it is used, either through further appropriations or by income generated by the activity that it finances. The use of funds of this type is common on state and local government levels. Under the revolving-fund system, income from certain sources is channeled into a separate treasury account for the purpose of specified expenditures. Objections to such funds are that they deprive the legislature of the privilege of reviewing expenditures and that the funds tend to isolate themselves or break away from the rest of government. The use of motor vehicle tax revenues for highways is an example of such a segregated or revolving fund. For further discussion, see Harold Groves, *Financing Government*, 6th ed., Holt, Rinehart and Winston, Inc., New York, 1965.

Right-to-Work Law A state law which makes it illegal for collective bargaining agreements to contain union-shop, maintenance-of-membership, preferential-hiring, or other clauses requiring compulsory union membership. After state legislatures were permitted to pass laws of this type by the Taft-Hartley Act of 1947, about twenty states, mostly in the South and the Middle West, passed right-to-work laws. Indiana, however, is the only major industrial state having a right-to-work law. The Taft-Hartley Act also provides that when a state prohibits the union shop, this prohibition shall be enforced even in establishments covered by Federal labor relations laws. The major effect of the right-to-work laws has been to outlaw the union shop. In practice, such laws have proved relatively ineffective, however, and have merely given rise to bootleg closed shops. See Albert Rees, *The Economics of Trade Unions*, The University of Chicago Press, Chicago, 1962; for an authoritative source on this subject, see Frederick Meyers, *"Right-to-Work" in Practice*, The Fund for the Republic, New York, 1959.

Risk The exposure of an investor to the possibility of gain or loss of money. His profit is his reward for assuming the risk of economic uncertainty, such as changes in consumer tastes or changes in technology. The financial risk is based on natural, human, and economic uncertainties. The risk involved in the first two type of uncertainties can be minimized by ensuring oneself against them, but there is no insurance against the risk of economic uncertainty. For further information, see Bion B. Howard and Miller Upton, *Introduction to Business Finance*, McGraw-Hill Book Company, New York, 1953; Harold Bierman and Seymour Smidt, *The Capital Budgeting Decision: Economic Analysis and Financing of*

Investment Projects, 2d ed., The Macmillan Company, New York, 1967; James L. Athearn, *Risk and Insurance,* 2d ed., Appleton-Century-Crofts, New York, 1969.

Risk Capital   *See Venture Capital.*

Robinson-Patman Act   A U.S. statute that outlaws certain types of price discrimination. Enacted in 1936 to strengthen the Clayton Antitrust Act, the Robinson-Patman Act made it illegal to sell goods more cheaply in one area than in another (geographical price discrimination) or to sell them at unreasonably low prices for the purpose of injuring and eliminating competitors (personal price discrimination). The main purpose of the act was to protect independent retailers and wholesalers by preventing unfair price discrimination by a seller in favor of certain purchasers who had large bargaining power. The act had the effect of curbing the preferential treatment that large chain stores were receiving from their suppliers through unwarranted quantity discounts. The basic principle of the act was that price differences should reflect only differences in cost; quantity discounts were justified only when they resulted in savings in cost and not when they were due to the exercise of market power. Lower prices were also justified when these were made in good faith to meet the equally low prices of a competitor. For further discussion of the Robinson-Patman Act, see *Robinson-Patman Act Symposium,* Commerce Clearing House, New York, 1946–1948; *Symposium on the Robinson-Patman Act,* Chicago Bar Association, Chicago, 1947; John Haslett, "Price Discriminations and Their Justification under the Robinson-Patman Act of 1936," *Michigan Law Review,* Ann Arbor, Mich., February, 1948, pp. 450–480.

Rollback Policy   A government policy establishing as a legal price an earlier and lower price than the existing one. Used extensively during World War II, the rollback grew out of the undesirable effects of a price-ceiling policy. If price inflation has already occurred when the price ceiling is set, it is difficult to impose the price level of any particular day, month, or year on current transactions. In general, the prices charged by manufacturers and dealers to their customers on a certain day are probably not in harmony with the costs of handling and purchasing their raw materials on that day. Thus, if input and sales prices are fixed at the prices of transactions on that day, manufacturers and dealers lose their profits and possibly incur deficits. On the other hand, sellers who adjust their prices to the current replacement costs of goods produced do not suffer from the system. Thus, the uniform fixing of prices observed at a particular moment discriminates against certain dealers and manufacturers. The rolling back of the prices of inputs during World War II eliminated this undesirable effect of controls. For example, if the base period for the price ceiling for retailers on suits and coats was March, 1942, wholesalers' and manufacturers' prices for the same articles were rolled back to levels prevailing in the autumn of 1941. In some cases, the rollback was combined with a subsidy to these producers and distributors to compensate them for the difference between the higher existing price and the rolled-back ceiling maximums. For an examination of these policies, see Seymour E. Harris, *Price and Related Controls in the United States*, McGraw-Hill Book Company, New York, 1945.

Rolling Readjustment The characteristic of a period of time when activity in some sectors of the economy is moving down and in others it is moving up, with the result that overall measures of economic activity do not change significantly. During a period of rolling readjustment, the various sectors of the economy begin their readjustment movements one at a time and not together; thus, a recession is avoided.

Rollover A method of refunding used by the U.S. Treasury Department. By this method, a new security offering is subscribed for in terms of a maturing obligation. Thus, a new issue can be paid for merely by turning in maturing holdings for the new issue. In this sense, the maturity rolls over. The alternative to the rollover method of refunding is to pay off the holders of the maturing debt and offer new issues for cash. For an example of how the rollover has worked in practice, see "Rolling over $12.5 Billion without Much Stretchout," *Business Week*, July 22, 1961, p. 99.

Roosa Plan A proposal by Robert B. Roosa for reforming the international monetary system. The plan consists of two steps. The main one would be the creation of a primary reserve asset—a fund unit. The second step would be the creation of a secondary reserve unit. Developed, convertible-currency countries would contribute their own currencies to a fund-unit account, upon which they would receive a checking-unit deposit which they could use to lend, invest, or make grants through payments to other monetary authorities or international financial institutions. For additional information, see Robert V. Roosa, *Monetary Reform for the World Economy*, Harper & Row, Publishers, Incorporated, New York, 1965.

Roundabout Production The use of less direct but more efficient means of production, usually first involving an investment in machinery or equipment. Robinson Crusoe might have nourished himself by wading out into the surf to catch fish bare-handed, but he found it more efficient to spend most of his time on shore, making and repairing fishing nets which did the catching unattended. A modern economy's production methods are increasingly roundabout; it has been estimated that only 10% of the U.S. work force in manufacturing industry is directly engaged in the production of consumer goods, while the rest either make the machines that produce consumer goods or make the machines that make machines. For the theoretical analysis of this trend, see Eugen von Böhm-Bawerk, *The Positive Theory of Capital*, G. E. Stechert & Company, New York, 1923.

Round Lot   The unit of trading on a stock exchange or any multiple of that unit of trading. The unit of trading on the New York Stock Exchange is 100 shares for most listed stocks (10 shares for some inactive stocks). Therefore, a round lot on the New York Stock Exchange is 100, 200, or 300 shares or any other multiple of 100 shares.

Runaway Inflation   *See Hyperinflation.*

Runaway Shop   A unionized business concern that moves to another state or another area to escape union demands. The question of whether any particular firm does or does not fit this category is frequently the subject of much debate. Labor leaders may insist that a particular firm is a runaway shop, while management insists that the primary motive behind the move was a tax concession, better access to raw materials, or greater proximity to markets. American trade unions have long faced great difficulties in establishing themselves in competitive industries in which firms can shift quickly from one part of the country to another. Firms in the garment industry, in which there is little capital investment, appear to have run away from union demands. Unless the union is alert it may suddenly discover that it has a large unemployment membership. The needle-trades unions, in particular, maintain efficient organizations to find runaway shops. See Leo Wolman, *The Ebb and Flow of Trade Unionism*, National Bureau of Economic Research, Inc., New York, 1936; Leo Troy, *Distribution of Union Membership among the States*, National Bureau of Economic Research, Occasional Paper 56, New York, 1957.

S

Sales Finance Company   *See Commercial Credit Company.*

Sales-Force-Composite Method   A type of sales forecasting that combines the views of salesmen on the sales outlook. Usually, each salesman estimates the future sales in his territory, and the various estimates are then scrutinized by higher executives to ensure that they are realistic. It is claimed that this method uses the knowledge of the men closest to the market, places responsibility with those who must produce results, and raises the confidence of the sales force in quotas that are developed from forecasts. Among the disadvantages of the method is the possibility that salesmen may be poor forecasters and may be inclined to underestimate sales in order to obtain lower quotas. See *Forecasting Sales,* National Industrial Conference Board, Studies in Business Policy no. 106, New York, 1963.

Sales Forecast   A prediction of the future sales of a given product or company. Sales forecasts often constitute a key element in the planning and control of a company's operations. Short-term forecasts are used to regulate production, inventories, and purchases, to budget expenses, and to plan cash requirements. They are also employed to set sales quotas and to direct sales efforts. Long-term sales forecasts are used in planning long-range financing and development. See Vernon G. Lippitt, *Statistical Sales Forecasting,* Financial Executives Research Foundation, New York, 1969; *Forecasting Sales,* National Industrial Conference Board, Inc., Studies in Business Policy no. 106, New York, 1963; Elmer C. Bratt, *Business Forecasting,* McGraw-Hill Book Company, New York, 1958, pp. 237–287.

Sales Potential   The maximum possible sales volume for an industry, a company, a product, or an area during a stated period. It is a sales target or goal. For example, the U.S. sales potential for aluminum is put at 6 million tons by 1975. For the XYZ Aluminum Company, the sales potential is 1 million tons, or 15% of the total market in that year. For aluminum product X, the sales potential is 300,000 tons, or 5% of the total market. For a detailed discussion of sales potential, see Francis E. Hummel, *Market and Sales Potentials*, The Ronald Press Company, New York, 1961.

Sales Tax A flat percentage levy on the selling price of an item. Sales taxes differ from excise taxes in that they are assessed on all, or almost all, commodities. They can be levied at any level of distribution. In some countries, France, for example, a tax (turnover tax) is collected each time that a commodity changes hands, but in the U.S. a sales tax is generally applied only once, usually at the retail level. The U.S. Federal government levies excises on more than sixty different items, but it has no sales tax. Such taxes are, however, of great importance to state and local governments. In 1969 these governments raised almost $29 billion from sales taxes or about 25% of total state revenues and more than 5% of local revenues. Sales taxes are frequently criticized as regressive, since they take a larger proportion of low than of high incomes, but when food is exempted, as it is in many states and localities, the regression tends to disappear. For a full discussion of the origins and effects of different types of sales taxes, see John F. Due, *Sales Taxation*, The University of Illinois Press, Urbana, Ill., 1957; for annual data on sales tax collections, see U.S. Department of Commerce, *Compendium of State Government Finances; ———, Compendium of City Government Finances;* for sales tax rates in individual states and communities, see *State Tax Reporter*, Commerce Clearing House, New York.

Sampling The process of selecting a segment of a population for the purpose of drawing inferences concerning the total population, or universe. The universe to be sampled, whether it is composed of people, payroll records, farms, or bank accounts, must consist of individuals so that sample units can be selected. The aim of sampling is simply to provide the required information with the minimum expenditure of time, effort, and money. In some cases, samples may provide more accurate results than a census or a complete enumeration if inexperienced workers take the census and make inaccurate reports. Two types of sampling are commonly used: (1) probability sampling, in which each unit is chosen with a known chance of being selected; and (2) nonprobability sampling, in which the selection of the sample may be based on convenience or judgment. There is always the risk that the selected sample may not be representative of the population, but only with probability sampling can the risk of relying on sample information be determined. For a simple explanation of the methods used in sampling, see M. J. Slonim, *Sampling in a Nutshell*, Simon and Schuster, Inc., New York, 1960; for sample theory, see M. H.

Hansen et al., *Sample Survey Methods and Theory*, John Wiley & Sons, Inc., New York, 1953, vol. I; for applications of sampling in business, see W. Edwards Deming, *Sample Design in Business Research*, John Wiley & Sons, Inc., New York, 1960.

Sampling, Convenience   The use of any handy group or chunk of the population or universe as the sample to be studied. Examples of convenience samples are workers in an office, houses in a block, a group of people interviewed on a street corner, or the top items in a carton. As an example of the last-named case, an aircraft manufacturer receives a shipment of 100,000 bolts, which to be usable must be strong enough to withstand a shearing force of 5,000 pounds. The manufacturer uses a convenience sample to test the strength of the bolts by selecting a few bolts from the top of each carton. It is conceivable, however, that the manufacturer of the bolts, knowing the testing procedures of the airplane manufacturer, placed all the strong bolts on the top of the carton. Thus, the convenience sample chosen by the aircraft manufacturer would not be representative of the complete shipment of bolts. With all types of samples, there is a possibility that the sample may not be representative of the population, but when convenience sampling is used, there is no way of knowing the extent of the risk of relying on sample information. Convenience sampling is often used in pilot studies and in studies in which sampling costs must be kept low. For applications of sampling in business, see W. Edwards Deming, *Sample Design in Business Research*, John Wiley & Sons, Inc., New York, 1960; see also M. H. Hansen et al., *Sample Survey Methods and Theory*, John Wiley & Sons, Inc., New York, 1953, vol. I.

Sampling, Judgment   The use of personal knowledge or experience in choosing a sample. Examples of judgment samples are the selection of a typical city's election results to determine the national trend or the choice of a group of companies considered representative of all companies, as in the McGraw-Hill Department of Economics' *Annual Surveys of Business' Plans for New Plants and Equipment*. Since probability theory is not employed in judgment sampling, standard errors of the sample estimates cannot be computed. For further discussion of judgment sampling, see W. Edwards Deming, *Sample Design in Business Research*, John Wiley & Sons, Inc., New York, 1960; see also M. H. Hansen et al., *Sample Survey Methods and Theory*, John Wiley & Sons, Inc., New York, 1953, vol. I.

Sampling, Probability   A method of sampling in which the likelihood of selecting each unit of the population or universe is known. Many methods are used in selecting probability samples. Let us suppose, for example, that a sample of factory workers is required for a study of income. When complete lists of factory workers are available, the sample units may be chosen randomly or systematically. Without such lists, we may select the sample in steps, first selecting a sample of areas from which to choose a sample of factories, which in turn yields a sample of workers. Whatever sampling procedure is used the selection of each unit is mechanical and has a specified probability. These probabilities are used as weights in calculating the income of factory workers and the standard errors of the estimated income. For a simple explanation of the methods employed in sampling, see M. J. Slonim, *Sampling in a Nutshell,* Simon and Schuster, Inc., New York, 1960; for applications of sampling in business, see W. Edwards Deming, *Sample Design in Business Research,* John Wiley & Sons, Inc., New York, 1960; for sample theory, see M. H. Hansen et al., *Sample Survey Methods and Theory,* John Wiley & Sons, Inc., New York, 1953, vol. I.

Sampling, Quota   A method of sampling in which definite numbers are selected from each class of the population. The quota assigned to each class is generally proportionate to its share of the population being surveyed. In some polls, for example, interviewers may be assigned quotas by age group and sex from different social and economic classes. The interviewers then select the specified number of respondents in each quota. This selection procedure can produce biased results, since interviewers are likely to choose respondents who are easy to reach and willing to be interviewed. Because random selection methods are not used for quota sampling, tolerance or sample precision cannot be computed. For further discussion of this method of sampling, see Frederick F. Stephan and Philip J. McCarthy, *Sampling Opinions: An Analysis of Survey Procedure,* John Wiley & Sons, Inc., New York, 1958.

Sampling, Simple Random (Unrestricted Random Sampling)   A method of sample selection in which each individual or sample unit is drawn independently and each individual has an equal chance of being chosen for a particular study. Numbers might be assigned to all individuals in the population or universe, and the sample units might be selected by drawing them from a hat or, more likely, by using published lists of random numbers. Generally, simple random sampling is not very simple, particularly when the population is large and the individuals are not numbered. For a discussion of random sampling, see M. J. Slonim, *Sampling in a Nutshell,* Simon and Schuster, Inc., New York, 1960; W. Edwards Deming, *Sample Design in Business Research,* John Wiley & Sons, Inc., New York, 1960; see also M. H. Hansen et al., *Sample Survey Methods and Theory,* John Wiley & Sons, Inc., New York, 1953, vol. I.

Sampling, Stratified   A method of sample selection in which the population is first divided into a number of strata and sample units are then chosen from each stratum. The stratification is accomplished so that all units in a given stratum are as nearly alike as possible. Each stratum is represented in the sample, the sample units being chosen by random methods. In the sample used for the *Current Population Survey,* which is conducted monthly by the U.S. Bureau of the Census, for example, all 3,100 counties in the U.S. are classified into 333 strata, and sample counties or groups of counties are chosen from each stratum. In the stratification, such characteristics as geographic area, population, income, occupation, and race are taken into account so that the counties in any one stratum are similar. For further discussion, see M. J. Slonim, *Sampling in a Nutshell,* Simon and Schuster, Inc., New York, 1960; W. Edwards Deming, *Sample Design in Business Research,* John Wiley & Sons, Inc., New York, 1960; see also M. H. Hansen et al., *Sample Survey Methods and Theory,* John Wiley & Sons, Inc., New York, 1953, vol. I.

Sampling, Systematic   A method of selecting units from a population or a universe by means of an interval pattern. A sample unit is chosen from the first interval and thereafter from every nth interval. In this case, n denotes the length of the interval, which might be every tenth individual on a list of numbered individuals or every card every one-eighth of an inch, moving from front to back, in a file drawer of cards. For numbered or ordered populations, systematic selection is quick, easy, and inexpensive. For further discussion, see M. J. Slonim, *Sampling in a Nutshell,* Simon and Schuster, Inc., New York, 1960; for applications in business, see W. Edwards Deming, *Sample Design in Business Research,* John Wiley & Sons, Inc., New York, 1960; for sample theory, see M. H. Hansen et al., *Sample Survey Methods and Theory,* John Wiley & Sons, Inc., New York, 1953, vol. I.

Sampling, Unrestricted Random   *See Sampling, Simple Random.*

Satisfice   The process of resolving a problem as satisfactorily as possible, given the various constraints on choices. This is an alternative to maximizing or optimizing production and profits. Suppose, for example, that one wants to produce 100 units of a given product in a day but that his productive facilities allow him to produce only 75 units. In order to produce the extra 25 units, he would have to expand his capacity, work the labor force overtime, or farm the extra units out to be produced by some other firm. Thus, he analyzes all options open to him and the costs associated with them to decide on a satisfactory profit position. This is the point on the supply-and-demand schedule where it just pays to produce the last unit of output, given the constraints. For additional information, see Herbert A. Simon, "Theories of Decision Making on Economics," *American Economic Review*, vol. XXVI, no. 4, pp. 243–283, American Economic Association, Evanston, Ill., June, 1959.

Saturation The relative absorption of a product or a service in a nation, region, or local area. For example, for electrical appliances in wired homes throughout the U.S., the saturation index as of January 1, 1971, ranged from 99.8% for refrigerators and 98.7% for black-and-white television sets to 14.4% for built-in ranges and 22.9% for food waste disposers. These statistics concerning the saturation of markets suggest that there is a small original market and a large replacement market for refrigerators and television sets and a large original market and a small replacement market for food waste disposers and built-in ranges. For statistics of the saturation of electrical appliances, see *Merchandising Week*, Billboard Publishing Company, New York, Feb. 22, 1971.

Saving The amount of current income which is not spent on consumption. A decision to save is basically a decision not to use up income but to hold it—in a bank, in securities, or in the form of cash. An individual may set aside current income for future consumption for a number of reasons: to build a reserve for emergency purposes, to accumulate funds for his old age, to protect his family, or to pay for a particular objective in the future, such as the education of children or the purchase of a home. A corporation also can save, usually by withholding part of its earnings from stockholders, in order to reinvest the money in the business. One of the most important factors influencing the level of personal saving is the size of family income; as income increases, the amount saved generally increases. Consumer saving also depends on expectations regarding future income; the greater the individual thinks his income will be in the future, the less incentive he has for rainy-day saving. The more certain this anticipated future income (e.g., from a safe job rather than from an uncertain one), the less motivation the individual has to accumulate a fund of savings. Furthermore, the degree to which present goods are desired over future goods and the care with which the future is anticipated also are important in determining the individual's saving habits. Another factor which may affect some types of saving is the rate of interest; the higher the rate of interest on invested funds, the greater the inducement to save. In the process of saving and providing for his own security, the individual is also providing a large part of the funds needed for business capital investment. For additional details on saving in the U.S., see Raymond W. Goldsmith, *A Study of Saving in the United States*, National Bureau of

Economic Research, Princeton University Press, Princeton, N.J., 1955; Irwin Friend, *Individual's Saving: Volume and Composition*, John Wiley & Sons, Inc., New York, 1954; —— and Stanley Schor, "Who Saves," *Review of Economics and Statistics*, vol. XLI, no. 2, part 2, pp. 213–248, Harvard University Press, Cambridge, Mass., May, 1959.

Savings and Loan Association   A cooperative savings organization through which savers can accumulate funds to purchase homes and borrowers can obtain home-mortgage money. Its basic purpose is to make it easier for its members to finance the purchase and repair of their homes. When a member puts money in a savings and loan association, he is buying stock in the association; by law, the association cannot accept deposits. When a member wants his cash, he must ask the association to buy back his shares. The association is obligated to repurchase his shares only as long as sufficient funds are available, however, since the member is a stockholder and not a creditor, as in a bank. The net earnings of the association are distributed to the stockholders as dividends on their investment. Savings and loan associations invest funds almost exclusively in home mortgages, especially for loans to members. They may receive charters either from Federal or from state governments. Federal associations must join the Federal Savings and Loan Insurance Corporation and the Federal Home Loan bank in their district, while state-chartered associations may do so if they wish. The Federal Home Loan banks provide additional liquidity to savings and loan associations by making loans to them against mortgages as collateral. In 1968 there were about 6,000 savings and loan associations in the U.S., with aggregate holdings of about $153 billion; they were the fastest-growing savings institutions in the country. For additional details, see *Savings and Loan Fact Book*, U.S. Savings and Loan League, Chicago, annually; *Savings and Loan Associations*, American Bankers Association, New York, 1958; H. Russell, *Savings and Loan Associations*, Matthew Bender & Company, Inc., Albany, N.Y., 1956.

Savings Ratio   The percentage that current savings is of current disposable income. Shifts and trends in the savings ratio are important in analyzing long-run trends in income and expenditures. Savings ratios that are based on data on consumer budgets provide information on savings patterns in different income and occupational classes at a given moment. For example, it has been found that the savings ratio is negative in the lowest income classes but rises steadily as income increases. The savings ratio is also used in analyzing the economic growth of developed and underdeveloped nations. Underdeveloped nations typically have a very low savings ratio, which makes investment very difficult. Further information on the last point may be found in Eugene Staley, *The Future of Underde-*

veloped Countries, Harper & Row, Publishers, Incorporated, New York, 1961; for historical data on savings and income from which the savings ratio can be computed, see U.S. Department of Commerce, *Survey of Current Business,* July issues; for the U.S. savings ratios, see *Economic Indicators,* prepared for the U.S. Joint Economic Committee by the Council of Economic Advisers, Government Printing Office, Washington, D.C., monthly.

Savings Ratio, Savings as Percent of Disposable Income, U.S.

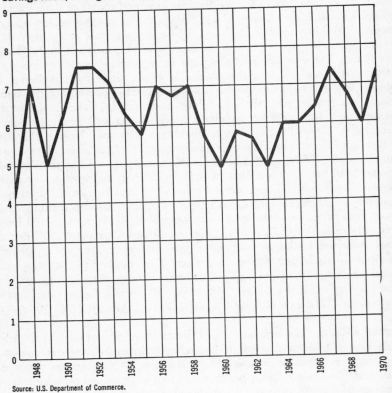

Source: U.S. Department of Commerce.

Say's Law of Markets A principle which states broadly that an economy's productive activity always generates demand sufficient to absorb the goods produced. According to a translation of the writings of Jean Baptiste Say, the French economist who originated this idea early in the nineteenth century, ". . . a product is no sooner created than it, from that instant, offers a market for other products to the full extent of its own value. . . . Thus, the mere circumstance of the creation of one product immediately opens a vent [market] for other products." Say's law held that an excess supply of goods or an excess demand for money tends to be self-correcting. Thus, a generally insufficient demand for an economy's products could not exist. Taken with other assumptions of classical economics, such as wage and price flexibility, Say's law produced an equilibrium model of the economy that ruled out the possibility of an extended recession or unemployment. This principle aroused disagreement among economists that has persisted into contemporary discussions, partially because Say's precise meaning was unclear. Among those who strongly disagreed with the principle were Thomas Robert Malthus and John Maynard Keynes, but the prevailing thought of the nineteenth century supported Say. For a fuller statement of Say's economics, see Jean Baptiste Say, *Treatise on Political Economy*, Wells and Lilly, Boston, 1821; for selections from the work, see *Readings in Economics*, Barnes & Noble, Inc., New York, 1949; see also William Fellner, *Modern Economic Analysis*, McGraw-Hill Book Company, New York, 1960, pp. 80–88; J. M. Keynes, *The General Theory of Employment, Interest, and Money*, Harcourt, Brace & World, Inc., New York, 1936, chap. 2; Joseph A. Schumpeter, *History of Economic Analysis*, Oxford University Press, Fair Lawn, N.J., 1954, pp. 615–625; for Malthus's opposing arguments, see Thomas R. Malthus, *Principles of Political Economy*, William Pickering, London, 1836; for a summary of the dispute, see Gardner Ackley, *Macroeconomic Theory*, The Macmillan Company, New York, 1961, chap. 5.

Scanlon Plan   A system of worker participation in planning to increase productive efficiency. This plan, which was developed by Joseph N. Scanlon, the president of a local of the United Steelworkers of America, offers no rigid formula but depends on the willingness of management to face criticism. All persons in the business organization—the workers, the foremen, and the management—are solicited for ideas on production methods and the problems of the business. These suggestions are then studied, evaluated, and applied when possible. Each member of the organization has a feeling of participation not only in criticizing management, but also in making constructive suggestions for improvement. The Scanlon Plan is based on the premise that the solution to business problems can be found within the organization by the people who know the situation rather than by outside experts. For additional details, see F. Lesieur (ed.), *The Scanlon Plan*, John Wiley & Sons, Inc., New York, 1958; see also George M. Schultz, "Worker Participation on Production Problems: A Discussion of Experience with the Scanlon Plan," *Personnel*, vol. XXVIII, no. 3, American Management Association, New York, November, 1951.

Scedasticity (Skedasticity) A word denoting dispersion, particularly as it is measured by variance. If the variance of a variable x is not constant but varies with the magnitude of another variable or over time, variable x is said to be heteroscedastic. If, instead, the variance is constant, variable x is said to be homoscedastic. For additional information, see Stefan Valavanis, *Econometrics*, McGraw-Hill Book Company, New York, 1959.

Scientific Socialism The Marxian doctrine of the inevitable movement of capitalist society toward self-destruction. The term scientific was used by Marx to distinguish his theories from those of the utopian Socialists. He believed that although they had found the correct goal of social movement, they did not pursue the correct route to that goal because they did not understand the nature of great social changes. Thus, their socialism was utopian and unscientific. Marx set out to create a science of all human history and social evolution and of the proper tactics to be used by the Socialist movement at each stage of history to guide and hasten the inevitable course of events. He thought that his theories were scientific because of his scientific proof of the inevitability of socialism. For details of Marx's scientific approach to history and society, see Karl Marx, *Capital*, Charles Kerr & Co., Chicago, 1906; see also Paul M. Sweezy, *The Theory of Capitalist Development*, Oxford University Press, Fair Lawn, N.J., 1942.

Scientific Tariff A levy whose duties exactly equalize foreign and domestic production costs. Defenders of a scientific tariff argue that domestic producers of some goods cannot meet foreign competition because of high costs and that a tariff should therefore be levied on the imported goods to offset the cost disadvantage of the home industry. For example, if the foreign costs of production were 50 cents lower than U.S. costs, the scientific duty that should be levied on each imported good would be 50 cents. The purpose of such a tariff would be to protect consumers by promoting fair competition. The basic fallacy of the scientific tariff is that if it were applied, it would abolish nearly all international trade, since the primary basis for trade lies in differences in production costs between nations. Furthermore, it would be very difficult to apply such a tariff in practice, since production costs of the same commodity vary widely from firm to firm and from region to region even within the same country, making it nearly impossible to calculate a single cost figure. The principle of the scientific tariff was written into two U.S. tariff acts, the Fordney-McCumber Tariff of 1922 and the Smoot-Hawley Tariff of 1930, in which the President was empowered to raise or lower tariffs by 50% to equalize the costs of production in the U.S. and competing foreign countries. For further information, see H. Austin Peck, *International*

Economics, Thomas Y. Crowell Company, New York, 1957; Charles P. Kindleberger, *International Economics,* 4th ed., Richard D. Irwin, Inc., Homewood, Ill., 1968.

Seasonal Adjustment   A statistical index of monthly or quarterly compensating factors used to correct a series of raw economic data for periodic climatic conditions and the existence of special holidays. Seasonal indices are expressed in terms of the percentage which each of the twelve

Examples of Seasonal Indices

	Stable	Moving	Stable	Moving
	1960		1961	
January	71.9	74.7	71.9	74.9
February	76.3	80.2	76.3	79.4
March	101.3	100.5	101.3	99.2
April	113.9	115.7	113.9	116.2
May	118.7	117.6	118.7	118.6
June	116.3	114.8	116.3	115.2
July	112.2	110.5	112.2	110.1
August	112.9	111.9	112.9	113.5
September	106.6	105.2	106.6	104.2
October	105.4	103.3	105.4	103.3
November	89.7	90.1	89.7	89.9
December	74.8	75.5	74.8	75.5
Total	1,200.0	1,200.0	1,200.0	1,200.0

monthly figures is of the average for the year. Seasonal adjustments are computed by various methods, such as the link-relative, monthly-means, and ratio-to-average methods. Seasonal adjustments may be stable (that is, they furnish a constant seasonal index for each month in every year) or moving (that is, they furnish a slightly different index for each month in every year). For the advantages and detailed methodology of computing seasonal adjustments, see Julius Shiskin, *Electronic Computers and Business Indicators,* National Bureau of Economic Research, Occasional Paper 57, New York, 1957.

Seasonally Adjusted Figures (Seasonally Compensated Figures)
Economic figures that are free from normal seasonal influences. Allowance is made statistically for the underlying month-to-month or quarter-to-quarter swings in the raw data of an economic series. The advantage of seasonally adjusted data is that the cyclical movement is not obscured by purely seasonal variations. For comparisons of unadjusted and seasonally

adjusted data and current methods of adjusting raw economic data, see Julius Shiskin, *Electronic Computers and Business Indicators*, National Bureau of Economic Research, Inc., Occasional Paper 57, New York, 1957.

Television-Set and Home-Radio Production, 1969 (1957–1959 = 100)

	Raw, Unadjusted Data	Seasonally Adjusted Data
January	158.9	151.5
February	164.1	156.0
March	162.6	164.4
April	143.0	158.9
May	144.3	151.9
June	143.8	150.6
July	111.1	143.0
August	152.1	144.9
September	158.0	143.6
October	166.7	141.3
November	143.4	126.2
December	99.7	109.6

Seasonal Unemployment Periodic loss of jobs caused by seasonal variations in the production of certain industries. The two main seasonal factors affecting output are weather and style changes. Certain industries, such as agriculture and building construction, are unable to operate during some periods of the year, while others, such as ice-cream and coal production, are subject to regular seasonal fluctuations in consumer demand. Fashion and trade customs, determining when the new year's models in automobiles, clothing, etc., are introduced, result in certain periodic slack periods. Peak seasons of general consumer demand, such as Christmas and Easter, also cause seasonal changes in employment and unemployment in specific industries. Although seasonal unemployment cannot be entirely eliminated, it is predictable, and thus the risks and hardships of seasonal layoffs can be reduced by planning ahead. Furthermore, although employees may be deprived of income in the off season, this type of unemployment is temporary, and employees are usually reemployed when the new season begins. Fixed annual wages and fill-in jobs are among the measures that are used to combat the effects of seasonal fluctuations. Changes in marketing policy, such as the staggering of introduction times for new annual models, are another approach to the problem. For further information, see W. S. Woytinski, *Employment and Wages in the United States*, The Twentieth Century Fund, New York, 1953, chaps. 24 and 25; Paul Casselman, *Economics of Employment and Unemployment*, Public Affairs Press, Washington, D.C., 1955; Lloyd G.

Reynolds, *Labor Economics and Labor Relations*, 5th ed., Prentice-Hall, Inc., Englewood Cliffs, N.J., 1970, pp. 121–122.

Seasonal Variation The more or less regular, month-to-month or quarter-to-quarter fluctuations that occur in almost any economic series of data because of periodic climatic conditions and special holidays. For example, television-set production in July is usually smaller than in any other month of the year because of plant shutdowns, vacations, and programming of generally poorer quality during the summer. For a description of seasonal variations, the advantages of eliminating them, and current methods of adjusting new economic data, see Julius Shiskin, *Electronic Computers and Business Indicators*, National Bureau of Economic Research, Inc., Occasional Paper 57, New York, 1957.

**Television-Set Production, 1969
(Thousands)**

January	960	July	614
February	1,002	August	877
March	1,235	September	1,167
April	865	October	984
May	845	November	888
June	1,070	December	764

Seat on the Exchange A membership in a stock exchange. The term originated when exchange members were actually seated as the traded securities were announced and the seated brokers made their bids and offers. Such seats are no longer provided, and exchange membership is merely referred to as a seat. As of 1971, there were 1,366 seats on the New York Stock Exchange, the largest U.S. exchange. A seat on the exchange may be sold, the price depending largely on the activity of the stock market (as an indication of the potential for profitable brokerage activity). In 1970, 154 seats were transferred in the New York Stock Exchange for prices ranging from $130,000 to $320,000. The lowest price at which a seat was ever sold on that exchange was $500 in the 1860s; the highest price ever received was $625,000 in 1929. Before a purchaser of a seat is admitted to exchange membership, he must be approved by the exchange and conform to its regulations. For additional information, see D. K. Eiteman, C. A. Dice, and W. J. Eiteman, *The Stock Market*, 4th ed., McGraw-Hill Book Company, New York, 1966; George L. Leffler and L. C. Farwell, *The Stock Market*, The Ronald Press Company, New York, 1963.

Secondary Boycott   An organized campaign to bring pressure to bear on an employer who is not directly involved in a labor dispute, with the aim of ultimately putting pressure on the employer with whom there is a dispute. A secondary boycott may take any of the following forms: a strike, a picket line, refusal by employees to work on certain products, or a campaign to convince consumers not to buy a certain product. The distinction between a primary and a secondary boycott is a legal one; in the U.S., most forms of the secondary boycott are considered unfair labor practices under the Taft-Hartley Act, and employers can sue unions for any damages suffered. The only legally acceptable secondary boycott is one whose objective is to reduce or to eliminate the undermining of union standards by nonunion competition. See U.S. Code, title 29, National Labor Management Act of 1947; Jack Barbash, *The Practice of Unionism*, Harper & Row, Publishers, Incorporated, New York, 1956.

Secondary Mortgage Market   *See Mortgage Market.*

Second-Best Theory   A theory that analyzes alternative suboptimal positions to determine the second best, when some constraint prevents an economy from reaching a Pareto optimum. In a general-equilibrium system, if one of the requirements for a Pareto optimum is unattainable, the other requirements, although attainable, may not lead to a second-best position. Thus, an optimum situation can be reached only by departing from all the Pareto conditions. For example, free-trade advocates have long argued that any reduction in tariffs will increase welfare, thereby getting closer to Pareto optimality. But a customs union that reduces tariffs between members can bring about production shifts that may reduce efficiency, thus moving further from Pareto optimality. See James Meade, *Trade and Welfare*, Oxford University Press, New York, 1955; Richard Lipsey and K. Lancaster, "The General Theory of Second Best," *Review of Economic Studies*, vol. XXIV, no. 63, pp. 11–32, Cambridge, England, 1956–1957.

Secular-Stagnation Thesis (Mature-Economy Thesis)   The theory that insufficient aggregate demand in advanced economies, such as those of the U.S. and Great Britain, is not merely a periodic, cyclical problem but a characteristic one. The secular-stagnation thesis, advanced by Alvin H. Hansen and John Maynard Keynes in the 1930s, was an attempt to explain the high unemployment and low investment of the Depression period. It was argued that the ingredients needed for a high rate of growth in a mature economy (greater advances in technology relative to population growth) may also result in a deficiency of aggregate demand necessary for full employment. Hansen believed that the massive U.S. private investment undertaken in the nineteenth century had been a result of population growth, the Western frontier, the industrial expansion associated with wars, and technical innovations. He thought that by the 1930s the U.S. had reached the status of a mature economy, with population growth declining, the frontier disappearing, the absolute volume of savings growing, and new technical innovations turning out to be capital saving. As a result, relatively few investment opportunities would be available, and a long-run trend of substantial unemployment would develop. Events since 1939 have proved that the Depression of the 1930s was, in fact, only a deep cyclical contraction which ushered in decades of economic growth in even the most mature industrial economies. Nevertheless, fears of secular stagnation are revived during each downturn. In the early 1960s, secular stagnationists pointed to the prevailing high unemployment rate in the U.S. as a confirmation of the stagnation thesis. For further information on the secular-stagnation thesis, see Alvin H. Hansen, *Full Recovery or Stagnation?*, W. W. Norton & Company, Inc., New York, 1938; Benjamin Higgins, "The Concept of Secular Stagnation," *American Economic Review*, vol. XL, no. 1, pp. 160–166, American Economic Association, Evanston, Ill., March, 1950; E. W. Swanson, "The Economic Stagnation Thesis, Once More," *Southern Economic Journal*, vol. XXII, no. 3, pp. 287–304, Southern Economic Association and University of North Carolina, Chapel Hill, N.C., January, 1956; Campbell R. McConnell, *Economics*, 4th ed., McGraw-Hill Book Company, New York, 1969.

Secular Trend (Economic Trend) A statistical term denoting the regular, long-term movement of a series of economic data. The secular trend of most economic series is positive, or upward, indicating growth, the angle of the trend depending on how fast or how slow the growth rate is. For example, since sales and production of chemicals grow faster than sales and production of food, the secular trend for chemicals is steeper than that for food, although the trend for both industries is upward. In a few cases, however, the secular trend of key economic series is important for business forecasting. For instance, after computing the secular trend for manufacturing production over a long period of years, it is possible to project the same rate of growth for a decade ahead and estimate the trend value of manufacturing output for that period. For the measurement of secular trend, see William A. Spurr and Charles Bonnini, *Statistical Analysis for Business Decisions*, Richard D. Irwin, Inc., Homewood, Ill., 1967.

Security   In finance, a legal document that establishes, represents, or evidences a right or rights to property. Although there are many different legal definitions of the term (e.g., in the U.S. Securities Act of 1933, the U.S. Internal Revenue Code, and various state laws), as ordinarily used, a security refers to a note, bond, option, stock, or evidence of indebtedness.

Seigniorage   The profit derived by the government from the coining of bullion. When the charge made by the government for coining bullion covers only the cost of coinage without a profit, it is called brassage. Seigniorage originally meant the share of the seignior, or lord, which he took to cover the expenses of coinage as well as a profit. Thus, money coinage was a profitable source of income for the nobility in the Middle Ages. Most modern governments do not use the seigniorage principle.

Selective Credit Control   A credit control designed to regulate the terms of a specific transaction. It differs from a general control in two fundamental respects. First, it applies to a specific transaction and is therefore personal in its effects, whereas a general control is impersonal. Secondly, a selective credit control curtails the demand for credit rather than the supply, as occurs under the application of more general controls. The primary purpose of controls of this type is to regulate areas that are not responsive to measures of general credit control. Thus, the high demand for stock-exchange loans in the 1920s, despite the high interest rates on such loans, revealed the necessity of having some sort of selective controls in this area. At the time of the U.S. entry into World War II and into the Korean conflict, when the prospect of war financing presented an obstacle to the vigorous application of general credit controls, selective measures were introduced to regulate consumer credit. Selective controls were necessary to curtail demand for consumer durables when the production of these goods was cut because of war production. In cases of consumer loans for stock purchases and for durables, the importance of nonbank lenders as a source of funds and the failure of high interest costs to dampen demand were of prime importance in favoring selective controls over general controls. A selective control operates by curtailing the use of credit in purchasing particular classes of goods. Among such controls were Regulation W for consumer credit, Regulation X for real estate credit, Regulations T and U for the financing of transactions in securities. The control operates by regulating specific aspects of the individual loan contract, such as minimum down payments and maximum maturity limitations. By raising the level of down payments and lowering the maximum maturity limitations, credit can be tightened. In the U.S., selective controls now exist only in the regulation of stock-exchange credit. For further information, see *Consumer Installment Credit,* 4 parts, Board of Governors of the Federal Reserve System and National Bureau of Economic Research, Inc., Washington, D.C., 1957; see also Carl E. Parry, *Selective Instruments of National Credit Policy,* Postwar Economic Studies, no. 8, Board of Governors of the Federal Reserve System, Washington, D.C., November, 1947.

Self-Employment A state of being gainfully employed on one's own account. Most members of professions (physicians, lawyers, etc.), farmers, and owners of small retail stores fall into this category. According to the U.S. Department of Labor, there were 71 million self-employed persons in the U.S. in April, 1971.

Sellers' Market A market situation in which demand is greater than supply at current prices. Because of the short supply, sellers have a favorable market position and can raise their prices and still sell their goods. Such a rise in prices will continue until supply and demand once again are equal at some price. When prices are relatively high in relation to past prices or producers' average costs, the existence of a sellers' market is indicated. In an extreme sellers' market, as during wartime shortages, it may be necessary to introduce rationing controls.

Seniority The status, secured by a worker's length of service, that determines certain employment rights. Length of service may be limited to a particular occupation in a particular department or expanded to take account of the full time that the employee has been working in the plant or for the company. Under a system of plantwide seniority, a chain of bumpings of workers from one job to another may take place when layoffs become necessary. A worker laid off in one department may displace a man in another department whose seniority is less than that of the first man, and, in turn, the second employee may bump a third worker in another department with still lower seniority. The procedure for layoffs is applied in reverse order to rehirings. Increasing emphasis on seniority rights in cases of layoffs and promotions may result in lower labor mobility. For additional details, see Lloyd G. Reynolds, *Labor Economics and Labor Relations,* 5th ed., Prentice-Hall, Inc., Englewood Cliffs, N.J., 1970.

Seniority Rule A provision in a labor contract that requires preferential treatment for workers having the longest service. One of the most common types of seniority rules covers layoffs and rehiring schedules: workers with the longest service are the last to be laid off during recessions and the first to be rehired in periods of recovery. An increasing number of U.S. labor contracts also make seniority a basis for promotion and transfer, workers who have the longest service being given first consideration for promotion or transfer to a more desirable job. Management frequently resists strict seniority rules on the ground that such rules promote inefficiency by preventing management from rewarding employees according to merit. Union officials, on the other hand, argue that seniority rules protect workers against arbitrary action and discrimination. For a discussion of the economic impact of seniority provisions, see Lloyd G. Reynolds, *Labor Economics and Labor Relations,* 5th ed., Prentice-Hall, Inc., Englewood Cliffs, N.J., 1970.

Separation of Ownership and Control   The phenomenon of modern corporate structure in which the power to control a corporation's business is in different hands from those of the persons who collectively own the corporation. This divorce of ownership from control results primarily from the diversification of corporate ownership among many small stockholders. For example, in 1970, 2.7 million different persons were shareholders of American Telephone and Telegraph, and no single owner held even 1% of the total. In a typical giant corporation, all management (officers and directors) usually holds only about 3% of the outstanding common stock. Because of the lethargy of the individual stockholder, who either does not exercise his voting rights or signs them over to the management by proxy, the control of management is largely unchecked in many corporations. This separation is not important if the actions of the control group (management) are in accordance with the wishes of the ownership group (shareholders). Management may, however, be less interested in maximum profits than in enhancing its own position and income through activities which are not in the interests of the corporation. Thus, separation of ownership and control may result in certain abuses by the control group. For additional details, see A. A. Berle and Gardiner Means, *The Modern Corporation and Private Property,* The Macmillan Company, New York, 1932.

Separation Rate (Layoff Rate)   The total number of quits, layoffs, discharges, and retirements during a specific period of time expressed as a percentage of total employment. Separations cover all types of employees, but they do not include workers out on strike. The separation rate is a significant indicator of overall business activity, which the National Bureau of Economic Research classifies as one of its leading indicators. When the separation rate begins to rise, business may be moving into a recession; when the rate declines, business may be on the road to recovery. For industry statistics and a more detailed definition of the separation rate, see U.S. Department of Labor, *Employment and Earnings,* monthly; for a discussion of the separation rate as an indicator of turning points of the business cycle, see R. C. Mendelssohn, "Three BLS Series as Business

Separation Rate in Manufacturing (Separations per 100 employees)

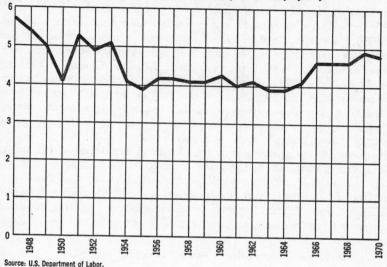

Source: U.S. Department of Labor.

Cycle Turn Signals," *Monthly Labor Review,* U.S. Department of Labor, September, 1959.

Serial Correlation   The correlation between observations of a time series and other observations of the same time series that either lead or lag by a specified time interval. Serial correlation crops up when observations overlap or are derived by interpolation and when the time interval is too short. A statistical test, based on the ratio of the mean-square successive difference to the variance, guards against the presence of serial correlation; that is, it indicates whether or not it is present and significant. For additional information, see Lawrence R. Klein, *An Introduction to Econometrics,* Prentice-Hall, Inc., Englewood Cliffs, N.J., 1962; Stefan Valavanis, *Econometrics,* McGraw-Hill Book Company, New York, 1959.

Services   The component of the gross national product that measures the output of intangible items. Services include such items as telephone service, railway, bus, and air transportation, private education, and radio and television repair. Since World War II, services have constituted the fastest-growing area of the U.S. economy, rising by 150% between 1957 and 1970 as compared with an increase of 119% for the economy as a whole. Since, in the national income accounts, this component cannot be estimated by the normal commodity-flow method, it is built up from a variety of statistical sources. The reliability of this series is impaired by the heavy reliance on periodic and sometimes infrequent source material. In 1950, for example, 23% of the value of services was based on comprehensive annual reports by government agencies and private sources; 55%, on periodic comprehensive sources, mainly from the Census of Business and Population; 13%, on sample information; and 9%, on miscellaneous sources. Imputed services provided by financial intermediaries are computed from annual reports received from various government sources. Private sources provide annual data for the expenses of handling life insurance, local transportation, and public utilities. Comprehensive periodic information is available from the Census of Population and Housing, the Census of Business, the Census of Agriculture, the Census of Religious Bodies, and the Biennial Survey of Education. The Census of Population and Housing and the Census of Agriculture are used to estimate the rental value of homes. Private research organizations and trade organizations provide the miscellaneous sources of data on expenditures for services.

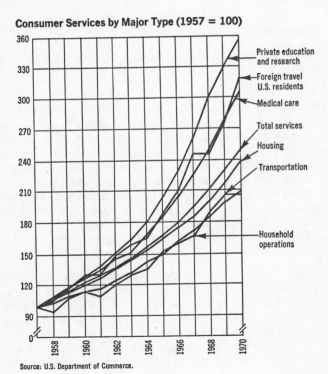

Consumer Services by Major Type (1957 = 100)

Source: U.S. Department of Commerce.

For further information, see Richard Ruggles and Nancy D. Ruggles, *National Income Accounts and Income Analysis*, 2d ed., McGraw-Hill Book Company, New York, 1956; U.S. Department of Commerce, *Survey of Current Business: National Income Supplement*, 1954.

Sherman Antitrust Act A U.S. Federal statute, enacted in 1890, that forbids all contracts in restraint of trade and all attempts at monopolization. The main purposes of the act were to prevent the exercise and growth of monopoly and to restore free enterprise and price competition. The Sherman Act made illegal "every contract, combination in the form of trust or otherwise, or conspiracy in restraint of trade or commerce among the several states" and declared that "every person who shall monopolize or attempt to monopolize . . . a part of the trade or commerce among the several states . . . shall be guilty of a misdemeanor." Thus, not only were all conspiracies in restraint of trade illegal, but all monopolies secured by other means, whether or not they restrained trade, were considered violations of the act. The Federal government was empowered to enforce the act, and violators were made subject to criminal penalties. No precise definitions of "restraint of trade" and "monopoly" were provided, however, and interpretation was left to the courts. In its early decisions, the U.S. Supreme Court ruled that the Sherman Act applied to every agreement in restraint of trade, but in the Standard Oil case of 1911 it formulated the rule of reason, which held that the Court would not forbid every contract having a restraining effect on trade but only those which constituted an unreasonable restraint. In later cases, whereas conspiracies to fix prices were judged illegal per se, other restraints of trade and attempts at monopolization as such were not ruled illegal unless an intent to monopolize or an abuse of power was judged. In recent years, there has been a shift in the Court's interpretation, so that the mere holding of monopoly power and conscious parallelism of action in oligopolistic markets (price leadership without formal agreements) are often considered violations of the Sherman Act. Although the act applied originally only to businesses engaged in interstate commerce, its scope has been progressively broadened, especially with the decisions involving the National Labor Relations Act in 1937, so that the antitrust laws are now applicable to nearly all firms in both interstate or intrastate commerce. For further information, see Vernon A. Mund, *Government and Business*, 3d ed., Harper & Row, Publishers, Incorporated, New York, 1960, chaps. 8, 9, and 10; *The Federal Antitrust Laws*, Commerce Clearing House, New York, 1952; Milton Handler, *A Study of Construction and Enforcement of the Federal Antitrust Laws*, Temporary National Economic Committee Monograph 38, Government Printing Office, Washington, D.C., 1941.

Shifting of Tax   The transfer of the tax burden from the original payer to someone else. A tax on a manufacturer can be shifted forward to the consumer by increasing the price of the goods sold by the amount of the tax. For example, a tax on an automobile manufacturer can be shifted forward to the consumer by a rise in car prices. A tax can be shifted backward by reducing the price of raw materials and other factors purchased. Thus, by cutting wages an employer can shift the burden of a tax on his firm. The extent to which a tax can be shifted depends on the nature of the tax, the economic environment in which it is levied, and the taxpayers' practices in taking advantage of the possibility of shifting. The only way in which a tax can be shifted is a change by business in the prices of the goods and services that are bought and sold. Thus, a purely personal tax, such as a poll tax or an inheritance tax, cannot be shifted. Neither can a tax on an economic surplus, such as rent or capital gains, be shifted. Among the market factors favorable to shifting are a less elastic demand, a more elastic supply, and a long period of time. For further information, see Harold Groves, *Financing Government*, 6th ed., Holt, Rinehart and Winston, Inc., New York, 1965; W. F. Ferger, "The Measurement of Tax Shifting, Economics and Law," *Quarterly Journal of Economics*, vol. LIV, pp. 429–454, Harvard University Press, Cambridge, Mass., May, 1940.

Shop Steward   The key individual in the handling of grievances in a unionized company. He is the lowest man in the elected union hierarchy and the link in day-to-day communication between the workers in the shop and front-line management personnel. As a rule, the steward is elected by the workers of his unit, which, in the case of a large plant is a department. Depending on the union, he may or may not receive special training; depending on individual contract arrangements, he may be relieved of all or part of his production duties. For a description of the shop steward's functions, see Leonard R. Sayles and G. Strauss, *The Local Union: Its Place in an Industrial Plant*, Harper & Row, Publishers, Incorporated, New York, 1953; see also Jack Barbash, *The Practice of Unionism*, Harper & Row, Publishers, Incorporated, New York, 1956.

Short Run   A time period that is not long enough for the firm to vary all factors of production. One factor of production, usually plant and equipment, is fixed in the short run, and the firm can change its level of output only by more or less intensively using its existing plant and equipment. Since virtually all costs of production would become fixed if a sufficiently short time period were taken, the short run must be long enough for the firm to vary its output as much as technology permits without changing the scale of the plant. In the long run, all factors of production, including the size or scale of the plant are variable. The concept of the short run is important to microeconomic theory because much of the theory of the firm and price theory uses cost curves and other analytical tools that assume a short-run time period. See Alfred Marshall, *Principles of Economics*, St. Martin's Press, Inc., New York, 1956; Jacob Viner, "Cost Curves and Supply Curves," *Zeitschrift für Nationalökonomie*, vol. III, 1931, reprinted in American Economic Association, *Readings in Price Theory*, Richard D. Irwin, Inc., Homewood, Ill., 1952; William Fellner, *Modern Economic Analysis*, McGraw-Hill Book Company, New York, 1960; Donald S. Watson, *Price Theory and Its Uses*, 2d ed., Houghton Mifflin Company, Boston, 1968.

Short Sale   The sale of stocks, bonds, foreign exchange, or commodities that the seller does not own. Short sellers believe that the price of a security, commodity, or foreign exchange will decline. They sell it hoping to cover, or buy it back at a lower price, and thereby make a profit on the transaction. Dealers frequently are technically short sellers in the ordinary course of their business. This happens when a customer wants to buy a stock, for example, which the dealer temporarily does not own. To service the customer, the dealer sells the stock, covering his short sale as soon as possible. Short selling of securities differs from that of commodities and foreign exchange. Securities sold short must be borrowed by the seller in order to deliver them to the buyer. After the seller covers, he returns the securities to the lender. In the case of commodities and foreign exchange, the short seller need not borrow because he has merely promised to deliver a certain amount of the commodity or foreign exchange at a specified date in the future. Normally, the short seller covers his sale before the time at which he would have to deliver. For further information, see George L. Leffler and L. C. Farwell, *The Stock Market*, The Ronald Press Company, New York, 1963; D. K. Eiteman, C. A. Dice, and W. J. Eiteman, *The Stock Market*, 4th ed., McGraw-Hill Book Company, New York, 1966, chap. 15; Paul Einzig, *Dynamic Theory of Forward Exchange*, St. Martin's Press, Inc., New York, 1961; Gerald Gold, *Modern Commodity Futures Trading*, Commodity Research Bureau, Inc., New York, 1959.

Short-Term Forecast   A projection which usually extends as much as six quarters ahead of the current period. For example, short-run forecasts made in January, 1971, could extend through the second quarter of 1972. Forecasts for the short term are more popular with business economists than those for the medium or the long term. A 1962 survey of the membership of the National Association of Business Economists showed that 95% of those who made forecasts prepared forecasts for the short run, 66% assessed medium-term prospects, and 72% studied the long-term outlook. One reason for the popularity of the short-run forecast is that the recent trend generally holds true over the short run. Occasionally, however, the economist making a short-term forecast must reckon with the fluctuations of the business cycle. Business forecasters most frequently use the indicator technique developed by the National Bureau of Economic Research. Not even judgment commands as much importance as indicators for short-run forecasts. Anticipations surveys rank third in usefulness in this type of forecasting. For a discussion of how far ahead business forecasters forecast and for short-term forecasting techniques and tools, see McGraw-Hill Department of Economics, report, Feb. 5, 1962; see also Elmer C. Bratt, *Business Forecasting*, McGraw-Hill Book Company, New York, 1958.

Sight Draft   *See Draft.*

Silver Certificate   A U.S. Treasury note in denominations of $1, $2, and $5. Silver certificates were backed by an equivalent number of silver dollars or by silver bullion in storage at West Point, New York. Silver certificates were first created under the Bland-Allison Act of 1878. The repeal of the Silver Purchase Act made it possible gradually to withdraw silver certificates from circulation. By early 1968, virtually all of them had disappeared. They are being replaced by Federal Reserve notes. See Lester V. Chandler, *The Economics of Money and Banking*, 5th ed., Harper & Row, Publishers, Incorporated, New York, 1969, p. 24.

Simulation Games for Business   Games used to provide experience for young executives by simulating the real-life operations of a business. Within the framework of a game, the executives are forced to cope with the same problems that face the top management of a company. The games are played with the help of computers, which make it possible to reproduce several years in the life of a business in one day. The rules of the game correspond as closely as possible to the realities of business economics. This type of gaming, which is referred to as operational gaming, attempts through simulation to provide a framework for trial-and-error decisions. The games' purpose is not to provide entertainment or a winner but to transfer the learning of a game situation to reality. For a discussion of business games and for instructions on how to play one, see G. R. Andlinger, "Business Games, Play One!" *Harvard Business Review*, pp. 115–125, Harvard Graduate School of Business Administration, Boston, March–April, 1958; R. C. Meier, *Simulation in Business and Economics*, Prentice-Hall, Inc., Englewood Cliffs, N.J., 1969.

Single Tax   A levy on a single category, used by the government as its sole source of revenue. The term single tax is usually associated with Henry George's proposal for the special taxation of land rents. Such a land-value tax would be an annual levy (100% or close to it) on the economic rent received by landowners. The proponents of the single tax argue that economic rents are a completely unearned surplus and that they ought not to go to landowners but should be used to finance government services. According to George, the use of the single tax would remove inequality and eliminate poverty. A single tax on land is also an instrument of developmental tax policy, since it removes all taxes from capital and labor and thus encourages the growth of these productive factors. Land rents are not the only type of unearned income, however, for all deviations from pure competition in other markets result in some type of surplus. The opponents of the single tax argue that a single tax is unfair, since it places all the tax burden on landowners, especially rural landowners, who are not necessarily rich but may be poor farmers. The tax would be applied only to economic rents and not to business rents due to improvements made on the land. In practice, this distinction between land and capital is hard to make, so that the application of a single tax would be very difficult to carry out. For further information, see Henry George, *Progress and Prosperity,* Random House, Inc., New York, 1938; Harry G. Brown, *The Economic Basis of Tax Reform,* Lucas Bros., Columbia, Mo., 1932.

Sinking Fund   A fund the purpose of which is the ultimate repayment, partial or complete, of a debt. The creation of a sinking fund is a method of amortizing a debt which has not matured. Payments into the sinking fund are usually based on a fixed annual sum, a fixed percentage of the bonds outstanding, or a fixed percentage of the annual profit, dividends, or sales of the corporation. Cash in the sinking fund may be invested until the bond issue reaches maturity or used at once to purchase and retire some of the outstanding bonds. Some sinking funds are provided for in a bond issue because they are required by law, as is the case for some railroad and other public-utility issues. Sometimes a sinking fund is agreed to as part of the provisions of a bond contract, since it increases the attractiveness of the bond and makes it easier to sell. Occasionally, a corporation with a strong financial position may start a sinking fund voluntarily. A sinking fund may also act as a check on the financial policies of management, since it requires the setting aside of payments for the fund before other cash payments may be made. For additional details, see Charles W. Gerstenberg, *Financial Organization and Management of Business,* 4th ed., Prentice-Hall, Inc., Englewood Cliffs, N.J. 1959.

Skedasticity   *See Scedasticity.*

Sliding Parity   *See Crawling Peg.*

Sluggish Year   A year in which the physical volume of goods and services and industrial production increase by less than 3%, consumer money income after taxes rises by less than 5%, and unemployment exceeds 5.5% of the labor force. In a sluggish business year, there are only modest purchases of consumer durable goods and capital goods. Since World War II, only 1960 and 1961 satisfy all these requirements in the U.S. The criteria given above are being used by many business economists to describe a sluggish business year.

Sluice-Gate Price   The minimum import price for poultry fixed by the European Economic Community's Council of Ministers on the basis of world market prices of feed grains and the cost of raising poultry for representative producers outside the Common Market. No imports are permitted below this price. In this manner, the Community can protect poultry production within the Community and avoid disturbances caused by offers of poultry at abnormally low prices from nonmember countries. For further information on the setting of minimum prices in the European Common Market, see *Treaty Establishing the European Economic Community, and Connected Documents,* title II, *Agriculture,* art. 44, Publishing Services of the European Communities, Brussels, 1957.

Slump   A temporary decline in the volume of general business, a specific industry, a company, or a product line. Generally, a slump is not due to any basic economic change. At the national level, it may occur because of a shift in tastes, such as the sudden increase in purchases of small foreign-made cars and the decline in purchases of large U.S.-made cars in the U.S. in 1958. At the company or product-line level, a slump can occur when a company decides to curtail its sales effort on an overall basis or for a specific product line.

Slutsky Equation   An econometric equation stemming from the demand calculus and dealing with economic value theory. It is often called the fundamental equation in the latter area. It separates the change in quantity demanded that is associated with a change in price into two parts: (1) the variation in quantity demanded that is due to income change and (2) the variation in quantity demanded that is a response to a price change for a constant level of utility. A final term in the equation depicts the substitution effect between two commodities. For additional information, see Lawrence A. Klein, *A Textbook of Econometrics*, Row, Peterson & Co., Evanston, Ill., 1953.

Slutsky's Proposition The moving average of a random series oscillates. This property is vital for the statistical analysis of business cycles. Since random time series are occasionally subject to runs similar to those encountered in tossing a true die (runs of fives or sixes), a moving average may reveal random oscillation that may be mistaken, for example, for a cyclical movement. This pitfall can be avoided by the use of correlograms and periodograms at an early stage of analysis. For additional information, see E. Slutsky, "The Summation of Random Causes as the Source of Cyclical Processes," *Econometrica*, vol. V, pp. 105–146, 1937; Stefan Valavanis, *Econometrics*, McGraw-Hill Book Company, New York, 1959.

Small Business A business that is owned and operated by relatively few persons, has a relatively small sales revenue, and possesses relatively little capital. The U.S. Department of Commerce defines a small business as including "any manufacturing plant which employs 100 persons or less, wholesale organizations with annual sales of less than $200,000, retail stores, service establishments, hotels, places of amusement and construction concerns with sales or receipts of less than $50,000." Much has been done to help the development of small businesses. In 1953 the Small Business Administration was established as the first independent agency of the U.S. government charged with the duty of fostering the interests of small business. For further information, see Joseph D. Phillips, *Little Business in the American Economy*, The University of Illinois Press, Ill., 1958; J. K. Lasser, *How to Run a Small Business*, 3d ed., McGraw-Hill Book Company, New York, 1963.

Small-Business Investment Company A privately owned corporation whose purpose is to provide long-term loans and equity capital to small businesses. Licensed and regulated by the Small Business Administration, small-business investment companies receive two type of assistance from the U.S. Federal government: (1) They can sell debentures to, or borrow from, the Small Business Administration, and (2) they qualify for certain preferential tax benefits. In order to receive funds from a small-business investment company, a firm must be considered small and convince the management of the company that its investment will be profitable. (A firm need not demonstrate that funds are unavailable from other sources because small-business investment companies, unlike the other credit programs of the Small Business Administration, are not lenders of the last resort. They are privately owned and are organized to make a profit, and they, not the government, select the firms they wish to lend money to or invest in.) The small-business investment company program was begun in August, 1958, and on June 30, 1972, 322 companies were in actual operation. Their capitalization ranged from $150,000 to almost $25,000,000 and averaged $1,000,000. By the same time, they had disbursed more than $2 billion to small-business concerns through approximately 40,000 separate financings. For a full description of the small-business investment company program and complete data on the companies' activities, see Small Business Administration, *Semiannual Reports,* Government Printing Office, Washington, D.C.

Small-Loan Company   *See Consumer Finance Company.*

Small-Loan Law   A law, enacted in many states of the U.S., that sets limits on the maximum rate of interest permissible on loans of less than $300. Interest rates fixed by general usury laws are usually too low to permit legitimate lenders to make small loans profitably, since the cost and risks on such loans are high. Small-loan borrowers, generally lower-income-class consumers, are often forced, in the absence of small-loan laws, to turn to loan sharks to borrow the money they need. Small-loan laws try to minimize the evils of loan sharks by authorizing interest rates on small loans sufficient to induce legitimate lenders to enter the small-loan business. The authorized small-loan rate, now controlled in two-thirds of the states, varies from 2½% to 3½%. The small-loan laws also provide for strict state supervision of the small-loan business. For additional details, see Louis Robinson and Rolf Nugent, *Regulation of the Small Loan Business,* Russell Sage Foundation, New York, 1935.

Smithsonian Agreement   An interim agreement on currency realignment among the Group of Ten at the Smithsonian Institution on December 18, 1971. The agreement included an increase in the U.S. gold price from $35 per ounce to $38. In addition, there occurred a general realignment of currency values resulting in effective upward revaluation (in terms of the dollar price of foreign currencies) of 16.88% for the Japanese yen, 13.58% for the German mark, and 11.57% each for the Dutch guilder and the Belgian franc. The Swiss franc, which had been revalued in May by 7.07%, was adjusted to provide an additional 6.36% effective revaluation and the Italians adjusted the gold parity of the lira downward slightly so that the net revaluation against the dollar was about 7.48%. Also the bands of allowable fluctuations were widened to 2¼% above and below the new par values. For additional information, see Tilford Gaines, "International Monetary Arrangements," *Economic Report,* Manufacturers Hanover Trust Company, January, 1972; for the European view of the Smithsonian agreement, see Juergen Ponto, "The Present World Currency Situation,"

The Conference Board Record, The Conference Board, New York, August, 1972.

Social Credit Movement   A movement whose purpose was to increase the purchasing power of the masses. The basis of the social credit approach, which was first proposed in 1919 by Clifford Hugh Douglas, a Scottish engineer, was that many of the advantages of modern technological efficiency were lost because the masses of workers could not buy all the goods produced for home consumption. The main reason for this disparity was an inadequate distribution of purchasing power coupled with the operation of the private banking system, which forced producers to increase their prices. The social credit remedy was the taking over by the central government of all monetary functions. In this way, the total purchasing power of society could be adjusted to the available supply of consumer goods. Credit would be very easy, enabling producers to lower their prices. Furthermore, national dividends would be issued periodically to consumers, further adding to their purchasing power. Every increase in production would be accompanied by an increase in the money supply. The social credit movement also adopted the ideas of technocracy, advocating that production be controlled by engineers and scientists rather than by entrepreneurs. For additional details, see Clifford H. Douglas, *Social Credit,* rev. ed., W. W. Norton & Company, Inc., New York, 1933; E. S. Holter, *The ABC of Social Credit,* Longmans, Green & Co., Ltd., Toronto, Canada, 1934; P. Mariet, *The Douglas Manual of Social Credit,* Longmans, Green & Co., Ltd., Toronto, Canada, 1934; J. Lewis, *Douglas Fallacies,* Chapman & Grimes, Inc., Boston, 1936.

Social Darwinism   *See Classical Liberalism.*

Socialism   An economic and political system the basis of which is the abolition of private property and the public ownership and operation of the means of production. Whereas capitalism recognizes the relatively unrestricted right of private ownership of productive factors, socialism reserves the ownership of factors for the community as a whole. Since there is no private ownership of the means of production (capital), there is no class of employers and no separate class of employees. Without private employers, there is no private profit motive, and thus the classic market forces for organizing production are not present. Large-scale government planning is therefore necessary to ensure the smooth functioning of the system. Another major aspect of socialism is the redistribution of income for the purpose of achieving equality for all. This welfare consideration is summed up in the phrase "from each according to his abilities, to each according to his needs." As distinct from communism, socialism advocates the peaceful and democratic extension of government ownership and the gradual transition from capitalism to complete socialism. There are many varieties of Socialist theory, including Christian, Fabian, guild, utopian, scientific, and Soviet socialism. For further information, see Ludwig von Mises, *Socialism: An Economic and Sociological Analysis,* The Macmillan Company, New York, 1936; Arthur C. Pigou, *Socialism versus Capitalism,* Macmillan & Co., Ltd., London, 1937; Joseph A. Schumpeter, *Capitalism, Socialism, and Democracy,* Harper & Row, Publishers, Incorporated, New York, 1942; Paul M. Sweezy, *Socialism,* McGraw-Hill Book Company, New York, 1949.

Social Overhead Capital *See Infrastructure.*

Social Security Program A public welfare program which seeks to reduce the threat to the economic security of the individual. Programs of this type attempt to reduce an individual's or a family's loss of income and welfare by providing cash benefits and needed services. There are three

Social Security Act Changes–Past and Future

			Maximum Tax Paid		
	Rate, % *	Wages Covered	Employee	Employer	Total
1937–1949	1	$ 3,000	$ 30.00	$ 30.00	$ 60.00
1950	1½	3,000	45.00	45.00	90.00
1951–1953	1½	3,600	54.00	54.00	108.00
1954	2	3,600	72.00	72.00	144.00
1955–1956	2	4,200	84.00	84.00	168.00
1957–1958	2¼	4,200	94.50	94.50	189.00
1959	2½	4,800	120.00	120.00	240.00
1960–1961	3	4,800	144.00	144.00	288.00
1962	3⅛	4,800	150.00	150.00	300.00
1963–1965	3⅝	4,800	174.00	174.00	348.00
1966 †	4⅕	6,600	277.20	277.20	554.40
1967	4⅖	6,600	290.40	290.40	580.80
1968	4⅖	7,800	343.20	343.20	686.40
1969–1970	4⅘	7,800	374.40	374.40	748.80
1971	5⅕	7,800	405.60	405.60	811.20
1972	5⅖	9,600	518.40	518.40	1,036.80
1973	5⅘	10,800	631.80	631.80	1,263.60
1974	5⅘	12,000	702.00	702.00	1,404.00

* Rate of tax paid by both employees and employers.
† Beginning with 1966, includes hospital insurance rate.

Social Security Benefits *
(In dollars)

Average Monthly Earnings	Primary Insurance Amount	Maximum Total Monthly Benefits for Family
250	115.00	202.40
300	127.10	240.00
350	140.40	280.80
400	153.60	322.40
450	165.00	354.40
500	177.50	374.80
550	189.90	395.60
600	204.00	415.20
650	218.00	434.40

* As of 1969.

main categories of economic insecurity which social security plans try to eliminate. One is the risk of physical inability to work, leading to a loss of earning power. Examples of this type are sickness, accidents, old age, and death. The second category is economic risk, primarily that of involuntary unemployment. The third factor which reduces individual welfare is the economic burden of a large family. All social security programs involve a transfer of resources to increase total national welfare. If the program is financed by progressive taxation, the transfer is from the rich to the poor. If it is financed primarily by the payments of workers and employers, the resources are transferred within the same class of persons, from the more fortunate to the less fortunate. The actual benefits may be distributed through old age, survivors, and disability payments; unemployment compensation; public relief; family allowances; and public health services. Social security programs of one sort or another have been undertaken by most industrial countries. Some nations, such as Great Britain and New Zealand, have developed a much more comprehensive and unified system of social security than others. For further information, see J. Henry Richardson, *The Economic and Financial Aspects of Social Security*, University of Toronto Press, Toronto, Canada, 1960; Eveline M. Burns, *Social Security and Public Policy*, McGraw-Hill Book Company, New York, 1956; Valdemar Carlson, *Economic Security in the United States*, McGraw-Hill Book Company, New York, 1962; Lewis Meriam, *Relief and Social Security*, The Brookings Institution, Washington, D.C., 1946.

Social Welfare Principle of Taxation   The principle that taxes should be levied in a way that will correct an unjust or improper distribution of income. The principle's adherents often argue that injustices may arise either through market forces or through inheritance, and they frequently favor progressive income taxes and inheritance taxes. See Richard A. Musgrave, *The Theory of Public Finance*, McGraw-Hill Book Company, New York, 1959.

Soft Currency   A national currency that is regulated by exchange control, thus limiting its convertibility into gold and other currencies. A nation places exchange controls on its currency because the official exchange rate overvalues the currency and it wishes to avoid the depreciation that would result from forced devaluation. Soft currency differs from hard currency, which is freely convertible. Nations export a smaller quantity of goods to a country when payment is in soft currency than if payment were in hard currency. For the same reason, prices of commodities often depend on whether payment is to be made in hard or soft currency. Nations with a soft currency find it difficult to make payment in hard currency because they must obtain most of their hard-currency balances through exports. Problems of this nature grow smaller as currencies become more freely convertible and as soft-currency countries increase their production of exportable commodities and exert greater control over internal inflation. Nations are sometimes willing to accept payment in soft currency because they desire to make payments easy for the debtor nation or because they receive some special trade benefit in return. See Raymond F. Mikesell, *Foreign Exchange in the Postwar World*, The Twentieth Century Fund, New York, 1954.

Soft Goods (Nondurable Goods)   Consumer items which last for only a short time. Among soft goods are such items as clothing, shoes, and drugs. According to the U.S. Department of Commerce, an item is nondurable if it is used up in less than three years. The criterion of lack of durability cannot be applied in all cases, however; for example, although clothing is classified as soft goods, a fur coat, which is categorized as clothing, obviously is expected to last well over three years. Soft goods are usually purchased when needed. Expenditures for soft goods grow approximately in line with population growth. In 1970, U.S. consumers purchased $265 billion worth of soft goods, which represented 43% of their total expenditures for goods and services. For a complete list of items classified as soft goods and U.S. consumer expenditures for each of them, see U.S. Department of Commerce, *Survey of Current Business: National Income Supplement*, July issues.

Soft Loan   A foreign loan repayable in the receiving country's own soft currency. Soft loans were considered a compromise between hard loans and grants. Countries receiving aid in soft-loan form were expected to use the money in a responsible manner because they would have to repay it; however, it was easier for the needy country to obtain a loan. Soft-loan aid was not effective, however, because the donors accumulated large reserves of the debtors' soft currency without being able to use it. Most U.S. lending agencies now make foreign loans repayable in dollars and regulate the ease or difficulty of repayment by means of the maturity of the loan and the interest rate. See Benjamin Higgins, *Economic Development*, W. W. Norton & Company, Inc., New York, 1959; Raymond F. Mikesell and Robert Allen, *Economic Research toward Less Developed Countries*, a study prepared for the Subcommittee on Economic Policy of the U.S. Joint Economic Committee, Government Printing Office, Washington, D.C., 1961.

Soil-Bank Program   A farm program, authorized by the Congress of the U.S. in the Agricultural Act of 1956, which was designed (1) to reduce production in order to cut crop surpluses and strengthen the market and (2) to build and protect soil and water resources as a backlog for the future. There are two major parts to the soil-bank program. Under the first part, the acreage reserve, farmers can earn payments for restricting their harvested acreage of basic crops, such as wheat, cotton, corn, rice, peanuts, and tobacco, below the established acreage allotments. Under the second part, the conservation reserve, farmers earn payments for shifting crop acreage to specific conservation practices. For general information on the soil bank, see Ezra T. Benson, *Farmers at the Crossroads*, The Devin-Adair Company, Inc., New York, 1956.

Solvency   The ability of a business firm to meet its debts. There are two senses in which the term solvency is used: actual solvency, which is the ability of the firm to cover all its liabilities in the event of liquidation; and technical solvency, which is the ability of the firm to pay its debts as they come due. A firm may be technically solvent yet may not be able to meet all its long-term debts in the case of liquidation; on the other hand, a business may be actually solvent yet have its funds so largely tied up in assets other than cash as to be unable to meet its current debts. A business must be technically solvent if it is to continue its day-to-day operations. A number of rough tests have been devised to analyze the technical solvency of a firm: the current ratio, or the ratio of current assets to current liabilities; the quick ratio, or the ratio of liquid assets (e.g., cash, receivables, and marketable securities) to total short-term debt; the inventory turnover; and working capital, or current assets minus current liabilities. The actual solvency of a firm may be judged by analyzing the ratio of tangible assets to total debt (current and noncurrent) and the ratio of tangible net worth to total debt. For further information, see Bion B. Howard and Miller Upton, *Introduction to Business Finance*, McGraw-Hill Book Company, New York, 1953.

Special Drawing Rights (SDRs) A new form of international liquid reserves to be used in the settlement of international payments among member governments of the International Monetary Fund. The SDR system was established at the Rio de Janeiro conference of 1967, and the first allocation of SDRs was made in 1970. Drawing rights were allocated among the IMF members according to their already-established quotas in the Fund. SDRs were created to augment the total of international liquidity available to meet international payments arising through trade and investment between nations. The SDR augments gold, the key international currencies, bilateral borrowing arrangements between nations, and borrowing facilities of the IMF to meet the growing needs for world liquidity. The first allocation of SDRs amounted to $3.4 billion. During the first basic period of SDR use, 1970–1972, the Fund created a total of $9.5 billion worth of SDRs. SDRs may be used only by governments who are members of the IMF. For additional information, see Thomas E. Davis, "The New International Monetary Plan in Perspective," *Monthly Review*, Federal Reserve Bank of Kansas City, Kansas City, February, 1968, pp. 11–18; Mordechai E. Kreinin, "Special Drawing Rights: What Are They? How Will They Function?" *Business Topics*, pp. 77–80, Michigan State University, Summer, 1970. For Statistics on SDRs, see International Monetary Fund, *Annual Report*.

Specialization The division of different productive activities among different individuals, industries, and regions. There is specialization, or division of labor, involved in the different operations needed for the production of a single good, as is the case in assembly-line production. Specialization can occur on the level of community production, as in the work of specialized craftsmen and tradesmen, and it can exist on a regional or national level, as in the concentration of one nation on the production of agricultural produce and another on the production of manufactured goods. Specialization is undertaken because it enhances productive efficiency and results in increased output at lower cost. It permits individual workers to take advantage of their different abilities, for each man works in the area in which he is most productive. Division of labor also results in the acquisition of appropriate skills which increase efficiency. Devoting all of one's time to a single operation or occupation also eliminates the loss of time involved in shifting from one job to another. The simplification of function resulting from specialization within a single productive process lends itself to mechanization and the use of labor-saving capital. Moreover, the specialization of industry may facilitate the invention and efficient use of machinery. Specialization of production on a regional basis permits the nonhuman resources, land and capital, to be used in the most efficient way. Just as a different relative endowment of personal abilities makes some individuals better suited for certain types of work than others, differences in the relative endowment of productive resources among various regions make regional specialization more efficient. There are, however, limits to the extent of industrial and regional specialization. Increasing costs which accompany the rising output may reduce the comparative advantage gained by specialization to a point at which it is no longer profitable to specialize. Furthermore, specialization is limited by the extent of the market for the good being produced. Inherent in the existence of specialization is the existence of interdependence, or the need of the specialized worker, industry, and region to rely on others for the production of the goods and services needed for daily life. Thus specialization is the basis for all trade—local, regional, and international. For further discussion, see Adam Smith, *The Wealth of Nations,* Random House, Inc., New York, 1937.

Specie   Gold and silver used to back paper currency and into which paper currency is redeemable. Paper currency promises payment in gold or silver on demand against presentation of the note. Specie is no longer legally in circulation in the U.S. except in the form of token silver coins, and Americans cannot redeem their dollars for gold.

Specific Cycle   Recurring alternations of expansion and contraction in individual business-cycle indicators. The specific cycle for an individual series may or may not coincide with the cycle in general business activity. For each indicator, the dates of the high and low points nearest the turning dates of the business cycle are selected as the specific turning dates. For further discussion of specific cycles, see Geoffrey H. Moore (ed.), *Business Cycle Indicators,* Princeton University Press, Princeton, N.J., 1961, vol. I.

Specific Tariff   An import duty which is levied on the basis of a unit of quantity or weight. This type of tariff is levied as a specific charge per unit of the good imported, e.g., 10 cents per book or 3 cents per pound. It differs from the ad valorem tariff, which is based on value and not on units. Specific tariffs provide a fluctuating amount of protection, since the protection afforded varies inversely with changes in the prices of imports. When import prices are rising, the burden on imports with specific tariffs generally falls; when prices are falling, the burden increases. Specific duties are generally easier to administer than ad valorem duties because it is not necessary to estimate the value of the import.

Spectral Analysis　In statistics and econometrics, a technique for isolating and estimating the durations and amplitudes of the cyclical components of time series. It results in separating the random from the systematic components of time series. For additional information, see Karl A. Fox, *Intermediate Economic Statistics,* John Wiley & Sons, Inc., New York, 1968.

Speculation　The act of knowingly assuming above-average risks with the hope of gaining above-average returns on a business or financial transaction. Speculation is usually applied to the buying and selling of securities, commodities, or foreign exchange in the hope that a profit will be made because of price changes. With the exception of the transactions of persons who ordinarily need foreign exchange or commodities for their businesses, all transactions in these markets are speculative because neither of these items pays dividends or interest; thus, price movements are the only way in which a profit can arise. In the securities markets, speculation is distinguished from investment by the motives or attitudes of the person involved. The investor is interested in safety of principal, a moderate but steady income, and possibly some growth in principal. In contrast, the speculator, by assuming large risks, forgoes safety of principal in the hope of quick (in most cases), large gains. Successful speculation requires money, knowledge of the market that is speculated in, cool nerves (the ability to view losses with equanimity), and some luck. Even though the economic and social consequences of speculation have been debated for a long time, no firm conclusions have resulted. See Alfred L. Bernheim, *The Security Markets,* The Twentieth Century Fund, New York, 1935; Paul Einzig, *Dynamic Theory of Forward Exchange,* St. Martin's Press, Inc., New York, 1961.

Spendable Average Weekly Earnings　Gross weekly pay of U.S. manufacturing production workers less Federal social security and income taxes. This statistical series is the nearest measure to actual take-home pay but exceeds it by the amount of certain deductions, such as union dues and insurance payments. Spendable earnings are computed for two categories of workers, those with no dependents and those with three dependents. Estimates are published in U.S. Bureau of Labor Statistics, *Monthly Labor Review.*

Spending Unit　All related persons living together in the same dwelling who pool their incomes to meet their major expenses. In some cases, a spending unit may be only one individual. Wife, husband, and children under the age of eighteen living at home are always considered members of the same spending unit. Other related persons in the household are separate spending units if they earn more than $15 per week and do not pool their incomes. In March, 1970, there were 63 million spending units in the U.S. The number and characteristics of spending units are important statistics in establishing market potentials for consumer durable goods, such as stoves and refrigerators. For incomes, savings, and intentions to buy based on the spending-unit concept, see *Consumer Attitudes and Inclinations to Buy,* University of Michigan Survey Research Center, Ann Arbor, Mich., periodically.

Spin-Off Method   A method used by a corporation to distribute to its own stockholders stock that it owns in another corporation. The term spin-off also refers to split-ups and split-offs. A spin-off occurs when company A transfers assets to company B for B's stock; then company A distributes its holdings of company B's stock to its stockholders. A split-up occurs when company A transfers some of its assets to company B for B's stock and the remainder of its assets to company C for C's stock. Company A distributes its holding of company B's and company C's stock to its stockholders in exchange for its own (company A's) stock. Thus, company A is liquidated. A split-off occurs when company A transfers certain assets to company B for B's stock, and then company A distributes B's stock to its own stockholders in exchange for some of its own stock. See Robert S. Holzman, *Corporate Reorganizations,* The Ronald Press Company, New York, 1955, pp. 8.21–8.24; *1970 Federal Tax Course,* Prentice-Hall, Inc., Englewood Cliffs, N.J., 1969.

Spot Market (Cash Market)   A market in which commodities are sold for cash and delivered immediately. The spot market, also known as the cash or physical market, consists of sellers who have the goods to be traded on hand, ready for immediate delivery, and of buyers who want the goods immediately. It is distinguished from the futures market, in which contracts for the future delivery of commodities are traded. Most ordinary trade takes place in spot markets. There are two main classes of spot markets, primary or local markets and central markets. Local markets develop in producing areas and center at local transportation points from which the commodities are shipped to the large central markets. Central markets, such as Chicago for grain or New Orleans for cotton, are the main centers of large-scale distribution of the primary commodities. In these central spot markets, trading is smoothed out by dealers, who act as intermediaries between the producers and the manufacturers who demand the goods. They bear most of the risk of exchange, buying and selling commodities in an attempt to make a profit from their transactions. For further information, see Julius Baer and E. Olin Saxon, *Commodity Exchanges and Futures Trading*, Harper & Row, Publishers, Incorporated, New York, 1949.

Spot Market, Central   *See Spot Market.*

Spot Market, Local   *See Spot Market.*

Spot Price (Cash Price)   The price quoted for the immediate sale and delivery of a commodity. The spot price is distinguished from the future price, which is the price quoted for the sale of commodities to be delivered at a future date. On grain markets, the spot price is also known as the cash price. Spot and future prices fluctuate together most of the time, since both spot and future markets respond to the same fundamental factors. The holders of futures can always convert their holdings into spot commodities if the price of futures falls in relation to the spot price and vice versa, and the future price will therefore generally be kept in line with the spot price. Often, dealers rely on the future market to determine the general level of spot prices and then express spot prices in terms of bids over or under the futures price; e.g., a spot price of wheat of "2 cents under September" means that if the future price of September wheat is $1.98, the spot price for wheat is $1.96. The interest of spot traders lies in obtaining the commodity on as favorable a basis relative to the futures as possible. For further information, see Julius Baer and E. Olin Saxon, *Commodity Exchanges and Futures Trading*, Harper & Row, Publishers, Incorporated, New York, 1949.

Spread   A contract that gives the holder the right to buy or sell a specified amount of stock for a designated time period at prices that are above and below the market price of the stock at the time the contract is written. It is a combination of a put and a call, with the added feature that the buy and sell prices are the current market price at the time that the contract is written. As in the case of the straddle, both parts of the spread can be exercised during the life of the contract. For further information, see D. K. Eiteman, C. A. Dice, and W. J. Eiteman, *The Stock Market*, 4th ed., McGraw-Hill Book Company, New York, 1966, p. 164.

Spread Effect   A stimulating effect which arises from international trade. The most important spread effect of a rise in the value of exports is its multiplier effect on per-capita income in the other sectors of the economy. This is brought about by a rise in the demand for all the economy's goods. The higher the level of economic development that a country has achieved, the stronger the spread effects will usually be, since the export sector is more closely linked with the rest of the economy. Some economists have argued that the spread effects of trade for under-developed countries are very weak and are usually outweighed by the backwash (unfavorable) effects, so that on the whole underdeveloped nations have been hurt and not helped by international trade. For additional details on the spread effects in underdeveloped countries, see H. Myint, "The Gains from International Trade and the Backward Countries," *Review of Economic Studies,* vol. XXII, no. 2, Oliver & Boyd Ltd., Edinburgh, 1955; Gunnar Myrdal, *Economic Theory and the Under-developed Regions,* Gerald Duckworth & Co., Ltd., London, 1957.

Stability   A condition of high-level economic activity with an absence of severe cyclical fluctuations. Basically, most economists would consider three aspects of economic activity relevant to the measurement of stability: production, employment, and prices. Since these three aspects tend to fluctuate together in a cyclical fashion, stability can be defined in terms of the absence of such fluctuations. Nevertheless, an absolute level of production cannot be consistent with full employment for more than a few days or months because it has to keep pace with growth and pro-ductivity gains; otherwise, the result would be a reduction in the employ-ment level. At least in its physical aspects, economic stability does not mean constancy. Therefore, a norm of physical stability must be stated in terms equal to population growth and productivity increases while instability is stated in terms of deviations from potential production. This implies a growth norm in order to have economic stability in a growing economy. In contrast to the definition of stable physical activity, that is, a condition of growing employment and production, when economists speak of stable prices, they usually mean a constant price level. If stable physical activity is a long-run trend, determined by population and productivity, stable prices are desirable. Thus, it is obvious that the absence of severe cyclical fluctuations is the major criterion of stability. For further information, see Robert A. Gordon, *Business Fluctuations,* 2d ed., Harper & Row, Publishers, Incorporated, New York, 1961; see also *Defense against Recession: Policy for Greater Economic Stability,* Com-mittee for Economic Development, New York, 1954; *The Quest for Stability,* Federal Reserve Bank of Philadelphia, Philadelphia, 1954.

Stagnation   An unsatisfactory rate of growth of real per capita product or income. Stagnation implies that real product or income is constant, declining or growing much less rapidly than it might. An economy may be subject to long-run or secular stagnation for two reasons. First, the growth rate of output may be less than the rate of population growth even though resources are fully employed. Secondly, although the economy may have the capacity for sufficient growth, insufficient aggregate demand may prevent the achievement of its potential. Some economists have argued that in a mature economy, such as those of the U.S. and Great Britain, a secular stagnation of the second type is setting in. The greater advances in technology relative to population growth are said to result not only in a greater capacity to produce, but also in an insufficient amount of aggregate demand, causing substantial long-run unemployment and stagnation. For further information, see Benjamin Higgins, "The Concept of Secular Stagnation," *American Economic Review,* American Economic Association, Evanston, Ill., March 1950; Alvin H. Hansen, *Full Recovery or Stagnation,* W. W. Norton & Company, Inc., New York, 1938.

Stagnation Theory   A theory, originated in the late 1930s, which states that the U.S. and some other industrialized nations have become "mature" because investment outlets that could absorb savings are lacking and, therefore, that these nations' economies stagnate. The foremost advocate of the stagation thesis was (and is) Alvin H. Hansen. Hansen argues that four factors caused a marked decline in U.S. investment outlets: (1) the rapid decline in population growth; (2) the closing of the frontier; (3) the lack of new industries, such as railroads, electric power, and the automobile, which could absorb massive doses of capital investment; and (4) the increasing importance of depreciation reserves which allowed corporations to finance their replacement capital needs without tapping new savings. Since expected savings would be greater than expected investment, national income would decline or, at best, remain stationary; the economy would not be growing but would be stagnating. This analysis led Hansen to recommend that government expenditures for such public works as slum clearance and education be increased to take up the slack and increase investment. Critics of the stagnation thesis argue that the rate of population growth had been declining long before the major economic slump in the 1930s, that the frontier had been declared closed before the twentieth century began, that there would be great new industries to absorb savings, and that depreciation allowances did not cover the capital needs of expanding corporations. See Alvin H. Hansen, *Fiscal Policy and Business Cycles,* W. W. Norton & Company, Inc., New York, 1941; ———, "The Stagnation Thesis," *Readings in Fiscal Policy,* American Economic Association, Richard D. Irwin, Inc., Homewood, Ill., 1955; George Terborgh, "The Bogey of Economic Maturity," *Fortune,* Time Inc., June, 1945.

Standard & Poor's Composite Index   An index of the prices of 500 listed industrial, railroad, and utility common stocks. The composite index is the best known of the 137 indices of securities prices computed and published by Standard & Poor's Corporation, the largest securities research organization in the U.S. It is a weighted, aggregative index expressed in relatives with an average value for the base period, 1941–1943, equal to 10. Weighting is based on each stock's relative market importance, which is determined by the number of shares outstanding. Thus, the price of each stock in the index is multiplied by the number of shares outstanding, the products are summed, and the total is divided by the value of the base period; this quotient is multiplied by 10 to arrive at the index figure. The composite index, with other Standard & Poor's indices, is published in Standard & Poor's Corporation, *Outlook,* New York. Many newspapers publish the daily high, low, and close for the index. Standard & Poor's Corporation, *Security Price Index Record,* New York, annually, gives historical records of all the firm's indices as well as a detailed discussion of the method of computation; for further discussion, see D. K. Eiteman, C. A. Dice, and W. J. Eiteman, *The Stock Market,* 4th ed., McGraw-Hill Book Company, New York, 1966, pp. 182–187.

Standard Deviation   A measure of the spread of a set of values around the arithmetic average. It is the tendency of the individual values to vary from the mean. Operationally, the standard deviation is the square root of the sum of the squares of the deviations of observed values from the arithmetic mean of a series divided by the number of items. In general, about two-thirds of the individual values turn out to be less than one standard deviation from the mean, about 95% are within two standard deviations, and virtually all (99.7%) are within three standard deviations. The standard deviation is easier to interpret than the variance, another measure of spread, because the former indicates the spread in the same units as the variable itself. For example, the standard deviation for a set of family-income values would be expressed in dollars of income, whereas the variance would be expressed in dollars of income squared. For further discussion of variability, see Robert Schlaifer, *Introduction to Statistics for Business Decisions,* McGraw-Hill Book Company, New York, 1961.

Standard Metropolitan Area   An integrated economic and social unit with a large volume of daily travel between its central city (with a population of 50,000 or more) and the outlying parts of the area. As of 1970, there were 247 standard metropolitan areas in the U.S. Each area consists of one or more complete counties except in New England, where towns are more significant than counties. An area may contain both highly industrialized counties and primarily residential counties if the latter contribute significantly to the industrialized counties' labor force and are socially and economically integrated with the central city in the area.

Population, number of establishments, income, and investment on a standard-metropolitan-area basis are important statistics for establishing market potentials. For a more detailed explanation of the standard-metropolitan-area concept and for statistics, see U.S. Department of Commerce, *United States Census,* 1970.

Standard Money *See Redemption.*

Standard of Living A composite of quantities and qualities of goods, such as food, clothing, and house furnishings, and services, such as housing, transportation, and medical care, which an economic unit (an individual, family, or group) considers essential. The standard is usually expressed in monetary terms, since prices of the various goods and services making up the standard are usually available. Costs of attaining the same standard of living vary from place to place and from time to time. Because the actual levels of living of families and individuals often fall far short of the standards of decency and comfort, perhaps the standard of living is also a social aspiration or good for many persons. For a detailed discussion of standard and levels of living, see S. Howard Patterson and Karl W. H. Scholz, *Economic Problems of Modern Life,* McGraw-Hill Book Company, New York, 1948.

State Bank A U.S. commercial bank operating under the authority of a state charter and under the supervision of a state banking commissioner. State banks outnumber national banks, which operate on Federal charters, by nearly 2 to 1, but since most of them are small, they hold less than 40% of all U.S. demand deposits. State banks may belong to the Federal Reserve System (although most do not) and may participate in the Federal Deposit Insurance Corporation (most do). Annual state banking statistics are published in Federal Deposit Insurance Corporation, *Assets, Liabilities and Capital Accounts: Commercial and Mutual Savings Banks,* Government Printing Office, Washington, D.C.

State Farm A type of farm, found in Communist countries, on which the means of production are owned and operated directly by the state in conjunction with hired labor. State farms thus differ from collective farms, on which production is carried out on the basis of cooperative organization among the farmers. See Harry Schwartz, *Russia's Soviet Economy,* Prentice-Hall, Inc., Englewood Cliffs, N.J., 1954, chap. 8, pp. 327ff.

Statics That part of economic theory which analyzes equilibrium positions. Statics concentrates only on the definition of equilibrium positions and the requirements for equilibrium and is not concerned with the path by which the equilibrium position is reached or the time it takes for equilibrium to be achieved. For example, the familiar supply-and-demand analysis of price and output determination is an application of economic statics, since the problem is only to determine the equilibrium level of price and output. Comparative statics is the study of movements from one equilibrium position to another as certain of the given variables change. The economic thinking of David Ricardo and John Stuart Mill is best described as comparative statics. For a discussion of the nature of static analysis, see Frank Knight, *On the History and Method of Economics,* The University of Chicago Press, Chicago, 1956, chap. 8; Kenneth E. Boulding, "In Defense of Statics," *Quarterly Journal of Economics,* Harvard University Press, Cambridge, Mass., November, 1955; Henry William Spiegel, *The Development of Economic Thought,* John Wiley & Sons, Inc., New York, 1952, pp. 602–611.

Stationary State   An economic process which merely reproduces itself from one period to the next. Classical economists, such as David Ricardo and John Stuart Mill, believed that technological innovations would be insufficient to offset the effects of diminishing returns, and that therefore a developing capitalist economy would move gradually toward the stationary state of a mature economic system. As investment increases, the rate of profit decreases (as a result of diminishing returns) until profits have fallen so low that there is no longer any incentive for new capital accumulation. In the classical stationary state, wages are at a subsistence level (biological or customary), net capital formation is zero, and the economy's production has reached its maximum level. For further discussion of the classical concept of the stationary state, see Mark Blaug, *Ricardian Economics,* Yale University Press, New Haven, Conn., 1958; Philip Charles Newman, *The Development of Economic Thought,* Prentice-Hall, Inc., Englewood Cliffs, N.J., 1952.

Statistician   An individual trained in statistical methods. Statisticians are found in a variety of fields, ranging from biometrics to business. The business statistician, in addition to having a working knowledge of statistical methods, must also possess an understanding of the economic principles involved in the operations with which he is concerned. The extent and character of his work are based on his position in the economic structure, that is, whether he works for a business firm, a trade association, a business research organization of a college or university, or the government; whether he is in a small or a large statistical department; and how far he has advanced up the occupational ladder.

Statistics The science of the collection and classification of facts used to facilitate the interpretation of numerical data that have been obtained from groups of individuals or from groups of observations of a single individual. The individuals can be nations, industries, firms, or consumers. Among the various statistical methods that are concerned with business and economics are measures of central tendency (averages), sampling and sampling error, correlation between two sets of related data, time series (business cycles), and game theory, which provides an optimum choice under different assumptions.

Sterling Area A group of countries that hold their international reserves in pounds sterling deposited with British banks. All members of the Commonwealth of Nations except Canada are in the sterling area, as are Iceland, the Republic of Ireland, Burma, Jordan, and Libya. During World War II many sterling-area countries accumulated large balances in London, and in most of the postwar period their use of these reserves was tightly controlled. By the mid-1950s, however, the restrictions were lifted, and balances held by foreigners in British banks became freely convertible. Figures on sterling balances are carried in *The Monthly Digest of Statistics,* Her Majesty's Stationery Office, London; *Bank of England Annual Report,* Bank of England, London.

Stochastic Independence In econometrics, a condition in which the random term (or error term) in one equation is not correlated with the random term in any other equation of a given econometric model and over the same time period. It follows that stochastic dependence is the relationship between random variables that are correlated. For additional information, see Stefan Valavanis, *Econometrics,* McGraw-Hill Book Company, New York, 1959.

Stochastic Model A formula or collection of formulas which describes the relationship between two or more economic variables, where specific statistical assumptions are made to allow for error. There is some probability that the model represents the exact but unknown relationship. Since the relationships are not entirely exact, an error term is specifically included in the equations of stochastic models to describe the special way in which the relationship between the dependent and independent variables is inexact. This relationship cannot be precise because models are necessarily incomplete; there may be errors in the basic data from which the stochastic models have been developed. Although many economists believe that there can be no specific representation of human interactions, which are subject to so many random disturbances, stochastic models are useful because they are shorthand representations of highly complex situations. For additional details, see Stefan Valavanis, *Econometrics*, McGraw-Hill Book Company, New York, 1959; Lawrence R. Klein, *A Textbook on Econometrics*, Harper & Row Publishers, Incorporated, New York, 1953; Edwin Kuh, "Econometric Models: Is a New Age Dawning?" *American Economic Review*, Supplement, vol. 55, pp. 362–369, May, 1965; E. Parzen, *Stochastic Processes*, Holden-Day, Inc., Publisher, San Francisco, 1962; L. Takacs, *Stochastic Processes*, John Wiley & Sons, Inc., New York, 1960.

Stock Dividend   Authorized but unissued shares of stock of a corporation that are paid to the stockholders as a dividend. In essence, a stock dividend simply changes the corporation's capital structure because the surplus, or retained earnings, account is reduced by the same amount as the capital stock account is increased. An example follows:

Capital Account

Before Stock Dividend		After 50% Stock Dividend	
Capital stock; 100,000 shares at $5 per share	$500,000	Capital stock; 150,000 shares at $5 per share	$750,000
Surplus	$500,000	Surplus	$250,000

The only effect that a stock dividend has on the stockholders is that they now own a greater number of shares, but each share's book value is lower and its market value is generally lower. Before the dividend, the book value (capital stock plus surplus divided by the number of shares) per share in the example given above was $10; after the dividend, it was $6.67. If we assume that the market value was $20 per share before the dividend, it would be, ceteris paribus, $13.33 per share after the dividend. There are two main reasons why directors declare stock dividends: (1) They want to lower the market value of the stock, perhaps to broaden ownership. (2) They want to conserve cash but still give the stockholders something. See Charles W. Gerstenberg, *Financial Organization and Management of Business*, 4th ed., Prentice-Hall, Inc., Englewood Cliffs, N.J., 1959, pp. 437–440; George L. Leffler and L. C. Farwell, *The Stock Market*, The Ronald Press Company, New York, 1963.

Stock Exchange   An organized marketplace in which securities (mainly stocks) are bought and sold. In the U.S., the term refers to sixteen centrally located trading places where brokers and dealers regulary meet to transact business for their own accounts and for their customers. These stock exchanges must register with the Securities and Exchange Commission (SEC) as national securities exchanges unless they have been specifically exempted by the SEC. As of 1970, there were thirteen national securities exchanges in the U.S.; three other stock exchanges were exempted from registration. The SEC regulates the stock exchanges, the securities listed on the exchanges, and the brokers and dealers doing business on the exchanges. The New York Stock Exchange is the largest stock exchange in the U.S., accounting for about 65% of the share-trading volume and nearly 80% of the dollar volume of trading on all national securities exchanges. For information on the SEC's regulation of stock exchanges, see U.S. Securities and Exchange Commission, *Annual Reports;* for statistical information on shares traded by exchanges, see U.S. Securities and Exchange Commission, *Statistical Bulletin,* monthly; for further information, see D. K. Eiteman, C. A. Dice, and W. J. Eiteman, *The Stock Market,* 4th ed., McGraw-Hill Book Company, New York, 1966; George L. Leffler and L. C. Farwell, *The Stock Market,* The Ronald Press Company, New York, 1963.

Stockholders' Equity   Total capital stock and retained earnings in a corporation. In accounting for the elements of stockholders' equity, emphasis is placed on the source of capital, that is, the amount of the stockholders' equity that was produced by stockholders' contributions and the amount that was produced by retained earnings. The ratio of net earnings to stockholders' equity is a popular measure of corporate success. Current statistics on stockholders' equity in manufacturing corporations appear in U.S. Federal Trade Commission and Securities and Exchange Commission, *Quarterly Survey of Manufacturing Corporations.*

Stock Option   A contract which gives the purchaser the privilege of buying or selling a specified amount of stock at a certain price within a stipulated period. Although puts, calls, spreads, straddles, and warrants are all stock options, the term stock option is usually used to refer to a type of compensation plan that corporations establish for some employees. Because U.S. personal income tax rates are sharply progressive, many corporations believe that the lure of higher salaries will not attract and hold key employees. Instead of giving such an employee a higher salary, a corporation gives him an option to buy the company's stock at the current market value (for example, at any time within ten years). Supposedly, the option gives the employee the incentive to work hard to help the company thrive because, if the company grows, the stock price will probably rise as well, thus increasing the value of the option. When the key employee thinks that the time is most advantageous, he can exercise his option. Moreover, if he sells the stock for a profit, the profit is treated as a capital gain, which means a lower tax liability for a high-salaried employee. See Robert Sheehan, "The Stir over Stock Options," *Fortune*, Time, Inc., October, 1962; Arch Patton, "Facts about Stock Options: A Survey," *Business Horizons*, Indiana University Graduate School of Business, Bloomington, Ind., Summer, 1962; Erwin N. Griswold, "Are Stock Options Getting Out of Hand?" *Harvard Business Review*, Harvard Graduate School of Business Administration, Boston, November–December, 1960.

Stock Right A privilege given to stockholders to purchase additional stock, in proportion to the amount that they own, at a price lower than that which nonstockholders must pay. As an example, a small corporation with 1,000 shares outstanding may wish to issue an additional 1,000 shares. The new issue can be sold through the distribution of rights, permitting, for each share presently held, the right to purchase an additional share, usually below the present market price. The premium between the market price and the subscription price (the lower price that existing stockholders pay for the additional shares) gives stock rights a definite value, and since the rights are transferable, the original holders may either use them or sell them to someone else. The value of each right can be determined by the following formula:

$$\frac{\text{market price on old stock (rights on)} \quad \text{minus} \quad \text{subscription price of new stock}}{1 \text{ plus number of rights required to buy 1 new share}}$$

Stockholders of record receive the rights on the day of issuance. Thereafter, the stock is traded ex rights, and the formula for the value of the rights is:

$$\frac{\text{market price on old stock (ex rights)} \quad \text{minus} \quad \text{subscription price of new stock}}{\text{number of rights required to buy 1 new share}}$$

For the corporation, the issuance of rights is a method of raising additional funds from existing stockholders, but it is more costly than open-market financing, or the sale at the current market price through investment bankers. Moreover, it can be a hazardous method. Despite the discount price placed on the new stock, there is always the risk that the market price for the old stock may decline below the subscription price during the stock offering. This ruins the issue, since it is then cheaper to buy the stock on the open market than to exercise the rights. Because of these high risks, standby underwriting agreements are often made to assure the corporation of success. For further information, see George L. Leffler and L. C. Farwell, *The Stock Market*, The Ronald Press

Company, New York, 1963; H. A. Finney and H. E. Miller, *Principles of Accounting*, 6th ed., Prentice-Hall, Inc., Englewood Cliffs, N.J., 1965; see also J. F. Childs, "A Technique of Offering Common Stock through Rights," *Public Utilities Fortnightly*, Public Utility Reports Inc., Washington, D.C., Nov. 11, 1954; G. H. Evans, Jr., "The Theoretical Value of a Stock Right," *Journal of Finance*, American Finance Association, New York, March, 1955.

Stock Split (Stock Split-Up)   A division of the capital stock of a corporation into a greater number of shares without affecting the total capital account but reducing the par or stated value of 1 share. For example, a corporation with 1 million shares of $10-par-value stock (total capital equals $10 million) splits its stock 2 shares for 1 share. After the split, the company has 2 million shares of $5-par-value stock (total capital remains $10 million). The distinction between a stock split and a stock dividend is that the former does not affect the surplus, or retained earnings, account, whereas the latter capitalizes surplus. The market value of the stock in the above example would, ceteris paribus, be halved after the split. Essentially, corporations split their stock to reduce its market value for two reasons: (1) They plan to issue additional stock and want the price to be lower so that the stock will be more readily marketable. (2) They want wider distribution of share ownership so that outsiders would find it more difficult to concentrate enough stock and gain control of the company. See Jules I. Bogen (ed.), *Financial Handbook*, 4th ed., The Ronald Press Company, New York, 1968.

Stop Order (Stop-Loss Order)   An order that a customer gives to his broker to buy or sell a certain amount of stock if the price of the stock rises to a certain price or higher (buy) or falls to a certain price or lower (sell). The main distinction between stop and limit orders is that the stop order becomes a market order if the price of the stock reaches the stated, or stop, price, whereas the limit order never becomes a market order. Stop orders are used to protect profits or to prevent large losses on either short sales or long purchases. An example of each on a long purchase follows: Let us assume that a person has bought stock at $20 per share. After a few months, the price has risen to $30 per share. To protect the greater part of this $10-per-share profit, the person puts a stop order to sell at $28. Now, if the stock begins to decline in price, the stop order becomes a market order at $28 per share, and the stock is sold at the best price available at that time. The bulk of the $10 profit is thus intact. If the price continues to rise, all that happens is that the person's profits keep increasing, and he can raise his stop price to protect his bigger profit. To prevent a large loss, a person can place a stop order to sell at $18 when he buys a stock at, say, $20 per share. If he is mistaken when he buys and the stock's price starts to decline, his stop order prevents a large loss; if the stock's price rises, nothing happens. There are two disadvantages to stop orders: (1) There is no guarantee that a person will be "stopped out" at the stop price because at that price the stop order automatically becomes a market order, which means that, if the price is declining rapidly, the actual sale price can be lower. (2) If a person places a stop order too close to the prevailing market price, a slight, temporary price dip can actuate the stop order, but subsequently the price may move upward. See George L. Leffler and L. C. Farwell, *The Stock Market*, The Ronald Press Company, New York, 1963.

Straddle   A contract that gives the holder the right to buy or sell a specified amount of stock at a certain price for a designated time period. It is simply a combination of a put and a call. If the holder exercises either part of his option, the other is not invalidated. Thus it is conceivable that both parts could be exercised during the life of the contract. For further information, see D. K. Eiteman, C. A. Dice, and W. J. Eiteman, *The Stock Market*, 4th ed., McGraw-Hill Book Company, New York, 1966, pp. 311–312.

Strategic Stockpile   Governmental storage of certain goods deemed strategic and vital to national defense. The purpose of stockpiling goods, set down in the Strategic and Critical Materials Stock Piling Act of 1946, was to "decrease and prevent wherever possible a dangerous and costly dependence of the U.S. upon foreign nations in times of national emergency." The determination of the degree to which a good is strategic depends on how vital it is to the defense effort, how it can be converted to military use, and whether its absence would cause a critical deficiency in the Soviet defense economy. As of March 31, 1971, the U.S. government had a strategic stockpile valued at about $7.0 billion, consisting primarily of metals (aluminum, nickel, tin) and other raw materials, such as rubber. For further information, see U.S. Office of Emergency Preparedness, *Stockpile Report of the Congress*, semiannually; Thomas C. Schelling, *International Economics*, Allyn and Bacon, Inc., Boston, 1958, chaps. 30 and 31.

Strike   A mutual agreement among workers to stop working in order to obtain or resist a change in working conditions. The workers do not quit their jobs but rather leave them temporarily. Strikes may involve a simple walkout or include picketing and, occasionally, even violence. They are most commonly caused by wage disputes. Many strikes result from unsatisfied demands for union recognition and from issues connected with union security or with working conditions, such as hours or work seniority or working rules. The number and duration of strikes at any time may depend on the financial condition of unions, the militancy of the labor movement, and the indifference of management. In addition, the number of strikes may depend on the machinery available for adjusting employer-employee disputes. Sit-down or stay-in strikes, in which strikers seize the property of the employer and prevent him from using it, are usually considered illegal. See E. T. Hiller, *The Strike: A Study of Collective Action,* The University of Chicago Press, Chicago, 1928; see also Harry Laidler, *What Do You Know about Labor?* The John Day Company, Inc., New York, 1956.

Strike Adjustment A technique for estimating and eliminating the effect of a prolonged strike before the seasonal factor is estimated. It is necessary because a prolonged strike which exerts a strong influence on a particular economic time series, such as automobile production, steel production, or carloading, may distort the seasonal pattern around the strike period.

Strikebreaker Any person who accepts work at a struck shop. The strikebreaker, or scab, as he is sometimes called, may be brought in to replace a worker out on strike, or he may be a worker who continues to work while the other workers are on strike. The introduction of outside strikebreakers is an attempt by the employer to break the strike and to force the workers to return to work. Labor violence, when it arises, is more likely to be directed against the strikebreakers than against management. The Taft-Hartley Act of 1947 guarantees the strikebreakers' right to continue working and makes it illegal for union members to restrain or prevent strikebreakers from crossing a picket line.

Structural Equation An equation making up all or part of the mathematical expression of an econometric model. Structural equations depict the pattern of relationships that is assumed to exist among the statistical variables involved in the model. Examples of structural equations accompanied by detailed explanations abound in most econometric textbooks.

Structural Unemployment The loss of jobs resulting from changes in the economic environment. Among the more important structural changes believed to have a significant effect on employment are changes in consumer tastes, the level of technology, population growth, and government policies. Long-term variations in consumer tastes and technology may cause the creation or disappearance of industries, resulting in unemployment. Population growth can affect unemployment by influencing both the demand for production and the supply of workers. The effect of government spending and tax policies on unemployment is increasing in importance as government assumes a larger role in the economy. For information on the effect of structural factors in unemployment, see League of Nations, "Economic Stability in the Post-War World," *Report of the Delegates on Economic Depression,* part II, Geneva, 1945, pp. 25–44; see also U.S. Joint Economic Committee, *Higher Unemployment Rates, 1957–1960: Structural Transformation or Inadequate Demand,* Government Printing Office, Washington, D.C., 1961; ———, *Unemployment, Terminology, Measurement and Analysis,* Government Printing Office, Washington, D.C., Nov. 29, 1961.

Subscription Right A privilege given to stockholders to purchase additional stock or convertible debentures at a price lower than that which nonstockholders must pay. Common law gave stockholders preemptive rights that entitled them to subscribe to new issues of stock before nonstockholders. Subsequent legislation changed the nature of these preemptive rights, so that corporate directors can now choose between offering new stock through a rights issue, or privileged subscription, or through the marketing efforts of securities underwriters. If the directors decide on privileged subscription, they send their stockholders a subscription warrant which gives them one subscription right for every old share of stock owned and describes the terms of the subscription. As long as these rights allow stockholders to purchase the new issue at a price lower than the current market value of the old stock, the rights have value and are traded on stock exchanges. Shareholders receiving rights can exercise them (pay the subscription price and get the number of shares of the issue to which they are entitled) or sell them. If stockholders for some reason fail to exercise or sell rights, they lose money. For further information, see Jules I. Bogen (ed.), *Financial Handbook,* 4th ed., The Ronald Press Company, New York, 1968; George L. Leffler and L. C. Farwell, *The Stock Market,* The Ronald Press Company, New York, 1963.

Subsidiary A business enterprise which is controlled by another corporation. Its shares are owned by the controlling company (holding or parent company). A subsidiary differs from a branch of the parent company in that it has its own corporate entity and its own corporate charter. The parent company forms a subsidiary either by purchasing the controlling share of an existing corporation or by setting up a new corporation and retaining the controlling share of its stock. When all the outstanding stock of the subsidiary is owned by the parent company, it is called a wholly owned subsidiary. A subsidiary owned and operated by two or more other corporations is a joint subsidiary. For example, railroad stations used by several different railroads are joint subsidiaries of the railroads. See Charles W. Gerstenberg, *Financial Organization and Management of Business,* 4th ed., Prentice-Hall, Inc., Englewood Cliffs, N.J., 1959.

Subsidiary Coin   A coin of a smaller denomination than the basic monetary unit of a country, which in the U.S. is the dollar and in the United Kingdom the pound sterling. In the U.S., all coins—silver, nickels, and pennies—of less than $1 in value are subsidiary. Coins not made of silver, such as the nickel and the penny, are also called minor coins. The main use of subsidiary coins is to facilitate payment of sums smaller than the basic monetary unit, as in minor retail sales. When coins of this type were first issued, they were freely coined and full bodied; that is, they contained their face value in metal. It was difficult, however, to keep an appropriate number of such coins in circulation, because when the market value of the metal fell, an overabundance of the metal was brought to the mint to be coined; when the market value rose, individuals melted the coins down. The solution was found by halting free coinage and making coins with an amount of metal smaller than their face value. Almost no subsidiary coins in the world today are full bodied. See Paul B. Trescott, *Money, Banking and Economic Welfare,* 2d ed., McGraw-Hill Book Company, New York, 1965; for the total amount of subsidiary coins in circulation, see *Federal Reserve Bulletin,* Washington, D.C., monthly.

Subsidy   A payment to individuals or businesses by a government for which it receives no products or services in return. The purpose of such payments is to make available a particular service or product at a price that the public can readily afford, when the service or product cannot otherwise be profitably supplied at this price. The particular service or product is considered essential to the public welfare, and the government therefore finds it necessary to subsidize the enterprise in order to keep it operating and producing the service or product. In the U.S., Federal subsidies are given to airlines to carry mail, to railroads and other means of public transportation for the transportation of commuters, to farmers under the current agricultural progam, and to the shipbuilding industry to build ships. The term subsidy has also been used to include governmental payments to other governments, now referred to as grants-in-aid. In fiscal 1970 and 1971, the cost of Federal subsidy programs was approximately $40 billion per year. For further information, see U.S. Joint Economic Committee, *The Economies of Federal Subsidy Programs,* Government Printing Office, Washington, D.C., 1971.

Subsistence Theory of Wages (Iron or Brazen Law of Wages) A theory of the late eighteenth and early ninetenth centuries that held that wages, in the long run, tend to equal the minimum amount necessary to support life. Based on the Malthusian doctrine of population, the reasoning behind the theory was as follows: Since the food supply cannot increase as rapidly as the population, the size of the population tends to be at a level that will just enable people to subsist. If wages fall below the amount necessary for subsistence, a greater number of people will die, a smaller amount of labor will be offered, and wages will rise. If wages rise above the subsistence level, a greater number of children will be born because families can afford them, a greater amount of labor will subsequently be offered, and wages will then fall. The theory was softened to some extent by the recognition that subsistence depends in part on customs and habits as well as on biological necessities, but most of the early economists who adhered to the subsistence theory were not optimistic that the standard of living would rise above the provision of bare physical necessities. Because of its lack of accord with reality in Europe and the U.S., this theory was generally abandoned at about the middle of the nineteenth century in favor of the wages-fund theory, which, in turn, has been superseded by the marginal-productivity theory of wages, the most widely accepted non-Marxian theory of the present time. For a classical statement of the subsistence theory, see David Ricardo, *Principles of Political Economy and Taxation,* John Murray (Publishers), Ltd., London, 1817, chap. 5; for a modern discussion of the theory, see Michael T. Wermel, *The Evolution of the Classical Wage Theory,* Columbia University Press, New York, 1939; Henry Smith, "The Minimal Economy," *The Economic Journal,* vol. 75, pp. 31–43, March, 1965.

Substantial-Labor-Surplus Market *See Substantial-Unemployment Area.*

Substantial-Unemployment Area (Substantial-Labor-Surplus Market) A classification of U.S. labor-market areas in which unemployment usually amounts to 6% or more of an area's labor force. This labor-market rating is assigned by the Bureau of Employment Security on the basis of information submitted by affiliated state employment security agencies, which draw upon the information available in local public employment offices. A high unemployment rate is not the sole criterion used to classify labor-market areas. Consideration also is given to the outlook for the area as reflected by employers' estimates of future labor needs and developments. Areas falling in the Bureau of Employment Security's Group D (an unemployment rate of 6 to 8.9%), Group E (9 to 11.9%), and Group

F (12% or higher) are regarded as areas of substantial unemployment or substantial labor surplus. Firms located in areas classified in these three categories are eligible for preference in bidding on government procurement contracts. Area classifications are issued in U.S. Bureau of Employment Security, *Area Labor Market Trends,* monthly.

Substitute Goods   *See Cross Elasticity.* For further information, see D. S. Watson, *Price Theory and Its Uses,* 2d ed., Houghton Mifflin Company, Boston, 1968.

Substitution Effect   When the price of a good is changed, people buy more or less of it, depending upon whether the price has fallen or risen. The change in the amount purchased when the price changes (and therefore the elasticity of demand) is attributable to two separate influences upon the purchaser: the substitution effect and the income effect. The desire of a consumer always to purchase more of a cheaper product and less of a more expensive product is the substitution effect. A discussion of the general nature of the substitution effect and an indifference-curve analysis of it may be found in D. S. Watson, *Price Theory and Its Uses,* 2d ed., Houghton Mifflin Company, Boston, 1968; a mathematical discussion of the substitution effect may be found in James M. Henderson and Richard E. Quandt, *Microeconomic Theory: A Mathematical Approach,* 2d ed., McGraw-Hill Book Company, New York, 1971.

Suburban Population   The persons inhabiting the area that lies outside a central city and is closely related to it. The suburban population is characterized by its daily flow into the city to work and back home from the city in the evening. The process of suburbanization has occurred at an accelerated rate in the twentieth century, and about 35% of the U.S. pop-

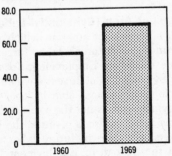

Suburban Population (Millions)

Source: U.S. Department of Commerce; Bureau of the Census.

ulation is classified as suburban. For information concerning the growth of suburban areas, see Warren S. Thompson, *The Growth of Metropolitan Districts in the United States 1900–1940*, Government Printing Office, Washington, D.C., 1948; see also Donald J. Bogue, *Metropolitan Decentralization: A Study of Differential Growth*, The Free Press of Glencoe, New York, 1950.

Sumptuary Tax   A levy that is imposed to reduce the consumption of harmful goods. The best current example is the tax on alcoholic beverages. In the Middle Ages, however, luxuries were often considered harmful, and taxes were imposed on them to discourage consumption. Taxes are now imposed on luxury items on the ground that those who buy them can best afford to pay an additional tax.

Super Gold Tranche   An automatic credit that can be drawn on by a member nation of the International Monetary Fund in addition to its regular gold tranche position. A nation's gold tranche position is equivalent to the 25% of its quota in the IMF which it deposits in gold with the Fund. This may be drawn on at will by the country to meet payments imbalances. The other 75% of a country's quota represents the amounts of its currency paid into the Fund and is divided into three credit tranches. Permission from the Fund is needed to draw on the credit tranche position. With each succeeding credit tranche, it becomes more difficult to draw on the Fund's facilities without making explicit promises as to government policies to be pursued to right the balance-of-payments position. However, borrowings from the Fund of a nation's currency give rise to an additional credit to the nation whose currency is being borrowed. The credit is equivalent to the amount by which the Fund's holdings of the nation's currency fall short of the 75% of quota originally paid in. This credit is the super gold tranche and may be drawn on in a manner similar to that in which the gold tranche position is drawn on. For additional information, see International Monetary Fund, *Annual Report*, 1969.

Supplemental Unemployment Benefit (SUB)   Any payment received by laid-off workers in the U.S. from private unemployment-insurance plans in addition to benefits provided by state unemployment-insurance plans. As of 1968, such plans covered 2.3 million workers, most of whom were in the automobile, glass, and steel industries. SUB originated in 1955 as a compromise between the positions of the United Automobile Workers, who demanded a guaranteed annual wage, and the Ford Motor Company. Plans of this type arise from collective bargaining agreements and are financed by employers. Typically, they increase a worker's income during a layoff from about 40 or 45%, the range most often provided by unemployment insurance, to 60 or 65% of base pay after taxes. In addition, SUB plans may pay the full 60 or 65% of basic take-home pay to workers whose rights to unemployment insurance have been exhausted. SUB plans increase the typical duration of unemployment benefits from 26 to 52 weeks. There are two basic types of plans: the funded, or insurance, type of plan; and the individual trust account or savings-arrangement type. Benefits are financed by the employer's contributions to the group or individual trust fund. When the fund is low, benefits may either be restricted to senior employees or be sharply curtailed for other employees. The introduction of SUB plans has made employers reluctant to hire additional employees and the unemployed less anxious to find new employment. An authoritative source on this subject is Sumner H. Slichter et al., *The Impact of Collective Bargaining on Management*, The Brookings Institution, Washington, D.C., 1960; see also Albert Rees, *The Economics of Trade Unions*, The University of Chicago Press, Chicago, 1962.

Supply   The ability and willingness of a firm to sell a good or service. The supply of a firm for a good or service is a schedule of the quantities of that good or service that the firm would offer for sale at alternative prices at a given moment in time. The supply schedule, or the listing of quantities that would be sold at different prices, can be shown graphically by means of a supply curve. The term supply refers to the entire schedule of possibilities and not to one point on the schedule. It is an instantaneous concept expressing the relationship of price and the quantity that would be willingly sold, all other factors being constant. Except for a monopoly market structure, adding the quantities offered for sale at the various possible prices, the supply schedule for all firms, or the market supply, can be derived. The monopolist's supply schedule is, in effect, the market supply schedule since he is the only seller. Supply schedules obviously depend upon the cost structures of firms. Assuming that firms attempt to maximize profits, the short-run supply curve is that portion of a firm's marginal-cost curve equal to, or greater than, average variable costs. In the long run (where all costs are variable) the supply curve is that portion of the marginal-cost curve equal to, or greater than, average costs. In the short run, the supply curve will always have a positive slope because of the law of diminishing returns. That is, the higher the price for a good or service, the larger the quantity that will be offered for sale. In the long run, the supply curve will rise if there are internal or external diseconomies of scale, it will be horizontal if there are constant returns to scale, and it will fall (negative slope) if there are internal or external economies of scale. The latter case implies that larger output means more efficient production and, hence, lower costs. Thus a firm would be willing to supply more at a lower price. The level of costs of producing a good or service—and therefore the supply schedule—depends on the state of technology which is embodied in the production function for that good or service and on the process of the required inputs. Any change in these determinants causes a shift in the whole supply schedule. For instance, if a technological advance results in the production of a larger output with unchanged inputs, the supply schedule shifts to the right; that is, at any given price the firm would be willing to supply a larger quantity for sale. If, on the other hand, the price of inputs increases, the supply schedule shifts to the left, and firms would be willing to supply smaller quantities at various prices. These changes should not be confused with a change in the quantity supplied, which describes merely the movement from one point to another along a given supply curve. See George J. Stigler, *The Theory of Price*, 3d ed., The Macmillan Company, New York, 1966; Jacob Viner, "Cost Curves and Supply Curves," in American Economic Association, *Readings in Price Theory*, Richard D. Irwin, Inc., Homewood, Ill., 1952; William Baumol, *Economic Theory and Operations Analysis*, Prentice-Hall, Inc., Englewood Cliffs, N.J., 1965, chap. 11.

Suppressed Inflation A situation in which inflationary pressures exist but, because of direct price controls and the rationing of goods, inflation does not take place. During World War II, the real income of U.S. Consumers rose substantially, but they could not increase their purchases of goods because the supply of consumer goods was limited. Price controls prevented the prices of consumer goods from rising as they ordinarily would have risen in a period of short supply and great demand. Thus, inflation was said to be suppressed during the period of controls, for prices rose immediately after the controls were removed. For a discussion of suppressed inflation, see Sumner H. Slichter, *What's Ahead for American Business*, Little, Brown and Company, Boston, 1951.

Surety Bond A contract between a principal and a responsible third party (surety) which makes the surety responsible for the principal's fulfillment of an obligation to the obligee (the party who is protected). For example, most persons who are arrested on a criminal charge can obtain their release from jail by getting a bail bond, which is a type of surety bond. The surety guarantees that the defendant (principal) will appear for trial (fulfill his obligation to the court, which is the obligee); if the defendant fails to appear, the full amount of the bond is payable by the surety. In addition to bail bonds, there are many kinds of surety bonds, including fiduciary bonds, which cover principals who are entrusted with the safekeeping of someone else's funds; contract bonds, which guarantee that a contracted piece of work is completed; and public-official bonds, which the law requires in order to secure the performance of persons elected to fill positions of public trust—tax collectors, treasurers, and so on. Fidelity bonds are actually surety bonds that specifically cover employers for their employees' dishonest acts. For further informaton, see Solomon S. Huebner and Kenneth Black, Jr., *Property Insurance,* Appleton-Century-Crofts, Inc., New York, 1957, chap. 31.

Surplus-Labor Market *See Labor-Shortage Area.*

Surplus Value The difference between a worker's wages and the value of the goods that he produces during a certain period. The term was used by Karl Marx to define the capitalist's profit. Marx maintained that the value of a particular commodity is the result solely of the labor involved in its production. Thus, he viewed surplus value as a measure of the exploitation of the working classes. Modern economists recognize that labor, although extremely important, is not the sole factor in production. Capital and managerial skills are equally important elements in the productive process and, like labor, are legitimately entitled to a return. The fact that the Soviet Union now strongly emphasizes investment in plants and equipment suggests that the Russians have come to believe that capital as well as labor adds to value. See Karl Marx, *Capital,* Charles Kerr & Company, Chicago, 1906; Eric Roll, *A History of Economic Thought,* 3d ed., Prentice-Hall, Inc., Englewood Cliffs, N.J., 1956, pp. 266–273; for a more recent exposition of surplus value, see Paul M. Sweezy, *The Theory of Capitalist Development,* Oxford University Press, Fair Lawn, N.J., 1942.

Surtax An additional tax levied on a tax base after a normal tax has been applied. A surtax is often used to achieve progressive taxation of income, the surtax being applied to income above a certain level. For example, in 1960 the normal Federal corporate income tax in the U.S. was 30% of all net income, and an additional surtax of 22% was imposed on all taxable income in excess of $25,000. Before 1954, the Federal personal income tax was based on a proportional normal tax (3% in 1951) on all income and a progressive surtax on incomes above a certain amount. Since 1954, the normal tax and surtax rates have been combined in a single schedule.

Survey A technique of gathering facts and attitudes related to various persons (consumers or businessmen) from a scientific sample of these persons that is considered representative of a larger group. The information is usually either of a quantitative nature or of a type which can be summarized in quantitative terms. The survey technique is one of the most-advanced marketing-research practices. Nevertheless, with the introduction of panel-research and motivation-research techniques, it has become less important as a marketing-research method. Examples of surveys are those of the U.S. Bureau of the Census and the Survey Research Center of the University of Michigan on consumers' plans to buy durable goods and those of the U.S. Department of Commerce, Securities and Exchange Commission, and McGraw-Hill Department of Economics on businessmen's plans to buy new plants and equipment. For general information concerning surveys and survey methods, see G. Katz et al., *Contributions of Survey Methods to Economics,* Columbia University Press, New York, 1954.

Sustainable Growth   A rise in per capita real income or per capita real gross national product that is capable of continuing for a long time. A condition of sustainable economic growth means that economic stagnation will not set in. Sustainable growth will provide employment for a growing population as well as greater individual well-being, thus promoting the economic welfare of the country. Many economists put the rate of sustainable growth in the U.S. at 2.7% per year. According to Walt W. Rostow, the condition of sustainable growth in a developing country follows the takeoff stage in its economic development. With its radical changes in production techniques and distribution of income, the takeoff perpetuates a new scale of investment, which, in turn, fosters a rising trend in per capita output. For further information, see Walt W. Rostow, "The Take-off into Self-sustained Growth," *Economic Journal,* vol. LXVI, no. 261, pp. 25–48, Royal Economic Society, London, March, 1956.

Swap Arrangement   An official arrangement between the central banks of two countries for standby credit to exchange holdings of each other's currencies. These standby arrangements help to limit potential problems caused by speculative runs on a nation's currency. The swap arrangement leads to a swap transaction when one of the two parties to the agreement requires a loan of the other party's currency. Swap transactions are generally temporary in nature, with the borrowing central bank generally pledged to repay the creditor within a three-month period. Swap transactions allow a central bank to intervene in the foreign-exchange market to defend its currency in the event of speculation on that nation's currency. The U.S. has by far the largest network of bilateral swap arrangements. In 1968, the U.S. Treasury arrangements and Federal Reserve System swap network amounted to $10.5 billion. During the same year, the total of all other such credit facilities among International Monetary

Fund members amounted to $5.8 billion. Between 1961 and 1968, the Federal Reserve System drew $6.3 billion in foreign currencies under its swap network and repaid nearly $5.9 billion. During this same period, the United Kingdom drew almost $7.2 billion in U.S. dollars under swap transactions and repaid $6.0 billion. For additional information, see Charles P. Kindleberger, *International Economics*, 4th ed., Richard D. Irwin, Inc., Homewood, Ill., 1968, pp. 451–452; for data on swaps, see International Monetary Fund, *Annual Report*.

Sweetheart Agreement   A substandard labor contract, negotiated by a dishonest union leader in return for private payments from an employer. Sweetheart agreements may be signed either by corrupt locals of national unions or by unions that have been established solely for the purpose of obtaining such agreements. Some employers have been accused of assisting in the organization of unions of the latter type to prevent the establishment of legitimate unions. Sweetheart agreements are a violation of the U.S. Federal labor relations laws, and a union engaging in these practices, if detected, will not be certified as a bargaining agent. For a discussion of sweetheart agreements and other corrupt labor practices, see Albert Rees, *The Economics of Trade Unions*, The University of Chicago Press, Chicago, 1962.

Swing Shift   A work shift beginning at or about 4 P.M. and continuing until midnight. Swing shifts are ordinarily worked only when an enterprise is operating twenty-four hours a day, using three shifts, each of which works eight hours. The term is also used to cover the workers in a plant operating seven days a week who staff the plant when the regular workers are given days off.

Sympathy Strike   A strike against a particular employer by a union with no direct grievance of its own in support of another union that is striking to achieve certain concessions from the employer. It is used as a means of demonstrating labor solidarity in an effort to apply additional pressure on the employer. As a rule, U.S. unions are wary of engaging in sympathetic strikes because of the substantial legal risks involved under the common law and the Taft-Hartley Act. See E. T. Hiller, *The Strike: A Study of Collective Action*, The University of Chicago Press, Chicago, 1928; U.S. Code, title 29.

Syndicalism   A form of socialism that aims both at public ownership of productive resources and at the elimination of central government. A syndicalist society is assumed to come about not as the result of an inevitable economic evolution but rather as a consequence of a supreme effort on the part of the working class led by a dedicated minority. The syndicalist movement originated before World War I because of working-class discontent with the failure of the French government to secure improved living conditions. Beginning as a thoroughly spontaneous revolt, it attracted many intellectuals, who gave it a philosophical and theoretical framework. The plan for the period after the expected workers' revolution against the government included (1) the establishment of trade unions (syndicats), through which all revolutionary actions including the ultimate one, the general strike, were to be organized, and (2) the joining of these unions into a federation that was to coordinate (but not dictate) internal union policies and the diplomatic representation of France in international affairs. Syndicalism lost much of its appeal in the 1920s, when working conditions in France improved and communism seemed to offer a more promising alternative. For an expression of the movement's philosophy, see Georges Sorel, *Reflections on Violence,* The Viking Press, Inc., New York, 1914; Allan G. Gruchy, *Comparative Economic Systems,* Houghton Mifflin Company, Boston, 1966, pp. 268–271.

T

Tableau Économique   A graphic picture of the general interdependence of the economic system introduced by François Quesnay for Louis XV in 1759. The *tableau économique* tries to show how the different sectors of the economy sell their goods to one another and how they spend the money received from these sales. It depicts the circular flow of goods in one direction and of purchasing power in the other direction, emphasizing the fundamental identity of output with income. Illustrating the mutual interdependence of industries, the *tableau* was based on the belief of the physiocrats that net production is derived only from the argicultural sector and that it all goes to the landlord in the form of rent. It was presented by Quesnay in the form of a numerical diagram (see the accompanying illustration). At the beginning of the period depicted, the farmers hold the entire money supply of 2 milliards. They pay this sum to the landowners for the rental of their land, and the landowners in turn spend the money on food (1 milliard) and other commodities (1 milliard). The artisans (producers of nonagricultural commodities) spend their total income of 2 milliards (1 milliard received from the landlords and 1 milliard received from purchases by farmers) on agricultural products. At the end of the period, the farmers have received 3 milliards of income and have spent 1 milliard, and they therefore hold the same amount as they started with. The 2 milliards are paid once more to the landlord as rent, and the cycle starts over again. For additional details, see Ronald L. Meek, "Tableau Économique," *Economica*, vol. XXVII, no. 108, pp. 322–347, London School of Economics and Political Science, London, November, 1960; A. Phillips, "The Tableau d'Économique as a Simple Leontief Model," *Quarterly Journal of Economics*, vol. LXIX, no. 1, pp. 137–144, Harvard University Press, Cambridge, Mass., February, 1955.

Tableau Économique, as Presented in Quesnay's Analyse (Millards)

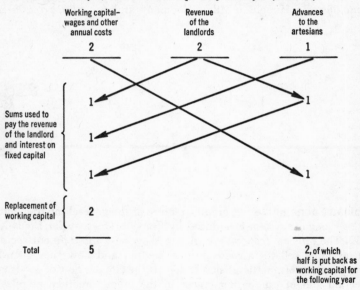

Taft-Hartley Act (Labor-Management Relations Act of 1947) The primary Federal statute regulating labor-management relations in the U.S. The act attempted to establish a new balance of power in the collective bargaining process after the Wagner Act of 1936 had freed labor unions from many impediments and permitted them to grow without, in the later opinion of Congress, adequate safeguards for management and for the individual worker. Under the Taft-Hartley Act, the role of government in labor disputes is to safeguard the public interest and not to take the part of either labor unions or management in their disputes. To this end, the act reorganized the National Labor Relations Board (NLRB) and established the Federal Mediation and Conciliation Service. It also listed unfair labor practices of employers and of labor unions that might be directed against each other or against the individual worker, made extensive provisions for determining union representation and collective bargaining procedures, and provided for court review of actions of the NLRB and for suits by and against labor organizations. In 1959 the act was amended by the Labor-Management Reporting and Disclosure Act (Landrum-Griffin Act). For details, see Wayne L. McNaughton and Joseph Lazar, *Industrial Relations and the Government*, McGraw-Hill Book Company, New York, 1954; Charles Gregory, *Labor and the Law*, W. W. Norton & Company, Inc., New York, 1961.

Take-Home Pay   The amount of money that an employee actually receives in each pay period. It excludes all items withheld, such as deductions for Federal, state, and city taxes, union dues, state disability tax, social security tax, payments on a retirement-annuity plan, and payments for life and health and accident insurance. Spendable average weekly earnings, or gross weekly pay less Federal social security and income taxes, is the published statistical measure nearest to take-home pay.

Takeoff in Economic Development   The critical point in the development of a national economy which marks the final disintegration of traditional society's resistance to steady economic growth and the liberation of the forces that establish expansion and progress as national goals. Walt W. Rostow, who views the takeoff as the most crucial period in a nation's economic history, indicates that it occurred in Great Britain in the two decades after 1783, in France and the U.S. in the several decades before 1860, in Germany in the third quarter of the nineteenth century, in Japan in the fourth quarter, in Russia and Canada at the turn of the twentieth century, and in India and China in the 1950s. In each case, the preconditions for rapid economic growth had been fulfilled: an adequate stock of social overhead capital had been installed, a surge of technological development had occurred in industry and agriculture, and dominant political power had come into the hands of persons who were committed to the pursuit of modernization and to a rapid rise of real output per capita as major objectives of national policy. Invariably, the takeoff is marked by an accelerated investment rate, the development of manufacturing industry, and the emergence of political, social, and institutional forces that favor continued growth as a means of raising incomes and the standard of living (always the overriding objective of underdeveloped countries). For a full discussion of this historical phenomenon, see Walt W. Rostow, *The Stages of Economic Growth: A Non-Communist Manifesto*, Cambridge University Press, New York, 1960.

Tariff (Customs Duty)   A tax on the importation and, rarely, on the exportation of particular goods, levied by a national government and payable to it when the item crosses the nation's customs boundary. Tariffs originated with the tolls that sovereigns collected on goods that moved into or through their territory. Instead of devices to raise revenue, import duties are now considered effective deterrents to imports that might endanger a domestic industry's sales or a nation's balance of international payments. Formerly, tariff schedules showed an absolute amount of duty to be paid on a variety of imported items, but, because of the frequent changes necessitated by inflation, the modern practice is to establish ad valorem tariffs, which show the duty as a percentage of the imported item's wholesale value. There is no question that an import duty tends to discourage imports; what is in doubt is whether this is in the interest of the tariff-levying country. Classical economists, beginning with John Locke and Adam Smith, have claimed that the artificial protection of certain domestic industries whose products could be bought cheaper abroad and the artificial limitation of the most efficient foreign producer's market result in a misallocation of resources that impedes the nation's and the world's economic welfare. This view is often disputed on political, military, and ethical grounds. The economic argument against it is generally based on one of three claims: (1) that a judicious tariff structure (the optimum tariff) can, if other countries do not retaliate by levying a tariff of their own, improve a country's commodity terms of trade, income terms of trade, or balance of payments; (2) that the concentrated injury to an important industry that loses its tariff protection outweighs the broadly scattered benefits of tariff reduction to the rest of the economy; and (3) that a new (infant) industry requires tariff protection while it is growing to the size and efficiency that will subsequently assure its success in a world of free trade. Since World War II, the trend has been away from tariffs as a tool of national policy. Most modern international tariff agreements aim at tariff reduction and generally provide for other means (especially international credits) to resolve the balance-of-payments, economic development, and other temporary national problems that once served as excuses for the introduction of higher tariffs. See P. T. Ellsworth, *The International Economy*, 4th ed., The Macmillan Company, New York, 1961; Charles P. Kindleberger, *International Economics*, 4th ed., Richard D. Irwin, Inc., Homewood, Ill., 1968.

Tax Anticipation Bills Short-term money-market instruments sold by the Treasury to smooth the inflow of tax payments from corporations. Large corporations generally accumulate funds for their quarterly tax payments throughout the quarter. They thus have some amount of idle cash which could be earning interest. Treasury bills are sold at a discount at public auction, maturing when taxes are due. They are accepted at maturity by the government as payment for tax liabilities. Corporations thus have a short-term investment for their funds, while the Treasury obtains the money in advance of the tax date. The Treasury determines the amount of tax anticipation bills to be sold and the frequency of sales, according to the Federal government's needs for funds during a specific fiscal period. Prices of the bills are determined by the bidding procedure. A large portion of the receipts of tax anticipation bills is credited to Treasury tax and loan accounts in comercial banks designated as special depositaries. Tax anticipation bills were first sold in 1951. Between 1952 and 1966 more than $80 billion worth of such Treasury bills were sold. The volume issued annually varied from about $800 million in 1953 to over $11 billion in 1967. See Jane F. Nelson, "Tax Anticipation Bills," in Jimmie R. Monhollon (ed.), *Instruments of the Money Market,* Federal Reserve Bank of Richmond, Richmond, Va., February, 1968.

Tax Avoidance An attempt to reduce tax liability. It involves choosing legal forms and handling affairs in such a way as to take advantage of a legally permissible alternate tax rate or an alternative method of assessing income. Tax avoidance, in contrast to tax evasion, is considered by many to be a legitimate aim, since it is not illegal but consists of exploiting the discrepancies and loopholes in the tax laws to the fullest extent. Among the more common methods of tax avoidance are the manipulation of capital gains and losses, the formation of holding companies to create artificial deductions, and the creation of multiple trusts for relatives and dependents. For further information on the mechanics of tax avoidance and proposals to tighten the Federal tax structure, see Lawrence H. Seltzer, *The Nature and Tax Treatment of Capital Gains and Losses,* National Bureau of Economic Research, Inc., New York, 1951; U.S. House of Representatives Committee on Ways and Means, *Tax Revision Compendium,* 1959.

Tax Base The objective basis on which a tax is imposed. The possible objects of taxation are almost endless, but some of the more common ones are income (income tax), property owned by the taxpayer (property tax), and the value of certain goods sold (sales tax). The specific nature of the tax base largely determines where the burden of each tax falls. Broadening the tax base refers to the application of the tax to a larger portion of the object already being taxed, usually by reducing previous exemptions. Erosion of the tax base refers to a narrowing of the tax base through an increase in the preferential treatment given to certain groups, usually by creating special exemptions and reducing tax rates. For further information on both the broadening and the erosion of the U.S. Federal tax base, see U.S. House of Representatives Committee on Ways and Means, *Tax Revision Compendium*, 1959, sections II and III.

Tax Burden   The final resting place of the tax levied. In effect, a statement of the tax burden is a statement of who pays the tax and in what amount. The problem of assessing the actual burden of a tax is complicated by the fact that the person who finally bears the tax is frequently not the person who pays it originally, since many taxes, especially those on businesses, may be shifted so that the real burden falls on the consumer. For further information on the distribution of the tax burden, see E. H. Plank, *Public Finance*, Richard D. Irwin, Inc., Homewood, Ill., 1953, chap. 8; A. Conrad, "On the Calculation of Tax Burdens," *Economica*, new series, vol. 2, pp. 342–348, London School of Economics and Political Science, London, November, 1955; Helen Tarasov, *Who Does Pay the Taxes?* New School for Social Research, New York, 1942, supplement IV.

Tax Court, U.S.   A special administrative court which hears and decides Federal tax cases. Originally set up under the Revenue Act of 1924, it is the first place for the U.S. taxpayer to turn in order to challenge administrative tax decisions of the Bureau of Internal Revenue. The court's rulings can be reviewed by the Court of Appeals and, in the case of a conflict of decisions, by the Supreme Court. Although created as an administrative body, the Tax Court is functionally incapable of making rules and acts primarily in a judicial role. For further information, see *Procedure and Practice before the Tax Court of the United States*, 14th ed., Commerce Clearing House, Inc., Chicago, 1954.

Tax Credit   A legal provision permitting U.S. taxpayers to deduct specified sums from their tax liabilities. A credit differs from a deduction in the following essential respect: It is subtracted after the total tax liability has been calculated, whereas a deduction is subtracted from the income subject to tax. Thus, a tax credit of a given amount is more valuable to a taxpayer than a deduction of the same amount. For example, a U.S. taxpayer who is in the 50% bracket of the Federal income tax reduces his total burden by $50 if he is allowed a $50 tax credit, but his total burden is reduced by only $25 if he is given a $50 deduction. Examples of tax-credit provisions in the U.S. Internal Revenue Code as of December 31, 1970, include (1) foreign tax credit, which allows taxpayers to credit against their U.S. tax the foreign tax on income from abroad, and (2) retirement income credit. For a discussion of the tax credits allowed to individuals by the U.S. Internal Revenue Code, see U.S. Treasury Department, *Your Federal Income Tax*, annually.

Tax Deduction   A legal provision permitting U.S. taxpayers to deduct specified expenditures from their taxable income. A deduction differs from a credit in the following essential respect: it is subtracted from the income subject to tax, whereas a credit is subtracted after the total tax liability has been calculated. Thus, a tax deduction of a given amount is less valuable to a taxpayer than a credit of the same amount. For example, a U.S. taxpayer who is in the 50% bracket of the Federal income tax reduces his total burden by $25 if he is allowed a $50 tax deduction, whereas his total burden is reduced by $50 if he is allowed a $50 credit. Examples of tax-deduction provisions in the U.S. Internal Revenue Code as of May 1, 1971, include (1) personal deductions for state and local taxes, interest on indebtedness, contributions to charitable organizations, medical expenses to the extent that these exceed 3% of adjusted gross income, and certain other specified items, such as losses from fire and theft and a part of the expenses of child care for working mothers; (2) business deductions for the ordinary and necessary expenses of carrying on any trade or business, including wages, salaries, interest, rent, and depreciation, which is the cost of plants and equipment either used up in production or rendered obsolete by time. For a detailed discussion of the deductions allowed to individuals by the U.S. Internal Revenue Code, see U.S. Treasury Department, *Your Federal Income Tax*, annually; for a discussion of the economic impact of tax deductions, see Harry Kahn, *Personal Deductions in the Federal Income Tax*, National Bureau of Economic Research, Inc., Princeton University Press, Princeton, N.J., 1960.

Tax Equalization   An adjustment made by central U.S. governmental units, such as states or counties, to assure an equitable distribution of property assessments among tax districts. When these central units use property taxes as a large source of revenue, they generally resort to tax equalization to prevent competitive undervaluation by local districts. Such undervaluation may be used by local areas to reduce their share of the taxes paid to the central unit. Tax equalization is carried out by central assessment, under which each district as a whole is valued by a central board of assessment and within each district individual lots are assessed totally, so that the sum of all the assessed property values in a district equals the centrally fixed assessment for that district. For additional details, see Harold M. Groves, *Financing Government*, 6th ed., Holt, Rinehart and Winston, Inc., New York, 1965.

Tax Equity A fair distribution of the tax burden. There are two aspects to tax equity: vertical equity, which is different treatment of persons in different relative positions; and horizontal equity, which is equal treatment for persons in equal positions even if they earn their income in different ways. Although equity is a universal goal in taxation, there is no unanimity of opinion as to the type of tax which results in the fairest distribution. There are three main approaches to achieving tax equity. The most common, the ability-to-pay doctrine, holds that an equitable tax is one under which the wealthy contribute proportionately more than the poor for government services. The obligation to pay is seen as a collective responsibility rather than a personal one. A different, more individualistic approach, the benefit theory, states that tax payments should be proportional to the benefits derived from government services. A third method, the sociopolitical method, would use the taxing power to redistribute income from the upper to the lower classes, placing almost all the burden on the rich and almost none on the poor. Political and administrative factors, however, require that other considerations, practicality and expediency, be added in placing the tax. The introduction of factors irrelevant to tax equity detracts from its fairness. For further information on the approaches to tax equity, see Richard A. Musgrave, *The Theory of Public Finance*, McGraw-Hill Book Company, New York, 1959, part 2; E. H. Plank, *Public Finance*, Richard D. Irwin, Inc., Homewood, Ill., 1953, chap. 8.

Tax Evasion An illegal attempt to avoid payment of taxes. Generally, a lax administration and high tax rates promote tax evasion. The more complex the tax laws and the greater the self-assessment required of taxpayers, the harder the tax laws are to administer and the easier they are to evade. The public attitude toward evasion is also important, for if public opinion is sympathetic to evasion, especially of unpopular taxes, tax evasion will be encouraged. For further details, see A. V. Tranter, *Evasion in Taxation*, George Routledge and Sons, Ltd., London, 1929.

Tax Exclusion A legal provision that permits taxpayers to exclude certain specified types of income from their taxable income. As of May 1, 1971, the U.S. Internal Revenue Code defined "gross income" as "all income from whatever source . . . except as otherwise provided. . . ." Among the most important exclusions as of that date were (1) veterans' pensions; (2) social insurance benefit payments; (3) workmen's compensation; (4) life insurance payments by reason of death; (5) employer contributions to employee pension, accident, or health plans; (6) interest on obligations of state and local governments; (7) gifts and inheritances; and (8) dividends received up to $50 per year per taxpayer. For a detailed discussion of deductions allowed individuals by the U.S. Internal Revenue Code, see U.S. Treasury Department, *Your Federal Income Tax*, annually.

Tax Exemption   A legal provision permitting taxpayers to deduct from their taxable incomes certain specified sums on a per capita basis. Exemptions in the U.S. Internal Revenue Code as of December 31, 1970, included (1) $625 for each taxpayer and each of his dependents, (2) an additional $625 if the taxpayer is sixty-five years of age or older, and (3) an additional $625 for blind persons. The basic exemption allowance was increased to $675 in 1971 and $750 in 1972. For a detailed discussion of exemptions allowed individuals by the U.S. Internal Revenue Code, see U.S. Treasury Department, *Your Federal Income Tax*, annually; for a discussion of the economic impact of exemptions, see Lawrence H. Seltzer, "The Place of the Personal Exemptions in the Present-Day Income Tax," *Tax Revision Compendium*, Tax Foundation, New York, 1959, vol. 1, pp. 493–514.

Tax Haven   A foreign country which offers low tax rates and other special advantages to corporations of other countries. In the U.S., tax laws formerly permitted a company to accumulate profits abroad tax-free, deferring the tax until the dividends were returned to the U.S. parent corporation. Thus, many large business firms formed foreign subsidiaries to take advantage of tax havens abroad. By shifting profits from one foreign company to another (e.g., through a holding company) and using companies in the low-tax countries to accumulate earnings, U.S. firms were able to save substantial amounts on taxes. Such tax havens as Switzerland, Panama, and Venezuela enabled corporations to accumulate capital more rapidly, made foreign financing easier, and allowed the use of foreign subsidiaries as a funnel for other investments. According to the Revenue Act of 1962, however, domestic corporations are no longer allowed a tax differential on dividend income received from foreign corporations in developed countries (this does not apply with respect to dividends received from corporations located in less-developed countries). For additional details, see "T-Men Eye Overseas Tax Havens," *Business Week*, Dec. 24, 1960; *Revenue Act of 1962*, Report 1881, U.S. Senate Committee on Finance.

Tax Incentive   The devising and arranging of taxes to provide positive encouragement to individuals and businesses and thus help achieve higher rates of economic activity for the nation. Such inducements in the U.S. take many forms, among which are exemptions and credits. For example, the 7% tax credit for investment in machinery and equipment, approved by Congress in 1962, was aimed at spurring capital investment. Thus, the tax system can be used to reward desirable economic conduct and penalize undesirable economic actions. For a more detailed discussion, See Harold M. Groves, *Postwar Taxation and Economic Progress*, McGraw-Hill Book Company, New York, 1946.

Tax Incidence The final resting place of the tax burden. By shifting the tax forward or backward, the burden of the original tax can be transferred from one person to another. The incidence of the tax falls on the person who cannot shift it any further. The only way in which to avoid the incidence of a tax is to remove oneself from its jurisdiction; e.g., to avoid the incidence of a property tax, one can sell the property. For further information on the nature of tax incidence and shifting, see Harry G. Brown, *The Economics of Taxation*, Holt, Rinehart and Winston, Inc., New York, 1934; W. F. Ferger, "The Measurement of Tax Shifting: Economics and Law," *Quarterly Journal of Economics*, Harvard University Press, Cambridge, Mass., May, 1940, pp. 429ff.; Otto von Mering, *The Shifting and Incidence of Taxation*, Richard D. Irwin, Inc., Homewood, Ill., 1942.

Tax Loophole An unintentional and unforeseen avenue of tax avoidance. Often the term tax loophole is not used in this narrow sense of an inadvertent oversight in the drafting of legislation; instead, it refers to a tax provision which gives a special advantage to an individual or a group. Such intentional tax loopholes may have as their main purpose the promotion of certain fields of activity through special tax incentives or may merely represent the legislative influence of pressure groups or lobbies. Some provisions in U.S. tax laws that were generally considered in this category as of July 1, 1971, were capital gains, depletion allowances, and executive expense accounts. For further information on tax loopholes in the Federal tax structure and proposals for reform, see U.S. House of Representatives Committee on Ways and Means, *Tax Revision Compendium*, 1959, sections I, II, and III.

Tax-Loss Carryback A legal provision permitting both corporations and unincorporated businesses to use the operating losses of one year to offset the profits of preceding years. Such provisions, it is argued, help reduce the tax-created risks of business, since a company that suffers a loss after having paid taxes in prior years can obtain a tax refund soon after losses appear. As of December 31, 1970, the U.S. Internal Revenue Code provided that operating losses, or ordinary losses, could be carried back for three years. For a full discussion of tax-loss carrybacks, see U.S. Internal Revenue Service, *U.S. Internal Revenue Code, 1954.*

Tax-Loss Carryforward   A legal provision permitting businesses and individuals to use the losses of one year to offset the income of succeeding years. Such provisions, it is argued, help reduce the tax-created risks of business and investment and thereby promote business activity and private investment. As of December 31, 1970, the U.S. Internal Revenue Code has provided that both capital losses and operating losses (ordinary losses) can be carried forward for five years. For a full discussion of tax-loss carryforwards, see U.S. Internal Revenue Service, *U.S. Internal Revenue Code, 1954.*

Tax Sharing   A practice whereby one level of government, such as a state, levies a tax and shares the proceeds with a lower level of government, such as a county or a town. Tax sharing has become a method of providing localities with sufficient funds for their growing needs. Usually, it is not accompanied by much central supervision, thus giving local units freedom to use the shared funds as they please. Two major problems arise in the distribution of the shared revenues. First, the apportionment of the funds among localities is often based on the origin of the tax receipts, but the origin sometimes cannot be determined accurately. Secondly, distribution based on origin often returns to the more wealthy districts a far greater proportion of the tax recepits than they can utilize efficiently while the poorer and more needy areas are somewhat neglected. For further information, see Alfred G. Buehler, *Public Finance,* McGraw-Hill Book Company, New York, 1940, chap. 29; M. Newcomer, "Revenue Sharing between Federal and State Governments, and between State and Local Governments," *Proceedings,* National Tax Association, Boston, 1936, pp. 275ff.

Technical Coefficient   *See Technological Coefficient.*

Technocracy   A program of social and economic reconstruction that proposed to place industrial engineers and scientists in control of economic life. The basic tenet of technocracy was that modern society with its technological advances was too complex to be run by politicians and entrepreneurs. According to the technocrats, control should be placed in the hands of those who had caused the revolution in technology, the engineers and scientists. The term technocracy, coined by William H. Smith in 1919, was defined as "a theory of social organization and a system of national industrial management." Others active in the technocratic movement were Walter Rautenstrach, Harold Loeb, and Felix Frazer. Technocracy had its greatest popularity in the later years of the depression, 1932 and 1933, and has since almost disappeared. For additiona details, see Howard Scott et al., *Introduction to Technocracy,* The John Day Company, Inc., New York, 1933; Allen Raymond, *What Is Technocracy?* McGraw-Hill Book Company, New York, 1933; Frank Arkright, *The ABC of Technocracy,* Harper & Row, Publishers, Incorporated, New York, 1933.

Technological Coefficient (Technical Coefficient)   In input-output analysis, the ratio of units of input to units of output. If a given production function is a straight line, changes in factor costs do not influence the technological coefficient because there is no possibility of substituting one factor for another in response to price changes. For additional information, see Karl A. Fox, *Intermediate Economic Statistics,* John Wiley & Sons, Inc., New York, 1968.

Technological Unemployment   The displacement of labor by machinery and improved methods of production. Technological unemployment is an inevitable aspect of a dynamic economy which is constantly striving for increased productivity, higher living standards, and higher wages. It usually affects both the quantity and the type of labor needed in the industry involved, decreasing the number of workers employed for the particular operation and often requiring new and different skills for the remaining workers. Those most affected by technological change are semi-skilled and unskilled industrial workers. Managerial employees, professional persons, and workers in the service industries are generally much less subject to technological unemployment. Not only may technological change cause considerable short-term unemployment, but unemployment may be prolonged if the new production methods do not lead to price reductions and new skills are not acquired by the displaced workers. To combat technological unemployment, many unions strongly oppose automation, condone featherbedding and make-work practices, and negotiate agreements that provide for generous dismissal benefits for displaced workers or the retraining and employment of displaced employees on new equipment. For further information, see Elmer Malloy, *Automation and Major Technological Change,* AFL–CIO, Industrial Union Department, Washington, D.C., 1958; S. E. Hill and Frederick Harbison, *Manpower and Innovation in American Industry,* Princeton University Press, Princeton, N.J., 1959; James Carey, *Challenge of Automation,* Public Affairs Press, Washington, D.C., 1955.

Technology   The science or body of knowledge applicable to the production of goods. It is generally acknowledged that modern technology was one of the most important conditions that led to the rise of the industrial system of modern capitalism. It was modern machinery, the product of technology, which made possible the rapid increase in the volume of production. The enormous increase in physical production is, in turn, the characteristic quality that has made capitalism a success. Thus, technology has made possible gains in individual and social wealth. For further information, see Richard L. Meier, *Science and Economic Development: New Patterns of Living,* The Technology Press of the Massachusetts Institute of Technology and John Wiley & Sons, Inc., New York, 1956; see also Robert A. Brady, *Organization, Automation, and Society: The Scientific Revolution in Industry,* University of California Press, Berkeley, Calif., 1961.

Terms of Trade   The relationship between the prices which a producer must pay and those which he receives for his products. An improvement in the terms of trade means that the producer's selling price has increased to a greater extent (or fallen to a lesser extent) than the price of the items that he needed, leaving him better off. This relationship is most frequently studied in the analysis of international trade. For instance, if the price of materials which Great Britain imports from Africa declines while the price of products which it exports to Africa rises (or falls to a lesser extent), the terms of trade are said to have moved in Britain's favor and against Africa. Unless big changes in the volume of trade develop, such movements benefit the British balance of payments. The terms of trade can be calculated mathematically; if the relationship between export and import prices in the base year is taken as 100, any improvement in the terms of trade causes the index to rise and any deterioration causes it to fall. In some cases, government policy is set by such an index. For example, if the U.S. agricultural parity price index, which measures the terms of trade for farmers with 1909–1914 as a base period, falls to a predetermined level, a governmental loan program automatically goes into operation. Although terms of trade usually apply to price relationships and are more accurately labeled commodity terms of trade, it is possible to employ analogous methods to determine income terms of trade, which indicate whether economic changes affect the real earnings of income recipients in one country (or one industry or one firm) favorably or adversely when compared with another. For a full discussion of the terms of trade, see Gottfried Haberler, *The Theory of International Trade,* The Macmillan Company, New York, 1950; Charles P. Kindleberger, *The Terms of Trade: A Case Study,* Massachusetts Institute of Technology, Cambridge, Mass., 1956.

Thin Corporation   A corporation that owes a large quantity of debt relative to its equity capital. When a corporation is judged thin according to the standards of the U.S. Tax Court, payment of interest on the debt owed a shareholder creditor is subject to the corporate profits tax, and repayment of the debt legally constitutes a dividend and is subject to ordinary income tax rates. Court decisions leave considerable doubt as to how high the debt-to-equity ratio must be in order for it to be judged too high, but ratios of 4 to 1 or less appear to be acceptable. For a discussion of some of the legal aspects of the thin-corporation doctrine, see Joseph Rabin, "The Clifford Case of the Thin Corporation," *Taxes,* p. 285, Commerce Clearing House, Inc., Chicago, April, 1956; for a discussion of the doctrine as an impediment to investments in small business, see Edwin S. Cohen, "Raising Venture Capital for Small and New Business," *Federal Tax Policy for Economic Growth and Stability,* 84th Cong., 1st Sess., 1955, p. 673.

Tied Loan   A foreign loan in which the borrower is required to spend the proceeds only in the country making the loan. The advantages of tied loans are that they stimulate employment and income in the creditor nation and do not affect the balance of payments of that country adversely. Underdeveloped countries, which are the main recipients of tied loans, however, sometimes resent limits on their freedom to use the money, especially when they are forced to pay higher prices in the lending nation than are available elsewhere. The chief U.S. agency offering tied loans to foreign countries is the Export-Import Bank of Washington. Whereas a considerable part of U.S. foreign aid has been tied, the trend is toward permitting borrowing nations to spend U.S. loans wherever they want. For additional details, see Robert Asher, *Grants, Loans, and Local Currencies,* The Brookings Institution, Washington, D.C., 1961.

Tie-in Sale   See *Tying Contract.*

Tight Money (Dear Money)   The term used to designate a policy of monetary restraint, conducted by the U.S. monetary authorities, which is designed to reduce the supply of credit, raise interest rates, and thus relieve inflationary pressures that have arisen because of excess demand. A change from an easy-money policy to a tight-money policy may take the form of positive actions, such as open-market sales, increases in required-reserve ratios, or increases in discount rates. Such a shift in policy can be passive, as in failing to increase reserves in the face of a rising demand for credit. As a result of open-market sales by the Federal Reserve System, the U.S. commercial banking system loses reserves and must make some adjustments in its asset portfolios. If there are no excess funds in the system, the banks must either borrow additional reserves from the Federal Reserve or restrict their earning assets by either curbing loans, disposing of securities, or adopting both measures. Long before they have exhausted their liquid assets and longer-term investments, however, most banks take measures to restrain the growth of their loan portfolios. They first satisfy requests for loans by good deposit customers with whom they have had a continuing relationship. Thereafter, restrictive measures include the reduction of the maturity of term loans that are granted, the stricter application of standards of credit worthiness, and the granting of less than the full amount of the loans that have been requested. The net free-reserve positions of Federal Reserve member banks, which are reported weekly by the Federal Reserve System and appear in Friday's newspapers, are an indication of the present monetary policy. It is generally agreed that free reserves of less than $150 million would indicate a degree of monetary restraint, while a position of negative free reserves would indicate a policy of very tight money. For a discussion of tight money during the 1950s, see Paul B. Trescott, *Money, Banking, and Economic Welfare*, 2d ed., McGraw-Hill Book Company, New York, 1965.

Time Deposit   Money held in the bank account of an individual or a firm for which the bank can require advance notice of withdrawal, usually a month to two months. Advance notice must be given for corporations' time deposits, but this requirement is almost always waived for individuals' deposits. Time deposits can be held in commercial and mutual savings banks. A 3 to 6% reserve on time deposits is required for all U.S. banks that belong to the Federal Reserve System. Reserves for other banks are subject to state law. In the U.S. at the end of 1970, time deposits in commercial and mutual savings bands totaled $301 billion. See Walter W. Haines, *Money, Prices and Policy*, 2d ed., McGraw-Hill Book Company, New York, 1966; for statistics on time deposits, see *Federal Reserve Bulletin*, Washington, D.C., monthly.

Time Draft   *See Draft.*

Time-Schedule Float   *See Float.* For further information, see John J. Klein, *Money and the Economy*, 2d ed., Harcourt, Brace & World, Inc., New York, 1970.

Time Series   A set of ordered observations of a particular economic variable, such as prices, production, investment, and consumption, taken at different points in time. Most economic series consist of monthly, quarterly, or annual observations. Monthly and quarterly economic series are used in short-term business forecasting. Before these series can be made useful as forecasting tools, seasonal fluctuations must be removed. For a detailed discussion of time series and time-series analysis, see

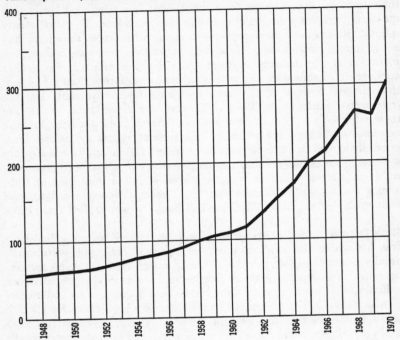

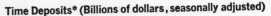

Time Deposits* (Billions of dollars, seasonally adjusted)

*Averages of daily figures, all December.

Source: Board of Governors, Federal Reserve System.

Frederick E. Croxton and Dudley J. Cowden, *Practical Business Statistics*, 3d ed., Prentice-Hall, Inc., Englewood Cliffs, N.J., 1960, chaps. 28–31.

Time-Series Analysis (Time-Series Decomposition) The process by which the components of an economic time series, such as production, investment, and consumption, are separated and isolated in order to study the fluctuations peculiar to each of them. Economic series are generally assumed to be composed of three mutually exclusive and exhaustive components: (1) The trend cycle consists of cumulative and reversible movements characterized by recurrent and aperiodic intervals of expansion and contraction (the cycle) and by longer-run drifts underlying the economy (the trend). The trend is usually characterized by longer movements than those of the cycle. (2) The seasonal represents the composite effect of climatic and institutional factors and is represented by fluctuations which are repeated more or less regularly each year. (3) The irregular, the residual which is left when the trend cycle and the seasonal have been removed from the original economic time series, consists of erratic real-world occurrences and measurement errors and is characterized generally by movements of less than six months' duration. Most methods of time-series analysis assume one of two models: the additive model, in which the three components are related additively; or the multiplicative model, in which the three components are related multiplicatively. For a detailed discussion of time series and time-series analysis, see Frederick E. Croxton and Dudley J. Cowden, *Practical Business Statistics*, 3d ed., Prentice-Hall, Inc., Englewood Cliffs, N.J., 1960, chaps. 28–31.

Time-Series Decomposition *See Time-Series Analysis.*

Time Study The determination of the time required by an experienced person working at a normal pace to do a specified task. Time-study methods are used most often in industry to determine production norms for incentive systems. In addition, they are employed to arrange schedules, plan work, and estimate labor costs. To carry out a time study, the operation under consideration must first be broken down into a large number of small steps or normal elements. The time required to carry out the individual elements of the job is then measured with a high degree of accuracy. The average times are converted to normal times by correcting them for the degree of effort and skill of each operator. The time required for the total operation is learned by adding the normal times for each element of the process and allowances for such factors as rest periods, miscellaneous delays, and clean-up periods. The final normal production standard can be expressed either as the number of standard minutes per unit of output or in terms of the number of units of output required per hour. For further information, see Harold B. Maynard et al., *Methods–Time Measurement*, McGraw-Hill Book Company, New York, 1948; Ralph Barnes, *Motion and Time Study*, 4th ed., John Wiley & Sons, Inc., New York, 1958; Gerald Nadler, *Motion and Time Study*, McGraw-Hill Book Company, New York, 1955; Phil Carroll, *Timestudy for Cost Control*, 3d ed., McGraw-Hill Book Company, New York, 1954.

Time Wage Rate A rate structure which provides for wage payments in terms of an hourly, weekly, or monthly time interval. Under a time-wage-rate system, the employee is paid on the basis of the time spent on the job rather than on the amount produced, which is characteristic of a piece-rate structure. A majority of the labor force, especially white-collar workers, is paid on the basis of time rates. Although it has been argued that a time wage rate does not stimulate the worker to his best effort and thus may result in higher costs of production, many types of works are not suitable for a piece rate, and all employers have minimum standards of performance for time-rate workers. There are three basic types of time-wage-rate systems: (1) personal-wage-rate structures, in which wage rates apply to persons rather than to jobs; (2) job-title-rate structures, in which wage rates pertain to the type of work performed rather than to the individual employed; and (3) job-evaluation structures, in which the wage rates depend on basic job attributes and requirements. For further information, see *Systems of Wage Payment*, National Industrial Conference Board, Inc., New York, 1930; Pearce Davis and Gerald Matchett, *Modern Labor Economics*, The Ronald Press Company, New York, 1954, chap. 19.

Tolerance   A measure of the precision of survey estimates, based on probability sampling, that indicates how close the estimate is to the figure that would have been obtained from a complete census using exactly the same methods of data collection. Sample tolerance is generally reported in terms of standard errors. For example, the odds are 2 to 1 that the survey estimate will not differ from the census count by more than one standard error. The odds are 19 to 1 that the difference will be less than two standard errors. Tolerance can only be calculated for a probability sample. For further discussion, see M. J. Slonim, *Sampling in a Nutshell*, Simon and Schuster, Inc., New York, 1960; W. Edwards Deming, *Sample Design in Business Research*, John Wiley & Sons, Inc., New York, 1960; see also M. H. Hansen et al., *Sample Survey Methods and Theory*, John Wiley & Sons, Inc., New York, 1953, vol. I.

Trade Acceptance   A draft for the purchase of goods which has been accepted by the purchaser. It is a demand by a creditor rather than a promise to pay by a debtor and thus has little value until the drawee indicates his intention to honor it by writing "accepted" across its face and signing it. Since the trade acceptance arises from the sale of merchandise which will itself be the source of funds, it is self-liquidating and can readily be discounted at a bank. In practice, the trade-acceptance form usually accompanies the shipment of goods to the buyer, who accepts it by signing his name and designating the bank at which is is payable. The buyer returns it to the seller, who may hold it until it matures or discount it at his bank. At maturity, the trade acceptance is treated in exactly the same manner as a check. Although the trade acceptance is a formal evidence of debt, eliminating misunderstanding with reference to the terms of repayment and providing the seller with a discountable credit instrument, it has largely been replaced by open-account credit as the major form of mercantile credit. For additional details, see William J. Shultz and Hedwig Reinhardt, *Credit and Collection Management*, 3d ed., Prentice-Hall, Inc., Englewood Cliffs, N.J., 1962.

Trade Association   An organization of companies in an industry that undertakes public relations work, disseminates industry statistics, and improves technology and management methods. Among well-known U.S. industry trade associations are the National Association of Manufacturers, American Iron and Steel Institute, American Petroleum Institute, Manufacturing Chemists' Association, and National Machine Tool Builders' Association. Contemporary trade associations are concerned largely with functions which have little to do with competition, but in the late 1920s trade associations often were organized to reduce the intensity of competition. This conclusion was pointed up in the comprehensive study of trade associations carried out by the Temporary National Economic Committee (TNEC) in 1941. For the TNEC study of associations, see Charles A. Pearce, *Trade Association Survey*, TNEC Monograph 18, Washington, D.C., 1941.

Trade Barrier   An artificial restraint on the free exchange of goods and services between nations. The most common types of trade barriers are tariffs, quotas, and exchange control. Such obstacles to trade are usually imposed by a country that wishes to protect domestic producers in their home market against foreign competition, better its terms of trade, reduce domestic unemployment, or improve its balance-of-payments position. The raising of trade barriers by one country often provokes other nations to retaliate with barriers of their own to maintain their overall trade position. Generally, the effect of a trade barrier is to reduce the volume of trade while increasing the domestic price of the protected good. Thus, it results in a relatively inefficient allocation of world resources and reduces the level of total world income and production. For further information, see Margaret S. Gordon, *Barriers to World Trade*, The Macmillan Company, New York, 1941; H. Heuser, *Control of International Trade*, Routledge & Kegan Paul, Ltd., London, 1939; Raymond F. Mikesell, *Foreign Exchange in the Postwar World*, The Twentieth Century Fund, New York, 1954.

Trade Credit   The credit that one nonfinancial firm extends to another. Trade credit may take a variety of forms. In the U.S., the most common variety arises from the practice of billing for the product shipped to a customer and allowing a certain time, ordinarily from ten to thirty days, as a maximum period for payment. Trade credit may also be extended through the purchase of a customer's accounts receivables or through trade acceptances. Sometimes, long-term loans are extended by one firm to another, generally with the expectation that the loan will increase the total business of both borrower and lender. Examples of this type of long-term trade credit are found in the automobile industry, in which manufacturers sometimes advance as much as 80% of the necessary capital to their dealers. Petroleum producers also frequently make long-term, low-interest loans to their dealers. For the most part, trade credit flows from large firms to small ones, but it is not uncommon for small manufacturers to offer open-account credit to large trade and service establishments. Many U.S. economists have suggested that trade credit helps small firms by serving as a substitute for bank loans during periods of tight money, but other observers contend that it is an inadequate substitute in two respects: (1) Trade credit may make the small firm excessively dependent on his large supplier. (2) It may enable the large supplier to undercut (either in price or credit terms) small suppliers that are in direct competition with it. For a discussion of trade credit in relation to small-business finance, see Robert S. Einzig, "Credit from Large to Small Business," in *Financing Small Business*, U.S. Senate Committee on Banking and Currency, 58th Cong., 1958.

Trade Discount   A percentage deduction from a bill or debt, such as a deduction given a purchaser for prompt payment of bills. A $10,000 purchase on 3/10-n/30 terms means that, if the bill is paid within ten days from the date of invoice, payment may be reduced by the trade discount of 3%. Otherwise, the total amount billed must be paid in thirty days. For further discussion, see Joel Dean, *Managerial Economics*, Prentice-Hall, Inc., Englewood Cliffs, N.J., 1962.

Trademark   Any word, name, symbol, or device used by a manufacturer or merchant to identify his goods and services and so distinguish them from competitive products. The trademark was mainly a result of the Industrial Revolution, when manufacturers began selling their products in national and international markets. Since earlier manufacturers had dealt directly with their customers, there was no doubt as to the products' source, but the development of widely dispersed markets required manufacturers to use some symbol, word, or mark as an identifying device. From the manufacturer's point of view, trademarks offer some advantages. If the manufacturer has already established a good reputation for his line of products, new products may be introduced under the same trademark and will thus be more readily accepted. The Lanham Trademark Act of 1946 codified and expanded U.S. trademark law, providing for registration at the U.S. Patent Office of certain types of trademarks. For information concerning trademarks and their relation to marketing theory, see Lewis K. Johnson, *Sales and Marketing Management*, Allyn and Bacon, Inc., Boston, 1957.

Trade Union   An association of workers who do the same kind of work. It bargains collectively on behalf of its members with single employers, business firms, or associations of employers. Trade unions are generally limited to skilled or semiskilled workers who have learned crafts. A carpenter's union, for example, is made up exclusively of carpenters. Trade unions differ from industrial unions, which include workers in a given industry regardless of the type of work that they do. Early unions in the U.S. were formed on the trade-union basis, and skilled workers were thus the first to be organized. In Great Britain, the legal definition of trade union includes employers' as well as employees' associations. British trade unions have long emphasized a wide variety of educational activities. They also may take part in politics and the operations of government, and most of them provide their members with benefits for sickness, old age, unemployment, and work stoppages due to labor disputes. See G. D. H. Cole, *An Introduction to Trade Unionism*, George Allen & Unwin, Ltd., London, 1953; Albert Rees, *The Economics of Trade Unions*, The University of Chicago Press, Chicago, 1962.

Trading Ring   *See Pit.*

Trading Stamp   A redeemable coupon which is given to consumers who make purchases in retail stores. Stamps of this type are saved and later traded in for gift merchandise at a store operated by the stamp company. The trading-stamp plan has been used in the U.S. primarily by supermarkets, gasoline stations, and drug stores to promote sales. In the hope that trading stamps will attract new customers and increase sales, thereby compensating for the original cost of the stamps, retail stores join a particular stamp plan and purchase trading stamps from the stamp company. Generally, a customer receives one trading stamp for each 10-cent purchase. When one retailer adopts a trading-stamp plan, his competitors are often forced to follow suit to retain their customers. The use of trading stamps may become especially important if a firm operates under such institutional rigidities as resale price-maintenance laws and nationally advertised prices. Trading stamps may then constitute a convenient price-cutting mechanism. The use of trading stamps has been upheld in the courts as not violating state fair-sales-practices laws. For further information, see Harvey Vredenberg, *Trading Stamps,* Indiana Business Report No. 21, Indiana University, Bureau of Business Research, Bloomington, Ind., 1956; Albert Haring and Wallace Yoder, *Trading Stamp Practice and Pricing Policies*, Indiana University Press, Bloomington, Ind., 1958; Otto A. Davis, "The Economics of Trading Stamps," *Journal of*

Business, vol. XXXII, no. 2, pp. 141–150, University of Chicago Graduate School of Business, Chicago, April, 1959.

Tradition-directed Economy A mode of economic organization in which the problems of production and distribution are solved by procedures devised in the distant past and rigidified by tradition. For example, the production problem may be solved by the hereditary assignment of the father's job to his sons. Until recent times, most economies were tradition-directed, and even now tradition is of major importance in many backward societies. Even in highly industrialized and modern economies, such as that of the U.S., tradition plays a major role in such things as tipping, allowances to minors, and bonuses based on length of service. See Robert L. Heilbroner, *The Making of Economic Society,* Prentice-Hall, Inc., Englewood Cliffs, N.J., 1962; Paul A. Samuelson, *Economics,* 7th ed., McGraw-Hill Book Company, New York, 1967.

Transactions Velocity *See Velocity of Money.* For an elementary textbook treatment, see Campbell R. McConnell, *Economics,* 4th ed., McGraw-Hill Book Company, New York, 1969.

Transfer Payment A government or business expenditure for which no goods or services are received in return. Most government transfer payments are of the nature of welfare payments, such as social security benefits, unemployment compensation, and relief payments. Certain other government subsidies, such as the farm price supports, are also considered transfer payments. In 1962 transfer payments of the U.S. government sector amounted to $34.1 billion, or 22% of all government expenditures. Since they represent a return of revenue to individuals, government transfer payments are considered negative taxes. Their effect is to redistribute income (e.g., from employed to unemployed or from city worker to farmer), and thus they alter the composition of private goods production in favor of the recipients of the payments. Business transfer payments are usually gifts or donations, such as corporate gifts to non-profit institutions; they amounted to $2.3 billion in the U.S. in 1962. For further information, see Valdemar Carlson, *Economic Security in the United States,* McGraw-Hill Book Company, New York, 1962.

Transformation Curve The locus of the output combinations of two goods that can be produced from a fixed total supply of resources. Each point on the transformation curve (also called the production-possibilities curve) depicts a possible distribution of output between two goods in a full-employment economy. The slope of the curve (always negative) is a measure of how much of one good Y must be given up to produce one additional unit of the other good X. The curve slopes downward to the right, indicating that to obtain more of one product X, a full-employment economy must always sacrifice some of the other product Y. The transformation curve is concave to the origin because of the law of increasing costs, since the factors of production are not completely adaptable to the two alternative uses. For additional details, see J. Black, "A Formal Proof of the Concavity of the Production Possibilities Function," *Economic Journal*, vol. LXVII, no. 265, pp. 133–135, Royal Economic Society, London, March, 1957; Paul A. Samuelson, *Economics*, 7th ed., McGraw-Hill Book Company, New York, 1967.

Transformation Curve

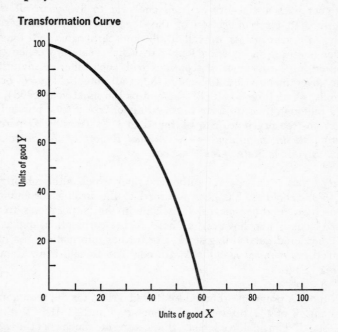

Units of good X

Transitory Income   *See Permanent-Income Hypothesis.*

Treasury Bill   The shortest-term security issued by the U.S. government. Sold to the public at weekly auctions, treasury bills usually mature in 91 or 182 days, although tax-anticipation bills, a special type designed to attract funds set aside for tax payments, can be issued for a period as long as one year. The government's high credit rating makes treasury bills exceptionally secure investments. They are especially attractive to commercial banks, nonfinancial corporations, foreign central banks, and other investors who want to earn interest on temporarily idle cash without fear of default. Because of the short maturities, treasury bill prices do not fluctuate as widely as those of other U.S. securities, but price changes do occur. One reason for fluctuation is that the Federal Reserve System frequently buys and sells large quantities of treasury bills in order to affect the cost and availability of bank loans. At mid-1968, more than $64 billion worth of treasury bills was outstanding. Detailed statistics on ownership, maturities, and prices are published in U.S. Treasury Department, *Treasury Bulletin,* monthly.

Treasury Note A government security issued by the U.S. Treasury Department with a maturity of from one year to five years. It is thus an intermediate-term obligation of the Treasury. Short-term securities maturing in a year or less are called bills and certificates, and long-term securities maturing in a period longer than five years are called bonds. The reason for the issuance of securities with such different maturities is that the government wishes to be able to tap all potential sources of loanable funds. As of June 30, 1968 (the end of the fiscal year 1968), there was $71 billion in treasury notes outstanding, or 25% of total public issues. Statistics on treasury notes can be found in U.S. Treasury Department, *Treasury Bulletin,* monthly; ———, *Annual Report of the Secretary of the Treasury on the State of the Finances.*

Treasury Stock That part of authorized stock which, although originally issued to stockholders, has been returned to the issuing corporation by gift, purchase, or other means. It is kept in the corporation's treasury. Treasury stock is not, however, an asset of the corporation, and it is no longer considered outstanding stock. For further information, see Jules I. Bogen (ed.), *Financial Handbook,* 4th ed., The Ronald Press Company, New York, 1968.

Triffin Plan A program proposed by Robert Triffin for the reorganization and expansion of the International Monetary Fund (IMF). With other economists, Triffin believed that the cause of much of the world's currency and payments problems lies in the inadequate growth of world liquidity and monetary reserves. This solution to the world liquidity problem, which is based on a plan introduced by John Maynard Keynes in 1943, is to internationalize the foreign-exchange reserves of all countries through an expanded export-import fund (XIMF). Member countries would deposit all their currency holdings of foreign exchange plus some gold with the XIMF, and their monetary reserves would then consist primarily of XIMF deposits. International accounts would be settled by the XIMF, which would simply credit or debit a nation's account with the fund. Besides short-term lending to members with balance-of-payments and reserve problems, the XIMF would increase international liquidity when necessary by making medium- and long-term investment loans, especially for development in underdeveloped countries. The XIMF would thus become a central bank for central banks, adjusting the supply of deposits (reserves) to meet the liquidity needs of the world economy. In addition to creating an international reserve currency, it would ease the pressure on the U.S. dollar as the key reserve currency. The Triffin Plan does not attack balance-of-payments problems directly but merely makes the financing of deficits easier. Moreover, there is a possibility that the plan would tend to have an inflationary bias. For further information, see Robert Triffin, *Gold and the Dollar Crisis,* Yale University Press, New Haven, Conn., 1961; ————, *Europe and the Money Muddle,* Yale University Press, New Haven, Conn., 1957; Seymour E. Harris (ed)., *The Dollar in Crisis,* Harcourt, Brace & World, Inc., New York, 1961, pp. 223–294.

Trough The low point of economic activity. Coming after a period of contraction and before a period of recovery, it is usually a short interval, lasting only a month or two. According to the National Bureau of Economic Research, the troughs in the five U.S. postwar recessions occurred in October, 1949, August, 1954, April, 1958, February, 1961, and November, 1970. For a detailed discussion of troughs, see Geoffrey H. Moore (ed.), *Business Cycle Indicators,* Princeton University Press, Princeton, N.J., 1961.

Trust Fund A fund of money or property administered by an individual or an organization for the benefit of another individual or organization. The trustee is the person or organization who is in charge of the fund, and the beneficiary is the person or group for whose benefit the fund was created. A trust fund can be established to provide income for beneficiaries during the life of the grantor or after his death, to benefit a charitable organization, to increase the value of property by placing it in the hands of a competent trustee, or to protect the trust property (e.g., for a minor). The primary duties of the trustee are to invest the principal of the fund and to distribute the benefits. The investment policies of the trustee may be specified by the individual setting up the trust, but if no specification is made, investment of trust funds in the U.S. is governed by state law. Although any adult may legally be appointed trustee of a trust fund, most trust services are performed by trust companies or commercial banks with trust departments. For additional details on trust funds, see George Clark, *Trusts,* 2 vols., The Bobbs-Merrill Company, Inc., Indianapolis, 1954; G. T. Stephenson, *Estates and Trusts,* Appleton-Century-

Crofts, Inc., New York, 1949; N. Gilbert Riddle, *The Investment Policy of Trust Institutions*, Business Publications Co., Chicago, 1934.

Turning Point The point in a business cycle at which the direction of economic activity reverses itself. There are two distinct turning points in each cycle, the upper turning point (the peak), when expansion comes to an end; and the lower turning point (the trough), when contraction changes into the beginning of expansion. Actually, the term turning zone is more apt than turning point, since there is usually a critical period of a few months which marks the end of a phase of expansion or contraction. The upper turning zone is usually marked by a peak (or perhaps a slight decline) in output and employment, a fall in stock and commodity prices, a greater-than-normal increase in inventories, and a change of business optimism into caution and perhaps even into pessimism regarding the short-term future. In the lower turning zone, these factors are reversed. In the postwar period, according to the National Bureau of Economic Research, the U.S. experienced upper turning points in November, 1948, July, 1953, July, 1957, May, 1960, and November, 1969, and lower turning points in October, 1949, August, 1954, April, 1958, February, 1961, and November, 1970. For a fuller discussion of the theory, measurement, and forecasting of turning points, see Robert A. Gordon, *Business Fluctuations*, 2d ed., Harper & Row, Publishers, Incorporated, New York, 1961; Arthur F. Burns and Wesley C. Mitchell, *Measuring Business Cycles*, National Bureau of Economic Research, Inc., New York, 1946; Geoffrey H. Moore (ed.), *Business Cycle Indicators*, vol. I, National Bureau of Economic Research, Inc., Princeton University Press, Princeton, N.J., 1961; see also L. C. Trueblood, "The Dating of Post-War Business Cycles," American Statistical Association, *Proceedings of the Business and Economics Section*, Washington, D.C., 1961, p. 16.

Turning Zone *See Turning Point.*

Turnover The number of times during a year that the inventory of a firm is sold. The annual stock turnover can be computed by dividing annual sales by the average inventory. Both inventory and sales figures should be valued consistently, that is, either at cost or at sale price. Generally, a firm with a higher annual rate of turnover has lower operating costs and earns a higher rate of net profit on its capital investment. It has been found that as the volume of sales of a firm increases, its rate of stock turnover also increases. For additional details, see Thomson Whitin, *The Theory of Inventory Management*, Princeton University Press, Princeton, N.J., 1953; Martin Starr and David Miller, *Inventory Control: Theory and Practice*, Prentice-Hall, Inc., Englewood Cliffs, N.J., 1962.

Turnover Tax A tax on transactions of goods and services at all levels of production and distribution. The turnover tax, also known as the general sales tax or the gross income tax, is more inclusive than the common retail sales tax, since it is levied every time that a good, whether finished or in the process of production, changes hands. Since the burden of any sales tax can usually be shifted forward by including it in the selling price of the good, the result of a general turnover tax is a tendency to pyramid the amount of the tax from one stage to another so that the final selling price of an article includes the sum of all the taxes paid on the good's materials during its production. Thus, when a turnover tax is in operation, it is to the advantage of producers to avoid as many independent transactions as possible in the process of producing a good. The turnover tax is an important source of revenue in the Soviet Union as well as in a number of European Common Market countries. It is also in use in a few U.S. states, such as Indiana, New Mexico, and West Virginia. For additional details, see Alfred G. Buehler, *General Sales Taxation,* The Business Bourse, New York, 1932.

Twentieth-Century Liberalism *See Reform Liberalism.*

Two-Stage Least Squares An econometric technique facilitating the restatement of a set of equations in a simultaneous model such that each equation of the model specifies a single endogenous variable as a function solely of exogenous variables and/or first-stage least-squares estimates of other endogenous variables involved in any equation. In effect, this technique recognizes that some endogenous variables act as explanatory variables in some equations and overcomes barriers to their use as explanatory variables by restating them in the form of predetermined variables. For additional information, see Karl A. Fox, *Intermediate Economic Statistics,* John Wiley & Sons, Inc., New York, 1968; Gerhard Tintner and Charles B. Millham, *Mathematics and Statistics for Economists,* Holt, Rinehart and Winston, Inc., New York, 1970.

Two-Tier Gold Mart A system incorporating two prices of gold instead of a fixed price. One price is the official gold payment at $35 per ounce in transactions made only between governments. The second is the freely set price through the supply-and-demand mechanism. In the latter case, gold is completely demonetized. Thus, speculators could buy gold at a free-market price above $35 per ounce. This technique, reintroduced by the U.S. in March, 1968, acts as a partial check on speculative operations in gold since the price is fixed for intergovernment payments. The two-tier system had been in existence prior to 1961, when it was eliminated and the London Gold Pool was established. Some economists feel that a wide gap between the official and free-market price of gold is intolerable. For more information, see Paul A. Samuelson, *Economics,* 8th ed., McGraw-Hill Book Company, New York, 1970, pp. 698–699.

Tying Contract (Tie-in Sale)   A transaction in which a seller insists on selling additional products (tied products) to a buyer who wishes to purchase a single key product (tying product). Examples of tying contracts in the U.S. are block bookings of motion pictures, in which a given number of Grade B pictures must go with Grade A films, and the Pullman Company's insistence on servicing only cars made by Pullman Standard. Although there are economies in booking motion pictures in groups and in standardizing sleeping cars, the Clayton Antitrust Act forbids tying contracts as a violation of market freedom. The present application of section 3 of the act forbids tying contracts if a seller has a near monopoly in the key product and a considerable volume of business in the additional products. For a discussion of tying products, see Simon N. Whitney, *Antitrust Policies,* The Twentieth Century Fund, New York, 1958, vol. II; for a statement of the theory of tie-in sales, see M. L. Burstein, "The Economics of Tie-in Sales," *Review of Economics and Statistics,* vol. XLII, Harvard University Press, Cambridge, Mass., February, 1960.

Unbalanced Growth   The growth of capital investment in different sectors of a developing economy at a different rate. Whereas a number of economists have favored plans of balanced investment for underdeveloped areas, others have argued that the resources required for a program of balanced growth are so large that a really underdeveloped country cannot support such a plan. What is really needed is a deliberate unbalancing of capital investment, concentrating on strategic industries and sectors which will induce growth in other areas. A chronic imbalance of investment may produce a faster rate of growth than a balanced program because of the incentives and pressures that it sets up in nonstrategic industries. Investment should be concentrated in industries with the greatest amount of forward linkage (encouraging investment in subsequent stages of production) and backward linkage (inducing investment in earlier stages of production). For additional details on the purposes and programs of unbalanced growth, see Albert O. Hirschman, *The Strategy of Economic Development,* Yale University Press, New Haven, Conn., 1958; Hans Singer, *The Concept of Balanced Growth and Economic Development: Theory and Facts,* University of Texas Conference on Economic Development, Austin, Tex., April, 1958; Tibor Scitovsky, "Growth: Balanced or Unbalanced," in Moses Abramovitz et al., *The Allocation of Economic Resources,* Stanford University Press, Stanford, Calif., 1959.

Underconsumption (Overproduction)   The manufacture of goods in excess of consumer demand. Under the conditions assumed by the classical economists and their successors, general overproduction is impossible. These conditions included free competition among buyers and sellers, no significant limitations on the knowledge of market conditions, a high degree of mobility in the supply of labor and capital, and the use of money only as a medium of exchange. The classical economists recognized that local disparities between supply and demand could exist in particular markets, and under certain conditions, but these, they said, would disappear in time as a result of adjustments in the whole system. This doctrine, which is attributed to Jean Baptiste Say, is referred to as Say's law of markets. The law was criticized severely by opponents who believed that these conditions were unrealistic and that, given different postulates, a situation was likely to develop which could be described as a state of general overproduction. For example, Say's law assumed that each sale must provide the wherewithal to make a purchase; hence, supply creates its own demand. Money, which is received in exchange for a good, can serve as a store of value as well as a medium of exchange, however, and under certain conditions there is likely to be a rush for liquidity and a hoarding of cash, producing a situation in which there is a lack of demand. Thomas Malthus was one of the first to attack the Say doctrine, stating that it was theoretically unsound and contrary to experience because "we see in almost every part of the world vast powers of production which are not put into action." Eventually, Say's law was disregarded, and theories relating underconsumption or overproduction to business cycles developed. These theories maintained that the capitalist system would result in excess production which would exceed the ability of people to consume, in a decline of prices to unprofitable levels, in increasing unemployment, and in the existence of depressed conditions until the excess production was absorbed. For further information concerning underconsumption business-cycle theories, see W. T. Foster and W. Catchings, *Profits*, Houghton Mifflin Company, Boston, 1925; J. A. Hobson, *The Economics of Unemployment*, George Allen & Unwin, Ltd., London, 1922; for criticisms of underconsumption theories, see E. F. M. Durbin, *Purchasing Power and Trade Depression*, Jonathan Cape, Ltd., London, 1933; Alvin H. Hansen, *Business Cycle Theory*, Ginn and Company, Boston, 1927; for a discussion of the concept of general overproduction, see H. Neisser, "General Overproduction: A Study of Say's Law of Markets," *Journal of Political Economy*, vol. 42, no. 4, pp. 433–465, The University of Chicago Press, Chicago, August, 1934; see also The Committee on Principles of Economics, *Principles of Economics*, Pitman Publishing Corporation, New York, 1959, pp. 552–556.

Underdeveloped Nation   A country in which per capita real income is relatively low compared with the per capita real incomes of industrial nations. Thus, an underdeveloped nation is a relatively poor country with per capita income under $500, or less than one-eighth that of the U.S. In general, there are several characteristics that are indicative of an underdeveloped area: (1) A very high proportion of the population is engaged in agriculture (usually between 70 and 90%). (2) There is evidence of considerable disguised unemployment and a lack of employment opportunities outside agriculture. (3) There is very little capital per head, and the condition of low per capita income requires existence at a near-subsistence level. (4) For the large mass of people, saving is practically nonexistent, while the savings that do exist are accumulated by the landholding class and do not further industry and commerce. For an examination of policies for economic development, see Edward S. Mason, *Economic Planning in Underdeveloped Areas: Government and Business*, Fordham University Press, New York, 1958; Benjamin Higgins, *Economic Development*, W. W. Norton & Company, Inc., New York, 1959.

Underdevelopment   A state or condition of economic development in a region or nation that lacks the facilities to initiate growth. A high proportion of such a nation's resources must be devoted to agriculture. The central fact about this stage of economic development is that a ceiling exists on the level of attainable output per capita. This ceiling results from the fact that the potentialities that flow from modern science and basic resources are either not available or not systematically applied. See Eugene Staley, *The Future of Underdeveloped Countries*, Harper & Row, Publishers, Incorporated, New York, 1961.

Underidentification   A condition that exists when it is not possible to estimate all parameters by means of the information supplied by a system of stochastic equations or when no parameters can be estimated. Most authorities equate the terms underidentified and not identified. In special cases it is possible to eliminate underidentification by introducing additional restrictions into the analysis. For additional information, see Karl A. Fox, *Intermediate Economic Statistics,* John Wiley & Sons, Inc., New York, 1968; Stefan Valavanis, *Econometrics,* McGraw-Hill Book Company, New York, 1959.

Underpopulation A condition of insufficient population for an area. In contrast to the case of an overpopulated area, an increase in population in an underpopulated area raises the standard of living by making it possible to utilize available resources more efficiently. In a nation experiencing underpopulation, there are a large land area and available resources in relation to the population. Man-land ratios, such as the number of persons per square mile or the acreage of arable land per capita, are crude measures of the degree of population concentration. Low man-land ratios or high arable-land–per capita ratios indicate underpopulation. Canada and Australia appear to be good examples of underpopulation.

Man-Land Ratios in Representative Countries

Country	Crude Density in Number of Inhabitants per Square Mile	Arable Land in Acres per Capita
U.S.	55	2.1
Canada	5	5.4
Argentina	23	2.5
Uruguay	39	1.8
Mexico	62	1.1
Australia	5	9.5
United Kingdom	590	0.3
Denmark	294	1.4
Netherlands	985	0.2
France	237	0.9
Spain	169	1.3
India	416	0.7
Philippines	312	0.8
Japan	710	0.1

SOURCE: UN Food and Agriculture Organization, *Production Yearbook,* 1970, UN Demographic Yearbook, 1971.

Underwriter Any person, group, or firm that assumes a risk in return for a fee, usually called a premium or commission. The term originated in sixteenth-century England, where shipowners and merchants would present written insurance proposals to individuals who conducted an insurance business in London coffeeshops. The insurers, acting as individuals, would sign their names *under* the proposal stating how much of the risk each would assume, if any, and what premium they would charge. Today, underwriter refers not only to the principal function of insurance companies but also to investment banks, which underwrite new issues of securities. That is, for a commission, the investment bank guarantees, or insures, that the issuer will receive a stipulated amount of money on a certain day. It is up to the underwriter to market the securities, and in the event of a weak market, he may be forced to reduce the price of the securities and take a loss. For additional information, see D. L. Bickelhaupt and J. H. Magee, *General Insurance,* 8th ed., Richard D. Irwin, Inc., Homewood, Ill., 1970; Investment Bankers Association of America, *Fundamentals of Investment Banking,* Prentice-Hall, Inc., Englewood Cliffs, N.J., 1949.

Undistributed Profits   *See Retained Earnings.*

Undistributed Profits Tax   A tax imposed on U.S. corporations (mostly holding or investment companies or relatively small corporations) which permitted their retained earnings to accumulate beyond the reasonable needs of business. Corporations held the profits and did not pay dividends so that their stockholders could postpone the personal income taxes that would have had to be paid if the dividends were paid out. Stockholders could get the accrued retained earnings out by selling part of their stock and paying a capital gains tax. The undistributed profits tax attempted to prevent this from taking place. The tax imposed is 27.5% of the accumulated taxable income not in excess of $100,000, plus 38.5% of the excess over $100,000. The exceptions, inclusions, and detailed definitions of the terms are in U.S. Internal Revenue Service, *U.S. Internal Revenue Code of 1954,* sections 531–537.

Unearned Revenue (Unearned Income)   In accounting, unearned revenue consists of collections received in advance for which goods and/or services will be provided in the future. For example, a magazine publisher receives checks from subscribers in payment of subscriptions for several years in advance. These collections are sometimes considered unearned income and are classified as current liabilities until they have been earned. In some cases, the liability may be split into two parts: (1) the estimated cost of liquidating the obligation and (2) the estimated profits which would be derived from liquidation (which is sometimes referred to as a deferred credit to income). The latter would be excluded from current liabilities, while the former would be included. For a brief discussion involving unearned income and its related expenses in determining income, see H. A. Finney and H. E. Miller, *Principles of Accounting*, 6th ed., Prentice-Hall, Inc., Englewood Cliffs, N.J., 1963; Paul Grady, *Inventory of Generally Accepted Accounting Principles for Business Enterprises*, American Institute of Certified Public Accountants, Inc., New York, 1965.

Unemployed Person In the U.S., anyone sixteen years of age or over who is not working and is looking for a job. Also counted among the unemployed are (1) those who are waiting to be called back to a job from which they have been laid off, (2) those who are waiting to report to a new job scheduled to begin within thirty days, and (3) those who are out of work but are not looking for a job because of temporary illness or because of a belief that no work is available in their line or in their community. Monthly estimates of U.S. unemployment are obtained through personal interviews in a sample of 50,000 households in 449 areas. These estimates are always larger than the number of persons eligible for unemployment insurance, which does not provide complete coverage. The number of unemployed in the U.S. has ranged from about 13 million in 1933 to less than 700,000 in 1944. From 1950 to 1970, unemployment averaged about 3.3 million. U.S. unemployment statistics are compiled monthly by the U.S. Department of Labor, which uses figures gathered by the U.S. Bureau of the Census in a particular week of each month. See U.S. Department of Labor, *Monthly Report on the Labor Force*. For changes in unemployment from 1800 to 1960, see Stanley Lebergott, *Manpower in Economic Growth*, McGraw-Hill Book Company, New York, 1964, pp. 164–190.

Unemployment Benefit A benefit distributed under an unemployment-compensation program. In the U.S., the amount of the benefit and its duration vary from state to state. Maximum benefits range from $40 to $123 per week and cover from twenty to thirty-four weeks. During the recessions of 1958 and 1961, the duration of unemployment benefits was increased. The national average of unemployment benefits in the recession month of October, 1958, was $30.45, or about 37% of the previous wages of the unemployed who were collecting benefits. The number of unemployed U.S. workers who receive benefits has fluctuated between 40 and 60% of the total number of unemployed. The main factors associated with this relatively low rate of coverage are the increasing number of unemployed workers who exhaust their benefit rights, the entrance into the labor market of a growing number of new workers, who receive no benefits while first unemployed, and an increasing number of disqualifications for benefits. Although unemployment benefits have some countercyclical effect, they have averaged less than 2% of total consumption expenditures. Nevertheless, these benefits, which were not available during the depression of the 1930s, help offset losses in purchasing power. For additional details, see Richard A. Lester, *The Economics of Unemployment Compensation*, Princeton University, Industrial Relations Section, Princeton, N.J., 1962; U.S. Department of Labor, *Adequacy of Benefits under Unemployment Insurance: A Staff Report Prepared for the Steering Committee of the Federal Advisory Council*, October, 1958; Joseph M. Becker, *The Adequacy of the Benefit Amount in Unemployment Insurance*, The W. E. Upjohn Institute for Employment Research, Kalamazoo, Mich., May, 1961; for current statistics on benefit payments under state programs, see U.S. Bureau of Employment Security, *The Labor Market and Employment Security*, monthly.

Unemployment Benefits

State	Maximum Weekly Unemployment Benefits	Maximum Duration, Weeks
Alabama	$50	26
Alaska	60–85	28
Arizona	50	26
Arkansas	50	26
California	65	26
Colorado	77	26
Connecticut	82–123	26
Delaware	65	26
District of Columbia	73	34
Florida	47	26
Georgia	50	26
Hawaii	86	26
Idaho	59	26
Illinois	45–88	26
Indiana	40–52	26
Iowa	61	26
Kansas	60	26
Kentucky	56	26
Louisiana	60	28
Maine	57	26
Maryland	65	26
Massachusetts	69–104	30
Michigan	53–87	26
Minnesota	57	26
Mississippi	40	26
Missouri	57	26

Unmployment Benefits (*continued*)

State	Maximum Weekly Unemployment Benefits	Maximum Duration, Weeks
Montana	42	26
Nebraska	48	26
Nevada	47–67	26
New Hampshire	60	26
New Jersey	72	26
New Mexico	58	30
New York	75	26
North Carolina	54	26
North Dakota	54	26
Ohio	47–66	26
Oklahoma	49	26
Oregon	55	26
Pennsylvania	60	30
Puerto Rico	46	20
Rhode Island	71–91	26
South Carolina	53	26
South Dakota	47	26
Tennessee	50	26
Texas	45	26
Utah	56	36
Vermont	61	26
Virginia	59	26
Washington	72	30
West Virginia	58	26
Wisconsin	72	34
Wyoming	56	26

SOURCE: U.S. Department of Labor.

Unemployment Compensation   *See Unemployment Benefit.*

Unemployment Rate   The number of jobless persons expressed as a percentage of the total labor force. The U.S. counts as unemployed anyone sixteen years of age and over who is out of work and would like a job even if he is doing little about finding one. Many other countries count as unemployed only those persons who are receiving unemployment compensation. These differences make international comparisons hazardous. Ranging from 3% in booms to 25% during the great depression of the 1930s, the U.S. unemployment rate since World War II has averaged about 4.5%, or slightly higher than the 4% rate usually regarded as full employment. The U.S. rate is compiled monthly by the U.S. Department of Labor, which uses survey figures gathered by the U.S. Bureau of the Census. See U.S. Department of Labor, *Monthly Report on the Labor Force;* for rates of many other countries, see Statistical Office of the United Nations, *Monthly Bulletin of Statistics,* New York.

Unemployment Rate (Percent)

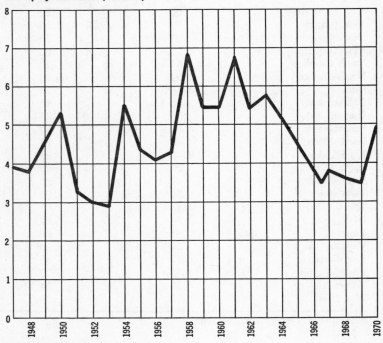

Source: U.S. Department of Labor.

Unfair Competition Deceptive, dishonest, or injurious methods of competition. Originally, the law against unfair competition was aimed at halting the passing off of one's goods as the goods of a competitor, but it now includes both actions which hamper, injure, or exclude competitors and concerted action to suppress competition. Among the common forms of unfair competition are cutthroat competition, price discrimination among types of goods and among firms, false and misleading advertising, tying arrangements, bribery, spying, intimidation, and other direct inter-ference with competitors. The Congress of the U.S. prohibited many forms of unfair competition in interstate commerce by adopting the

Federal Trade Commission Act of 1914. In 1938 the jurisdiction of the Federal Trade Commission was extended by the Wheeler-Lea Act to protect customers against unfair business practices, primarily against misrepresentation of products. For additional details, see John P. Miller, *Unfair Competition,* Harvard University Press, Cambridge, Mass., 1941; Milton Handler, "Unfair Competition and the Federal Trade Commission," *George Washington Law Review,* George Washington University, Washington, D.C., January, 1940, pp. 399–426; Vernon A. Mund, *Government and Business,* 3d ed., Harper & Row, Publishers, Incorporated, New York, 1960, chap. 13.

Unfair Labor Practices Actions on the part of employers which discourage or discriminate against union membership and actions on the part of unions which discourage or discriminate against nonunion personnel that have been outlawed by the National Labor Relations Act. Discriminatory hiring policies, the influencing of the choice of unions by their employees, and a refusal to bargain with union representatives are some of the practices forbidden to management. Forcing management to discriminate in favor of union members or of particular unions, engaging in secondary boycotts, and requiring featherbedding practices of the employer are some of the practices forbidden to unions. Complaints by either side are filed with the National Labor Relations Board, whose general counsel has sole power to investigate them and to prosecute. See Wayne L. McNaughton and Joseph Lazar, *Industrial Relations and the Government,* McGraw-Hill Book Company, New York, 1954; Lloyd G. Reynolds, *Labor Economics and Labor Relations,* 5th ed., Prentice-Hall Inc., Englewood Cliffs, N.J., 1970.

Unified Budget A Federal budget which covers financial transactions of two principal kinds of funds—Federal funds and trust funds. It combines the receipts and outlays for both types of funds after deducting the transactions that flow between them. By and large, it measures the transactions of the government with the public. It is more comprehensive than either the administrative budget or the cash budget, the latter of which does not include all transactions of government trust-fund accounts. For additional details, see *The Budget of the United States Government, Fiscal Year 1972,* U.S. Government Printing Office, Washington, D.C., 1971.

Union Label An identification tag attached to a product to indicate that the item was made in a union shop by a union worker. Many union members and their relatives buy only products with union labels. According to union members, the union label is a sign of good workmanship.

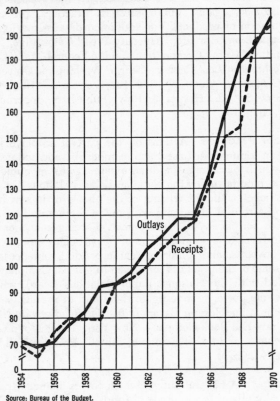

Unified Budget, Receipts and Outlays for the Fiscal Years, 1954-1970 (Billions of dollars)

Source: Bureau of the Budget.

Union Shop A plant or establishment in which all workers must join the union within a specified time after hiring (usually thirty days). The key distinction between a union shop and a closed shop is that the former gives the employer freedom to hire anyone, whereas the latter restricts his choice to persons who are already members of the union. The union-shop arrangement is the only form of union-security provision that is growing rapidly in importance in the U.S. In 1946 only 17% of the nation's collective bargaining agreements provided for the union shop, but by 1959 the proportion had increased to 74%. There are two important reasons for the increase: (1) the Taft-Hartley Act of 1947, which prohibited the closed shop; and (2) the change in the steel industry from maintenance of membership to the union shop. For statistics, see *Union*

Security and Checkoff Provisions in Major Union Contracts 1958–59,
U.S. Department of Labor Bulletin No. 1272; for a discussion of the
union shop, see Joseph Shister, *Economics of the Labor Market,* 2d ed.,
J. B. Lippincott Company, Philadelphia, 1956.

Unit Banking System   A banking system in which banks are individual
incorporated or unincorporated entities that are not affiliated with any
other member of a system. The banking system of the U.S. was founded
on the unit banking doctrine, but the credit needs of a growing country
demanded that the system become more highly concentrated. Nevertheless, defenders of the unit banking system placed many obstacles in the
path of greater concentration, such as laws which were intended to protect unit banks from the competition of branch banks. For example, the
McFadden-Pepper Act of 1927 permitted national banks to establish
branches in the metropolitan areas of the parent bank but forbade them
to establish branches in towns of less than 25,000 population, permitting
one branch in a town of 50,000 population and not more than two
branches in towns of 100,000 population. Advocates of branch banking
and unit banking still argue about advantages and disadvantages of each
system. For further information on the structure of unit banking and a
critical comparison with the branch banking system, see David A. Alhadeff,
Monopoly and Competition in Banking, University of California Press,
Berkeley, Calif., 1954.

Unit Investment Trust   An investment company that is organized under
a trust indenture or a similar instrument, does not have a board of directors, and issues only redeemable securities which represent an undi-
vided interest in a unit of specified securities (underlying securities).
Companies of this type were quite popular in the U.S. in the 1920s, when
they were also called fixed trusts, because the underlying securities could
be changed only under certain conditions. After the stock-market crash of
1929, however, unit trusts became almost obsolete. Subsequently, they
regained the interest of investors but in a somewhat different form. Almost all the unit investment trusts now registered with the Securities and
Exchange Commission are associated with open-end investment companies (mutual funds). Known as contractual plans or front-end-load
plans, they give the small investor the opportunity to accumulate shares
in the mutual fund (underlying securities) by contractually obligating
themselves to pay a certain amount of money each month for a certain
number of years. The investor can drop out of the program (redeem his
shares) at any time, but unless he remains in it for at least a few years,
commissions, which are paid at the beginning of the program (front-end
load), can be staggering. See U.S. Securities and Exchange Commission,

Annual Reports; Investment Company Act of 1940; Commission on Interstate and Foreign Commerce, *Report of the Securities and Exchange Commission on the Public Policy Implications of Investment Company Growth,* December, 1966.

Unlisted Security Any security that is not registered with a stock exchange. Although some unlisted securities are traded on stock exchanges that give unlisted trading privileges, most are bought and sold in the over-the-counter market. No accurate totals of the number of unlisted securities in the U.S. are available, but there is little question that many more securities are unlisted than are listed. Unlisted securities include all municipal, state, and revenue obligations, some government securities (some government securities are listed at times on the New York Stock Exchange, but extremely few are ever traded there), and most corporate bonds and preferred and common stocks. Most corporations that do not list their securities are not able to do so, because they do not meet the listing requirements of the stock exchanges. Some corporations, such as the large commercial banks and insurance companies, prefer not to list their securities even though they could meet the exchanges' requirements. See George L. Leffler and L. C. Farwell, *The Stock Market,* The Ronald Press Company, New York, 1963; Irwin Friend et al., *The Over-the-Counter Securities Markets,* McGraw-Hill Book Company, New York, 1958.

Unsecured Loan A loan made without security or other legal claim upon specific property to satisfy the debt. An individual or a business firm must have an excellent past operating record, be in good financial condition, and have strong prospects in order to borrow money on this basis. It is the most economical and the most desirable method of financing working capital. The unsecured loan is made simply by signing a promissory note.

Urban Population Residents of cities and the suburbs surrounding cities. Before the 1950 census, the urban population of the U.S. was defined almost entirely on the basis of municipal incorporation and size of place and was contrasted with the rural population, or country dwellers. The definition included as urban all places incorporated as muncipalities and having a population of 2,500 or more. In 1950, however, the Bureau of the Census adopted a new concept of urban population to include the urban fringe, whether or not suburbs were incorporated. It has been suggested that the Bureau move even further in this direction and adopt a fourfold urban-rural system of classification, including urban, suburban, village and open-country nonfarm, and rural farm classifications. For further information, see Donald J. Bogue, *The Population of the United States*, The Free Press of Glencoe, New York, 1959; see also R. M. Williams, "Fluctuations in Urban Growth: Some Comparative Data and Analysis," *Regional Science Association Proceedings*, University of Pennsylvania, Wharton School, Philadelphia, 1955.

Urban Population (Millions)

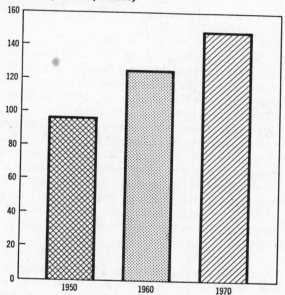

Source: U.S. Department of Commerce; Bureau of the Census.

Urban Renewal The redevelopment and improvement of urban areas in the U.S. It involves the cooperative action of government and private business to reshape the structure of the nation's cities to meet the demands of a constantly growing and changing urban population. The most pressing problem being attacked by urban renewal programs is the spreading of slum areas in many large cities. Urban renewal includes slum clearance and rehabilitation, prevention of blight, relocation, low-cost public housing projects, and an attack on the city housing problem in general. It began with the passage of the Housing Act of 1949, which provided Federal assistance to cities for the betterment of urban housing. In 1954 the act was amended to provide for a broader and more comprehensive approach to the problem of slums and urban redevelopment.

Some states also have undertaken urban renewal programs, providing their cities with the funds and technical assistance necessary for urban planning and development. One authority places the total bill for urban renewal at about $2,150 billion over a twenty-year period. For additional details, see Peter Wagner, *The Scope and Financing of Urban Renewal and Development*, National Planning Association, Washington, D.C., 1963; see also John W. Dyckman and Reginald R. Isaacs, *Capital Requirements for Urban Development and Renewal*, McGraw-Hill Book Company, New York, 1961; James Q. Wilson, *Urban Renewal*, The M.I.T. Press, Cambridge, Mass., 1967.

User Charge   A levy paid by a user of a public transportation system. It is applied so that those who obtain the benefits of transportation improvements provided by the government repay the cost to the government. User charges generally take the form of tolls, license fees, or fuel taxes and are levied at Federal, state, and local levels. The main burden of user charges falls on highway and waterway traffic. Controversy arises over the amount of user charges, the basis of measuring user benefit (e.g., distance traveled, number of passengers, load weights, etc.), and differential treatment of different types of vehicles (e.g., different charges for cars and trucks on toll roads). For further information, see Emery Troxel, *Economics of Transport*, Holt, Rinehart and Winston, Inc., New York, 1955, chap. 11; Beatrice Aitchison, *Charges for Private Use of Federally-Provided Transportation Services and Facilities*, Government Printing Office, Washington, D.C., 1953.

Use Tax   A tax levied in the U.S. on the initial utilization of a good as opposed to one levied on its sale. It was devised by states to offset the loss of sales taxes through the purchase of goods outside their boundaries and to remove the disadvantage to local businesses of competing with out-of-state firms. The tax is imposed on taxable items which have been bought out of the state, and the amount is usually equal to the sales tax. Since a use tax is almost impossible to collect on small items, its applicability is generally limited to purchases of such items as automobiles, which are reported to the state by the owners in order to obtain licenses. Some cities levy use taxes, but the collection problem there is even more difficult than in the case of states. Revenue derived from use taxes is small, and their main importance lies in helping to make sales taxes effective. Since most reports on state and city tax revenues list the revenues derived from sales and use taxes together, it is difficult to determine the exact revenues derived from use taxes alone. See John F. Due, *Sales Taxation*, The University of Illinois Press, Urbana, Ill., 1957; Maurice Cris, *The Use Tax*, Public Administration Service, Chicago, 1941.

Usury   An excessive rate of interest. During the Middle Ages, all interest was called usury, and all usury was deemed a crime. In the contemporary U.S., usury means an overly high rate of interest, the term overly high being defined by state law. The maximum legal limits range from 6 to 30%, although in many states the statutes do not apply to corporate borrowing. Penalties for breaking usury laws vary from forfeit of the excess interest to loss of the entire loan.

Utility   The ability of a good or a service to satisfy human wants. Utility expresses the relationship between goods and a man's pleasures or pains. It is the property possessed by a particular good or service which affords an individual pleasure or prevents pain during the time of its consumption or the period of anticipation of its consumption. For example, a sirloin steak which a man is eating has utility for him, and so had the same steak when it was in his refrigerator before he broiled it. The utility of a good is said to vary in intensity with the intensity of the pleasure that it creates. The degree of utility of a good, however, varies constantly. For example, the first and second steaks may provide equal amounts of utility, but a third steak may result in diminishing utility and perhaps even in pain. Utility thus is not proportional to the quantity or type of the good or service consumed. For further discussion of utility, see W. Stanley Jevons, *The Theory of Political Economy*, 5th ed., Kelley and Millman, Inc., New York, 1957, chap. 3; see also Alfred Marshall, *Principles of Economics*, 8th ed., Macmillan & Co., Ltd., London, 1920.

Utopian Socialism   An early type of socialism which advocated the direction of production by workingmen's associations and producers' cooperatives. Utopian, or associational, socialism is nonscientific in that it concerns itself not primarily with a critical analysis of society but with definite plans for establishing utopian ideas. The utopian Socialists did not advance any plan of state ownership of the means of production but endeavored to establish small, autonomous, voluntary local communities of workers living together. The members of these communities would pool their assets, each member giving his best service to the group and all sharing the fruits of their production according to their needs. There would be no need for a central coercive government because these ideal cooperative communities would eliminate poverty, discontent, etc. A number of the prominent utopian Socialists—Robert Owen, Charles Fourier, and Louis Blanc—were active in the late eighteenth and early nineteenth centuries in attempts to win acceptance for their doctrines and in the foundation of model colonies in Europe and the U.S. Their extremely unrealistic programs were never taken very seriously, however, and the movement soon disappeared. For further information, see Harry Laidler, *Social-Economic Movements*, Thomas Y. Crowell Company, New York, 1944; G. D. H. Cole, *A History of Socialist Thought*, 4 vols., St. Martin's Press, Inc., New York, 1956–1958.

V

Vacancy Rate, Homeowner The percentage of the total units in the homeowner inventory that are available for sale. The total homeowner units consist of owner-occupied units, vacant units sold and awaiting occupancy, and vacant units available for sale. Excluded are vacant units that are dilapidated, seasonal, or held off the market. The data are reported quarterly by the Census Bureau.

Vacancy Rate, Rental The percentage of the total known number of rental housing units that are available for rent. Vacant units available for rent include units offered for rent and for rent or sale. The total number of rental units is composed of renter-occupied units, vacant units rented but not yet occupied, and vacant units available for rent. Excluded are vacant units that are dilapidated, seasonal, or held off the market. The data are reported quarterly by the Census Bureau.

Value The price commended by a good or service in the market. The concept of value is ordinarily used in economics to denote value in exchange. That is, the exchange value of a good is expressed as a quantity of other goods or money which must be exchanged to obtain one unit of the given good. The value of a commodity depends upon two elements: its desirability and its scarcity—the familiar factors of supply and demand. If a good is desirable (because of its usefulness, its aesthetically pleasing qualities, or any other reason), it has value for the individual. However, since the worth of a good to an individual decreases as it becomes more abundant (because of the law of diminishing marginal utility), value also depends upon the good's scarcity. To have value in exchange, a good must be both desirable and scarce. If it is not desired by anyone, no one will be willing to exchange any good or money for it no matter how scarce it is, and its exchange value will be zero. If the good is abundant, no matter how desirable it is (e.g., air), everyone has as much of it as he wants, and no one will pay for it. Thus, it will have no exchange value. For further information, see J. R. Hicks, *Value and Capital*, 2d ed., Oxford University Press, Fair Lawn, N.J., 1946; H. K. Neibyl, "The Need for a Concept of Value in Economic Theory," *Quarterly Journal of Economics*, vol. LIX, no. 2, pp. 201–216, Harvard University Press, Cambridge, Mass., February, 1940; Richard Ruggles, "The Value of Value Theory," *American Economic Review*, supplement, vol. XLIV, no. 2, pp. 140–151, May, 1954; C. E. Ferguson and Juanita M. Kreps, *Principles of Economics*, 2d ed., Holt, Rinehart and Winston, Inc., New York, 1965, pp. 90–91.

Value Added by Manufacture The difference between the value of goods and the cost of materials or supplies that are used in producing them. Value added is derived by subtracting the cost of raw materials, parts, supplies, fuel, goods purchased for resale, electric energy, and contract work from the value of shipments. It is the best money gauge of the relative economic importance of a manufacturing industry because it measures that industry's contribution to the economy rather than its gross sales. According to the 1958 *Census of Manufactures*, for example, the U.S. machine-tool industry had shipments of $697 million, while the men's dress-shirt and pajama industry had shipments of $996 million. This would imply that the latter was of greater importance than the former, but the value added by the two industries was almost precisely the same: $430 million for the machine-tool industry and $431 million for the dress-shirt and pajama industry. For detailed statistics on value added by manufacture, see U.S. Department of Commerce, *1967 Census of Manufactures;* for examples of how value added is used as a tool in economic analysis, see E. B. Alderfer and H. E. Michl, *Economics of American Industry*, 3d ed., McGraw-Hill Book Company, New York, 1957.

Value-added Tax (VAT) A tax on the value added. The principle of this tax is that the person paying for goods or services pays tax thereon and collects tax on his sales. The base of the tax measures essentially the value of the productive services claimed by the taxpayer in the conduct of his business. The net effect is that taxes paid are credited against taxes collected, and only the balance is payable to the taxing authority. The tax is rebated on exports and imposed on imports. Border taxes in Europe are substantial and will grow in importance. Several members of the

Common Market and EFTRA have value-added taxes. This type of tax is currently being proposed for the U.S. because of our balance-of-international-payments problem and because of the present heavy burden of income taxes. It is generally assumed that a value-added tax will be passed on to consumers and shifted forward. For additional details on the pros and cons of a value-added tax, see "The Report of the President's Task Force on Business Taxation," *Business Taxation*, Washington, September, 1970, pp. 61–82.

Variable Cost   Costs that vary directly in response to changes in the volume of production. Costs of this type include payments for labor, raw material, and all other variable resources. For many manufacturing firms, some portions of the electrical power consumption will be a variable cost. Other portions of the electrical consumption of the firm will represent fixed costs for lighting administrative offices, running accounting machines, and other purposes not associated directly with production. By definition, variable costs are zero when no output is being produced, and fixed costs are the only costs being incurred at that time. See D. S. Watson, *Price Theory and Its Uses*, 2d ed., Houghton Mifflin Company, Boston, 1968, for an economic treatment of variable costs; for an accounting treatment of variable costs, see Charles H. Griffin, Thomas H. Williams, and Glenn A. Welsch, *Advanced Accounting*, Richard D. Irwin, Inc., Homewood, Ill., 1966.

Variable Proportions, Law of   *See Diminishing Returns, Law of.*

Variable-Span Diffusion Indices   A collection of diffusion indices, each with a different time span, such as three months, six months, or nine months. For any given index, the time span is fixed. A diffusion index is usually computed over one-month spans, but similar measures can be computed over intervals of two months, three months, or any number of months. For further discussion, see Geoffrey H. Moore and Julius Shiskin, "Variable Span Diffusion Indexes and Economic Forecasting," a paper presented at the Sixth Annual Forecasting Conference, American Statistical Association, New York Chapter, Apr. 17, 1964.

Variance   A measure of the spread of a set of values. It is the tendency of the individual values to vary from the mean. Operationally, a variance is the sum of the squares of the deviations of observed values from the arithmetic mean of a series divided by the number of items. For example, the variance for a set of family-income values would be expressed in terms of dollars of income squared. Since it is easier to interpret the measure of spread expressed in the same units as the variable itself, however, the statistical measure of spread generally used in economic analysis is the standard deviation, which is the square root of the variance. For further information on the subject of variability, see Robert Schlaifer, *Introduction to Statistics for Business Decisions,* McGraw-Hill Book Company, New York, 1961.

Variate-Difference Method   A technique for the analysis of time series whose variations stem from a systematic and a random (error) component. If the systematic component (some smooth function of time) can be described by a polynomial, the systematic component can be eliminated by successive differencing, and thus the random component may be isolated. This method has rather limited applications largely because the mathematical solution of a system can rarely be described by a polynomial. For additional information, see Lawrence R. Klein, *Econometrics,* Row, Peterson & Company, Evanston, Ill., 1953.

Vector   *See Matrix.*

Veil-of-Money Concept   The concept that money is neutral. Since goods are actually exchanged for goods, money transactions are only a veil that hides the underlying real processes. When people cannot see through the veil of money and consider money as having value in itself, a money illusion is said to exist. In the classical view, money was completely neutral, so that any changes in the money supply affected only the absolute price level and not any of the real variables of the system, such as the level of output. This concept, however, is valid only in comparing different full-employment equilibrium situations. When the economy is underemployed, money is no longer neutral and changes in the money supply can affect the real variables. For additional details, see A. C. Pion, *The Veil of Money,* St. Martin's Press, Inc., New York, 1949; Don Patinkin, *Money, Interest and Prices,* Harper & Row, Publishers, Incorporated, New York, 1956.

Velocity of Money   The number of times that an average dollar is spent during a specific period, usually one year. The velocity of money depends on the average length of time people hold their money, and it can be calculated by dividing the total dollar volume of sales by the total money supply in circulation. Since World War II, the velocity of money has been slowly rising. If the velocity of money rises, people are holding smaller cash balances and are spending their money sooner after they receive it. The transactions velocity is closely related to the level of economic activity; as economic activity expands, idle balances are reduced, increasing the velocity of money, and the expansion of loans puts the new money into the hands of active spenders. The reverse is true in terms of declining business activity. It has generally been found that the transactions velocity also varies directly with the level of interest rates. A concept closely related to the transactions velocity is the income velocity of money, which is the number of times that money moves from one income recipient to another. It can be derived by dividing the total national product by the money supply. In 1965 the income velocity of money was 4.15. The transactions velocity of money, which has also been rising steadily in the postwar period, was 13.4 in 1962. For data on money velocity and further theoretical explanation, see Paul McGouldrick, "A Sectoral Analysis of Velocity," *Federal Reserve Bulletin,* Washington, D.C., December, 1962; Howard S. Ellis, "Some Fundamentals in the Theory of Velocity," *Quarterly Journal of Economics,* vol. 52, p. 431, Harvard University Press, Cambridge, Mass., May, 1938; J. W. Angell, "The Components of the Circular Velocity of Money," *Quarterly Journal of Economics,* vol. 51, no. 2, pp. 224–272, Harvard University Press, Cambridge, Mass., February, 1937; William J. Frazer, Jr., *The Demand for Money,* The World Publishing Company, Cleveland, 1967; Campbell R. McConnell, *Economics,* 4th ed., McGraw-Hill Book Company, New York, 1969.

Venture Capital, Outside New stock issues. Such issues play a key role in business finance, but because of the growing importance of internal funds in financing capital expenditures, outside venture capital has become less important. In the U.S. in the mid-1920s, new stock issues provided more than 20% of the funds needed; by the 1960s, their share had dropped well below 10%. Nevertheless, growing companies often must turn to new stock issues to meet a major part of their needs for investment funds, and outside venture capital is required by many small and medium-sized firms to survive and prosper. For further information, see *Business Needs for Venture Capital,* report for the Electric Bond and Share Company, McGraw-Hill Department of Economics, New York, December, 1949; Elvin F. Donaldson and John K. Pfahl, *Corporate Finance,* 3d ed., The Ronald Press Company, New York, 1969.

Venture Capital (Risk Capital) The money supplied by stockholders either from plowed-back earnings or from new stock purchases. It provides the bulk of the funds needed for industrial progress, either by developing new corporations or by financing new ventures for existing firms. Venture capital is also needed as a cushion to support business borrowing. Bankers and investors will not lend money to a company with an inadequate margin of equity capital. For further discussion, see *Business Needs for Venture Capital,* report for the Electric Bond and

Share Company, McGraw-Hill Department of Economics, New York, December, 1949; Elvin F. Donaldson and John K. Pfahl, *Corporate Finance*, 3d ed., The Ronald Press Company, New York, 1969, pp. 432–434.

Verification   In econometrics, the process of setting up criteria for measuring the reliability of experimental results and using such criteria in deciding whether to accept or reject the economic theory or hypotheses being tested by means of the available data and an econometric model. For additional information, see Stefan Valavanis, *Econometrics*, McGraw-Hill Book Company, New York, 1959.

Vertical Integration   The operation of a single firm at more than one stage of production. The most comprehensive type of vertical integration would include productive stages from the processing of the raw material to the completion and distribution of the finished product. For example, some steel producers mine coal and iron ore, ship the ore in their own boats to their plants, make pig iron, convert the iron into steel, shape the steel into semifinished and finished products, and distribute and export the products to final consumers. A single company organized vertically can often carry out the entire production process more efficiently than a number of individual firms, each of which handles one stage of the process. One reason for this situation is that technologically complementary processes can be brought together in a single plant with a resulting gain in efficiency. Moreover, economies may result from the improved coordination of output rates at various production stages. Vertical integration may also eliminate substantial shipping costs and payments to middlemen. It may not be economical in all industries, however, for the characteristics of the productive process and the nature of the demand for the goods produced at various stages play a large role in determining the suitability of vertical integration for a particular firm. For further information, see Joe S. Bain, *Industrial Organization*, 2d ed., John Wiley & Sons, Inc., New York, 1968.

Vertical Labor Mobility   *See Labor Mobility.*

Vested Interest   An individual's claim to property or to the free exercise of a certain activity. When a vested interest is given legal sanction, it becomes a vested right, enforceable against other individuals or the state. A vested interest may also be a legally enforceable claim to a future benefit. For example, a worker has a vested interest in his share of social security benefits which he expects to receive at retirement.

Visible Item of International Trade   An international transaction in which there is a movement of tangible goods. Examples of visible items are commodity imports, such as coffee and tea, and commodity exports, such as machinery and airplanes. Visible items differ from invisible items, such as tourist expenditures, personal remittances, and shipping, banking, and insurance charges. Statistics on the dollar volume and quantities of visible items of U.S. international trade are collected by the Bureau of Foreign Commerce of the U.S. Department of Commerce and reported in its *Foreign Trade Bulletin*.

Vital Statistics   The statistics of life: data on births, marriages, divorces, and deaths. These statistics are important in projecting estimates of future population. In the U.S. in 1970, there were 3,718,000 live births, 2,179,000 marriages, and 1,921,000 deaths. For current vital statistics, see U.S. Public Health Service, National Statistics, *Monthly Vital Statistics Report*, Government Printing Office, Washington, D.C.; for historical data, see U.S. Bureau of the Census, *Statistical Abstract of the United States*, 1963.

Wage Control   Centralized control and stabilization of wages. During national emergencies, such as wars, normal economic relations are disrupted to so great an extent that it may be necessary to institute governmental control over wages to prevent inflation. Wage control is usually undertaken by freezing wages as of some date and then requiring permission before any changes may be made. Wage adjustments may be permitted to remove inequities that may have been present at the time of the freeze and to compensate for any rise in the cost of living. The U.S. has occasionally resorted to some form of wage stabilization, the strongest control occurring during World War II, when a National War Labor Board was created to settle wage disputes and stabilize wages. The Office of Economic Stabilization was established to coordinate the various wage and price controls. The Board, which was in operation until the end of the war, handled more than 460,000 applications for wage increases affecting 29 million workers. Wages were frozen for 90 days on August 15, 1971 in order to halt inflation. After November 13, 1971, the Pay Board attempted to hold wage increases to no more than 5.5% per year. For further information on the U.S. experience with wage control, see Martin Stoller and J. S. Zeisel, "Economics of the Wage Freeze: Wartime Wage Control in the U.S.," *National Industrial Conference Board Business Record,* February, 1958; U.S. Department of Labor, *The Termination Report: National War Labor Board,* Washington, D.C., 1948; John Dunlop and Arthur Hill, *The Wage Adjustment Board,* Harvard University Press, Cambridge, Mass., 1950; H. Henig and S. H. Unterbergen, "Wage Control in Wartime and Transition," *American Economic Review,* p. 319, American Economic Association, Evanston, Ill., June, 1945; for an example of wage control in another country, see Ellen Bussey, "Experience with Wage Controls in the Netherlands," *Monthly Labor Review,* U.S. Department of Labor, Washington, D.C., September, 1958.

Wage Rate The rate of pay received by a worker on the basis of some unit, such as an hour, a week, or a unit of product produced or sold. A schedule of established wage rates constitutes the basic wage structure of an individual firm or an industry. There are two basic types, time-rate structures and incentive-rate structures. Time-wage employees receive a fixed sum of money per unit of time, whereas incentive workers receive compensation that varies with output. For further information, see R. C. Smith and M. J. Murphy, *Job Evaluation and Employee Rating,* McGraw-Hill Book Company, New York, 1946; see also J. K. Louden, *Wage Incentives,* Harvard University Press, Cambridge, Mass., 1960.

Wages-Fund Theory A mid-nineteenth-century theory which held that wages are determined by (1) a fixed sum of capital set aside by employers for the payment of wages and (2) the number of workers. Essentially a restatement of the subsistence theory of wages, the wages-fund theory emphasized the short-run possibility of wages' rising above the subsistence level. Because the theory was based on the proposition that a predetermined fund irrevocably set aside for wages must be divided among a definite number of workers, however, it led most of its adherents to the following conclusion: In the long run, reductions in the population are the only effective means of raising wages much above the subsistence level. The wages-fund theory was generally abandoned during the latter part of the nineteenth century, primarily because it was recognized that wages could be paid from current production as well as from a given fund. In the early twentieth century, it was gradually replaced by the marginal-productivity theory of wages, the most widely accepted non-Marxian theory of the present time. For a classical statement of the wages-fund theory, see John Stuart Mill, *Principles of Political Economy,* J. W. Parker, London, 1848, book III; F. W. Taussig, *Wages and Capital: An Examination of the Wages Fund Doctrine,* D. Appleton & Company, Inc., New York, 1896, reprinted by Augustus M. Kelley, Publishers, New York, 1968; for a history and analysis of the theory, see Michael T. Wermel, *The Evolution of the Classical Wage Theory,* Columbia University Press, New York, 1939.

Wagner Act   *See National Labor Relations Act.*

Warrant   An option which gives the holder the privilege of purchasing a certain amount of stock at a specified price for a stipulated period. There are two types of warrants, stock-purchase warrants and subscription warrants. Stock-purchase warrants (also called option warrants) are sometimes issued with or attached to bonds, preferred stock, and infrequently, common stock. They entitle the holder to buy common stock in the same corporation at a certain price. Some of these warrants limit the right to buy to a specified period; others are perpetual. Stock-purchase warrants are sometimes attached to the underlying issue and cannot be detached; their value is a part of the bond or preferred stock. Others are detachable, sometimes after a waiting period, and frequently have inherent value which depends on the current price of the common stock. These are traded in the same manner as other securities. This type of warrant is generally used to make the bonds or preferred stock more attractive to the investor; if the company thrives, he has an opportunity to gain through the purchase of the common stock. Subscription warrants are used with privileged subscriptions to new issues of common stock. Common stockholders in many corporations have preemptive rights to subscribe to that proportion of any new issue of common stock equivalent to the proportion of the corporation that they owned before the issue. Before the stock is issued, the common stockholders receive subscription warrants which indicate the number of rights that they have and which serve as evidence of their right to subscribe to the new issue. For further information, see Jules I. Bogen (ed.), *Financial Handbook,* 4th ed., The Ronald Press Company, New York, 1968; Charles W. Gerstenberg, *Financial Organization and Management of Business,* 4th ed., Prentice-Hall, Inc., Englewood Cliffs, N.J., 1959.

Wash Sale   A fictitious sale of a security or a commodity. Wash sales, which are now illegal in the U.S., were formerly used to create the illusion that a stock or a commodity was being actively traded even though no real changes in ownership occurred. The manipulator hoped to drive the price up and thereby profit. Wash sales could be accomplished in several ways: (1) Two brokers could agree to simulate a sale on the exchange by agreeing on price and amount but without exchanging money or securities. (2) A speculator could give matched orders to two brokers, one to buy and one to sell the same amount of stock at the same price. (3) A person could sell securities to a friend, retrieve the securities, and pay back the friend. The U.S. Internal Revenue Service also considers a transaction a wash sale if a stockholder sells and then buys back the same stock within less than thirty days. The stockholder is not allowed to apply the capital gains or capital loss tax rate to such a sale. See D. K. Eiteman, C. A. Dice, and W. J. Eiteman, *The Stock Market*, 4th ed., McGraw-Hill Book Company, New York, 1966, pp. 552–555.

Watered Stock Common stock which a corporation issues without receiving full payment for it. The formal value of outstanding stock therefore exceeds the proceeds from its sale. Apparently, the term dates back to a time when Daniel Drew (who later became a stock-market manipulator) drove cattle to market after giving them salt but no water with their feed. Then he would water them heavily, which increased the cattle's weight and his profits. The watering of stock was prevalent in the U.S. in late nineteenth and early twentieth centuries; even the United States Steel Company was involved in watering stock in 1901. Stock watering was condemned because it was thought to hurt the corporation's credit and discriminate against the public, since watered stock usually went to insiders. The practice of watering stock declined as corporate financial practices improved, government regulations were enacted, and the issuance of no-par stock made the practice obsolete. Watered stock is now unimportant because earnings and not the book value of assets determine the market value of stock. See George L. Leffler and L. C. Farwell, *The Stock Market*, The Ronald Press Company, New York, 1963.

Webb-Pomerene Act (Export Trade Act) A Federal statute which exempts associations of exporters from the antitrust laws. Enacted by Congress in 1918, the Webb-Pomerene Act permits American firms to form organizations for the purpose of conducting export trade and exempts them from the jurisdiction of the antitrust laws, provided that the associations do not restrain trade within the U.S. The export associations are required to file detailed information with the Federal Trade Commission and are subject to periodic investigation by the Commission. The Webb-Pomerene Act was adopted mainly to enable small American exporters to compete successfully with foreign selling cartels and to present a united front against foreign buying cartels. In practice, however, small business has benefited little from participation in export associations, and large exporting enterprises have been able to concentrate their power even more thoroughly under the Export Trade Act. As of 1964, about fifty export associations operated under the provisions of the act; they handled about 10% of total U.S. exports. For further information, see Sidney Diamond, "The Webb-Pomerene Act and Export Trade Associations," *Columbia Law Review*, New York, November, 1944, pp. 805–835; Leslie Fournier, "Webb-Pomerene Law," *American Economic Review*, pp. 18–33, American Economic Association, Evanston, Ill., March, 1932; "Small Business and the Webb-Pomerene Act," *Report of the Foreign Trade Subcommittee of the Special Committee to Study Problems of American Small Business*, Senate Subcommittee Print No. 11, 79th Cong., 2d Sess., 1946.

Welfare Economics A theoretical branch of economics which is concerned with the application of ethical standards of evaluation to economic systems. The actual socioeconomic goals are assumed and are not determined by economic analysis. For example, the primary social goals for a welfare evaluation of the operation of an economic system might be maximum freedom of choice for individuals, an equitable distribution of income, and optimum standards of living for all individuals as determined by their preferences and restricted only by available resources and technology. An optimum solution in welfare economics is usually considered one in which the welfare of the greatest number of people is maximized and not the profits of an individual or a firm. Much of the analysis of welfare economics has been accomplished in the area of maximizing consumer satisfaction. For any given distribution of income, the optimum allocation of resources occurs under competitive marginal-cost pricing. The optimum adjustment of production in terms of consumer preferences is obtained only if the marginal rate of substitution between each two goods that are consumed is equal to the marginal rate of transformation of the two goods in production. For a fuller statement on welfare economics, see Arthur C. Pigou, *The Economics of Welfare*, 4th ed., Macmillan & Co., Ltd., London, 1932; A. P. Lerner, *The Economics of Control*, The Macmillan Company, New York, 1944; J. de V. Graff, *Theoretical Welfare Economics*, Cambridge University Press, New York, 1957; Tibor Scitovsky, *Welfare and Competition*, Richard D. Irwin, Inc., Homewood, Ill., 1957; Kenneth E. Boulding, "Welfare Economics," in Bernard F. Haley (ed.), *Survey of Contemporary Economic Theory*, Richard D. Irwin, Inc., Homewood, Ill., 1952, vol. II; William J. Baumol, *Welfare Economics and the Theory of the State*, Harvard University Press, Cambridge, Mass., 1965; Ian M. Little, *Critique of Welfare Economics*, Oxford University Press, Fair Lawn, N.J., 1957.

Welfare State   A private economy in which large-scale governmental action emphasizes social benefits. Welfare-state goals include maintenance of a minimum living standard for all citizens, production of social goods and services, control of the business cycle, and adjustment of total output to allow for social costs and revenues. Since the New Deal, the welfare-state aspect of U.S. government has been increasing. The growth in public services involves a transition from an individualistic economy to a mixed public-private economy. The welfare state is not socialistic; rather, it involves governmental expenditures and the use of fiscal policy to adjust aggregate demand to the productive capacity of the private economy. While the government makes large expenditures, private enterprise carries out actual production. Among the instruments of the modern welfare state are progressive taxation, social security, unemployment insurance, farm-support programs, and government-sponsored housing programs. Other nations, such as Great Britain and the Scandinavian countries, have moved further in the direction of the welfare state than has the U.S. An example of this is the cradle-to-the-grave welfare assistance program operated by the British government. For further information on the benefits and costs of the welfare state, see Francis M. Bator, *The Question of Government Spending,* Harper & Row, Publishers, Incorporated, New York, 1960; Henry C. Wallich, *The Cost of Freedom,* Harper & Row, Publishers, Incorporated, New York, 1960.

White-Collar Worker   A worker who engages in a job requiring ordinary attire. White-collar occupations generally do not require much physical effort. Among white-collar workers are professional persons, business managers and proprietors, and clerical and sales workers. In the U.S., there has been a marked increase since World War II in the ratio of white-collar to blue-collar employees. In 1955 the number of white-collar workers in the country for the first time approximately equaled the number of blue-collar workers. The U.S. Department of Labor has predicted that white-collar workers will outnumber blue-collar workers by 47 million to 31 million by 1980. For a study of the white-collar worker, see C. Wright Mills, *White Collar: The American Middle Class,* Oxford University Press, Fair Lawn, N.J., 1951.

Wholesale Price Index   A monthly measure of changes in wholesale prices that is compiled by the U.S. Bureau of Labor Statistics. The index includes a representative group of 2,000 commodities, ranging from crude rubber, cotton, and iron ore to finished apparel, tires, and machinery. The importance assigned to individual items depends on dollar shipments which are frequently revised, but the index does not take full account of quality changes. The base period for the index is 1967, and current prices are expressed as a percentage of the 1967 average. Indices are prepared for major industries, product classes, and individual items as well as for 2,000 commodities. All are released in U.S. Bureau of Labor Statistics, *Wholesale Prices and Price Index,* monthly.

Wholesale Price Index (1967 = 100)

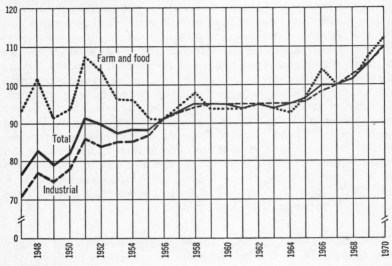

Source: U.S. Department of Labor.

Wholesaler A merchant who is engaged in purchasing goods from producers, primarily for resale to other business firms for their own use or for final sale to consumers. The wholesaler thus acts as an intermediary between producers and users of the many products of industry; hence, he frequently is referred to as a middleman. Product lines carried by wholesalers range from basic farm products to complex machine tools. In playing his role in the economy, the wholesaler performs a variety of functions, including the storage, transportation, and servicing of the goods required by his customers. For detailed statistical information and other facts concerning wholesale operations, see U.S. Bureau of the Census, "Wholesale Trade Summary Statistics," *1967 Census of Business,* vol. III; see also M. R. Warshaw, *Effective Selling through Wholesalers,* University of Michigan, Ann Arbor, Mich., 1961.

Wholesale Sales Sales of all establishments engaged in selling to retailers, jobbers, or businesses rather than to consumers. Wholesale trade classifications are based on the standard industrial-classification definitions used in U.S. censuses of business. Because of the position of wholesale trade in the distribution of the national economy, sales figures are most meaningful when they are used with similar data for manufacturing and retail trade. There is a considerable amount of duplication in the sales of manufacturers, wholesalers, and retailers, and some attempts have been made to eliminate it. For example, wholesalers' sales exclude the operations of manufacturers' sales branches and offices and the marketing stations of petroleum refiners, since the sales of these establishments are covered in the manufacturing series. Wholesale sales are an important economic indicator, since they reflect the level of economic activity at an intermediate stage of the distributive process. The monthly data of the U.S. Bureau of the Census on wholesale trade are based on reports of a sample of respondents. Wholesale sales in the U.S. totaled about $250 billion in 1970. For current statistics, see U.S. Bureau of the Census, *Wholesale Trade Reports,* monthly.

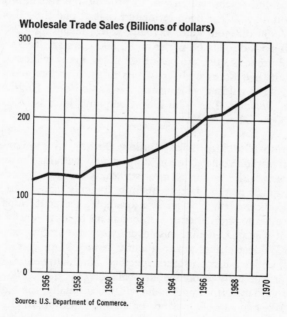

Wholesale Trade Sales (Billions of dollars)

Source: U.S. Department of Commerce.

Widening of Margins   A technique to allow exchange rates to fluctuate around their par values within a range of about 2 to 3% on either side of parity (smaller band) or 4 to 5% (broader band). A widening of the range provides central banks with greater leeway in managing their currencies and increases the risks for speculation. Some economists believe this technique would deal effectively with short-run disturbances and would curb speculation in foreign exchange by making possible losses as well as gains. However, they think it would not solve the problem created by long-run disparities of inflation rates in different countries. For additional information, see Paul A. Samuelson, *Economics,* 8th ed., McGraw-Hill Book Company, New York, 1970.

Wildcat Bank An unsound bank chartered under the laws of various states of the U.S. during the chaotic banking period between 1816 and 1863. This type of bank was permitted to issue bank notes against a multitude of assets, including mortgages, bonds, and personal loans. The refusal of the Federal government to permit continuance of the national bank resulted in the establishment of many banks, named wildcats because they "were located in the depths of the forests where there were few human habitations, but plenty of wildcats." These banks were purposely located in the wilderness to prevent the redemption of their worthless currency. It has been estimated that at one time there were in circulation 7,000 different kinds of bank notes, including 1,700 issues of banks which existed solely on paper and 3,800 counterfeit issues. Because of the lack of proper security to back their notes, many wildcat banks were forced to shut their doors with great loss to stockholders and depositors. For a sketch of the wildcat banking era, see Noble Foster Hoggson, *Epochs in American Banking,* The John Day Company, Inc., New York, 1929, pp. 129–143.

Wildcat Strike (Quickie Strike; Outlaw Strike) A spontaneous strike action taken without official union support and without the due process that characterizes the calling of most strikes. A wildcat strike is designed to achieve quick results, but frequently its only aim is to dramatize unsettled conditions in a plant. For example, garment-industry strikes have been called to strengthen the enforcement of a previously concluded agreement if it appeared that employers were attempting to violate the agreement. Wildcat strikes are frequently termed stoppages so that they may not fall under a ban on strikes specified in an agreement. Many such stoppages are actually spontaneous walkouts by the workers without direction or guidance from union officials. Occasionally, the real object of a wildcat strike may not be demands on an employer but an effort to make union leadership conform to the policies and ideas of the workers. See Jack Barbash, *The Practice of Unionism,* Harper & Row, Publishers, Incorporated, New York, 1956; E. T. Hiller, *The Strike: A Study of Collective Action,* The University of Chicago Press, Chicago, 1928.

Withholding Tax   A Federal or state tax withheld by U.S. employers from the wages and salaries of workers at the time of payment. A fixed percentage is withheld from each pay check. This method of taxation has been characterized as "pay as you go," since the taxes needed to run the governments are paid from current earnings. Among the advantages of the withholding method of tax collection are prompt payment to the governments and lack of complaint on the part of the workers because they never possess the money that is withheld. Among the disadvantages are the additional paper work required of the companies withholding funds. For a more detailed discussion, see Harold M. Groves, *Postwar Taxation and Economic Progress*, McGraw-Hill Book Company, New York, 1946.

Woman Power   Women as a labor resource. As of 1969, there were about 30 million women in the U.S. labor force, constituting one-third of the nation's work force. Working wives had doubled in numbers over two decades and now accounted for well over 50% of the female labor force. Single women workers totaled over 6 million, and widowed, divorced, or

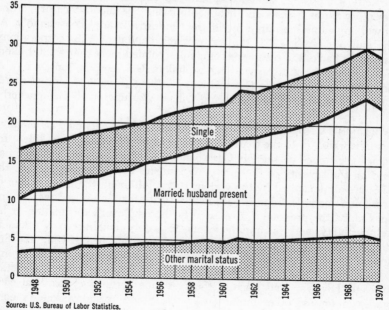

Growth of the Female Labor Force, 1947-1970 (Millions)

Single

Married: husband present

Other marital status

Source: U.S. Bureau of Labor Statistics.

separated women workers more than 5 million. According to the 1960 census, women were represented in all of the 479 occupations reported They play a particularly important role in manufacturing and service occupations, clerical and sales work, and the professions and management. Only slightly more than one-third of the U.S. women who work, however, hold full-time jobs throughout the year. About one-third hold full-time jobs but do not work throughout the year, and one-third work during part or all of the year on a part-time basis, which is defined as less than thirty-five hours a week. For further information, see U.S. Department of Labor, *1962 Handbook on Women Workers,* Bulletin 285, 1963; National Manpower Council, *Womanpower,* Columbia University Press, New York, 1957; see also Ingrid C. Kildegaard, "Working Wives," *Journal of Advertising Research Foundation,* vol. 3, no. 2, New York, June, 1963.

Working Capital, Net   The excess of current assets over current liabilities. These excess current assets are available to carry on business operations. As demand increases in prosperous times, a large volume of working capital is needed to expand production. When demand falls off, a smaller amount of working capital is necessary to operate at a lower rate of capacity. Companies should maintain the flow of funds from cash into inventory through sales and again into cash. The amount or proportion of working capital required by different industries varies considerably. At the end of March, 1971, the net working capital of U.S. corporations, excluding banks and insurance companies, totaled more than $220 billion. For current statistics on working capital in U.S. corporations, see U.S. Securities and Exchange Commission, *Working Capital of United States Corporations,* Government Printing Office, Washington, D.C., quarterly.

Workmen's Compensation   Cash and medical benefits paid by employers to workers, or to the dependents of workers who have been killed, for injuries sustained on the job. Cash benefits are based on the worker's pay and on the severity of the injury. Workmen's compensation laws in the U.S. are administered by the various states. Although the primary aim of workmen's compensation is economic security for the injured worker and his family, the program has resulted in the employer's recognition of his responsibility and in improvements in safety conditions. Workmen's compensation is the oldest social security program in the U.S.; the first group of states passed workmen's compensation laws in 1911; and Mississippi completed the list in 1948. The plans vary greatly from state to state, however, and some of them exclude certain occupational categories or impose other limitations, while others make workmen's compensation programs voluntary for certain classes of employers. Workmen's compensation is financed by insurance. Most states permit the use of private insurance companies, but some insist on a state insurance fund. Two authoritative texts on the subject are H. M. Sommers and A. R. Sommers, *Workmen's Compensation*, John Wiley & Sons, Inc., New York, 1954; Marshall Dawson, *Problems of Workmen's Compensation Administration*, U.S. Department of Labor Bulletin 672, 1940.

Work Rules Any rule, right, or responsibility embodied in a labor contract. The scope of work rules can be extended to include employment conditions not mentioned in the contract but which have become traditional through their continued and uniform observance over the years. In a more limited sense, the term refers to a condition of employment that affects both job security and production efficiency. Controversy over work rules in U.S. contract negotiations includes the problems of work assignment, application of seniority, rearrangement of job functions, manning requirements, incentive rates, and standards of efficiency. Disagreement over the specific nature of the work rules, especially those pertaining to job security, shop conditions, and the work load, is a major cause of strikes, especially in industries in which automation and other modern technological improvements are being introduced. For further information see Solomon Barkin, "Work Rules: A Phase of Collective Bargaining," *Labor Law Journal*, pp. 375ff., Commerce Clearing House, Chicago, Ill., May, 1961; William Gomberg, "The Work Rules and Work Practices Problem," *Labor Law Journal*, pp. 643ff., Commerce Clearing House, Chicago, Ill., July, 1961; "The Evolution of Work Rules and Their Effects on Employment," part X, *Proceedings of the Fourteenth Annual Meeting*, Industrial Relations Research Association, Madison, Wis., 1961.

Workweek, Average The number of weekly hours per factory worker for which pay has been received, including paid holidays, vacations, and sick leaves. In the U.S., workweek figures cover full-time and part-time production and related workers who receive payment for any part of the pay period ending nearest the fifteenth of the month. Because of the increasing amount of paid holidays, vacations, and sick leaves, the paid workweek exceeds the number of hours actually worked per week. The average-workweek series compiled from payroll data by the U.S. Bureau of Labor Statistics differs from the series of weekly hours actually worked that is compiled from household surveys by the U.S. Bureau of the Census. It also differs from the standard or scheduled workweek because such factors as absenteeism, part-time work, and stoppages make the average workweek lower than the standard workweek. The average workweek for all manufacturing reflects shifts in importance as well as changes in the workweek in component industries. The average workweek is a significant indicator of overall business activity, which the National Bureau of

Economic Research classifies as one of its many leading indicators. The workweek turns up or down more rapidly than employment because decisions about the length of the workweek are usually made by foremen who operate on a more flexible level than managements that determine

Workweek–All Manufacturing(Hours)

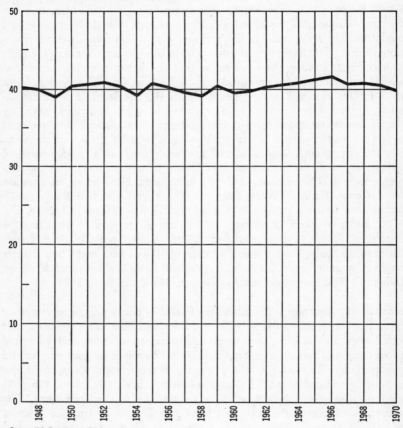

Source: U.S. Department of Labor.

shifts in hiring practices. For industry statistics and a more detailed explanation of the techniques of collection of workweek data, see U.S. Department of Labor, *Employment and Earnings,* monthly; for a discussion of the workweek as an indicator of turning points of business cycles, see R. C. Mendelssohn, "Three BLS Series as Business Cycle Turn Signals," *Monthly Labor Review,* U.S. Department of Labor, September, 1959;

Gerhard Bry, *The Average Workweek as an Economic Indicator,* National Bureau of Economic Research, Occasional Paper 69, New York, 1959.

Write-down   The partial reduction of the book value of an asset or assets to take account of the capital that has been irretrievably lost through the permanent decline in the asset's value. The effect of writing down assets subject to depreciation is to increase the profits of future periods to the extent that the depreciation expense is lowered in those periods. For further information, see J. F. Bradley, *Fundamentals of Corporation Finance,* Holt, Rinehart and Winston, Inc., New York, 1955, pp. 513–515.

Write-off   The act of removing an asset from the books of a company. The term write-off is related to write-down, but the latter is more closely associated with the partial reduction of the book value of the asset rather than with removing the asset from the books entirely. For information on accounting procedures in writing off fixed assets, see H. A. Finney and H. E. Miller, *Principles of Accounting,* 6th ed., Prentice-Hall, Inc., Englewood Cliffs, N.J., 1965.

Write-up   The process by which an asset's book value is increased to its present appraised value. Prior to 1940, this process was common in the U.S. and was accomplished by making an offsetting credit to capital surplus, appraisal surplus, or appreciation surplus. Some accountants objected to the term surplus as applied to these unrealized increments in value and preferred to use an account title, such as unrealized increment in valuation of fixed assets. In 1940 the American Institute of Certified Public Accountants' Committee on Accounting Procedure issued a bulletin containing the following statement: "Accounting for fixed assets should normally be based on cost, and any attempt to make property accounts in general reflect current values is both impracticable and inexpedient." Thus, the practice of writing up values is now considered an improper one, possibly leading to abuse and creating many problems in connection with property taxation and valuation bases for regulatory purposes.

Y

Yardstick A term applied in the U.S. to the electric power rates established by the government-owned and -financed corporation, the Tennessee Valley Authority (TVA). The low rates charged by this corporation were to serve as an experiment to learn if they would increase demand and income and to ascertain their effect on profits. It was hoped that such rates would induce privately owned electric companies to reduce their own rates. The TVA electric-rate yardstick has aroused a great deal of controversy. Some have pointed to the drastic revisions in utility rates that have taken place since 1933 as evidence of the effectiveness of such a yardstick policy. Others say that other factors account for the reduction of rates and that the use of TVA rates as a yardstick is not fair. They cite such things as the fact that TVA pays no interest but that such costs are borne instead by the taxpayer. The government-owned corporation also pays a smaller amount of taxes than private utilities do. For example, in 1947, TVA paid in lieu of taxes to local governments (to compensate for local tax losses caused by the project) about 4% of its total revenues, whereas private companies paid taxes totaling about 19% of revenues. Both taxes and interest are costs of production. Thus, it has been argued by some that TVA rates serve as a somewhat shortened yardstick and that they would have to be doubled if TVA were required to compete on an equal basis with private utilities. For a statement of the argument, see "Does the TVA Constitute a True Yardstick?" *Edison Electric Institute Bulletin*, New York, March, 1935, pp. 77–80; see also David E. Lilienthal, *T.V.A.: Democracy on the March*, Harper & Row, Publishers, Incorporated, New York, 1953.

Yield The percentage that is derived from dividing the annual return from any investment by the amount of the investment. For instance, a $10,000 investment in common stocks that pays $500 in annual dividends yields 5%. Similarly, a bond purchased for $1,000 that returns $40 a year yields 4%. The term yield is used to describe the rate of return on any investment. Current yield is a somewhat similar term that means the percentage derived from dividing the annual return from an investment by the current cost of that investment. For example, if a person buys a piece of real estate for $20,000 that returns $2,000 a year, his yield is 10%. If, however, it now costs $30,000 to buy this piece of real estate and there has been no change in the amount of the return, the current yield is 6.7%. For statistics on the yields on various securities investments, see *Federal Reserve Bulletin,* Washington, D.C., monthly; U.S. Securities and Exchange Commission, *Monthly Statistics Bulletin;* for additional details, see T. M. Simpson et al., *Mathematics of Finance,* 3d ed., Prentice-Hall, Inc., Englewood Cliffs, N.J., 1951; see also *Yield and Interest Tables: Bonds and Stocks,* Financial Publishing Company, Boston, 1938.

Part 2

ORGANIZATIONS

Advertising Research Foundation (ARF) A nonprofit organization composed primarily of U.S. advertisers, advertising agencies, and advertising media. Its basic purpose is to further scientific practices and promote greater effectiveness in advertising and marketing through objective and impartial research. ARF seeks to develop new research methods and techniques, analyze existing techniques and define their proper applications and limitations, and establish research standards and criteria. As a specific aid to accomplishing these objectives, the foundation offers consultative and professional guidance for the conduct of research studies, supervises the technical aspects of advertising-research projects, and appraises published research studies. It also collects and disseminates data on advertising and marketing. Created in 1936 under the sponsorship of the American Association of Advertising Agencies and the Association of National Advertisers, both of which continue to support the ARF as founder members, the foundation is governed by a board of directors, the composition of which gives equal representation to advertisers, advertising agencies, and advertising media. Membership is composed of more than 400 organizations. The ARF is supported primarily by leading U.S. advertisers, agencies, and media organizations, but academic institutions, research organizations, advertisers, agencies, and media located outside the U.S. participate as associate members. Annual conferences of the ARF provide a meeting place where advertising and marketing people may obtain information about new developments and ideas in advertising and marketing research. The ARF has issued and released to its members more than 300 reports and papers, including recommended standards for research techniques, directories, bibliographies, and comprehensive reports based on thousands of interviews. It also publishes a bimonthly *Journal of Advertising Research*. ARF headquarters are located at 3 East 54th Street, New York, N.Y. 10022.

Advisory Committee on Labor-Management Policy A U.S. committee whose purpose is to make recommendations on policies to "promote free and responsible collective bargaining, industrial peace, sound wage and price policies, higher standards of living, and increased productivity." Created by an executive order issued by President John F. Kennedy on February 16, 1961, it consists of twenty-one members, seven of whom represent management, seven labor, and seven (including two Cabinet members) the public. The Committee provides a place at which union leaders and employers can discuss their problems and the effects of their actions on the national economy without the bitterness that may arise at the bargaining table. It studies general issues and problems and avoids involvement in specific labor negotiations. Since its establishment, the Committee has issued various reports concerning unemployment and automation. For its report on automation, see U.S. Department of Labor, *Monthly Labor Review*, Washington, D.C., February, 1962, pp. 139–144.

Agency for International Development (AID)   An agency of the U.S. Department of State which administers economic aid under the U.S. foreign assistance program (military assistance is administered by the Department of Defense). Created by the Foreign Assistance Act of September, 1961, AID combines the functions of the International Cooperation Administration and the Development Loan Fund and certain local-currency lending activities of the Export-Import Bank of Washington. The broad purpose of U.S. foreign assistance is to help other countries maintain their independence and achieve economic progress and political stability under increasingly free and democratic institutions. Under the Marshall Plan, which ended in 1952, 89% of U.S. foreign aid was in the form of grants, but loans have become much more important in recent years, averaging 52% of total AID assistance during the period 1962–1969. As a share of gross national product, U.S. economic assistance through AID has declined from 2.1% during 1949, the first full year of the Marshall Plan, to only 0.16% in the fiscal year 1969. Economic assistance is extended mainly in the form of commodities (99% of which are obtained in the U.S.), technical services by U.S. experts, and training, in the U.S. or other countries, of foreign nationals. Although some fifty-six countries received AID funds in 1969, 87% of the amounts programmed for countries were concentrated in only fifteen nations considered best able to use it. A record commitment of $45 million was made during 1969 on a high-priority basis to family-planning and population programs in twenty-nine countries and to other countries through support of international organizations working in the population field. Recognizing that private enterprise must play an important role in the economic progress of nations overseas, AID encourages and promotes overseas investment opportunities for the U.S. business community and helps develop private enterprise within the countries aided. Assistance to U.S. investors is extended through (1) dollar loans for well-conceived investments for which financing is not available on reasonable terms from other sources, (2) local-currency (Cooley) loans of proceeds from the sale of U.S. agricultural commodities, (3) investment surveys, and (4) investment guarantees. Publications of AID include *U.S. Foreign Assistance,* an annual statistical compilation; *Operations Report,* semiannually; *Annual Report.*

Agricultural Marketing Service (AMS)   An agency of the U.S. Department of Agriculture which operates under a broad mandate to service the marketing of farm products. The AMS deals with both the physical and the economic aspects of marketing, providing services, research, and regulation to help get the products of U.S. farms to consumers in the best possible condition and in the most efficient and least costly manner. Many of these services are furnished in cooperation with state departments of agriculture or other state and local agencies. AMS services may be grouped in five major categories:

1. *Facilities services* (standards, grading, inspection, and market news) to help the nation's marketing machinery run as smoothly and as efficiently as possible.
2. *Marketing research* to obtain practical answers to marketing problems, such as ways of holding down marketing costs, means of reducing waste and spoilage, improved ways of handling, storing, and transporting farm products, and improved means of measuring and protecting quality.
3. *Regulation* by means of Federal laws designed to preserve fair play and free and open competition in the marketplace, assure safe storage of farm products, and prevent misrepresentation.
4. *Food distribution* to expand markets for farm products and help share the nation's abundance with the undernourished and the underprivileged.
5. *Other related services* to strengthen farmers' bargaining power through such programs as marketing agreements and orders, surplus removal (mainly for perishable products), and acreage-marketing guides (containing advice on amounts to plant); help obtain fair and reasonable transportation rates and services for farmers and shippers; and aid states in establishing useful marketing programs and services. The AMS originated with the Office of Markets in May, 1913.

Major AMS publications include *Agricultural Marketing,* monthly; *Checklist of AMS Publications; USDA's Agricultural Marketing Service . . . What It is . . . What It Does?,* PA–513, monthly; *Services for You . . . from USDA's Agricultural Marketing Service,* PA–570.

Air Transport Association of America (ATA)   An organization whose primary purpose is the betterment of the U.S. airline business. In general, it does everything in its power to serve the interests and welfare of its members and the public at large. The Air Transport Association was formed in January, 1936, when seventeen airlines met in Chicago and drew up a set of objectives. As of 1970, membership stood at thirty-two scheduled airlines. These airlines are classified as domestic trunk lines, which operate between the major traffic centers within the U.S.; domestic local-service lines, which connect smaller traffic points with one another and with the major centers served by the trunk lines; international and overseas lines, which operate between the U.S. and other countries; intra-Hawaii and intra-Alaska lines, which operate between points in the two new states; helicopter lines, which connect post offices, suburbs, and airports in the metropolitan centers of Los Angeles, New York, and Chicago; and all-cargo lines, which carry freight in regularly scheduled service between points in the U.S. and between the U.S. and Europe and the Caribbean area. The ATA unifies the various interests of these groups and provides a "bank" for the deposit of the combined knowledge and experience of all U.S. scheduled airlines, particularly in the safety field. The major publications of the ATA are *Facts and Figures,* an annual review of the air-transport year, and *Orientation and Destination of Airline Traffic Survey,* published quarterly. *Facts and Figures* is free; the other publication is available through the ATA at a charge. ATA headquarters are located at 1000 Connecticut Avenue, N.W., Washington, D.C. 20036.

Alliance for Progress   Originally planned as a ten-year cooperative effort of twenty of the American republics to accelerate the economic and social development of the participating countries of Latin America. Its objectives and machinery were outlined in the Charter of Punta del Este, signed on August 17, 1961, by ministerial representatives of the twenty American republics, who had been called together in a special meeting of the Inter-American Economic and Social Council. Cuba attended the meeting but did not sign the Charter. (In 1965 the U.S. extended its commitment for as long as necessary to meet the Charter's goals.) The Alliance, which grew out of the Operation Panamerica proposed in 1958 by President Juscelino Kubitschek of Brazil, actually resulted from a speech made by President John F. Kennedy to Latin American diplomats at the White House on March 13, 1961. The Charter of Punta del Este called for a substantial and sustained growth of per capita income capable of assuring self-sustaining development for the Latin American nations. It was estimated that this would involve an annual rate of economic growth of not less than 2.5%. Others of the Charter's twelve fundamental goals are more equitable distribution of national income, balanced diversification of national economic structures, acceleration of the process of rational industrialization, a raising of the levels of agricultural productivity, encouragement of programs of comprehensive agrarian reform, elimination of adult illiteracy, a minimum increase of five years in life expectancy, increases in the construction of low-cost houses, maintenance of stable price levels, strengthening of existing agreements on economic integration, and development of cooperative programs to prevent excessive fluctuations in exchange earnings from exports. The Charter estimated that the achievement of these goals would require $20 billion in external assistance over the ten-year period. Latin America itself was expected to supply 80% of the total resources needed. The U.S. declared in the Charter that it would provide "the major share" of the $20 billion in external assistance, chiefly in public funds. It was hoped that private U.S. investment over the ten years would total $3 billion; the rest of the estimated $20 billion in external funds would be contributed by international credit institutions and public and private investments of other industrialized nations. The machinery of the Alliance is based on the preparation of national development plans by each of the Latin American nations. These plans can be reviewed by a committee of nine economists established within the Organization of American States (OAS). Once the committee has approved them, the plans can be submitted for external financing to interested governments and international agencies. The bulk of U.S. assistance for the achievement of the goals of the Alliance is administered by the Bureau for Latin America of the Agency for International Development (AID). Other U.S. agencies whose credits support the achievement of the goals of the Alliance include the Export-Import Bank of Washington, Food for Peace, and the Peace Corps. The Inter-American Development Bank, besides its regular resources, administers the Social Progress Trust Fund, which is entirely supplied by the U.S. AID, and other U.S. agencies issue press releases on their work. An annual meeting of the participating nations, at which progress during the previous year is analyzed, produces detailed documents that are available through the OAS.

American Association for the Advancement of Science (AAAS) The general U.S. scientific society interested in the advancement of the physical, biological, and social sciences. Its activities are devoted largely to matters that concern several different disciplines or the whole scientific community. Its membership totals 128,000. Nearly all the state and regional academies of science and 260 national or regional scientific and professional societies are affiliates of the AAAS. The aims of the association are to further the work of scientists, facilitate cooperation among them, improve the effectiveness of science in the promotion of human welfare, and increase public understanding and appreciation of the

importance and promise of scientific methods in human progress. The AAAS publishes the weekly magazine *Science,* a quarterly bulletin, a quarterly newsletter dealing with the problems in science education, and a series of technical symposia. AAAS headquarters are located at 1515 Massachusetts Avenue, N.W., Washington, D.C. 20005.

American Bankers Association (ABA)　An organization whose purpose is to promote the usefulness of U.S. banks. In meeting the needs of banking, the activities of the association have been constantly changing and expanding to reflect the development of new services available from banks, new techniques in bank operations, problems of administration and management, and relationships between banks and the public, the government, and other components of the economy. Working groups of the association include national bank, state bank, savings, and trust divisions; a state association section; the American Institute of Banking section; twenty-four standing committees; and numerous subcommittees, commissions, departments, and special-service groups. Each of these groups specializes in its field, issuing studies, reports, and informative bulletins and holding meetings throughout the nation to permit the exchange of information and ideas among members. The ABA was organized in 1875 at a meeting of bankers in the town hall at Saratoga Springs, New York. Its membership represents more than 97% of the state and national banks in the U.S. At the close of the association year 1969, its total membership comprised 18,503 banks and branches, including 128 members in other countries. The governing body of the ABA is its annual convention, which is held every autumn. Between conventions, an executive council is in charge of association affairs, and between meetings of the council control is vested in an administrative committee. Day-to-day activities and coordination of the working groups are carried on by a permanent staff at the national headquarters. For many years, the ABA has emphasized the importance of educational programs for bank personnel. Its American Institute of Banking offers courses through chapters and study groups in 570 cities and towns and by correspondence throughout the nation. With a membership of 218,483 and 100,132 students enrolled in its classes, it is one of the world's largest adult education organizations. Specialized and graduate-level bankers schools include the Stonier Graduate School of Banking at Rutgers University, the National Trust School at Northwestern University, the National Automation School at Purdue University, the National Commercial Lending School at the University of Oklahoma, the National Mortgage School at Ohio State University, and the National Instalment Credit School at the University of Oklahoma; various personnel courses are also offered. All these educational activities are coordinated by a banking education committee. Besides the reports of the working groups that are issued as the need arises, the association publishes the monthly *Banking Magazine* as its official journal. It also publishes specialized periodicals, such as the AIB *Bulletin* and the *Protective Bulletin*. ABA national headquarters are located at 90 Park Avenue, New York, N.Y., 10016; its Washington office is at 815 Connecticut Avenue, N.W., Washington, D.C. 20006.

American Book Publishers Council, Inc. The trade association of general book publishers in the U.S. The 180 companies making up its membership produce 95% of all general books published in the country. The council's purposes are (1) to foster, develop, and improve trade conditions in the book-publishing industry through research and study of increased outlets for books; (2) to report to the industry on trends and changes with respect to book publications, copyrights, and other matters of general importance to those engaged in publishing and generally to report to its members on the greater dissemination of knowledge and increasing demand for reading and for books; (3) to serve as a medium for the interchange of ideas with respect to publication, sale, copyright, and other matters of interest to book publishers in the U.S. and other countries and to other persons engaged in the production and distribution of copyrightable material; and (4) to aid members with respect to insurance plans and to supply information regarding credit, taxes, postage, freight, and other matters pertinent to the publishing industry. Management of the council's affairs is vested in a fifteen-member board of directors and an executive committee. The council maintains liaison with other associations serving the book industry, with the National Book Committee, with the American Library Association, and with many professional educational organizations. It is a member of the International Publishers Association. The council was organized in 1946 as an outgrowth of the Council on Books in Wartime, which functioned during World War II. Its headquarters are located at 1 Park Avenue, New York, N.Y. 10016.

American Bureau of Metal Statistics A nonprofit statistical bureau sponsored by the most important producers of copper, lead, and zinc in the U.S., Canada, Mexico, Chile, and Peru. While the bureau is not connected in any way with the U.S. government, there is constant and close cooperation with government departments with mutual benefit. The bureau was formed in 1920. Its chief activity is the collection and publication of statistics on the principal nonferrous metals. The data thus compiled, which are published in the bureau's *Year Book*, provide voluminous statistical information for market analysis, research, and industry surveys. The *Year Book* is available by purchase only. In addition, the Bureau issues monthly and quarterly reports on a subscription-fee basis. Its headquarters are located at 50 Broadway, New York, N.Y. 10004.

American Business Press, Inc. (ABP) A trade association representing the publishers of specialized industrial, business, professional, and trade publications and newspapers. Originally founded in 1906 as the Federation of Trade Press Associations, it was created by the merger of Associated Business Publications and National Business Publications in 1965. It exists today as the only association representing publishers of independent, tax-paying business periodicals. It is dedicated to the advancement of better business communication and better publishing management. The ABP is the united voice of business publishing in Washington and on the campus. Through its Business Press Advertising Bureau it seeks to further business-publication advertising effectiveness, to foster more extensive use of business-publication advertising, and to help member publishers' salesmen sell. As of March, 1970, ABP membership totaled 110 companies publishing a total of 527 audited business publications. Its headquarters are located at 205 East 42d Street, New York, N.Y. 10017.

American Economic Association An organization of persons interested in the study of economics or the economic aspects of political and social questions. The association was organized in 1885 at Saratoga, New York. From then until about 1910, its membership was confined largely to college and university teachers of economics, but with the growing general interest in the subject of economics after the turn of the century, it began to attract an increasing number of members from business and professional groups. Membership now exceeds 19,000 individuals, plus 7,000 subscribers. The three major purposes of the association are (1) the encouragement of economic research, especially the historical and statistical study of the actual conditions of industrial life; (2) the issuance of publications on economic subjects; and (3) the encouragement of perfect freedom of economic discussion. The association as such takes no partisan attitude, nor does it commit its members to any position on practical economic questions. Its publications are the *American Economic Review* (first published in 1911), including the *Papers and Proceedings* of the annual meetings, and the *Journal of Economic Literature*. The *Review* contains several lead articles, communications, and notes. The *Journal* contains original articles, book reviews, and bibliographical listings, as well as abstracts of articles from other economics periodicals. In addition, occasional monographs on economic subjects are issued as supplements to the *Review*. In cooperation with Richard D. Irwin, Inc., the association sponsors the publication of a series of volumes of republished articles in selected fields. The association's headquarters are located at 629 Noyes Street, Evanston, Ill. 60201.

American Economic Foundation A publicly supported educational organization, founded in 1939, for semantic research in the area of economic communications with emphasis on the correction of popular misunderstandings regarding the basic factors of production and the allocation of resulting income between those factors. The procedure is to reduce elemental economic ignorance and establish a common arithmetical base for realistic collective bargaining. The work is unique because the vocabulary is unique. The foundation's best-known publications are the economic primer *How We Live* and its summary, *The Ten Pillars of Economic Wisdom.* From these has sprung a substantial body of educational material consisting of books, pamphlets, editorials, films, and visual aids for use in employee communications, in teacher seminars, in group discussions, and with the general public under the title "The Do-It-Yourself Program of Economic Self-Education." The foundation's headquarters are located at 51 East 42d Street, New York, N.Y. 10017.

American Farm Bureau Federation An independent, nongovernmental, voluntary organization of U.S. farm and ranch families united for the purpose of analyzing their problems and formulating action to achieve educational improvement, economic opportunity, and social advancement, thereby promoting the national welfare. The Farm Bureau is local, statewide, national, and international in scope and influence and is nonpartisan, nonsectarian, and nonsecret in character. The Farm Bureau movement grew out of an attempt to improve agricultural income through the use of better farming methods. Between 1911 and 1918, several state land-grant colleges sent county agents who were trained agriculturists to work with farmers in seeking to improve their methods of raising crops and livestock. After the passage of the Smith-Lever Act by Congress in 1914, the work was aided by Federal and state funds. At the end of World War I, county farm bureaus in several states set up state organizations. Then in March, 1920, representatives of 28 state farm bureaus met in Chicago and formed the American Farm Bureau Federation. By December, 1969, it had 1,865,854 member families in 49 states (excluding Alaska) and Puerto Rico. It is financed by membership dues, and membership is on a family basis. There are more than 2,800 organized county farm bureaus; within a state, they are typically federated to form a state farm bureau. Individual farm-family members, through study and discussion, evolve the policies and programs which they wish to support through their local, county, state, and national organizations. During the depression of the 1930s, the Farm Bureau played an important part in developing emergency legislation which emphasized soil-conservation programs, acreage-control legislation, and price-support loans for certain farm commodities. Since World War II, the Farm Bureau has sought changes in national farm legislation that would place greater reliance on the market-price system in achieving a balance between production and demand. The Farm Bureau has an extensive commodity program concerned with the specific commodity problems of its members. It employs research and promotion to increase the use of foods, promote the extension of animal agriculture, and increase the use of farm products in industry. Services to members include fire, automobile, general farm liability, and life insurance. In addition, cooperative purchasing of farm supplies and cooperative marketing are important services in many states. The American Farm Bureau Federation publishes a weekly newsletter for leaders and a monthly magazine, the *Nation's Agriculture*, which is circulated to each member farm family. National headquarters are located at Merchandise Mart Plaza, Chicago, Ill. 60654.

American Federation of Labor–Congress of Industrial Organizations (AFL-CIO)

A federation of autonomous unions which does not engage directly in collective bargaining nor in the formulation of bargaining objectives but which develops and compiles general economic data for use by unions, serves as a clearinghouse of information, and prepares analyses of national economic affairs which it presents to Congress and the administration on behalf of the labor movement as a whole. The purposes of the AFL-CIO, as set forth in its constitution, are to advance generally the interests of workers and to promote the best interests of the nation. The AFL-CIO serves as the political and legislative arm of the labor movement on both a national and a state level. This does not, of course, preclude parallel or complementary operations by affiliated unions when they so desire. The AFL-CIO has also established standards with respect to ethical practices, racial equality, and jurisdictional questions which are binding on all affiliated unions. Failure to adhere to the ethical practices code caused the expulsion of three unions, including the International Brotherhood of Teamsters, in 1957. The power of the AFL-CIO to act on both jurisdictional and civil rights matters was materially strengthened at its 1961 convention. The federation was established in 1955 by a merger of the formerly separate AFL and CIO. The American Federation of Labor represented mostly craft unions; the Congress of Industrial Organizations, mostly industrial unions. The AFL-CIO comprises 120 affiliated national and international unions and some 18% directly affiliated local unions; the total membership is 13.6 million.

Structurally, the AFL-CIO includes 6 trade or industrial departments, 50 state central bodies, and more than 750 local central bodies. Major AFL-CIO publications are the weekly AFL-CIO *News* and the monthly *American Federationist,* which includes reports on economics, collective bargaining, and educational matters. AFL-CIO headquarters are located at 815 Sixteenth Street, N.W., Washington, D.C. 20006.

American Finance Association   A nonprofit U.S. professional society in the field of finance. It attempts to improve public understanding of financial problems, to provide for an exchange of financial ideas through the distribution of a periodical and other media, and to encourage the study of finance in colleges and universities. The association was organized informally in 1940 as a professional society in which financial theory could be tested against practice and practice against theory. Instrumental in its formation were economists and professors of finance who were interested in exchanging ideas and the results of research. Chartered as a corporation in 1952, the association is affiliated with the Economic and Allied Social Science Association. The association has more than 5,000 members and subscribers, who are either professors in colleges and universities or financial economists, bankers, treasurers, analysts, or other individuals interested in financial problems. The latter group represents more than 400 business concerns. The association is active in many areas of finance, particularly business finance, consumer finance, insurance, international finance, investment, money and banking, public finance, and real estate finance. Its publication is *Journal of Finance,* issued five times per year. The association's headquarters are located at the Graduate School of Business Administration, New York University, 100 Trinity Place, New York, N.Y. 10006.

American Gas Association   The national trade association of the U.S. natural-gas industry. Its activities include providing information on sales, finance, utilization, research, management, and safety; making available the consulting services of a staff of experts; developing operating standards and equipment specifications; promoting employee and public safety; conducting research and development programs; testing gas appliances at its Independence, Ohio, and Los Angeles laboratories; and conducting promotional campaigns and extensive advertising. Complete documentation on the industry is available in the association's library at headquarters. The association holds an annual convention and many regional and special conferences. It has a large program of publications, including AGA *Monthly, Proceedings* of the convention, *Gas Facts, Rate Service, Directory of Approved Appliances,* and newsletters, committee reports, promotional and publication informational bulletins, research reports, and technical manuals. The association was formed in 1918 by the merger of the American Gas Institute and the National Commercial Gas Association. It now has a membership of 6,000 companies and individuals and a staff of 320. Its members include distributors of natural gas, pipeline companies, and their employees. The association's headquarters are located at 1515 Wilson Boulevard, Arlington, Va. 22209; offices are also maintained in Hollywood, California.

American Iron and Steel Institute   A nonprofit organization of members of the iron and steel industry in the Western Hemisphere. It is dedicated to serving the industry by engaging in activities of common interest. The institute's principal purposes are (1) to promote the interests of the iron and steel industry or any part or branch thereof, (2) to collect statistics and other information concerning the industry, (3) to engage in investigation and research, (4) to provide a forum for the exchange of information and the discussion of problems relating to the industry, and (5) to promote the use of iron and steel. Recognizing the need for such activities, the ironmasters of the U.S. organized the American Iron Association in 1855. At the end of the Civil War, this association was reorganized, and its name was changed to American Iron and Steel Association. The American Iron and Steel Institute was organized in 1908, and in 1912 it took over the work of the association. The institute was created on a basis broader than that of either of its predecessor organizations. As of February, 1970, it had seventy-nine company members, of which nine were in Canada, sixty-five in the U.S., three in South America, and two in Mexico. There are also more than 2,600 individual members, of whom about 85% are present or past employees of company members of the institute. The institute publishes a periodical, *Steel Facts;* a *Yearbook;* an *Annual Statistical Report;* a *Directory of Iron and Steel Works of the United States and Canada;* numerous statistical reports; literature pertaining to steel products; and technical and engineering information. Its headquarters are located at 150 East 42d Street, New York, N.Y. 10017.

American Management Association (AMA)   A nonprofit educational organization dedicated to the advancement of management as a profession in the U.S. by developing an organized body of knowledge on the subject. It was organized in 1923 as an outgrowth of several predecessor organizations, including the National Personnel Association. By means of more than 1,100 meetings a year—conferences, seminars, and courses—the AMA performs as an informational clearinghouse for executives on the principles and methods of management. Meetings are held in eleven areas of management: general management, personnel, finance, administrative services, insurance, manufacturing, marketing, packaging, international management, purchasing, and research and development. In addition, the AMA issues numerous bulletins, reports, and research studies on management and publishes six well-known periodicals and services: *Personnel; Management Review;* the *Manager's Letter;* the *Management News; Supervisory Management;* the *Executive Compensation Service.* It also maintains an extensive library through which source materials are made available to its 32,000 members. The American Foundation for Management Research was established in 1960 by an initial grant from the American Management Association. The AMA makes no profit and does no lobbying. It is interested solely in the development of management as a profession and in keeping business leadership abreast of the times by a continual exchange of experience and ideas. Its headquarters are located at 135 West 50th Street, New York, N.Y. 10020; other offices and operations are located in Saranac Lake and Hamilton, N.Y.; San Francisco, Calif.; and Montreal, Canada. An affiliate, the International Management Association, operates in São Paulo, Brazil, and Brussels, Belgium.

American Marketing Association An organization of U.S. market researchers, marketing educators, and individuals engaged in marketing activities in business and government, the basic objective of which is the advancement of science marketing. The American Marketing Association, formed by a merger of the American Marketing Society and the National Association of Marketing Teachers on January 1, 1937, dates from 1915, with the establishment of the National Association of Advertising Teachers. It operated as a nonprofit, unincorporated association until June 22, 1951, when its members voted a change to the status of a nonprofit corporation incorporated in the state of Illinois, operating under the same name, American Marketing Association. At the time of the merger, the new organization had 600 members; by 1970 membership had grown to 18,000. In addition to membership in the national organization, 80% of the members also maintain membership in one of the association's chapters, of which there are fifty-three in the U.S. and four in Canada. The chapters offer a wide variety of programs, including conferences, seminars, workshops, and marketing game sessions. In addition, the national association conducts numerous seminars in specialized marketing problem areas, an annual membership conference, and a conference for marketing educators. It publishes two quarterly journals, books, monographs, and technical papers. The association's headquarters are located at 230 N. Michigan, Chicago, Ill. 60601.

American Mathematical Society A professional society devoted to the furtherance of pure and applied mathematics. It serves its membership by the publication of over 251 books and journals, by the provision of cataloging and indexing services, by the sponsorship of technical gatherings (meetings, symposia, institutes, and seminars), and by the cooperation with other similar organizations in joint projects. Journals published by the society include the *Transactions of the American Mathematical Society* and the *Proceedings of the American Mathematical Society*, both of which publish the results of original research; the *Bulletin of the American Mathematical Society*, which is the official journal of the society; *Mathematics of Computation*, which is devoted to advances in numerical analysis, the application of computational methods, mathematical tables, high-speed calculators, and other aids to computation; *Mathematical Reviews*, an abstracting and reviewing journal covering the world literature of mathematical research; three journals of Russian translations—*Soviet Mathematics—Doklady, Mathematics of the USSR—Sbornik*, and *Mathematics of the USSR—Izvestija*; and the *Notices of the American Mathematical Society*, which is the news journal of the society. The society also publishes *Contents of Contemporary Mathematical Journals*, which contains the tables of contents of about 240 mathematical journals, as part of the information services offered by the society. The *Mathematical Offprint Service*, another information service, offers a service to the mathematical community by providing offprints in all areas of mathematics which are of specific interest to the individual mathematician. The Society's headquarters are located at 321 South Main Street, Providence, R.I.; the mailing address is P.O. Box 6248, Providence, R.I. 02904.

American Paper Institute A permanent coordinating organization for the U.S. paper and pulp industry. Its objectives include public service through research, dissemination of pertinent information, elimination of discriminatory and unfair business practices, and promotion of integrity in advertising and other high ethical standards. The association was founded in 1878 under the name American Paper and Pulp Association. Its name was changed in 1969. Consisting of twelve divisional associations, each serving particular needs of producers of various grades or commodities of pulp and paper, it functions through an executive staff of specialists. To deal with overall industry problems and those relating to two or more divisions, the association has set up committees concerned with all matters of industry import, such as power and water resources, research coordination, technical developments, finances, international trade, public affairs, community relations, industrial relations, market research and classification, and definitions of pulp, paper, and paperboard products and terms. More than 300 experts in these and other fields participate in the deliberations of the committees. Association policy, however, is set by its executive committee and board of governors, based largely upon the conclusions reached by these groups. It has developed a comprehensive statistical program. Its periodical publications include *Monthly Statistical Summary, including Fact Sheet,* monthly; *Paper Production Ratio Report,* weekly; *Statistics of Paper,* annually; *Capacity Survey,* annually; *A Capital and Income Survey of the United States Paper Industry,* annually; *United States Paper Production, Imports, Exports and Consumption,* annually; *Imports of Wood Pulp by Grades and Country of Origin,* monthly. The association's headquarters are located at 122 East 42d Street, New York, N.Y. 10017; there is also a Washington office.

American Petroleum Institute   A trade association representative of the U.S. oil industry and all its segments. The institute's basic objectives are (1) to afford a means of cooperation with the government in all matters of national concern; (2) to foster foreign and domestic trade in American petroleum products; (3) to promote, in general, the interests of the petroleum industry in all its branches; and (4) to promote the mutual improvement of its members and the study of the arts and sciences connected with the petroleum industry. The activities of the institute lie mainly in the areas of production, transportation, refining, marketing, science and research, equipment and procedural standardization, and public and environmental affairs. The largest single budget item for each year has been for funds expended in research. All research is undertaken through colleges, universities, and other qualified agencies, and all findings and patents have been dedicated to the public. Created in 1919, the institute was an outgrowth of the National Petroleum War Service Committee, which coordinated the oil industry's efforts during World War I. The institute has approximately 7,500 individual members and 400 company members. It holds a large number of regional and national meetings each year, mostly of a scientific or technical nature. It tabulates and publishes statistical information, such as the *Weekly Statistical Bulletin* and *Petroleum Facts and Figures.* The institute's headquarters are located at 1271 Avenue of the Americas, New York, N.Y. 10020

American Psychological Association (APA)   An organization of qualified psychologists in the U.S., the purpose of which is to advance psychology as a science, as a profession, and as a means of promoting human welfare. It attempts to further these objectives by holding annual meetings, publishing psychological journals, and working toward improved standards of psychological training and service. The association was founded in 1892 and incorporated in 1925. In order to give recognition to the specialized interests of different psychologists, the APA includes twenty-nine divisions. Among them are the Division of General Psychology, Division of Evaluation and Measurement, Division of Personality and Social Psychology, the

Society for the Psychological Study of Social Issues, Division of Maturity and Old Age, Division of Consumer Psychology, and the Division of Philosophical Psychology. There are three classes of membership: associate, member, and fellow. APA headquarters are located at 1200 Seventeenth Street, N.W., Washington, D.C. 20036.

American Society for Quality Control (ASQC) An educational and scientific organization dedicated to the art and science of quality control and its application to industry and business. Its primary function in the field of education is the encouraging of colleges and other educational institutions to include courses in quality control, reliability, sampling, and any other statistical techniques in their curricula. In addition, it conducts courses and seminars throughout the U.S. and Canada and encourages meetings and conferences. Founded in 1946, the society now has a membership of more than 22,000, primarily centered in the North American continent but having members around the world. As an aid to industry and the general public, it publishes a monthly journal, *Quality Progress;* and a quarterly, *Journal of Quality Technology.* Jointly with the American Statistical Association, it publishes *Technometrics,* a quarterly journal for the physical, chemical, and engineering sciences. ASQC headquarters are located at 161 West Wisconsin Avenue, Milwaukee, Wis. 53203.

American Statistical Association A nonprofit U.S. professional organization whose objectives are to foster statistics and its application, promote unity and effectiveness of effort among all concerned with statistical problems, and increase the contribution of statistics to human welfare. The American Statistical Association, one of the oldest professional organizations in the U.S., was organized in 1839 in Boston. Since its founding, the methods of statistics have expanded to a point at which they pervade almost every field of human activity. They are essential to the vast compilation of data, the facts from which analyses, forecasts, and decisions are derived. The publications of the American Statistical Association are as follows:

Journal of the American Statistical Association, quarterly, published continuously since 1888. Virtually every major scientific advance in statistical methodology has been recorded in the *Journal,* which publishes material on both theoretical and applied aspects of statistics, including the application of statistical theories to new fields and problems.

American Statistician, the news magazine for the profession. Established in 1947, it appears five times yearly and carries articles of current interest in addition to news about the association's activities, meetings of other societies, conferences, international statistical activities, Federal statistical activities, etc. Both the *Journal* and the *American Statistician* are sent to members as part of the membership dues.

Technometrics, quarterly, a journal of statistics for the physical, chemical, and engineering sciences. Established in 1959, *Technometrics* is sponsored jointly by the American Statistical Association and the American Society for Quality Control. Members of the two societies may subscribe at a special-member rate.

Proceedings of the Business and Economic Statistics Section and *Proceedings of the Social Statistics Section* of the American Statistical Association, annually. These volumes contain the papers and discussions presented at the sessions of each section during the annual meeting of the association and are available at a special price to members of the association.

The association also publishes from time to time special monographs. In cooperation with the institute of Mathematical Statistics and the Biometric Society (Eastern North American Region), it has published a brochure, *Careers in Statistics*, which gives information on the educational requirements and opportunities for careers in statistics and is designed for high school seniors, college undergraduates, teachers, vocational-guidance counselors, etc. This brochure is available free from the American Statistical Association. The association's headquarters are located at Suite 640, 806 Fifteenth Street, N.W., Washington, D.C. 20005.

American Trucking Associations, Inc. (ATA) The national federation of the organized U.S. trucking industry. It comprises fifty-one state trucking associations (including the District of Columbia) and twelve independent and autonomous conferences, each representing a special class or type of truck operation. The federation and its state affiliates bear full responsibility for national policies, national planning, and national activities in connection with all matters of interest or concern to the trucking industry in general. These common interests include taxation; safety; equipment and maintenance; sizes and weights; municipal, county, state, and Federal regulations and controls; highways and related problems; and public appreciation of and good will toward trucks and trucking service. ATA was formed at Chicago in 1933 as the result of a merger of the American Highway Freight Association and the Federated Truck Associations of America. The rapid growth of the motor-carrier industry had made it clear to the operators that a single, effective organization, nationwide in scope, was needed, and the movement toward national federation was further spurred by Federal regulation of trucking operations. First came the National Recovery Administration's Code of Fair Competition, in 1933, and two years later the passage of the Motor Carrier Act, which brought highway transport under the jurisdiction of the Interstate Commerce Commission. The official publication of ATA is *Transport Topics*, a weekly tabloid-sized newspaper. ATA headquarters are located at 1616 P Street, N.W., Washington, D.C. 20036.

Association for Computing Machinery   An organization of individuals and firms in the U.S. that are interested in information processing. Its purposes are to advance the sciences and arts of information processing, including the study, design, development, construction, and application of modern machinery-computing techniques and appropriate languages for general information processing, for scientific computation, for the recognition, storage, retrieval, and processing of data of all kinds, and for the automatic control and simulation of processes; and to promote the free interchange of information about the sciences and arts of information processing among specialists and the public in the best scientific and professional tradition. The association was founded in 1947. Its publications are *Journal of the Association for Computing Machinery*, quarterly, devoted to research papers; *Communications of the ACM*, monthly, devoted to reports of work in progress and topics of immediate interest; *Computing Reviews*, bimonthly, devoted to critical reviews of books and papers in the computing field. The association's headquarters are located at 211 East 43d Street, New York, N.Y. 10017.

Automobile Manufacturers Association (AMA)   An organization of the major U.S. manufacturers of passenger cars, motor trucks, and motor coaches. Its three basic functions are (1) the maintenance of services that can be more efficiently or effectively rendered on an industrywide basis than on a company basis; (2) the collection of factual information on the manufacture, distribution, and use of motor vehicles and the widespread dissemination of such information; and (3) cooperative activity with other industrial, social, and governmental groups in reaching solutions in the public interest for public problems arising from the manufacture and use of passenger cars and commercial vehicles. One of the world's most complete libraries on automotive subjects is maintained by the AMA in Detroit and serves as a constant and accurate source of automotive information for AMA members, researchers, authors, and representatives of news media. The AMA has fostered motor vehicle safety, improved highways, parts standardization, patent cross-licensing, and other developments aimed primarily at helping the industry and highway transportation to serve the nation. It has been instrumental in establishing and supporting such organizations as the Automotive Safety

Foundation, the Society of Automotive Engineers, the National Safety Council, and the National Highway Users Conference. The present association was established in 1913 by a merger of the Automobile Board of Trade and the National Association of Automobile Manufacturers. It called itself the National Automobile Chamber of Commerce until 1934, when the present name was adopted. The majority of AMA publications are single editions and consist chiefly of informational booklets or research studies. There are two annual statistical handbooks, *Automobile Facts and Figures and Motor Truck Facts;* and a quarterly magazine, *Automotive Safety.* The AMA main headquarters are located at 320 New Center Building, Detroit, Mich. 48202. There are also branches at 366 Madison Avenue, New York, N.Y. 10017 and 1710 H Street, N.W., Washington, D.C. 20036.

B

Bank for International Settlements (BIS) A company *sui generis* whose objectives are to promote the cooperation of central banks, provide additional facilities for international financial operations, and act as a trustee or agent in international financial settlements that are entrusted to it under agreements with the parties concerned. The BIS was founded in 1930 in execution of the Hague Agreements. Its authorized capital amounts to 1,500 million Swiss gold francs. This capital is divided into 600,000 shares with a nominal value of 2,500 gold francs each, of which 448,325 shares, paid up to the extent of one quarter, have been issued. About four-fifths of these shares are owned by central banks (in the main European central banks), and about one-fifth by private individuals. Privately held shares can be transferred only with the agreement of the BIS and the consent of the central bank concerned. The general meeting is composed of the central banks of the countries in which the shares were issued. The rights of representation and of voting are completely independent of the ownership of shares. The administration of the bank is vested in its board of directors, which consists of eight governors of

European central banks and five other members. The board elects a president and appoints a general manager and the other members of the management. In order to enable the BIS to carry out its international functions, it was granted certain immunities under its Constituent Charter, the Hague Agreements of 1930, and the Brussels Protocol of 1936. It is exempt from all Swiss taxes on its capital, reserves, or profits. In addition, the bank, its property, and the assets entrusted to it are immune from expropriation, requisition, restrictions on the export or import of gold or currencies, and other similar measures. The extent of the bank's operations has grown considerably. On March 31, 1969, its balance-sheet total amounted to 14,643 million gold francs. A priority dividend of up to 6% per annum is payable, and a maximum further dividend of 3% may be paid. The bank performs a fourfold task. First, it is a bank, its operations being carried out mainly with central banks. Second, it is an agent or trustee in connection with international financial settlements. Third, the bank serves as a meeting place for the governors of central banks, especially European central banks. Finally, the BIS is a center for research and information on economic and monetary matters. The best-known example of this part of the bank's work is its Annual Report. The bank also prepares numerous other documents, mainly for distribution to central banks. Its headquarters are located in Basel, Switzerland.

Battelle Memorial Institute (Columbus Laboratories)   An independent research organization whose economists carry out contract research for sponsors in industry and government in a wide range of technical and socioeconomic areas. Research in business strategy related to changing technology embraces technological forecasting, market and product planning, diversification and expansion, economic feasibility of new products or processes, long-range planning, plant location, searches for new products, utilization of raw materials and by-products, transportation and distribution analyses, and economic simulation modeling. Most of the technical economists have an educational background and experience in business and economics with prior training in different technical fields. Computer simulation models, relevance trees, economic models, and other techniques are applied as appropriate to sponsors' needs. In socioeconomic research, Battelle's methodology ranges from econometrics and mathematical economics to "soft" approaches such as urban land-use planning. Research for sponsoring groups (the Federal government, state and regional organizations, and local governments and community action agencies) ranges from macro input-output analyses for developed economies; through intermediate analyses, such as the benefits and costs of regional environmental control; to the micro, such as the evaluation of a multichurch-sponsored center for ecumenical renewal and planning.

A major group-sponsored study involving input-output methodology has been under way at Battelle since 1964. Called "Aids to Corporate Thinking," this program is aimed at projecting—to 1985—the economies of the United States, the United Kingdom, and each of the Common Market countries. A distinctive feature of economic research at Battelle is the use of interdisciplinary research teams, combining the skills of economists with those of the scientific and engineering staff. Its Columbus Laboratories are located at 505 King Avenue, Columbus, Ohio 43201.

Benelux An economic union of Belgium, the Netherlands, and Luxembourg, the objective of which is to bring about a full merger of the economies of the three nations. Plans were originally made in 1944, by their governments-in-exile in London, to establish an economic union once World War II was over. A Belgium-Luxembourg Economic Union had been in existence since 1923. In the years immediately following the war, however, numerous difficulties hindered the establishment of a union of the three countries. The first step was finally taken on January 1, 1948, when they established a customs union with a uniform tariff for all goods reecived from other countries and abolished all duties among themselves. This union was one of the first notable steps toward economic integration in Europe, leading eventually to the European Common Market, which now includes the three Benelux countries. Although the members of Benelux have made great progress toward economic unification, the free movement of labor, coordination of social security programs, and standardization of postal and transportation rates, they have not as yet achieved their goal of total internal unity. They have found it difficult to coordinate national finance and commerce, with the result that 20% of internal trade is still subject to tariffs. There are also wide differences in excise taxes. The Benelux case illustrates the many difficulties that arise when an attempt is made to remove national trade barriers which have existed for many years. For further information, see Raymond F. Mikesell, "Lessons of Benelux and the European Coal and Steel Community for the European Economic Community," *American Economic Review*, vol. XLVIII, no. 2, American Economic Association, Evanston, Ill., May, 1958; J. E. Meade, *Negotiations for Benelux: An Annotated Chronicle, 1943–1956*, Princeton Studies in International Finance, no. 6, Princeton University Press, Princeton, N.J., 1957; ———, "Benelux: The formation of the Common Customs," *Economica*, London School of Economics and Political Science, London, August, 1956.

Board of Governors of the Federal Reserve System A policy-making and supervisory agency of the Federal Reserve System of the U.S. The seven members of the Board are appointed to fourteen-year terms by the

President with Senate confirmation. The Board determines general monetary, credit, and operating policies for the System as a whole and formulates the rules and regulations necessary to carry out the purposes of the Federal Reserve Act. It sets reserve requirements, margin requirements, and the maximum rates of interest that member banks can pay on deposits, and it reviews and determines the discount rates set by the district banks. The Board has broad supervisory powers with respect to Federal Reserve banks and member banks. It acts as the chief spokesman for the Federal Reserve System, which it represents in most of its dealings with other governmental and congressional agencies. For further information, see *The Federal Reserve System: Purposes and Functions,* 1963.

Board of Trade A Department of the British government responsible for the promotion and regulation of trade and commerce. It is a committee of the Privy Council and has been in existence since 1766. The Board was reorganized in 1969, and its functions now cover overseas commercial relations and export promotion, consumer protection, aviation, and shipping, as well as the sponsorship of service industries, distributive trades, newspapers, and publishing. Its statistics division prepares reports and analyses of overseas trade and other economic statistics. It compiles index numbers of the volume and unit values of exports and imports; collects data on, and prepares indices of, wholesale prices; and prepares and publishes statistics relating to shipping, civil aviation, tourism, retail trade and consumer debt, and stocks and capital expenditures (actual and forecast) of the distributive and service trades, as well as statistics and information on overseas investment and items in the invisible account of the balance of payments, the financial accounts of companies, etc. Through the Business Statistics Office it also collects and issues the results of the censuses of production and the quinquennial censuses of distribution and the annual inquiries into the service and distributive trades, and it collects many statistics issued in the Business Monitor series. For further information on available economic statistics, see reports of the British Information Service, 845 Third Avenue, New York, N.Y. 10022.

Brookings Institution A nonprofit organization of the U.S. that is devoted to nonpartisan research, education, and publications in economics, government, foreign policy, and the social sciences generally. Its research role is that of independent analyst and critic, committed to publishing its findings for the information of the public. In its conferences and other activities, its function is to serve as a bridge between the academic community and leaders in public and private affairs by bringing new knowledge to the attention of decision makers and affording scholars a practical insight into policy issues. The institution was incorporated on December

8, 1927, to merge the activities of three antecedent organizations: the Institute for Government Research, founded in 1916; the Institute of Economics, established in 1922; and the Robert Brookings Graduate School of Economics and Government, organized in 1924. The consolidated organization was named in honor of Robert Somers Brookings (1850–1932), a St. Louis businessman whose leadership was central in the development of the earlier institutions. Brookings is maintained largely by endowment and by private support. Its work is carried out by three research programs, a publications program, a computer center, and an advanced-study program which conducts educational conferences and other activities for government officials and for executives from business, labor, and the professions. As a national center for the study of public problems, the institution conducts a variety of activities which foster research. Specialists in and out of government are brought together to explore research needs in special problem areas. Research fellowships for advanced graduate students are awarded for study at Brookings, and research professorships are granted to teachers of economics or business in liberal arts colleges. Guest appointments are extended to visiting scholars, and conference facilities are made available to members of other nonprofit organizations devoted to education and research. The institution's publications, on a continuing basis, are the *Annual Report* and a quarterly *Bulletin*. Recent Brookings books are Dankwart A. Rustow, *A World of Nations: Problems of Political Modernization*, 1967; Ruth B. Russell, *The United Nations and United States Security Policy*, 1968; Ernest H. Preeg, *Traders and Diplomats*, 1970; Kermit Gordon (ed.), *Agenda for the Nation*, 1968; James L. Sundquist, *Politics and Policy: The Eisenhower, Kennedy and Johnson Years*, 1969; Richard E. Caves and Associates, *Britain's Economic Prospects*, 1968; Joseph A. Pechman, Henry J. Aaron, and Michael K. Taussig, *Social Security: Perspectives for Reform*, 1968; Charles L. Schultze, *The Politics and Economics of Public Spending*, 1969; Arthur N. Okun, *The Political Economy of Prosperity*, 1970. The institution's headquarters are at 1775 Massachusetts Avenue, N.W., Washington, D.C. 20036.

Bureau of the Census   A bureau of the Social and Economic Statistics Administration of the U.S. Department of Commerce. It conducts censuses of population and housing every ten years and of agriculture, business, governments, manufacturers, mineral industries, and transportation at five-year intervals. Its sample surveys determine current trends in many fields, including population and housing characteristics, construction activity, retail and wholesale sales and service receipts, manufacturing, and governments. In addition, it compiles detailed statistics on U.S. foreign trade from import and export firms. The Bureau collects and processes data for other government agencies and makes special tabulations of its data for many users. A decennial census of the population, required by the U.S. Constitution as a basis for the allocation of representatives in Congress, has been taken by the Federal government since 1790. U.S. marshals (reporting to the President in the first census and to the Secretary of State in the next five censuses) and their assistants were early enumerators; specially appointed supervisors, who chose enumerators, first served in 1880. A temporary organization was set up for each census from 1790 to 1900. In 1902, Congress established the first permanent Census Office, making it possible to collect data in the decennial interim. Even the first census in 1790 was not a simple head count; data on the age of men provided a measure of military and labor resources. When census takers were directed by Congress, in the 1840 census act, to collect "all such information in relation to mines, agriculture, commerce, manufactures, and schools, as will exhibit a full view of the pursuits, industry, education, and resources of the country," the U.S. Census took a major step toward its broad role of fact finder for the nation. The Bureau of the Census issues reports from its census and surveys and many special publications. Census reports are listed in a quarterly, *Catalog of United States Census Publications*, and are available in many libraries. A selected list of special Bureau publications follows:

Statistical Abstract of the United States, annual one-volume basic reference source.
County and City Data Book, one-volume collection of data from major censuses and other sources.
Historical Statistics of the United States: Colonial Times to 1957, more than 8,000 time series on major aspects of the nation's development, in one volume.
County Business Patterns, employment, payrolls, and reporting units, compiled from social security tax reports.

Bureau of Economic Analysis (BEA)   A branch of the U.S. Department of Commerce which engages in economic analysis, utilizing for this purpose primarily the national-economic-accounting data which it originates. BEA was formerly known as the Office of Business Economics (OBE). There is no other official source of the gross national product, national income, or U.S. balance of international payments. The national accounts provide the framework for most overall economic anaylsis both by government and by business firms. BEA carries a major share of the responsibility for such analysis within the Department of Commerce. Of these aggregates, the oldest is the U.S. balance of international payments, which was developed from a concept into a working set of international economic accounts beginning in 1921. Hence, BEA derived its legislative authority through the Bureau of Foreign and Domestic Commerce, but it was established as a separate unit in 1945. Pursuant to a Senate resolution, the national income accounts became a primary BEA responsibility in 1932. Since then, the scope, detail, and frequency of issue of both the whole and each component part have been increased sufficiently to maintain the position of the U.S. not only as the pioneer but also as the world leader in this field. Gross national product was developed as a separate but coordinate national economic account in 1940, in response to the urgent need for such economic intelligence in the planning of America's war effort. In addition to tracing the flow of final products, BEA has developed 140,000 interindustry relationships which afford a detailed description of the U.S. industrial structure, showing what each industry buys from every other industry and how a change in demand affects every industry. The detailed input-output structure of the U.S. economy has been made available on magnetic tape for computer processing. A wealth of regional economic data is also available in machine-readable form. BEA measures personal income, by type of income and by industrial source, for the 50 states, 223 metropolitan areas, and about 2,650 nonmetropolitan-area counties. The availability of data for these latter two types of areas gives the series great flexibility in terms of regional classification. Personal income provides the most comprehensive measure of economic activity, consumer purchasing power, and economic welfare available on a geographic basis. The industrial detail in which personal income is measured makes the series especially useful in analyzing causes of economic change in local areas. The monthly *Survey of Current Business*, the major vehicle for the dissemination of analytical data and results produced in OBE, was instituted about 1921. The forty pages of business statistics which appear regularly in each issue are carried back, with explanatory notes, in a *Business Statistics Supplement* published in alternate years. To cast further light upon movements shown by the basic accounts data, BEA has developed auxiliary series in certain other more specific economic areas. One of these is the survey taken quarterly for about twenty-five years to report expected business expenditures for new plants and equipment. BEA is responsible for the statistical indicators program, including the issuance of *Business Conditions Digest*. BEA also publishes monographs to provide authoritative data on a comprehensive and timely basis. Issued as supplements to the *Survey of Current Business*, they cast additional light on component areas of the national accounts or sum of trends and methodology. Recent titles include *Input-Output Structure of the U.S. Economy* (vol. I, *Transactions Data for Detailed Industries;* vol. II, *Total Requirements for Detailed Industries*), 1963; *U.S. Business Investments in Foreign Countries*, 1966; *U.S. Mer-*

chandise Exports and Imports, mid-1920s through 1968; *The National Income and Product Accounts of the United States,* 1929 to 1965. BEA publications are available from the Superintendent of Documents, Government Printing Office, Washington, D.C. 20402, or any field office of the U.S. Department of Commerce.

Bureau of Employment Security   A bureau of the U.S. Department of Labor that has responsibility for two major programs, the U.S. Employment Service, which was established in the Department under the Wagner-Peyser Act of June 6, 1933; and the Unemployment Insurance Service, which was first established as the Bureau of Unemployment Compensation by the Social Security Board. Within the framework of the Federal-state system, the U.S. Employment Service is responsible, through its affiliated state employment services and their 1,900 local public employment offices, for the following:

1. Providing a nationwide employment service for employees and employers, which includes placement, counseling, aptitude testing, and other services for all applicants, including young persons, older workers, veterans, and the handicapped, and placement and related services to employers in both farm and nonfarm establishments.
2. Providing for the development and initiation of manpower training and retraining activities for the existing and potential work force of the U.S.
3. Developing and carrying out programs to reduce and prevent the adverse effects of automation on the labor force.
4. Developing and maintaining the capability of meeting the needs for civilian manpower in national emergencies or other disasters.
5. Providing labor-market and related information to labor, management, government, and the public.

In the calendar year 1962, the public employment service placed approximately 6.7 million persons in nonfarm jobs and 8.5 million in farm jobs, provided counseling service to 2 million persons, and gave about 2 million vocational-aptitude tests. Within the framework of the Federal-state system, the Unemployment Insurance Service is responsible for guiding and assisting state employment security agencies in the following:

1. Providing soundly financed and administered state unemployment-insurance programs for the workers of the U.S., geared to the demands of a changing economy.
2. Providing labor-market and related information pertinent to the unemployment-insurance program.
3. Studying and developing public income-insurance programs for non-work-connected disabilities.

The Bureau is also responsible for administering, through the state employment-security agencies, programs of unemployment insurance for Federal workers and ex-servicemen, allowances for trainees, and adjustment-assistance allowances for workers adversely affected by import activities. In the calendar year 1962, approximately $2.6 billion in unemployment-insurance benefits were paid to unemployed workers covered by the Federal-state unemployment-insurance laws, and average weekly insured unemployment was 1,783,000. The major publications of the Bureau are *Employment Security Review,* monthly; *Labor Market and Employment Security,* monthly; *Area Labor Markets Trends,* monthly; *Insured Unemployed,* monthly; *Farm Labor Market Developments,* monthly; *Employment and Wages,* quarterly; *Annual Report; Job Guide for Young Workers,* biennially; *Dictionary of Occupational Titles; Comparison of State Unemployment Insurance Laws,* biennially; *Benefit Series Service,* monthly.

Bureau of Labor Statistics   A bureau of the U.S. Department of Labor that serves as the Federal government's principal fact-finding agency in the field of labor economics. Its major programs provide statistics and analyses of employment, unemployment, manpower, productivity and technological developments, wages, industrial relations, work injuries, price trends, costs and standards of living, foreign labor conditions, and economic growth. The Bureau obtains its information from workers, businessmen, and other government agencies, all of whom supply the data voluntarily because of their interest in and need for the analyses and summaries which ensue. The Bureau's research projects, in turn, grow out of the needs of these same groups as well as the needs of Congress, Federal and state governments, and the Department of Labor. Its research is oriented toward the Department of Labor's objectives of promoting the welfare of wage earners, improving their working conditions, and advancing their opportunities for profitable employment. A Bureau of Labor, predecessor of the Bureau of Labor Statistics, was established in the Department of the Interior by act of June 27, 1884, and organized in January of the following year. In 1913, after several changes in status, it became the Bureau of Labor Statistics in the newly created U.S. Department of Labor. The Bureau has eight field offices, located in Boston, New York, Philadelphia, Atlanta, Chicago, Dallas, Kansas City, and San Francisco. Its chief official, a nonpolitical Presidential appointee, is the Commissioner of Labor Statistics. The Bureau conducts a training program for economists, statisticians, and other labor officials from economically developing countries. This program is sponsored by the Department of State through the Agency for International Development. The information collected by the Bureau through field surveys and other means is issued in special bulletins and reports, in several periodicals, and in press releases.

The major periodicals are the *Monthly Labor Review* (which began publication in July, 1915), *Employment and Earnings,* and the *Occupational Outlook Quarterly.* Two other monthly periodicals are *Current Wage Developments* and *Labor Developments Abroad.* An *Occupational Outlook Handbook,* providing guidance material on major occupations, and a *Directory of National and International Labor Unions in the United States* are two biennial publications. A handbook, *Economic Forces in the United States,* is compiled especially for visiting foreigners.

Bureau of Mines   A bureau of the Department of Interior. A series of disastrous coal-mine explosions in the first decade of the twentieth century resulted in the organization of the Bureau of Mines in 1910. Aside from its responsibilities for inspecting mines, much of the Bureau's work consists of research and development in five major areas of inquiry: mining, minerals, fuels, helium, and health and safety. Results of this research and related investigations are published by the Bureau in its own series of *Reports of Investigations* and *Information Circulars* and in articles appearing in a broad spectrum of trade and technical journals. The Bureau also conducts a variety of economic and statistical studies, undertaken primarily to serve as a guide to research planning but also to provide valuable data for national policy makers, industry, and the general public. Information on production, supply, consumption, distribution, and other aspects of domestic and foreign mineral industries is published for metals, nonmetals, and mineral fuels. Statistics on injuries and employment in the U.S. mineral industries also are published. The most important of the Bureau's statistical and economic reports is the annual three-volume *Minerals Yearbook,* which summarizes significant developments in mineral industries for successive calendar years and presents information on production, consumption, trade, and utilization of mineral materials. *Mineral Industries Surveys* present data similar to those published in the *Yearbook,* but they are issued more frequently, appearing at various intervals (weekly, monthly, and quarterly) during the year. Of special interest is *Mineral Facts and Problems,* an encyclopedic reference volume covering the history, geology, mining, preparation, and use of scores of mineral and fuel commodities. This volume, published in the Bureau's *Bulletin* series, is brought up to date every five years. Statistical and economic reports on mineral trade throughout the world are the monthly *Mineral Trade Notes* and *International Coal Trade* and the *International Petroleum Annual.* Accident and injury statistics are reported in the monthly *Coal Mine Injuries and Coal Mine Fatalities* and the annual *Health and Safety Surveys.* The Bureau is organized into three functional categories: (1) The staff, planning, administrative, and information functions support all the Bureau activities; (2) compliance and enforcement obligations and powers are vested in the Deputy Director—Health and Safety; and (3) research, resource, and environmental activities are the responsibilities of the Deputy Director—Mineral Resources and Environmental Development.

Bureau of the Mint A bureau of the U.S. Treasury Department. It exchanges silver bullion for silver deposits, assays gold and silver bullion samples for certification to determine the correct fineness, manufactures and distributes domestic coins, safeguards the government's holdings of monetary metals, and compiles and analyzes general data of worldwide scope relating to gold, silver, and coins. The U.S. Mint was established by act of Congress on April 2, 1792, and was placed under the supervision of the Secretary of State. The Bureau of the Mint was established by the Coinage Act of 1873 and was placed under the Treasury Department. It reports annually to the Secretary of the Treasury on all Mint operations for the fiscal year, including in its report estimates of domestic and foreign production of gold and silver monetary statistics pertaining to the U.S. and most of the other countries of the world. The Mint's field institutions are the U.S. Mint, Philadelphia, Pa. 19106; U.S. Mint, Denver, Colo. 80204; U.S. Assay Office, San Francisco, Calif. 94102; U.S. Assay Office, New York, N.Y. 10005; U.S. Bullion Depository (gold), Fort Knox, Ky.; and U.S. Bullion Depository (silver), West Point, N.Y. 10996.

Bureau of Public Roads A bureau of the U.S. Department of Transportation's Federal Highway Administration. It carries out the responsibilities and authority of the Secretary of Transportation with respect to Federal and Federal-aid highway construction, administration, and research. The Bureau administers Federal legislation providing for the improvement, in cooperation with the several states, of roads in the Federal-aid primary, secondary, and interstate highway systems and urban extensions thereof; for the survey and construction, in cooperation with the Forest Service, of roads in the forest highway system; for the survey and construction, in cooperation with the Central American republics, of the Inter-American Highway; and for other programs as authorized. In cooperation with the Department of State and other Federal agencies, the Bureau provides assistance and advice to foreign governments in various phases of highway engineering and administration. Public Roads conducts a program of research on all phases of highway improvement and safety and highway transportation as a basis for the development of progressive highway engineering and administrative practices. The Bureau was created in October, 1893, as the Office of Road Inquiry under the authority of the Agricultural Appropriation Act for the fiscal year 1894. On July 1, 1918, it became the Bureau of Public Roads.

Under the reorganization effected on July 1, 1939, the Bureau was transferred to the Federal Works Agency, and its name was changed to Public Roads Administration. On August 20, 1949, however, it was transferred to the Department of Commerce and once again became the Bureau of Public Roads. On April 1, 1967, the Bureau became a part of the newly formed Department of Transportation. In the field, division offices discharge the responsibilities of the Bureau at the local level. Division offices are located in all states, the District of Columbia, and Puerto Rico. These divisions are grouped under nine Federal Highway Administration Regional Offices. The Bureau publishes *Public Roads,* bimonthly; *Highway Statistics,* annually.

Bureau of Reclamation   A bureau of the U.S. Department of the Interior. It was created in 1902 as the Reclamation Service under the Reclamation Act. Its original purpose was to reclaim the arid and semi-arid land of the Western United States so that the unproductive dry-land acres of the wide plains could provide food and settlement opportunities for the settlers streaming from the East. This purpose has since been broadened to include the generation of hydroelectric power and the provision of municipal and industrial water supplies, flood control, fish and wildlife conservation, water quality control, and recreational opportunities. Technical assistance is provided to other countries in connection with the development and utilization of water resources. By 1969 the Bureau had completed 269 dams and dikes which impounded water in 214 reservoirs in the seventeen Western states that it serves. These reservoirs have a storage capacity of 132.2 million acre-feet of water. In 1968 the various projects delivered water for the irrigation of nearly 8.4 million acres, which produced crops valued at more than $1.8 billion. They also furnished nearly 1.9 million acre-feet of water for municipal and industrial use. Outdoor recreation was provided on 1.7 million acres of water surface and along 11,000 miles of shoreline for 49.5 million visitors to the Bureau's 232 recreation areas. In fiscal 1969 project power plants generated 43 billion kilowatthours of hydroelectric energy. Of the nearly $5.9-billion investment in Reclamation project facilities, nearly 90% will be repaid to the government by the users of the water and electric power supplied by the projects. The Commissioner issues an annual report summarizing the accomplishments of the Bureau for the year. In addition, the agency publishes a quarterly magazine, *Reclamation Era,* as well as a number of pamphlets and books which deal with different aspects of its work and with its individual major projects. The Bureau of Reclamation consists organizationally of the Commissioner's office in Washington, D.C., the Chief Engineer's office in Denver, seven regional offices, and project and other operating offices in the regions.

Business and Defense Services Administration (BDSA) The arm of the U.S. Department of Commerce that is oriented to the nation's business and industrial economy on a commodity-by-commodity and industry-by-industry basis. Established on October 1, 1953, BDSA is organized along commodity-industry lines to provide business services to most U.S. manufacturing and distribution industries, to stimulate business and industrial development, and to prepare and execute plans for industrial-mobilization readiness. Basically, BDSA has four major program areas of activity: industrial analysis, international commodities, industrial mobilization, and business and government services. The *industrial-analysis program* is concerned for the most part with economic impact studies which identify the key factors influencing the effectiveness with which industries, workers, and communities respond to economic changes. It explores the variables that affect particular growth industries and industries in decline in an effort to pinpoint cause-and-effect relationships. Through its *international-commodities program*, BDSA engages in international-commodity intelligence, brings foreign-market opportunities to the attention of American businessmen, and advises businessmen regarding financial and loan sources for foreign trade. BDSA has the chief responsibility in the Federal government for maintaining *industrial-mobilization readiness*. It constantly assesses the availability of materials that may be required in an emergency and is equipped to act quickly if the need arises. In the field of *business and government services*, BDSA serves as a focal point for businessmen in their dealings with other government agencies and provides assistance through periodic reports and analyses of commodity, industry, and trade conditions. The hard core of BDSA operations consists of twenty-two industry and commodity divisions which cover some 400 industries. These divisions are staffed by experts who furnish commodity-industry intelligence and expertise and serve as the points of contact with their respective industries. These specialists develop basic information on production, consumption, inventories, markets, technological developments, and other factors which affect the economic position of business and industry. They also produce analytical reports for use by business, industry, and government relating to conditions and levels of business activity, current and projected production trends, and market outlooks. The principal publications issued by BDSA on a continuing basis are the *U.S. Industrial Outlook*, annually; *Marketing Information Guide*, monthly; *Chemicals*, quarterly; *Copper*, quarterly; *Construction Review*, monthly; *Containers and Packaging*, quarterly; *Pulp, Paper and Board*, quarterly. Other significant publications are *Water and Wastewater Facilities, 1955–1980; Growth Pacesetters in American Industry, 1958–1968; Bibliography on Marketing to Low-Income Consumers.*

Business Council for International Understanding (BCIU) A non-profit organization supported by seventy-nine U.S. corporations, BCIU concentrates on (1) international government-business relations and (2) the U.S. business presence abroad. Closely cooperating with, but independent of, the State and other government departments, it has selectively planned many thousands of company consultations for American companies with virtually every U.S. ambassador and many other senior Washington and embassy officers. In another application of the industry consultations, BCIU often arranges individual and group participation of numerous other business organizations, for their mutual benefit as well as that of the foreign service officer or visiting statesman or business leader. It is currently increasing its attention also to visiting statesmen and business leaders from abroad and, with them, is working toward more productive high-level dialogue with other countries. The council sponsors a course for key international executives several times each year at the American University in Washington, along the lines of a private "foreign service institute." BCIU has also pioneered in recruiting and programming the voluntary assistance of U.S. industry experts to developing countries (notably in the Dominican Republic after the fall of Trujillo). It was one of the original proponents of the Overseas Private Investment Corporation, with a mixed public-private board and staff, which materialized in 1970. In a longer-range version of its industry consultation program, BCIU worked out a program that enables a senior foreign service officer to spend more than six months with several American companies for the purpose of learning at firsthand about problems and problem solving in the age of the multinational company. Its headquarters are located at 420 Lexington Avenue, New York, N.Y. 10017.

C

Cabinet Committee on Economic Policy A group of top-level presidential advisers which serves as a forum for discussion of, and recommendations on, economic matters. The work of the Committee is coordinated by the Chairman of the Council of Economic Advisers. It includes the President; the Vice President; the Chairman of the Council of Economic Advisers; the Secretaries of the Treasury, Agriculture, Commerce, Labor, and Housing and Urban Development; Counselors to the President; the Director of the Office of Management and Budget; and the Deputy Under Secretary of State for Economic Affairs. The Cabinet Committee considers a broad spectrum of business and economic issues and reviews the findings of various of its subcommittees. During 1969, the President appointed subcommittees to study and make recommendations on such problems as agricultural trade, post-Vietnam economic planning, antitrust laws, interest-rate ceilings, and Federal lending policies. President Nixon established the Cabinet Committee early in 1969. See *The Annual Economic Report of the President,* Government Printing Office, Washington, D.C., 1970 and 1971.

Casualty Actuarial Society An organization of actuaries in the U.S. and Canada who are employed by insurance companies, rate-making organizations, and state insurance departments. Its aim is the promotion of actuarial and statistical science, as applied to the problems of insurance other than life insurance, by means of personal intercourse, the presentation and discussion of appropriate papers, and the collection of a library. The society has two grades of membership, associate and fellow. Membership is attained by passing a series of examinations for each grade which are held annually in various cities in the U.S. and Canada. In addition, the first two parts of the associateship examination are joint identical examinations held in May and November of each year and are jointly sponsored by the Casualty Actuarial Society and the Society of Actuaries. Organized in 1914 as the Casualty Actuarial and Statistical Society of America, the society received its present title on May 14, 1921. At the November, 1950, meeting, its constitution and bylaws were amended to enlarge the scope of the society to include all lines of insurance other than life insurance. The effect of this amendment was to include fire and allied lines of insurance. The principal publication is the *Proceedings,* issued annually. In addition, the society has put forth a few publications designed to aid students in studying for its examinations when the subject matter of such examinations is not readily available from other sources. The society's headquarters are located at 200 East 42d Street, New York, N.Y. 10017.

Catholic Economic Association An organization of individuals (not necessarily Roman Catholics) who are interested in the ethical implications of economic problems. Its primary purpose is the scientific discussion of economic problems requiring a knowledge both of economic science and Christian social philosophy. The association's aims and objectives are (1) to evaluate in the light of Christian moral principles the assumptions, methods, objectives, and relationships of economic science; (2) to discuss problems of economic policy, the solution of which requires a knowledge both of economic science and of Christian social principles; (3) to assist in the formulation of practical programs for the application of Christian social principles; and (4) to foster and encourage research, writing, and publication and to meet at regular intervals for the achievement of the objectives listed above. Members, who come from all areas of economic life, include teachers and administrators of colleges and universities, businessmen, government administrators, union and labor experts, members of the clergy, lawyers, accountants, journalists, and others who are interested in the application of the social teaching of the Catholic Church to economics and to present-day problems. Annual meetings are held during the Christmas season in conjunction with the American Economic Association and allied organizations. The *Review of Social Economy* is the official organ of the association. Its headquarters are located at the College of Saint Teresa, Winona, Minn. 55987.

Center for Research on Utilization of Scientific Knowledge   *See Institute for Social Research.*

Center for the Research and Documentation of Consumption (CREDOC)   A non-profit-making organization created and controlled by the government of France. Its functions are to establish data on consumption in France for use in national accounts, to carry out research into consumer behavior, and to make forecasts of consumer demand. When the Center was created in 1953, it was attached to the Productivity Commissariat, an independent body, but it is now heavily involved with the drafting of the French economic plans. A new development in the Center's work is the carrying out of studies of urban development on a contract basis for local authorities. Its headquarters are located at 30 Rue Astorg, Paris 8, France.

Central American Common Market   An organization of five Central American countries—Costa Rica, El Salvador, Guatemala, Honduras, and Nicaragua—that has a program providing for progressive regional development by means of the expansion of the markets of each of the countries, the stimulation of production, the exchange of goods and services, the raising of standards of living, and the employment of the respective populations with the objective of reestablishing Central American unity. The program of Central American economic integration began in 1951 through governmental action by the several countries and the cooperation of the

Economic Commission for Latin America of the United Nations, which has headquarters in Mexico. After many technical studies and much intensive activity, the five countries were by 1960 making final preparations to permit realization of a common market. Simultaneously, projects were undertaken in the area of the infrastructure (transportation, hydroelectric systems, etc.), industry, agriculture, and animal husbandry. By means of the General Treaty of Central American Economic Integration, signed by the member nations on December 3, 1960, three organizations were created to guide the movement: the Central American Economic Council, composed of economic ministers of each of the participating nations, whose function is the direction and coordination of economic matters; the Executive Council, with supervisory functions and with representatives designated by each of the contracting countries, which concerns itself with the application and administration of the treaty; and the Permanent Secretariat, which is associated with both the Central American Economic Council and the Executive Council to pass final judgment on the correct application of the terms of the agreement. The main financial institution of the CACM is the Central American Bank of Economic Integration (CABEI). A monthly newsletter supplying information on the activities of the Central American economic integration program is published by the Permanent Secretariat, which is located in Guatemala City, Guatemala.

Central Institute of Statistics   A special institute of the Italian government that possesses juridical, functional, and financial autonomy under the direct authority of the President of the Council of Ministers. Established by an act of July 9, 1926, and modified by an act of May 27, 1929, it has sole authority and responsibility for the statistical documentation of the demographic, social, and economic life of Italy. In particular, it carries out general censuses of population, housing, industry and trade, agriculture, and any other statistical inquiry of interest to the country; compiles and publishes statistical data and information; coordinates statistical programs of other governmental bodies; and makes special statistical inquiries on behalf of government departments, associations, and other bodies. Some of the Institute's main publications are the monthly *Statistical Bulletin, Indicators,* and *Foreign Trade Statistics;* the quarterly *National Inquiry on Labor Force;* and the annual *Italian Statistical Yearbook* and *Italian Statistical Abstract.* Other special statistical yearbooks deal with demography, health, social security, education, culture, law enforcement, agriculture, forestry, climate, livestock raising, fishing and hunting, industry, building and public works, internal trade, work, and migration. The Institute's headquarters are located at 16 Via Cesare Balbo, Rome, Italy.

Central Statistical Office   A department forming part of the British Cabinet Office. In 1940 the statisticians in the Central Economic Information Service were separated from the economists in the group. The economists were formed into the Economic Section, which worked under the Lord President of the Council and subsequently were shifted to the Treasury. Through the work of the Central Statistical Office, the use of statistical methods developed rapidly, most significantly in the field of national income.

Centre de Recherches et de Documentation sur la Consommation   *See Center for the Research and Documentation of Consumption (CRE-DOC).*

Chamber of Commerce of the United States of America   A federation, composed of local, state, and regional chambers of commerce and of trade and professional associations, business firms, corporations, and individuals, that is dedicated to the philosophy of limited government, dispersal of economic and political power, individual freedom, free competitive markets, and steady economic progress in the U.S. It works toward ten specific goals: (1) to strengthen and improve the competitive enterprise system; (2) to keep the economy dynamic and expanding, create new job opportunities, and raise the level of living of the American people; (3) to preserve the representative form of government, with proper checks and balances and with limitations on its powers; (4) to encourage the solution of local and national problems through voluntary organized action and thus to reduce intervention by government; (5) to reduce less essential government spending; (6) to halt inflation by eliminating the causes of inflation; (7) to equip and encourage businessmen and others to be better-informed, more active, and more responsible citizens; (8) to emphasize the worth and dignity of the individual; (9) to advance the political and economic interests of the U.S. in world affairs; and (10) to keep the country productive and strong against the threat of war. The chamber was formed upon the recommendation of President William Howard Taft, who saw the need for a central source to provide government with the benefit of the thinking and experience of the business community on national problems and issues. A meeting of representatives of commercial and trade associations was held in Washington in April, 1912, when the first steps were taken to organize the national chamber. By 1969, there were nearly 4,000 organization members and more than 37,000 business members. The underlying membership is made up of about 5 million individuals and firms. The chamber provides much service to its members. Most of its resources are devoted to research, economic education, policy making, and action programs. It is involved in the field of economic education through several packaged courses, and it also offers a course in nonpartisan political action. The chamber publishes many studies for its members and others on current topics, such as *After Vietnam; Business & the Future; The Metropolitan Enigma; Rural Poverty & Regional Progress in an Urban Society; Business and the Consumer.* In addition, it publishes a number of periodicals, including *Nation's Business,* monthly; *Washington Report,* biweekly; *Association Letter,* monthly; *Chamber of Commerce Newsletter,* monthly; *Congressional Action,* weekly; *Here's the Issue,* biweekly. Its headquarters are located at 1615 H Street, N.W., Washington, D.C. 20006.

Chicago Board of Trade   The world's largest grain exchange. The board itself does not buy or sell, nor does it set prices. It is the marketplace in which 1,402 members efficiently buy and sell for themselves or as representatives of their firms for thousands of customers. There are two interrelated markets, the cash market and the futures market. In the cash market, the largest in the world for corn and soybeans, grain is bought and sold by samples graded according to Federal standards by licensed inspectors. The futures market deals in contracts for future delivery. Futures trading in grain developed at the Board of Trade to fulfill a need, and about 90% of the world's grain-futures trading is done at this exchange, as well as trading in several nonfarm commodities. The exchange operates under strict rules and regulations established by the membership and is licensed as a contract market by the U.S. Department of Agriculture. The commodities traded are wheat, soybeans, corn, oats, rye, soybean oil and meal, iced broilers, silver, and plywood. The Board of Trade was established in 1848 to collect buyers and sellers at a central point. It specifies the quality of a commodity that may be delivered on futures trades and spells out all terms of a complete contract. In the pits, traders complete the contract, specifying the commodity, amount, price, delivery month, and name of the buyer or seller. The Board of Trade publishes *Hedgings Highlights* and numerous publications on commodities. Headquarters are located at 141 West Jackson Boulevard, Chicago, Ill. 60604.

Civil Aeronautics Board (CAB)   An independent agency of the U.S. government. It encourages and develops an air transport system properly adapted to the present and future needs of the foreign and domestic commerce of the U.S., of the Postal Service, and of the national defense. It regulates air transportation in such a manner as to recognize and preserve the inherent advantages of such transportation, assure the highest degree of safety, foster sound economic conditions, and improve the relations between, and coordinate transportation by, air carriers. It promotes adequate, economical, and efficient service by air carriers at reasonable charges and without unjust discrimination, undue preferences or advantages, or unfair or destructive competitive practices. It promotes safety in air commerce and encourages and promotes development of civil aeronautics. The major publications of CAB are *Quarterly Airline Industry Economic Report*, covering combined traffic, capacity, and financial information concerning the carriers, and *CAB Chart Book of Airline Economic Trends*.

Commission on International Commodity Trade   A functional body of the United Nations concerned with intergovernmental consultation or action on commodity problems. It was set up in 1954 under the Economic and Social Council to examine measures designed to avoid excessive fluctuations in the prices of, and volume of trade in, primary commodities and to keep under review the world market situation for such commodities. In 1958, however, the Commission was reconstituted to study and analyze developments and trends in international commodity trade and movements in the terms of trade and the effect of such developments on the position of countries participating in international commodity trade, particularly with regard to the less-developed countries.

Commission on Money and Credit   A private commission sponsored by the Committee for Economic Development to study the U.S. monetary system. It undertook a three-year study of the public and private financial institutions, policies, and practices of the U.S., which was completed in 1961. Although the commission found that no "wholesale overhaul of our financial structure" was needed, it recommended that many small changes be put into effect. It proposed that the President be given increased power to coordinate national economic policy, that there be a closer relationship between the administration and the Federal Reserve Board, and that the Board be strengthened by giving it control of open-market operations, discount-rate policy, and reserve requirements. It also recommended elimination of the debt limit, the 25% gold backing required for Federal Reserve notes, and the interest ceiling on long-term, government-guaranteed mortgage credit. It indicated that commercial and savings banks should be allowed greater flexibility in their investment policies and that all commercial banks should be required to join the Federal Reserve System. For additional details on the proposals of the Commission on Money and Credit, see *Money and Credit: The Report of the Commission on Money and Credit*, Prentice-Hall, Inc., Englewood Cliffs, N.J., 1961; U.S. Joint Economic Committee, *Review of the Report of the*

Commission on Money and Credit, Government Printing Office, Washington, D.C., 1961.

Committee for a National Trade Policy (CNTP)   A voluntary, bipartisan organization to promote understanding of the issues facing the U.S. in its trade relations with other nations. It is supported by more than 2,000 corporations, national and local organizations, and individuals throughout the U.S. The committee is the only organization that is concerned solely with the development of a trade-expansion policy in the national interest. The CNTP advocates a reciprocal reduction of trade barriers through multilateral negotiations as a basis for the expansion of U.S. trade that is necessary to the continued economic growth of the nation. It attempts to serve as a catalyst in developing public support for an enlightened trade policy, as a clearinghouse and source of information and educational material, and as a focal point for the expression of public and business opinion in support of a liberal trade policy. The committee publishes a monthly newsletter, *Trade Talk.* Its headquarters are located at 1028 Connecticut Avenue, N.W., Washington, D.C. 20036.

Commodity Exchange Authority (CEA)   An agency of the U.S. Department of Agriculture which regulates futures trading and pricing on commodity exchanges. Federal regulation in this field began with the Commodity Exchange Act of 1922, which applied to grain exchanges. In 1936 and subsequently, the Congress of the U.S. amended the legislation to cover cotton, wool, eggs, potatoes, soybeans, fats and oils, livestock and livestock products, and other specified commodities. Predecessor agencies of the Commodity Exchange Authority, which was established in 1947, were the Grain Futures Administration and the Commodity Exchange Administration. The CEA supervises trading in regulated commodities on the Chicago Board of Trade, Kansas City Board of Trade, Minneapolis Grain Exchange, New York Cotton Exchange, New York and Chicago mercantile exchanges, and ten other exchanges designated as contract markets under the Commodity Exchange Act. The major purposes of regulation are the prevention of price manipulation, market corners, and dissemination of false and misleading crop and market information affecting commodity prices. Other responsibilities are to protect traders against cheating, fraud, and abusive practices in commodity transactions; to safeguard the handling of traders' margin money and equities by preventing the misuse of such funds by brokers; and to assure the benefits of exchange membership to farmer cooperatives. The CEA also has responsibility for investigating trading and market operations and providing information, statistics, and reports to the public on futures trading and marketing and conditions that affect the markets. Regulatory projects of the agency include overseeing the trading rules and standards which contract markets are required to maintain and the annual registration of about 1,000 floor brokers on the exchanges and about 340 futures commission merchants with approximately 2,500 principal and branch offices throughout the U.S. The agency regularly audits futures commission firms as a safeguard against the misuse of traders' funds by brokers. It also provides daily supervision of trading on the exchanges and the continuous surveillance of trading and analysis of market conditions. The agency's statistical yearbook, *Commodity Futures Statistics*, is a source of information on the volume of trading, open contracts, deliveries on futures contracts, speculative and hedging participation in the markets, and other basic data. There are also daily and monthly reports on market activity and market composition.

Commonwealth Bureau of Census and Statistics   An organization of the Australian government. It was created in 1906 and has the authority to collect and publish statistical information, to determine the soundness of the statistical methods used in the government, and to make a regular inspection of all statistical work done by various governmental departments. Among its principal publications are *Official Year Book of the Commonwealth of Australia; Pocket Compendium of Australian Statistics; Demography; Overseas Trade; Australian National Accounts; Census of Population and Housing 1966; Building and Construction; Banking and Currency; Manufacturing Industries; Manufacturing Commodities; Rural Industries; Non-Rural Industries* (all annually); and the *Quarterly Summary of Australian Statistics; Monthly Review of Business Statistics; Digest of Current Economic Statistics* (monthly).

Community Facilities Administration   *See Housing and Home Finance Agency (HHFA).*

Confederation of British Industry (CBI)   An organization which acts as the spokesman for, and representative of, British productive industry and in some respects British business as a whole both in Great Britain and overseas. Incorporated by Royal Charter, it was created in 1965 to combine the roles previously played by the long-established British Employers' Confederation, the Federation of British Industries, the National Association of British Manufacturers, and also the Industrial Association of Wales and Monmouthshire. Membership includes companies, employers' organizations, trade associations and commercial associations (together representing many thousands of companies), and most of the nationalized industries. Its objectives are to formulate policy and provide a united voice for industry and business on a comprehensive span of economic, trading, and technical subjects, including the field of industrial relations; to provide its members with a wide range of individual services in the U.K. and overseas; and to promote activities designed to assist industry and business, e.g., education, research, and overseas trade—including European integration, productivity, conservation problems, investment policy, and long-term forward planning, i.e., the shape and place of U.K. industry in the world ahead. An important part of the confederation's task is to promote and publicize the viewpoints of industry and business as widely as possible at home and overseas. The organization has nine regional offices in England and offices in Scotland, Wales, and Northern Ireland. It is represented in some 100 centers overseas. Much work is done on the problems of small firms. The CBI's four monthly computerized *Industrial Trends Survey* is widely recognized as giving the most up-to-date picture of prevailing business conditions in the U.K. Its headquarters are located at 21 Tothill Street, Westminster, London SW1, England.

Confederazione Generale dell' Industria Italiana *See General Association of Italian Industry*.

Conference Board (CB) An independent, nonprofit institution of the U.S. and Canada which studies the various social, economic, and business problems relating to and affecting industry and disseminates facts and conclusions based on careful and unbiased investigation. Supplementing its research are its conference, seminar, and educational activities. CB is specifically prohibited by its charter from attempting to influence legislation of any kind. As an organization, it has no opinions and makes no predictions. Its sole purpose is to promote prosperity and security by assisting in the effective operation and sound development of voluntary productive enterprise. The work of CB is made possible through the support of more than 4,200 subscribing associates, including business organizations, trade associations, government bureaus, labor unions, libraries, individuals, and colleges and universities. As the National Industrial Conference Board, CB was conceived in 1916 by a group of American business leaders who were hampered by a lack of accurate, impartial business and economic information. Out of the compelling need for a reliable, independent business research agency, Conference Board was established as the National Industrial Conference Board. In 1954, it set up an office in Montreal to extend its program to Canada and to provide a clearinghouse for business and economic information between the two countries. Periodically during the year CB publishes *Studies in Business Economics,* which are examinations of current economic issues affecting business, and various *Technical Papers*, which are basic studies of significant economic problems. Also issued periodically are *Studies in Business Policy*, which are reports of business practices and experiences in the fields of advertising, finance, marketing, production, sales, foreign trade, and related management areas; *Studies in Personnel Policy*, which are reports and analyses based on company experiences in personnel management and labor relations; and *Studies in Public Affairs*, which examine trends and developments affecting the environment in which business operates. Monthly, CB publishes *The Conference Board Record*, a business magazine circulated among CB associates and qualified nonassociates. The board's offices are located at 845 Third Avenue, New York, N.Y. 10022.

Conference on Economic Progress   A nonprofit, nonpolitical organization engaged solely in economic research, education, and the publication of studies related to full employment and full production in the U.S. Organized in 1954, it issues basic studies on a periodic rather than on a regular basis. Sixteen reports have been issued, as follows:

Toward Full Employment and Full Production, 1954.
A National Prosperity Program for 1955, 1955.
Full Prosperity for Agriculture, 1955.
The Gaps in Our Prosperity, 1955.
Consumption: Key to Full Prosperity, 1957.
Wages and the Public Interest, 1958; a broad study of the wage problem, stressing the need to restore full employment and production.
The "Recession": Cause and Cure, 1958; an analysis of the factors leading up to the 1958 recession and an outline of a program for realizing full-prosperity potentials.
Toward a New Farm Program, 1958; an analysis of the farm problem in the perspective of the whole American economy and a presentation of goals for full prosperity for agriculture, meshed with overall full-prosperity goals.
Inflation: Cause and Cure, 1959; an analysis of factors underlying recent price rises and a program for combining price stability and optimum economic growth.
The Federal Budget and "The General Welfare," 1959; a discussion of what the U.S. can afford and needs to do through 1964 in the fields of education, health services, and various welfare and social security programs.
Tight Money and Rising Interest Rates, 1960; an analysis of the cost to the nation of excessive interest rates and their relation to the low rate of economic growth, recessions, and high unemployment levels of recent years.

Food and Freedom, 1960; an analysis of U.S. farm production potentials in relation to U.S. needs at home and acute food and fiber shortages in the free world, together with a proposal of programs for better-managed farm-product supply, geared to domestic and world needs and combined with a parity level for American farm income.

Jobs and Growth, 1961; a study of the magnitude and costs of the current unemployment problem and an outline of a program to restore maximum employment, production, and purchasing power.

Poverty and Deprivation in the United States, 1962; a detailed picture of income distribution in the U.S. and the consequences of the poverty and deprivation which now afflict two-fifths of the nation, together with a proposal of programs for lifting low living standards.

Key Policies for Full Employment, 1962; a discussion of causes of the low rate of economic growth and of rising unemployment levels in the U.S. during the preceding nine years, together with a proposal of private and public economic policies needed to maximize employment and production.

Taxes and the Public Interest, 1963; an analysis of the relation of present tax policies to the slowdown in the rate of economic growth and to the increase of unemployment in recent years, together with a proposal of changes in these policies which would contribute to the maintenance of high levels of production and employment.

The conference's headquarters are located at 1001 Connecticut Avenue, N.W., Washington, D.C. 20006.

Conseil National du Patronat Français   A horizontal and vertical organization of French employers in the business community. Its primary purpose is to promote free enterprise. The aims of the Patronat are to defend the interests of the business community, propose further economic advances in France and in the European Common Market as a whole, and form areas of agreement on the best ways to expand the French economy and living standards. The Patronat represents the interests and views of about 900,000 small, medium-sized, and large enterprises which together employ more than 7 million persons. In effect, it is a kind of supreme council of French business interests, being composed of 514 industrial and commercial federations and 114 regional associations. The individual executive and his staff can receive business, financial, technical, and social services from the Patronat. The Patronat is an outgrowth of the Confederation of French Employers, which itself was an outgrowth of the Confederation of French Manufacturers. The Confederation of French Employers was dissolved in 1940 during the Vichy regime. After the liberation of France in 1944, a meeting of local and industrial business associations was held to form a national organization, but it was not until June, 1946, that the bylaws of the Patronat were approved. The Patronat publishes a monthly magazine, *Patronat Français,* which includes the latest economic data and analyses. Its headquarters are located at 31 Avenue Pierre Premier de Serbie, Paris 16, France.

Consumer and Marketing Service (C&MS)   An agency of the U.S. Department of Agriculture. It administers broad marketing service, consumer protection, regulatory and related programs and activities of the Department, including assigned civil defense and defense mobilization activities. Many of these services are furnished in cooperation with state departments of agriculture or other state and local agencies. C&MS services may be grouped into eight major categories:

1. *Market news.* This service provides current, unbiased information to producers, processors, distributors, and others to assist them in the orderly marketing and distribution of farm commodities. Information is collected and disseminated on supplies, demand, prices, movements, locations, quality, condition, and other market data on farm products in specific markets and marketing areas.
2. *Standardization, inspection, grading, and classing.* U.S. standards for grades, such as U.S. No. 1, U.S. Choice, and U.S. Grade A, have been developed by this service for most of the important farm commodities. While the use of most standards is voluntary, their application for some commodities is mandatory, such as those for grain and cotton moving in interstate commerce on the basis of grade; for apples, pears, grapes, and plums destined for exports; for tobacco sold on designated markets; and for products stored on the basis of grades under authority of the U.S. Warehouse Act.
3. *Consumer protection.* C&MS also administers inspection programs to insure the wholesomeness of domestic, imported, and exported meat and poultry products. Standards are established and labels are approved for meat and poultry products. Continuous supervision is exercised over further processing of meat and poultry products to assure wholesomeness and truthful labeling and to prevent adulteration or deceptive practices.
4. *Freight-rate services.* C&MS has the responsibility for obtaining fair and reasonable rates and essential services necessary to efficient transportation of agricultural commodities and farm supplies.
5. *Marketing regulatory programs.* C&MS administers several programs to protect producers, handlers, and consumers of agricultural commodities from financial loss resulting from careless, deceptive, or fraudulent marketing practices.
6. *Marketing agreements and orders.* These programs help to establish

and maintain orderly marketing conditions for certain commodities and their products such as milk, fruits, vegetables, tobacco, nuts, and hops.

7. *Surplus removal, export, and diversion programs.* Under Section 32 of the Agricultural Adjustment Act, C&MS makes payments to commercial exporters and others to encourage exports of surplus commodities and makes payments to encourage diversion of surplus commodities from normal channels of trade to new markets and new uses.

8. *Plentiful foods.* C&MS administers a cooperative effort to encourage the consumption of agricultural products that face marketing difficulties. Working through producer groups, trade associations, news media, and institutional feeding operations, this program calls attention to foods in the case of which the return to the producer is threatened by a supply that is larger than the market can readily absorb in the absence of special merchandising efforts.

Controllers Institute of America   *See Financial Executives Institute (FEI).*

Cost-of-Living Council   A group of government officials organized to administer the ninety-day freeze on wages and prices. It was established on August 15, 1971, and on October 15, 1971, it was directed to establish program policy during Phase 2 of the Economic Stabilization Program and to correlate the activities of the Price Commission, the Pay Board, and the Internal Revenue Service during the administration of the program.

Council for Technological Advancement   *See Machinery and Allied Products Institute (MAPI).*

Council of Economic Advisers   A three-member board which advises the President of the U.S. on national economic policy. Established under the Employment Act of 1946, the Council has as its primary role "to develop and recommend to the President national economic policies to foster and promote free competitive enterprise, to avoid economic fluctuations . . . and to maintain employment, production and purchasing power." The Council also assists the President in the preparation of his annual economic report, gathers information on economic conditions, appraises the economic programs and activities of the Federal government, and makes economic studies at the President's request. It publishes each January the *Annual Report to the President by the Council of Economic Advisers.* See also Edward S. Flash, Jr., *Economic Advice and Presidential Leadership,* Columbia University Press, New York, 1965.

Council of Mutual Economic Assistance (COMECON)   An international economic organization, founded by the USSR and the Communist countries of Eastern Europe in 1949, which has the stated purpose of raising living standards. Prior to 1956, however, the Council served primarily to channel reconstruction goods to the USSR and to prevent the Communist countries of Europe from seeking U.S. Marshall Plan aid. Since then, its major emphasis has been on the coordination of long-range production planning and the exchange of goods among Eastern European countries. Among the areas in which it has encouraged cooperation are pipelines, electric power, and telephones. COMECON has also enabled its members to participate in bulk buying from non-Communist countries, promoted multilateral trade among member countries, and broadened facilities for aid to underdeveloped non-Communist countries. Between 1949 and 1961, trade among member countries increased from less than one-third to two-thirds of their total foreign trade. The population of COMECON countries is 311 million, or more than the combined populations of the European Common Market and the European Free Trade Area.

Council of State Governments   A joint agency of the fifty U.S. state governments, founded in 1933. Its purpose is to strengthen state government and its public services and to preserve its role in the American Federal system; to assist the states in improving their legislative, administrative, and judicial practices; to promote state-local and interstate cooperation; and to facilitate Federal-state relations. The Council conducts research on state programs and problems, maintains an inquiry and information service, consults at state direction with Federal officials and congressional committees on matters of Federal-state concern, and holds national and regional metings during which legislators and state officials survey and deal with common problems. Among its publications are a monthly newsletter, *State Government News;* a quarterly journal, *State Government;* and *The Book of the States,* a biennial reference work, which contains summaries of developments within the states, including detailed data on state revenues, expenditures, and debt. The Council's headquarters are located in Lexington, Kentucky.

Council on Foreign Relations   A private, nonpartisan, and nonpolitical organization of the U.S., the purposes of which are as follows: (1) to study problems of foreign policy, particularly long- and intermediate-range problems, in the hope of throwing new or additional light on the difficult questions with which the U.S. must cope; (2) through study groups, which work with council authors, and through off-the-record meetings to help council members maintain and deepen their knowledge and understanding of the problems of U.S. foreign policy; and (3) through *Foreign Affairs* and other publications to increase information on and understanding of foreign-policy issues in the U.S. and other countries. The council was founded in 1921 as a result of a merger of two groups of Americans, an earlier Council on Foreign Relations which had been formed in 1918 to provide a forum for distinguished foreigners visiting the U.S.; and a group of men, most of whom had played a part in the Paris Peace Conference of 1919, who wanted to create an organization to study international affairs. Membership is limited to 1,600, and all members must be American citizens. Affiliated with the council are thirty-three committees on foreign relations throughout the U.S. The council publishes a quarterly, *Foreign Affairs*, and three annual volumes, *Political Handbook and Atlas of the World*, edited by Richard P. Stebbins, and *The United States in World Affairs* and *Documents on American Foreign Relations*, written and edited, respectively, by Richard P. Stebbins. In addition, it publishes each year a number of books on major issues of U.S. foreign policy. Among the most important of these in the 1950s and 1960s have been William Diebold, Jr., *The Schuman Plan and Trade and Payments in Western Europe;* Henry A. Kissinger, *Nuclear Weapons and Foreign Policy;* John C. Campbell, *Defense of the Middle East;* A. Doak Barnett, *Communist China and Asia;* Edwin Lieuwen, *Arms and Politics in Latin America.* The council has also inaugurated a series of short policy books aimed at presenting authoritative analyses and recommendations on important foreign-policy problems. Among these books are Ernest A. Gross, *The United Nations;* Adolf A. Berle, *Latin America;* John C. Dreier, *The Organization of American States* and *The Hemisphere Crisis;* Christian A. Herter, *Toward an Atlantic Community.* The Council's headquarters are located at 58 East 68th Street, New York, N.Y. 10021.

Cowles Foundation   A U.S. foundation for economic research which operates as an integral part of Yale University. It has as its purpose the conduct and encouragement of research in economics, finance, commerce, industry, and technology, including problems of the organization of these activities. It seeks to foster the development of logical, mathematical, and statistical methods of analysis for application in economics and related social sciences. The Cowles Foundation continues the work of the Cowles Commission for Research in Economics, which had been founded in 1932 by Alfred Cowles at Colorado Springs, Colorado. The commission moved to Chicago in 1939 and was affiliated with the University of Chicago until 1955. In that year, the professional research staff of the commission accepted appointments at Yale University and, along with other members of the Yale Department of Economics, formed the research staff of the newly established Cowles Foundation. Publications assume a variety of forms and include discussion papers, reprints, and monographs. Among the monographs are Alan S. Manne and Harry M. Markowitz, *Studies in Process Analysis: Economy-Wide Production Capabilities;* Gerard Debreu, *Theory of Value: An Axiomatic Analysis of Economic Equilibrium;* Harry M. Markowitz, *Portfolio Selection: Efficient Diversification of Investments;* William C. Hood and T. C. Koopmans, *Studies in Econometric Method;* T. C. Koopmans, *Activity Analysis of Production and Allocation;* Kenneth J. Arrow, *Social Choice and Individual Values.* A complete list of titles of papers and monographs in print is contained in the periodic *Report of Research Activities,* which is available on request from the foundation. The foundation's office is at 30 Hillhouse Avenue, New Haven, Conn. (the mailing address is Box 2125, Yale Station, New Haven, Conn. 06520).

Department of Commerce   A department of the Federal government of the U.S. which was created to promote the domestic and foreign commerce of the nation. The principal units of the Department that deal primarily with economics are the Office of Economic Affairs, the Bureau of the Census, the Bureau of Economic Analysis, the Business and Defense Services Administration, the Bureau of International Commerce, and the Economic Development Administration. The Office of Economic Affairs is headed by the Assistant Secretary for Economic Affairs, who is chief economist for the Department and provides policy direction and general supervision for the Bureau of the Census and the Bureau of Economic Analysis. The Bureau of the Census takes a census of population and housing every ten years and censuses of business, manufacturing and mineral industries, agriculture, transportation, and governments every five years. In addition, the Bureau keeps up to date some of the more important statistics on population, housing, retail and wholesale trade, U.S. international trade, construction, manufacturers' shipments and orders, defense expenditures, and major economic indicators, as well as data on state and local governments. Data on the labor force, collected monthly, provide estimates of employment and unemployment for the Labor Department. Manufacturing and trade surveys include annual canvasses, a series of reports for selected industries, and weekly and monthly reports on sales of retail stores and merchant wholesalers. Statistics on U.S. foreign trade show exports and imports by commodity and country. The Bureau of Economic Analysis interprets and analyzes domestic and international data and provides periodic textual and statistical views of the U.S. economy. The Bureau computes gross national product, which measures the nation's total output of goods and services, and the U.S. balance of payments, which shows the transactions between the U.S. and other countries by major categories. It also publishes reports on the various components of GNP such as consumer, business, and government expenditures; personal income; business investment; business profits; farm income; etc. Input-output tables published at intervals of several years by BEA show the interrelationships between major industries and the probable impact of a given economic change on various industries. In addition, the Bureau is responsible for regional economic analysis and for the preparation of key business indicators such as plant and equipment expenditures and inventory and sales expectation surveys. It also periodically conducts surveys of U.S. private capital investment abroad and foreign investment in the U.S. The twenty-three industry divisions of the Business and Defense Services Administration collect and analyze economic information on specific industries and develop domestic and foreign marketing data. Industry experts and professional economists cooperate in conducting growth studies to analyze industry trends and identify factors influencing favorable growth rates. The Bureau of International Commerce helps to shape U.S. foreign economic policies in regional economic affairs and East-West economic relations. It is concerned with the international trade policy of the U.S., international commodity problems, and international financial policies. In addition, it analyzes and reports on economic conditions in other countries and publishes world trade statistics. These functions are carried out by the Bureau's Office of Commercial and Financial Policy, Office of Regional Economics, and Office of Export Control. The Economic Development Administration conducts programs to help create permanent new jobs and stimulate economic growth in areas of the nation with severe unemployment and low-income problems. The agency makes loans and grants to help local communities provide public facilities essential to growth, and it makes business loans to help establish or expand private enterprise. It also provides technical and planning assistance and conducts research to help overcome barriers to economic growth. Major regularly issued publications of the Department of Commerce that deal with economics are as follows: Bureau of Economic Analysis—*Survey of Current Business,* monthly; Bureau of the Census—*Business Conditions Digest,* monthly; *Defense Indicators,* monthly; *Construction Activity,* monthly; *Consumer Buying Intentions,* quarterly; Economic Development Administration— *Economic Development,* monthly. It also issues numerous reports on trade; housing starts, sales, and vacancies; population characteristics; and consumer income, as well as data on state and local governments and various industries.

Department of Economic Research of the American Medical Association   A department which seeks to apply economic concepts and theory objectively, logically, and systematically to the analysis of the health-services marketplace. This research focuses upon the health-care production function, the cost function, system relationships to the national economy, and other special topics. Analysis of the production function involves substitutability and complementarity of factors of production and organization structure as an implicit factor input. Financing mechanisms and components of cost are included in analysis of the cost function. Relationships of the health-care system to inflation, overall economic growth, and public policy also are investigated, in addition to special problems such as innovation and planning in health-care delivery. This department is located at 535 North Dearborn Street, Chicago, Ill. 60610.

Department of Health, Education, and Welfare   A department of the Federal government of the U.S. It was established to improve administration of governmental responsibilities in the fields of health, education, and social security. It was created on April 11, 1953, replacing the Federal Security Agency, which had been established in 1939 to administer programs in the fields of health, education, and economic security. The Department's seven major agencies are the Health Services and Mental Health Administration (1968), the National Institutes of Health (1948), the Food and Drug Administration (1907), the Environmental Health Service (1970) (these four agencies constitute the reorganized Public Health Service, which began in 1798), the Office of Education (1867), the Social Security Administration (1935), and the Social and Rehabilitation Service (1967). The Health Services and Mental Health Administration helps expand the organization and delivery of health services at the community level through programs of comprehensive health planning, regional medical programs, community mental health centers, and health-services research and development. The National Institutes of Health support and conduct biomedical research into the causes and prevention of diseases, administer health manpower training grants, and communicate biomedical information to the medical and health professions. The Food and Drug Administration enforces Federal laws designed to ensure the purity, safety, and truthful labeling of foods, drugs, and cosmetics, and it clears manufacturers' evidence of the safety of new drugs, food and color additives, and pesticide residues on crops. The Environmental Health Service directs the national effort to restore and maintain an environment conducive to the health and well-being of every American, including activities in air pollution, solid wastes, radiation, occupational health, and urban problems. The Office of Education collects and publishes educational statistics and information and supports programs, ranging from kindergarten to the postgraduate level, developed by state educational agencies, local school districts, colleges, and other educational agencies and institutions. The Social Security Administration administers the Federal system of old age, survivors, and disability insurance and Medicare. The Social and Rehabilitation Service administers the Department's major social service, rehabilitation, and public assistance programs, including Medicaid and aid for the aged, the mentally and physically disabled, the blind, and needy families with dependent children. Each of the Department's agencies publishes documents dealing with its programs. The Department's overall publications are *Annual Report of the U.S. Department of Health, Education, and Welfare; Catalog of HEW Assistance;* and *People Working for People.*

Department of Housing and Urban Development   The principal Federal agency responsible for programs concerned with housing needs and urban renewal and development. Authorized by Public Law 89-174, September 9, 1965, the Department came into existence on November 9, 1965, when it replaced the Housing and Home Finance Agency and absorbed the programs previously administered by that agency and its constituent Federal Housing Administration, Public Housing Administration, Urban Renewal Administration, and Community Facilities Administration. The Department was created in response to America's urbanization and to the increasing importance of housing and urban development in the national life. HUD's programs are channeled through communities, urban areas, states, and private and public agencies and sponsors. Through loans, grants, mortgage insurance, subsidies, and technical assistance, the Department helps communities to meet the nation's housing and urban development needs. Its principal programs help to provide decent housing for low-income and moderate-income families, special assistance for housing for elderly and handicapped people, and housing needed by colleges and university students; they help rebuild slum and blighted areas and encourage and support plans for orderly metropolitan growth. Broad authority for operating decisions is vested in regional and area offices. Its major publication is *Housing and Urban Development Trends,* monthly.

Department of Labor   A department of the Federal government of the U.S. It undertakes measures to advance the welfare of wage earners, their working conditions, and their employment opportunities. The Department, which has a key role in efforts to promote the greatest use of the nation's manpower and to increase the employability of the jobless and the under-employed, administers youth and adult programs which offer a wide range of work-experience, training, and career-related services. Among these are institutional and job training programs under the Manpower Development and Training Act; work-incentive provisions of the Social Security Act to help people move from welfare rolls to permanent jobs; the Concentrated Employment Program, which brings together community resources to aid the poor and disadvantaged; and Job Opportunities in the Business Sector, a program conducted in cooperation with the National Alliance of Businessmen. The Department is also responsible for certain programs authorized under the Economic Opportunity Act, including Public Service Careers, Operation Mainstream, and Neighborhood Youth Corps. Other programs administered by the Department are the Job Corps, a residential program of human renewal for out-of-school and out-of-work young men and women; a special employment service for veterans; apprentice training; and certification of immigrants for employment in the U.S. The Department also supervises the nation-wide employment-service and unemployment-insurance systems. In addition to its activities under manpower legislation, the Department administers other laws concerning workers, including the Fair Labor Standards Act, which regulates minimum wages and overtime pay and provides for equal pay for equal work; the Public Contracts Act; the Labor-Management Reporting and Disclosure Act; and several statutes providing workmen's compensation for job-related injuries. The Department also gathers and publishes data on employment and unemployment, wages and hours of work, prices and the cost of living, work injuries, and labor relations. In addition, it develops policies and programs to promote the welfare of over 31 million women in the labor force, advances foreign policy objectives of the government in the international labor field, and administers the Federal government's program of equal employment opportunity in government contracts and federally assisted construction projects. Bureaus and offices of the Department include the Manpower Administration's U.S. Training and Employment Service, Unemployment Insurance Service, Bureau of Apprenticeship and Training, and Job Corps;

the Labor-Management Services Administration's Office of Labor-Management and Welfare-Pension Reports, Office of Labor-Management Policy Development, Office of Labor-Management Relations Services, and Office of Veterans' Reemployment Rights; the Wage and Labor Standards Administration's Women's Bureau, Wage and Hour Division, Bureau of Labor Standards, Bureau of Employees' Compensation, and Office of Federal Contract Compliance; and the Bureau of Labor Statistics. Among the Department's major publications are the *Manpower Report of the President: A Report on Manpower Requirements, Resources, Utilization, and Training; Monthly Labor Review; Occupational Outlook Handbook,* biennially; *Occupational Outlook Quarterly; Consumer Price Index,* detailed report, monthly; *Manpower* magazine, monthly; *1969 Handbook on Women Workers;* the *Dictionary of Occupational Titles;* the *Directory of National and International Labor Unions.*

Department of the Church and Economic Life of the National Council of Churches A department of the National Council of Churches whose chief function is the promotion of the study of the ethical issues that are involved in every phase of economic life. It is a long-range, persistent effort to promote understanding of what is involved in economic affairs and of the ways in which the Christian conscience affects decisions that every person has to make, whether as head of a family, consumer, employer, jobholder, professional man, government official, or citizen. The department enlists the active participation of lay persons, particularly those who deal with economic problems at first hand. Its conferences are noteworthy for furnishing a meeting place where men and women who are frequently on opposite sides of the economic struggle can exchange ideas with the single purpose of understanding how their Christian faith can help them fulfill their mutual responsibilities in economic affairs. A representative sampling of its published study documents and monographs includes F. Ernest Johnson (ed.), *Ethics and Economics in Society,* 11 vols., Harper & Row, Publishers, Incorporated, New York; *In Search of Maturity in Industrial Relations: Some Long-Range Ethical Implications of the 1959–60 Dispute in the Steel Industry; Learning to Know and Use the Peaceful Atom in Our Daily Lives: A Guide for Church People; Christian Principles and Assumptions for Economic Life; The Churches and Persistent Pockets of Poverty in the U.S.A.,* a report on a consultation on that subject; *Christians in a Rapidly Changing Economy.* In addition, the department issues two periodicals, each of which appears at least once annually, and it maintains a library and reference service covering economic, ethical, and related matters, which issues a *Library Bulletin.* The department's headquarters are located at 475 Riverside Drive, New York, N.Y. 10027.

Dominion Bureau of Statistics The central statistical agency of Canada. It compiles, analyzes, and publishes statistical information on the commercial, industrial, financial, social, and general conditions of the Canadian people. In addition, it conducts a census of population and agriculture at periodic intervals. The Bureau was established by the Statistics Act of 1918. Among its publications are *Canada Year Book; Canadian Statistical Review,* monthly. Its headquarters are located in Ottawa, Canada. Statistical reports on Canada may be obtained from the Canadian Information Service, 1251 Avenue of the Americas, New York, N.Y. 10020.

E

Econometric Society An international society for the advancement of economic theory in its relation to statistics and mathematics. Its main object is the promotion of studies which aim at a unification of the theoretical-quantitative and empirical-quantitative approaches to economic problems and which are penetrated by constructive and rigorous thinking similar to that which has come to dominate the natural sciences. The society was founded on December 31, 1930, by a small and distinguished group of American and European economists, statisticians, and mathematicians. In the following year, the first European meeting was held in Lausanne, and the first American meeting in Washington. With the founding of the Cowles Commision for Research in Economics (now the Cowles Foundation) in 1932, a proposal was made that the commission support the activities of the Econometric Society and enable it, among other things, to publish a journal. This proposal was adopted, and the first issue of *Econometrica* was published in 1933. Membership now exceeds 3,000, and the circulation of *Econometrica* exceeds 6,890 in over ninety countries. The main activities of the society are the bimonthly publication of *Econometrica* and the conduct of scientific conferences and meetings. Each year, two meetings are held in the

United States and one in Europe; conferences are also organized in other parts of the world. A world congress of econometricians is held every five years. The society's headquarters are located at Yale University; its mailing address is Box 1264, Yale Station, New Haven, Conn. 06520.

Economic and Social Council (ECOSOC) A body of the United Nations that endeavors to promote higher standards of living, full employment, and conditions of economic and social progress and development in its member nations. The council is organized to solve international economic, social, health, and related problems. Thus, it makes or initiates studies and reports on international economic, social, cultural, educational, health, and related matter and presents recommendations on such matters. The council consists of eighteen members elected by the General Assembly for staggered three-year terms.

Economic Commission for Africa (ECA) An economic commission of the United Nations, dealing with the regional economic problems of Africa. Set up under the Economic and Social Council in 1958, it has fifteen members and eight associate members. The Commission has standing committees on trade, natural resources and industrialization, and physical planning. In addition, it has an expert committee on social development and a working party on public administration.

Economic Commission for Asia and the Far East (ECAFE) An economic commission of the United Nations, dealing with the regional economic problems of Asia and the Far East. Set up in 1947 under the Economic and Social Council, it has twenty-four members and two associate members. Its subsidiary bodies consist of a committee on industry and natural resources, with subcommittees on iron and steel, electric power, and mineral resources development, and working parties on cottage and small-scale industries and on housing and building materials.

Economic Commission for Europe (ECE) An economic commission of the United Nations, dealing with the regional economic problems of Europe. Set up in 1947 under the Economic and Social Council, it has twenty-nine members. Switzerland, a non-United Nations member, participates in a consultative capacity. The Commission's subsidiary bodies consist of committees on coal, electric power, housing, industry and materials, inland transport, steel, manpower, timber, development of trade, and agricultural problems.

Economic Commission for Latin America (ECLA) An economic commission of the United Nations, dealing with the regional economic problems of Latin America. Set up in 1948 under the Economic and Social Council, it has twenty-four members. It has a trade committee and a Central American economic cooperation committee. Under the trade committee, working groups on the regional market and on central banks have been established, while under the Central American economic cooperation committee subcommittees on trade, statistical coordination, transport, electricity, and housing, building, and planning have been established.

Economic Council of Canada   An independent organization, detached from government, whose aims are to plot the potential growth and prospective problems of the Canadian economy in order to assist forward planning in both the private and public sectors. Government itself is not represented on the council, as in the case of Great Britain's National Economic Development Council, and the council members do not serve as staff consultants to the head of the government, as in the case of the American Council of Economic Advisers. Established by Parliament in 1964, the council reports to the Prime Minister for administrative purposes, but its reports on the Canadian economy are released directly to the public. In addition to its regular *Annual Reviews,* the council also issues special reports in response to requests from the federal government that it study particular matters (such as competition policies and so-called incomes policies), and it also publishes numerous technical background papers prepared by its own research staff and consultants. There are twenty-eight members of the council, including three full-time members. Business, labor, and consumers are strongly represented, and there are also a few academicians. The council's headquarters are in Ottawa, Canada.

Economic Planning Agency   A Japanese governmental organization whose principal tasks are the establishment and implementation of the long-range Japanese economic plan; the establishment of fundamental economic policies and of the principle of an annual economic program; the coordination and adjustment of economic policies which concern two or more administrative agencies; the analysis and research of domestic and foreign economic movements and the preparation of annual and monthly economic reports; and the fundamental research and study of the economic structure and of economic fluctuations, as well as the preparation of national income statistics by Economic Research Institute. After World War II, in August, 1946, the Economic Stabilization Board was established under the immediate control of the Prime Minister, with a view to establishing and directing rehabilitation programs for the postwar Japanese economy. Then, several reorganizations and redesignations took place as economic rehabilitation and economic self-support were attained and an economic development stage evolved. In July, 1955, the group was reorganized into the Economic Planning Agency, under which the Economic Research Institute was established in June, 1958, as an auxiliary organ. Among Economic Planning Agency's annual publications are *Economic Survey* (English version available); *National Income Report* (summary in English available); *Annual Report on Economic Outlook* (English version available); *Livelihood White Paper;* among its monthly reports are *Monthly Economic Report* (summary in English available); *Japanese Economic Statistics* (English version available); irregular reports, such as *Economic Research Series* (excerpted English version available). Its headquarters are located at Kasumigaseki, Chiyoda-ku, Tokyo, Japan.

Economics and Finance Department of the Association of American Railroads

A fact-finding agency serving as the statistical and economic clearinghouse for the U.S. railroad industry in matters of common interest. Functions include the compilation, tabulation, and analysis of statistics and other forms of economic inquiry. Its surveys and publications in the field of transportation economics are made available not only to the railroads but also to government agencies, teachers, students, businessmen, and business organizations. The department's transportation library is open to all interested persons. Major publications issued on a continuing basis are as follows:

Railroad Review and Outlook, annually. Discusses various factors currently affecting the U.S. railroad industry, including the national economic situation, traffic trends, employment and wages, material prices, rates and fares, and legislation, with statistical tables and charts.

Indexes of Railroad Material Prices and Wage Rates, quarterly. Shows annual indices of charge-out prices and wage rates and quarterly indices of spot prices of railroad fuel, material, and supplies.

Property Investment and Condensed Income Account, annually. Shows investment in transportation property, working capital, average net investment, net railway-operating income, rate of return, and net income of individual Class I railroads.

Operating and Traffic Statistics, annually. Includes selected statistics of freight-train, passenger-train, and yard-service performance; motive power; car equipment; and traffic data of individual Class I railroads.

Railroad Mileage by States, triennially. Gives a summary of the mileage operated by individual railroads in each state and the District of Columbia.

Railway Revenues and Expenses, quarterly (monthly prior to 1962). Gives a tabulation of revenues, expenses, and net railway-operating income of individual Class I railroads, with a summarized income account of all Class I railroads combined.

Revenues, Expenses and Freight Traffic, annually. Shows freight revenue, freight-service expenses, and other freight-service statistics of individual Class I railroads.

Statistics of Railroads of Class I in the United States, annually. Presents selected financial, operating, and traffic statistics for recent years on Class I railroads as a whole.

Yearbook of Railroad Facts, annually. Pocket-size summary of the railroad industry in the U.S. and its long-term and short-term trends.

The association's headquarters are located in the American Railroads Building, Washington, D.C. 20036.

Edison Electric Institute (EEI)   A U.S. trade association of investor-owned electric light and power companies. It has the following objectives: the advancement in the public service of the art of producing, transmitting, and distributing electricity and the promotion of scientific research in this field; the ascertainment and dissemination of factual information, data, and statistics on the electric industry to its members and to the public; the extension of assistance to its operating company members to enable them to generate and sell electric energy at the lowest possible price commensurate with safe and adequate service, giving due regard to the interests of consumer, investor, and employee. Organized in 1933, the institute continues to serve as a forum in which electric-utility people meet to discuss developments in all phases of their business. Most of the work of EEI is done by its many committees, which are composed principally of electric-utility men and women from its member companies. The working committees of EEI consist of six divisions: general; engineering and operating; sales; accounting; public, employee, and investor relations; and research. General publications include the monthly *EEI Bulletin,* which contains articles of general interest to utilities and their management personnel. The economics and statistics department compiles a monthly *Data of Interest,* which consists of recent statistics which may be of interest or value to power companies. Among the EEI's periodical publications are *Electric Utility Industry Statistics in the United States; Weekly Electric Output Index; Pocketbook of Electric Industry Statistics; I Want to Know about the Electric Industry; Power and Progress; Farm Electrifications; Sales Planner; Semi-Annual Electric Power Survey;* various manuals and reference books. EEI headquarters are located at 750 Third Avenue, New York, N.Y. 10017.

Electronics Industries Association (EIA)   A national organization of U.S. electronic manufacturers, originally organized in 1924 as the Radio Manufacturers Association, which "supports and strives to advance the defense of our country, the growth of our economy, the progress of technology, and all interests of the electronics industry compatible with the public service. It operates at all times within the framework of law, ethics, and the national interest." The association has grown in membership and services, particularly since 1950, and now includes manufacturers from all important segments of the electronics industry. Its major divisions deal with consumer products, military products, industrial electronics, and parts, tube, semiconductor, lasers, and distributor products. Departments of the EIA provide membership services: engineering, marketing services, international, industrial relations, public affairs, public relations, and military relations. Among the technical achievements of the EIA have been the development of standards for the transmission of monochrome and color television and for FM stereophonic broadcasting. The association is recognized as the authority for marketing statistics and as the spokesman for the electronics industries in Congress and with Federal agencies. Significant reports published recently include *The Post Vietnam Defense and Space Market Environment* and *Future Communications Systems via Satellites Utilizing Low-Cost Earth Stations*. Long interested in the allocation and use of scarce radio frequencies, the EIA has cooperated with the Institute of Electrical and Electronics Engineers in a number of studies under the supervision of the Joint Technical Advisory Counsel (JTAC). Regular EIA publications include *Annual Trade Directory, Weekly Report, Industrial Relations Digest, International News, Annual Reports, Yearbook* (a summary of industry statistics), and various technical bulletins. The EIA has also published *Electronics: Your Chance to Shape the Future*, and it prepared the text of a manual on the selection and use of language-laboratory facilities, which was published by the U.S. Office of Education. EIA headquarters are located at 2001 I Street, N.W., Washington, D.C. 20006.

European Common Market (European Economic Community; EEC)

An economic union consisting of the following countries and their overseas dependencies: Italy, the Federal Republic of Germany, Belgium, Luxembourg, France, and the Netherlands, with Greece as an associate member. Created by the Treaty of Rome on March 25, 1957, the EEC went into effect on January 1, 1959. Its major purposes are (1) the gradual elimination of all trade barriers on goods exchanged between member countries, (2) the removal of restrictions on capital and labor movements between members, (3) the creation of the European Development Bank to provide capital for developing areas within the union, (4) greater political cooperation among the members, and (5) a joint trade policy and a common tariff toward nonmembers. EEC's external trade is greater than that of the U.S. and is considerably larger than that of the European Free Trade

Association (EFTA). In July, 1961, Great Britain applied for talks with the EEC with a view to full membership. In the following months, all EFTA members acted to seek participation in the integration of Europe. After the breakdown of negotiations with Britain in January, 1963, however, the negotiating conference ceased work on all applications until 1970. Great Britain's application was accepted in 1971. For a comprehensive study of the Common Market, see Emile Benoit, *Europe at Sixes and Sevens,* Columbia University Press, New York, 1961; for current statistics, see *OEC Statistical Bulletin,* Organization for Economic Cooperation and Development, Paris, monthly.

European Free Trade Association (EFTA; Outer Seven)   A group of countries that have agreed to eliminate tariffs among themselves. They include Austria, Denmark, Norway, Portugal, Sweden, Switzerland, and the United Kingdom, with Finland as an associate member. The association was created in November, 1959, by the Stockholm Convention, which leaves each member country in full control of its foreign economic policy and of its tariffs toward nonmembers. EFTA was established to give these countries outside the Common Market some of the benefits of economic integration without, however, requiring either political cooperation or joint economic policies. Its external trade is about as great as that of the U.S. and very close to that of the European Common Market. In July, 1961, Great Britain, after consultation with its fellow EFTA members, applied for talks with the EEC with a view to full membership. In the following months, all EFTA members acted to seek participation in the integration of Europe. This negotiating conference ceased work on all applications after the breakdown of negotiations with Great Britain in January, 1963. The major obstacles to the merger with the Common Market at that time were Britain's economic ties to the Commonwealth of Nations and the wide divergence between the groups over agricultural policy. However, Great Britain's application was accepted in 1971. For a comprehensive study of EFTA, see Emile Benoit, *Europe at Sixes and Sevens,* Columbia University Press, New York, 1961; for current statistics, see *EFTA Bulletin,* EFTA Information Office, Washington, D.C., monthly.

European Parliament   A single legislative body serving the European Coal and Steel Community (ECSC), the European Common Market, and the European Atomic Energy Community (Euratom). Its actual powers are largely consultative. Although it did not officially come into existence until March, 1958, it first took form as the Common Assembly in April, 1951, with the signing of the Treaty of Paris establishing the ECSC. When the Common Market and Euratom were established in March, 1957, a convention was signed that transferred the powers of the ECSC

Common Assembly to one legislative body. Members of the European Parliament are appointed by and from the national parliaments of the six member nations. France, the Federal Republic of Germany, and Italy each have 36 delegates, Belgium and the Netherlands each have 14, and Luxembourg has six, or 142 delegates in all. The delegates sit by party (the Christian Democrats, the Liberals, and the Socialists) and not by country in fulfillment of one of the first decisions of the former Common Assembly. Each year, the Parliament elects a president and eight vice presidents. The mainspring of the European Parliament's influence is found in its thirteen standing committees, which are concerned, respectively, with political affairs, external trade, agriculture, social affairs, internal market, economic and financial affairs, relations with underdeveloped countries, transport, energy, research and cultural affairs, health protection, administration and budget, and legal affairs. The committee system allows small groups to prepare reports on specific fields as working documents for the Parliament. These reports are then debated and put to the vote in a full session of Parliament. The committees also hold periodic hearings with the Community executives, providing the Community with expert information and advice when needed. Some of the Community policies that have been debated by the Parliament are (1) the negotiations for the entry of Great Britain into the Common Market, (2) action on the second convention of association of the African states and the Malagasy Republic with the Common Market, (3) a definition of Common Market relations with Latin America, (4) the state of preparation for multilateral tariff negotiation in the framework of the General Agreement on Tariffs and Trade, and (5) the development of a common energy policy. The Parliament meets in Strasbourg, France.

European Payments Union (EPU)   An intra-European payments union designed "to promote and free the flow of intra-European trade through a freely automatic multilateral system which permits each member of the Union to offset its deficit with any participating country against its surplus with any other country of the group." The EPU came into being on July 1, 1950, by agreement of the members of the Organization for European Economic Cooperation. It was intended to be a temporary system to assist the European countries until they could complete their recovery from the effects of World War II. The Union functioned much like a clearinghouse, requiring monthly reports from member countries on their bilateral deficits or surpluses with each other. These deficits and surpluses were then offset against one another to arrive at a total surplus or deficit position for each country, which was then added to, or subtracted from, its previous position. Each country was assigned a quota that was based on its total intra-European transactions in 1949. The account of each country was settled monthly with payment partly in gold and partly by credit up to the extent of the quota. All deficits beyond the quota required payment in gold. Thus, no nation could settle unlimited balances through the EPU. The EPU successfully provided Europe with currency convertibility during the postwar period of economic redevelopment. It was terminated on December 27, 1958, and was succeeded by the European Monetary Agreement. For further information, see *Ninth Report of the Organization for European Cooperation: A Decade of Cooperation; Achievements and Perspectives*, Organization for European Economic Cooperation, Paris, April, 1958, chap. 4; see also H. Austin Peck, *International Economics*, Thomas Y. Crowell Company, New York, 1957.

Export-Import Bank of the United States (Eximbank) An independent agency of the U.S. government whose purpose is to help finance and facilitate U.S. foreign trade. Established in 1934 as a District of Columbia banking corporation, it was reincorporated in 1945 and operates under the broad flexible provisions of the 1945 act, as amended. Eximbank is a somewhat unique organization in that it conducts an international banking program with public funds. It was the first public agency, national or international, to arrange credits for the capital equipment required for large-scale economic development projects on a global basis. Primarily concerned with stimulating the sale of U.S. products overseas, Eximbank finances the purchase of U.S. capital equipment, materials, and services by foreign governments or private entities. Its loans must be spent in the U.S. and are repayable in dollars, plus interest on terms appropriate for the goods. In addition to dollar financing, the bank provides U.S. exporters with guarantees and insurance on their foreign accounts receivable. By its statutes, Eximbank is required, in all lending and guarantee operations, to assure itself of a reasonable ability of the borrower to meet his commitments. In addition, the law directs the bank to supplement and encourage private capital interests and not to compete with them. To perform its functions, Eximbank has a capital stock of $1 billion, which is held by the U.S. Treasury, and, in addition, has been granted authority to borrow up to $6 billion from the Treasury. Although the objective of the Bank is to facilitate U.S. foreign trade, a fortunate side effect has been the earning of dividends for the U.S. taxpayer through the collection of interest loans. In twenty-nine years of operations around the world, the Bank paid $738.4 million to the Treasury in interest and dividends and accumulated reserves of more than $800 million above operating expenses. In assisting the export sale of U.S. goods and equipment, the Bank disbursed nearly $9 billion during this period to American manufacturers and exporters. In keeping with the dictum not to compete with private capital, the bank received participation in its lending program from private banks and financial institutions amounting to $800 million. Eximbank lending has financed U.S. industrial and agricultural equipment for every major geographical region of the world. Authorized credits for the overseas sale of U.S. goods and equipment include $750 million for electric power development, $1.9 billion for transportation and communications, $540 million for mining development, $1.4 billion for agriculture and forestry machinery, $820 million for general industrial machinery, $290 million for water-supply and irrigation projects, and $3.1 billion to foreign governments in the form of trade emergency loans. As the result of this activity, thousands of U.S. manufacturers and exporters have received overseas orders. In addition, between the end of World War II and the establishment of the Marshall Plan, the bank administered the government's reconstruction program for Europe, which entailed the lending of billions of dollars for the purchase of U.S. goods. Eximbank's offices are located at 811 Vermont Avenue, N.W., Washington, D.C. 20571.

"Fanny Mae"   *See Federal National Mortgage Association (FNMA).*

Farm Credit Administration   An independent agency of the U.S. government that supervises the land-bank system and intermediate credit banks. The Farm Credit Act of 1933 authorized farmers to organize production-credit associations as a source of operating credit by discounting farmers' notes with the intermediate credit banks and also provided for banks for cooperatives to finance farmers' marketing and purchasing cooperatives. In 1939 the Farm Credit Administration became an agency of the Department of Agriculture, but it was again made an independent agency of the executive branch of the government by the Farm Credit Act of 1953. The Administration operates under policies established by a thirteen-member, part-time Federal Farm Credit Board. Twelve of the members, one from each Farm Credit district, are appointed by the President, who considers nominations from the organizations using the banks in each district; the thirteenth member is appointed by the Secretary of Agriculture. The expenses of the Administration are paid from assessments against the banks and associations that it supervises. Loan funds are obtained principally from the sale of consolidated bonds and debentures to the investing public by each group of banks. These securities are not guaranteed by the government either as to principal or as to interest. The Farm Credit Administration releases an annual report each year.

Farm Credit System An organization of United States financial institutions which provides credit services adapted specifically to the needs of farmers and their cooperatives. Under the supervision of the Farm Credit Administration, the cooperative Farm Credit System functions through twelve Farm Credit districts throughout the U.S. Within each district are a Federal Land bank and local Federal land-bank associations, through which farmers obtain long-term real estate loans; a Federal intermediate credit bank and local production-credit associations, which provide short- and intermediate-term operating loans; and a bank for cooperatives, from which farmers' marketing, purchasing, and service cooperatives can obtain operating, commodity, and facility loans. Activities of the three banks in a district are coordinated through a district Farm Credit board. The original authority for the organization of the nationwide cooperatvie Farm Credit System was contained in the Federal Farm Loan Act, enacted by Congress in 1916, which created the Federal Land Bank system as a source of farm-mortgage credit. The Agricultural Credits Act of 1923 authorized the establishment of Federal intermediate credit banks to discount farmers' notes for banks and other lending institutions. The System was originally capitalized by the Federal government. This capital, which totaled $683 million at its peak and in 1963 amounted to $199 million, is being replaced with member capital ($466 million in 1963), with the ultimate objective of complete farmer ownership. Complete farmer ownership was achieved in December, 1968, when all the government capital was repaid. During 1969, the System lent $10.7 billion and had $13.2 billion of loans outstanding. Bulletins and circulars describe the organization and functions of the System, and numerous statistical reports and releases are prepared throughout the year.

Farmer Cooperative Service A service of the U.S. Department of Agriculture. It conducts research studies, maintains an advisory service, and engages in educational activities to assist the nearly 3 million U.S. farmers who use cooperatives to market farm products, purchase farm supplies, and obtain business services. Its work covers cooperative management, organization, policies, merchandising, product quality, costs, efficiency, financing, and membership. In addition, it helps nationals of other countries to learn about U.S. farmer cooperatives. The Service had its beginning in the Office of Markets, which was formed in 1913 in the U.S. Department of Agriculture. In 1926 the Cooperative Marketing Act authorized the Cooperative Marketing Division to promote knowledge of cooperative principles and practices. Subsequently, this division was transferred to the Federal Farm Board and then to the Farm Credit Administration. In December, 1953, this function was transferred to the Department of Agriculture as an agency, Farmer Cooperative Service. It cooperates with other agencies in the Department of Agriculture, with other Federal departments, the banks for cooperatives of the Farm Credit System, the land-grant colleges, extension services, state departments of agriculture, and teachers of vocational agriculture in helping farmers improve their cooperatives. Its research and educational publications are available to the public. A monthly magazine, *News for Farmer Cooperatives*, carries research and educational articles of interest to farmer cooperatives in the U.S. and other countries. A publication which normally appears every year is *Research Report: Statistics of Farmer Cooperatives*. Other major publications are *Farmer Cooperatives in the U.S.*, Bulletin 1; *Cooperatives in Agribusiness*, Educational Circular 33; *How to Start a Cooperative*, Educational Circular 18; *Farmer Cooperatives . . . Farm Business Tools*, Agricultural Information Bulletin 275; *How Farm Marketing Cooperatives Return Savings to Patrons*, Research Report 7; and *Financial Structure of Farmer Cooperatives*, Research Report 10.

Farmers' Educational and Cooperative Union of America   *See National Farmers Union.*

Federal Aviation Administration (FAA)   A part of the U.S. Department of Transportation whose purpose is "to provide for the regulation and promotion of civil aviation in such manner as to best foster its development and safety, and to provide for the safe and efficient use of the airspace by both civil and military aircraft. . . ." The roots of the FAA go back to 1926, when the first Air Commerce Act was passed. This act established an Aeronautics Branch in the Department of Commerce for the purpose of regulating the then new business of air transportation, licensing pilots, developing air-navigation facilities, promoting flying safety, mapping airways, and furnishing flight information to those who needed it. Further regulatory steps created the Civil Aeronautics Authority and then the Civil Aeronautics Administration. The formation of the FAA on January 1, 1959, brought together in one organization the Civil Aeronautics Administration, the Airways Modernization Board, and the safety-rule-making function of the Civil Aeronautics Board (the Board itself continued as an independent agency). The FAA was created to meet the need for one central organization with the ability and responsibility to fulfill the requirements of the fast-growing aviation community. Its responsibilities and activities encompass all of the U.S. and its possessions and touch upon international areas in which U.S. flag carriers operate, providing the around-the-clock services necessary to assure the safety and regularity of air travel. The Agency is responsible for developing and operating a common (civil-military) air-traffic control system, writing safety rules and regulations, allocating and regulating air space, and conducting research and development. It also certificates airmen and aircraft, is responsible for installation and operation of air-navigation facilities, and provides guidance and financial assistance for the construction of airports.

Federal Communications Commission (FCC)   An independent agency of the U.S. government. It is responsible for regulating interstate and foreign communications by radio, television, wire, and cable. Created on June 19, 1934, the function of the FCC is to provide for the orderly development and operation of broadcasting services and rapid, efficient nationwide and worldwide telegraph and telephone service at reasonable rates. It promotes the safety of life and property through the use of wire and radio communications and employs communications facilities for strengthening the national defense. With jurisdiction over communications in the fifty states, Guam, Puerto Rico, and the Virgin Islands, the Commission cooperates with various government agencies concerned with wire and radio communication in international and national matters. It also cooperates with state regulatory commissions in telegraph and telephone matters. The FCC does not regulate the Federal government's use of radio. In its regulation of broadcasting, the Commission has jurisdiction over AM and FM radio, UHF and VHF television (both commercial and educational), and cable television (CATV). It also regulates aviation, ship, amateur, and various forms of business and citizens' radio services. It considers applications for construction permits and licenses for all classes of nongovernment radio stations. The Commission also assigns frequencies, sets operating power, designates call signs, and inspects transmitting equipment and regulates its use. It passes on license renewals and changes in ownership of radio and television broadcasting stations, which, under the Communications Act of 1934, are licensed to serve the public interest, convenience, and necessity. The Commission, usually at license renewal time, reviews the overall performance of a station to determine whether it has lived up to its obligations and the promises made when it was licensed to operate. In the common-carrier field, which includes telephone, telegraph, cable, microwave, and satellite communications, the FCC sets regulations and supervises charges, practices, and classification of services. It licenses radiotelephone and radiotelegraph circuits and assigns frequencies for their operation. The Commission also prescribes and reviews accounting practices, acts on requests for mergers, and considers applications for construction of new facilities and changes in service. In international matters, the FCC is responsible for domestic administration of the telecommunications provisions of treaties and international agreements. Under State Department auspices, the Commission participates in international conferences concerned with communications matters. It licenses radio and cable circuits from the U.S. to foreign points and regulates operating companies. It also licenses radio stations on American planes and ships in international service. The FCC is administered by seven commissioners—not more than four of whom may be members of the same political party—appointed by the President with the approval of the Senate. A commissioner's appointment is usually for a seven-year term. One of the commissioners is designated chairman by the President. A chairman's tenure is at the pleasure of the President. Among FCC publications are the *Annual Report* and *Statistics of Communications Common Carriers.*

Federal Crop Insurance Corporation   An agency of the U.S. Department of Agriculture that plans and administers the crop-insurance program. The Federal Crop Insurance Corporation was created by Congress in 1938 to fill a long-existing need. The aim of Congress was "to promote the national welfare by improving the economic stability of agriculture." Benjamin Franklin had suggested, in 1788, "an office of insurance for farms against the damage that may occur to them from storms, blight, insects, etc. A small sum paid by a number would repair such losses and prevent much poverty and distress." In asking for crop-insurance legislation, following the tragic drought years of the 1930s, President Franklin D. Roosevelt stated that crop insurance would "help to protect the income of individual farmers against the hazards of crop failure, . . . stabilize farm buying power and contribute to the security of business and employment." In order to produce a crop, the American farmer must invest up to 80% of his expected gross return, or the equivalent of four years' profit. This investment is subject to a wider variety of unavoidable risks than any other business. Federal crop-insurance indemnities have been paid for more than 120 causes of crop damage, including drought, plant disease, and insect infestation. These can wipe out or severely damage not only a single farmer's crop but a substantial part of the farm production of a county, a state, or a region. With the loss of the equivalent of up to four years' profits, a serious economic blight strikes both the farmers and all those who share in the money that the affected farmers would normally spend. In areas stricken by crop disasters, bank credit necessarily tightens up, farm and rural business bankruptcies increase, and the whole economy is hurt. Crop insurance is intended to counteract this situation. Its effectiveness varies with the percentage of farmers in an area who buy crop-insurance policies to protect their production costs. The Federal Crop Insurance Corporation publishes its *Annual Report to Congress.*

Federal Deposit Insurance Corporation (FDIC)   An independent corporation of the U.S. government whose major purposes are to insure the deposits of all banks entitled to benefits under the law, to act as receiver for closed national banks as well as for closed state banks when appointed by state authorities, and to promote the continuance or development of sound banking practices. The FDIC insures deposits up to a maximum of $20,000 for each depositor. At the end of 1969 about 97% of all incorporated banks of deposit in the U.S. were participating in Federal deposit insurance. The FDIC was created by the Banking Act of 1933, and Federal deposit insurance became effective on January 1, 1934. From January 1, 1934, to December 31, 1969, the Corporation made disbursements to protect 1,673,000 depositors in 482 banks in serious financial difficulties. Full recovery was made available to 99.7% of these depositors, disbursements in these cases totaling $475.0 million. Estimated recoveries of $419.3 million have reduced the Corporation's potential loss of funds in all insurance transactions to about $55.7 million. FDIC's income is derived from assessments on insured banks and from investments; it receives no appropriations from Congress. By statute, insured banks are assessed annually one-twelfth of 1% of assessable deposits and are credited with two-thirds of their annual assessments after deductions for losses and expenses incurred during the year by the Corporation. For 1969, the effective net assessment rate was about one-thirtieth of 1%. On December 31, 1969, the Corporation's Deposit Insurance Fund amounted to $4,051 million. The FDIC is authorized to borrow not more than $3 billion outstanding at any one time from the U.S. Treasury, and the Secretary of the Treasury is authorized and directed to lend up to this amount to the Corporation on such terms as may be fixed by the Corporation and the Secretary when, in the judgment of the board of directors of the FDIC, such funds are required for insurance purposes. The FDIC has never exercised this borrowing power. The Corporation is managed by a three-member board of directors. The Comptroller of the Currency is an ex officio member; the other members are appointed by the President for six-year terms with the advice and consent of the Senate. The FDIC publishes an annual report of its operations to Congress. It also publishes an annual *Report to Insured Banks,* describing its financial operations, and *Assets, Liabilities, and Capital Accounts,* a semiannual report containing data for all banks. Copies of these reports are sent to each insured bank and are available to the public on request.

Federal Home Loan Bank Board   An independent agency of the U.S. Government. It supervises the $168-billion savings and home-financing industry and is the country's major private source of funds to finance the construction and purchase of homes. The Board is headed by a three-member board, appointed by the President for four-year terms and confirmed by the Senate. The Federal Savings and Loan Insurance Corporation, a permanent government corporation under direction and supervision of the Board, protects aganst loss the funds of some 45 million savers in over 4,400 insured member institutions. Insurance protection is provided up to a maximum of $20,000 for each saver in each insured institution. A saving and loan association's membership in the Federal Home Loan Bank System assures the homeowner-borrower that the institution to which he applies is a dependable source of economical home financing. This System, directed by the Board in Washington and working through the Federal Home Loan Banks in twelve districts, makes available long- and short-term credit to about 4,800 member thrift and home-financing institutions. Funds loaned to these institutions represent proceeds of the sale of consolidated notes and bonds in the open money market. Major publications of the Federal Home Loan Bank Board that are available on request are *Annual Report, Combined Financial Statements* of Member Institutions of the Federal Home Loan Bank System, *List of Member Institutions—FSLIC* Insured, *Source Book* of Savings and Homefinancing, *Trends in the Savings and Loan Field, Summary of Savings Accounts* by Bank Districts, States, SMSA's, Counties, annually; *Estimated Home Mortgage Debt and Financing Activity, Federal Savings and Loan Insurance Corporation—Financial Statements, Real Estate Foreclosure Report,* quarterly; *Savings and Mortgage Activity—Selected Balance Sheet Data* separately reported for all operating savings and loan associations and for FSLIC-insured savings and loan associations, *The Journal of the Federal Home Loan Bank Board, Interest Rates and Other Characteristics of Conventional First Mortgage Loans,* monthly.

Federal Home Loan Bank System   *See Federal Home Loan Bank Board.*

Federal Intermediate Credit Banks   Twelve banks, one in each Farm Credit district of the U.S., which do not lend directly to farmers and stockmen but make loans to, and discount agricultural paper for, production-credit associations, state and national banks, agricultural credit corporations, livestock loan companies, banks for cooperatives, and Federal Land banks. The banks obtain the funds that they use in their lending operations mainly from sales to the public of short-term consolidated collateral-trust debentures. The banks were authorized by the Agricultural Credit Act of 1923, and before January 1, 1957, they were entirely government owned. The Farm Credit Act of 1956 provided, however, for the gradual retirement of government-owned capital stock as private capital and surplus reserves were built up to support the financial operations of the banks. Complete farmer ownership was achieved in December, 1968, when all the government's investment in the banks was repaid.

Federal Maritime Commission An independent agency of the U.S. government established to administer the broad regulatory provisions of the various shipping acts. Its principal areas of responsibility are as follows: (1) It regulates rates, fares, and practices of common carriers by water in the domestic offshore trade and in the foreign commerce of the U.S. In addition, it regulates charges, classifications, and tariffs in the domestic offshore trade and passes on the reasonableness of rates and fares in this trade. (2) It regulates practices of ocean-freight forwarders and of terminal operators furnishing terminal facilities for, or in connection with, a common carrier by water, and it licenses independent ocean-freight forwarders and supervises their practices. (3) It approves, disapproves, cancels, or modifies conference and other agreements between common carriers by water in the foreign and domestic offshore trade of the U.S. and supervises actions taken pursuant to such agreements. (4) It approves or disapproves contract rate systems used by common carriers by water or conferences of such carriers in foreign commerce. (5) It makes rules and regulations affecting shipping in the foreign trade to meet conditions unfavorable to shipping which result from foreign laws, rules, or regulations or from competitive methods used by foreign-flag carriers. (6) It hears complaints of alleged violations of the various provisions of the Shipping Acts and decides whether or not a violation has occurred. In appropriate circumstances, it awards reparations for injuries. (7) It requires evidence of adequate financial responsibility from owners or charterers of American or foreign vessels, having accommodations for fifty or more passengers and embarking at U.S. ports, to pay judgments for personal injury or death or to indemnify passengers holding tickets in the event of nonperformance of a voyage. The Federal Maritime Commission was established on August 12, 1961. The authority for its operations stems from the following legislation: Shipping Acts,

1916, as amended; Intercoastal Shipping Act, 1933, as amended; Merchant Marine Act, 1920, as amended; and Merchant Marine Act, 1936, as amended. The Commission is composed of five commissioners who are appointed by the President for five-year terms with the advice and consent of the Senate. Not more than three of the commissioners may be appointed from the same political party. The President designates one of them to serve as Chairman of the Commission. The Commission's only publication on a continuing basis is its *Annual Report*.

Federal Mediation and Conciliation Service   An independent agency of the U.S. government charged with promoting labor-management peace. It plays a dual role of preventing and settling collective bargaining disputes between employers and organizations of employees. Federal law requires that notices of disputes be filed with the Service if no agreement has been reached thirty days in advance of the termination or reopening of a labor contract. Receipt of the notice alerts the Service to the possibility of labor conflict so that a commissioner may be assigned to investigate and inquire whether aid will be needed. The commissioner's job is not to take sides but, by listening, reviewing, analyzing, advising, and suggesting, to help point the way for the disputants to find a solution to their problems. The Service is also actively engaged in preventive, or creative, mediation. This involves consultation with labor and management to help them improve relations during the term of labor contract agreements and be better prepared to handle amicably the eventual renewal of the contract. Originally a bureau of the Department of Commerce, the Service became part of the Department of Labor when that Department was established in 1913. When the Labor-Management Relations Act of 1947 (Taft-Hartley Act) was adopted, the Service was transferred from the Department of Labor to its present independent status. The Service is headed by a Director appointed by the President. It maintains a staff of some 265 skilled mediation commissioners in seven regional offices and more than seventy-five field offices located in principal industrial centers. The commissioners represent a balanced cross section of industrial life, about one-third having backgrounds in organized labor, one-third in management, and one-third in the professions and in government. They are all pledged to a completely neutral role as representatives of the public interest. The Service publishes an *Annual Report*.

Federal National Mortgage Association (FNMA; "Fannie Mae")   An instrumentality of the U.S., FNMA is a government-sponsored corporation, owned entirely by private stockholders. It is subject to regulation by the Secretary of Housing and Urban Development. FNMA provides supplementary assistance to the nationwide secondary market for mortgages guaranteed by the Administrator of Veterans' Affairs (VA) or insured by the Federal Housing Administration, Department of Housing and Urban Development (FHA), or Farmer's Home Administration, Department of Agriculture (FHDA). Originally chartered as a government-owned corporation in 1938, FNMA was rechartered by the Congress in 1954 as a mixed-ownership (government and private) corporation. In September, 1950, it was transferred from its status as a subsidiary of the Reconstruction Finance Corporation to the Housing and Home Finance Agency, and in September, 1965, it was transferred as an entity to the newly created Department of Housing and Urban Development. In September, 1968, FNMA was partitioned into two corporations: Government National Mortgage Association (GNMA), to remain within the Department of Housing and Urban Development as a wholly government-owned corporation, and the present Federal National Mortgage Association, to operate as a government-sponsored corporation owned entirely by private stockholders. FNMA is income-producing and completely self-supporting. Its publications are quarterly *Financial Statements* and *Annual Report*. FNMA headquarters are located at 1133 Fifteenth Street, N.W., Washington, D.C. 20005.

Federal Open Market Committee A committee of Federal Reserve System officials which governs the open-market purchases and sales of U.S. government securities and other authorized assets with a view to accommodating commerce and business and with regard for their effect on the general credit situation of the U.S. The Committee's meetings constitute a forum for exploring all aspects of the economy's performance and discussing ways in which the Federal Reserve System's influence over the cost and availability of bank credit can be used most effectively to promote such national economic goals as a high rate of economic growth, high employment, reasonable price stability, and a favorable balance of international payments. Operations in foreign exchange, which are coordinated with similar Treasury operations, are directed at maintaining the strength of the dollar in its role as a key international currency. The Federal Open Market Committee developed from an informal investment committee set up by the Federal Reserve Banks in early 1922 to centralize purchases and sales of U.S. government securities on behalf of the Federal Reserve Banks. This committee began later in 1922 to make policy recommendations from time to time to the several Reserve Banks, and the Banking Act of 1933 gave a successor advisory group statutory recognition as the Federal Open Market Committee. The Banking Act of 1935 gave the Committee statutory control over all open-market operations and provided that its membership include (as it does at present) the seven members of the Board of Governors of the Federal Reserve

System, the president of the Federal Reserve Bank of New York, and four of the eleven other Federal Reserve Bank presidents, chosen in rotation. Under the Committee's direction, a manager of the System's open-market account conducts operations in U.S. government securities and banker's acceptances, and a special manager for foreign-currency operations conducts activity in the foreign field. Both managers are also officers of the Federal Reserve Bank of New York, through which operations are conducted. A record of the policy actions taken by the Committee at each meeting, including the votes on the decisions and a résumé of the basis for them, is released approximately ninety days following the date of the meeting and is subsequently published in the *Federal Reserve Bulletin* as well as in the *Annual Report* of the Board of Governors of the Federal Reserve System. The *Monthly Review* of the Federal Reserve Bank of New York contains an article on the money market, which treats open-market operations briefly each month. Also available from the New York Bank are these booklets: Paul Meek, *Open Market Operations,* for the general reader; Robert V. Roosa, *Federal Reserve Operations in the Money and Government Securities Markets,* for those who wish a more detailed treatment of the subject.

Federal Power Commission (FPC)   An independent agency of the U.S. government that licenses non-Federal hydroelectric power projects and regulates the interstate wholesale rates of electric utilities and their securities, mergers and consolidations, acquisitions, and accounts. To assure an abundant supply of electric energy throughout the U.S. with the greatest possible economy and with regard to the proper use and conservation of natural resources, the FPC is empowered and directed to divide the country into regional districts for the voluntary interconnection and coordination of facilities for the generation, transmission, and sale of electric energy. It also has jurisdiction over the interstate transportation and sale of natural gas. The FPC regulates natural-gas companies in much the same way it regulates electric utilities, including the exercise of jurisdiction over rates and accounts. Until June 4, 1954, the Commission had held that its jurisdiction did not extend to companies engaged solely in the production and gathering of natural gas, but the U.S. Supreme Court then ruled that independent producers selling natural gas in interstate commerce were subject to FPC rate and certificate jurisdiction. In this decade the FPC is concerned not only with assuring an adequate, low-cost supply of electric power and natural gas but also with serving society's need for energy in an environment compatible with a high quality of life in the twentieth century. Created in 1920 to administer the provisions of the Federal Water Power Act, the FPC was composed of the Secretaries of War, Interior, and Agriculture. It was reorganized in 1930 as an independent agency with five full-time commissioners appointed by the President with the advice and consent of the Senate. Commissioners serve five-year terms, one term expiring each year. Not more than three of them may be members of the same political party. The Chairman is named by the President, and the Vice Chairman is elected annually by the Commission. Major FPC publications, all published annually, include *Statistics for Interstate Natural Gas Pipeline Companies; Statistics of Privately-Owned Electric Utilities; Statistics of Publicly-Owned Electric Utilities; Typical Electric Bills; Steam-Electric Plant Construction Costs and Annual Production Expenses; Hydroelectric Plant Construction Costs and Annual Production Expenses.*

Federal Reserve System   A nationwide system consisting of the Board of Governors, the Federal Open Market Committee, the twelve Federal Reserve Banks and their twenty-four branches, the Federal Advisory Committee, and the member banks. Its purpose is to foster a flow of additional money that will facilitate orderly economic growth, a stable dollar, and long-run balance in our international payments. Before the establishment of the Federal Reserve System, the U.S. suffered from an irregular flow of credit and money that contributed to unstable economic development. Following a monetary crisis of unusual severity in 1907, Congress appointed a National Monetary Commission to determine what should be done. After considering the results of the Commission's study as well as the recommendations of other authorities, it passed the Federal Reserve Act on December 23, 1913. Because of experience in the late 1920s and early 1930s, the powers of the Federal Reserve System were strengthened materially by the banking acts of 1933 and 1935. At the base of the System are the Federal Reserve's 6,000 member banks. All national banks must be members; state-chartered banks may become members. Although fewer than half of the commercial banks in the U.S. are members of the System, these banks hold nearly 85% of all commercial bank assets. At the top of the System's structure is a nonpartisan seven-member Board of Governors in Washington, appointed by the President with Senate approval. The Board's prime function is the formulation of monetary policy. It has the power to approve changes in the discount rates that Reserve banks charge for loans to member banks. Its other responsibilities include the authority to vary the percentage of deposits that the member banks must keep as reserves, to set margin requirements governing credit for the purchase of securities, and to establish maximum interest rates that can be paid on time and savings deposits. The Board supervises the operations of the Federal Reserve Banks, and the individual members are also members of the Federal Open Market Committee. Through the Reserve banks and their branches, the Federal Reserve System performs a variety of services, including the distribution of currency and coin, the clearance and collection of checks, and the transfer of bank funds by telegraph from one part of the country to another. It also has broad responsibilities for the examination and regulation of the operation of its member banks. The Board of Governors publishes the *Federal Reserve Bulletin,* monthly; *Federal Reserve Chart Book on Financial and Business Statistics,* monthly; and *Annual Report, The Federal Reserve System: Purposes and Functions.* These are all available from the Board of Governors of the Federal Reserve System, Washington, D.C. 20551. Each Federal Reserve bank publishes its own monthly review of business conditions, an annual report, and occasional pamphlets on topics of special interest.

Federal Savings and Loan Insurance Corporation *See Federal Home Loan Bank Board.*

Federal Savings and Loan System *See Federal Home Loan Bank Board.*

Federal Statistical Office An independent central authority of the Federal Republic of Germany within the Federal Ministry of the Interior. Its main functions are the technical and methodological preparation of Federal statistics; the promotion of their uniformity and comparability; the collection, compilation, and presentation of the data; and the establishment of national accounts. The Federal Statistical Office has close contacts with the Conference of European Statisticians, the Statistical Office of the European Communities, and the Statistical Office of the United Nations. Among its important publications are *Statistisches Jahrbuch* (Statistical Yearbook), *Wirtschaft und Statistik* (Economics and Statistics), *Statistischer Wochendienst* (Weekly Information on Statistics), and *Survey of German Federal Statistics.* Its headquarters are located at 11 Gustav Stresemann Ring, 62 Wiesbaden, Federal Republic of Germany.

Federal Statistics Users' Conference (FSUC) A nonprofit organization composed of users of Federal statistics from business, labor, trade associations, nonprofit research organizations, and state and local governments. Founded in 1956, its objective is to promote Federal statistical programs of optimum usefulness at minimum cost. It provides a forum where statistics users from different sectors of the economy can meet to discuss and define their common needs for information from Federal sources. It is also a vehicle by which these common needs may be made known to the producers of Federal statistics, and it provides a service to its members by keeping them informed of developments affecting the quantity and quality of Federal statistics they use. It is engaged in a continuing effort to get the Federal government to define more clearly priority needs for statistical improvement, to better coordinate Federal statistics programs, and to make more effective use of existing resources as ways of promoting more adequate statistical information while encouraging economy, discouraging duplication, and holding down the paper-work burden on respondents to statistical questionnaires. The conference has a number of committees working on different problems of importance to members. Committees include (1) Anticipations and Intentions Statistics, (2) Balance of Payments and Foreign Market Statistics, (3) Long Range Improvements in Federal Statistics, (4) Demographic Statistics, (5) Agricultural Statistics, (6) Federal Construction and Housing Statistics, (7) Federal Distribution Statistics, (8) Federal Government Expenditures Statistics, (9) Manpower Statistics, (10) National Economic Accounts, and (11) Transportation Statistics. The conference maintains close contacts with the Bureau of the Budget and major statistics-producing agencies. Congressional committees dealing with statistics programs and problems frequently ask the conference to find out user views on statistical programs or problems which are of concern to Congress. The annual meeting, special conferences devoted to particular statistical programs or problems, the work of conference committees, and direct inquiries to members are devices used to obtain the views of statistics users for these purposes. It publishes a monthly *Newsletter* and special reports on topics of current importance to Federal statistics users. The conference's headquarters are located at 1523 L Street, N.W., Washington, D.C. 20005.

Federal Trade Commission (FTC)   An independent regulatory agency created in 1914 by the Federal Trade Commission Act with authority to prevent unfair methods of competition and unfair and deceptive acts or practices in commerce. It was established because of congressional concern that maintenance of a free economy could not be achieved solely by prosecution in the Federal courts of "full-blown" combinations in restraint of trade and monopolies violative of the Sherman Antitrust Act. The FTC was made responsible for halting, in their incipiency, business practices which had the capacity to hinder or prevent competition. The FTC also prosecutes discriminatory practices violative of the Clayton Act, as amended by the Robinson-Patman Act, and, concurrently with the Department of Justice, unlawful mergers and acquisitions. Of increasing recent importance, the FTC is charged with protection of the nation's consumers from acts and practices, including advertising, which are fraudulent, deceptive, or misleading. The FTC is additionally responsible for preventing the interstate marketing of dangerously flammable fabrics, for requiring consumer creditors to make true credit-cost disclosures, and for regulating the packaging and labeling of consumer commodities to prevent consumer deception and to facilitate value comparisons. Through rules, regulations, and cooperative procedures the Commission provides authoritative guidance to business and industry on what is lawful under the laws administered by the FTC. In its economic reporting work, the FTC gathers, analyzes, and makes available to the Congress, the President, and the public factual data on business and competitive conditions. Examples of FTC economic publications in recent years are *The Use of Games of Chance in Food and Gasoline Retailing* (1968), *Automobile Warranties* (1968), and *Corporate Mergers* (1969). The FTC also publishes, in collaboration with the Securities and Exchange Commission, the *Quarterly Financial Report for Manufacturing Corporations,* which presents a composite income statement and balance sheet for all active U.S. manufacturing corporations by industry and asset size. Its *Annual Report to Congress* covers its accomplishments during the preceding fiscal year, outlines its functions and responsibilities under the various acts which it administers, gives the texts or relevant portions of the statutes pertaining to the FTC, describes in detail the organization of the Commission, and lists its investigations and reports since 1915. The FTC consists of five members appointed by the President and confirmed by the Senate for a term of seven years. Not more than three of the commissioners are permitted by the FTC's organic act to be members of the same political party. One commissioner is designated by the President as chairman of the FTC, who is responsible for the executive and administrative functions of the agency.

Federation des Industries Belges *See Federation of Belgian Industries.*

Federation of Belgian Industries The representative organization of Belgian industry on the national level. Its aim is to advance the idea of a free-enterprise economy for Belgium. The federation's essential task is to elucidate and defend the views of industrial circles on all major economic and social problems and to speak effectively on behalf of industry at the national and industrial level. While it is both an organization of action and an organization of documentation, its real justification and usefulness are evident in its actions, which serve not only the interests of its members but those of the nation. As an organization of documentation, the federation has been able to develop specialized research services based on its access to reliable sources of industrial information. In addition, it takes an active part in the work of organization, both public and private, official and unofficial, and national and international. In conjunction with the public authorities and with nationally and industrially federated trade-union organizations, it seeks solutions conducive to maintaining and furthering social peace and the economic prosperity of Belgium. Created in 1946 as a successor to the Comité Central Industriel, which was founded in 1895, the federation covers a large number of professional associations, representing all sectors of Belgian industrial activity. It is a confederation of some 35,000 industrial enterprises associated in member federations, whose actions it coordinates in a spirit of close cooperation and freely accepted discipline. Federation publications are the *Bulletin,* thrice monthly, which provides a liaison between the organization and the industrial endeavors of the country; *Industrie,* monthly, which is intended for managers, economists, sociologists, and scientists. Headquarters are located at 4 Ravenstein, Brussels, Belgium.

Financial Executives Institute (FEI)   A U.S. management organization whose objectives are to serve as an effective spokesman for the business community by (*a*) isolating in advance those problems and issues which might in time affect business or the environment in which it operates and (*b*) preparing and presenting forceful recommendations for action by business and professional groups and governmental agencies; (2) to develop a superior body of knowledge of advanced financial management techniques, ethics, and philosophy; (3) to aid all financial executives in broadening their knowledge of these techniques, ethics, and philosophies and to participate actively and successfully in the full range of business activities; and (4) to provide a medium for, and to stimulate, the healthy exchange of ideas and experience between the business, government, and academic communities. Established in 1931, FEI now has a membership of more than 6,800 financial executives of leading business concerns. An annual conference and six area conferences are held each year. The institute publishes research studies, position papers, and a monthly magazine, *Financial Executive.* Headquarters are located at 50 West 44th Street, New York, N.Y. 10036.

Food and Agriculture Organization of the United Nations (FAO)   An international agency of the United Nations whose chief aims are to increase food production throughout the world and to improve the nutrition of the world's peoples, leading to better standards of living. To achieve these aims, FAO continually reviews the conditions of world food and agriculture and supplies governments with facts and figures relating to nutrition, agriculture, forestry, and fisheries and with appraisals and forecasts relating to the production, distribution, and consumption of their products. It also promotes and recommends national and international action that is aimed at increasing production in agriculture, fisheries, and forestry; improving education and administration in these fields; improving the processing, marketing, and distribution of agricultural products; conserving national resources; promoting adequate agricultural facilities; and furthering policies with respect to agricultural commodity arrangements. Upon request, FAO furnishes technical assistance to members in all these fields. The Organization grew out of the United Nations Conference on Food and Agriculture, which was held in Hot Springs, Va., in 1943. At this conference, 44 nations agreed to work together to promote freedom from want and thus contribute toward a lasting peace. The first of the post-World War II international agencies, FAO was formally founded at Quebec, Canada, on October 16, 1945, when 42 governments ratified its constitution. At present, FAO has 121 member nations. Continuing publications of FAO are *The State of Food and Agriculture; Monthly Bulletin of Agricultural Economics and Statistics; Unasylva; Yearbook of Forest Products; Yearbook of Fishery Statistics; World Fisheries Abstracts; FAO Trade Yearbook; FAO Production Yearbook; Fertilizers: An Annual Review of World Production, Consumption and Trade; The FAO Plant Protection Bulletin; Food and Agriculture Legislation; Cocoa Statistics;* and *CERES, FAO Review.* The North American regional office of FAO is located at 1325 C Street, S.W., Washington, D.C. 20437.

Food and Nutrition Service (FNS)   An agency of the U.S. Department of Agriculture. It was organized in 1969 to concentrate administration of food programs in the national drive to end hunger in the U.S. Cash grants, donated foods, and technical assistance are provided to state and local government agencies for a number of interrelated activities that may be divided into two broad areas—child food service programs for schools and institutions and food or food stamps for low-income families. The child nutrition programs include school lunches, school breakfasts, and meals for children in nonschool group activities such as day-care centers and summer recreation programs. Some Federal funds are available to help poor schools and organizations buy kitchen and serving equipment to start or expand food services for needy children. Food help for needy families is provided through the food-stamp program and the direct donation of foods; both activities are carried out through state and local government agencies. The aim is to end poverty-caused hunger and malnutrition by providing food or the means to buy food to poorly paid workers, the elderly, and the handicapped. Principal FNS publications include PA-948, *Child Nutrition Programs;* PA-930, *Food Stamp Program;* PA-667, *USDA's Food Donation Programs;* and *Food and Nutrition News,* monthly. FNS also publishes numerous pictorial and simply worded flyers and leaflets, some in both English and Spanish, to inform poor people about the programs.

Forecasting Section, Economics and Finance Ministry   An organization of the French government which acts as a general source of information for the Ministry of Economics and Finance and issues all statistical data prepared by the economics and financial services. It has responsibility for making economic analyses of current problems and offers technical assistance with regard to all problems connected with economic forecasting. It was created as SEEF in 1952 to provide detailed national income and expenditure accounts and annual economic budgets to act as a framework for economic policy making. In 1962, however, many of its tasks concerned with national accounting were turned over to the National Institute of Statistics and Economic Studies. In 1965, it succeeded SEEF. It publishes a review, *Statistiques et études financières*. Its headquarters are located at 6 Avenue de l'Opéra, Paris 1, France.

Foundation for Economic Education, Inc.   A nonprofit, nonpolitical organization of the U.S. that was founded to champion the free market, private property, and a philosophy of limited government. In an attempt to combat the trend toward governmental intervention in human affairs, it carries out a program of disseminating information on the free-enterprise system through its various publications. Among them is a monthly magazine, the *Freeman*. The foundation also sponsors seminars on economic education. Its headquarters are located at Irvington on the Hudson, N.Y. 10533.

G

General Confederation of Italian Industry   A nonpolitical body whose aims are to analyze problems of interest to all industries or some particular sectors, to protect manufacturers' interests in the economic and labor field, and to represent industry in its relations with public and private institutions as well as with international agencies. It is made up of associations or groups of enterprises. These associations are of two types: (1) national trade associations and (2) regional associations. At present the confederation membership comprises 205 associations, of which 99 are trade associations and 106 are regional associations, totaling about 100,000 member firms with about 3 million employees. It began its activity in 1919, availing itself of the experience of Federazione Industriale Piemontese and of a previous Confederazione Italiana dell' Industria that remained in operation until the beginning of World War I. Its major publications are *Rivista di Politica Economica* (Review of Economic Policies), which provides studies of different branches of economics; *Annuario* (Yearbook), a complete review of economic and industrial problems of the year; *Rassegna di Statistiche del Lavoro* (Summary of Labor Statistics), a report of statistics of the labor market in Italy and abroad; *Gazzetta della Piccola Industria* (Small Industries' Gazette), a monthly publication dealing with the economic and labor problems of small enterprises. In 1961, it started to publish a research series, of which twenty-one volumes in Italian and four volumes in English have been released. Its headquarters are located at Piazza Venezia, 11, Rome, Italy.

General Commissariat of the Plan An agency of the French government. It is almost independent, although it is part of the Prime Minister's office and has close links to the Ministry of Finance. Acting as a bridge between the public and private sectors, it obtains a concerted point of view on the future of the French economy and is able to formulate a course of action to make the economic plan work. The agency receives the cooperation of about 3,500 persons who are drawn from all sectors of the economy but mostly are businessmen. These persons staff twenty-five committees, twenty of which deal with specific areas of the economy and five of which cut across all sectors, covering finance, labor, research, productivity, and regional development. Each government ministry is represented on the committees that concern it. The plan for 1962–1965, for example, was set up in four stages. The first stage, purely governmental, involved the Commissariat and the economic section of the Ministry of Finance, which outlined three plans for the gross national product with breakdowns for twenty-eight major sectors, for labor needs, and for exports and imports. The plans were based on annual growth rates of 3, 4.5, and 6%. In the next stage, the plans were discussed with the government and with an assembly of leaders of industry, labor, farmers, consumers, and other nonpolitical groups. The tentative goal was set at 5%, and the government planners developed a new plan. In the third stage, the twenty-five committees and subgroups corrected the plan from the point of view of technical assumptions concerning labor, investment, and market prospects at home and abroad and the expansion plans of individual companies. In the fourth stage, the industry reports and the government plan were combined; the growth rate was then put at 5.5%. This plan was sent to the Cabinet, which adopted it as a general guide to official economic policy, and to the National Assembly for approval.

Gosplan   The state planning commission of the U.S.S.R. It is charged with developing the general economic plan, which serves as a guide for factory and farm production and other economic activity in the Soviet Union. Gosplan's recommendations are embodied in a national economic plan, which describes in detail the economic goals of the U.S.S.R. for a specified period, usually one and five years. Its recommendations must be approved by the Supreme Soviet, the elective governing body of the U.S.S.R. Measures for carrying out the plans advanced by Gosplan are formulated by the Council of Ministers of the U.S.S.R., an appointive body which is constitutionally responsible to the Supreme Soviet. For a further discussion of Soviet planning and Gosplan's role, see Harry Schwartz, *Russia's Soviet Economy*, Prentice-Hall, Inc., Englewood Cliffs, N.J., 1954, chaps. 4 and 5.

Group of Ten   A group of ten leading industrial nations, formed to provide cooperation in maintaining a smoothly functioning international monetary system. The combined monetary reserves of the group are a second line of defense, behind the International Monetary Fund, against balance-of-payments pressures on convertible currencies. Under the Group of Ten, the General Agreements to Borrow were established in 1962. Under the GAB a fund of $6 billion worth of currencies was set up. This fund can be drawn on by central banks of any member nation through the IMF. Drawings must be approved by individual creditor nations and do not correspond to the automatic drawing rights of the International Monetary Fund. The Group of Ten consists of the United States, the United Kingdom, Belgium, Canada, France, West Germany, Italy, Japan, the Netherlands, Sweden, and the observer nation of Switzerland. For additional information, see Alvin H. Hansen, *The Dollar and the International Monetary System*, McGraw-Hill Book Company, New York, 1965.

Ifo-Institut für Wirtschaftsforschung An independent, nonprofit research organization having the legal status of a registered society; the institute is located in Munich. The functions of the Ifo-Institut include the following:

1. Observation, analysis, and forecasts of short- and long-term economic trends; studies of economic and fiscal policies; observation of foreign economies
2. Market observation and structural studies of industry, the building sector, agriculture, wholesale and retail trade, handicrafts and allied trades, transport and traffic; survey of regional economic structures
3. Preparation of long-run growth projections for the various sectors and subsectors of the economy on the basis of the institute's own long-term projections for the national product and its components
4. Determination of cost and output structures of individual branches of the economy in the form of input-output analyses; carrying out of management polls, particularly the application of the new "Konjunkturtest" (business survey) and "Investitionstest" (investment survey) methods developed by the Ifo Institute; preparation of market and trade-cycle analyses in very brief form for important individual markets ("Konjunkturspiegel," or business activity reflector) and sectors of the economy ("Investitionsberichte," or investment reports)
5. Studies of the economic problems of African developing countries

The Ifo-Institut is financed by the subscriptions of its members, fees for commissioned work, and private and public grants. All native-born persons and legal entities may become members of the Ifo-Institut. Each member fixes his own contribution (at least DM300 per year). Ifo-Institut issues the following periodicals: *Ifo-Schnelldienst*, weekly; *Wirtschaftskonjunktur*, quarterly; *Ifo-Studien*, annually. Its headquarters are located at 5 Poschingerstrasse, Munich, 27, Federal Republic of Germany.

IIT Research Institute (IITRI) An independent contract research organization, serving government and industry, whose work encompasses virtually all the physical and biological sciences and their related technologies. Founded in 1936, it was formerly known as the Armour Research Foundation of the Illinois Institute of Technology. An extremely broad spectrum of research and engineering is performed at IITRI, from fundamental studies of physical phenomena to planning and product development. This mixture of basic and applied research stems directly from IITRI's major goals: scientific excellence in the pursuit of new knowledge and the translation of this knowledge into useful applications. The principal research areas are chemistry, computer sciences, electronics, life sciences, engineering, mechanics, metals, ceramics, physics, product development, law-enforcement science and technology, environmental and waste utilization, olfactronics and odor sciences, and space technology. Research projects for industrial and government sponsors encompass almost every field of science and experimental engineering. With more than 1,000 research projects a year, the institute's annual research volume exceeds $27 million, making it one of the largest contract research organizations in the U.S. IITRI publishes *Frontier,* a biannual scientific magazine featuring articles written by staff members and distributed without charge to scientists, government officials, industrialists, and business leaders. In addition, IITRI scientists and engineers publish almost 300 research papers and articles each year. IITRI is located at 10 West 35th Street, Chicago, Ill. 60616.

Institute for Social Research of the University of Michigan An institute that was conceived as a mechanism by which sustained research programs could be conducted in a variety of academic disciplines, with resources permitting the conduct of studies of considerable size. It is composed of three research centers: the Survey Research Center, the Research Center for Group Dynamics, and the Center for Research on Utilization of Scientific Knowledge. The Survey Research Center was organized at the University of Michigan in 1946. After the Research Center for Group Dynamics came to the university in 1948, the Institute for Social Research was established with the two centers as its constituent parts. The third center of the institute was established in 1964. The Survey Research Center is concerned primarily with the utilization and development of the sample survey in advancing theory and knowledge in the social sciences. It is interested in a wide range of research problems representing a number of fields, including economic behavior and attitudes, organizational behavior and human relations, communications and influence, political behavior, and mental health. The economic-behavior program has carried out surveys to determine the distribution among different population groups of income and income change, U.S. government savings bonds, bank deposits, amounts saved, amounts borrowed, home ownership and home purchases, installment debt, consumer inventories, and frequency of travel by rail and plane. These studies have yielded both descriptive material and a knowledge of fundamental relationships based on complex analyses. Two studies conducted by the program have extended over many years. The oldest is the survey of consumer finances, conducted annually since 1946, which collects statistics on the distribution of consumer income, assets, debts, and major transactions. A book, *1960 Survey of Consumer Finances,* summarized fifteen years of consumer statistics. The second sequential study consists of the periodic surveys of consumer attitudes, which are designed to measure the changes in consumer optimism and confidence and are used by many governmental and business organizations. These surveys measure the complex motivational forces that influence the American people to buy or save. Such knowledge significantly increases the accuracy of short-term forecasts as to the probable level of business activity. Since 1955 a series of surveys has measured trends in the travel market—the persons who travel, their preferred means of traveling, the length and cost of their business and vacation trips, and their general attitudes and motivations toward travel. These data appear in a series of publications called *The Travel Market.* The Research Center for Group Dynamics is engaged in the development of a basic science of groups. Through an integrated program of social research, theories and techniques are being developed for studying such properties of groups as cohesiveness, communication, norms, leadership, decision making, and productivity. The center uses a variety of methods in its investigations of group behavior. Studies are made of natural groups, such as those found in communities, schools, or industry, as well as of groups assembled for experimental purposes. The Center for Research on Utilization of Scientific Knowledge investigates and attempts to reduce the gap between what is known and what is being utilized and applied in our society. This center studies the processes of science utilization, the spread of new knowledge, ways of training practitioners to apply research findings effectively in their respective fields, and the value and ethical issues in the use of scientific knowledge. The headquarters of the institute are located in Ann Arbor, Mich. 48103.

Institute of Life Insurance   An organization of U.S. life insurance companies. It has two broad objectives: (1) to make available basic information about the life insurance business, its operations, and its services in order to broaden the public's understanding of life insurance; and (2) to transmit public attitudes about life insurance to the insurance business so that companies and agents can render better and more effective service. The institute is supported by life insurance companies which represent nearly 95% of the assets of the business in the U.S. To help perform its duty as the central source of information, it is constantly engaged in the gathering of data about life insurance. Its division of statistics and research is responsible for the collection and tabulation of industrywide aggregates and other performance statistics, which are published in one or more publications and are distributed by other divisions of the institute to their specialized publics. The division has also embarked on a program of research in the social sciences, which has as its primary emphasis the study of the family in the changing U.S. society. Other research projects include the surveying and evaluation of public opinion and other consumer surveys which attempt to determine attitudes toward life insurance as well as characteristics of life insurance owners. Among the institute's publications are the annual *Life Insurance Fact Book,* which is based primarily on data gathered by the division of statistics and research and serves as a reference volume. The monthly *Tally of Life Insurance Statistics* features an article on a current survey or analysis of statistics relevant to life insurance as well as monthly reports of benefit payments and assets of the life insurance companies, quarterly data on stockholdings, and state distributions of death payments. Other publications include a folder, *Group Insurance Coverages in the United States;* the pamphlet *Life Insurance Buying,* an analysis of the characteristics of buyers of new ordinary insurance policies; and *Decade of Decision,* which was written by Jerome B. Cohen of the City University of New York, and describes life and health insurance by means of a case-study approach. The institute's headquarters are located at 277 Park Avenue, New York, N.Y. 10017.

Institute of Management Sciences   An international nonprofit scientific society whose objectives are to identify, extend, and unify scientific knowledge that contributes to the understanding and practice of management. To this end, it conducts meetings, conferences, and symposia, publishes journals and monographs of special interest, and encourages research in the management sciences. Among its subject areas are planning, simulation and gaming, mathematical models, business information systems, organization theory, control systems, and research and development management. The institute was organized in December, 1953, and incorporated in the state of California. Its membership of more than 6,200 consists of managers, educators, scientists, and students in more than eighty-three countries. There are chapters in twenty-five areas, including Japan, the United Kingdom, and Norway, outside the United States; a Western European section; and twelve colleges of individuals with specific interests. The institute is governed by a council of eighteen. It publishes *Management Science*, monthly, which reports basic research in theory and applications. The institute conducts two meetings each year, one international and one American; one of the meetings every third year is held outside the United States. It contributes to the support of research at the Center for Operations Research & Econometrics at the University of Louvain, in Belgium. The Institute may be reached through P.O. Box 6112, Providence, R.I. 02904.

Institut National de la Statistique et des Etudes Economiques *See National Institute of Statistics and Economic Studies (INSEE).*

Institut National de Statistique *See National Institute of Statistics.*

Inter-American Development Bank An international financial institution organized in 1960 to foster the economic progress of its member countries in Latin America. Membership consists of the U.S. and nineteen Latin American countries. The Bank was established with two completely separate resources: its ordinary capital resources, subscribed at $813,160,000 (of this, $381,580,000 has been fully paid in and $431,580,000 is callable); and its Fund for Special Operations, subscribed at $146,316,000. In addition, since 1961 the Bank has administered $394,000,000 of the $500,000,000 Social Progress Trust Fund which the U.S. government established to promote social development in Latin America as part of the Alliance for Progress program. The Bank makes loans to member countries, to political subdivisions of these countries, and to public and private enterprises. The loans are made either for specific projects or to development banks and institutions in member countries for relending for projects which are not large enough to warrant direct credits from the Bank. Loans to private borrowers are made with or without governmental guarantees. With its ordinary resources, the Bank makes loans which are repayable in the currency disbursed. Thus, dollar loans made with the ordinary resources must be repaid in dollars. The Bank can increase its ordinary resources by selling bonds in the world's financial markets. Loans made from the Fund for Special Operations may be repayable in the currency of the borrower. Loans from the Fund may be used for projects which are not directly productive but which are vital to the long-term development of Latin American countries. With the resources of the Social Progress Trust Fund, the Bank extends loans for projects in the field of land settlement and improved land use, housing for low-income groups, community water-supply and sanitation facilities and advanced education and training. The Bank made its first loan in

February, 1961. Up to December 11, 1962, it had approved 133 loans for a total of $602.8 million. The basic authority of the Bank is vested in its board of governors, composed of one governor and one alternate appointed by each member country for five-year terms. The board meets once a year in the capital of a different member country. The day-to-day conduct of the Bank's operations is entrusted to its board of executive directors, the president of the Bank, and the executive vice president. The board of directors functions continuously at the Bank's headquarters. It is composed of seven directors representing the member countries. Approximately two-thirds of the Bank's staff consists of Latin American citizens and one-third of U.S. citizens. For details of the Bank's operations, see Inter-American Development Bank, *Annual Report*. The Bank's headquarters are located at 808 Seventeenth Street., N.W., Washington, D.C. 20025.

Interdistrict Settlement Fund (Gold Settlement Fund)   A part of the Federal Reserve System of the U.S. under the control of the Board of Governors in Washington which facilitates check clearing and transfers of funds between banks in different Federal Reserve districts. Its only assets are gold certificates deposited in the Fund by the twelve Federal Reserve banks, and its only liabilities are the corresponding deposits. A Federal Reserve bank clears an interdistrict check by crediting its member bank's account with the amount of the check and sending it to the Federal Reserve bank in whose district it belongs. This bank debits the account of the member bank on whom the check was drawn, and it owes the first Federal Reserve bank the amount of the check. This is balanced by means of the Interdistrict Settlement Fund. The Fund credits the first bank with the amount and debits the second. In practice, the settlement comes at the end of each day, when each Federal Reserve bank notifies the Fund of the amount owed to it by the other Federal Reserve banks and owed by it to them, and the accounts are credited and debited accordingly. See Donald L. Kemmerer, *The ABC of the Federal Reserve System,* Harper & Row, Publishers, Incorporated, New York, 1950.

Internal Revenue Service   An agency of the U.S. Treasury Department. It determines, assesses, and collects internal revenue taxes and enforces the internal revenue laws and such related statutes as the Federal Alcohol Administration Act and the Federal Firearms Act. The Service's mission is to achieve the highest possible degree of voluntary compliance with Federal tax laws and to maintain the highest degree of public confidence in its integrity and efficiency. Prior to the establishment of the agency in 1862, the nation had relied on internal taxation only in two brief periods. These were from 1791 to 1802, to pay Revolutionary War debts, and from 1813 to 1817, to finance the War of 1812. The Civil War and the Revenue Act of 1862 marked the beginning of a permanent Federal tax-collecting organization. While personal income taxes were a feature of the 1862 act, this form of taxation was dropped in 1872. From then until the passage in 1913 of the Sixteenth Amendment, which authorized an income tax, internal tax collections were derived primarily from excises on alcohol and tobacco products. Since 1913, revenues from income taxes have provided the major share of the government's tax revenue. Gross Internal Revenue collections for the fiscal year 1969 were $187.9 billion. Individual income taxes amounted to $97.4 billion, corporation income taxes to $38.3 billion, employment taxes to $33.1 billion, excise taxes to $15.5 billion, and estate and gift taxes to $3.5 billion. The Internal Revenue Service is decentralized, the responsibility for Federal tax administration being generally vested in fifty-eight district directors. As of June, 1970, there were seven regional offices, each headed by a regional commissioner to supervise the district directors in his region. The major publications of the Service are the Commissioner's *Annual Report; Internal Revenue Bulletin; Reports on Revenue Collections; Statistics of Income; Your Federal Income Tax; Tax Guide for Small Business; Farmer's Tax Guide; Employer's Tax Guide.*

International Association for Research in Income and Wealth An international society whose main object is the furthering of research on the definition and measurement of national income and wealth, social accounting and its use in economic budgeting, international comparisons, aggregations of national income and wealth, problems of statistical methodology connected therewith, and related matters. The association was founded in September, 1947, in conjunction with a meeting of the International Statistical Institute in Washington, D.C., by a group of individuals who were then actively engaged in national-income-accounting research. The first general meeting of the association was held in September, 1949, in Cambridge, England. Financial support for the association during the periods 1949–1961 was provided by the Nuffield Foundation and the Rockefeller Foundation. Each of the biennial meetings resulted in the publication of a volume of papers (*Income and Wealth,* series I–XI). In addition, eight volumes of the *Bibliography of Income and Wealth* were published for the period 1937–1960. Four special regional conferences were held with funds provided by the Rockefeller Foundation, and these resulted in regional volumes for Africa, Latin America, Asia, and the Middle East. In 1962, the association moved its headquarters from the National Institute of Economic Research in England to Yale University. The Yale Economic Growth Center has provided support for the association since January, 1962. In an effort to provide better dissemination of research in the field of income and wealth, a quarterly journal, the *Review of Income and Wealth*, was substituted for the biennial conference volumes in January, 1966. Membership in the association now exceeds 250, and the circulation of the *Review* exceeds 1,250 in over thirty countries. The main activities of the association are the quarterly publication of the *Review* and the conduct of biennial conferences. The association's headquarters are located at Yale University; its mailing address is Box 2020, Yale Station, New Haven, Conn. 06520.

International Bank for Reconstruction and Development An international banking institution affiliated with the United Nations. Known popularly as the World Bank, it operates primarily by making loans, in cases in which private capital is not available on reasonable terms, to finance productive investments in member countries. It also provides a wide variety of technical assistance to its members. The bank may lend to member governments, governmental agencies, or private enterprises; if the borrower is not a goverment, the guarantee of the member government concerned is required for the loan. Founded at the Bretton Woods Conference in July, 1944, the bank began operations in June, 1946. Its membership consists of the governments of member countries, each of which subscribes to its capital stock in accordance with the country's economic strength. As of December 31, 1969, 112 countries were members of the bank, and the total subscribed capital was $23,066 million, of which 10% had been paid in. The paid-in capital, however, was never intended to finance all the bank's operations. Lending funds have been drawn mainly from the sale of its bonds (more than $8,069 million, of which $4,303 million was outstanding on December 31, 1969) in the capital markets of the world, from the sale of parts of its loans (about $2,343 million), and from earnings and repayment of loans (about $1,953 million). By December, 1969, the Bank had made 657 loans, totaling more than $13,115 million, to finance projects in 88 member countries. The distribution of bank lending was as follows: Africa, $1,873 million; Asia, $4,297 million; Australia, $418 million; New Zealand, $98 million; Europe, $2,435 million; Western Hemisphere, $3,794 million; and IFC, $200 million. Major publications, especially those issued on a continuing basis, are the *Annual Report—The World Bank/IDA; Summary Proceedings of Annual Meetings; The World Bank Group* (1969 ed.); *World Bank Atlas* (population, per capita product, and growth rates), 1969; *The World Bank, IDA, and IFC Policies and Operations.* The bank's offices are located at 1818 H Street, N.W., Washington, D.C. 20433.

International Brotherhood of Teamsters An independent international union with a membership of over 2 million, which, in addition to truck drivers, includes a large number of workers in warehousing and food processing as well as in every important industry in the country. The union began in 1888 when 1,200 drivers scattered throughout the Central states amalgamated their eighteen locals into the Team Drivers International Union. Since then, the union has grown in size and diversity to become the largest single labor organization in the world. In November, 1969, the peak membership month for the union, local unions paid per capita tax to the international union on 2,041,345 members. The basic unit is the local union, which usually is chartered on craft or class jurisdictional lines, although a general local may include workers from several jurisdictions. When three or more locals are located in a given geographical area, they are affiliated with a joint council, of which there are approximately fifty. Additionally, locals are affiliated with state conferences where they exist, and all are affiliated with one of four area conferences geographically divided to include all the U.S., Canada, and Puerto Rico. The union is structured with area conference and international trade divisions. Local unions enjoy autonomy. The supreme governing body of the international union is the international convention convened every five years. The general executive board is composed of a general president, a general vice president, a general secretary treasurer, and twelve area vice presidents, all elected in convention. The union's official journal is the *International Teamster,* published monthly. Headquarters are at 25 Louisiana Avenue, N.W., Washington, D.C. 20001.

International Confederation of Free Trade Unions (ICFTU)   A world trade-union body organized in 1949 for the purpose of remaining free from Communist influence. At the time that the confederation was organized, it included 70 trade unions in 53 countries with about 50 million members; by 1961 it had 135 affiliates in 107 countries and territories with 56.5 million members. All affiliates are autonomous. U.S. unions are represented by the AFL-CIO and the United Mineworkers. The ICFTU opposes all forms of dictatorship and totalitarianism. Its chief function is educational, with emphasis on underdeveloped countries, and it has created colleges for training labor leaders in Calcutta, India, and Kampala, Uganda, and is considering a college in French-speaking Africa. Another activity is the International Solidarity Fund, which disburses donations from union members to victims of strikes, mine disasters, earthquakes, and other misfortunes. Publications include *Free Labor World,* monthly; *Information Bulletin,* bimonthly; *Economic and Social Bulletin.* ICFTU headquarters are located in Brussels, Belgium; offices are maintained in New York, Geneva, and various cities in Latin America, Asia, and Africa.

International Development Association (IDA)   An affiliate of the International Bank for Reconstruction and Development (World Bank) that provides funds to less-developed countries whose ability to make effective use of capital is greater than their capacity to assume and repay debts on conventional terms. It was established in September, 1960. Principles similar to those of the World Bank are followed by IDA in appraising projects and in negotiating credits, but it lends money for a similar but sometimes wider range of purposes than the bank does. The development credits which IDA has extended have been for terms of fifty years and bear no interest. A service charge of three-quarters of 1% per annum, payable on the amounts withdrawn and outstanding, is made to meet IDA's administrative costs. Membership in IDA is open to member countries of the World Bank; by December, 1969, 104 countries had joined IDA, raising its total subscriptions to $1,014 million. IDA's total resources as of December 31, 1969, amounted to $3,176.6 million. The bulk of IDA's usable resources comes from subscriptions and additional contributions from the eighteen richer member countries and from transfers from the World Bank itself. From the beginning of its operations in November, 1960, to December 31, 1969, IDA extended 178 development credits amounting to more than $2,292 million to fifty-one countries in Africa, Asia, the Middle East, Europe, and the Western Hemisphere. Major publications are the *Annual Report—The World Bank/IDA; Summary Proceedings of Annual Meetings; The World Bank Group* (1969 ed.); *World Bank Atlas* (population, per capita product, and growth rates), 1969; *The World Bank, IDA, and IFC Policies and Operations.* IDA offices are located at 1818 H Street, N.W., Washington, D.C. 20433.

International Finance Corporation (IFC) IFC was established in 1956 by its member governments to supplement the work of the International Bank for Reconstruction and Development (World Bank). An affiliate of the World Bank, IFC is a separate legal entity with its own funds and staff. Its purpose is to further economic development by encouraging the growth of productive private enterprise in its developing member countries. In association with private investors, IFC assists in financing, without a government guarantee, private enterprises and private development finance companies, where sufficient private capital is not available on reasonable terms. It promotes the international flow of private capital and encourages the growth of capital markets in the developing countries. Most IFC investments consist of a share subscription plus a long-term loan. Some consists of a share subscription only, when there is no need for an IFC loan. Less often, when the equity is provided by other investors but loan funds are not available from other sources on reasonable terms, IFC will make a straight loan. It may then require a bank guarantee, demand a rate of interest higher than it would otherwise ask, or seek some other means of limiting or compensating for its risk. IFC's authorized capital is $110 million. On January 1, 1970, approximately $107 million was fully paid in by ninety-two member countries. In addition, IFC had a reserve against losses of $54 million derived from accumulated earnings. As of January 1, 1970, IFC had made 187 commitments totaling $377.4 million to 135 private enterprises in forty member countries. Of this total, $41.7 million was standby and underwriting commitments. Major publications are the *IFC Annual Report; IFC General Policies*, a sixteen-page booklet (in English, French, German, Italian, Portuguese, and Spanish); *Summary Proceedings of Annual Meetings; Financial Statements;* and *Facts about IFC*, which includes a summary of IFC investments and standby and underwriting commitments. IFC offices are located at 1818 H Street, N.W., Washington, D.C. 20433.

International Labour Organisation (ILO)   A specialized agency of the United Nations with primary responsibility in the labor field. It was founded in 1919 by the Treaty of Versailles as an affiliate of the League of Nations. While its original purpose was to develop labor standards for application in various countries, its operations have materially broadened in scope to include concern for all social and economic questions affecting employment and labor standards. The ILO has a unique tripartite structure in which each member nation appoints two government delegates and one each from employers and from labor. Since the U.S. joined the agency in 1934, its nomination for the worker delegate has been made by the AFL-CIO, while the U.S. Chamber of Commerce nominates the employer delegate. The U.S.S.R. was a member from 1934 to 1939, when it dropped out; it renewed its membership in 1954. The ILO functions through three bodies: the International Labour Conference, which is composed of delegates from all member nations, and is the basic legislative and policy-making body; the Governing Body, which is composed of forty-eight members elected by the government and by workers' and employers' groups of the conference and which handles problems between annual conferences; and the International Labour Office, which is the administrative group. Over the years, the ILO has enacted conventions, which are draft multilateral treaties that require ratification by a member nation before they become binding upon that nation; recommendations, which are guides to the member nations in establishing labor standards, and less formal instruments known as resolutions, memorandums, and statements, which have no binding effect on a nation. In addition, the ILO has engaged in direct technical assistance, consisting mainly of advice and training in economic development fields; in making available fellowships or scholarships for the study of modern methods; and in the organization of clinics and seminars on a regional basis. It has become the United Nations implementing agency in the labor and social development fields for the European Economic

Community and the European Coal and Steel Community. In 1946, the ILO became responsible for its own financing. Since 1951 the U.S. contribution has been about 25%; that of the U.S.S.R., about 10%; that of Great Britain, about 9.4%; and that of France, about 6%. African nations have emerged as an important factor in the ILO, accounting for more than one-fourth of the membership. ILO headquarters are located in Geneva, Switzerland.

International Monetary Fund An international financial institution affiliated with the United Nations which provides funds to its member nations as they are needed. It promotes a freer system of world trade and payments as a means of helping its members to achieve economic growth, high levels of employment, and improved standards of living. The Fund is a continuing forum for the consideration of foreign-exchange problems, in which members are encouraged to avoid the use of restrictive practices and to maintain an orderly pattern of exchange rates. A request for Fund assistance is considered in the light of the member's fiscal and monetary policies and its cooperation with the Fund's principles. In a foreign-exchange crisis, the Fund may be the largest source of quickly available credit, since its directors are prepared to act on an emergency request within seventy-two hours. The Fund has also played a part in longer-range programs of fiscal and monetary reform, both in the planning efforts and in subsequent financing. Its financial assistance takes the form of a foreign-exchange transaction. The member pays the Fund an amount of its own money equivalent, at the par value agreed upon with the Fund, to the amount of foreign currency that it wishes to draw. The member is expected to "repurchase" its own currency from the Fund within three (at the outside, five) years by a payment of gold or dollars or some other currency acceptable to the Fund. Each member of the Fund is assigned a quota, which approximately determines its voting power and the amount of foreign exchange that it may draw from the Fund. On April 30, 1970, the Fund's assets totaled more than $21 billion. A new facility of special drawing rights in the Fund went into operation on January 1, 1970. On that date, nearly $3.5 billion worth of SDRs were distributed as a new reserve asset, supplementing gold and foreign currencies. The amount was increased by $3 billion on January 1, 1971, and again on January 1, 1972, and may be further increased in the future by decision of participating countries. The highest authority of the Fund is exercised by its board of governors, on which each member country is represented by a governor and an alternate governor. The board has delegated many of its powers to the executive directors. The five members with the highest quotas each appoint one of the Fund's executive directors, and thirteen directors are elected by the other members, making a total of eighteen.

The articles of agreement of the Fund were formulated at the United Nations Monetary and Financial Conference held at Bretton Woods, New Hampshire, on July 1 to 22, 1944. The agreement has been in force since December 27, 1945, when it was signed by twenty-nine governments, representing 80% of the original quotas in the Fund. As of April 30, 1970, there were 115 member countries. The Fund's publications include the *Annual Report; Annual Report on Exchange Restrictions; International Financial Statistics,* a monthly statistical bulletin; *Balance of Payments Yearbook; Staff Papers,* three times yearly; *International Financial News Survey,* weekly.

Interstate Commerce Commission (ICC)   An independent agency of the U.S. government which provides for Federal regulation of transportation facilities (except airlines). Congress created the Commission on February 4, 1887. Its original authority was extremely limited, but early developments indicated the need for enlarging and strengthening its powers, and Congress adopted amendments intended to accomplish this objective. The first major addition to the law, the Hepburn Act of 1906, provided for the enforcement of ICC orders and extended its jurisdiction to include express companies, pipelines (except water and gas), and sleeping-car companies. Reflecting the growing importance of buses and trucks in interstate commerce, the Motor Carrier Act of 1935 (now part II of the Interstate Commerce Act) gave the ICC authority to regulate interstate transportation of passengers and property by motor carriers. The Transportation Act of 1940 extended ICC jurisdiction to water carriers operating in interstate commerce along the coasts, between the coasts, and on inland waterways (part III of the act). The 1940 legislation also made numerous changes in parts I and II of the act and established the present national transportation policy. The ICC has also been affected by numerous other acts, including several of the early 1900s that dealt with railroad safety. However, this function was transferred to the Department of Transporation on April 1, 1967; the Transportation Act of 1920, which extended the ICC's authority over rates; and a 1942 amendment, which provided for regulations of freight forwarders. The most recent amendments, those contained in the Transportation Act of 1958, reduced the number of agricultural commodities exempt from ICC regulation when transported by motor carrier; authorized the Commission to permit the discontinuance of passenger trains or service under certain conditions in addition to its existing authority to authorize the abandonment of railroad lines. The commissioners are appointed by the President for seven-year terms. Pursuant to the President's Reorganization Plan No. 1 of 1969, the chairman is designated by the President from among its members. Major ICC publications are *Decisions of ICC; Interstate Commerce Acts Anno-*

tated; Annual Reports of ICC; Transport Statistics in United States; Accounting Regulations; Report of Section of Railroad Safety; Report of Director of Locomotive Inspection.

Investment Bankers Association of America (IBA)   A voluntary, unincorporated association of investment bankers and securities dealers of the U.S. and Canada, which was organized in 1912. Its nearly 680 member organizations (individual proprietorships, partnerships, corporations, and commercial banks) underwrite and deal in all types of securities. They maintain more than 2,400 branch offices in addition to their main offices. These places of business are located in leading commercial centers and smaller communities throughout the U.S. and Canada. Investment banking's primary function is to channel the savings of millions of persons into productive use by industry and governmental units. As underwriters, investment bankers purchase the stocks and bonds of issuers seeking new funds for resale to individual and institutional investors. Such issuers are either corporations or state and municipal governments. The purpose of the association and its eighteen regional groups is to serve the industry, its customers, and the general welfare in any appropriate way. It fosters a high standard of conduct in business relations and provides a number of programs and services for its members. It also promotes activities to inform the public about the securities business, principles of sound investing, and the U.S. economic system. Through its officers, committees, and staff, the IBA endeavors to keep members advised of significant developments affecting their interests and those of investors. The quarterly *IBA Statistical Bulletin* is a recognized source of data on the municipal-bond market. From time to time, reports are published on various industries, on government, municipal, and corporate securities, and on other investment-related subjects. The association's officers and committees speak for its members on significant issues of the day. The IBA cooperates with and advises various governmental agencies and legislative bodies at both national and state levels on matters affecting the investment community. With its constituent groups, it provides a variety of training programs for the industry: collegel-level classroom and correspondence courses for registered representative candidates; the Institute of Investment Banking, an executive development program; and seminars on operations management and management functions for industry executives. IBA headquarters are located at 425 Thirteenth Street, N.W., Washington, D.C. 20004.

Investment Company Institute   A voluntary organization of the U.S. investment-company industry. It provides a medium through which its members may consult with one another and with governmental agencies and through which they may keep informed of developments in connection with pertinent laws and administrative rulings. The organization conducts a public information program and a research program providing statistical and other information about the industry to the members, governmental agencies, and the public. The institute's membership consists of open-end investment companies (mutual funds), investment advisers to these funds, and underwriters of their shares. Assets of its mutual-fund members represent more than 90% of the assets of all mutual funds in the U.S. The institute's history began with its informal organization in 1940, when the National Committee of Investment Companies was established by combining informal groups representing open-end and closed-end investment companies. It was reorganized in 1941 as a permanent organization, under the name National Association of Investment Companies, with the adoption by the members of a memorandum of association. In 1961 the members decided to change its name to Investment Company Institute and to expand its membership to include investment advisers and underwriters. The institute operates under the direction of the officials of its member companies. A twenty-seven-member board of governors elected by the members is responsible for its overall program. The institute's publications include *Mutual Fund Fact Book; Mutual Fund Shares: An Aid to Attorneys; Mutual Fund Shares: An Aid to Profit Sharing and Pension Plans; Professional Money Management for the Professional Man through Mutual Funds; Planning Your Retirement through Mutual Funds; Planning for College Education through Mutual Funds; The Money Managers: Professional Instrument through Mutual Funds; A Woman's Guide to Mutual Funds; The Mutual Fund Shareholder: A Comprehensive Study; Investing Made Easy; Annual Report.* Its headquarters are located at 1775 K Street, N.W., Washington, D.C. 20006.

Istituto Centrale di Statistica   *See Central Institute of Statistics.*

Istituto Nazionale per lo Studio della Congiunture   *See National Institute for the Study of Economic Trends.*

Italian Union of Chambers of Commerce, Industry, and Agriculture
A voluntary association of Italian chambers of commerce. It coordinates the activities that the chambers of commerce, industry, and agriculture are called upon to carry out in connection with their tasks and aims. Its purpose is to strengthen the chamber-of-commerce system. The union calls meetings and congresses for the study of problems concerning the Italian economy and takes the initiative in favor of economic progress. Among its publications are *Sintesi Economica* (Economic Analysis); *Compendio Economico Italiano* (Economic Survey of Italy), in Italian,

French, and English; Vera Cao-Pinna, *Le prospettive dei consumi alimentari in Italia, 1965–1970–1975* (Outlook for Food Consumption in Italy, 1965–1970–1975), Rome, 1962; *La Carta Commerciale d'Italia*, Giuffrè, Milano, 1968; *I conti economici regionali 1965–1968*, Abete, Roma, 1970. Its headquarters are located at 21, Piazza Sallustio, Rome, Italy.

J

Joint Committee on the Economic Report *See Joint Economic Committee.*

Joint Council on Economic Education An independent, nonprofit, nonpartisan, educational organization founded in 1949 to encourage, coordinate, service, and improve economic education in the nation's schools and colleges. Its program is designed to provide teachers with training in economics emphasizing the structure of economic knowledge, as distinct from the objectives and applications of the science, and to assist them in finding techniques to convey this knowledge in the classroom. Improvement in teaching methods is facilitated by continuous research and curriculum development programs carried out in cooperation with selected schools, school systems, and colleges around the country. Through its College and University Program, the Joint Council not only encourages professional economists and educators to work together to improve the preparation of future teachers but also encourages them to work with school systems in developing means for including economic understandings in the existing curriculum. The Joint Council's principal medium for expanding and improving economic literacy is a network of 46 affiliated, but autonomous, councils on economic education functioning at the state level; 58 centers for economic education on college and university campuses; and over 140 school systems contractually participating in the Developmental Economic Education Program (DEEP). The Joint Council and its affiliated councils prepare and distribute such material as (1) descriptions of classroom practices for all grade levels; (2) resource units or teachers' guides; (3) overall curriculum designs for economic education, grades 1 through 12; (4) bibliographies; and (5) filmstrips exploring major facets of the U.S. economy. Some recent titles published include *Learning Economics through Children's Stories; Handbook for Curriculum Change: Guidelines; Steps for a Balanced Economy; DEEP 1969: Perspectives on a 5-Year Experiment in Curriculum Change; Study Materials for Economic Education in the Schools; Economic Stabilization Policies.* With the advice of members of the American Economic Association's Committee on Economic Education, the Joint Council publishes the semiannual *Journal of Economic Education,* the only publication devoted exclusively to reporting major developments in the teaching of economics. The Joint Council is directed by educators and governed by a seventy-member board of trustees elected from the teaching profession, business, labor, and farm and research organizations. It is the only organization in the field formally affiliated with the American Economic Association, the American Association of Colleges for Teacher Education, and major professional groups in the National Education Association. Its headquarters are located at 1212 Avenue of the Americas, New York, N.Y. 10036.

Joint Economic Committee   In the U.S. government, the congressional counterpart of the Council of Economic Advisers. The Joint Economic Committee of the Congress, created under the Employment Act of 1946, was established to assist the President in gathering authoritative information concerning economic trends, to appraise programs in the light of the declared policy of the act, and to recommend national economic policies, within the framework of the free competitive system, for avoiding economic fluctuations and diminishing the effects thereof. Its function is to make a continuing study of economic developments and national economic policies with a view to coordinating these programs in order to further the stated objectives of the act. This function is carried out through studies and reports on specific economic issues. At the beginning of each Congress, a report containing findings and recommendations with respect to the main proposals made by the President is filed with Congress as a guide to the committees dealing with legislation. The Joint Economic Committee, which was known under the original act as the Joint Committee on the Economic Report, is composed of ten members of the Senate and ten members of the House of Representatives, the majority party in each case being represented by six members and the minority party by four members. The committee issues *Economic Indicators,* a monthly publication which is prepared for it by the Council of Economic Advisers and is supplied to each member of Congress and to subscribers throughout the

U.S. who are interested in timely and authoritative information on economic trends; an annual economic report reviewing the President's economic program as presented to Congress; reports of hearings on a wide variety of economic subjects. Typical of the reports of hearings are studies of the administration of monetary policy, the adequacy of government statistics, the problems of economic growth, the impact of foreign economic policy on the domestic economy of the U.S., the economics of public expenditure.

L

Life Insurance Association of America An organization of U.S. life insurance companies whose functions are as follows: (1) to consider any matter of general concern to the welfare and interests of life insurance policyholders and the life insurance business; (2) to consider important measures that may be introduced from time to time in legislative bodies for the purpose of preparing public statements recommending adoption or rejection; (3) to promote economy and efficiency in the general administration of life insurance companies; (4) to engage in research and other activities in furtherance of its purposes. The association, which was organized in 1906, was formerly known as the Association of Life Insurance Presidents. Its constitution provides for a chairman, who is elected annually, and for a board of directors of fifteen executives of life insurance companies, five being elected each year to serve for three-year terms. The association's only publication available to the public is the *Economic and Investment Report,* issued annually by the vice president and chief economist of the association. Its headquarters are located at 277 Park Avenue, New York, N.Y. 10017.

M

Machinery and Allied Products Institute (MAPI) The economic research organization and national spokesman for the U.S. capital goods and allied products industries, which produce the facilities of production, distribution, transportation, communications, and commerce. MAPI, organized in 1933, and its affiliate, the Council for Technological Advancement (CTA), are dedicated to the advancement of the public welfare and the interests of producers of industrial equipment through a better understanding, by government, industry, and the general public, of the role of capital goods in furthering the economic progress of the U.S. In carrying out this objective, MAPI-CTA conducts research in the economics of capital goods and capital formation and investment and in modern management techniques in such areas as marketing, industrial relations, manufacturing, international operations, finance, and insurance. The products of this research are published in bulletins, memorandums, brochures, and books. In its publications program, the institute has traditionally emphasized a systematic approach to business investment decisions, the need for adequate capital recovery provisions in the U.S. tax code, and other policies necessary to maintain a dynamic economy. Among major institute publications in this area are *Business Investment Management: A MAPI Study and Manual; Underdepreciation from Inflation: A Ghost Returns; Accelerated Depreciation as an Offset to Inflation; Inflation and Corporate Profits; A Favorable Climate for Productive Investment.* The institute's quarterly publication, *Capital Goods Review,* is addressed largely to questions of capital formation and investment, including recently such topics as the effects of inflation on equity returns, the effects of inflation on lenders and borrowers, and the cost of borrowed capital. Other recent works of institute research include *The New Economics; Products Liability and Reliability: Some Management Considerations; The Automation Hysteria; The Government Contractor and the General Accounting Office.* MAPI offices are located at 1200 Eighteenth Street, N.W., Washington, D.C. 20036.

Magazine Publishers Association (MPA)   A U.S. organization devoted to advancing the interests of all magazines in all departments. It serves publishers and aspects of publishing wherever there are common problems which can be solved or common needs for information which can be met by joint effort. MPA represents the magazine industry among groups with allied interests: advertisers, advertising agencies, national and local business organizations, educators, students, and national and local civic or public bodies and organizations. It provides an industry voice to ensure recognition of magazines for their content, their power in the marketplace, and their influence on the thoughts, tastes, and actions of Americans as well as to counter legislative and administrative attacks on publishing and advertising. The association stimulates the use of magazines for reference, pleasure, information, and inspiration; sponsors programs that increase circulation through constructive selling; and makes possible the effective participation of all publishers in the advancement of the printed word and the promotion of increased use of magazine advertising. MPA's membership of about 400 includes large and small magazines of both general and specialized interest. Its headquarters are located at 575 Lexington Avenue, New York, N.Y. 10022.

Manufacturing Chemists' Association, Inc. (MCA)   A nonprofit membership corporation, including U.S. and Canadian manufacturers of chemicals who sell a substantial portion of the chemicals which they produce to other companies. The term chemicals is interpreted to exclude most fringe areas, as well as products of mixing, formulating, or compounding operations which do not involve a change in chemical structure. Charter members in 1872, when the association was founded, consisted of seventeen U.S. manufacturers engaged principally in the production of sulfuric acid. By 1969, MCA included about 190 members, representing more than 90% of the production capacity of basic industrial chemicals within the U.S. and Canada. Although many members function in direct competition, MCA provides a channel through which they may treat industry-wide problems cooperatively in the public interest. The association is engaged in some thirty-five basic activities pertinent to the chemical industry, and about twenty-five technical and functional committees assist and advise it in implementing specific programs. Major committee activities are concerned with industry-wide problems in safety and occupational health; precautionary labeling; packaging and transportation of hazardous substances; abatement of pollution and development of air-quality, water-resources, and solid-waste management; research into the characteristics, use, and handling of plastics; international trade and tariffs; chemically reactive metals and alloys; public relations; industrial relations; and economic aspects of the industry. Among other areas of committee concern are food additives, education, insurance, nuclear energy, patents, tax policy, legal and medical advice, and sponsored research on a variety of topics in various institutions. In addition to two general meetings of members each year, there are numerous technical conferences and symposia on the various activity areas. In addition, MCA participates in technical conferences sponsored by allied organizations. It also maintains a close affiliation with state and Federal government agencies and with national and foreign organizations whose activities are of significance to the chemical industry. A wide variety of publications includes more than 400 items of technical literature and numerous periodical membership bulletins on industry developments, legislative trends, and business conditions. MCA headquarters are located at 1825 Connecticut Avenue, N.W., Washington, D.C. 20009.

Ministère de l'Economie et des Finances, Direction de la Prévision *See Forecasting Section, Economics and Finance Ministry.*

Mortgage Bankers Association of America (MBA) An organization representing the principal investor and lending interests in the field of mortgage financing in the U.S. It provides its membership with industry-wide standards. Organized in 1914, the Mortgage Bankers Association of America comprises more than 2,000 independent mortgage-banking firms, commercial and mutual savings banks, insurance companies, and title companies. MBA holds an annual Convention each autumn, three annual mortgage conferences in different sections of the country; two conferences for senior executives, cosponsored by MBA and New York University in the East and by MBA and Southern Methodist University in the West; and numerous technical seminars, symposia, and clinics. Schools of mortgage banking, sponsored at Northwestern University and Stanford University, offer a three-year program consisting of three one-week summer sessions on campus, plus two interspersed eleven-month home-study programs. A correspondence school for nonmanagement personnel in the field of mortgage banking has also been established. The association sponsored the creation of the MBA Research and Educational Trust Fund to promote scientific research in the field of mortgage banking by the issuance of grants to universities engaged in such research. MBA publishes a monthly magazine, the *Mortgage Banker;* three textbooks on mortgage banking; technical manuals and special reports; a quarterly, *National Delinquency Survey;* a *Directory of Members,* listing all member firms, including their mortgage personnel; *FHA: Payments at a Glance,* giving FHA payments on all ten- to forty-year loans; standardized mortgage forms for the industry. Its headquarters are located at 111 West

Washington Street, Chicago, Ill. 60602. An office maintained in Washington, D.C., issues a monthly, *Washington News Letter; Quarterly Economic Report; Letters to Members,* covering Federal matters with which the mortgage industry is concerned. This office also arranges for members of MBA to appear before congressional committees considering legislation of interest to the mortgage industry.

N

National Aeronautics and Space Administration (NASA)   An independent agency of the U.S. government whose purpose is to direct the aeronautical and space activities sponsored by the Federal government with the exception of those activities concerned primarily with the development of weapons, military operations, or the defense of the U.S. Created by an act of Congress, NASA was established on October 1, 1958. Among its major objectives are the expansion of human knowledge of phenomena in the atmosphere and space; the improvement of the usefulness, performance, speed, safety, and efficiency of aeronautical and space vehicles; the development and operation of vehicles capable of carrying instruments, equipment, supplies, and living organisms through space; the establishment of long-range studies of the potential benefits to be gained from the utilization of aeronautical and space activities for peaceful and scientific purposes, as well as the opportunities for, and the problems involved in, such utilization; and the most effective utilization of the scientific and engineering resources of the U.S. For the fiscal year 1971, the NASA budget was $3.3 billion, as compared with its top $5.3 billion in 1965.

National Association of Business Economists (NABE)   An organization of more than 1,500 U.S. economists who work for private business organizations. The NABE was organized in April, 1959, to serve the needs of the rapidly increasing number of economists employed in private firms. Full-time government, academic, or trade-union economists are not eligible for membership. The specific objectives of the NABE are (1) to provide a forum for the discussion of the problems of practicing business economists; (2) to provide a means of communication between the business community and collegiate schools of business, government, and economists in other fields; (3) to bring into sharper focus the contribution which trained economists can make in the business firm; and (4) to stimulate discussion and research in matters of public policy affecting the business community and business policies affecting the national economy. NABE carries out its objectives through a variety of activities. The programs of the two-day annual meeting are focused directly on topics of interest to the practicing business economist, and the association also sponsors one-day seminars devoted to a thorough examination of single topics, such as international issues facing U.S. business, antitrust problems, and communications problems. NABE publishes *Business Economics* four times a year. The association sponsors an internship program for college students who wish to work in business during the summer, a data-clearinghouse project which permits the exchange of ideas with academic economists, and a placement service. The association's mailing address is P.O. Box 28038, Washington, D.C. 20005.

National Association of Manufacturers (NAM)   An organization of U.S. manufacturing companies whose aims are as follows: (1) to promote the industrial interests of the U.S.; (2) to foster the domestic and foreign commerce of the U.S.; (3) to improve relations between employer and employee; (4) to protect individual liberty and the rights of employer and employee; (5) to disseminate information among the public with respect to the principles of individual liberty and ownership of property; and (6) to support legislation in furtherance of these principles and to oppose contrary legislation. The NAM was organized on January 22, 1895, by some 600 manufacturers who met in Cincinnati as a consequence of an editorial in a trade paper (*Dixie Manufacturer*) calling on manufacturers to join in forming a National Association of Manufacturers for the promotion of trade and commerce. Major NAM publications are *NAM Reports; Review of Legal Developments; Law Department Memo; Service for Company Publications; Industrial Press Service; Program Notes,* for women's clubs; *Dateline,* for the clergy. Its headquarters are located at 277 Park Avenue, New York, N.Y. 10017.

National Association of Mutual Savings Banks   An organization created in 1920 to provide an effective means for the "common protection and common advancement" of the mutual savings banks of the U.S. It represents savings banks in national affairs and in matters relating to Federal government policies and programs, and it conducts educational, research, informational, and other service activities on behalf of its member banks. Membership in the association represents more than 99% of the $75-billion total assets of the savings-banking industry. A board of directors, composed of elected representatives of the several geographic areas as well as the small and large institutions, is the governing body that establishes overall policies, authorizes programs, and approves the annual budget. An executive committee acts on an interim basis between quarterly meetings of the board. Among the association's various departments are the following:

1. *Bank Operations,* which develops manuals, reports, and surveys dealing with bank operations, electronics, insurance, savings bank life insurance, and new services.
2. *Education,* which conducts, under the direction of the Committee on Education and Management Development, the Graduate School of Savings Banking at Brown University, the Management Development Program at the University of Massachusetts, the technical Schools of Special Studies, and the Seminar for Presidents.
3. *Information,* which seeks to create greater understanding of the basic structure and objectives of savings banking, maintains close relations with the press, and issues the association's official publication, *Savings Bank Journal.*
4. *Legal,* which analyzes and interprets all legal aspects of the national association's activities, assists in the preparation of materials for presentation to regulatory authorities and to the Congress and acts to coordinate tax-ruling activities affecting the industry.
5. *Research,* which collects, analyzes, and disseminates information on historical and current trends in savings banking; savings, money, and capital markets; and the nation's economy.
6. *Washington Office,* which maintains liaison between the national association and the Federal government.

An *Annual Report,* describing savings-banking trends and summarizing association activities, is issued at the time of the association's annual conference, in May; the *National Fact Book* is issued annually in mid-June; the *Annual Directory and Guide* appears in September. At the request of the Commission on Money and Credit, the association prepared *Mutual Savings Banking: Basic Characteristics and Role in the National Economy,* Prentice-Hall, Inc., Englewood Cliffs, N.J., 1962. The association's headquarters are located at 200 Park Avenue, New York, N.Y. 10017.

National Association of Purchasing Management A cooperative U.S. service agency and a forum in which purchasing men analyze mutual problems and exchange information. Its basic objectives are (1) to foster and promote the interchange of ideas and cooperation among its members; (2) to develop and apply more efficient purchasing methods and practices; (3) to collect and disseminate information of benefit to its members; (4) to correct trade abuses; (5) to encourage the institution of courses in schools and colleges for the practical training of purchasing agents; and (6) to strive by every legitimate means to advance the purchasing profession. From its foundation in 1915, the association has developed into a national organization representing more than 20,000 members in 111 local affiliated associations. Early in its history, it adopted principles and standards of purchasing practice which are generally accepted as a basic ethical code for purchasing. The regular publication of the association that is sent to members is the semimonthly *Bulletin,* a digest of pertinent and timely business and commodity information. An important monthly feature of the *Bulletin* is the report of the association's business survey committee, an opinion survey of business conditions by approximately 200 purchasing executives who are carefully selected with respect to location and industry. A loose-leaf ring binder, "Guide to Purchasing," in which current and future literature and studies are consolidated, is provided each member. It is supplemented quarterly on subjects that will keep members abreast of the latest developments in purchasing and materials management. A quarterly publication, *Journal of Purchasing,* presents concepts from business statistics, economics, engineering, behavioral science, and any discipline which contributes to the advancement of purchasing knowledge. The association's headquarters are located at 11 Park Place, New York, N.Y. 10007.

National Association of Real Estate Boards (NAREB) An organization of U.S. real estate boards and state associations whose purposes are to provide information, education, and research; to establish ethical standards; and to further sound public policies affecting real estate. It is recognized as the spokesman of organized real estate in the U.S. When the association was founded in Chicago in 1908, its membership consisted of 120 men who represented nineteen boards and one state association with a combined membership of 1,435; by 1970 it had 91,631 members and more than 1,576 boards. Only members of NAREB may use the term realtor, which was adopted in 1916 and registered as the association's trademark in the U.S. Patent Office. NAREB has a long history of promoting home ownership and protecting property owners. It was a prime mover in the establishment of the Home Owners Loan Corporation, the Home Loan Bank System, the mortgage-insurance program of the Federal Housing Administration, and the Federal National Mortgage Association. From its beginning, it campaigned for real estate license laws in each state, and it is now trying to have these laws strengthened. One of NAREB's outstanding accomplishments has been the establishment of the "Build America Better" program, designed to help communities wipe out blighted areas, with emphasis on conservation and rehabilitation in urban renewal. More recently the association has successfully launched its "Make America Better" program, in which realtors work in a wide variety of civic activities to solve the pressing problems of the cities and towns. The association has a large real estate library and a nationally known research department. Through its local boards and state associations, it provides educational courses and conferences and cooperates in the presentation of university courses in real estate. NAREB has nine affiliates, most of which emphasize education in specialized fields. They are the American Institute of Real Estate Appraisers, the Institute of Real Estate Management, the National Institute of Farm and Land Brokers, the American Society of Real Estate Counselors, the American chapter of the International Real Estate Federation, the Executive Officers Council (board executives), and the Women's Council. Two of their publications are the *Appraisal Journal* and the *Journal of Property Management,* both quarterly professional magazines. *Realtor's Headlines,* a weekly newsletter, is published by NAREB. The association's headquarters are located at 1300 Connecticut Avenue, N.W., Washington, D.C. 20006.

National Association of Securities Dealers, Inc. An organization of brokers and dealers in the U.S. over-the-counter securities market. The association resulted from legislation passed by Congress in 1938 for the purpose of regulating this market. Its objectives are (1) to adopt, administer, and enforce rules of fair practice and rules to prevent fraudulent and manipulative acts and practices and, in general, to promote just and equitable principles of trade for the protection of investors; (2) to promote self-discipline among members and to investigate and adjust grievances between the public and members and between members; (3) to provide a medium through which members may confer, consult, and cooperate with governmental and other agencies in the solution of problems affecting investors, the public, and the investment-banking and securities business; and (4) to promote through cooperative effort the investment-banking and securities business, to standardize its principles and practices, to promote therein high standards of commercial honor, and to encourage and promote among members observance of Federal and state securities laws. The association's only publications on a continuing basis are the *NASD Manual* and a newsletter. Its headquarters are located at 888 Seventeenth Street, N.W., Washington, D.C. 20006.

National Better Business Bureau, Inc. A nonprofit corporation established by legitimate U.S. businesses in 1912 to protect themselves and the public from advertising or selling practices which are fraudulent, misleading, or unfair, where these exist on a regional or national scale. The bureau's membership is representative of all phases of business and all sections of the country. The bureau is affiliated with 140 local better business bureaus in key cities in the U.S., Canada, Latin America, and Israel. Each bureau is autonomous, but all exchange information and cooperate in the public interest. The National Better Business Bureau also provides a protective service to approximately 800 chambers of commerce in small communities that do not have local bureaus. It supplies its membership and the public with factual information about the reliability of national advertisers and the validity of advertising claims. An effort is made to adjust complaints. More than 100,000 inquiries and complaints are received by the bureau annually. A division of solicitations reports on organizations soliciting contributions or membership subscriptions from business. The bureau seeks to obtain the correction of advertising or selling practices which, upon investigation, are found to be false, misleading, or unfair. Voluntary cooperation is received from advertisers or their agencies in more than 90% of the cases. Facts are supplied to government agencies where necessary. Advertising and selling codes are promulgated on an industrywide basis, and approximately 300 bulletins dealing with advertisers and advertising practices are published each year. The bureau also publishes a loose-leaf service, supplemented and revised each month, entitled *Do's and Don'ts in Advertising Copy*, which is used by advertisers, agencies, and media in the preparation and acceptance of copy. This service is sold on a subscription basis. The bureau's headquarters are located at 230 Park Avenue, New York, N.Y. 10017.

National Bureau of Economic Research, Inc. A private, nonprofit corporation of the U.S. formed, according to its charter, "to conduct, or assist in the making of exact and impartial investigations in the field of economic, social and industrial science, and to this end to cooperate with governments, universities, learned societies, and individuals." It is not a government agency nor an adjunct of a university, nor does it sell its research services. Organized to determine the facts bearing upon major economic problems, the bureau makes every effort to determine these facts objectively and to interpert them impartially. It devotes its attention to topics of national importance and selects for study those topics that appear susceptible to scientific treatment. The bureau is governed by a board of directors, who are chosen to reflect different economic and social points of view and represents widely differing spheres of activity. Members include persons from industry and labor; banking and finance; professional associations of economists, economic historians, accountants, and statisticians; and economists from universities. Advisory committees aid in planning specific projects and review the progress of investigations. The Universities-National Bureau Committee for Economic Research and the Conference on Research in Income and Wealth plan and organize conferences, securing the cooperation of many specialists on the subjects selected. The results of the bureau's research are made available to all through the publication of its studies. Between 1920, the date of the bureau's founding, and 1963, 200 books and about 140 occasional, technical, and other papers were published. Hard-bound books are published for the bureau by the Princeton University Press; the bureau itself issues its other works. The current program of the bureau includes studies of economic growth, national income, consumption, and capital formation, business cycles, financial institutions and processes, and international economic relations. The bureau has been instrumental in the development of many basic economic measures and indices now in wide use, such as national income and capital-formation estimates. Its work on this subject in the 1920s and 1930s led to the establishment of regular reports of gross national product and its components by the Department of Commerce. Publications in this field include *The National Economic Accounts of the United States: Review, Appraisal, and Recommendations* (1958); Simon Kuznets, *Capital in the American Economy: Its Formation and Financing*, 1961; Raymond W. Goldsmith, *The National Wealth of the United States in the Postwar Period*, 1962. Earlier work by Solomon Fabricant and others in indices of production and of the productivity of labor and capital was capped in 1961 by John W. Kendrick, *Productivity Trends in the United States*. The bureau's work on indicators for business-cycle analysis, tested for more than twenty-five years, is summed up in Geoffrey H. Moore (ed.), *Business Cycle Indicators*, 2 vols., 1961. The monthly *Business Cycle Developments*, published by the Department of Commerce, uses the bureau's methods and results. A bureau study by Julius Shiskin, *Signals of Recession and Recovery*, 1961, describes and analyzes it. A publication in the field of studies of shifts in the distribution of income and wealth in the U.S. is Robert J. Lampman, *The Share of Top Wealth-Holders in National Wealth, 1922–56*, 1962. Comprehensive records of corporate bonds as investments have been developed in W. Braddock Hickman, *Corporate Bond Quality and Investor Experience*, 1958; and other volumes. Monthly estimates of consumer installment credit outstanding are now published by the Board of Governors of the Federal Reserve System, but the work of the bureau in this field is continuing; a new study is Paul Smith, *Cost of Providing Consumer Credit*.

The bureau's headquarters are located at 261 Madison Avenue, New York, N.Y. 10016.

National Bureau of Standards (NBS) A Federal research agency established by Congress in 1901 and operating under the U.S. Department of Commerce. Its central mission is to provide national leadership in the development and use of accurate and uniform techniques of physical measurement. The three major elements of this mission are (1) to provide the central basis for the national measurement system through the development and maintenance of standards of physical measurement, determination of important physical constants which may be used as standards, and international correlation of the national standards and definitions of the units of measurement; (2) to promote accurate and uniform measurements through calibration services, development of transfer standards and instruments, development and distribution of standard materials, encouragement of other standards laboratories, and cooperation in the formulation of standard codes and specifications; and (3) to provide data on the properties of materials which are of importance to science and industry and which are not available elsewhere of sufficient accuracy. These data are the result of selected measurements made by the Bureau and of a program of surveying and critically evaluating data obtained in other laboratories. In addition, the Bureau has been assigned special responsibilities within the government for the fields of radio propagation, data processing, building technology, hydraulics, and cryogenic (low-temperature) engineering. In support of its various programs, NBS conducts research in physics, chemistry, mathematics, and engineering. It maintains major laboratories at Washington, D.C., and Boulder, Colorado, as well as twenty-six field stations in the U.S. and other countries. The results of Bureau research are made available through a large number of publications, including the three-section *Journal of Research* and the *Technical News Bulletin,* and the nonperiodical Applied Mathematics Series, monographs, handbooks, technical notes, special publications, Building Science Series, monographs, National Standard Reference Data Series, product standards, and Federal Information Processing Standards Publications (FIPS PUBS).

National Economic Council, Inc. A politically oriented U.S. organization dedicated to the preservation of human liberty, including the maintenance and invigoration of private enterprise, rights of property, and American independence. The purposes stated in its charter are (1) to stimulate and develop the economic life of the U.S. and of the several states; (2) to encourage Federal, state, and local governments to practice wise economy in public spending; (3) to urge all persons versed in practical affairs as well as in other fields of endeavor to take an active part in public affairs, thereby contributing to the people the benefit of their experience and judgment; (4) to aid in developing an informed public opinion on the major political, social, and economic problems of the U.S. and an understanding by public officials of the importance and needs of private enterprise under the U.S. system of government; (5) to encourage a balanced economy within the U.S. in conformity with the principles of constitutional liberty; (6) to stimulate respect for the Constitution and the country's laws; and (7) to stand at all times for the freedom and independence of the U.S. The council employs tested and available modern methods to reach actual and potential leaders of public thought and the American people as a whole. The semimonthly *Economic Council Letter* furnishes information to thousands of readers; brief reviews of books are included from time to time. The *Economic Council Papers*, published occasionally, contain special articles on current issues or reprints of important articles and speeches which need wider circulation. The council's headquarters are located at 230 Park Avenue, New York, N.Y. 10017.

National Economic Development Council (NEDDY) An organization of the British government. It was established in 1962 to achieve better coordination and cooperation in the formulation of economic policy. It is composed of the Prime Minister and five other ministers (Chancellor of the Exchequer, President of the Board of Trade, Minister of Technology, Secretary of State for Employment and Productivity, and Secretary of State for Economic Affairs), six representatives of management, six representatives of trade unions, two chairmen of nationalized industries, the Chairman of the National Board for Prices and Incomes, two independent members, and the Director General of NEDO. Its tasks are as follows: to examine the economic performance of the nation with particular concern for plans for the future in both private and public sectors of industry; to consider what the obstacles to quicker growth are, what can be done to improve efficiency, and whether the best use is being made of resources; and to seek agreement upon ways of improving economic performance, competitive power, and efficiency. Its publications may be obtained in the U.S. from the British Information Service, 845 Third Avenue, New York, N.Y. 10022.

National Economic Development Office (NEDO) An independent organization of Great Britain, financed by public funds. The office is organized into three main divisions—industrial, commercial, and administrative. The industrial division services the twenty-one economic development committees for different sectors of industry and the other groups working on special projects. The economics division is concerned mainly with studying aspects of economic growth and planning and with preparing papers for discussion by NEDDY on a wide range of economic problems. It also provides advice and economic statistics for the twenty-one economic development committees. NEDO is headed by a director general who is answerable to the National Economic Development Council.

National Electrical Manufacturers Association (NEMA) The largest U.S. trade organization for manufacturers of electrical products. Its membership of approximately 500 companies produces most of the electrical equipment sold in, or exported from, the U.S. NEMA was organized in 1926 through the merger of several organizations of electrical manufacturers, the oldest of which had been in existence since 1908. It is now organized into seven semiautonomous divisions, dealing with lighting equipment, industrial electronics and communications equipment, industrial equipment, building equipment, insulating materials, wire and cable, and utility equipment. Projects developed by NEMA members are geared to the specific interests of a group, section, or division and are implemented through a staff of approximately 112 persons. The association offers opportunities for electrical manufacturers to meet under legal and proper auspices to discuss their mutual problems and to conduct cooperative activities beneficial to themselves, the industry, and the public. NEMA is the medium used to take prompt and effective action on national legislation and Federal regulations affecting electrical manufacturers. NEMA assists its members to operate more efficiently and profitably by preventing restrictive local and state legislation which suppresses markets; by providing a necessary and helpful exchange of useful information on statistical and other phases of the electrical-manufacturing industry; by developing and promoting the use of product standards; by promoting the expanded use of electricity and electrical products; and by establishing a spirit of cooperative effort among members to improve products, enlarge distribution, and increase efficiency in the use of electrical products. The association publishes the *NEMA Report; Standards Council Executive Report; Government News Bulletin; Guide to NEMA Standards;* and those standards publications listed in the *Guide*. Its headquarters are located at 155 East 44th Street, New York, N.Y. 10017.

National Farmers Union (Farmers' Educational and Cooperative Union of America) An organization representing the U.S. family farmer in agricultural matters. It numbers some 250,000 farm-family members, or more than 750,000 individual members in forty-four states. The organization's business activites include several national and state mutual insurance companies. Its National Casualty Company is rated "A" by Best's Insurance Service; its life company has a "Recommended" rating from Best's. It is the union's belief that a stable and prosperous agriculture will be accomplished through a combination of educational, cooperative, and legislative forces. The educational program includes the publication of national and statewide newspapers and special materials informing members on agricultural and other matters; and a junior educational program, conducted by the national organization and every state organization, which includes family and individual study programs and summer camps. The union has been a champion of the cooperative movement since its inception. Its members own and operate a greater number of farmer cooperatives than the members of any other organization. These include two of the largest farmer cooperatives in the world, the Farmers Union Grain Terminal Association and the Farmers Union Central Exchange, both with headquarters in St. Paul, Minnesota. The National Farmers Union has been a leader in the development of effective and efficient cooperative practices and has championed measures protecting cooperatives; it is directly responsible for the passage of the Capper-Volstead Act, called the "Cooperative Bill of Rights." In the legislative field, the National Farmers Union's basic goals are a stable and fair income for family farmers comparable to that received in nonfarm industry, commodity programs based on supply management or production in line with need; retention of farm families on the land and encouragement of young people to stay on farms, and international programs of cooperation and development. The organization was established at Point, Texas, on August 28, 1902. Some of the measures first proposed or otherwise championed by the National Farmers Union include the parcel post system, the Federal Reserve Act, the graduated income tax, the Federal Farm Loan Act and subsequent Farm Credit programs, the Reclamation Act, the Packers and Stockyards Act, the Agricultural Adjustment Act, the Rural Electrification Administration, Federal crop insurance, the Employment Act of 1946, the rural telephone program, special school lunch and milk programs, the food-stamp program, and Food for Peace. The organization's headquarters are located at 12025 East 45th Avenue (P.O. Box 2251), Denver, Colo. 80201; it also has an office in Washington, D.C.

National Foreign Trade Council   A private, nonprofit U.S. business association whose overall objective is the promotion and protection of American foreign commerce through the expansion of trade and investment abroad under a system of free, private, competitive enterprise. The spokesman of the U.S. international business community, the council contributes to the establishment of sound commercial policies; provides a forum for the continuing exchange of ideas among world-minded business executives; and serves as a catalyst in the development of common solutions to international business problems. The council was organized in Washington on May 28, 1914, by a resolution of the First National Foreign Trade Convention that called for the creation of a National Foreign Trade Council "to coordinate the foreign trade activities of the nation." It is maintained by funds subscribed by member companies. Member firms, which represent a broad cross-section of industries throughout the country, comprise manufacturers, exporters and importers, petroleum, mining, and agricultural enterprises, retailers, banks, railroads, airlines, steamship companies, publishers, insurance companies, and allied industries. Council publications include the weekly news digests *Noticias*, covering Latin America, and *Breve*, for Europe, and bulletins and memorandums covering developments at home and abroad affecting U.S. foreign trade and investment; all are restricted to members. The council also publishes the Declaration of the National Foreign Trade Convention each year, a glossary of foreign trade terms and other educational memorandums, which has limited general distribution. Its headquarters are located at 10 Rockefeller Plaza, New York, N.Y. 10020.

National Income Commission (NIC)   An independent British organization dealing with the public and private sectors of the economy of Great Britain. Its tasks are to inquire into questions of pay or other conditions of employment in the public and private sectors, to examine settlements over pay or conditions of employment referred to it by the British government, and to report from time to time on the need for the government to act in fulfillment of its pledge to restrain growth in profits if restraint in earned incomes led to undue growth in total profits.

National Institute for the Study of Economic Trends (ISCO)   A public body, though completely free with regard to its technical and scientific methods. Its specific purpose is to analyze the current economic situation and particularly to promote and foster the study of problems relating to the Italian economy. It cooperates with the government in the analysis of current domestic and international economic problems and with reference to international organization. It is also charged with drawing up the "General Report on the Economic Situation of the Country," which is submitted every year to the Parliament by the Ministers of Budget and Treasury. It drafts twice a year a "Report on the Current Developments of the Italian Economic System," which is discussed in a general meeting by the Consiglio Nazionale dell'Economia e del Lavoro (CNEL). In agreement with the European Economic Community, and in line with similar surveys carried out by the Common Market countries, it carries out monthly business surveys among the Italian industrial companies. It was established in Rome in 1959. Its major publications are *Congiuntura Italiana*, monthly; *Congiuntura Estera*, monthly; and monthly analytical papers dealing with particular aspects of current economic developments (prices, foreign trade, etc.). Its headquarters are located at Via Palermo 24, Rome, Italy.

National Institute of Statistics An administrative organization within the framework of the Belgian Ministry of Economic Affairs. A complete centralization of all Belgian statistical services was established by order of King Leopold III on August 7, 1939. It covered (1) the execution of the periodical general censuses and surveys and the production of all the statistics of the state with the exception of surveys limited to specialized subjects, (2) the centralization of the publication of all statistical inquiries, and (3) the scientific and technical study of all statistics consigned to its care and the supervision of the production of these statistics. By a decree of February 24, 1831, the first administrative service for collecting statistical data had been established in the Belgian Home Office under the name of Bureau de Statistique Générale. This name was changed to Administration de la Statistique Générale in 1924, to Office Central de Statistique in 1932, and to Institut National de Statistique in 1946. Its principal publications are *Bulletin de statistiques* (Bulletin of Statistics); *Statistiques demographiques; Statistiques du commerce et des transports; Statistiques industrielles; Statistiques agricoles; Annuaire statistique de la Belgique* (Statistical Yearbook); *Bulletin mensuel du commerce extérieur de l'union économique belgoluxembourgeoise*. The Institute's headquarters are located at 44 Rue de Louvain, Brussels, Belgium.

National Institute of Statistics and Economic Studies (INSEE) An organization of the French government whose most important objectives are to observe demographic, social, and economic phenomena; to coordinate all statistical activities of the French government; to collect and process statistics on prices, production, and employment; to prepare demographic and economic studies; to study the total economy as well as individual sectors; to plan studies of regions, the nation, and the world; to prepare estimates of national income and to provide short- and longer-run forecasts of national income in order to draw up the economic budget for the nation and for the various French longer-run plans; and to assure liaison with statistical organizations of other nations and with international statistical groups. The Institute, which was created by law in 1946, inherited the task of the Statistique Générale de France, which dated back to the end of the eighteenth century. It issues weekly, monthly, and annual publications, including *Bulletin mensuel de statistique* (Monthly Bulletin of Statistics); *Études et conjonture* (Studies of the Economic Situation in France and Other Nations); *Annuaire statistique de France* (French Annual Statistical Report). Its headquarters are located at 29 Quai Branly, Paris 7, France.

National Labor Relations Board (NLRB) An independent agency of the U.S. government which administers the nation's principal labor relations law. This statute, the National Labor Relations Act, generally applies to all interstate commerce except railroads and airlines, which are covered by the Railway Labor Act. In its statutory assignment, the NLRB has two principal functions: (1) to prevent and remedy unfair labor practices whether by unions or by employers and (2) to conduct secret-ballot elections in which employees decide whether unions will represent them in collective bargaining. In either function, the NLRB can act only when it is formally requested to do so. Individuals, employers, or unions may initiate cases by filing charges of unfair labor practices or petitions for employee-representation elections. The agency has five board members and a general counsel, each of whom is appointed by the President with the consent of the Senate. Since its creation in 1935, the NLRB has processed a quarter of a million unfair-labor-practice cases and has conducted more than 160,000 secret-ballot employee self-determination elections in appropriate worker groups. Among NLRB publications are *Digest of Decisions of the NLRB; Annual Report; Layman's Guide to Basic Law; Summary of the National Labor Relations Act.* It has headquarters at 1717 Pennsylvania Avenue, N.W., Washington, D.C. 20570.

National League of Insured Savings Associations An organization representing savings and loan associations in the U.S. The league was organized "for the purpose of bringing about a proper understanding of the savings and loan industry and its objectives and close cooperation with legislative committees, government and state authorities and others, so as to better serve its members in the public interest." Named the National Savings and Loan League when it was founded in 1943, the National League of Insured Savings Associations adopted its present name in 1958 so that the distinguishing functions of the league would be more clearly understood by both industry and the interested public. Since its foundation, the league has become a permanent savings and loan organization; has sponsored legislation which has enabled savings and loan associations to grow in size from $4 billion to more than $80 billion; has achieved greater recognition of savings and loan associations in government and among the leaders of the Congress; and has launched an intensive program to create savings and loan associations in the underdeveloped half of the world: Latin America, Africa, and Asia. The league has always maintained a small membership on the theory that a small, highly mobile organization often can accomplish results that are not always possible with a larger group. It transmits important savings and loan developments to its membership through its weekly *National Newsletter,* monthly *National League Journal,* and other specialized publications, such as the *Savings and Loan Tax Bulletin* and the *Economic Memorandum.* Its executive offices are located at 1200 Seventeenth Street, N.W., Washington, D.C. 20006.

National Lumber Manufacturers Association A nonprofit organization of the U.S. whose basic purposes are to develop new markets for wood; preserve existing markets for wood; advance the interests of lumber manufacturers, their customers, and consumers of lumber; improve lumber services to the public; and maintain a healthy atmosphere within which the industry can operate in the public interest as an important segment of free enterprise. The association was formed at St. Louis, Missouri, in December, 1902, when representatives from the Far West, New England, the South, and other timber-producing regions gathered to form a federation of regional associations which would speak with a single voice and provide the means for mutual action. Major publications issued by the association on a continuing basis are *Lumber Letter,* weekly; *Quarterly Reporter; National Wood Promotion Program Weekly Review; Lumber Industry Facts,* biannually; *NLMA Directory and Policies,* annually; *Finger Tip Facts and Figures,* monthly.

National Machine Tool Builders' Association A nonprofit trade association consisting of about 190 U.S. companies engaged in the design and construction of machine tools. The membership of the association accounts for about 85% of the productive capacity of the machine-tool industry in the U.S. The purposes of the organization are to promote the lawful interests of the machine-tool industry in the direction of good business ethics, to improve methods of production and marketing, to promote research and development within the industry, and to better acquaint the government and the public with machine tools and their direct relationship to the U.S. productive capacity. The association was founded in 1902. Through a subsidiary corporation, National Machine Tool Builders' Show, Inc., a machine-tool show is sponsored every two years; annual sales-training conferences are conducted; and seminars are held on the numerical control of machine tools, legal and tax matters, and other activities of general interest. While the association does not publish a periodical, the machine-tool community is apprised of industry events through correspondence, brochures, bulletins, and other media. The association cooperates with other industries and with governmental agencies in matters pertaining to the machine-tool industry, collects and disseminates monthly information on machine-tool orders and shipments, and participates in activities that promote a continued and orderly growth of the industry. Its activities, which are directed by a board of directors working through twenty-two committees, twenty groups, and two councils, cover the broad range of the industry's management, technical, and marketing problems. The association's headquarters are located at 2139 Wisconsin Avenue, N.W., Washington, D.C. 20007.

National Mediation Board   An independent agency of the U.S. government, the main duties of which include mediating disputes involving rates of pay, rules, or working conditions and determining the representatives of employees for collective bargaining purposes. Among other duties are the appointment of neutrals to arbitration boards and similar tribunals and, under certain conditions, the interpretation of the meaning of an agreement reached through mediation. The National Mediation Board was created by the 1934 amendment to the Railway Labor Act, which established procedures designed to resolve peacefully disputes between common carriers by rail and by air and other employees. The Board is composed of three members, who are appointed by the President with the advice and consent of the Senate. Its administrative affairs are handled by an executive secretary. The Board is assisted by a staff of mediators whose appointments are subject to U.S. Civil Service regulations. Among the Board's publications are the *Annual Report; Administration of the Railway Labor Act; Interpretations Issued by the National Mediation Board; Determinations of Craft or Class.*

National Municipal League   A nonprofit, nonpartisan educational association of individuals and organizations devoted to the improvement of state and local government through an informed, participating citizenry. It was organized in 1894 by Louis D. Brandeis, Charles Francis Adams, Theodore Roosevelt, and other prominent Americans to act as a clearing-house of information for private citizens, public officials, educational institutions, and local civic organizations seeking to strengthen state and local institutions. The league conducts and promotes research in problems of government and effective citizenship. Its National Conference on Government, held annually since 1894 in various cities, is attended by approximately 1,000 civic, educational, business, professional, and other leaders from all parts of the U.S. and usually from other nations. Its committees and staff prepare model laws, charters, administrative systems, and pamphlets setting the highest governmental standards and practices. Best known of the league's major publications are the *Model*

City Charter and *Model County Charter* and the ten-book series of the State Constitutional Studies project, including the *Model State Constitution*. Contemporary specialized studies provide comparative data on primary election laws, legislative apportionment, and county, metropolitan, and other current governmental problems. The league has been a leader in the development of improved financial-management practices and expenditure controls for local governments. It maintains a specialized library and publishes a monthly periodical, the *National Civic Review,* which serves as a forum for the exchange of ideas for civic leaders and as a working tool for students of government. Each year, the league (and *Look*) present the All-America Cities Awards to eleven communities in which intelligent citizen action has achieved significant progress. The league's offices are located at 47 East 68th Street, New York, N.Y. 10021.

National Planning Association (NPA) A nonprofit, nonpolitical organization which studies methods for the full utilization of the productive resources of the U.S. to give the American people the highest possible material and cultural standards of living. It does not limit its efforts to national problems but may also study international, governmental, economic, and social problems. Incorporated in the District of Columbia in 1934 as a voluntary, scientific, educational, economic, and philanthropic organization, NPA is governed by a forty-member board of trustees, consisting of representatives of labor, finance, industry, commerce, and agriculture. Reports and statements on matters of significant concern are prepared by the steering committee of the board and the four standing committees: the agriculture, business, and labor committees on national policy and the committee on international policy. NPA has sponsored reports on such topics as Canadian-American relations, full-employment policies, social security, competitive coexistence, national goals and resources, national security, arms control, government organization, and overseas development. Special research projects, oriented toward policy formulation, are carried out under special committees composed of NPA leaders, other qualified and interested citizens, and technical experts. In addition, some 800 U.S. leaders advise the association as members of its national council, and a public membership of more than 3,000 individuals, corporations, and groups participates in and contributes to the work of NPA. NPA's continuing publications include the monthly *Looking Ahead;* and the National Economic Projections Series and Regional Economic Projections Series, subscription services which provide, on a continuing basis, detailed analyses of the prospects for economic growth. Its headquarters are located at 1606 New Hampshire Avenue, N.W., Washington, D.C. 20009.

National Resource Analysis Center   A unit of the Office of Emergency Preparedness. It provides the analytical base for OEP's policy, planning, and programming activities in support of the agency's national security responsibilities. It develops and maintains a complete capability of monitoring, evaluating, and projecting the status of the nation's resources and economy to meet all types of national emergency; identifies and analyzes past and future resource deficiencies and strengths; and conducts and supports comprehensive research and systems analyses to support decisions on alternative emergency preparedness policies, plans, and programs. It analyzes support judgments and decisions on emergency production programs, strategic materials, stockpile and import policies, economic recovery, and mobilization planning in general. It also develops and applies economic and political analyses, mathematical models, simulation techniques, operations research, and other scientific methods for predicting, forecasting, and testing alternative solutions in an emergency environment.

National Savings and Loan League   *See National League of Insured Savings Associations.*

National Science Foundation (NSF)   An independent agency in the executive branch of the U.S. government, operating with funds appropriated by Congress. The purpose of the Foundation is to strengthen research and education in the mathematical, physical, medical, engineering, social (including economics), and other sciences. NSF also develops and disseminates information on scientific resources and manpower. In the area of scientific research, NSF awards research grants and contracts —primarily to universities and other nonprofit institutions; funds national research centers; and maintains national research programs, including the International Biological Program, Global Atmospheric Research Program (jointly with ESSA), Weather Modification, International Decade of Ocean Exploration, Ocean Sediment Coring, Earthquake Engineering, and Arctic and Antarctic Research Programs. The Foundation provides institutional support to colleges and universities for comprehensive improvements in science programs. In the field of science education, NSF awards graduate and postdoctoral fellowships in the sciences and engineering; supports graduate student traineeships at educational institutions; and develops and funds programs for improving science education at the elementary, secondary, and college levels with special institutes to improve the competence of teachers, projects and modernize materials of instruction and courses of study, and projects for high-ability secondary and college students. The Foundation administers the National Sea

Grant Program, which provides for the strengthening of research, education, and training in the marine sciences. Other activities of NSF include developing and supporting the use of computers in research and science education, developing and funding programs for improving the dissemination of scientific information, planning and developing international scientific programs, supporting the exchange of U.S. and foreign scientists, and developing policies for the promotion and utilization of science and science education. Continuing series of NSF publications include *National Patterns of Research and Development Resources; Federal Funds for Research and Development and Other Scientific Activities; Federal Support to Universities and Colleges; Research and Development in Industry; American Science Manpower; Annual Report.* For further information, contact the Office of Government and Public Programs, National Science Foundation, 1800 G Street, N.W., Washington, D.C. 20550.

National Tax Association A nonpolitical, nonsectarian, and nonprofit organization of the U.S. and Canada that is concerned with taxation and public finance. It is essentially an educational organization. Its research is conducted by study committees, which make their reports at annual conferences. The association was founded in Columbus, Ohio, in 1907, and conferences have been held annually since that date except in the war years of 1918 and 1945. Delegates attend the conferences from the several states of the U.S., its possessions, and the District of Columbia as well as the provinces of Canada. These conferences form a common meeting ground for discussion, resolution, and action of academic representatives, administrators (Federal, state, and local), and practitioners in the field of taxation, including the tax executives of corporations. The association's publications consist of an annual volume of the *Proceedings* of the conference, which contains the papers presented at the conference and discussion on them. The *National Tax Journal*, which is issued quarterly, contains articles written by eminent authorities in the field of taxation and public finance, including economists, professors, practitioners, and administrators. The association's headquarters are located at 905 Payne-Shoemaker Building, Harrisburg, Pa. 17101.

O

Office of Economics A functional group of the Canadian Department of Industry, Trade and Commerce. It consists of four branches—General Analysis, Investment Analysis, Market Analysis, and Productivity—and conducts studies on various aspects of the Canadian economy and markets abroad to provide analytical background, briefing, and advice for use by the Department and government. It carries out these functions by the continuous examination of the developing economic situation within Canada, the periodic examination of developments in major segments of industry, and the preparation of market information pertaining to individual industries or commodities, the analysis of capital investment in Canada and abroad, and the study and analysis of industrial productivity. The Office of Economics is located in Ottawa, Canada.

Office of Management and Budget An independent office of the U.S. government established to provide the President with the services of a professional staff agency headed by a director who is chosen without Senate confirmation. The Office has seven general functions: (1) preparation and execution of the budget; (2) improvement of government organization and administrative management; (3) development of efficient coordinating mechanisms to implement government activities and to expand interagency cooperation; (4) improvement of budgeting, accounting, and other aspects of financial management; (5) development of programs to recruit, train, motivate, and deploy career personnel of the Federal government; (6) improvement of Federal statistics and management information systems; and (7) assessment of program objectives, performance, and efficiency. It was established in the Executive Office of the President pusuant to Reorganization Plan No. 2 of 1970. By Executive Order No. 11541 of July 1, 1970, all functions transferred to the President by part I of the plan were delegated to the Office of Management and Budget. As a means of dealing with government-wide management problems, the Office has five divisions: Organization and

Management Systems, Program Coordination, Executive Development and Labor Relations, Legislative Reference, and Statistical Policy and Management Information Systems. To assist the President in the preparation and execution of the Federal budget, to evaluate the effectiveness of Federal programs, and to maintain the working relationships with all the agencies of the Federal government, the Office relies on its eight program and budget divisions: Budget Review, Evaluation, National Security Programs, International Programs, Economics, Science and Technology Programs, Natural Resources Programs, Human Resources Programs, and General Government Programs. While each division is assigned a field in which it takes leadership, all divisions of the Office share responsibility, in varying degrees, for the performance of the Office's functions. The major publications of the Office of Management and Budget are *The Budget of the United States Government; The Budget in Brief; Special Analyses.*

Operations Research Society of America (ORSA)   A professional organization for American operations research, providing persons who are interested in this field with facilities for the interchange of competence for work known as operations research. It encourages and develops aspirants to the profession. Since the society's formation in May, 1952, membership has grown to more than 7,200, about one-half of whom are from business and industry, one-fourth from military operations-research groups, and one-fourth from universities, government agencies, etc. There are twelve active local sections and five student sections. In addition, there are six technical sections in the fields of cost effectiveness, educational sciences, health applications, military applications, space sciences, and transportation science. The society annually awards the Lanchester Prize ($2,000) for the best paper on operations research published in the English language during the year. Its headquarters are located at Baltimore, Md. 21202. Recent publications sponsored by ORSA are Julius S. Aronofsky, *Progress in Operations Research,* John Wiley & Sons, Inc., New York, 1969, vol. 3; David B. Hertz & Jacques Melese, *Proceedings of the Fourth International Conference on Operational Research,* John Wiley & Sons, Inc., New York, 1968.

Organization for Economic Cooperation and Development (OECD)   An international intergovernmental organization, successor to the Organization for European Economic Cooperation (OEEC). The OECD promotes policies designed (1) to achieve the highest sustainable economic growth and employment and a rising standard of living in member countries, while maintaining financial stability, and thus to contribute to the development of the world economy; (2) to contribute to sound economic expansion in member and nonmember countries in the process of economic development; and (3) to contribute to the expansion of world trade on a multilateral, nondiscriminatory basis in accordance with international obligations. Recognizing that the OEEC, created in 1948 to implement the Marshall Plan, had successfully achieved the objectives of European recovery, and considering that broader cooperation would make a vital contribution to the peaceful and harmonious relations of the people of the world, the governments of twenty countries—Austria, Belgium, Canada, Denmark, France, the Federal Republic of Germany, Greece, Iceland, Ireland, Italy, Luxembourg, the Netherlands, Norway, Portugal, Spain, Sweden, Switzerland, Turkey, the United Kingdom, and the U.S.—signed the constituent convention on December 14, 1960. The convention was duly ratified by the required number of national parliaments by September 30, 1961. Since that time, the admission of Japan (1964) and Finland (1969) has brought the number of member countries to twenty-two. The supreme body of the organization is the Council, which may meet at the level of ministers or at the level of their alternates (permanent delegations). Within the limits of the convention, the Council is in fact a permanent conference in which the economic problems of the member countries are constantly reviewed. The Council may establish such subsidiary bodies (committees, subcommittees, working parties) as may be required for the achievement of the aims of the organization. A secretary general, appointed by the Council and responsible to it, serves as chairman of the Council meetings at sessions of the permanent representatives. The secretary general and the secretariat headed by him assist the Council and the other bodies of the organization in the execution of the work by submitting proposals, conducting research, issuing publications, etc. The OECD prepares and distributes publications on general economics, statistics, trade, aid to less-developed areas, industrial sectors, energy, agriculture, basic raw materials, science, technology, etc. OECD headquarters are located at the Château de la Muette, Rue André-Pascal, Paris 16, France; the U.S. center is located at 1750 Pennsylvania Avenue, N.W., Washington, D.C. 20006.

Organization for European Economic Cooperation   *See Organization for Economic Cooperation and Development (OECD).*

P

Pay Board   A fifteen-member tripartite board consisting of business, labor, and public representatives whose function it is to set and administer wage and salary policies. The Board was established on October 28, 1971, and officially functions under the Economic Stabilization Program of the Executive Office of the President. Its initial standard for average wage and salary adjustments was 5.5%, and it applied to pay adjustments provided for in contracts entered into or pay practices established after November 13, 1971. It is located at 2000 M Street, N.W., Washington, D.C. 20508.

Population Association of America   An organization of professional demographers in the U.S. Its purpose is the promotion of the improvement, advancement, and progress of the human race by means of research with respect to problems connected with human population, in both its quantitative and its qualitative aspects, and the dissemination and publication of the results of such research. To this end, it holds scientific meetings, stimulates research, and promotes high professional standards; sponsors publications concerned with demography; and cooperates with other national or international organizations in the scientific study of population. The association was formally established in 1932 and chartered in 1937. It issues three publications: *Population Index,* a quarterly journal devoted to the annotation of books and articles on human fertility and mortality, the size and spatial distribution of the population, marriage, divorce, the family, migration, demographic and economic interrelations, population policies, methods of population research, and related subjects; *Demography,* a quarterly journal containing reports of current research on population; and *P.A.A. Affairs,* a quarterly newsletter reporting on the activities of the association, its officers and committees, and events of professional interest. An annual meeting is held in April. Its address is P.O. Box 14182, Benjamin Franklin Station, Washington, D.C. 20044.

Population Reference Bureau, Inc. A private nonprofit educational organization founded in 1929 by a group of biologists, sociologists, and economists. The bureau is the world's oldest organization devoted to population awareness. Its special role is to speak of the threat which man's increasing numbers poses to human environments, human dignity, and human survival. The bureau believes that the population problems of industrialized and developing countries require a careful presentation of the demographic and ecological facts, an assessment of their meaning, and a voluntary change in mores. Founded in 1929, the bureau issues *Population Bulletins, Profiles, Selections,* ancillary textbooks, an annual *World Population Data Sheet,* and other publications. It consults with other groups in the United States and abroad and operates an information service, library, and international program with emphasis on Latin America. A list of publications is available from the Population Reference Bureau, Inc., 1755 Massachusetts Avenue, N.W., Washington, D.C. 20036.

Price Commission A seven-member commission consisting of public members only whose function is to hold increases in prices and rents, on the average for the whole nation, to no more than 2½% per year. The commission is dependent on the voluntary compliance of citizens for achievement of this goal. The commission was established on October 28, 1971, and officially functions under the Economic Stabilization Program of the Executive Office of the President.

Production-Credit Associations *See Farm Credit System.*

Public Affairs Institute A nonprofit, nonpartisan research institution of the U.S. which provides facts to persons who can use them in creating opinion and shaping national policies. It covers ten major fields: agriculture; business; education; elections and political trends; government, fiscal, and taxation; health and welfare; international relations; labor; national defense; and resources and conservation. The institute publishes memorandums, pamphlets, research papers, books, and a weekly newspaper column, "Washington Window." Its headquarters are located at 312 Pennsylvania Avenue, S.E., Washington, D.C. 20003.

Public Health Service A component of the U.S. Department of Health, Education, and Welfare. The PHS consists of four operating agencies: the Health Service and Mental Health Administration, the National Institutes of Health the Environmental Health Service, and the Food and Drug Administration. These agencies work with states and communities; national, state and local organizations; educational and research institutions; and private industry to prevent and control disease, to conduct health research, and to provide health services, education, and information. The PHS also cooperates with foreign governments and international organizations in carrying out studies and activities that improve health throughout the world. The Public Health Service is directed by the Surgeon General, who is the principal deputy to the Assistant Secretary for Health and Scientific Affairs. A predecessor agency, the Marine Hospital Service, was established in the Treasury Department in 1798. It became the Public Health Service in 1912. Among the principal publications are *Public Health Reports,* monthly; *Journal of the National Cancer Institute,* monthly; *Vital Statistics of the United States,* annually; *Monthly Vital Statistics Report; Morbidity and Mortality Weekly Report; Health Statistics from the United States National Health Survey.*

R

Railroad Retirement Board   An independent agency in the executive branch of the U.S. government which administers a comprehensive social insurance system for the nation's railroad workers and their families, providing protection against the loss of income resulting from old age, disability, death, unemployment, and temporary sickness. Under the Railroad Retirement Act, benefits are payable to workers with at least ten years of railroad service who retire because of old age or disability, to their eligible wives, and to surviving widows, children, and parents of deceased employees. Under the Railroad Unemployment Insurance Act, benefits are payable for up to a fiscal year to unemployed or sick railroad workers who earned at least $1,000 in the preceding calendar year. The Railroad Retirement acts of 1935 and 1937 and the Carriers' Taxing Act of 1937 (now the Railroad Retirement Tax Act) are the foundations of the present retirement system. The unemployment-insurance system was first established by the Railroad Unemployment Insurance Act, enacted in 1938 and effective on July 1, 1939. These acts were amended several times. The retirement system is financed by payroll taxes levied in equal amounts on the employers and employees under the Railroad Retirement Tax Act—except for railroad retirement supplemental annuities, which are financed by a tax on employers only. The 1970 tax rate is 9.55% of the first $650 of each employee's monthly earnings. The maximum tax rate, 10.65%, is to be reached in 1987. The costs of the unemployment-insurance system are borne entirely by employers through separate payroll taxes. The tax rate for a calendar year depends on the balance in the unemployment-insurance account on the preceding September 30; the maximum rate is 4% of the first $400 of each employee's monthly earnings. The Board gives direct assistance and information to applicants for benefits and operates a free placement service for unemployment-insurance claimants. The Railroad Retirement Board is composed of three members appointed by the President; two are chosen on the basis of recommendations made by representatives of employees and employers, respectively, while the third member, the chairman, represents the public interest. Publications include the *Monthly Benefit Statistics*, *Annual Report*, and a variety of informational leaflets, pamphlets, and releases. The Board's headquarters are located at 844 Rush Street, Chicago, Ill. 60611; seven regional and ninety-two district offices are located in railroad centers throughout the nation.

RAND Corporation An independent nonprofit research organization of the U.S. that is engaged in the systematic interdisciplinary analysis of problems of national security and public welfare. It originated in work begun in 1946 on U.S. Air Force Project RAND, a long-range defense research activity. The corporation was formally established in November, 1948. Besides operating Project RAND under contract with the Air Force, it conducts research for other defense agencies and for the Atomic Energy Commission, the National Aeronautics and Space Administration, and the Agency for International Development. In addition, research on policy isssues in education, poverty, environmental pollution, health, housing, transportation, and other aspects of public welfare (now more than 20% of the program) is undertaken through contracts or grants from New York City, such agencies as the Office of Economic Opportunity and the National Institutes of Health, and private foundations; corporation funds are also used for such research. Three of RAND's ten technical departments carry out research directly related to economics. The economics department conducts studies of national strategy, including strategic goals and the various avenues of their achievement. Other research areas are decision-making processes in large organizations, research and development, economic and social development in the less-developed countries, and such problems of urban society as unemployment among low-income youth, the economics of health care, and the opportunities and options for cable television. (In 1969, the New York City/RAND Institute was formed as part of a program of applied urban research for that metropolitan area.) The resource analysis department develops improved tools for analyzing weapon-system costs and the impact of resource inputs on alternative total military force mixes. In the domestic area, it is studying alternative future transportation systems for regional development of the "northeast corridor" and possible future configurations of the securities transactions industry. The management sciences department studies weapon-system scheduling, inventory, and support problems and consults on information and management systems of the Air Force. In the area of public welfare, it has completed studies of employment, urban housing, and transportation. Published RAND research is made available to the public through a system of some 150 depository collections in major libraries throughout the U.S. and in several foreign countries. Its headquarters are located at 1700 Main Street, Santa Monica, Calif. 90406.

Reconstruction Finance Corporation   A U.S. government corporation organized to aid in financing agriculture, commerce, and industry, to encourage small business, to help maintain economic stability, and to assist in promoting maximum employment and production. It began operations on February 2, 1932, at the depth of the depression. Effective July 1, 1939, it was grouped with other agencies to form the Federal Loan Agency. During the 1940s and early 1950s, its functions were transferred to other agencies. Its lending powers were terminated on September 28, 1953, and it was abolished on June 30, 1957.

Regional Science Association   An international association for the advancement of regional analysis and related spatial and areal studies. It operates as an objective, scientific organization without political, social, financial, or nationalistic bias. The association's main objectives are to foster the exchange of ideas and promote studies focusing on the region and utilizing tools, methods, and theoretical frameworks specifically designed for regional analysis as well as concepts, procedures, and analytical techniques of the various social and other sciences. It supports these objectives by promoting acquaintance and discussion among its members and with scholars in related fields, by stimulating research, by encouraging the publication of scholarly studies, and by performing services to aid the advancement of its members and the field of regional science. The headquarters of the association are located at the Wharton School, University of Pennsylvania, Philadelphia, Pa. 19104.

Renegotiation Board An independent agency of the U.S. government whose main function is to conduct renegotiation proceedings with contractors in order to eliminate excessive profits on defense and space contracts and related contracts. The Board was created by the Renegotiations Act of 1951. Between 1951 and June 30, 1969, 3,883 determinations of excessive profits made by the Board came to nearly $1 billion before adjustment for Federal income and excess profit tax credits. Between 1951 and June 30, 1969, voluntary refunds and price reduction reported by contractors in connection with renegotiation proceedings resulted in a savings of $1.3 billion.

Research Center for Group Dynamics *See Institute for Social Research of the University of Michigan.*

Research Institute of Industrial and Labor Relations and Technological Change (ISRIL) A nonprofit association organized mainly to study industrial and social relations in the broad context of a modern economy. It was founded in Rome in 1962 by a group of experts on industrial and labor relations, operations research, industrial engineering, sociology, and the economy. It has been engaged in studying the following fields: The industrial enterprise, development factors, the labor market, and the system of industrial relations. Among the publications of the institute are *Productivity and the Technological Gap* and *Economic Development and Urban Growth in Italy*. The institute is located at 24 Via Velletri, Rome, Italy.

Resources for the Future, Inc. A nonprofit, tax-exempt organization of the U.S. that is concerned with research and education in the development, conservation, and use of natural resources and the improvement of the quality of the environment. Established in 1952 with the cooperation of the Ford Foundation, it has received most of its support since that time from that foundation. It was decided at the outset that the organization could make its greatest contribution through studies in the social science fields. This program has been carried out through research by a small central professional staff and grants to other tax-exempt organizations. Most of the studies, especially the earlier ones, have dealt with U.S. resource problems, but some worldwide resource problems and problems relating particularly to the less-developed countries have also been examined. Since 1964 there has been a special program of Latin American studies. In addition to research work, the organization has a fellowship program supporting doctoral dissertations on problems involving natural resources. The following major publications have resulted from the research program: Hans H. Landsberg et al., *Resources in America's Future;* Harold J. Barnett and Chandler Morse, *Scarcity and Growth;* Sam H. Schurr et al., *Energy in the American Economy, 1850–1975;* Marion Clawson et al., *Land for the Future;* Clawson Knetsch and Jack L. Knetsch, *Economics of Outdoor Recreation;* Allen V. Kneese and Blair T. Bower, *Managing Water Quality;* Harvey S. Perloff and Lowdon Wingo (eds.), *Issues in Urban Economics;* Wilbur R. Thompson, *A Preface to Urban Economics.* In addition, there are numerous other books, an *Annual Report,* and a leaflet, *Resources,* issued three times a year. Nearly all RFF's books are published by, and available from, The Johns Hopkins Press. Headquarters of Resources for the Future, Inc., are located at 1755 Massachusetts Avenue, N.W., Washington, D.C. 20036.

Royal Statistical Society A U.K. organization of professional statisticians (some 20% of whom are from outside the U.K.) whose main objectives are the collection and publication of statistical material, the continuation of its statistical library, the development of statistical theory and methodology, the application of statistical methods to ever-widening fields, the improvement and extension of statistical material collected by official and unofficial bodies and its publication, and the advancing of the realization of the importance of statistics in central and local governments. It was founded in 1834 under the title of Statistical Society of London, and a charter of incorporation was granted in 1887. Membership consists of fellows and honorary fellows. The society publishes three types of journals: Series A (general) contains papers read and discussed at general meetings of the society, Series B (methodological) contains papers read and discussed at the meetings on research methods, and Series C is concerned with practical applications of statistical methods. Its headquarters are located at 21 Bentinck Street, London W 1, England.

Rubber Manufacturers Association, Inc. An organization of close to 200 rubber manufacturers located in the U.S. These manufacturers fabricate every type of rubber product and account for about 80% of the country's rubber consumption. Founded in 1900, the association endeavors to promote in all lawful ways the commercial interests of its members, including the compilation of statistical and other factual industry data; the establishment of standards, and the furtherance of industry public relations and a liaison between the industry and government and related industries. The organization functions through product divisions representing the major items or types of products made by its members and through service committees dealing with matters of general interest to all rubber manufacturers. The product groups include such items as tires, industrial rubber products, flooring, druggists' and stationers' sundries, heels and soles, footwear, latex foam products, and molded and extruded articles. The association publishes monthly, quarterly, and annual reports and surveys regarding the production and distribution of various rubber products. Its headquarters are located at 444 Madison Avenue, New York, N.Y. 10022.

Rural Electrification Administration (REA) A lending agency in the U.S. Department of Agriculture, REA makes self-liquidating loans to qualified borrowers to finance electric and telephone service in rural areas. The loans bear 2% interest and are repayable over a maximum period of thirty-five years. Part of each electric consumer's and telephone subscriber's monthly payments for service is used to pay off the government loans. Congress annually determines the amount of funds REA may lend. In the field of rural electrification, REA finances the construction and operation of generating plants, electric transmission and distribution lines, or systems for the furnishing of initial and continued adequate electric service to persons in rural areas not receiving central-station service. Loans are made to cooperatives, public power districts, other public bodies, and electric companies. Abiding by REA's "area coverage" policy, borrowers design their systems to serve entire rural areas and give the same consideration to less densely settled sections that is given to the more populous areas. The criterion is not that an individual line or section be self-supporting but that the system, as a whole, be feasible. REA has been making electric loans since 1935, the year the agency was created by executive order of the President. At that time only 10.9% of U.S. farms had electric service. Today 98.4% of the 2.9 million farms are electrified. REA-financed electric systems serve about half of these farms. As of January, 1970, REA had approved $7.1 billion in loans to 1,098 electric borrowers to serve 6.8 million consumers over 1.7 million miles of line in forty-six states, the Virgin Islands, and Puerto Rico. The REA telephone loan program, authorized by Congress in 1949, provides loans to telephone companies and to cooperative, nonprofit, limited-dividend, or mutual associations for the purpose of financing the improvement and expansion of telephone service in rural areas. In 1950, according to U.S. Bureau of the Census figures, 38.2% of the farms in the U.S. had telephone service, but much of this service was inadequate and of poor quality. An estimated 82% of the nation's farms now have telephone service, and most of this service is automatic. REA telephone borrowers provide dial service to more than 2 million subscribers in forty-six states and are operating about 520,000 route miles of line. As of January, 1970, REA had approved almost $1.7 billion in telephone loans to 630 commercial companies and 235 cooperatives. The following publications are available from the Rural Electrification Administration: *Annual Report of the REA Administrator; National Summary of the Rural Electrification Loan*

Program; National Summary of the Telephone Loan Program; List of REA-Financed Electric Systems; List of REA-financed Telephone Systems; Annual Report of Energy Purchased by REA Electric Borrowers; List of REA-financed Generating Plants; Quarterly Statistical Bulletins (REA electrification and telephone loan programs). The *Annual Statistical Report: Rural Electrification Borrowers* and the *Annual Statistical Report: Rural Telephone Borrowers* are available from the Superintendent of Documents, U.S. Government Printing Office, Washington, D.C. 20402.

S

Securities and Exchange Commission (SEC) An independent agency of the U.S. government which administers the Federal securities laws, whose objectives are the protection of the investing public. The enactment of these laws, beginning in 1933, followed congressional disclosure of malpractices in the securities markets which, by seriously undermining the confidence of investors in securities, threatened stagnation of the capital-formation process essential to continued industrial growth. Under the laws, securities may not be offered for public sale in interstate commerce unless disclosure is provided, through prior registration with the SEC and the delivery of a prospectus to investors, of pertinent financial and other corporate information so that the securities may be realistically evaluated. Periodic disclosure of similar information is required of companies whose securities are listed on the major exchanges throughout the country as well as a few thousand additional companies in which there is a substantial public investor interest and whose shares are traded over the counter. Moreover, these companies must comply with certain disclosure rules when they solicit proxies from their shareholders, and their management officials and holders of more than 10% of the stock must report monthly on their holdings of, and transactions in, their companies' equity securities. In addition, the short-swing trading profits of these persons in such securities may be recovered by the issuing company, thus tending to curb misuse of inside information. The exchanges as well as brokers and dealers engaged in an over-the-counter securities business must register with the Commission and make their trading practices conform to regulations prescribed for investor protection. The laws prohibit fraud, manipulation, and other abusive practices and empower the SEC to investigate complaints or other indications of securities violations and to invoke sanctions against violators, including revocation of registration, injunction, and criminal prosecution. The laws also provide for SEC regulation of various activities of mutual-fund and other investment companies as well as companies comprising registered electric and gas utility holding-company systems. In addition to its administrative orders, decisions, and rules, the Commission issues a daily *News Digest* (available on a subscription basis from the Government Printing Office), which contains a summary of such administrative actions and a résumé of all new stock-offering proposals for which registration statements are filed. It also publishes various statistical and other economic data, including weekly reports on round- and odd-lot transactions on the New York and American Stock Exchanges; a weekly stock price index; quarterly reports on individuals' savings, plant and equipment expenditures of U.S. business, corporate working capital, balance-sheet and income data for U.S. manufacturing corporations, and new securities offerings; and an annual study on corporate pension funds. A monthly summary of insider-trading reports and a monthly statistical bulletin are available for subscription from the Government Printing Office, Washington, D.C.

Small Business Administration (SBA) An agency of the U.S. government created by Congress solely to advise and assist the nation's small businesses. The significance of SBA's activities and programs can be gauged by the fact that more than 4.5 million business concerns, or 95% of all American businesses, are classified as small. The SBA serves small business in these ways: (1) by lending money to small businessmen, directly or in participation with banks; (2) by licensing, regulating, and helping to finance privately owned small business investment companies; (3) by helping small business to secure a fair share of government contracts and surplus government property; (4) by providing information and assistance in the field of management; (5) by assisting small businesses which are victims of disasters; (6) by developing and presenting helpful material in the foreign-trade field; and (7) by providing production and products assistance. Historically, SBA can trace a broken-line ancestry back to the Smaller War Plants Corporation (SWPC), which existed during World War II. Again, during the Korean conflict, when a need arose to bring the full productive capacity of the nation's small businesses into a rapid defense buildup, the Small Defense Plants Administration (SDPA) was established. Congress recognized that small firms, while forming such an important part of the American economy, were at a serious disadvantage, both in an emergency and in peacetime, in competition with large companies in securing financing, in doing business with the Federal government, in obtaining expert managerial advice, etc. Thus, SDPA was transformed into a new agency, the Small Business Administration, with broadened authority to assist all types of small business, including manufacturers, retailers, service establishments, and construction firms. The SBA issues a number of publications which describe in detail its various activities. The most comprehensive is *SBA, What It Is, What It Does*. Another publication is the *Federal Handbook for Small Business*, sponsored jointly by SBA, the White House Committee on Small Business, and the Senate and House Committees on Small Business, which provides information on all Federal programs of interest to small business. Other helpful SBA publications are *SBA Business Loans; Long-Term Capital for Small Business; Building Business, Building Jobs; U.S. Government Purchasing, Specifications and Sales Dictionary; Selling to the U.S. Government; SBA Management and Research Assistance; SBA Disaster Loans*. SBA publications and further information on SBA services may be obtained from any of SBA's sixty field offices or from SBA, Washington, D.C. 20416.

Social and Economic Statistics Administration (SESA) An organization formed within the U.S. Department of Commerce to consolidate the statistical activities of the Bureau of the Census and the Bureau of Economic Analysis (formerly the Office of Business Economics). SESA was established on January 1, 1972, in order to bring the Commerce Department's major statistical programs in line with the overall Federal statistical system proposed by President Nixon as a Department of Economic Affairs.

Social Science Research Council A nonprofit corporation of the U.S. which has as its purpose the advancement of research in the social sciences. It was incorporated on December 27, 1924, to advance research in the social sciences. There are thirty members of the board of directors, twenty-one of whom are elected or appointed from panels nominated by the executive committee of the board from seven national scientific societies: the American Anthropological Association, the American Economic Association, the American Historical Association, the American Political Science Association, the American Psychological Association, the American Sociological Association, and the American Statistical Association. The rest are appointed by the board. The council publishes *Items* (quarterly), which reports on its work. Its headquarters are located at 230 Park Avenue, New York, N.Y. 10017.

Social Security Administration An agency of the U.S. Department of Health, Education, and Welfare which administers the Federal old age, survivors, and disability insurance program (commonly called social security). Its Commissioner also has responsibility for the Bureau of Hearings and Appeals, which has delegated authority to conduct administrative and judicial reviews of appeals from decisions relating to claims for benefits, lump-sum payments, and earnings records under the program. The Bureau of Federal Credit Unions, which charters, conducts examinations of, and supervises Federal credit unions, also comes under the Commissioner's jurisdiction. The Social Security Act, approved on August 14, 1935, with nine major amendments thereafter, is the legal base of the social insurance program under which nine out of ten Americans are protected against loss or sharp reduction of income that may stem from severe disability, untimely death, or retirement in old age. At the end of 1962, more than 18 million men, women, and children were receiving more than $1 billion in monthly benefits, and new claims were being received at the rate of nearly 300,000 a month. The maintenance of earnings records, upon which eligibility for and the size of benefits depend, is an important part of the social security system. Individual earnings records are kept up to date at the national headquarters in Baltimore, Maryland, by means of electronic-data-processing and microfilm-storage methods. A wide range of free publications explaining the social security programs in all its aspects is available in each of the Social Security Administration's 613 district offices located in the fifty states, the District of Columbia, and Puerto Rico. In addition, reports of specialized studies of beneficiary characteristics, trends in the national economy, etc., as derived from earnings and payment records, medical statistics gathered in the administration of the disability program, and controlled surveys among beneficiaries are published from time to time and are made available on request to individuals and organizations with common interests in these areas. A monthly publication, the *Social Security Bulletin,* contains technical articles and reviews of current developments in social insurance and related fields with emphasis on comparative statistics.

Society for Industrial and Applied Mathematics (SIAM) A U.S. association of mathematicians and scientists throughout the world whose purpose it is to stimulate the application of mathematics to science and industry. Recognizing the gap in a professional structure where the rapid expansion of industrial research had created a need for basic analytical thought and new mathematical methods, SIAM developed new media to bridge this gap and foster the exchange of ideas among all who are interested in the applications of mathematics. It enjoys increasing support from industry and from the scientific and academic communities, and it now has approximately 4,000 individual members and 250 industrial and academic memberships. SIAM sponsors the John Von Neumann Lectures, administers a visiting lecturer program, and, with the support of the National Science Foundation (NSF), the Atomic Energy Commission (AEC), the Office of Naval Research (ONR), and the Air Force Office of Scientific Research (AFOSR), has sponsored special international symposia on various topics in mathematics. Beginning with a single publication, *SIAM Journal on Applied Mathematics* (at present published eight times a year), the society now issues five additional publications: *SIAM Review* (quarterly), *SIAM Journal on Control* (quarterly), *SIAM Journal on Numerical Analysis* (quarterly), *SIAM Journal on Mathematical Analysis* (quarterly), and *SIAM Newsletter* (bimonthly). In addition, SIAM translates cover-to-cover the Russian quarterly journal *Teoriya Veroyatnostei i ee Primeneniya* (Theory of Probability and Its Applications). With the support of NSF, SIAM has also published two simultaneous cover-to-cover translations of anniversary volumes published by the U.S.S.R. Academy of Sciences honoring N. I. Muskhelishvili and L. I. Sedov. SIAM publishes the *SIAM 'Symposium Series*, which are casebound collections of selected invited and contributed papers from symposia held in conjunction with SIAM's national and fall meetings. Headquarters are located at 33 South Seventeenth Street, Philadelphia, Pa. 19103.

Society of Actuaries   A body of professional U.S. actuaries whose qualifications are symbolized by the passing of certain examinations leading to the degree of associate and fellow. Its primary purpose is to encourage the development and application of logical analysis and technical methods to the solution of problems in the fields of insurance and the related fields of social welfare. The society was formed in 1948 as a result of the merger of two earlier bodies. The first of these dates back to 1889, at which time all its members were life insurance companies. A periodical, the *Transactions*, is published three times yearly for the purpose of recording papers, discussions, comments, book reviews, etc., that arise from the society's meetings. Over the years, the society has also developed a substantial library covering its field of interest; this library has been turned over to the College of Insurance in New York, where it is available to persons engaged in the insurance business. The office of the society is located at 208 South La Salle Street, Chicago, Ill. 60604.

Stanford Research Institute (SRI)   A nonprofit organization performing contract research for industry, government, and foundations. Its fields of interests are in the physical and life sciences, economics and management sciences, and engineering (principally electronics). Established in 1946 by a group of West Coast business leaders, in cooperation with the trustees of Stanford University, to provide Western industry with a center where diversified research could be performed, it now serves clients throughout the U.S. as well as overseas. Since its founding, SRI has completed about 7,000 research projects representing contracts for about $465 million, about 35% of which were done for business organizations, foundations, and other private clients. Its research programs in economics and management sciences range from agricultural economics to water-resource economics, from chemical process industries' economics to marketing and distribution economics, and from behavioral sciences research to long-range planning. SRI headquarters and main laboratory are located at 333 Ravenswood Avenue, Menlo Park, Calif. 94025. The institute also has a major laboratory at 820 Mission Street, South Pasadena, Calif. 91031, where research in economics, the physical sciences, environmental pollution, and agriculture is conducted.

Statistical Commission   A functional body of the Economic and Social Council of the United Nations which develops national statistics and improves their comparability among nations. It consists of twenty-four members. After consultation with national governments, it sets up guiding principles, definitions, concepts, and methods, taking into account current statistical practices and economic problems. The commission has been concerned with a standard international-trade classification for export and import statistics; an international standard industrial classification of all economic activities; a system of national accounts; population, housing, and industrial censuses; vital statistics; basic industrial statistics; distribution statistics; price statistics; index numbers of industrial production; and national income statistics.

Statistical Office of the United Nations   The statistical section of the United Nations Secretariat. The central statistical gathering agency of the UN, it also assists governments in carrying out statistical practices by publishing methodological studies and guides and manuals. The Statistical Office arranges for international seminars, conferences, and training centers at which statisticians from underdeveloped countries meet for consultation among themselves and with experts from statistically more developed countries. It publishes *Monthly Bulletin of Statistics; Statistical Yearbook; Demographic Yearbook; Yearbook of National Accounts Statistics in Two Volumes.*

Statistisches Bundesamt   *See Federal Statistical Office*

Survey Research Center   *See Institute for Social Research of the University of Michigan.*

Tariff Commission An independent agency of the U.S. government that serves the President and Congress chiefly as a fact-finding advisory body in tariff and trade matters. Created in 1916 by act of Congress, the agency is headed by six commissioners who are appointed by the President and confirmed by the Senate for terms of six years, one term expiring each year. Not more than three commissioners may be members of the same political party. The chairman and vice chairman are designated annually by the President. The Commission's activities may be divided into general fact-gathering functions and functions involving specific investigations under special statutory directives. Examples of the latter are as follows: Under the Trade Expansion Act of 1962, the Tariff Commission is required to advise the President of the probable economic effect of duty reductions proposed in trade-agreement negotiations. Under the same statute, the Commission, in specified circumstances, is required to determine and report to the President on whether increased imports of an article, resulting in major part from trade-agreement concessions, are the principal factor causing or threatening serious injury to a domestic industry or to a firm or are the principal factors causing or threatening significant unemployment or underemployment of the workers in a firm or subdivision thereof. Section 22 of the Agricultural Adjustment Act designates the Commission as the agency to conduct investigations to determine and report to the President on whether imports materially interfere with a government agricultural program. Under the Antidumping Act of 1921, the Commission, whenever advised by the Treasury that foreign merchandise is being sold in the U.S. at less than its fair value, determines whether a domestic industry is being injured by imports of such merchandise. Most publications of the Tariff Commission are reports on investigations that it has conducted; these reports are issued on a one-time basis. Major publications of the Commission that belong to a series include *Annual Report of the United States Tariff Commission; Operation of the Trade Agreements Program* (annual report); *Tariff*

Schedules of the United States, Annotated; Synthetic Organic Chemicals: U.S. Production and Sales (annual report); *Imports of Benzenoid Chemicals and Products* (annual report). The Tariff Commission has its main office in Washington, D.C.; it also maintains an office in the Customs House in New York.

Tax Foundation, Inc.   A private, nonprofit organization of the U.S. engaged in research and citizen education on all aspects of government spending, taxation, and debt. It was established in 1937. Its purpose is to aid in the development of more efficient government at all levels— Federal, state, and local. The foundation is not a pressure group and does not attempt to influence legislation at any government level; it believes that good government is the responsibility of all the people. The foundation provides legislators and other public officials with factual data at their request. It furnishes research studies and information services to state and local research associations and other citizen groups and supplies periodicals and studies to college economics and public finance classes. A tax-exempt research and educational organization under provisions of the Internal Revenue Code, the foundation receives its support in voluntary contributions and subscriptions from more than 1,500 individuals and business firms. The foundation's major periodicals are *Tax Review*, monthly; *Monthly Tax Features;* and *Library Bulletin.* Over the past five years, the foundation has published about thirty-five studies on such topics as tax credits; government employment, pay, and benefits; corporation income taxes; nontax revenues; city income taxes; urban mass transportation; Medicaid; social security; fiscal policy; revenue sharing; public financing of higher education; state expenditure controls; and earmarked state taxes. The foundation also publishes a reference handbook, *Facts and Figures on Government Finance*, biennially. Its offices are located at 50 Rockefeller Plaza, New York, N.Y. 10020.

Tennessee Valley Authority (TVA)   A corporation of the U.S. government established to carry out a broad program of resource development in the Tennessee River watershed, an area covering parts of seven states. Established on May 18, 1933, TVA is headed by a board of three directors reporting directly to the President and Congress. Much of the agency's work is accomplished with the participation of state and local governments and institutions. TVA has constructed twenty-two dams on the Tennessee River and its tributaries, which, together with a number of acquired dams and several owned by a private corporation, are operated as a multiple-use river-control system. It regulates floods in the Tennessee and lower Ohio and Mississippi River basins, provides a 650-mile navigation channel, and produces electricity. The system also provides subsidiary benefits, such as recreational opportunities, improved water supplies, and fish and wildlife propagation. TVA supplies electric power wholesale to 161 locally owned and operated retail-distribution systems which serve 2 million customers in a service area covering about 80,000 square miles. It also supplies large amounts of electricity to government atomic-energy plants and other Federal agencies concerned with national defense, space exploration, and aeronautical research. Rapid growth in the region's use of electricity has required construction of coal-fired and nuclear power plants in addition to TVA's hydroelectric capacity. At Muscle Shoals, Alabama, TVA operates a large fertilizer-development center. New and improved fertilizers developed there are used in educational programs to foster conservation agriculture in the Tennessee Valley and throughout the U.S. State agricultural colleges and other agencies cooperate in this program. Forest development is conducted in cooperation with other agencies to improve the economic value of the valley's forests and provide for watershed protection. TVA publications include *Annual Report of the Tennessee Valley Authority; Bibliography for the TVA Program; Facts about TVA Operations; TVA Today; Short History of the Tennessee Valley Authority*. Its administrative headquarters are located at Knoxville, Tenn. 37900.

Troika A group of economic policy advisers to the President of the U.S. This group includes the Secretary of the Treasury, the Director of the Office of Management and Budget (OMB), and the Chairman of the Council of Economic Advisers. They meet approximately once a week to discuss economic policy matters. Two additional tiers of high-ranking policy advisers are part of the Troika's advisory machinery. The second tier consists of a second member of the Council of Economic Advisers, the Economist for OMB, and the Assistant Secretary of the Treasury for Economic Policy. The third tier is comprised of senior staff economists from the three agencies. The third tier meets regularly to appraise the economic outlook and to draw policy implications for review by the second tier and final use by the members of the Troika themselves. Frequently, the Chairman of the Board of Governors of the semiautonomous Federal Reserve System meets with members of the Troika, forming the Quadriad. See *The Annual Economic Report of the President,* Government Printing Office, Washington, D.C., February, 1971.

Twentieth Century Fund A research foundation which undertakes timely, critical, and analytical studies of major economic, political, and social institutions and issues. Nonprofit and nonpartisan, the fund was founded in 1919 and endowed by Edward A. Filene. Originally a grant-giving foundation, the fund began in the 1930s to devote its full resources to its own program of research in such areas as international relations, urban problems, and the arts. Book-length fund studies are published by commercial and university presses only after they have been accepted by the fund staff. The fund also publishes staff papers and reports on current issues. It has recently begun including original films as part of its research program. To inform the public about the results of its studies, the fund operates a public information program which includes the publication of a newsletter. Current fund projects include studies nearing completion on the impact of mutual funds and institutional investors on the American economy, an audit of the Alliance for Progress, and a study of art museums. Other projects under way are concerned with the major philanthropic foundations, the military-industrial establishment, the Constitution, the renewal of American political parties, and UN specialized agencies. Task forces are studying international satellite communications, performing arts centers, public employee strikes, and financing congressional campaigns. Recently published studies concern trade policy, economic development in Asia, and the impact of television on presidential campaigns. The fund's headquarters are located at 41 East 70th Street, New York, N.Y. 10021.

U

Unemployment-Insurance Service   An agency of the Department of Labor's Manpower Administration which is responsible for (1) assisting state employment-security agencies in providing soundly financed and administered state unemployment-insurance programs for the nation's workers, geared to the demands of a changing economy; (2) providing labor-market and related information pertinent to the unemployment insurance program; (3) analyzing data on unemployment-compensation coverage, contributions, benefit rights, and benefit payments state by state and for the nation as a whole; and (4) studying and developing policy recommendations about other governmental or private income maintenance programs that may affect the unemployment-insurance system. It also arranges with state employment-service agencies for payment of training allowances under the Manpower Development and Training Act. UI reviews state administration of unemployment insurance to determine whether individuals are denied benefits to which they are entitled under the state law and under agreements with the Secertary of Labor to carry out Federal unemployment-compensation programs for former Federal civilian employees and ex-servicemen. Between July 1, 1968, and June 30, 1969, approximaely $2 billion in unemployment-insurance benefits were awarded to 4.1 million claimants. Major publications of the Unemployment-Insurance Service are *Significant Provisions of UI State Laws; Comparison of UI State Laws,* revised semiannually; *UI Tax Rates,* annually; *Benefit Series Service,* monthly; *Unemployment Insurance Statistics,* monthly.

United States Savings and Loan League and Affiliates   A trade association for the U.S. savings and loan business. Its primary objectives are (1) to advance the interests of savings and loan associations and cooperative banks; (2) to assist, through educational and other means, the promotion of thrift; (3) to encourage private investment in, and purchase of, homes; (4) to devise and promote, through educational means, safe and equitable ways of conducting the business of savings associations; and (5) to improve the statutes and regulations affecting the business. The league was founded in 1892. More than 5,000 associations and cooperative banks, which together hold 95% of the industry's assets, are members of the league. Closely affiliated organizations, the Advertising Division, Inc., and the American Savings and Loan Institute, are integral parts of its organization. The Advertising Division, a self-supporting agency, caters primarily to savings associations and offers highly specialized advertising materials, programs, and consulting services. The American Savings and Loan Institute offers its nearly 32,000 members a variety of educational programs. In addition to home-study correspondence courses, classroom instruction is offered by 168 institute chapters located throughout the U.S. A Graduate School of Savings and Loan and executive development programs are offered for managerial personnel. Affiliated with the institute are the Accounting Divisions, Inc., which develops standard forms, methods, and accounting systems; and the Society of Savings and Loan Controllers, which promotes the professional standing and knowledge of association controllers and internal auditors. League publications include *Savings and Loan News,* monthly, which describes operational, legislative, and competitive developments in the business; *Federal Guide; Legal Bulletin; Fact Book, Directors Digest; Management Digest; Quarterly Letter, Trends Report.* Economic and research studies and specific operational manuals are also available to members. Among textbooks offered are *Savings and Loan Principles; Savings Accounts; Mortgage*

Lending; Savings and Loan Accounting. The league's executive offices are located at 221 North La Salle Street, Chicago, Ill. 60600.

U.S. Arms Control and Disarmament Agency   An independent agency of the U.S. government which has the broad responsibility for the conduct of studies relating to arms control and disarmament. The Agency's Economics Bureau conducts economic studies dealing with the impact of defense and disarmament on the U.S. economy, industries, regions, and employment, and it analyzes the economic aspects of matters affecting the international climate for arms control and disarmament. The bulk of the domestic research is conducted under contracts with persons or organizations outside the Agency. Classified and unclassified research reports are prepared. Among the unclassified reports published is the annual report, *World Military Expenditures.*

U.S. Customs   A bureau of the U.S. Treasury Department. Founded in 1789, its principal duties include the assessment and collection of all duties, taxes, and fees due on merchandise imported into the U.S.; the direction of certain navigation laws and treaties; and the combating of smuggling and frauds on the revenue. Since Customs is located at the U.S. borders and at inland ports of entry, it works with, and aids in enforcing the laws and regulations of, the Immigration and Naturalization Service, the Public Health Service, the plant and animal quarantine activities of the Department of Agriculture, Foreign Assets Control, the Department of Commerce, and many other government agencies whose functions involve the entrance or exit of people or merchandise into or out of the U.S. Revenues from Customs provided the major share of the U.S. income until 1916, when Congress passed income tax legislation. In fiscal 1969, the Bureau of Customs handled 227 million people arriving in the U.S., processed $34 billion in imported merchandise, and collected $3.257 billion at a cost of $3.08 per each $100 collected. In fiscal 1969, Customs seized over 57,000 pounds of marijuana, over 311 pounds of heroin, nearly 200 pounds of cocaine and other narcotics, over 600 pounds of hashish, and nearly 5 million 5-grain units of dangerous drugs, and it made a total of over 28,000 other seizures of merchandise and 6,200 arrests of persons involved in smuggling and frauds on the revenue. The Bureau is divided into nine regions, which include 42 customs districts, over 400 ports and stations, and 8 offices in foreign countries. U.S. Customs publications include *Exporting to the United States, U.S. Import Requirements; Prospective Imports-Customs Duty; Import Quota; Marking of Country of Origin, Alcoholic Beverages.* Customs also issues *Customs Hints* for both residents and nonresidents and other informative booklets and folders for travelers.

U.S. Office of Education   An agency of the U.S. Department of Health, Education, and Welfare. It identifies needs, evaluates resources, and provides professional and financial assistance in order to enhance the quality and broaden the scope of the nation's educational system. The Office is engaged primarily in (1) administering Federal programs of aid to education covering all levels from preschool to postdoctoral study, such as financial assistance to colleges and college students, grants for innovative approaches to educational problems, and funds in support of research and demonstration projects to advance instructional techniques; (2) collecting and disseminating information and statistics resulting from research and other information regarding the condition of education in the U.S.; and (3) providing technical and consultative assistance to educational agencies and institutions and to states and local communities. The U.S. Office of Education was established in 1867 and has been part of the Department of Health, Education, and Welfare since 1953. It publishes a prize-winning magazine, *American Education,* issued ten times a year and containing articles on current problems and programs in education throughout the country. A catalog of other publications of the Office may be obtained from the Information Center, U.S. Office of Education, 400 Maryland Avenue, S.W., Washington, D.C. 20202.

U.S. Training and Employment Service   An agency of the Department of Labor's Manpower Administration which is responsible for providing leadership to the state employment-security agencies and for developing training and work-experience programs designed to relieve unemployment and promote maximum utilization of the nation's manpower. The U.S. Training and Employment Service (USTES) combines the activities of the former Bureau of Employment Security and the Bureau of Work-Training Programs. The 2,200 local offices of the state employment service processed nearly 10 million new applications between July 1, 1968, and June 30, 1969. Approximately 7,500,000 nonagricultural job openings were listed. The employment service made 5,500,000 nonagricultural placements—many in training or work-experience programs. It also made 4,819,000 agricultural placements. Client groups include the disadvantaged and hard-core unemployed, farmers and rural workers, veterans, youth, older workers, the underemployed, welfare recipients, minority-group members, handicapped persons, aliens, professional and technical personnel, and employers. Applicants receive job and personal counseling, referral to training or job opportunities, and supportive services to help with various medical, legal, or child-care problems. USTES is responsible for administering youth and adult programs which offer a broad range of work-experience, training and career-related services in rural and urban centers. It also coordinates employment-security activities with other government agencies and the public and advises the legislative and executive branches of government on employment-security matters. In order to facilitate sound program planning, it collects and analyzes operational and economic data related to employment-service programs. The major publications of USTES are *Dictionary of Occupational Titles, Area Trends in Employment and Unemployment,* monthly; *Employment and Wages,* quarterly; *Employment Service Statistics,* monthly; *Job Guide for Young Workers; Farm Labor Developments,* periodically.

United Transportation Union (UTU)   An international organization of workers in the transportation industry including railroad operating and nonoperating employees, bus company employees, and others. UTU represents over 85% of all railroad engine and train crews and is the largest transportation union affiliated with the AFL-CIO. The aims and purposes of the union are to promote the general welfare of the membership; to advance their social, moral, political, economic, and intellectual interests; and to provide for their families. The UTU was formed on January 1, 1969, by the merger of four of the oldest unions in the U.S.: the Brotherhood of Railroad Trainmen, the Brotherhood of Locomotive Firemen and Enginemen, the Order of Railway Conductors and Brakemen, and the Switchmen's Union of North America. All the predecessor brotherhoods were organized as craft unions and insurance organizations in the late 1800s, when railroad work was so dangerous that employees were not able to get insurance protection for their families. The union still provides fraternal insurance for members. A desire for labor unity brought a membership referendum vote supporting the merger which formed UTU. Membership totals 265,000 workers in 2,000 locals. The union maintains effective grievance, legislative, and public relations departments and publishes a weekly membership newspaper called the *UTU News.* The international headquarters are located in Cleveland, Ohio.

Urban Land Institute (ULI)   An independent, nonprofit U.S. research organization whose interests and activities cover the entire field of urban planning, growth, and development. It was incorporated in 1936 under the laws of the state of Illinois. Among its principal purposes are to study and interpret trends in real property and to seek their orientation in the changing economic, social, and civic needs of the U.S.; to study principles and methods by which urban land can be developed and improved more efficiently; and to act as a clearinghouse for the dissemination of case materials, monographs, and technical journals. ULI undertakes certain applied research programs under contract and in association with such groups as the Federal Housing Administration, the National Association of Home Builders, and the International Council of Shopping Centers. Such programs are geared to the housing and shopping center industries and have direct practical applications. Much of the institute's work is carried on by three councils: the Community Builder's Council, the Industrial Council, and the Central City Council. These councils pay particular attention to the major fields of urban land development: residential, industrial, and commercial. They offer a unique service to cities, civic organizations, and private corporations through panel studies that bring to bear on specific downtown, industrial, and suburban problems the talents of a highly informed and experienced group of men. The panels review and evaluate plans and proposals and make recommendations on procedures and actions to be taken. ULI also is carrying forward a program of basic research geared to uncovering the fundamental relationships between taxation and land use. Four monographs have appeared under this program. Other publications are *Urban Land,* monthly, covering news and trends of interest in land development; *Land Use Digest,* a monthly newsletter to ULI members; technical bulletins, periodically; research monographs, periodically; *Community Builders Handbook; Operation Shopping Centers; Standard Manual of Expense Accounts for Shopping Centers; The Dollar and Cents of Shopping Centers.* ULI headquarters are located at 1200 Eighteenth Street, N.W., Washington, D.C. 20036.

Urban Renewal Administration *See Housing and Home Finance Agency.*

Verbond der Belgische Nijverheid *See Federation of Belgian Industries.*

Veterans Administration (VA) An independent agency of the U.S. government whose purpose is to administer laws authorizing benefits for former members of the nation's armed forces and for the dependents and beneficiaries of disabled and deceased veterans. These benefits include disability and death compensation and pensions, vocational rehabilitation and education, hospital and outpatient care, nursing home care, domiciliary and restoration care, life insurance for both veterans and servicemen, guaranteed or insured and direct loans to veterans, prosthetic and other appliances for disabled veterans, special housing and conveyances for severely disabled veterans, a guardianship program for certain incompetent veterans and dependents of veterans, emergency officers' retirement pay, and other benefits and services for veterans and their dependents as authorized by law. The VA was established by an executive order of the President on July 21, 1930, in accordance with an act of Congress dated July 3, 1930, which authorized the President to consolidate all Federal agencies then dealing with veterans' affairs. The order consolidated into a single agency the Bureau of Pensions, the U.S. Veterans' Bureau, and the National Home for Disabled Volunteer Soldiers. The VA mantains 166 hospitals, 6 independent outpatient clinics, 6 restoration centers, 16 domiciliaries, 63 nursing home care units, 57 regional offices, 6 data processing centers, 30 VA offices, and 2 insurance centers throughout the 50 states, the District of Columbia, Puerto Rico, and the Republic of the Philippines. Since the first veterans' benefit was approved by the Pilgrims of Plymouth Colony in 1636, providing that any soldier injured in defense of the colony "shall be maintained competently by the Colony during his life," a grateful nation has not neglected the welfare of its servicemen and their dependents. The fiscal year 1970 budget of over $7.7 billion distributed throughout the U.S. fulfilled the VA's charge "to care for him who shall have borne the battle and for his widow, and his orphan." The principal VA publications of interest are the *Annual Report of the Administrator of Veterans Affairs* and the VA Fact Sheet IS-1, *Federal Benefits for Veterans and Dependents,* which is a summary of benefits administered by the agency and is updated annually after each session of Congress. The latter publication is available at VA offices.

Z

Zinc Institute A nonprofit national trade association of the U.S. zinc industry. Founded in 1918, the institute collects and distributes information related to the uses of zinc. Its sources of information are research and close contacts with the zinc industry. Distribution is accomplished by educational programs, consultation, publications, and technical publicity. The institute's services are available without charge to anyone who is interested in the utilization of zinc and zinc-coated products. Among its major publications are *Annual Review of the Zinc Industry in the United States; Zinc: The Science and Technology of the Metal, Its Alloys and Compounds; Zinc: A Mine to Market Outline.* The institute's headquarters are located at 292 Madison Avenue, New York, N.Y. 10017. It has field offices in Detroit, Michigan; Lafayette, Indiana; and Toronto, Ontario.